TEACHERS DISCOVERING COMPUTERS
INTEGRATING TECHNOLOGY
in the
CLASSROOM

Gary B. Shelly
Thomas J. Cashman
Randolph E. Gunter
Glenda A. Gunter

COURSE TECHNOLOGY
ONE MAIN STREET
CAMBRIDGE MA 02142

Thomson Learning™

SHELLY
CASHMAN
SERIES®

Australia • Canada • Denmark • Japan • Mexico • New Zealand • Philippines
Puerto Rico • Singapore • South Africa • Spain • United Kingdom • United States

TEACHERS DISCOVERING COMPUTERS
INTEGRATING TECHNOLOGY
in the
CLASSROOM

CONTENTS

CHAPTER 3

Software Applications for Education

SPECIAL FEATURE **3.44**

Creating a Teachers Web Page

CHAPTER 4

Hardware Applications for Education

SPECIAL FEATURE **4.46**
Buyer's Guide 2000
How to Purchase, Install, and Maintain a Personal Computer

CONTENTS

Preface

In 1998, the Shelly Cashman Series® team produced *Discovering Computers 98: A Link to the Future, World Wide Web Enhanced* for the Introduction to Computers course. This textbook became an instant best-seller. Its popularity was due to (1) the integration of the World Wide Web; (2) the currency of the materials; (3) its readability; (4) extensive exercises; (5) supplements; and (6) the ancillaries that allow an instructor to teach the way he or she wants to teach.

Realizing that all of the proven enhancements used in the *Discovering Computers 98* book could be molded into a new textbook specifically designed for teaching educational technology to current and future K-12 teachers, counselors, and administrators, the Shelly Cashman Series team has produced *Teachers Discovering Computers: Integrating Technology in the Classroom*.

Objectives of This Textbook

This book in intended for use in a one-quarter or one-semester undergraduate or graduate level introductory computer course for educators. Students will finish the course with a solid understanding of educational technology, including how to use computers, how to access information on the World Wide Web, and most importantly how to integrate computers and educational technology into classroom curriculum. This book also can be used in inservice training workshops that train teachers, administrators, and counselors how to use and effectively integrate educational technology. The objectives of this textbook are as follows:

- Present practical, efficient ways to integrate technology resources and technology-based methods into everyday practices
- Provide students with an understanding of the concepts and skills outlined in the International Society for Technology in Education (ISTE) technology standards for all teachers
- Present the fundamentals of computers and educational technology in an easy-to-understand format
- Use the World Wide Web as a repository of the latest information and as an educational resource and learning tool for K-12 education
- Provide information on both Macintosh computers and PCs
- Give students an in-depth understanding of why computers are essential tools in society, business, and K-12 education
- Provide students with the knowledge of using educational technology with diverse student populations
- Offer numerous examples of how to use educational technology in various subject areas and with students with special needs
- Explain the responsible, ethical and legal use of technology, information, and software resources students must understand
- Provide students with knowledge of technology that enhances their personal and professional productivity

Distinguishing Features

Teachers Discovering Computers: Integrating Technology in the Classroom includes the following distinguishing features.

The Proven Shelly and Cashman Pedagogy

More than three million students have learned about computers using Shelly and Cashman computer fundamental textbooks. With World Wide Web integration and interactivity, streaming up-to-date, educational technology-related CNN videos, extraordinary visual drawings and photographs, unprecedented currency, and the Shelly and Cashman touch, this book will make your introductory computer course for teachers exciting and dynamic, an experience your students will remember as a highlight of their educational careers. Students, teachers, and course instructors will find this to be the finest textbook they have ever used.

World Wide Web and CNN Enhanced

Teachers Discovering Computers continues the Shelly and Cashman tradition of innovation with its extensive integration of the World Wide Web. The purpose of integrating the World Wide Web into the book is to (1) offer students additional information and currency on topics of importance; (2) make available alternative learning techniques with Web-based streaming audio and up-to-date, educational technology-related CNN videos; (3) underscore the relevance of the World Wide Web as a basic information tool that can be used in all facets of K-12 education and society; and (4) offer instructors the opportunity to organize and administer their campus-based or distance-education-based courses on the Web using CyberClass. The World Wide Web is integrated into the book in four central ways:

- End-of-chapter pages and many of the special features in the book have been stored as Web pages on the World Wide Web. While working on an end-of-chapter page, students can display the corresponding Web page to obtain additional information on a term or exercise, explore the vast resources the Web has for education, or get an alternative point of view. The end-of-chapter Web pages provide students with thousands of links to additional sources of information; sources that have been evaluated for appropriateness and are maintained by a team of educators. See page xiv for more information.

- *Teachers Discovering Computers* uses streaming audio on the Web in the end-of-chapter InBrief sections, streaming up-to-date, educational technology-related CNN videos on the Web in the end-of-chapter AtTheMovies sections, and in the Interactive Labs in the end-of-chapter NetStuff sections.

- Throughout the text, marginal annotations titled WebInfo provide suggestions on how to obtain additional information via the World Wide Web on an important topic covered on the page. The textbook Web site provides links to these additional sources of information.

- CyberClass Web-based teaching and learning system as described on page xiii. This textbook, however, does not depend on Web access in order to be used successfully. The Web access adds to the already complete treatment of topics within the book.

A Visually Appealing Book that Maintains Student Interest

Using the latest technology, the pictures, drawings, and text have been artfully combined to produce a visually appealing and easy-to-understand book. Many of the figures show a step-by-step pedagogy, which simplifies the more complex computer and educational technology concepts. Pictures and drawings reflect the latest trends in computer and educational technology. Finally, the text was set in two columns, which research shows is easier for students to read. This combination of pictures, step-by-step drawings, and text sets a new standard for education textbook design.

Latest Educational Technology and Computer Trends

The terms and examples of educational technology described in this book are those your students will encounter when using computers in the school setting as well as at home. The latest educational software packages and programs are shown throughout this book.

Macintosh Computers and PCs

Unlike many businesses, both Macintosh computers and PCs are used in the K-12 school environment. The textbook addresses both computer platforms and describes the appropriateness and use of educational software for both Macintosh computers and PCs.

Shelly Cashman Series Interactive Labs

Eighteen unique, hands-on exercises, allow students to use the computer to learn about computer technology. Students can step through each Lab exercise in about 15 minutes. Assessment is available. The Interactive Labs are described in detail on page xv. These Labs are available free on the Web (see page 1.34) or on CD-ROM for an additional cost (ISBN 0-7895-5750-9 for Macintosh users and ISBN 0-7895-5749-5 for PC users).

End-of-Chapter Exercises

Unlike other books on educational technology fundamentals, a major effort was undertaken in *Teachers Discovering Computers* to offer exciting, rich, and thorough end-of-chapter materials to reinforce the chapter objectives and assist you in making your course the finest ever offered. As indicated earlier, each and every one of the end-of-chapter pages is stored as a Web page on the World Wide Web to provide your students in-depth information and alternative methods of preparing for examinations. Each chapter ends with the following:

- **InBrief** This section summarized the chapter material for the purpose of reviewing and preparing for examinations. Links on the Web pages provide additional current information. With a single click on the Web page, the review section is read to the student using streaming audio.

- **KeyTerms** This list of the key terms found in the chapter together with the page number on which the terms are defined will aid students in mastering the chapter material. A complete summary of all key terms in the book, together with their definitions, appears in the Index at the end of the book. On the Web page, students can click terms to view a definition and a picture, and then click a link to visit a Web page that provides supplemental information.

- **AtTheMovies** In this section, students complete exercises that require them to click photographs on the Web page to view streaming up-to-date CNN videos. These videos, which present educational technology-related topics, reinforce the chapter or provide extended knowledge of important concepts.

- **CheckPoint** Matching and short-answer questions, together with a figure from the chapter that can be labeled, are used to reinforce the material presented within the chapter. Students accessing the Web page answer the questions in an interactive forum.

- **TeacherTime** In this section, students will gain an appreciation of the value that technology and the World Wide Web has for K-12 education by visiting exciting educational Web pages and completing suggested curriculum integration tasks. The Web pages provide links to further challenge students on a vast array of interesting teacher-related topics.

- **CyberClass** These exercises have students connect to the CyberClass Web page where they complete tasks that include online flash cards; practice tests; e-mail; bulletin board activities; visiting and evaluating Web sites; and CyberChallenge.

- **EdIssues** The use of computers and other technologies in education is not without its controversial issues. At the end of each chapter, several scenarios are presented that challenge students to critically examine their perspective of the use of technology in K-12 education and society in general. Other non-technology related scenarios allow students to explore many current controversial issues in education; for example, school violence. The Web pages provide links to challenge students further.

- **NetStuff** To complete their introduction to computers, students need to interact with and use computers. A series of interactive lab exercises, software tutorials, Windows and Macintosh exercises, and other tasks allow students to learn computer skills and software programs by completing hands-on exercises on the Web. The last NetStuff exercise sends students into an educational chat room where they can discuss engaging issues and topics presented in the book with other education students throughout the world.

Timeline 2000: Milestones in Computer History

A colorful, highly informative ten-page timeline following Chapter 1 steps students through the major computer technology developments over the past 50 years, including the most recent advances.

Guide to World Wide Web Sites

More than 100 popular Web sites are listed and described in a general guide to Web sites that follows Chapter 2. These sites are organized into general categories, such as Entertainment, Health and Medicine, Government and Politics, Shopping, and more.

Creating a Teacher's Web Page

Following Chapter 3, a fourteen-page project provides students with instructions on how to create a basic teacher's Web page using Netscape Composer. By completing this step-by-step project, students will acquire many of the skills needed to create educational Web and curriculum pages.

Buyer's Guide 2000: How to Purchase, Install, and Maintain a Personal Computer

A thirteen-page guide following Chapter 4 introduces students to purchasing, installing, and maintaining a desktop or laptop computer.

Creating a HyperStudio Project

Following Chapter 5, a twelve-page project provides students with step-by-step instructions on creating a basic HyperStudio stack.

Guide to Educational Sites and Professional Organizations

More than 80 popular education-related Web sites are listed and described in a guide to educational Web sites that follows Chapter 6. These sites are organized into 21 categories, such as Art, Chemistry, Foreign Language, and Mathematics.

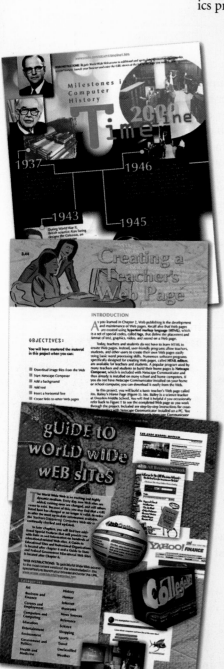

Guide to State and Federal Government Educational Web Sites

The federal government, state governments, and state institutions and organizations offer a multitude of Web resources for K-12 teachers and students. Educational resources provided by more than twenty-five federal government agencies and all fifty states and the District of Columbia are listed and described in a guide that follows Chapter 8.

Instructor's Support Package

A comprehensive instructor's support package accompanies this textbook in the form of two CD-ROM packages for both the Macintosh computer and PC platforms. The two packages titled Teaching Tools (ISBN 0-7895-5752-5 for Macintosh users and ISBN 0-7895-4639-6 for PC users) and Course Presenter (ISBN 0-7895-5751-7 for Macintosh users and ISBN 0-7895-5646-4 for PC users) are described in the following sections. Both packages are available free to adopters through your Course Technology representative or by calling one of the following telephone numbers: Colleges and Universities, 1-800-648-7450; High Schools, 1-800-824-5179; and Career Colleges, 1-800-477-3692.

Teaching Tools

The Teaching Tools for this textbook include both teaching and testing aids. The contents of the Teaching Tools CD-ROM are listed below.

Instructor's Manual

The Instructor's Manual is made up of Microsoft Word files. The files include the following for each chapter: chapter objectives; chapter overview; detailed lesson plans with page number references; teacher notes and activities; answers to the exercises; test bank (100 true/false, 50 multiple-choice, and 70 fill-in-the-blank questions per chapter); and figure references. The actual figures used in the textbook are available in the Figures in the Book ancillary. The test bank questions are numbered the same as in Course Test Manager. You can print a copy of the chapter test bank and use the printout to select your questions in Course Test Manager. You also can use your word processing software to generate quizzes and exams from the test bank.

Figures in the Book

Illustrations for every picture, table, and screen in the textbook are available in electronic form. Use this ancillary to present a slide show in lecture or to print transparencies for use in lecture with an overhead projector. If you have a personal computer and LCD device or projection system, this ancillary can be an effective tool for presenting lectures.

Powerful Testing and Assessment Packages

Course Test Manager for the PC and WesTest for the Macintosh are powerful testing and assessment packages that enable instructors to create and print tests from the text bank. In addition, with Course Test Manager, instructors with access to a networked computer lab (LAN) can administer, grade, and track tests online. Students also can take online practice tests, which generate customized study guides that indicate where in the text students can find more information for each question.

Interactive Labs

These Interactive Labs are the non-audio versions of the eighteen hands-on Interactive Lab exercises. Students can step through each lab in about fifteen minutes to solidify and reinforce computer concepts. Assessment requires students to answer questions about the contents of the Interactive Labs.

Interactive Lab Solutions

This ancillary includes the solutions for the Interactive Labs assessment quizzes.

Course Presenter with Figures, Animations, and CNN Video Clips

Course Presenter is a multimedia lecture presentation system that provides PowerPoint slides for every subject in each chapter. Use this presentation tool to present well-organized lectures that are both interesting and knowledge-based. Eight presentation files are provided for the book, one for each chapter. Each file contains PowerPoint slides for every subject in each chapter together with optional choices to show any figure in the chapter as you introduce the material in class. Twenty-four current, two- to three-minute, computer-related CNN video clips and dozens of animations that reinforce chapter material also are available for optional presentation. Course Presenter provides consistent coverage for multiple lecturers.

Supplement

One additional supplement can be used in combination with *Teachers Discovering Computers: Integrating Technology in the Classroom*. This supplement reinforces the computer and educational technology-related concepts presented in the book.

Shelly Cashman Series Interactive Labs with Audio on CD-ROM

The Shelly Cashman Series Interactive Labs with Audio on CD-ROM (ISBN 0-7895-5750-9 for Macintosh users and ISBN 0-7895-5749-5 for PC users) may be used in combination with this textbook to augment your students' learning process. See page xv for a description of each lab. These Interactive Labs also are available at no cost on the Web by clicking the appropriate button on the NetStuff exercise pages (see page 1.34).

Acknowledgments

The Shelly Cashman Series would not be the most successful computer textbook series ever published without the contributions of outstanding publishing professionals. First, and foremost, among them is Becky Herrington, director of production and designer. She is the heart and soul of the Shelly Cashman Series, and it is only through her leadership, dedication, and tireless efforts that superior products are produced.

Under Becky's direction, the following individuals made significant contributions to this book: Doug Cowley, production manager; Ginny Harvey, series specialist and copyeditor; Ken Russo, Web designer and cover designer; Ellana Russo, graphic artist; Marlo Mitchem, associate production editor; Nancy Lamm and Marilyn Martin, proofreaders; Sarah Evertson of Image Quest, photo researcher; Jeanne Busemeyer, CNN video editor; and Cristina Haley, indexer.

Special thanks go to Richard Keaveny, managing editor; Jim Quasney, series consulting editor; Lora Wade, product manager; Erin Bennett, associate product manager; Francis Schurgot, Web product manager; Marc Ouellette, associate Web product manager; and Erin Runyon, editorial assistant.

Our sincere thanks go to Betty Hopkins, designer of this book. Betty executed the magnificent photo and art treatment and performed the entire initial layout and typography. Special thanks go to our talented graphic artists, Mike Bodnar, for rendering the outstanding illustrations, Stephanie Nance and Mark Norton for the design of the Special Feature sections; and Jeanne Black, Quark expert and layout artist.

Thanks go to Patti Abraham, Diane Murphy, Eileen Atkinson, Donna Baumbach, and James Russett for reviewing the manuscript; Vicki Rath, Rita Kienle, and Julie Kittrell for reviewing and assisting in the development of the end-of-chapter materials and special features; and Darrell Ward of *Hyper*Graphics Corporation for the development of CyberClass. We hope you find using this book an exciting and rewarding experience.

Gary B. Shelly

Thomas J. Cashman

Randolph E. Gunter

Glenda A. Gunter

CYBERCLASS — A WEB-BASED TEACHING AND LEARNING SYSTEM

CyberClass is a Web-based teaching and learning system that adopters of *Teachers Discovering Computers: Integrating Technology in the Classroom* can use in a traditional campus setting or distance learning setting. CyberClass is available in three levels so you can choose the one that best fits your course needs.

CyberClass Level I is free to adopters of this book and includes (1) 25 interactive flash cards per chapter that serve as a self-study aid to help students master chapter content; (2) practice tests that enable students to test their mastery of a chapter; includes study guide feedback; and (3) a link to this book's award-winning Web site.

CyberClass Level II is available for an additional cost and includes (1) a customizable and secure Web site that the instructor can use to organize and administer a campus-based or distance learning-based course; (2) access to all CyberClass Level I capabilities; (3) posting class syllabi for students to read; (4) posting class assignments for students to read; (5) the capability of sending messages to and receiving messages from class members and instructors; (6) an option to submit assignments electronically to instructors; (7) access to a student bulletin board; (8) posting of hot links for class members; (9) electronic flash cards for every bold term in the book, organized by chapter; (10) CyberChallenge, a self-study game; and (11) a class administrative system that includes Web-based testing and class rosters.

CyberClass Level III is available for an additional cost and includes (1) all the capabilities of Level I and Level II; (2) audio-conferencing, which allows instructor and students to meet for Web-based lectures; and (3) live assessment, which allows instructors to send questions real-time to students who then respond back immediately.

Notes to the Student

If you have access to the World Wide Web, you can obtain current and additional information on topics covered in this book in the three ways listed below.

WebInfo

For more information on Macintosh computers, visit the Teachers Discovering Computers Chapter 1 WebInfo page **(www.scsite.com/tdc/ ch1/webinfo.htm)** and click Macintosh.

Figure 1

1. Throughout the book, marginal annotations called WebInfo **[Figure 1]** specify subjects about which you can obtain additional current information. Enter the designated URL and then click the appropriate term on the Web page.
2. Each chapter ends with eight sections titled InBrief, KeyTerms, AtTheMovies, CheckPoint, TeacherTime, CyberClass, EdIssues, and NetStuff. These sections in your book are stored as Web pages on the Web. You can visit them by starting your browser and entering the URL given in the instructions at the top of the end-of-chapter pages. When the Web page displays, you can click links or buttons on the page to broaden your understanding of the topics and obtain current information about the topic.
3. Use CyberClass as described on the previous page.

Each time you reference a Web page from *Teachers Discovering Computers,* a sidebar displays on the left. To display one of the end-of-chapter exercises **[Figure 2]**, click the chapter number and then click the exercise title in the sidebar. To display one of the Special Features, click the desired Special Feature title in the sidebar.

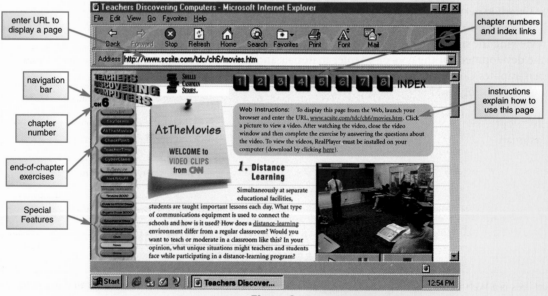

Figure 2

TO DOWNLOAD PLAYERS

For best viewing results of the Web Pages referenced in this book, download the Shockwave and Flash Player. To play the audio in the InBrief section and view the video in the AtTheMovies section at the end of each chapter, you must download the RealPlayer. Follow the steps below:

Shockwave and Flash Player — (1) Launch your browser; (2) enter the URL, `www.macromedia.com`; (3) click the Get Shockwave Flash button; (4) click download shockwave; (5) if you are using Microsoft Internet Explorer, scroll down and click the AUTOINSTALL button; if you are using Netscape Navigator, scroll down and click the DOWNLOAD NOW button; and (6) respond to the dialog boxes. With Microsoft Internet Explorer, the AUTOINSTALL button will update your system automatically. With Netscape Navigator, you must launch Explorer and then double-click the downloaded file to update your system.

RealPlayer — (1) Launch your browser; (2) enter the URL, `www.real.com`; (3) click the FREE RealPlayer G2 button; (4) click RealPlayer G2; (5) click Free RealPlayer; (6) step through and respond to the forms, requests, and dialog boxes; (7) when the File Download dialog box displays, click Save this program to disk; (8) save the file to a folder and remember the folder name; and (9) launch Explorer and then double-click the downloaded file in step 8.

Shelly Cashman Series Interactive Labs with Audio

Each of the eight chapters in this book includes the NetStuff exercises, which utilize the World Wide Web. The fourteen Shelly Cashman Series Interactive Labs described below are included as exercises in the NetStuff section. These Interactive Labs are available on the Web (see page 1.34) or on CD-ROM. The CD-ROM version (ISBN 0-7895-5750-9 for the Macintosh and ISBN 0-7895-5749-5 for the PC) is available for a small additional cost. A non-audio version also is available at no extra cost on the Shelly Cashman Series Teaching Tools CD-ROM that is available free to adopters. Each lab takes students approximately 15 minutes to complete using a personal computer and helps them gain a better understanding of a specific subject covered in the chapter.

Shelly Cashman Series Interactive Labs with Audio		
Lab	*Function*	*Page*
Using the Mouse	Master how to use a mouse. The Lab includes exercises on pointing, clicking, double-clicking, and dragging.	1.34
Using the Keyboard	Learn how to use the keyboard. The Lab discusses different categories of keys, including the edit keys, function keys, ESC, CTRL, and ALT keys and how to press keys simultaneously.	1.34
Connecting to the Internet	Learn how a computer is connected to the Internet. The Lab presents using the Internet to access information.	2.49
The World Wide Web	Understand the significance of the World Wide Web and how to use Web browser software and search tools.	2.49
Word Processing	Gain a basic understanding of word processing concepts, from creating a document to printing and saving the final result.	3.43
Setting Up to Print	See how information flows from the system unit to the printer and how drivers, fonts, and physical connections play a role in generating a printout.	3.43
Understanding the Motherboard	Step through the components of a motherboard. The Lab shows how different motherboard configurations affect the overall speed of a computer.	4.45
Configuring Your Display	Recognize the different monitor configurations available, including screen size, display cards, and number of colors.	4.45
Maintaining Your Hard Drive	Understand how files are stored on disk, what causes fragmentation, and how to maintain an efficient hard drive.	4.45
Understanding Multimedia	Gain an understanding of the types of media used in multimedia applications, the components of a multimedia PC, and the newest applications of multimedia.	5.39
Scanning Documents	Understand how document scanners work.	5.39
Working at Your Computer	Learn the basic ergonomic principles that prevent back and neck pain, eye strain, and other computer-related physical ailments.	6.40
Exploring the Computers of the Future	Learn about computers of the future and how they will work.	8.41
Keeping Your Computer Virus Free	Learn what a virus is and about the different kinds of viruses. The Lab discusses how to prevent your computer from being infected with a virus.	8.41

Shelly Cashman Series – Traditionally Bound Textbooks

The Shelly Cashman Series presents the following computer subjects in a variety of traditionally bound textbooks. For more information, see your Course Technology representative or call one of the following telephone numbers: Colleges and Universities, 1-800-648-7450; High Schools, 1-800-824-5179; and Career Colleges, 1-800-477-3692. For Shelly Cashman Series information, visit Shelly Cashman Online at **www.scseries.com**

COMPUTERS	
Computers	Discovering Computers 2000: Concepts for a Connected World, Web and CNN Enhanced
	Discovering Computers 2000: Concepts for a Connected World, Web and CNN Enhanced Brief Edition
	Teachers Discovering Computers: Integrating Technology in the Classroom
	Discovering Computers 98: A Link to the Future, World Wide Web Enhanced
	Discovering Computers 98: A Link to the Future, World Wide Web Enhanced Brief Edition
	Exploring Computers: A Record of Discovery 2e with CD-ROM
	Study Guide for Discovering Computers: A Link to the Future, World Wide Web Enhanced
	Brief Introduction to Computers 3e (32-page)

WINDOWS APPLICATIONS	
Microsoft Office	Microsoft Office 97: Introductory Concepts and Techniques, Brief Edition (6 projects)
	Microsoft Office 97: Introductory Concepts and Techniques, Essentials Edition (10 projects)
	Microsoft Office 97: Introductory Concepts and Techniques (15 projects)
	Microsoft Office 97: Advanced Concepts and Techniques
Microsoft Works	Microsoft Works 4.5* • Microsoft Works 3.0*
Windows	Microsoft Windows 98: Essential Concepts and Techniques
	Microsoft Windows 98: Introductory Concepts and Techniques
	Microsoft Windows 98: Introductory Concepts and Techniques Web Style Edition
	Microsoft Windows 98: Complete Concepts and Techniques
	Microsoft Windows 98: Comprehensive Concepts and Techniques
	Introduction to Microsoft Windows NT Workstation 4
	Microsoft Windows 95: Introductory Concepts and Techniques (96-page)
	Introduction to Microsoft Windows 95 (224-page)
	Microsoft Windows 95: Complete Concepts and Techniques
Word Processing	Microsoft Word 97* • Microsoft Word 7*
	Corel WordPerfect 8 • Corel WordPerfect 7 • WordPerfect 6.1*
Spreadsheets	Microsoft Excel 97* • Microsoft Excel 7* • Microsoft Excel 5*
	Lotus 1-2-3 97*
Database	Microsoft Access 97* • Microsoft Access 7*
Presentation Graphics	Microsoft PowerPoint 97* • Microsoft PowerPoint 7*

PROGRAMMING	
Programming	Microsoft Visual Basic 6: Complete Concepts and Techniques*
	Microsoft Visual Basic 5: Complete Concepts and Techniques*
	Microsoft Visual Basic 4 for Windows 95* (available with Student version software)
	QBasic • QBasic: An Introduction to Programming • Microsoft BASIC
	Structured COBOL Programming

INTERNET	
Internet	The Internet: Introductory Concepts and Techniques (UNIX)
Browser	Netscape Navigator 4: An Introduction
	Netscape Navigator 3: An Introduction
	Microsoft Internet Explorer 4: An Introduction
	Microsoft Internet Explorer 3: An Introduction
Web Page Creation	HTML: Complete Concepts and Techniques*
	Microsoft FrontPage 98: Complete Concepts and Techniques*
	Netscape Composer
	JavaScript: Complete Concepts and Techniques*

SYSTEMS ANALYSIS	
Systems Analysis	Systems Analysis and Design, Third Edition

DATA COMMUNICATIONS	
Data Communications	Business Data Communications: Introductory Concepts and Techniques, Second Edition

*Also available as an Introductory Edition, which is a shortened version of the complete book

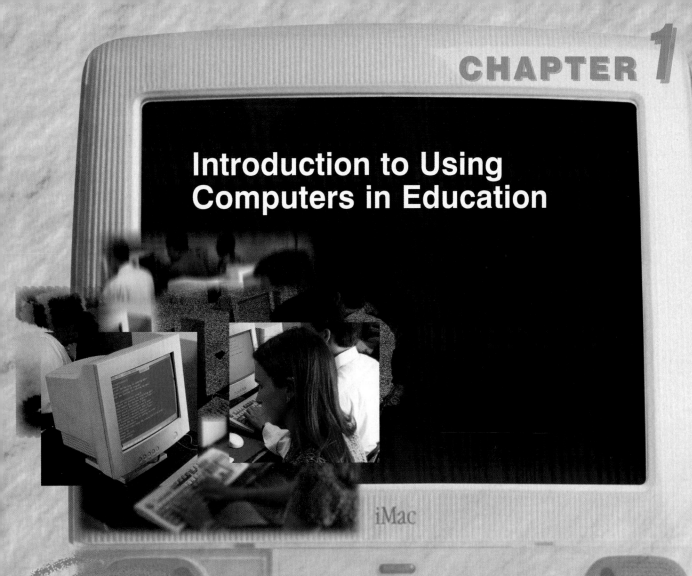

Introduction to Using Computers in Education

Objectives

After completing this chapter, you will be able to:

- Explain the difference between computer, information, and integration literacy
- Define and describe computers and their functions
- Identify the major components of a computer
- Explain the four operations of the information processing cycle: input, process, output, and storage
- Explain how speed, reliability, accuracy, storage, and communications enable computers to be powerful tools

- Differentiate among the various categories of software
- Explain the purpose of a network
- Discuss the uses of the Internet and the World Wide Web
- Explain why computer technology is important for education
- Provide examples of how computers are changing the way we teach and learn

COMPUTERS PLAY AN ESSENTIAL ROLE IN HOW INDIVIDUALS WORK, LIVE, AND LEARN. Organizations of all sizes — even the smallest schools and businesses — rely on computers to help them operate more efficiently and effectively. At home, work, and school, computers help people do work faster, more accurately, and in some cases, in ways that previously were not possible. People use computers at home for education, entertainment, information management, and business purposes. They also use computers as tools to access information and to communicate with others around the world. In the classroom, computers and computer-related technologies can have a profound influence on the way teachers instruct and students learn. Even the activities that are part of your daily routine, typing a report, driving a car, paying for goods and services with a credit card, or using an ATM, can involve the use of computers.

As they have for a number of years, computers continue to influence the lives of most individuals. Today, teachers in K-12 schools are educating students who will spend all of their adult lives in the technology-rich twenty-first century. To help schools better educate students, the federal government, state governments, and school districts are spearheading massive funding efforts to equip classrooms with computers, connectivity to networks, and access to the Internet and the World Wide Web. Teachers in these classrooms must prepare themselves to utilize both current and emerging computer technologies.

The purpose of this book is to help you understand how computers work and how you can use computers and the Internet to gather, organize, and analyze information to make informed decisions. Chapter 1 introduces you to basic computer concepts, such as what a computer is, how it works, and how teachers and administrators integrate computers into K-12 education. As you read, you also will begin to understand the vocabulary used to describe computers and educational technology. While you are reading, remember that this chapter is an overview and that many of the terms and concepts that are introduced are presented in detail in later chapters.

What Is a Personal Computer?

WebInfo

For more information on Macintosh computers, visit the Teachers Discovering Computers Chapter 1 WebInfo page

(www.scsite.com/tdc/ch1/webinfo.htm) and click Macintosh.

A **personal computer**, or **PC**, is a computer designed for use by one person at a time. Many people associate the term personal computer or PC, with computers that use Microsoft Windows, which is a popular operating system used on many of today's computers. All personal computers, however, do not use Windows. Apple Macintosh computers, for example, which use a different operating system, **Mac OS**, still are a type of personal computer. Why the confusion?

In 1981, IBM Corporation released its first personal computer, the IBM Personal

Computer **[Figure 1-1]**. The IBM Personal Computer was an instant business success and quickly became known by its nickname — the PC. For marketing reasons, IBM allowed other companies to copy its computer design; therefore, many companies started making IBM-compatible computers. These computers were called IBM-compatible because they used software that was the same as or similar to the IBM PC software. All subsequent IBM computers and IBM-compatibles were called PCs.

Figure 1-1 The original IBM Personal Computer introduced in 1981.

Three years after the introduction of the first IBM PC, the Apple Computer Company introduced the **Macintosh computer [Figure 1-2]**. Macintosh computers could accomplish many of the same tasks as IBM PCs, but were very different. For one, the Macintosh computer used a pointing device called a mouse. Macintosh computers were incompatible with the IBM PC because they used different software than the IBM and IBM-compatible computers. As a result, a distinction developed between the terms Macintosh and PC, even though Macintosh computers are personal computers. This distinction and confusion between the two types of computers continues today.

Businesses, homes, and K-12 schools today use dozens of different models of Apple and IBM-compatible personal computers. To avoid confusion in this textbook, personal computers that use Microsoft Windows will be referred to as *PCs* and all Macintosh personal

Figure 1-2 Apple Computer Company introduced the Macintosh computer in 1984.

[a] Apple Macintosh (Mac)

[b] Dell (PC)

Figure 1-3 Figure 1-3a shows a typical Macintosh computer system and Figure 1-3b shows a typical PC system.

computers will be referred to as Macintosh computers **[Figure 1-3]**. When this book refers to the terms personal computer, desktop computer, or computer, the subject matter being discussed is applicable to Apple, IBM, and IBM-compatible computers. Most of the concepts and terms covered in this textbook are applicable to all types of personal computers.

Computer, Information, and Integration Literacy

Today, the vocabulary of computing is all around you. Before the advent of computers, memory was an individual's mental ability to recall previous experiences; storage was a place for out-of-season clothing; and communications was the act of exchanging opinions and information through writing, speaking, or sign language. In today's world, these words and countless others have taken on new meanings as part of the vocabulary used to describe computers and their uses.

When you hear the word, computer, initially you may think of computers used in schools to perform activities such as create flyers, memos, and letters; manage student rosters and calculate grades; or track library books. In the course of a day or week, however, you encounter many other computers. Your home, for instance, can contain a myriad of electronic devices, such as cordless telephones, VCRs, handheld video games, cameras, and stereo systems including small computers.

Computers help you with your banking when you use automatic teller machines (ATMs) to deposit or withdraw funds. When you buy groceries, a computer tracks your purchases and calculates the amount of money you owe; it even may generate coupons customized to your buying patterns.

Even your car is equipped with computers that run the electrical system, control the temperature, and run sophisticated anti-theft devices.

Experts anticipate that by the year 2010, all occupations will involve the use of computers on a daily basis **[Figure 1-4]**. As the world of computers advances, it is essential that you gain some level of **computer literacy**; that is, you must have a knowledge and understanding of computers and their uses.

Information literacy means knowing how to find, analyze, and use information. Information literacy is the ability to gather information from multiple sources, select relevant material, and organize it into a form that will allow the user to make decisions or take specific actions.

Students must learn to make informed decisions based on information obtained in all areas of their lives. For example, suppose you decide to move to a new city and need a place to live. You could find a home by driving around the city looking for a house or apartment within your price range that is close to school or work. As an information literate person, however, you might search for a home using the Internet, which is a global network of computers that contains information on a multitude of subjects. Using these resources to locate potential homes before you leave will make your drive through the city more efficient and focused.

How do computers relate to information literacy? They relate because, increasingly, information on housing, cars, and other products, as well as information on finances, school systems, travel, and weather, is accessible by computers. For example, with communications equipment, you can use a computer to connect to the Internet to access information on countless topics. Once you have accessed the desired information, computers can help you analyze and use that information.

While computer and information literacy are very important for educators, today's teachers also must use computers as a tool to facilitate learning. Teachers must be able to assess technology resources and plan classroom activities using available technologies. These skills are part of **integration literacy**, which is the ability to use computers and other technologies combined with a variety of teaching and learning strategies to enhance students' learning. Integration literacy means that teachers can determine how to match appropriate technology to learning objectives, goals, and outcomes.

Understanding how to integrate technology into classroom curriculum successfully relies on a solid foundation of computer and information literacy.

As an educator, computers will affect your work and your life every day — and will continue to do so in the future. Today, school administrators use computers to access and manage information and teachers use computers to enhance teaching and learning. The computer industry continually is developing new uses for computers and making improvements to existing technologies. Learning about computers and their applications will help you to function effectively in society and become a better facilitator of learning.

Figure 1-4 Computers are present in every aspect of daily living — in the workplace, at home, in the classroom, and for entertainment.

CHAPTER 1

WebInfo

For details on new opportunities in Educational Technology, visit the Teachers Discovering Computers Chapter 1 WebInfo page

(www.scsite.com/tdc/ch1/webinfo.htm)

and click Opportunities.

What Is a Computer and What Does It Do?

A **computer** is an electronic machine, operating under the control of instructions stored in its own memory, that can accept data (input), manipulate the data according to specified rules (process), produce results (output), and store the results for future use.

Data is a collection of unorganized facts, which can include words, numbers, images, and sounds. Computers manipulate and process data to create information. **Information** is data that is organized, has meaning, and is useful. Examples are reports, newsletters, a receipt, a picture, an invoice, or a check. In **Figure 1-5**, data is processed and manipulated to create a check.

Data entered into a computer is called **input**. The processed results are called **output**. Thus, a computer processes input to create output. A computer also can hold data and information for future use in an area called

storage. This cycle of input, process, output, and storage is called the **information processing cycle**.

A person who communicates with a computer or uses the information it generates is called a **user**.

The electric, electronic, and mechanical equipment that makes up a computer is called **hardware**. **Software** is the series of instructions that tells the hardware how to perform tasks. Without software, hardware is useless; hardware needs the instructions provided by software to process data into information.

The next section discusses various hardware components. Later in the chapter, categories of software are discussed.

The Components of a Computer

A computer consists of a variety of hardware components that work together with software

Figure 1-5 Data is processed into information. In this example, the company name, the date, the number of cameras, and cost per camera each represents data. These items are processed into information, which in this case is a check.

to perform calculations, organize data, and communicate with other computers.

These hardware components include input devices, output devices, a system unit, storage devices, and communications devices. **Figure 1-6** shows some common computer hardware components.

Input Devices

An **input device** allows a user to enter data and commands into the memory of a computer. Three commonly used input devices are the keyboard, the mouse, and a microphone.

A computer keyboard contains keys that allow you to type letters of the alphabet, numbers, spaces, punctuation marks, and

other symbols. A computer keyboard also contains special keys that allow you to perform specific functions on the computer.

A mouse is a small handheld device that contains at least one button. The mouse controls the movement of a symbol on the screen called a pointer. For example, moving the mouse across a flat surface allows you to move the pointer on the screen. You also can make choices and initiate processing on the computer by using a mouse.

A microphone allows you to speak to the computer in order to enter data and control the actions of the computer.

Figure 1-6 Common computer hardware components include a keyboard, mouse, microphone, system unit, disk drives, printer, monitor, speakers, and a modem.

CHAPTER 1

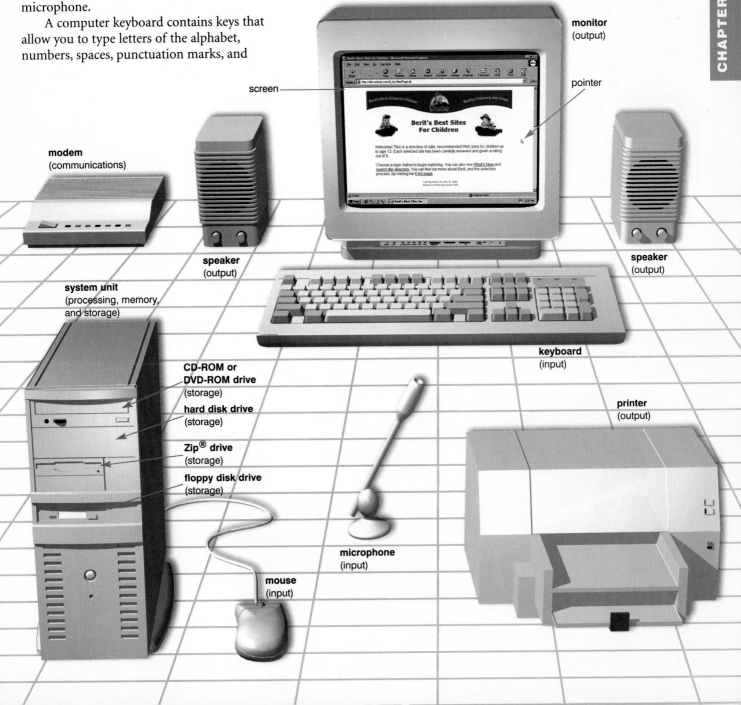

Output Devices

An **output device** is used to convey the information generated by a computer to a user. Three commonly used output devices are a printer, a monitor, and speakers.

A printer produces text and graphics, such as photographs, on paper or other hard-copy medium. A monitor, which looks like a television screen, is used to display text and graphics. Speakers allow you to hear music, voice, and other sounds generated by the computer.

System Unit

The **system unit** is a box-like case made from metal or plastic that houses the computer electronic circuitry. The circuitry in the system unit usually is part of or is connected to a circuit board called the motherboard.

Two main components on the mother-board are the central processing unit (CPU) and memory. The **central processing unit (CPU)**, also called a **processor**, is the electronic device that interprets and carries out the instructions that operate the computer.

Memory is a series of electronic elements that temporarily holds data and instructions while they are being processed by the CPU.

Both the processor and memory are chips. A chip is an electronic device that contains many microscopic pathways designed to carry electrical current. Chips, which usually are no bigger than one-half inch square, are

packaged so they can be connected to a motherboard or other circuit boards **[Figure 1-7]**.

Some computer components, such as the processor and memory, reside inside the system unit; that is, they are internal. Other components, such as the keyboard, mouse, microphone, monitor, and printer, are located outside the system unit. These devices are considered external. Any external device that attaches to the system unit is called a **peripheral device**.

Storage Devices

Storage holds data, information, and instructions for future use. Storage differs from memory, in that it can hold these items permanently, whereas memory holds these items only temporarily during processing operations. A **storage medium** (media is the plural) is the physical material used to store data, instructions, and information. One commonly used storage medium is a disk, which is a round, flat piece of plastic or metal on which data is encoded, or written.

A **storage device** is the mechanism used to record and retrieve data, information, and instructions to and from a storage medium. Storage devices often function as a source of input because they transfer items from storage into memory. Four common storage devices are a floppy disk drive, a hard disk drive, a CD-ROM drive, and a DVD-ROM drive. A disk drive is a device that reads from and may write onto a disk.

Figure 1-7 Computer chips are packaged so they may be connected to a circuit board.

A floppy disk consists of a thin, circular flexible disk enclosed in a plastic shell. A floppy disk stores data and information using magnetic patterns and can be inserted into and removed from a floppy disk drive **[Figure 1-8]**. A floppy disk drive reads from and writes to a floppy disk. A Zip® disk is a higher-capacity floppy disk that can store the equivalent of about 70 floppy disks.

A hard disk provides much greater storage capacity than a floppy disk. A hard disk usually consists of several circular disks on which data, information, and instructions are stored magnetically. Sealed in an airtight case, hard disks are often housed inside the system unit.

Another type of disk used to store data is a compact disc **[Figure 1-9]**. A compact disc (CD) stores data using microscopic pits created by a laser light. One type of compact disc is a CD-ROM. A newer type of compact disc is a DVD-ROM, which has a tremendous storage capacity — enough for a full-length movie. To use a DVD-ROM, you need a disk drive called a DVD-ROM drive.

Communications Devices

A **communications device** enables a computer to exchange data, information, and instructions with another computer. Communications devices transmit data and information over transmission media, such as cables, telephone lines, or other means used to establish a connection between two computers. A modem is a communications device that enables computers to communicate via telephone lines. Although modems are available as both internal and external devices, most are internal; that is, contained within the system unit.

Why Is a Computer So Powerful?

A computer's power derives from its capability of performing the **information processing cycle** (input, process, output, and storage) with speed, reliability, and accuracy; its capacity to store large amounts of data and information; and its capability of communicating with other computers.

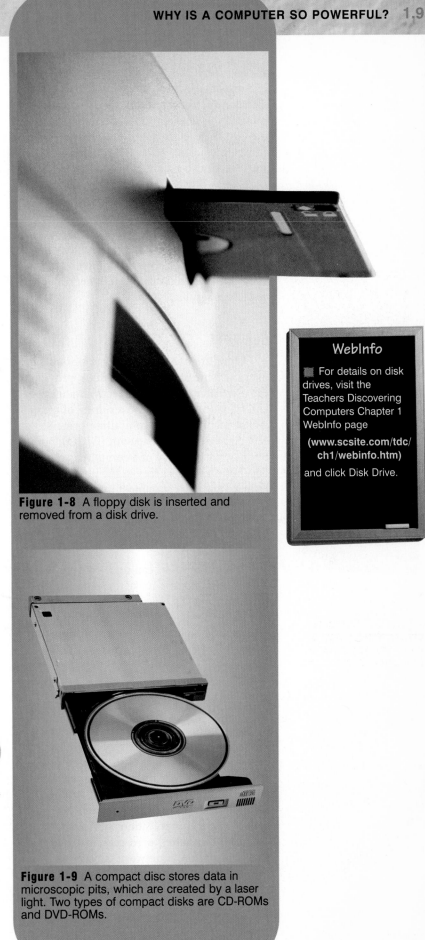

Figure 1-8 A floppy disk is inserted and removed from a disk drive.

WebInfo

For details on disk drives, visit the Teachers Discovering Computers Chapter 1 WebInfo page **(www.scsite.com/tdc/ ch1/webinfo.htm)** and click Disk Drive.

Figure 1-9 A compact disc stores data in microscopic pits, which are created by a laser light. Two types of compact disks are CD-ROMs and DVD-ROMs.

Speed

Inside the system unit, operations occur through electronic circuits. When data and information flow along these circuits, they travel at close to the speed of light. As a result, computers process billions of operations in a single second.

Reliability

The electronic components in modern computers are dependable because they have a low failure rate. The high reliability of their components enables computers to produce consistent results.

Accuracy

Computers can process large amounts of data and generate error-free results, provided the user enters the data correctly. If a user enters inaccurate data, the resulting output will be incorrect. This computing principle, called garbage in, garbage out (GIGO), points out that the accuracy of a computer's output depends on the accuracy of the input. In fact, human mistakes cause most instances of computer errors.

Storage

Many computers can store enormous amounts of data and make this data available for processing when needed. Using current storage methods, a computer can transfer data from storage to memory quickly, process the data, and then store the processed data for future use.

Communications

Most computers today can communicate with other computers. Computers with this capability can share any of the four information processing cycle operations, input, process, output, and storage, with another computer. For example, two computers connected by a communications device such as a modem can share stored data, instructions, and information. A **network** consists of two or more computers connected together via communications media and devices. As

mentioned, the most widely known network is the Internet, linking together millions of businesses, government installations, educational institutions, and individuals.

Home computer users increasingly are using the Internet to access other computers and to obtain or transfer information on practically any subject. Today, millions of people routinely send and receive messages using **electronic mail** (**e-mail**), which is the electronic exchange of messages to and from other computer users. The Internet also allows individuals to access a global network of computers to gather information, send e-mail and other types of messages, and obtain products and services **[Figure 1-10]**.

Computer Software

Software, also called a **computer program** or simply a **program**, is a series of instructions that tells the hardware of a computer what to do. For example, some instructions direct the computer to allow you to input data from the keyboard and store it in memory. Other instructions cause data stored in memory to be used in calculations such as adding a series of numbers to obtain a total. Some instructions compare two values stored in memory and direct the computer to perform alternative operations based on the results of the comparison; and some instructions direct the computer to print a report, display information on the monitor, draw a color graph on the monitor, or store information on a disk.

Before a computer can perform, or **execute**, a program, the instructions in the program must be placed, or loaded, into the memory of the computer. Usually, they are loaded into memory from storage. For example, a program might be loaded from the hard disk of a computer into memory for execution.

When you purchase a program, such as one that contains legal documents, you will receive one or more floppy disks, one or more CD-ROMs, or a single DVD-ROM on which the software is stored **[Figure 1-11]**. To use this software, you often must **install** the software on the computer's hard disk.

WebInfo

For more information on computer accuracy, visit the Teachers Discovering Computers Chapter 1 WebInfo page **(www.scsite.com/tdc/ch1/webinfo.htm)** and click GIGO.

Figure 1-10 The Internet is a worldwide collection of networks that links together millions of businesses, the government, educational institutions, and individuals.

Figure 1-11 When you buy software, you receive media such as floppy disks, CD-ROMs, or a DVD-ROM.

CHAPTER 1

Sometimes, a program can be loaded in memory directly from a floppy disk, CD-ROM, or DVD-ROM so you do not have to install it on a hard disk first.

When you buy a computer, it usually has some software already installed on its hard disk. Thus, you can use the computer as soon as you receive it.

Figure 1-12 illustrates the steps for running a computer program.

Software is the key to productive use of computers. With the correct software, a computer is an invaluable tool.

Software can be categorized into two types: system software and application software. The following sections describe these categories of software.

Figure 1-12 When you want to execute a program, the program instructions must be transferred from storage to memory. This figure shows the steps involved to execute a flight simulator program on a CD-ROM.

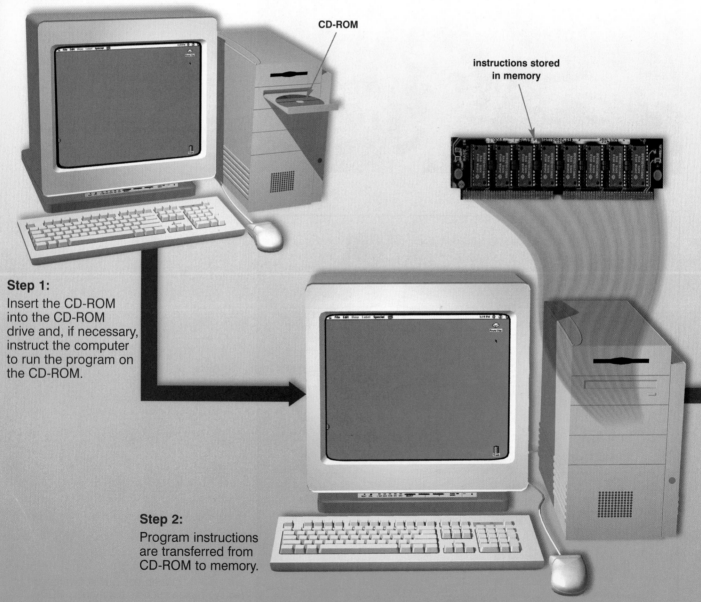

CD-ROM

instructions stored in memory

Step 1:
Insert the CD-ROM into the CD-ROM drive and, if necessary, instruct the computer to run the program on the CD-ROM.

Step 2:
Program instructions are transferred from CD-ROM to memory.

System Software

System software consists of programs that control the operations of a computer and its devices. System software also serves as the liaison between a user and the computer's hardware. Two types of system software are the operating system and utility programs.

Operating System   One of the more important programs on a computer, the **operating system** contains instructions that coordinate all of the activities of hardware devices. The operating system also contains instructions that allow you to run application software.

When you start a computer, the computer loads, or copies, the operating system into memory from the hard disk. The operating system remains in memory while the computer runs and allows you to communicate with the computer and other software. Many of today's PCs use a popular operating system called **Microsoft Windows [Figure 1-13a on the next page]**; many Macintosh computers

Step 3:
The program executes and the screen displays graphics that simulate flying an aircraft.

WebInfo

For more information on the Windows graphical user interface, visit the Teachers Discovering Computers Chapter 1 WebInfo page

(www.scsite.com/tdc/ch1/webinfo.htm)

and click GUI.

CHAPTER 1

use a unique operating system called the Macintosh operating system, or **Mac OS** [Figure 1-13b].

User Interface   All software has a **user interface**, which is the part of the software with which you interact. The user interface controls how you enter data and instructions. The user interface also controls how the computer presents information on the screen. Many of today's software programs use a **graphical user interface**, or **GUI** (pronounced *gooey*), which allows you to interact with the

software using visual items such as icons. An **icon** is a small image that represents a program, an instruction, or some other object. **Figure 1-14a** shows the Windows graphical user interface and **Figure 1-14b** shows the Mac OS graphical user interface.

Utility Programs   A **utility program** is a type of system software that performs a specific task, usually related to managing a computer, its devices, or its programs. An example of a utility program is an uninstaller, which removes a program previously installed on a

Figure 1-13 PCs use the Windows operating system, while Apple computers use the Macintosh operating system (Mac™ OS).

[a] PC operating system

[b] Apple Macintosh operating system

computer. Most operating systems include several utility programs for managing disk drives, printers, and other devices. You also can buy stand-alone utility programs to perform additional computer management functions.

Application Software

Application software consists of programs designed to perform specific tasks for users. When you think of the different ways people use computers in their careers or personal lives, you are thinking of examples of application software. Educational, business, and scientific computer programs are all examples of application software.

Popular application software includes word processing, spreadsheets, database, and presentation graphics. Word processing software allows you to create documents such as letters and reports. Spreadsheet software allows you to calculate numbers arranged in rows and columns. Teachers and schools use spreadsheet software for gradebooks, lesson plans, and other school-related tasks. Database

CHAPTER 1

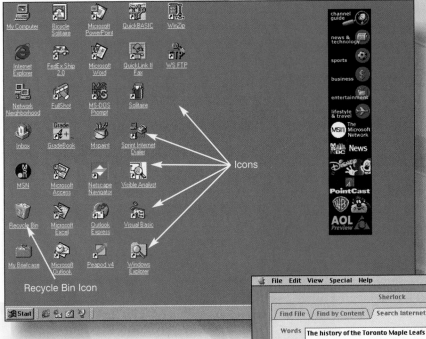

[a] Windows graphical user interface

Figure 1-14 Graphical user interfaces such as Microsoft Windows [Figure 1-14a] or Apple's Mac OS [Figure 1-14b], make computers easier to use. The small pictures, or symbols, on the screen are called icons. The icons represent programs, folders, files, or documents. The icons are selected by using a mouse or other pointing device.

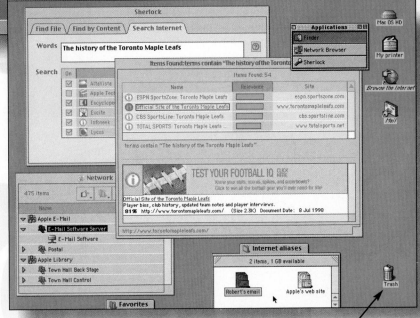

[b] Macintosh graphical user interface

Trash icon

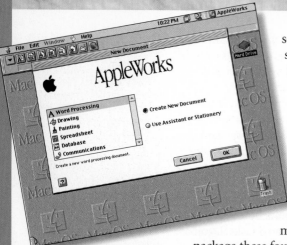

Figure 1-15
AppleWorks (previously called ClarisWorks) is a popular suite used by teachers and students primarily on Macintosh computers and includes word processing, spreadsheet, database, presentation graphics, and communications software.

WebInfo

For more information on shareware, freeware, and evaluation software, visit the Teachers Discovering Computers Chapter 1 WebInfo page **(www.scsite.com/tdc/ch1/webinfo.htm)** and click Shareware.

software allows you to store data in an organized fashion, as well as to retrieve, manipulate, and display that data in a meaningful form. With presentation graphics software, you can create electronic slides for use when giving classroom presentations.

Computer software manufacturers frequently package these four applications together as a single unit, called a software suite. A software suite contains individual software applications sold in the same box for a price that is significantly less than buying the applications separately [**Figure 1-15**].

Many other types of application software exist, thus enabling users to perform a variety of tasks. Some widely used software applications include: reference, education, and entertainment; desktop publishing; photo and video editing; multimedia authoring; network, communications, electronic mail, and Web browsers; accounting; school and student record keeping; and personal information management. Each of these applications is discussed in future chapters.

Packaged Software

Packaged software is designed to meet the needs of a variety of users, not just a single user, school, or business. Programs required for common educational, business, and personal applications are available for purchase off the shelf from software vendors or stores that sell computer products. You also can purchase packaged software on the Internet [**Figure 1-16**].

Custom Software   Sometimes a user or organization with unique software requirements cannot find packaged software that meets all of its needs. In this case, the user or organization can use **custom software**, which is a program developed at a user's request to perform specific functions. For example, a state Department of Education may design a custom gradebook and attendance program for use by its school districts.

Shareware and Freeware   **Shareware** is software distributed to a user free for a trial period. If you want to use a shareware program beyond the trial period, the person or company that developed the program expects you to send a small fee. When you send this small fee, the developer registers you to receive service assistance and updates. **Freeware** is software provided at no cost to a user by an individual or company. Thousands of inexpensive shareware and freeware programs are available for download from the Internet.

Software Development

People who write software programs are called **computer programmers** or

Figure 1-16 You can buy packaged software programs from computer stores, office equipment suppliers, retailers, and the Internet.

programmers. Programmers write the instructions necessary to direct the computer to process data into information. Programmers must place the correct instructions in the right sequence so the program performs the desired actions. Complex programs can require hundreds of thousands of program instructions. Many programmers use a programming language to write computer programs.

When writing complex programs for large businesses, programmers often follow a plan developed by a systems analyst. A **systems analyst** manages the development of a program, working with both the user and the programmer to determine and design the program.

Networks and the Internet

A **network** is a collection of computers and devices connected together via communications media and devices such as cables, telephone lines, modems, or other means. When you connect your computer to a network, you are online with the network.

Businesses and schools continue to network their computers so users can share **resources**, such as hardware devices, software programs, data, and information. Sharing resources saves time and money. For example, instead of purchasing one printer for every Macintosh and PC in a computer lab, schools can connect a single printer and all the computers using a local area network, or LAN. The network enables all of the computers within a lab to access the same printer.

Increasingly more schools and businesses are networking their computers. These networks can be relatively small or quite extensive. A local area network (LAN) is a network that connects computers in a limited geographic area, such as a school computer laboratory, business office, or group of adjacent buildings **[Figure 1-17]**. A wide area network (WAN) is a network that covers a large geographical area, such as one that connects the district offices of a statewide school system or the offices of a national corporation **[Figure 1-18]**.

Figure 1-17 A local area network (LAN) enables two separate computers to share the same printer.

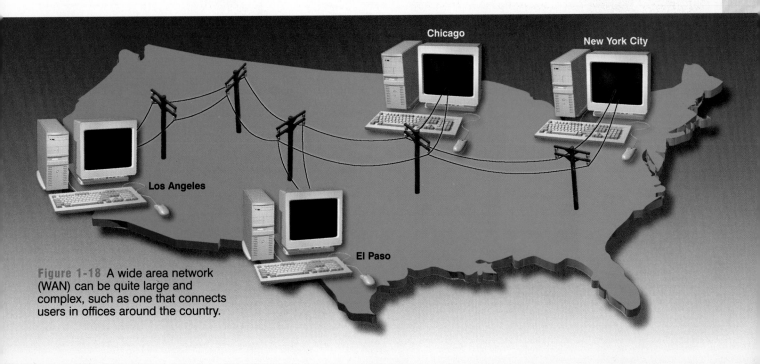

Chicago

New York City

Los Angeles

El Paso

Figure 1-18 A wide area network (WAN) can be quite large and complex, such as one that connects users in offices around the country.

CHAPTER 1

The world's largest network is the **Internet**, which is a worldwide collection of networks that links together millions of businesses, governments, educational institutions, and individuals using modems, telephone lines, and other communications devices and media. More than 90 million users around the world access the Internet for a variety of reasons [Figure 1-19]. For teachers, the Internet opens doors to a myriad of educational activities including the following:

- Sending messages to other connected users, including teachers and students

- Accessing a wealth of information, including curriculum and lesson plans, activities, and teacher's guides

- Joining an educational community to collaborate with teachers and students around the world

- To access sources of educational content such as encyclopedias, online museums, magazines, and other project collections

Most users connect to the Internet in one of two ways: through an Internet service provider or using an online service. An Internet service provider (ISP) is an organization that supplies connections to the Internet for a monthly fee. Like an ISP, an online service provides access to the Internet, but it also provides a variety of other specialized content and services such as financial data, hardware and software guides, news, weather, legal information, and numerous similar commodities. For this reason, the fees for using an online service usually are slightly higher than fees for using an ISP. Two popular online services are

Figure 1-19 Users access the Internet for a variety of reasons: to send messages to other connected users, to access a wealth of information, to shop for goods and services, to meet and converse with people around the world, and for entertainment.

America Online and The Microsoft Network (MSN).

One of the more popular parts of the Internet is the **World Wide Web** (**WWW**), also called the **Web**. The Web portion of the Internet consists of computer sites that contain billions of documents called Web pages. A Web page is a document that contains text, graphics, sound, animation, or video, and has built-in connections, or links, to other documents. Web pages are stored on computers throughout the world. A Web site is a collection of related Web pages that you can access electronically for information on thousands of topics. You access and view Web pages using a software program called a Web browser. The more popular Web browsers are Netscape Navigator and Microsoft Internet Explorer. **Figure 1-20** illustrates one method of connecting to the Web and displaying a Web page.

Figure 1-20 One method of connecting to the Web and displaying a Web page.

Step 1:
Use your modem to make a local telephone call to a commercial online service, such as The Microsoft Network (MSN).

Step 2:
The Web browser displays on your screen.

Step 3:
Enter the address of the Web site you wish to visit.

Web address

Step 4:
A Web page displays on your monitor.

Why Use Computer Technology in Education?

WebInfo

For more information on the International Society for Technology in Education (ISTE), visit the Teachers Discovering Computers Chapter 1 WebInfo page (www.scsite.com/tdc/ch1/webinfo.htm) and click ISTE.

In any society, educators have the ability to make an enormous positive contribution. Making such a contribution is a challenge and teachers must willingly embrace new teaching and learning opportunities. Educators are beginning to recognize that they must teach future leaders and citizens of our society the technologies that will be a major part of their future.

Technology is everywhere and integrated into every aspect of individuals' lives. Today's educators must provide students with the skills they will need to excel in a technology-rich society. Parents no longer are urging schools to incorporate technology into the classroom; they are insisting on it. When used appropriately, technology has the potential to enhance students' achievement and assist them in meeting learning objectives.

Technology can support learning in many ways. Using technology in the classroom, for example, can be motivational. Teachers have found that using modern computers or computer-related technologies can capture and hold students' attention. Computers also can provide many unique, effective, and powerful opportunities for teaching and learning. These opportunities include skill-building practice, real-world problem solving, interactive learning, discovery learning, and linking learners to instructional resources.

Computers also support communications beyond classroom walls, thus enabling schools and communities to provide an environment for cooperative learning, for development of high-order thinking skills, and for solving complex problems. As demonstrated by these examples, computers, when placed in the hands of teachers and students, can provide unique, effective, and powerful opportunities for many different types of instruction and learning.

Several leading national and international organizations support education and educators in the use of technology. One such organization is the **International Society for Technology in Education** (**ISTE**), which is a nonprofit group that promotes the appropriate use of technology to support and improve teaching and learning. ISTE, with over 6,000 members and a network of regional affiliates whose membership exceeds 40,000, has been instrumental in developing a set of fundamental technology concepts and skills for the **National Council for Accreditation of Teacher Education** (**NCATE**). NCATE is the official body for accrediting teacher education programs. As you work through this textbook and its related Web site, you will gain an understanding of the concepts and skills outlined in the ISTE standards **[Figure 1-21]**.

International Society for Technology in Education

ISTE Recommended Foundations in Technology for All Teachers

I.   Foundations. The ISTE Foundation Standards reflect professional studies in education that provide fundamental concepts and skills for applying information technology in educational settings. All candidates seeking initial certification or endorsements in teacher preparation programs should have opportunities to meet the educational technology foundations standards.

A. Basic Computer/Technology Operations and Concepts. Candidates will use computer systems to run software; to access, generate and manipulate data; and to publish results. They will also evaluate performance of hardware and software components of computer systems and apply basic troubleshooting strategies as needed.

  1. Operate a multimedia computer system with related peripheral devices to successfully install and use a variety of software packages.
  2. Use terminology related to computers and technology appropriately in written and oral communications.
  3. Describe and implement basic troubleshooting techniques for multimedia computer systems with related peripheral devices.
  4. Use imaging devices such as scanners, digital cameras, and/or video cameras with computer systems and software.
  5. Demonstrate knowledge of uses of computers and technology in business, industry, and society.

B. Personal and Professional Use of Technology. Candidates will apply tools for enhancing their own professional growth and productivity. They will use technology in communicating, collaborating, conducting research, and solving problems. In addition, they will plan and participate in activities that encourage lifelong learning and will promote equitable, ethical, and legal use of computer/technology resources.

  1. Use productivity tools for word processing, database management, and spreadsheet applications.
  2. Apply productivity tools for creating multimedia presentations.
  3. Use computer-based technologies including telecommunications to access information and enhance personal and professional productivity.
  4. Use computers to support problem solving, data collection, information management, communications, presentations, and decision making.
  5. Demonstrate awareness of resources for adaptive assistive devices for students with special needs.
  6. Demonstrate knowledge of equity, ethics, legal and human issues concerning the use of computers and technology.
  7. Identify computer and related technology resources for facilitating lifelong learning and emerging roles of the learner and the educator.
  8. Observe demonstrations or uses of broadcast instruction, audio/video conferencing, and other distant learning applications.

C. Application of Technology in Instruction. Candidates will apply computers and related technologies to support instruction in their grade level and subject areas. They must plan and deliver instructional units that integrate a variety of software, applications, and learning tools. Lessons developed must reflect effective grouping and assessment strategies for diverse populations.

  1. Explore, evaluate, and use computer/technology resources including applications, tools, educational software, and associated documentation.
  2. Describe current instructional principles, research, and appropriate assessment practices as related to the use of computers and technology resources in the curriculum.
  3. Design, deliver, and assess student learning activities that integrate computers/technology for a variety of student group strategies and for diverse student populations.
  4. Design student learning activities that foster equitable, ethical, and legal use of technology by students.
  5. Practice responsible, ethical and legal use of technology, information, and software resources.

Figure 1-21 Summary of the International Society for Technology in Education (ISTE) recommended educational technology foundations standards for all teachers.

An Example of How One School Uses Computers

To illustrate how a typical school might use computers and other computer-based technologies, this section takes you on a visual and narrative tour of a typical day at Ridgedale High School, home of the Fighting Tigers. Ridgedale High School is taking advantage of the Federal Communications Commissions **Education Rate**, or **E-Rate**, program, which is a government initiative designed to provide discounts to schools and libraries on all communications services, including network installation and Internet access.

All of the computers at Ridgedale High School are part of a local area network that allows teachers and students to share information with one another and with others around the world. First, Ridgedale networked the computers in all three of its computer labs. Two of these labs contain 30 PCs and the third lab contains 30 Macintosh computers. The school then installed at least two computers connected to the Internet in each classroom. Ridgedale High School also maintains a Web site to provide up-to-date information for students, teachers, and parents [Figure 1-22].

As the day starts, students are hurrying down the halls toward their classrooms, trying to reach them before the first period bell rings. For these students, the day is just beginning. For the administrators, teachers, and staff of Ridgedale High School, their day started much earlier.

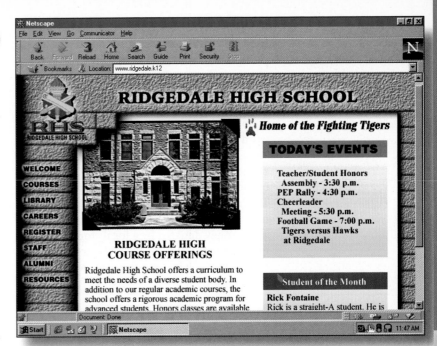

Figure 1-22 Ridgedale High School's Web site allows teachers, students, and parents to have direct access to extensive and up-to-date school-related information.

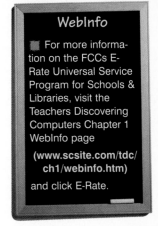

WebInfo

For more information on the FCCs E-Rate Universal Service Program for Schools & Libraries, visit the Teachers Discovering Computers Chapter 1 WebInfo page

(www.scsite.com/tdc/ch1/webinfo.htm)

and click E-Rate.

Figure 1-23 The superintendent shows her staff the final touches of the school district's Five-Year Technology Plan. She will use the charts and graphs to present the plan at the next school board meeting.

Superintendent

Early this morning, Dr. Helen Hartley, superintendent of Washington County Public School District, put the final touches on the district's Five-Year Technology Plan [Figure 1-23]. Dr. Hartley is very interested in the progress of the district's Technology Committee, whose members include administrators, teachers, media specialists, technology coordinators, and business partners from the community.

While pleased with the work the committee has accomplished thus far, the superintendent has found that, as more technology initiatives are launched, the committee's planning meetings are becoming too long

(and are hard to fit into the extremely busy schedules of the members). To help with this problem, Dr. Hartley asked the district Webmaster and network specialist, Bob Still, to develop an interactive template for the committee's Web page. Now, all the committee members can access the page with their password and work on their sections of the report.

Dr. Hartley has several other items to attend to and people to visit before heading to Ridgedale High School for the 3:30 P.M. Teacher/Student Honors Assembly. Ridgedale's new presentation system, which was purchased with money donated by a local store, would be up and running for the assembly and Dr. Hartley was looking forward to seeing the presentation.

Principal

Mr. Tony Hidalgo, the principal at Ridgedale High School, starts his day by completing several administrative tasks, which he accomplishes by sending several e-mail messages to teachers and staff. He sends an e-mail message to Ms. Jenny Marcus, Ridgedale's technology coordinator, to remind her to install and test the new presentation system before the Teacher/Student Honors Assembly. Mr. Hidalgo also sends an e-mail message to Dr. Hartley requesting an update on his latest budgeting request — $4,300 for new educational software for the math and science teachers and $1,150 for new computer software to run the school's security system **[Figure 1-24]**. He also updates Dr. Hartley on his plans to provide teachers with hands-on training on the school's four new desktop presentation systems.

Finally, before the students start to arrive, Mr. Hidalgo sends an e-mail message to all teachers and staff reminding them that the Teacher/Student Honors Assembly begins promptly at 3:30 P.M. Mr. Hidalgo finishes his early morning administrative tasks in time to walk the halls and greet students arriving for school.

School Secretary

When she first started at Ridgedale High School, Ms. Clara Rich, the school secretary, spent much of her day answering and routing incoming telephone calls. Last year, however, the school board approved the installation of a computerized telephone system that routes calls directly to the appropriate person. Ms. Rich's day now starts in a different manner, as she checks her e-mail and voice mail messages to determine if any teachers are going to be late or absent. If necessary, Ms. Rich accesses the school's teacher database to identify potential substitute teachers.

Next, Ms. Rich uses the school's inventory database to check the quantities of certain supplies and confirm delivery of recent purchases **[Figure 1-25]**. Ms. Rich reviews the customized certificates she has created for the Honors Assembly. She is sure the certificates, which she created using her desktop publishing program and the school's color printer, will impress students, teachers, and parents.

Figure 1-24 Mr. Hidalgo is pondering the wording of his important e-mail message to the Superintendent.

Figure 1-25 By using various databases, the school secretary easily can locate potential substitute teachers, manage equipment purchases, inventory, and supplies.

Technology Coordinator

Ms. Jenny Marcus, technology coordinator, arrives early to attend to several items and browse the Web to locate information on installing and testing the new presentation system. Jenny has several questions that she is unable to find answers for on the company's Web site. By accessing its technical assistance chat room, she is able to talk directly with a technician. The technician promptly answers most of her questions, but several deal with individual decisions that the principal needs to approve before the installation can be completed. Jenny calls and leaves a message on Mr. Hidalgo's voice mail asking if they can meet in her office at 10:00 A.M. to resolve these details **[Figure 1-26]**.

Cafeteria Manager

Ms. Kim Johnson, the cafeteria manager, starts working at 6:00 A.M. making sure the computerized purchasing and inventory system is ready to use for her morning training session. Ms. Johnson knows her staff is excited about the new system, which includes a database to track purchases, inventory, and student favorites, and keeps accurate records of students enrolled in the school lunch program **[Figure 1-27]**.

Media Specialist

Mr. Chris Finley, the media specialist, arrives at school very early because many students need access to media center resources before first period classes begin. While the students are searching the online catalog for materials, both in their own media center and other centers in the district, Mr. Finley completes his final preparations for Mrs. Acosta's tenth grade class **[Figure 1-28]**. Mr. Finley and Mrs. Acosta work together to create activities that help students learn history while sharpening their research skills.

After confirming that all of the center's computers are up and running, Mr. Finley starts gathering resources for Mrs. Acosta's students; including books, CD-ROMs, DVD-ROMs, and videotapes. He also plans to create bookmarks to related Internet sites later today, when no groups are scheduled to

Figure 1-26 The technology coordinator leaves a voice message for the principal after she has gathered technical information on the new presentation system from the World Wide Web.

Figure 1-27 The cafeteria manager is enthusiastic about her new purchasing and inventory system. Here, she shows her staff how the new computer program will save time and money.

Figure 1-28 After locating electronic resources, textbooks, and other materials in the school media center, the media specialist works with students on their research projects.

use the media center. Mr. Finley hopes to enter all the new materials into the computer-based catalog and circulation system by the end of the week. Students then can check out books and other center materials using the bar code scanner.

Teachers

Early the same day, Mrs. Ana Acosta uses presentation graphics software to put the finishing touches on the PowerPoint presentation she created to introduce her class to their research assignments **[Figure 1-29]**. Mrs. Acosta plans to start class by showing a video that Mr. Finley obtained through the state's interlibrary loan program. The video shows how history students across the country are using technology to create their own projects. She also created a research project overview using a software package called HyperStudio.

graphics, sounds, buttons, and animation on a variety of cards. Students click buttons to move through the HyperStudio cards and learn more about related concepts. Mrs. Acosta plans to have her students create their own HyperStudio stacks to document their projects.

Mr. Victor Reamy is in his classroom preparing for his advanced placement biology class. He is having his students work on their class projects in groups of three. Each group has access to the new laptop computers the school has received from an educational science improvement grant. The students' first computer-based assignment is to visit an excellent biology Web site he has found. Then, each group uses the laptops to run experiments, log their research findings, type their findings into a report, and create presentations for the class **[Figure 1-30]**.

Figure 1-30 Students create projects, experiments, research reports, and papers using a group laptop computer.

Figure 1-29 Using presentation graphics software, a teacher instructs her students on how to do their research assignment.

HyperStudio is a multimedia authoring program based on the concept of cards and stacks of linked cards. Creating a HyperStudio project involves entering text; importing or creating original backgrounds; and inserting

At the other end of school, two of the physical education instructors, Mrs. Rita Simpson and Mr. Gary Roberts, are installing and testing video equipment so they can tape gymnastics routines for personal and class evaluation of techniques. Mr. Roberts, who also is the girl's soccer coach, taped last week's soccer game and wants to show the soccer team how they can improve for the state finals competition next week.

The school recently purchased new software so students can evaluate their running techniques, cardiovascular activity, and nutritional needs. Today, many of

WebInfo

For more information on HyperStudio, visit the Teachers Discovering Computers Chapter 1 WebInfo page

(www.scsite.com/tdc/ ch1/webinfo.htm)

and click HyperStudio.

CHAPTER 1

Mr. Roberts's students will be entering the data into databases to keep track of their personal fitness [Figure 1-31].

Figure 1-31 Physical education students are entering personal information into a software program that will monitor and chart their personal fitness.

Parent

Using her home computer, Catherine Rosa accesses Ridgedale's Web site to check the time of the Teacher/Student Honors Assembly [Figure 1-32]. While she was looking up the time, Catherine notices a new graphic that reads, We Need Your Support! Curious, she clicks the graphic and links to a Web page requesting parent volunteers to chaperone the girl's soccer team on their trip to the state finals. Catherine sends an e-mail message to Mr. Roberts, stating that she gladly will chaperone on the trip. Catherine then quickly browses through the state Department of Education Web site to read the latest information released on Ridgedale High School before heading to the school for the assembly.

Figure 1-32 A parent of a Ridgedale High School student logs onto the school's Web site to find out the start time for a special event.

Community

Kevin Lee, a seventy-two-year-old, retired construction worker, starts his day by reading e-mail messages from sixteen-year-old Brian Johnson, a student at Ridgedale High School [Figure 1-33]. Kevin and Brian communicate online regularly as part of a program called Seniors Online. Seniors Online is a school program designed to match students with special needs with senior citizens, who serve as mentors. Each week Kevin, along with thirteen other senior citizens, visits the school to work with a student, one on one.

The students teach the senior citizens how to use a computer, send and receive e-mail messages, and browse the Web. Their mentors, in turn, help the students understand the challenges and opportunities they likely are going to experience after they graduate from high school. The interaction between the seniors and students with special needs is a remarkable success story.

The students send e-mail messages to their mentors to seek advice or just to share everyday news. For seniors such as Kevin, learning to use a computer is a great experience, but working directly with the students is the most rewarding experience of all.

Figure 1-33 A successful program at Ridgedale High School matches senior citizens with students with special needs. In this photo, a retired construction worker is checking his e-mail for a message from his new friend.

Summary of an Introduction to Using Computers in Education

This chapter presented a broad introduction to concepts and terminology related to computers and computers in education. You now have a basic understanding of what a computer is and how it processes data into information. You also have seen some examples of how computers are being used in K-12 schools and integrated into classroom settings. Reading and learning the concepts in this chapter will help you understand these topics as they are presented in more detail in future chapters.

www.scsite.com/tdc/ch1/brief.htm

InBrief

- InBrief
- KeyTerms
- AtTheMovies
- CheckPoint
- TeacherTime
- CyberClass
- EdIssues
- NetStuff

SPECIAL FEATURES

- TimeLine 2000
- Guide to WWW Sites
- Buyer's Guide 2000
- Educational Sites
- State/Federal Sites
- Chat
- News
- Home

Web Instructions: To display this page from the Web, launch your browser and enter the URL, www.scsite.com/tdc/ch1/brief.htm. Click the links for current and additional information. To listen to an audio version of this InBrief, click the Audio button below the title, InBrief, at the top of the page. To play the audio, RealPlayer must be installed on your computer (download by clicking here).

1. Personal Computers

A **personal computer**, or **PC**, is a computer designed for use by one person at a time. Macintosh computers and PCs are the two primary types of personal computers used in schools, businesses, and homes. Apple Computer Company manufactures Macintosh computers; several companies manufacture PCs.

2. Computer, Information, and Integration Literacy

As the world of computers advances, it is essential that you gain some level of **computer literacy**; that is, you should have a knowledge and understanding of computers and their uses.

Information literacy means knowing how to find, analyze, and use information. In addition, teachers must know how to integrate technology into K-12 curriculum, or integration literacy. **Integration literacy** is the ability to use computers and other technologies combined with a variety of teaching and learning strategies to enhance students' learning of required basic skills.

3. Computers, Data, Information, and Processing

A **computer** is an electronic machine, operating under the control of instructions stored in its own memory, that can accept data (input), manipulate the data according to specified rules (process), produce results (output), and store the results for future use. **Data** is a collection of unorganized facts, which can include words, numbers, pictures, and sounds. **Information** is data that is organized, has meaning, and is useful, such as a report, graphic, newsletter, invoice, check, video, or photograph. **Processing** is the activity of organizing data into information. Computers perform four basic operations: input, process, output, and storage. Computer professionals often refer to these four operations as the **information processing cycle** because a computer performs these actions repeatedly while the computer is running.

4. Computer Components

A computer consists of a variety of hardware components that work together with software to carry out various computer activities. These hardware components include input devices, output devices, a system unit, storage devices, and

communications devices. An **input device** allows a user to enter data and commands into the memory of a computer. An **output device** is used to convey the information generated by a computer to the user. The **system unit** is a box-like case made from metal or plastic that houses the computer circuitry. A **storage device** is the mechanism used to record and retrieve data, information, and instructions to and from a storage medium. A **communications device** enables a computer to exchange data and information with another computer.

5. Computer Power

A computer's power derives from its capability of performing the **information processing cycle** (input, process, output, storage) with speed, reliability, and accuracy; its capacity to store large amounts of data and information; and its capability of communicating with other computers.

6. Computer Software

Software, also called a **computer program** or simply a **program**, is a series of instructions that tells the hardware of a computer what to do. System software and application software are the two main categories of software. **System software** consists of programs that control the operations of a computer and its devices. **Application software** consists of programs designed to perform a specific task for a user.

7. Networks

A **network** is a collection of computers and devices connected together via communications media and devices such as

cables, telephone lines, modems, or other means. Businesses and schools <u>network</u> their computers so users can share **resources**, such as hardware devices, software programs, data, and information. Sharing resources saves time and money.

8. The Internet

The world's largest network is the **Internet**, which is a worldwide collection of networks that links together millions of businesses, the government, educational institutions, and individuals. Millions of people use the <u>Internet</u> to gain information, send messages, and obtain products or services. The **World Wide Web** (**WWW**), or **Web**, portion of the Internet consists of computer sites, called Web sites that can be accessed electronically for information on thousands of topics.

9. Computer Technology and Education

When used appropriately, technology has the potential to enhance students' achievement and assist them in meeting learning objectives. Networked computers allow communications <u>beyond classroom walls</u>, thus enabling schools and communities to provide an environment for cooperative learning, development of high-order thinking skills, and solving of complex problems. Computers can provide unique, effective, and powerful opportunities for many different types of instruction and learning. Several leading national and international organizations, including the **International Society for Technology in Education** (**ISTE**) support education and educators in the use of technology.

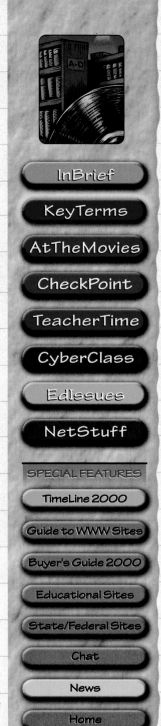

InBrief

KeyTerms

AtTheMovies

CheckPoint

TeacherTime

CyberClass

EdIssues

NetStuff

SPECIAL FEATURES

TimeLine 2000

Guide to WWW Sites

Buyer's Guide 2000

Educational Sites

State/Federal Sites

Chat

News

Home

KeyTerms

Web Instructions: To display this page from the Web, launch your browser and enter the URL, www.scsite.com/tdc/ch1/terms.htm. Scroll through the list of terms. Click a term to display its definition and a picture. Click KeyTerms on the left to redisplay the KeyTerms page. Click the TO WEB button for current and additional information about the term from the Web. To see animations, Shockwave and Flash Player must be installed on your computer (download by clicking <u>here</u>).

application software **[1.15]**
central processing unit (CPU) **[1.8]**
communications device **[1.9]**
computer **[1.6]**
computer literacy **[1.4]**
computer program **[1.10]**
computer programmers **[1.16]**
custom software **[1.16]**

data **[1.6]**

Education Rate (E-Rate) **[1.21]**
electronic mail (e-mail) **[1.10]**
execute **[1.10]**

freeware **[1.16]**

graphical user interface (GUI) **[1.14]**

hardware **[1.6]**
HyperStudio **[1.24]**

icon **[1.14]**
information **[1.6]**
information literacy **[1.4]**
information processing cycle **[1.6, 1.9]**
input **[1.6]**
input device **[1.7]**
install **[1.10]**
integration literacy **[1.5]**
Internet **[1.18]**
International Society for Technology in Education (ISTE) **[1.20]**

Macintosh computer **[1.2]**
Mac OS **[1.2, 1.14]**
memory **[1.8]**
Microsoft Windows **[1.13]**

National Council for Accreditation of Teacher Education (NCATE) **[1.20]**
network **[1.10, 1.17]**

operating system **[1.13]**
output **[1.6]**
output device **[1.8]**

packaged software **[1.16]**
peripheral device **[1.8]**
personal computer (PC) **[1.2]**
processor **[1.8]**
program **[1.10]**
programmers **[1.17]**

resources **[1.17]**
run **[1.12]**

shareware **[1.16]**
software **[1.6, 1.10]**
storage **[1.6]**
storage device **[1.8]**
storage medium **[1.8]**
system software **[1.13]**
system unit **[1.8]**
systems analyst **[1.17]**

user **[1.6]**
user interface **[1.14]**
utility program **[1.14]**

Web **[1.19]**
World Wide Web (WWW) **[1.19]**

www.scsite.com/tdc/ch1/movies.htm

AtTheMovies

WELCOME to VIDEO CLIPS from CNN

Web Instructions: To display this page from the Web, launch your browser and enter the URL, www.scsite.com/tdc/ch1/movies.htm. Click a picture to view a video. After watching the video, close the video window and then complete the exercise by answering the questions about the video. To view the videos, RealPlayer must be installed on your computer (download by clicking here).

InBrief

KeyTerms

AtTheMovies

CheckPoint

TeacherTime

CyberClass

EdIssues

NetStuff

SPECIAL FEATURES

TimeLine 2000

Guide to WWW Sites

Buyer's Guide 2000

Educational Sites

State/Federal Sites

Chat

News

Home

1. Computers and Education

Students' exposure to computers goes back to early childhood in many cases. Your students even may have used quite a few of the available hardware accessories and software features in their classroom courses. Now Intel is partnering with education to make it possible for students to know how computers and microprocessors work rather than just how to use them. Intel's "The Journey Inside" is bringing hands-on computer training to teachers to take back to their classrooms. According to the video, who is eligible for Intel's program? Explain how the program works. Do you see a use for it in any of your courses if you could adapt it to your students' age group?

2. Personal Computers for Students

When purchasing a personal computer, should you choose the cheapest option? According to the video, a "good college computer" should have 32 MB of memory, 4 GB of hard disk storage, a 233 or 266 MHz CPU, and a 56K modem. What do you think of this recommendation? If you were a student and had a choice, would you buy a desktop or a laptop computer? Why? In addition to the computer, what accessories might you purchase? Would you determine what accessories to buy based on the software you would need to run to complete your course of study in a class? As a teacher, have you actively integrated computers into your curriculum? Does your school require students to own their own computers? Does it provide Internet access?

3. Apple Computer

What is the name of Apple's newest personal computer? What does this name mean? List several ways in which this computer is different from other personal computers. The new computer does not come with a floppy disk drive (although you can purchase an external floppy disk drive). If you were to buy this computer, would you need an external floppy disk drive? Does this computer cost more or less than a comparable IBM personal computer?

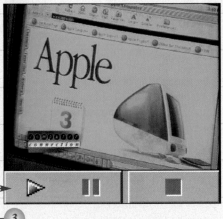

www.scsite.com/tdc/ch1/check.htm

CheckPoint

Web Instructions: To display this page from the Web, launch your browser and enter the URL, www.scsite.com/tdc/ch1/check.htm. Click a blank line for the answer. Click the links for current and additional information. To experience the animation and interactivity, Shockwave and Flash Player must be installed on your computer (download by clicking here).

InBrief

KeyTerms

AtTheMovies

CheckPoint

TeacherTime

CyberClass

EdIssues

NetStuff

SPECIAL FEATURES

TimeLine 2000

Guide to WWW Sites

Buyer's Guide 2000

Educational Sites

State/Federal Sites

Chat

News

Home

1. Label the Figure

Instructions: Identify each element of an information system by placing the correct label on the numbered lines.

7. _____
6. _____
5. _____
1. _____
2. _____
3. _____
4. _____

2. Matching

Instructions: Match each term from the column on the left with the best description from the column on the right.

____ 1. software
____ 2. input devices
____ 3. output devices
____ 4. storage device
____ 5. information

a. data that is organized has meaning and is useful, such as a report, newsletters, a receipt, a picture, an invoice or a check

b. allows a user to enter data and commands into the memory of a computer

c. examples include CD-ROM drives, floppy disk drives, and hard disk drives

d. conveys information generated by a computer to a user; examples include printers, monitors, and speakers

e. a series of instructions that tells the hardware how to perform tasks

3. Short Answer

Instructions: Write a brief answer to each of the following questions.

1. What is the difference between computer literacy, information literacy, and integration literacy? _____

2. What are the components of a Macintosh computer or PC? How does each component contribute to information processing? _____

3. What capabilities make a computer a powerful tool? Describe each. How does a computer's ability to communicate enhance a computer's power? _____

4. What is computer software? How is system software different from application software? _____

5. Briefly summarize why computers should be used in K-12 schools? _____

www.scsite.com/tdc/ch1/time.htm

TeacherTime

InBrief

KeyTerms

AtTheMovies

CheckPoint

TeacherTime

CyberClass

EdIssues

NetStuff

SPECIAL FEATURES

TimeLine 2000

Guide to WWW Sites

Buyer's Guide 2000

Educational Sites

State/Federal Sites

Chat

News

Home

Web Instructions: To display this page from the Web, launch your browser and enter the URL, www.scsite.com/tdc/ch1/time.htm. Click the links for current and additional information.

1. Computers dramatically have changed the way people access information. For example, avid newspaper readers now can turn to Web sites offered by their favorite newspapers and tabloids. Some of the more recognizable names include *The Boston Globe*, *Los Angeles Times*, *The Miami Herald*, *New York Times*, *USA TODAY*, and the *National Enquirer*; or you can search a Web site that will allow you to find your hometown newspaper online. How is the online rendering of a periodical different from the printed version? How are they similar? What are the advantages and disadvantages of each? Do you see a use for these online newspaper resources in your classroom? Why?

2. As the automobile led to the end of the horse and buggy, will the growth of the Internet lead to the demise of printed media? Probably not; in fact, booksellers are turning to the Internet to promote their products. Many online bookstores sell books, videos, and games. Some of these are Amazon.com, Barnes & Noble College Bookstores, and Books-A-Million, or you can visit a bookstore directory that links and describes dozens of top bookstore sites and book publishers. Visit a bookstore Web site and compare searching for a book online to finding a book in a traditional bookstore. Try looking for a particular title, a book by a certain author, and books on a specific subject. What are the advantages and disadvantages of shopping for a book online? How likely would you be to buy a book through a bookstore Web site? Why or why not?

www.scsite.com/tdc/ch1/time.htm

TeacherTime

InBrief

KeyTerms

AtTheMovies

CheckPoint

TeacherTime

CyberClass

EdIssues

NetStuff

SPECIAL FEATURES

TimeLine 2000

Guide to WWW Sites

Buyer's Guide 2000

Educational Sites

State/Federal Sites

Chat

News

Home

3. The health care industry had made significant breakthroughs during the past few years, and continued advances are expected in many health-related areas. For example, major prescription drug companies currently are developing/testing more than 1,000 new medicines. The Web offers an up-to-date source for information on virtually every area of health care. You can locate current information on diseases and other health aliments such as migraines. People can obtain an abundance of important information in a very short period of time, such as the latest treatment options. Visit the following medical site and research one specific area of health care that is of personal importance to you.

4. As new ways of learning in the classroom evolve, K-12 textbook publishers have begun to enhance their books with content-related Internet and World Wide Web products and services. From a teacher's standpoint, these textbook-related Web services have the potential to be important resources for teaching and learning. The information provided by publishers varies greatly from Web site to Web site and from publisher to publisher. Which of the following publishers do you think provide appropriate teacher resources, Allyn & Bacon, McGraw-Hill, Prentice-Hall, South-Western, or Steck-Vaughn? Why?

5. Are you or someone you know planning to tie the knot soon? With the Web, you can plan your wedding without ever leaving the comforts of home. This site gives information for men (tricks for getting a girl's ring size, a guide to bow ties for dummies) and women (gift ideas for bridesmaids and wedding-gown pictures). You even can bid on inexpensive honeymoon travel packages. Have you ever wondered why brides wear white or just how the wedding tradition came about? Sites on the Web can help you find the answer.

Married in White, you have chosen right
Married in Grey, you will go far away
Married in Black, you will wish yourself back
Married in Red, you will wish yourself dead
Married in Green, ashamed to be seen
Married in Blue, you will always be true
Married in Pearl, you will live in a whirl
Married in Yellow, ashamed of your fellow
Married in Brown, you will live in the town
Married in Pink, your spirit will sink

www.scsite.com/tdc/ch1/class.htm

CyberClass

InBrief

KeyTerms

AtTheMovies

CheckPoint

TeacherTime

CyberClass

EdIssues

NetStuff

SPECIAL FEATURES

TimeLine 2000

Guide to WWW Sites

Buyer's Guide 2000

Educational Sites

State/Federal Sites

Chat

News

Home

Web Instructions: To display this page from the Web, launch your browser and enter the URL, www.scsite.com/tdc/ch1/class.htm. To start Level I CyberClass, click a Level I link on this page or enter the URL, www.cyber-class.com. Click the Student button, click *Teachers Discovering Computers* in the list of titles, and then click the Enter a site button. To start Level II or III CyberClass (available only to those purchasers of a CyberClass floppy disk), place your CyberClass floppy disk in drive A, click Start on the taskbar, click Run on the Start menu, type a:connect in the Open text box, click the OK button, click the Enter CyberClass button, and then follow the instructions. If you are using a Macintosh, see your instructor.

1. Flash Cards (<u>Level I</u>, Level II, and Level III)

Click Flash Cards on the Main Menu of the CyberClass Web page. Click the plus sign before the Chapter 1 title. Click What Is a Personal Computer and answer all the cards in that section. Then, click Computer, Information, and Integration Literacy and answer the cards in that section. If you have less than 85% correct, continue to answer cards in other sections until you have more than 85% correct. All users: Answer as many more Flash Cards as you desire. Close the Electronic Flash Card window and the Flash Cards window by clicking the Close button in the upper-right corner of each window.

2. Practice Test (<u>Level I</u>, Level II, and Level III)

Click Testing on the Main Menu of the CyberClass Web page. Click the Select a book box arrow and then click Teachers Discovering Computers. Click the Select a test to take box arrow and then click the Chapter 1 title in the list. Click the Take Test button. If necessary, maximize the window. Take the practice test and then click the Submit Test button. Click the Display Study Guide button. Review the Study Guide. Scroll down and click the Return To CyberClass button. Click the Yes button to close the Study Guide window. If your score was less than 80%, click the Take another Test button to take another practice test. Continue taking tests until your score is greater than 80%. Then, click the Done button.

3. Web Guide (<u>Level I</u>, Level II, and Level III)

Click Web Guide on the Main Menu of the CyberClass Web page. When the Guide to World Wide Web Sites page displays, click Computers and Computing. Take a tour of the Computer Museum. In particular, review the history of computers. When you are finished, close the window and then prepare a brief report on your tour.

4. Assignments and Syllabus (Level II and Level III)

Click Assignments on the Main Menu of the CyberClass Web page. Ensure you are aware of all assignments and when they are due. Click Syllabus on the Main Menu of the CyberClass Web page. Verify you are up to date on all activities for the class.

5. CyberChallenge (Level II and Level III)

Click CyberChallenge on the Main Menu of the CyberClass Web page. Click the Select a book box arrow and then click Teachers Discovering Computers. Click the Select a board to play box arrow and then click Chapter 1 in the list. Click the Play CyberChallenge button. Maximize the CyberChallenge window. Play CyberChallenge until your score for a complete game is 500 points or more. Close the CyberChallenge window.

6. Hot Links (Level II and Level III)

Click Hot Links on the Main Menu of the CyberClass Web page. Review the sites in the Hot Links section and then write a brief report indicating which site you like best and why.

InBrief

KeyTerms

AtTheMovies

CheckPoint

TeacherTime

CyberClass

EdIssues

NetStuff

SPECIAL FEATURES

TimeLine 2000

Guide to WWW Sites

Buyer's Guide 2000

Educational Sites

State/Federal Sites

Chat

News

Home

EdIssues

Web Instructions: To display this page from the Web, launch your browser and enter the URL, www.scsite.com/tdc/ch1/issues.htm. Click the links for current and additional information.

1. School Violence

Numerous polls have shown that school safety is now the number-one concern of both parents and teachers. National leaders are calling the increase in school violence a national crisis. Do you agree that school violence should be the main concern of parents? One popular answer to the dramatic increase in the incidences of school violence is to build protective nets around the nation's schools; including fences, metal detectors, high-tech video surveillance, body searches, and armed guards. Do you agree with this solution? Other political and educational leaders stress that turning our schools into armed camps is not the solution. Instead, schools and communities must address and attempt to find solutions for the causes of school violence. Do you agree with this solution? If so, what are some of the causes of school violence? What would you suggest to reduce the incidences of school violence?

2. Possible Child Abuse

During your student internship, you notice that nine-year-old Juan Gonzales has bruises all over his arms and legs. He has been one of your more inquisitive students, but lately you have noticed that he has become moody, seems uninterested in class, and his grades are falling. The school nurse casually informs you that she has noticed that Juan has been losing weight the past couple of months. You suspect that Juan may be a victim of child abuse. You ask your supervising teacher what you should do and she says, "Oh! He is the son of a member of the school board; I am sure he is just growing and is at a clumsy age." You really like the school and would like to work there after graduation. Do you tell someone or do you ignore it? If so, who do you tell? What else could you do?

3. Technology Funding

Experts are estimating that approximately $30 billion from all sources, public and private, will be spent on computers, networks, software, and Internet access for America's public schools during the next five years. The federal government's goal is to have every K-12 classroom wired to the Internet in the near future. Proponents of this massive funding for K-12 technology argue that if American students are to be prepared properly for employment in a high-tech world, the nation's schools must be equipped with modern computers, networks, and high-speed Internet access. Opponents disagree with spending massive amounts of funds on technology for our schools. They argue that to date, technology has not led to increased test scores and is a waste of money. Opponents state that these funds could better be spent to reduce class size, attract better teachers, purchase up-to-date textbooks, and improve older schools. Can you see why both sides think they are right? Do you think schools should decrease funding for computers and increase funding in other important areas?

4. The Digital Divide

Surveys show that the number of American households that contain a multimedia computer and Internet access is growing at a incredible rate. The rate of growth, however, is disproportionate among economically well-off Americans and minorities, poor Americans, seniors, and those living in rural areas. Government leaders have called this disproportionate trend disturbing, others have called it an American tragedy. A 1998 report showed that 41 percent of white families own a personal computer, but only about 19 percent of black and Hispanic families do. As schools continue to install networks and modern computers, many experts are warning that this digital divide will seriously impact how some students learn in technology-enriched classrooms. Do you agree? If you agree, do you think educators should address this problem. Can you do anything to help reverse this potentially damaging trend? What about community, state, and federal political leaders — can or should they get involved?

www.scsite.com/tdc/ch1/net.htm

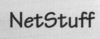

Web Instructions: To display this page from the Web, launch your browser and enter the URL, www.scsite.com/tdc/ch1/net.htm. To use the Using the Mouse lab or the Using the Keyboard lab from the Web, Shockwave and Flash Player must be installed on your computer (download by clicking here).

USING THE MOUSE LAB

1. Shelly Cashman Series Using the Mouse Lab

a. To start the Shelly Cashman Series Using the Mouse Lab from the World Wide Web, enter the URL, www.scsite.com/sclabs/menu.htm or display the NetStuff page (see instructions at the top of this page) and then click the USING THE MOUSE LAB button. If you are running the Interactive Labs from a CD-ROM, hard disk, or network, see your instructor for the startup procedures and then follow the instructions below.

b. When the Shelly Cashman Series IN THE LAB screen displays **[Figure 1-34]**, if necessary, maximize the window and then follow the instructions on the screen to start the Using the Mouse lab. When the Using the Mouse screen displays, if necessary, maximize the window, and then read the objectives.

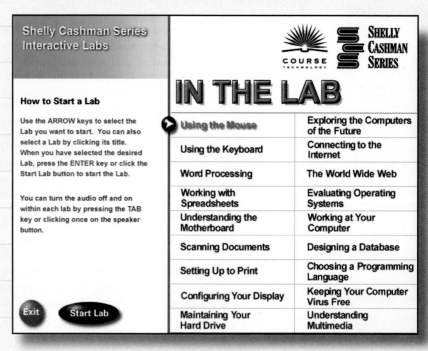

Figure 1-34

c. If assigned, follow the instructions on the screen to print the questions associated with the lab and hand in your answers to your instructor.

d. Follow the instructions on the screen to continue in the lab.

USING THE KEYBOARD LAB

2. Shelly Cashman Series Using the Keyboard Lab

Follow the appropriate instructions in NetStuff 1 above to start and use the Using the Keyboard lab, except click the USING THE KEYBOARD LAB button.

InBrief

KeyTerms

AtTheMovies

CheckPoint

TeacherTime

CyberClass

EdIssues

NetStuff

SPECIAL FEATURES

TimeLine 2000

Guide to WWW Sites

Buyer's Guide 2000

Educational Sites

State/Federal Sites

Chat

News

Home

www.scsite.com/tdc/ch1/net.htm

NetStuff

InBrief

KeyTerms

AtTheMovies

CheckPoint

TeacherTime

CyberClass

EdIssues

NetStuff

SPECIAL FEATURES

TimeLine 2000

Guide to WWW Sites

Buyer's Guide 2000

Educational Sites

State/Federal Sites

Chat

News

Home

IMPROVING MOUSE SKILLS

3. Improving Mouse Skills on a Macintosh or PC

Both Macintosh and PC operating systems include simple games, such as Jigsaw Puzzle or Solitaire, which are designed to help users learn mouse skills. To learn more about improving mouse skills, click the IMPROVING MOUSE SKILLS button and complete the exercise.

INTRODUCTION TO MACINTOSH COMPUTERS AND PCs

4. Introduction to Macintosh Computers and PCs

Many software packages provide an introductory tour that offers an overview of the program. These tours usually cover any new features and provide tips on using the software; some even use audio and video to enhance the introductory tour. To learn more about taking an introductory tour of your personal computer operating system, click the INTRODUCTION TO MACINTOSH COMPUTERS AND PCS button and complete the exercise.

INFORMATION LITERACY

5. Information Literacy

Today, most people believe that knowing how to use a computer is a basic skill necessary to function successfully in society. Information literacy is knowing how to find, analyze, and use information. Click the INFORMATION LITERACY button to increase your understanding of it and to complete this exercise.

WEB CHAT

6. Web Chat

Everyone who works with computers has experienced moments of enormous frustration — incomprehensible error messages, software glitches that produce unanticipated results, or even the entire system freezing up. Many people feel reactions to computer problems tend to be more extreme than reactions to problems with other tools they use. If you are viewing this page on the Web, click the accompanying picture to see how one individual handled a problem with his computer. Do computer problems make people angrier than problems with other tools? Why? How can people reduce their frustration when dealing with computer problems? Click the WEB CHAT button to enter a Web Chat discussion related to this topic.

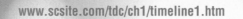

WEB INSTRUCTIONS: *To gain World Wide Web access to additional and up-to-date information regarding this special feature, launch your browser and enter the URL shown at the top of the page you want to view.*

Milestones in Computer History

Timeline 2000

1937

Dr. John V. Atanasoff and Clifford Berry design and build the first electronic digital computer. Their machine, the Atanasoff-Berry-Computer, or ABC, provides the foundation for advances in electronic digital computers.

1943

During World War II, British scientist Alan Turing designs the Colossus, an electronic computer created for the military to break German codes. The computer's existence is kept secret until the 1970s.

1946

Dr. John W. Mauchly and J. Presper Eckert, Jr. complete work on the first large-scale electronic, general-purpose digital computer. The ENIAC (Electronic Numerical Integrator And Computer) weighs thirty tons, contains 18,000 vacuum tubes, occupies a thirty-by-fifty-foot space, and consumes 160 kilowatts of power. The first time it is turned on, lights dim in an entire section of Philadelphia.

1945

Dr. John von Neumann writes a brilliant paper describing the stored program concept. His breakthrough idea, where memory holds both data and stored programs, lays the foundation for all digital computers that have since been built.

1.37

1951 The first commercially available
electronic digital computer, the UNIVAC I
(UNIVersal Automatic Computer), is introduced by
Remington Rand. Public awareness of computers
increases when the UNIVAC I, after analyzing only
5 percent of the popular vote, correctly predicts
that Dwight D. Eisenhower will win the
presidential election.

The IBM 305
RAMAC system
is the first to use
magnetic disk for
external storage.
The system provides
storage capacity
similar to magnetic
tape that previously
was used, but
offers the advantage
of semi-random
access capability.

1957

1947 William Shockley,
John Bardeen, and
Walter Brattain invent the transfer
resistance device, eventually called
the transistor. The transistor would
revolutionize computers, proving
much more reliable than
vacuum tubes.

1953 The IBM model
650 is one of the
first widely used computer systems.
Originally planning to produce only
50 machines, the system is so successful that eventually IBM manufactures more than 1,000. With the
IBM 700 series of machines, the
company will dominate the main-
frame market for the next decade.

FORTRAN
(FORmula TRANslation),
an efficient, easy-to-
use programming
language, is intro-
duced by John Backus.

1952

Dr. Grace Hopper
considers the
concept of reusable
software in her paper,
"The Education of a
Computer." The paper
describes how to
program a com-
puter with symbolic
notation instead
of the detailed
machine lan-
guage that had
been used.

Core memory,
developed in the
early 1950s, pro-
vides much larger
storage capacity
than vacuum
tube memory.

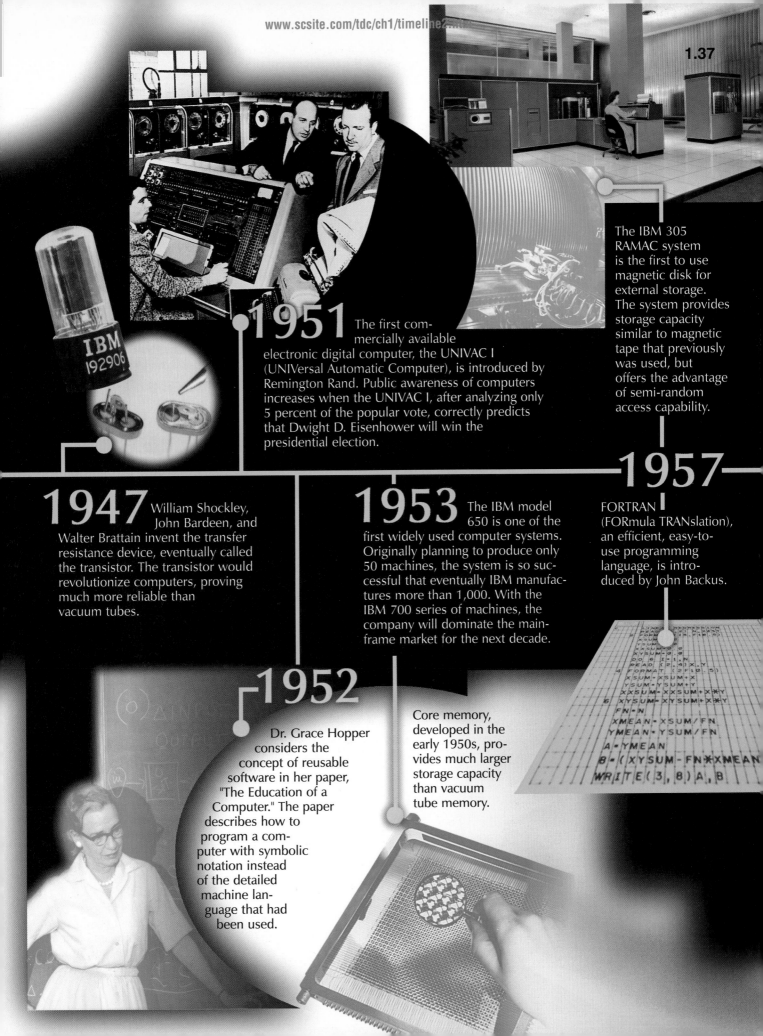

8

Dr. John Kemeny of Dartmouth leads the development of the BASIC programming language. BASIC will be widely used on personal computers.

Computers built with transistors mark the beginning of the second generation of computer hardware.

COBOL, a high-level business application language, is developed by a committee headed by Dr. Grace Hopper. COBOL uses English-like phrases and runs on most business computers, making it one of the more widely used programming languages.

Digital Equipment Corporation (DEC) introduces the first mini-computer, the PDP-8. The machine is used extensively as an interface for time-sharing systems.

958

1960

1965

1964

959

re than 200 pro-mming languages e been created.

M introduces two aller, desk-sized mputers: the IBM)1 for business and IBM 1602 for entists. The IBM)2 initially is called CADET, but IBM ps the name when mpus wags claim it n acronym for, Can't d, Doesn't Even Try.

The number of computers has grown to 18,000.

Third-generation computers, with their controlling circuitry stored on chips, are introduced. The IBM System/360 computer is the first family of compatible machines, merging science and business lines.

1968

Alan Shugart at IBM demonstrates the first regular use of an 8-inch floppy (magnetic storage) disk.

In a letter to the editor titled, "GO TO Statements Considered Harmful," Dr. Edsger Dijsktra introduces the concept of structured programming, developing standards for constructing computer programs.

Computer Science Corporation becomes the first software company listed on the New York Stock Exchange.

CSC STOCK PRICE
NYSE/COMPOSITE
Corrected Data for Dividends

DATE	PRICE	HIGH	LO
1/02/68	2.83	2.97	2
1/03/68	2.60	2.81	2
1/04/68	2.61	2.62	2
1/05/68			
1/08/68	2.54	2.60	
1/09/68	2.55	2.60	
1/10/68	2.46		
			30,100
			13,500
	2.51		23,400
	2.48		7,800
	2.49		18,800
	2.50		

IBM

Under pressure from the industry, IBM announces that some of its software will be priced separately from the computer hardware. This unbundling allows software firms to emerge in the industry.

The ARPANET network, a predecessor of the Internet, is established.

1969

Dr. Ted Hoff of Intel Corporation develops a microprocessor, or microprogrammable computer chip, the Intel 4004.

1971

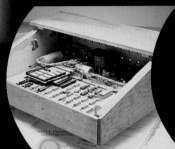

1970

Fourth-generation computers, built with chips that use LSI (large-scale integration) arrive. While the chips used in 1965 contained as many as 1,000 circuits, the LSI chip contains as many as 15,000.

1975

MITS, Inc. advertises the first microcomputer, the Altair. Named for the destination in an episode of *Star Trek*, the Altair is sold in kits for less than $400. Although initially it has no keyboard, no monitor, no permanent memory, and no software, 4,000 orders are taken within the first three months.

1976

Steve Wozniak and Steve Jobs build the first Apple computer. A subsequent version, the Apple II, is an immediate success. Adopted by elementary schools, high schools, and colleges, for many students the Apple II is their first contact with the world of computers.

Ethernet, the first local area network (LAN), is developed at Xerox PARC (Palo Alto Research Center) by Robert Metcalf. The LAN allows computers to communicate and share software, data, and peripherals. Initially designed to link minicomputers, Ethernet will be extended to personal computers.

1.40

VisiCalc, a spreadsheet program written by Bob Frankston and Dan Bricklin, is introduced. Originally written to run on Apple II computers, VisiCalc will be seen as the most important reason for the acceptance of personal computers in the business world.

The first public online information services, CompuServe and the Source, are founded.

The IBM PC is introduced, signaling IBM's entrance into the personal computer marketplace. The IBM PC quickly garners the largest share of the personal computer market and becomes the personal computer of choice in business.

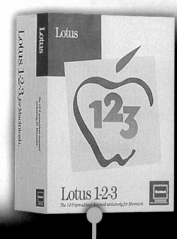

Lotus Development Corpor is founded. Its spreadsheet software, Lotus 1-2-3, whic combines spreadsheet, grap and database programs in c package, becomes the best-program for IBM personal computers.

1979

1981

1983

1980

1982

Alan Shugart presents the Winchester hard drive, revolutionizing storage for personal computers.

3,275,000 personal computers are sold, almost 3,000,000 more than in 1981.

Instead of choosing a person for its annual awarc *TIME* magazine names the computer Machine of the Year for 1982, acknowledg the impact of computers on society.

3,275,000

IBM offers Microsoft Corporation co-founder, Bill Gates, the opportunity to develop the operating system for the soon-to-be announced IBM personal computer. With the development of MS-DOS, Microsoft achieves tremendous growth and success.

Hayes introduces the 300 bps smart modem. The modem is an immediate success.

COMPAQ

Compaq, Inc. is founded to develop and market IBM-compatible PCs.

While working at CERN, Switzerland, Tim Berners-Lee invents an Internet-based hypermedia enterprise for information sharing. Berners-Lee will call this innovation the World Wide Web.

IBM introduces a personal computer, called the PC AT, that uses the Intel 80286 microprocessor.

Several personal computers utilizing the powerful Intel 80386 microprocessor are introduced. These machines perform processing that once only large systems could handle.

1987

1984

1989

Hewlett-Packard announces the first LaserJet printer for personal computers.

1988

Microsoft surpasses Lotus Development Corporation to become the world's top software vendor.

The International Society for Technology in Education (ISTE) is formed. The mission of ISTE is to help K-12 classroom teachers and administrators share effective methods for enhancing student learning with new classroom technologies. Today, ISTE has more than 6,000 members and a network of regional affiliates with a membership that exceeds 40,000.

Apple introduces the Macintosh computer, which incorporates a unique, easy-to-learn, graphical user interface.

1.42

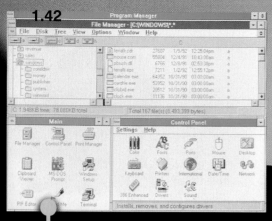

Microsoft releases Windows 3.1, the latest version of its Windows operating system. Windows 3.1 offers improvements such as TrueType fonts, multimedia capability, and object linking and embedding (OLE). In two months, 3,000,000 copies of Windows 3.1 are sold.

Several companies introduce computer systems using the Pentium® microprocessor from Intel. The Pentium® chip is the successor to the Intel 486 processor. It contains 3.1 million transistors and is capable of performing 112,000,000 instructions per second

Jim Clark and Marc Andreessen found Netscape and launch Netscape Navigator 1.0, a browser for the World Wide Web.

1992 — 1993 — 1994

AskERIC (Educational-Resources Information Center) starts up as a project of the ERIC Clearinghouse on Information and Technology at Syracuse University. Today, the federally funded AskERIC provides an extensive and searchable database of documents and resources; educators can send questions on any educational topic to AskERIC and receive a response within 48 hours.

The White House launches its Web page. The site includes an interactive citizens' handbook and White House history and tours.

Marc Andreessen creates a graphical Web browser called Mosaic. This success leads to the organization of Netscape Communications Corporation.

The Clinton Administration creates the Telecommunications and Information Infrastructure Assistance Program (TIIAP),which supplies grants to public institutions to fund the installation of advanced communications technologies. Over the next four years, TIIAP awards 378 grants of approximately $118 million in federal grant funds, which are matched by more than $180 million in nonfederal funds.

Good Morning

Welcome to the White House

N C S A
MOSAIC
X Window System • Microsoft Windows • Macintosh

Microsoft releases Windows 95, a major upgrade to its Windows operating system. Windows 95 consists of more than 10,000,000 lines of computer instructions developed by 300 person-years of effort. More than 50,000 individuals and companies test the software before it is released.

President Clinton launches a two-billion dollar, five-year, Technology Literacy Challenge — a program designed to catalyze and leverage state, local, and private sector efforts so American schools can provide students with the skills they need to succeed in the next century.

The Summer Olympics in Atlanta makes extensive use of computer technology, using an IBM network of 7,000 personal computers, 2,000 pagers and wireless devices, and 90 industrial-strength computers to share information with more than 150,000 athletes, coaches, journalists, and Olympics staff members, and millions of Web Users

1995

Sun Microsystems launches Java, an object-oriented programming language that allows users to write one application for a variety of computer platforms. Java becomes one of the hottest Internet technologies.

Two out of three employees in the United States have access to a personal computer, and one out of every three homes has a PC. Fifty million personal computers are sold worldwide and more than 250,000,000 are in use.

1996

President Clinton signs the Telecommunications Act of 1996 into law. The Act's Universal Service clause requires that schools and libraries are provided affordable telecommunication services.

An innovative technology called webtv combines television and the Internet by providing viewers with tools to navigate the Web.

1.44

Intel introduces the Pentium® II processor with 7.5 million transistors. The new processor, which incorporates MMX™ technology, processes video, audio, and graphics data more efficiently and supports applications such as movie-editing, gaming, and more.

The Federal Communications Commission approves the Education Rate (E-Rate) discount program to provide K-12 schools and all public libraries with discounted telecommunications services. FCC Chairman Hundt describes the E-Rate program as, "the biggest, single national effort to change education in K-12 classrooms in the history of our country."

DVD (Digital Video Disc), the next generation of optical disc storage technology, is introduced. DVD can store computer, audio, and video data in a single format, with the capability of producing near-studio quality. By year's end, 500,000 DVD players are shipped worldwide.

Microsoft ships Windows 98, an upgrade to Windows 95. Windows 98 offers improved Internet access, better system performance, and support for a new generation of hardware and software. In six months, more than 10,000,000 copies of Windows 98 are sold worldwide.

1997

1998

Deep Blue, an IBM supercomputer, defeats world chess champion Gary Kasparov in a six-game chess competition. Millions of people follow the 9-day-long rematch on IBM's Web site.

Apple and Microsoft sign a joint technology development agreement. Microsoft buys $150,000,000 of Apple stock.

E-commerce, or electronic commerce – the marketing of goods and services over the Internet – booms. Companies such as Dell, E*TRADE, and Amazon.com spur online shopping, allowing buyers to obtain everything from hardware and software to financial and travel services, insurance, automobiles, books, and more.

Fifty million users are connected to the Internet and World Wide Web.

More than 10,000,000 people take up telecommuting, the capability of working at home and communicating with an office via computer. More and more firms embrace telecommuting to help increase productivity, reduce absenteeism, and provide greater job satisfaction.

Apple Computer introduces the iMac, the latest version of its popular Macintosh computer. The iMac abandons such conventional features as a floppy disk drive but wins customers with its futuristic design, see-through case, and easy setup. Consumer demand outstrips Apple's production capabilities, and some vendors are forced to begin waiting lists.

Intel releases its Pentium III processor, which provides enhanced multimedia capabilities.

Microsoft introduces Office 2000, its premier productivity suite, offering new tools for users to create content and save it directly to a Web site without any file conversion or special steps.

1999

1998

The International Society for Technology in Education (ISTE) develops a set of fundamental technology standards for all teachers. The standards are adopted by the National Council for Accreditation of Teacher Education (NCATE).

2000

The Millennium Bug, Year 2000 Bug, or Y2K Bug has the potential to cause serious financial losses. On 1 January 2000, dates are read by non-compliant computers as 01/01/00, a year that is indistinguishable from 1900 or 3000, and some computer hardware and software will operate according to the wrong date. Y2K affects computer chips embedded in switchboards, automatic teller machines, video recorders, lifts, and security systems in the new millennium.

The Department of Justice's broad antitrust lawsuit asks that Microsoft offer Windows 98 without the Internet Explorer browser or that it bundle the competing Netscape Navigator browser with the operating system.

... our own ...

... cenaries to ...

... civil...

... selves by ...

... fare, is an und...

... ve been answered by ...

...tions to our British ...

...ration and settlem...

... dly interrupt...

... of America, in Gen...

... solemnly publish and ...

... that all political connect...

... Peace, contract Alli...

... a firm reliance ...

CHAPTER 2

Communications, Networks, the Internet, and the World Wide Web

Objectives

After completing this chapter, you will be able to:

- Define communications
- Identify the basic components of a communications system
- Describe how and why network computers are used in schools and school districts
- Explain how the Internet works
- Describe the World Wide Web portion of the Internet
- Specify how Web documents are linked to one another
- Explain the use of Web browser software

- Explain how to use a Web search tool to find information
- Identify several types of multimedia products available on the Web
- Explain how Internet services, such as e-mail, FTP, Telnet, newsgroups, and chat rooms work
- Describe the educational implications of the Internet and the World Wide Web
- Describe how to connect to the Internet and the World Wide Web

COMMUNICATIONS AND NETWORKS ARE THE FASTEST GROWING AREAS OF COMPUTER TECHNOLOGY. Adding tremendously to this growth is the popularity of the Internet and the World Wide Web (also called the Web or WWW), which is a service of the Internet that supports graphics and multimedia. Together, the Internet and the World Wide Web represent one of today's most exciting uses of networks. Already, these networks have changed the way people gather information, conduct research, shop, take classes, and collaborate on projects.

Businesses encourage you to browse their Web-based catalogs, send them e-mail for customer service requests, and buy their products online. The government publishes thousands of informational Web pages to provide individuals with materials such as legislative updates, tax forms, and e-mail addresses for members of Congress. Colleges even give *tours* of their campuses on the Web, accept applications online, and offer classes on the Internet.

Communications, networks, and the Internet also have dramatically changed the way teachers instruct and students learn. Today, communications media and networks are breaking down the walls of a classroom, allowing students to view the world beyond where they live and learn. The Internet is expanding beyond the covers of a textbook to include interactive, up-to-date, Web-based content. Never before has any technology opened so many opportunities for learning.

The future will bring even more exciting applications of these technologies. Federal and state governments, private businesses, and organizations are investing billions of dollars in Internet-related hardware and software for K-12 schools. As a result of this substantial investment, public schools are equipping their classrooms with multimedia computers and providing teachers and students with access to the Internet. This chapter discusses communications, networks, the Internet, and the World Wide Web; explains how they work; and reviews how teachers and administrators can use these technologies to communicate, obtain almost unlimited educational information, and enhance student learning.

What Is Communications?

Communications, sometimes called **telecommunications**, refers to the transmission of data and information between two or more computers using a communications channel such as standard telephone lines. The ability to communicate information instantly and accurately is changing the way people conduct business and interact with each other and the way students are learning. Electronic mail (e-mail), voice mail, fax (facsimile), telecommuting, online services, videoconferencing, Internet, and the World Wide Web are examples of applications that rely on communications technology **[Figure 2-1]**.

Figure 2-1 Telecommuting allows you to work from your home or some other location away from the classroom or school.

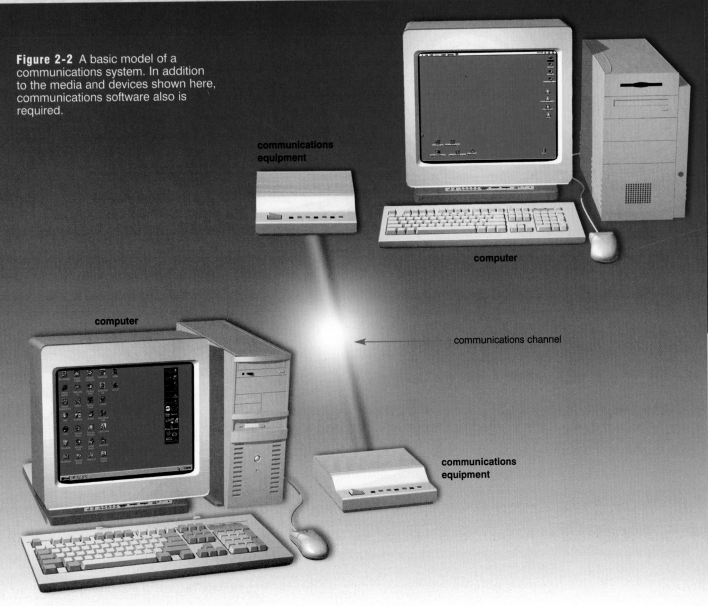

Figure 2-2 A basic model of a communications system. In addition to the media and devices shown here, communications software also is required.

CHAPTER 1

Communications Networks

A communications **network** is a collection of computers and other equipment organized to share data, information, hardware, and software. **Figure 2-2** shows a basic communications system that consists of the following equipment:

■ Two computers, one to send and one to receive data

■ Communications devices that send and receive data

■ A communications channel over which data is sent

This basic model also includes **communications software**, which is programs that manage the transmission of data between computers.

A **communications channel** is the path that data follows as the data is transmitted from the sending equipment to the receiving equipment in a communications system. Communications channels are made up of one or more **transmission media**, which is the physical materials or other means used to establish a communications channel. The most widely used transmission media are twisted-pair cables. Standard telephone lines in your home also use twisted-pair cables. **Twisted-pair cable** consists of pairs of plastic-coated copper wires twisted together **[Figure 2-3]**. Other examples of transmission media include coaxial cable, fiber-optic cable, microwave transmission, communications satellites, and wireless transmissions.

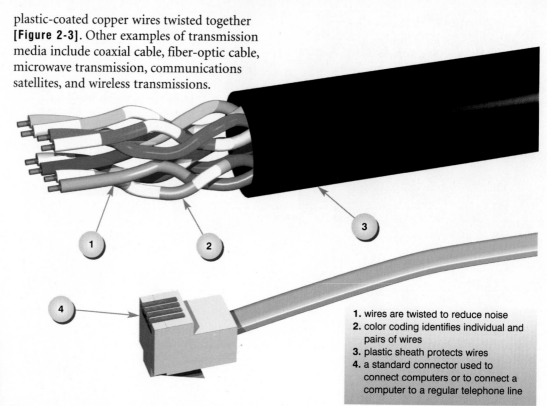

1. wires are twisted to reduce noise
2. color coding identifies individual and pairs of wires
3. plastic sheath protects wires
4. a standard connector used to connect computers or to connect a computer to a regular telephone line

Figure 2-3 Twisted-pair cables often are used to connect personal computers with one another or a personal computer to a regular telephone line. It is inexpensive and easily installed.

WebInfo

For details on modems, visit the Teachers Discovering Computers Chapter 2 WebInfo page **(www.scsite.com/tdc/ch2/webinfo.htm)** and click Modem.

Figure 2-4 A modem converts digital signals into analog signals and vice versa.

Digital signals are individual electrical pulses that a computer uses to represent data. Telephone equipment originally was designed to carry only voice transmission, which is comprised of a continuous electrical wave called an **analog signal**. For telephone lines to carry data, a communications device called a **modem** converts digital signals into analog signals.

The word modem comes from a combination of the words, *modulate*, to change a digital signal into sound or analog signal, and, *demodulate*, to convert an analog signal into a digital signal **[Figure 2-4]**. Computers at both the sending and receiving ends of this communications channel must have a modem for data transmission to occur. At the sending computer, a modem converts digital signals from a computer to analog signals for transmission over regular telephone lines. At the receiving computer, a modem converts analog signals back to digital signals.

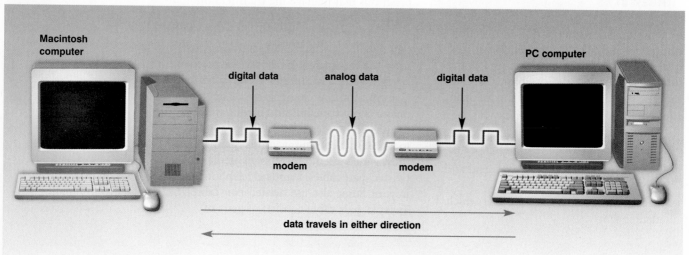

Macintosh computer

digital data   analog data   digital data

modem   modem

PC computer

data travels in either direction

An **external modem [Figure 2-5]** is a stand-alone, or separate, device that attaches to a computer with a cable and a telephone jack, or socket, with a standard telephone cord. An **internal modem [Figure 2-6]** is built on a circuit board that is installed inside a computer and attaches to a telephone socket using a standard telephone cord.

Most computers purchased for home use include internal modems that can transmit data at rates up to approximately 56,000 bits per second (56K modem). Today, many

external modem

Figure 2-5 An external modem is a stand-alone device that enables a computer to transmit information over a standard telephone line.

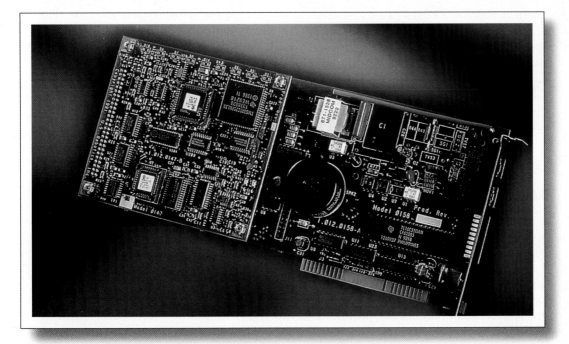

Figure 2-6 An internal modem performs the same functions as an external modem but is mounted inside the computer.

schools and businesses are making the transition from the use of modems to connectivity through networking. Networked computers contain a network interface card [**Figure 2-7**]. **Network interface cards** connect computers directly to a school or business network without using a modem. Networks are classified as either local area networks or wide area networks.

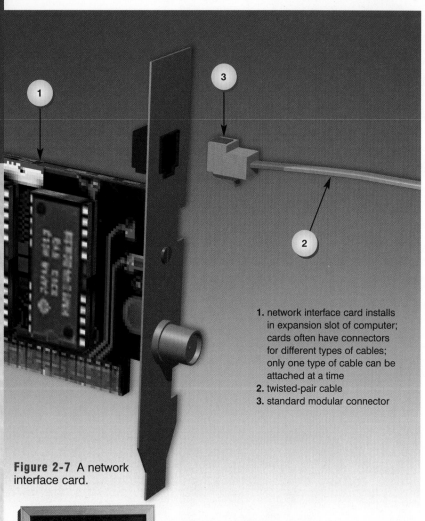

Figure 2-7 A network interface card.

1. network interface card installs in expansion slot of computer; cards often have connectors for different types of cables; only one type of cable can be attached at a time
2. twisted-pair cable
3. standard modular connector

Local Area Networks

A **local area network (LAN)** is a communications network that covers a limited geographical area such as a school, an office, a building, or a group of buildings. A LAN consists of a number of computers connected to a central computer, or server. A **server** manages the resources on a network and provides a

centralized storage area for software programs and data.

Wide Area Networks

A **wide area network (WAN)** covers a large geographical region (such as a city or school district) and uses regular telephone cables, digital lines, microwaves, wireless systems, satellites, or other combinations of communications channels. A WAN can consist of numerous local area networks organized into one larger network. For example, a large school district may establish a WAN that consists of dozens of local area networks, each LAN representing an individual school.

Networking the Classroom, School, and District

Due to extensive federal, state, and local funding, a majority of schools and school districts in the United States are networking their computers or upgrading older networks. Schools are installing high-speed networks for two reasons: to share hardware and software resources and to enable communications among and between schools and other organizations.

A school network server connects all of the computers located within a school. Recall that a *server* is a computer that can store large amounts of data and information and stores the network software that manages resources on the local area network. Typically, any teachers and students who use the network can access software and data on the server, although school or network administrators can limit access to specific records and software applications.

As an example of how a school district might network its computers, consider the Washington County Public School District, which consists of one high school (Ridgedale High School), two middle schools (Dresden and Fall Hills Middle Schools), and three elementary schools (Acorn, Johnson, and Martin Luther King Elementary Schools).

Martin Luther King Elementary School is a small school with fourteen classrooms. Each classroom has three modern Macintosh computers and a printer connected to a local area network [Figure 2-8]. Also connected to Martin Luther King's local area network is a computer lab that contains twenty-four networked Macintosh computers and four additional computers that are used by school administrators and staff. In total, Martin Luther King Elementary School's local area network consists of 70 Macintosh computers and numerous printers all connected to a central server [Figure 2-9].

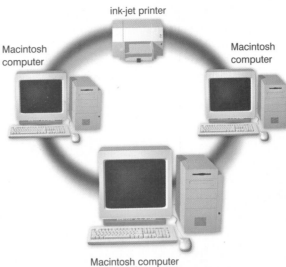

Figure 2-8 In each classroom, three Macintosh computers and a printer are connected to the school network.

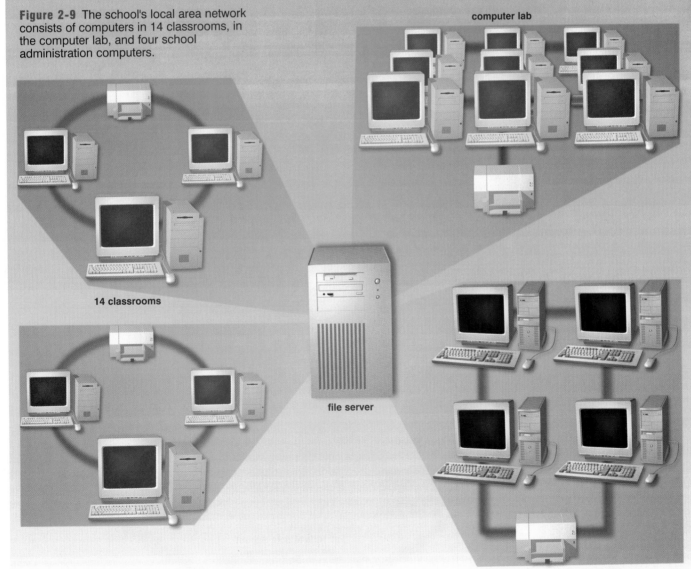

Figure 2-9 The school's local area network consists of computers in 14 classrooms, in the computer lab, and four school administration computers.

The local area network at Martin Luther King Elementary and the district's five other school LANs are connected to a large-capacity server and its associated equipment located at the Washington County Public School District's Central Office. Together, these networks form a wide area network that contains more than 600 networked Macintosh computers and PCs **[Figure 2-10]**.

Figure 2-10 The school district's wide area network consists of the local area networks of six member schools all connected to a file server located at the district's central office.

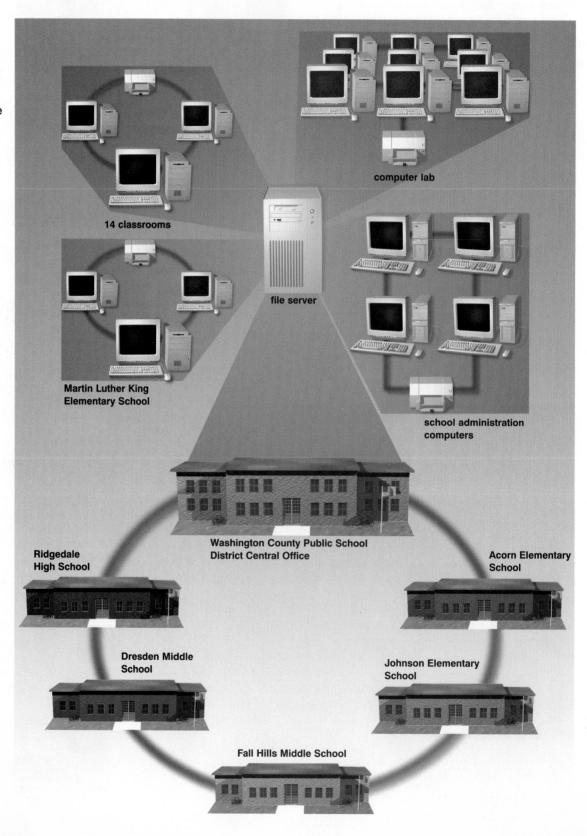

computer lab

file server

14 classrooms

Martin Luther King Elementary School

school administration computers

Washington County Public School District Central Office

Ridgedale High School

Acorn Elementary School

Dresden Middle School

Johnson Elementary School

Fall Hills Middle School

The Benefits of Computer Networks in Education

Just a few years ago, schools in America typically did not network their computers. Today, school districts are installing high-speed networks both at the school and district level. In doing so, K-12 schools obtain many important benefits.

One benefit of networking is that administrators, teachers, and students can share computer hardware, software, and data resources available throughout the school district. For example, administrators can maintain all student records and information securely at one central location. Teachers and administrative staff who have a need for access to student records can access various student information databases from just about any networked computer at any location.

By far, the most important benefit of networking school computers is that administrators, teachers, and students instantly can access the unlimited educational resources available on the Internet and communicate with other educators and students all over the world [Figure 2-11]. In brief, networking a school offers limitless possibilities for teaching and learning. Without question, the introduction of networks and the Internet into today's schools will have a dramatic impact on the next generation of teachers and students.

Figure 2-11 The Internet is useful as a tool to hold students' attention and even amaze them.

What Is the Internet?

You have learned that a network, such as the one installed at Martin Luther King Elementary School, is a collection of computers and devices connected via communications devices and media. Recall also that the world's largest network is the **Internet,** which is a worldwide collection of networks that link together millions of businesses, governments, educational institutions, and individuals using modems, telephone lines, and other communications devices and media [Figure 2-12]. Each of these networks provides resources and data that add to the abundance of goods, services, and information accessible via the Internet.

Networks that comprise the Internet, also called the **Net**, consist of federal, regional, local, and international networks. Public or private organizations own individual networks that constitute the Internet, no single organization owns or controls the Internet. Each organization on the Internet is responsible only for maintaining its own network.

WebInfo

For an overview of the Internet, visit the Teachers Discovering Computers Chapter 2 WebInfo page

(www.scsite.com/tdc/ch2/webinfo.htm)

and click Internet.

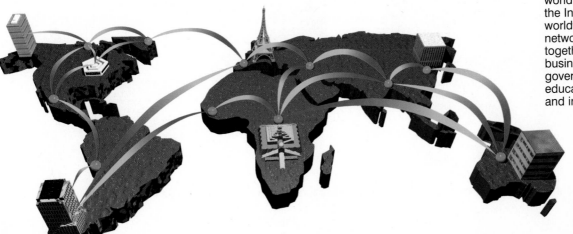

Figure 2-12 The world's largest network is the Internet, which is a worldwide collection of networks that link together millions of businesses, governments, educational institutions, and individuals.

Today, more than 90 million users around the world connect to the Internet for a variety of reasons. **Figure 2-13** illustrates sites on the Internet that represent some of the following uses.

■ To access a wealth of information, news, research, and educational material
■ To conduct business or complete banking and investing transactions
■ To access sources of entertainment and leisure, such as online games, magazines, and vacation planning guides
■ To shop for goods and services

■ To meet and converse with people around the world in discussion groups or chat rooms
■ To access other computers and exchange files
■ To send messages to or receive messages from other connected users

To allow you to perform these and other activities, the Internet provides a variety of services, such as the World Wide Web, electronic mail (e-mail), file transfer protocol (FTP), Telnet, newsgroups, mailing lists, and chat rooms. These services along with a

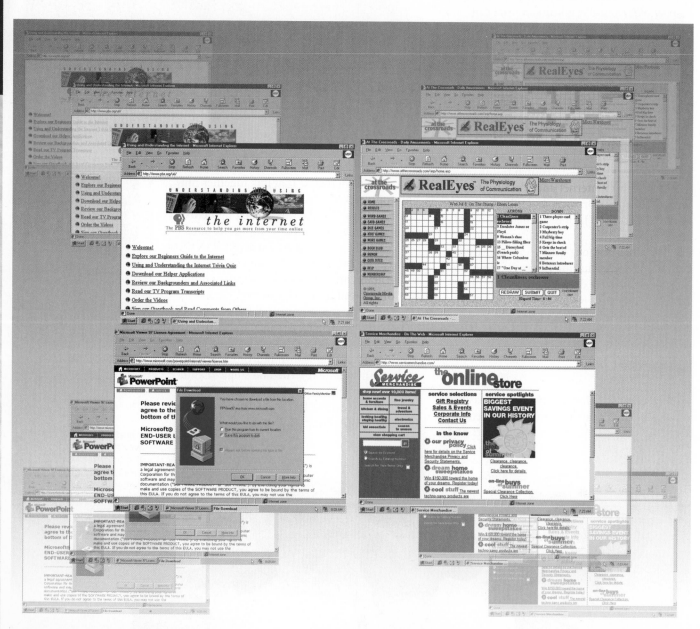

Figure 2-13 A number of reasons why more than 90 million users around the world connect to the Internet.

discussion of the history of the Internet and how the Internet works are explained in the following sections.

History of the Internet

Although the history of the Internet is relatively short, its growth has been explosive [Figure 2-14]. The Internet has it roots in a networking project of the U.S. Department of Defense's **Advanced Research Projects Agency (ARPA)**. ARPA's goal was to build a network that (1) would allow scientists at different locations to share information and collaborate on military and scientific projects and (2) could function even if part of the network were disabled or destroyed by a disaster such as a nuclear war. That network, called **ARPANET**, became functional in September 1969, effectively linking together scientific and academic researchers in the United States.

The original ARPANET was a wide area network consisting of four main computers, one each located at the University of California at Los Angeles, the Stanford Research Institute, the University of California at Santa Barbara, and the University of Utah. Each of these four computers served as the network's host. A **host** is the main computer in a network of computers connected by communications links. A host often stores and transfers data and messages on high-speed communications lines and provides network connections for additional computers.

As researchers and others realized the great benefit of using ARPANET's electronic mail to share information and notes, ARPANET underwent phenomenal growth. By 1984, ARPANET had more than 1,000 individual computers linked as hosts (today, more than 35 million host computers exist on the Internet).

To take further advantage of the high-speed communications offered by ARPANET,

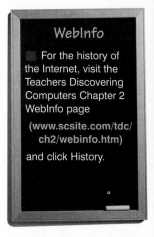

WebInfo

For the history of the Internet, visit the Teachers Discovering Computers Chapter 2 WebInfo page (www.scsite.com/tdc/ch2/webinfo.htm) and click History.

CHAPTER 2

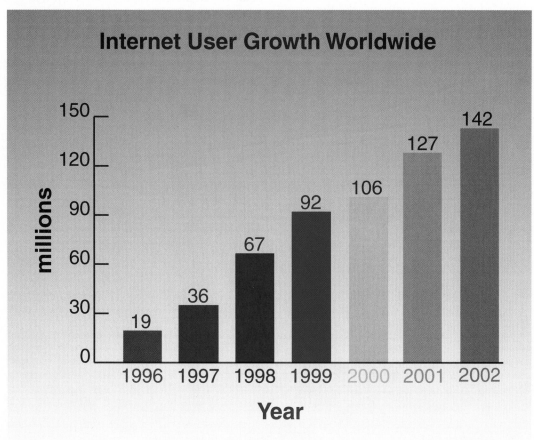

Internet User Growth Worldwide

source: eStats

Figure 2-14 The growth of the Internet has been explosive.

organizations decided to connect entire networks to ARPANET. In 1986, for example, the **National Science Foundation (NSF)** connected its huge network of five supercomputer centers, called **NSFnet,** to ARPANET. This configuration of complex networks and hosts became known as the Internet.

Because of its advanced technology, NSFnet served as the major backbone network of the Internet until 1995. A **backbone** is a high-speed network that connects regional and local networks to the Internet. Other computers then connect to these regional and local networks to access the Internet. A backbone thus handles the bulk of the communications activity, or **traffic**, on the Internet [Figure 2-15].

In 1995, NSFnet terminated its backbone network on the Internet to return to a research network. Today, a variety of corporations, commercial firms, and other companies operate the backbone networks that provide access to the Internet. These backbone networks, telephone companies, cable and satellite companies, educational institutions, and the government all contribute extensive resources to the Internet. As a result, the Internet is a truly collaborative entity.

Over the years, the total number of computers connected to the original network increased steadily and within the last few years, explosively. Today, experts estimate that tens of millions of computers distribute information over the Internet, including those at many K-12 schools. The percentage of American K-12 classrooms connected to the Internet is increasing dramatically.

How the Internet Works

Computers connected to the Internet work together to transfer data and information around the world. When a computer sends data over the Internet, the computer's software divides the data into small pieces, called **packets**. The data in a packet might be part of an e-mail message, a file, a document, or a request for a file. Each packet contains the

Figure 2-15 This map was prepared by the National Science Foundation and shows the major U.S. Internet connections.

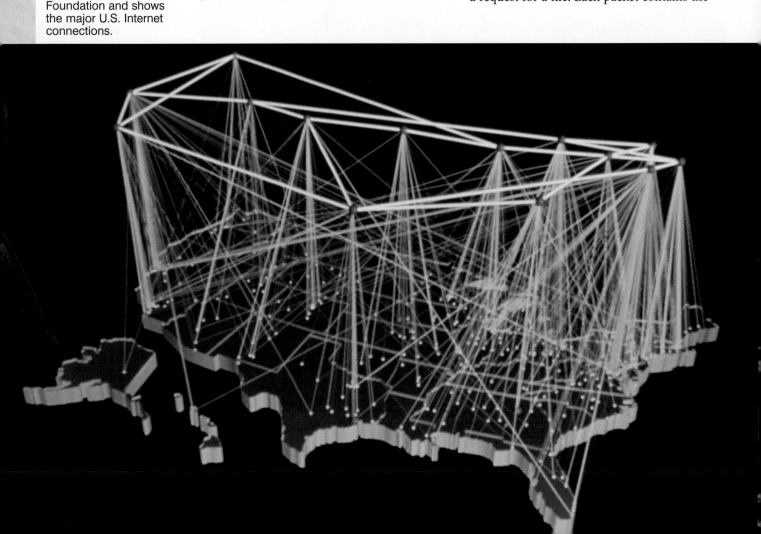

data, as well as the recipient (destination), origin (sender), and sequence information needed to reassemble the data at the destination. Packets travel along the fastest path available to the recipient's computer via hardware devices called **routers [Figure 2-16]**.

If the most direct path to the destination is overloaded or not operating, routers send the packets along an alternate path. Although each packet may arrive out of sequence, the destination computer uses the sequence information contained in each packet to reassemble the original message, file, document, or request. **Packet switching** is the technique of breaking a message into individual packets, sending the packets along the best route available, and reassembling the data.

For a technique such as packet switching to work, all of the devices on the network must follow certain standards or protocols. A **communications protocol** specifies the rules that define how devices connect to each other and transmit data over a network. The protocol used to define packet switching on the Internet is **transmission control protocol/Internet protocol (TCP/IP)**.

Data sent over the Internet travels over networks and communications lines owned and operated by many companies. You can connect to these networks in one of several ways. Some users connect to the Internet through an Internet service provider or an online service, using a modem to establish a connection by dialing a specific telephone number. Organizations such as schools and businesses often provide Internet access for students and employees by connecting their own network to an Internet service provider. Some school districts and states also provide Internet services for teachers and administrators so they can access the Internet from their homes.

Internet Service Providers versus Online Services

An **Internet service provider (ISP)** is an organization that has a permanent connection to the Internet and provides temporary connections to individuals and companies for a fee. The most common ISP fee arrangement is

WebInfo

For a list of Internet Service Providers, visit the Teachers Discovering Computers Chapter 2 WebInfo page

(www.scsite.com/tdc/ ch2/webinfo.htm)

and click ISP.

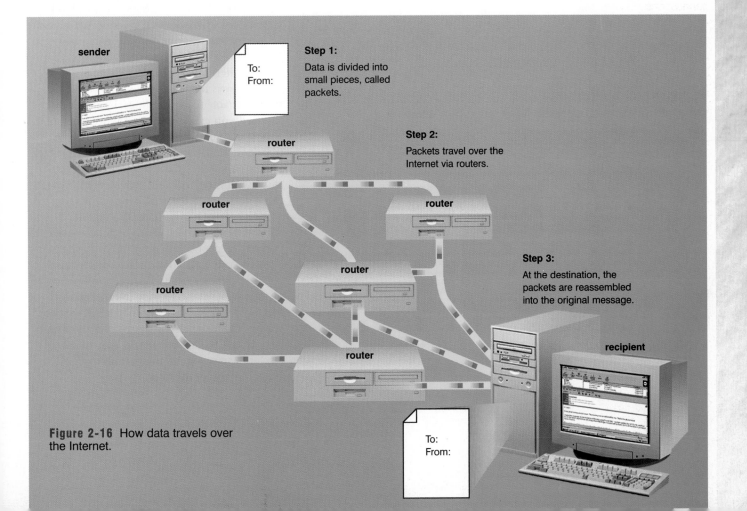

Step 1:
Data is divided into small pieces, called packets.

Step 2:
Packets travel over the Internet via routers.

Step 3:
At the destination, the packets are reassembled into the original message.

sender

router

router

router

router

router

router

router

recipient

To:
From:

To:
From:

Figure 2-16 How data travels over the Internet.

a fixed amount usually about $20 per month for an individual account. For this amount, most ISPs allow users unlimited Internet access.

Two types of ISPs exist: local and national. A **local ISP** usually provides one or more telephone numbers limited to a small geographic area. A **national ISP** is a larger business that provides local telephone numbers in most major cities and towns nationwide. Because of their size, national ISPs offer more services and generally have a larger technical support staff than local ISPs. The most important consideration when selecting an ISP is to be sure that it provides a local telephone number for Internet access, so you can avoid paying long-distance charges for the time you are connected to the Internet.

Like an ISP, an **online service** provides access to the Internet, but such online services also have members-only features that offer a variety of special content and services **[Figure 2-17]**. Typical content and services include news, weather, educational information, financial information, hardware and software guides, games, and travel information. For this reason, the fees for using an online service usually are slightly higher than fees for an ISP. The most popular online services are America Online (AOL) and The Microsoft Network (MSN).

Connecting to the Internet

When connecting from home or from the road while traveling, individuals typically use dial-up access to connect to the Internet. With **dial-up access**, you use your computer and a modem to dial into an ISP or online service over regular telephone lines. The computer at the receiving end, whether at an ISP or online service, also uses a modem. Dial-up access provides an easy way for mobile and home users to connect to the Internet to check e-mail, read the news, and access other information. Because dial-up access uses standard telephone lines, the speed of the connection is limited.

Newer technologies such as Integrated Services Digital Network (ISDN), cable modems, and digital subscriber line (DSL) offer an alternative to dial-up access over regular telephone lines and provide users with higher-speed Internet connections. Unfortunately, ISDN, cable modem support, and DSL are not available in all areas. **Integrated Services Digital Network** (**ISDN**) is a worldwide digital communications network. ISDN lines are almost five times faster than a modem on a standard telephone line. Disadvantages of ISDN are that it requires a separate telephone line in your home and can be complicated to configure.

An alternative is to use a **cable modem**, which allows for high-speed Internet access through cable television lines. Using a cable modem, you can connect to the Internet at speeds of 100 to 1,000 times faster than telephone modems. Increasingly more U.S. cable television networks are developing partnerships with Internet cable providers to provide these high-speed Internet connections.

Another option is to install a **digital subscriber line (DSL)**, which became available to businesses, schools, and home users during mid-1998 and uses data communications technology. Depending on the level of services requested by the user, DSL can provide Internet access speeds up to 25 times faster than a 56K modem. Having a DSL digital connection will allow business, school, and home users to take full advantage of the current and future multimedia enhancements of the Internet.

Figure 2-17 American Online is a popular online service that provides a multitude of services to millions of users.

The Internet Backbone

The inner structure of the Internet works much like a transportation system. Just as highways connect major cities and carry the bulk of the automotive traffic across the country, the main communications lines that have the heaviest amount of traffic (data packets) on the Internet are collectively referred to as the **Internet backbone**. In the United States, the communications lines that make up the Internet backbone intersect at several different points. National ISPs use dedicated lines to connect directly to the Internet. Smaller, regional networks lease lines from local telephone companies to connect to national networks. These smaller, slower speed networks extend out from the backbone into regions and local communities like roads and streets. **Figure 2-18** illustrates how all of the components of the Internet work together to transfer data over the Internet to and from your computer.

Figure 2-18 How data might travel the Internet.

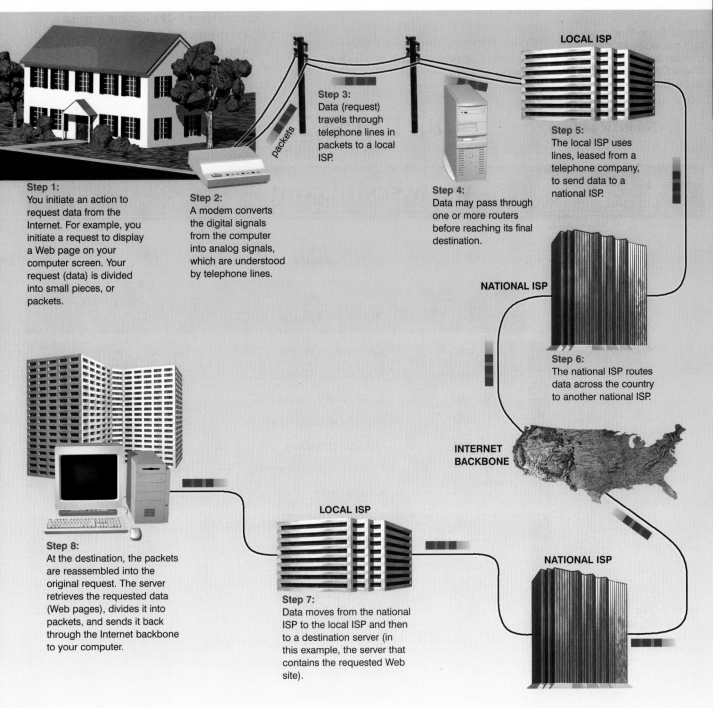

Step 1:
You initiate an action to request data from the Internet. For example, you initiate a request to display a Web page on your computer screen. Your request (data) is divided into small pieces, or packets.

Step 2:
A modem converts the digital signals from the computer into analog signals, which are understood by telephone lines.

Step 3:
Data (request) travels through telephone lines in packets to a local ISP.

LOCAL ISP

Step 4:
Data may pass through one or more routers before reaching its final destination.

Step 5:
The local ISP uses lines, leased from a telephone company, to send data to a national ISP.

NATIONAL ISP

Step 6:
The national ISP routes data across the country to another national ISP.

INTERNET BACKBONE

Step 8:
At the destination, the packets are reassembled into the original request. The server retrieves the requested data (Web pages), divides it into packets, and sends it back through the Internet backbone to your computer.

LOCAL ISP

Step 7:
Data moves from the national ISP to the local ISP and then to a destination server (in this example, the server that contains the requested Web site).

NATIONAL ISP

CHAPTER 2

Internet Addresses

The Internet relies on an addressing system much like to that of the postal system to send data to a computer at a specific destination. Each computer's location on the Internet has a specific numeric address consisting of four groups of numbers. Because these all-numeric computer addresses are difficult to remember and use, the Internet supports the use of text-based names that represents the numeric address. The text version of a computer address is called a **domain name**. **Figure 2-19** details both the numeric and the domain name of the Shelly Cashman Series Web site. The components of a domain name are separated by periods, each of which is referred to as a dot.

For domestic Web sites, the rightmost portion of the domain name contains a domain type abbreviation that identifies the type of organization that maintains the Web site. The rightmost portion of a university Web site, for example, would be .edu, which denotes it as a site operated by an educational institution. The domain names for some K-12 school sites include the abbreviation, .k12, followed by the abbreviation for the school's state. For international Web sites, the domain name also includes a country code, such as *.us* for the United States and .uk for the United Kingdom. **Figure 2-20a** lists the original domain type abbreviations and several recent additions. **Figure 2-20b** lists several country code abbreviations.

Figure 2-19 The numeric address and domain name for the Shelly Cashman Series® Instructional Web site.

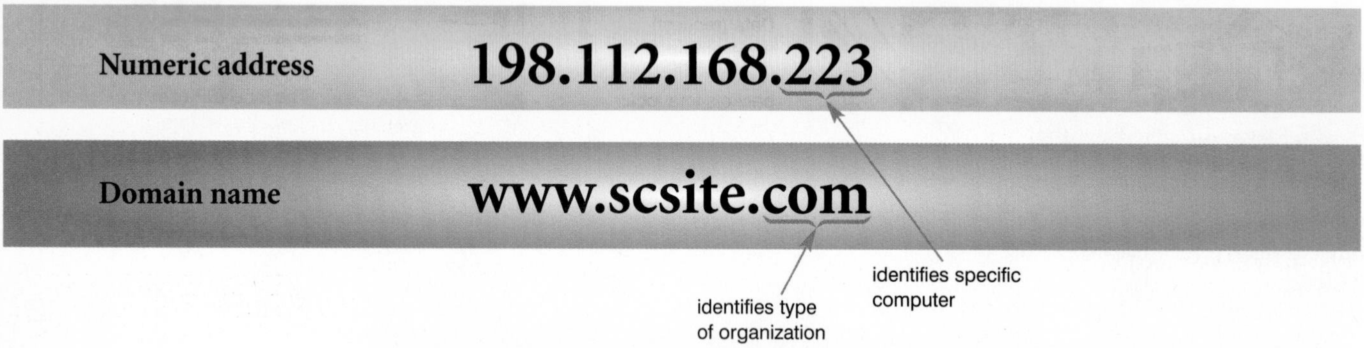

Numeric address	198.112.168.223

Domain name	www.scsite.com

identifies type of organization

identifies specific computer

Domain Abbreviations

	Domain Abbreviations	Type of Organization
Original	com	Commercial organizations, businesses, and companies
	edu	Educational institutions
	gov	Government institutions
	mil	Military organizations
	net	Network providers
	org	Non-profit organizations
	k12	K-12 schools
Newer	arts	Arts and cultural-oriented entities
	firm	Other businesses or firms
	info	Information services
	nom	Individuals or families
	rec	Recreation/entertainment sources
	store	Merchants and businesses offering goods to purchase
	web	Groups emphasizing Web activities

Figure 2-20a This table lists the original domain abbreviations commonly used today and examples of newly created ones.

Country Code Abbreviations

Abbreviations	Country
au	Australia
ax	Antarctica
ca	Canada
de	Germany
dk	Denmark
fr	France
jp	Japan
nl	Netherlands
se	Sweden
th	Thailand
uk	United Kingdom
us	United States

Figure 2-20b A partial list listing of country code abbreviations.

The World Wide Web

Although many people use the terms World Wide Web and Internet interchangeably, the World Wide Web is just one of the many services available on the Internet. The World Wide Web actually is a relatively new aspect of the Internet. While the Internet has been in existence since the late 1960s, the World Wide Web came into existence less than a decade ago — in the early 1990s. Since then, however, it has grown phenomenally to become the most widely used service on the Internet.

The **World Wide Web** (**WWW**), or simply **Web**, consists of a worldwide collection of electronic documents that have built-in hyperlinks to other related documents. These **hyperlinks**, also called **links**, allow users to navigate quickly from one Web page to another, regardless of whether the Web pages are located on the same computer or on different computers in different countries. A **Web page** is an electronic document viewed on the Web. A Web page can contain text, graphics, sound, and video, as well as hyperlinks to other Web pages. A **Web site** is a collection of related Web pages. Most Web sites have a

starting point, called a **home page**, which is similar to a book cover or table of contents for the site and provides information about the site's purpose and content.

Each Web page on a Web site has a unique address, called a **Uniform Resource Locator** (**URL**). As shown in **Figure 2-21**, a URL consists of a protocol, domain name, and sometimes the path to a specific Web page. Most Web page URLs begin with **http://**, which stands for **hypertext transfer protocol**, the communications protocol used to transfer pages on the Web. You access and view Web pages using a software program called a Web browser, or browser.

WebInfo

For an overview of the World Wide Web, visit the Teachers Discovering Computers Chapter 2 WebInfo page

(www.scsite.com/tdc/ch2/webinfo.htm)

and click WWW.

http://www.discoveryschool.com/schrockguide/index.htm

1. protocol — used to transfer data; for Web pages is always http:// (hypertext transfer protocol)
2. domain name — identifies computer that stores Web pages; often, but not always, begins with www
3. directory path — identifies where Web page is stored on computer
4. document name — name of Web page

Figure 2-21 The components of a Uniform Resource Locator (URL).

The Web pages that comprise a Web site are stored on a server, called a Web server. A **Web server** is a computer that delivers (serves) requested Web pages.

For example, when you enter the URL http://www.scsite.com/index.htm in your browser, your browser sends a request to the server whose domain name is scsite.com. The server then fetches the page named index.htm and sends it to your browser.

Web servers can store multiple Web sites. For example, many Internet service providers grant their subscribers storage space on a Web server for their personal, school, or company Web site.

How a Web Page Works

A Web page **[Figure 2-22]** is a hypertext or hypermedia document residing on an Internet computer that can contain text, graphics, video, and sound. A **hypertext** document contains text hyperlinks to other documents. A **hypermedia** document contains text, graphics, video, or sound hyperlinks that connect to other documents.

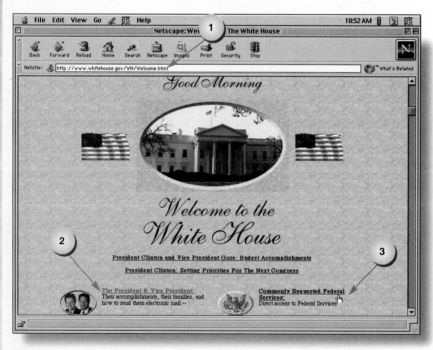

1. address of Web page; also called location or URL
2. different color indicates document associated with this hypertext link has been viewed
3. pointer positioned over a hypertext link changed shape to a hand with a pointing finger

Figure 2-22 An example of a Web page.

Three types of hyperlinks exist. **Target hyperlinks** link to another location in the same document. **Relative hyperlinks** link to another document on the same Internet computer. **Absolute hyperlinks** link to another document on a different Internet computer that could be across the country or across the world.

Hypertext and hypermedia allow students to learn in a nonlinear way. Reading a book from cover to cover is a linear way of learning. Branching off and investigating related topics as you encounter them is a nonlinear way of learning, also known as **discovery learning**. For example, as a student, you might learn about geology and want to learn more about mining. On the Web, you can click different links to access documents about mining, which then might stimulate your interest in old mining towns. You then could take a virtual tour and explore an old mining town, which might inspire you to read about a particular person who made his or her fortune in mining. The discovery learning experience described in this example — in which students branch from one related topic to another in a nonlinear fashion — is powerful and effective.

The Web's capability to support such learning makes it an interesting place to explore and positions it as a valuable tool for teaching and learning. Exploration offers great opportunities for discovery learning. As students' interest inspires them to learn more, the Web allows them to continue to explore for additional sources of information on any given topic. **Web surfing** is displaying pages from one Web site after another and is like using a remote control to jump from one TV channel to another.

A **Webmaster** is the individual responsible for developing Web pages and maintaining a Web site. Webmasters and other Web page developers create and format Web pages using **hypertext markup language (HTML),** which is a set of special codes, called **tags**, that define the placement and format of text, graphics, video, and sound on a Web page. Because HTML can be difficult to learn and use, many other user-friendly tools exist for **Web publishing**, which is the development and maintenance of Web pages. Today, many teachers are applying user-friendly tools to publish and maintain their own classroom Web pages **[Figure 2-23]**. You will learn how to create your own Web page using a popular Web creation software program in Chapter 3. You also will learn how to create and integrate curriculum pages into your lesson plans in Chapters 6 and 7.

Web Browser Software

As just discussed, you access and view Web pages using a software program called a Web browser. A **Web browser** or **browser** is a program that interprets HTML and displays Web pages and enables you to link to other Web pages and Web sites. **Figure 2-24** shows the HTML source document used to create the teacher's Web page shown in **Figure 2-23**. Your Web browser translates the source document with HTML tags into a functional Web page.

The first Web browsers used only text commands and displayed only text-based documents. In 1993, Marc Andreessen, a student at the University of Illinois, created a graphical Web browser called Mosaic. **Mosaic** displayed documents that included graphics and used a graphical interface. The graphical interface, just as it did with other application software programs, made it easier and more enjoyable to view Web documents and contributed to the rapid growth of the Web. Andreessen later

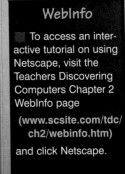

WebInfo

To access an interactive tutorial on using Netscape, visit the Teachers Discovering Computers Chapter 2 WebInfo page (www.scsite.com/tdc/ch2/webinfo.htm) and click Netscape.

CHAPTER 2

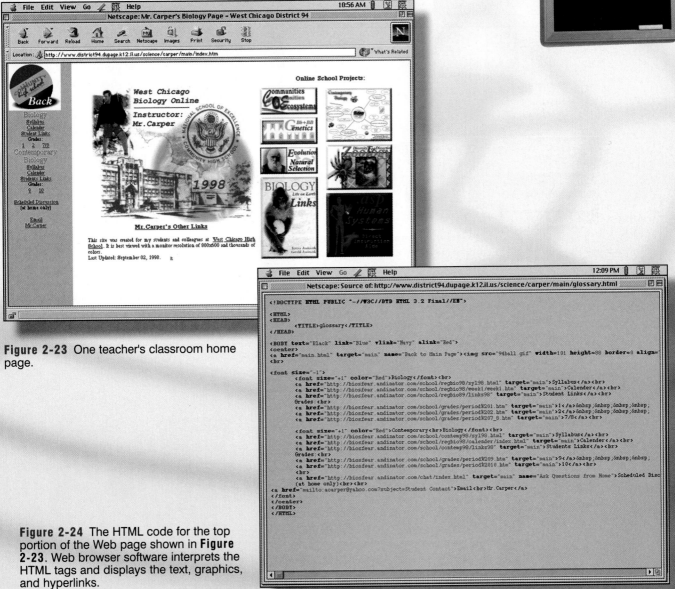

Figure 2-23 One teacher's classroom home page.

Figure 2-24 The HTML code for the top portion of the Web page shown in **Figure 2-23**. Web browser software interprets the HTML tags and displays the text, graphics, and hyperlinks.

CHAPTER 2

WebInfo

To access an interactive tutorial on using Internet Explorer, visit the Teachers Discovering Computers Chapter 2 WebInfo page

(www.scsite.com/tdc/ ch2/webinfo.htm)

and click Explorer.

became one of the founders of Netscape Communications Corporation, a leading Internet software company that developed the Netscape Navigator Web browser **[Figure 2-25]**. Another popular Web browser is Microsoft Internet Explorer **[Figure 2-26]**.

Before you can use a Web browser to view pages on the World Wide Web, your computer has to connect to the Internet through an Internet service provider or online service. When the browser program opens, it retrieves and displays a home page. As discussed earlier, home page often is used to describe the first page at a Web site. The same term describes

the Web page designated as the page to display each time you launch your browser. Most browsers utilize the manufacturer's Web page as the default home page, but you may change your browser's home page at any time. Many teachers, for example, set their browsers to display their school's home page when they launch their browser.

Once the browser retrieves a Web page using the page's URL, it can take anywhere from a few seconds to several minutes to display the page on your computer screen. The speed with which a Web page displays depends on the speed of the Internet connection and your computer and the amount of graphics on the Web page. To speed up the display of pages, Web browsers let you turn off the graphics and display text only.

Browsers display hyperlinks to other documents either as underlined text of a different color or as a graphical image. When you position the mouse pointer over a hyperlink, the mouse pointer changes to a small hand with a pointing finger. Some browsers also display the URL of the hyperlinked document at the bottom of the screen. You can display the document by clicking the hyperlink with a pointing device or by typing the URL in the location text box of the Web browser. To remind you that you have seen a

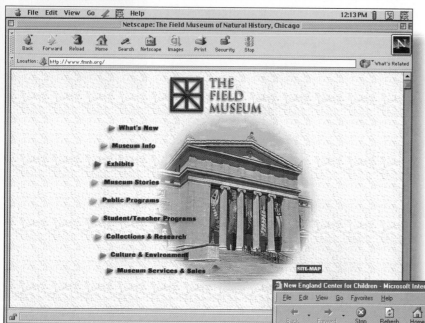

Figure 2-25 Netscape Navigator Web browser viewed on a Macintosh computer.

WebInfo

To access an interactive tutorial on using bookmarks, visit the Teachers Discovering Computers Chapter 2 WebInfo page

(www.scsite.com/tdc/ ch2/webinfo.htm)

and click Bookmarks.

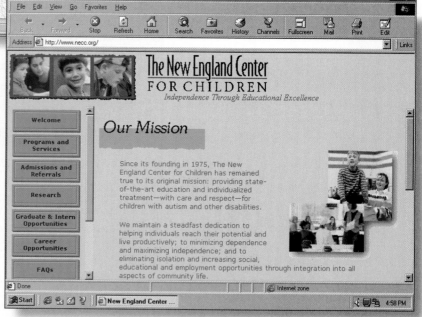

Figure 2-26 Microsoft Internet Explorer Web browser viewed on a PC.

document, some browsers change the color of a text hyperlink after you click it.

Two ways to keep track of Web pages you have viewed are a history list and a bookmark list. A **history list** records the pages viewed during the time you are online, also known as a session. If you think you might want to return to a page in a future session, you can record its location with a bookmark. A **bookmark** consists of the title and URL of a page. Bookmark lists, also called **favorites**, are stored on your computer and may be used in future Web sessions. Bookmark and history lists allow you to display a Web page quickly by clicking the name in the list.

Searching for Information on the Web

Searching for information on the Web can be challenging due to the sheer volume of content on the Web. In addition, no central menu or catalog of Web site content and addresses exists. Many companies, however, do provide search tools and maintain organized directories of Web sites to help you locate specific information. **Search tools** enable users to locate information found at Web sites all over the world **[Figure 2-27]**. Two basic types of search tools exist: search engines and search directories.

A **search engine** is a specific type of search tool that finds Web sites, Web pages, and Internet files that match one or more keywords you enter. Some search engines look for simple word matches and others allow for more specific searches on a series of words or an entire phrase. Search engines do not actually search the entire Internet (such a search would take an extremely long time). Instead, they search an index or database of Internet sites and documents. Search tool companies continuously update their databases. Because of the explosive growth of the Internet and because search engines scan different parts of the Internet and in different ways, performing the same search using different search engines often will yield different results.

Many search engines also provide search directories. A **search directory** is a type of search tool that allows users to navigate to areas of interest without having to enter keywords. Surfing search directories is a simple matter of following the links to the

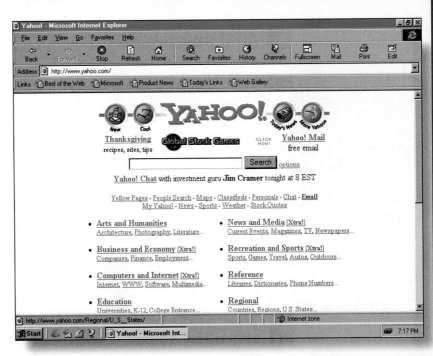

Figure 2-27 Yahoo! is a popular search engine.

specific topic you are looking for. Search directories are usually organized in categories such as education, sports, entertainment, or business. Search tools that cover a specific discipline, such as education, also are available on the Web.

Multimedia on the Web

Most Web pages include more than just formatted text and hyperlinks. In fact, some of the more exciting Web developments involve **multimedia**, which is the combination of graphics, animation, audio, video, and virtual reality (VR). A Web page that incorporates color, sound, motion, and pictures with text has much more appeal than one with text on a plain background. Combining text, audio, video, animation, and sound brings a Web page to life, increases the types of information available on the Web; expands the Web's potential uses; and makes the Internet a more entertaining place to explore. Although multimedia Web pages often require more time to open because they contain large files such as video or audio clips, the pages usually are worth the wait.

Most browsers have the capability of displaying basic multimedia elements on a

WebInfo

To access an interactive tutorial on using search engines, visit the Teachers Discovering Computers Chapter 2 WebInfo page

(www.scsite.com/tdc/ch2/webinfo.htm)

and click Search Engines.

WebInfo

For links to many popular education-related search engines, visit the Teachers Discovering Computers Chapter 2 WebInfo page

(www.scsite.com/tdc/ch2/webinfo.htm)

and click Education Search Engines.

Web page. Sometimes, however, your browser needs an additional program called a plug-in or helper application, which extends the capability of the browser. **Plug-ins** run multimedia elements within the browser window, while **helper applications** run multimedia elements in a window separate from the browser.

You can download plug-ins and helper applications free from many Web sites [Figure 2-28]. In fact, Web pages that use multimedia elements often include links to Web sites containing the required plug-in or helper application. Most browsers include commonly used plug-ins, but users often have to update their browsers as new plug-ins become available.

The following sections discuss multimedia Web developments in the areas of graphics, animation, audio, video, and virtual reality.

Popular Plug-In / Helper Applications

Plug-In / Helper Application	Description	Web Site URL
Acrobat Reader	View, navigate, and print Portable Document Format (PDF) files — documents formatted to look just as they look in the print medium	www.adobe.com
Shockwave and Flash Player	Experience dynamic interactive multimedia, graphics, and streaming audio	www.macromedia.com
QuickTime	View animation, music, audio, video, and VR panoramas and objects directly in a Web page	www.apple.com
RealPlayer	Live and on-demand near-CD-quality audio and newscast-quality video; streams audio and video content for faster viewing	www.real.com
Liquid MusicPlayer	Listen to and purchase CD-quality music tracks and audio CDs over the Internet; the first commercially viable and legally responsible system for this type of multimedia	www.liquidaudio.com
ichat	Access thousands of different chat rooms to chat with more than eight million ichat users	www.acuity.com
Cosmo Player	View 3-D and other virtual reality applications written in Virtual Reality Modeling Language (VRML)	cosmosoftware.com

Figure 2-28 Plug-ins and helper applications can extend the multimedia capability of Web browsers. Users usually can download them free from the manufacturers' sites.

Graphics Graphics were the first media used to enhance the text-based Internet. The introduction of graphical Web browsers allowed Web page developers to incorporate illustrations, logos, and other images into Web pages. Today, many Web pages use colorful graphical designs and images to convey messages [Figure 2-29].

The two more common file formats for graphical images found on the Web are JPEG (pronounced JAY-peg) and GIF (pronounced jiff or giff). **Figure 2-30** lists these and other file formats used on the Internet.

The Web contains thousands of image files on countless subjects that you can download at no cost and use for noncommercial purposes. Because some graphical files can be time consuming to download, some Web sites use thumbnails on their pages. A **thumbnail** is a small version of a larger graphical image,

CHAPTER 2

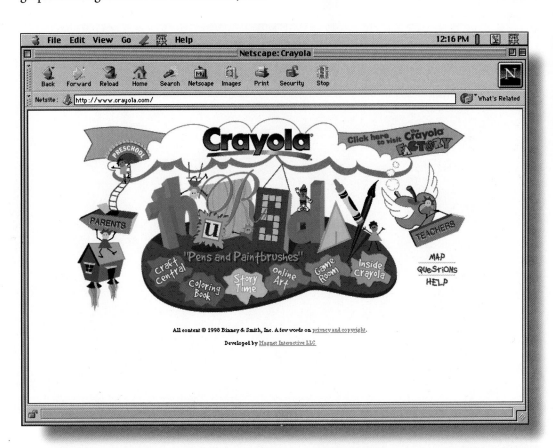

Figure 2-29 Many Web pages use colorful graphic designs and images to convey their messages.

Graphics Formats Used On the Internet

Acronym	Name	File Extension
JPEG (pronounced JAY-peg)	Joint Photographic Experts Group	.jpg
GIF (pronounced jiff or giff)	Graphics Interchange Format	.gif
PNG (pronounced ping)	Portable Network Graphics	.png
TIFF	Tagged Image File Format	.tiff
PCX	PC Paintbrush	.pcx
BMP	Bitmap	.bmp

Figure 2-30 Graphics formats used on the Internet.

that usually you can click to display the full-sized image **[Figure 2-31]**.

Animation **Animation** is the appearance of motion created by displaying a series of still images in rapid sequence. Animated graphics make Web pages more visually interesting and draw attention to important information or links. For example, text that is animated to scroll across the screen, called a **marquee** (pronounced mar-KEE), can serve as a ticker to display stock updates, news, school sports scores and events, or weather **[Figure 2-32]**.

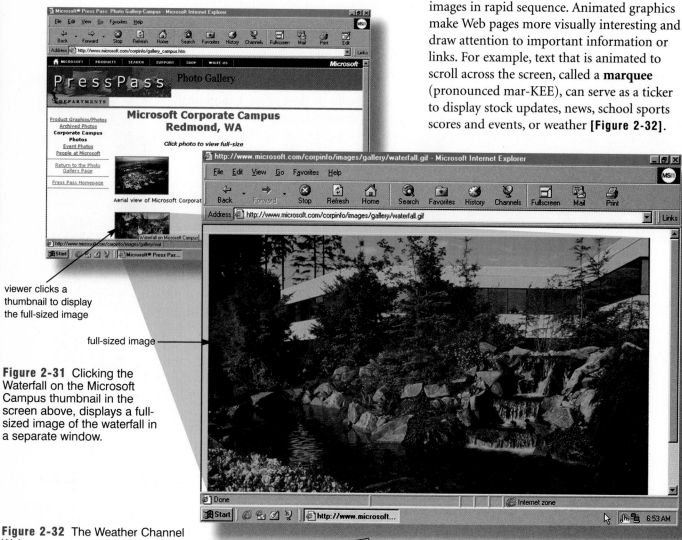

viewer clicks a thumbnail to display the full-sized image

full-sized image

Figure 2-31 Clicking the Waterfall on the Microsoft Campus thumbnail in the screen above, displays a full-sized image of the waterfall in a separate window.

Figure 2-32 The Weather Channel Web page uses a marquee to display weather forecasts in cities around the country.

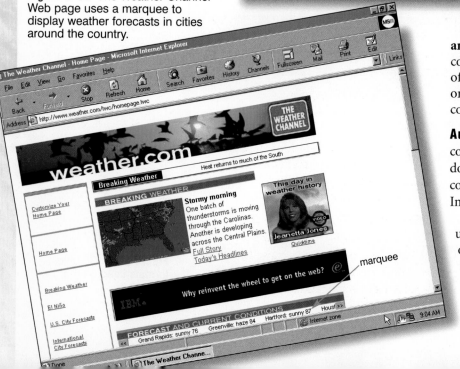

marquee

One popular type of animation, called an **animated GIF**, is a group of several images combined into a single GIF file. An abundance of education-related animations are available on the Web, many that you can download or copy at no cost.

Audio Simple **Web audio applications** consist of individual sound files that a user must download completely before playing. Two common formats used for audio files on the Internet are **WAV** and **AU**.

More advanced Web audio applications use streaming audio. **Streaming** is the process of transferring data in a continuous and even flow. Streaming is important because most users do not have fast enough Internet connections to download large audio files quickly. **Streaming audio** enables you to listen to the sound file as it downloads to your computer.

Many radio and television stations use streaming audio to broadcast music, interviews, talk shows, sporting events, music videos, news, live concerts, and other segments **[Figure 2-33]**. One accepted standard for transmitting audio data on the Internet is **RealAudio**.

telephone software and your computer's sound card digitize and compress your conversation and then transmit the digitized audio over the Internet to the called parties. Software and equipment at the receiving end reverse the process so they can hear what you have said, just as if you were talking on a telephone.

Some of today's Web browsers include Internet telephone software, such as CoolTalk and NetMeeting. In addition to Internet telephony, many of these products offer additional services such as a whiteboard to display

RealPlayer is used for streaming audio

Figure 2-33 Many radio and television stations use streaming audio. National Public Radio (NPR) transmits audio data in RealAudio, which is a component of RealPlayer.

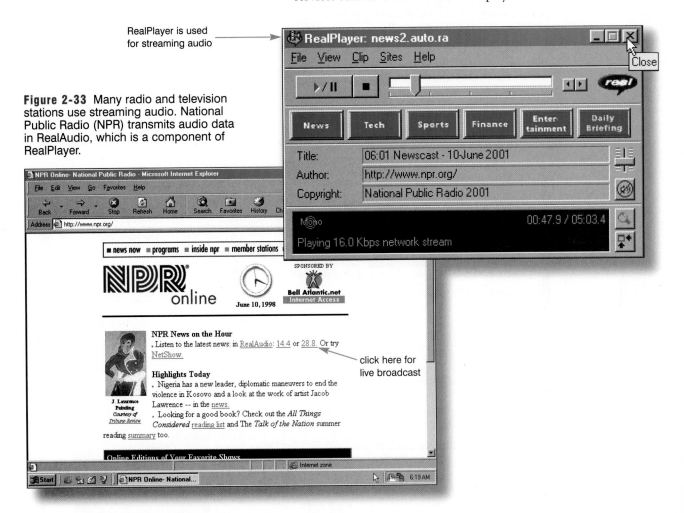

click here for live broadcast

Internet telephone service, also called **audioconferencing** and **Internet telephony** enables you to talk to other people over the Web. Internet telephony uses the Internet (instead of a public telephone network) to connect a calling party and one or more called parties. Internet telephone service thus allows you to talk to friends or colleagues for just the cost of your Internet connection. As you speak into a computer microphone, **Internet**

drawings, diagrams, and other graphics; chat tools so you can type text messages; and even videoconferencing so you can see images of the meeting participants.

Video   Like audio, simple **Web video applications** consist of individual video files, such as movie or television clips, that a user must download completely before viewing. Because video segments usually are large and take a long time to download, they often are short.

Streaming video allows you to view longer or live video images as the video file downloads to your computer. A widely used standard for transmitting video data on the Internet is **RealVideo**. Like RealAudio, most Web browsers support RealVideo.

Streaming video has the potential to create new possibilities for learning. As the speed of the Internet increases dramatically over the next few years, students from even the most remote schools will have access to thousands of full-motion videos from all over the world.

Streaming video also allows you to conduct Internet videoconferences, which works much like Internet telephony. Video-conferencing software and a computer's video capture card digitize and compress the video images and sounds. Internet software divides the data into packets and sends the data over

the Internet. Equipment and software at the receiving end assemble the packets, decompress the data, and present the image and sound as video. As with traditional videoconferencing, live Internet videoconferences can be choppy and blurry depending on the speed of the communications link. As noted, many products that support Internet telephony also have videoconferencing capabilities, thus allowing for face-to-face conversations over the Internet [**Figure 2-34**].

Virtual Reality   **Virtual reality** (**VR**) is the simulation of a real or imagined environment that appears as a three-dimensional (3-D) space. On the Web, VR involves the display of 3-D images that you can explore and manipulate interactively. Using special VR software, a Web developer can create an entire 3-D site that contains infinite space and depth called a **VR world**. A VR world, for example,

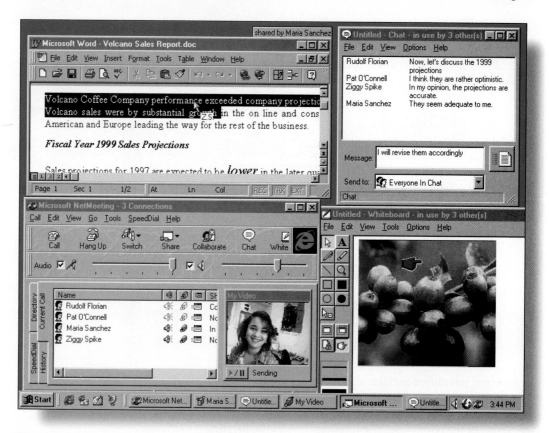

Figure 2-34 NetMeeting, which is included with Internet Explorer, offers Internet telephony.

might show a room with furniture. You can walk through such a VR room by moving your pointing device forward, backward, or to the side. To view a VR world, you may need to update your Web browser by downloading a VR plug-in program.

Games are a popular use of virtual reality, but VR has many practical applications as well. Companies can use VR to showcase products or create advertisements **[Figure 2-35]**. Architects create VR models of buildings and rooms to show their clients how a construction project will look before construction begins. Virtual reality also opens up a world of learning opportunities. Science educators, for example, can create VR models of molecules, organisms, and other structures for students to examine. Students also can take virtual tours of historical sites located all over the world. Several schools even use VR to allow parents to take a virtual tour of the school from their home.

Other Internet Services

Although the World Wide Web is the most talked about service on the Internet, many other Internet services are available. These services include e-mail, FTP, Telnet, newsgroups, mailing lists, and chat rooms. Each of these services is discussed in the following sections.

drag box to
rotate chair

Figure 2-35 VR has many practical applications. In this online catalog, you can change the color of the chair and rotate it — just as if you were in a catalog showroom.

click to change
color of chair

E-mail

E-mail (**electronic mail**) is the transmission of messages and files via a computer network. E-mail was one of the original features of the Internet, enabling scientists and researchers working on government-sponsored projects to communicate with their colleagues at other locations. Today, e-mail enables administrators, teachers, and students to communicate with millions of Internet users all over the world. E-mail quickly is becoming a primary communications method for both personal and business use [**Figure 2-36**].

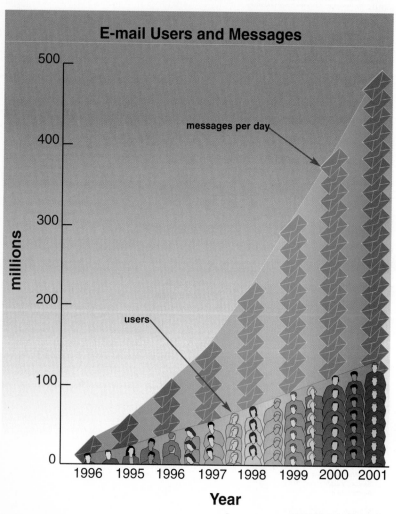

Figure 2-36 The number of e-mail users and e-mail messages as indicated by this graph, has grown phenomenally during the past several years.

Using an **e-mail program**, you can create, send, receive, forward, store, print, and delete messages. When you receive an e-mail

message, your Internet service provider's software places the message in your personal **mailbox**. Your mailbox is a storage location usually residing on the computer that connects you to the Internet, such as the server operated by your ISP. A **mail server** is a server that contains user's mailboxes and associated e-mail messages. Most ISPs and online services provide an Internet e-mail program and a mailbox on a mail server as a standard part of their Internet access services.

An **e-mail address** is a combination of a user name and a domain name that identifies the user so he or she can receive messages [**Figure 2-37**]. Your **user name** is a unique combination of characters that identifies you, and it must differ from other user names located on the same mail server. Your user name sometimes is limited to eight characters and often is a combination of your first and last names, such as the initial of your first name plus your last name. You may choose a nickname or any combination of characters for your user name, but others may find unusual combinations harder to remember.

Although no complete listing of Internet e-mail addresses exists, several Internet sites list addresses collected from public sources. These sites also allow you to list your e-mail address voluntarily so others may find it. The site might prompt you for other information, such as the high school or college from which you graduated, so others can determine if you are the person they want to reach.

FTP

File transfer protocol (FTP) is an Internet standard that allows you to exchange files with other computers on the Internet. For example, if you click a link on a Web page in your browser window that begins to download a file to your hard disk, you probably are using FTP [**Figure 2-38**].

An **FTP server** is a computer that allows users to upload and download files using FTP. An FTP server contains one or more FTP sites. An **FTP site** is a collection of files including text, graphics, audio, video, and program files. Some FTP sites limit file transfers to individuals who have authorized accounts (user names and passwords) on the FTP server. Many corporations, for example, maintain FTP sites for their employees.

CHAPTER 2

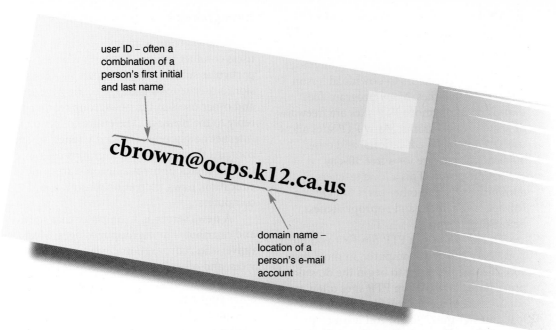

user ID – often a
combination of a
person's first initial
and last name

cbrown@ocps.k12.ca.us

domain name –
location of a
person's e-mail
account

Figure 2-37 An example of an Internet e-mail address. Sometimes, the underscore character separates sections of the user's name; for example, cindy_brown@ocps.k12.ca.us.

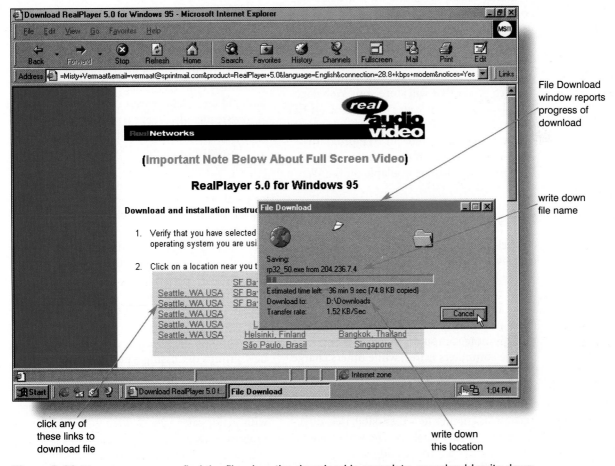

File Download
window reports
progress of
download

write down
file name

click any of
these links to
download file

write down
this location

Figure 2-38 To ensure you can find the file when the download is complete, you should write down the file's name and the location of the hard disk on which the file is being saved.

Other FTP sites allow **anonymous FTP**, whereby anyone can transfer some, if not all, available files. Many educational sites, for example, have FTP sites that use anonymous FTP to allow educators to download lesson plans and other files. Many program files located on anonymous FTP sites are freeware or shareware programs. Many FTP sites allow users to download educational and other application software for a free 30-day evaluation period. This allows teachers, administrators, and other users to evaluate software for content and appropriateness before purchasing.

To view or use an FTP file, first you must download it to your computer. In most cases, you click the file name to begin the download procedure. Large files on FTP sites often are compressed to reduce storage space and download transfer time. Before you use a compressed file, you must expand it with a decompression program, such as WinZip. Such programs usually are available at the FTP site or are packaged with the file you download.

In some cases, you may wish to **upload**, or copy, a file to an FTP site. For example, once you create a personal Web page, you need to upload the Web page from your computer to the Web server that will store your Web page. To upload files from your computer to an FTP site, you use an FTP program. Many Internet service providers include an FTP program when you subscribe to their service. Several FTP programs also are available on the Web.

Telnet

Telnet is a program or command that enables you to connect to a remote computer on the Internet. To make a Telnet connection to the remote computer, you must enter a user name and password. Once connected, your computer acts like a terminal directly linked to the remote computer. Access to many remote computers is free, while others charge a fee. For convenience, some remote computers provide you with a Telnet program.

Some uses of Telnet include connecting to a remote computer to access databases, directories, and library catalogs. The widespread use of Internet service providers and Web browsers, however, has reduced the need to log directly into remote computers using Telnet.

Newsgroups

A **newsgroup** is an online area in which users conduct written discussions about a particular subject. To participate in a discussion, a user sends a message to the newsgroup and other users in the newsgroup read and reply to the message. The entire collection of Internet newsgroups is called **Usenet**, which contains thousands of newsgroups on a multitude of topics. Some major topic areas include education, news, recreation, business, and computers.

A **news server** is a computer that stores and distributes newsgroup messages. Most universities, corporations, ISPs, online services, and other large organizations have a news server. Some newsgroups require you to enter your user name and password to participate in the discussion. These types of newsgroups are used when the messages on the newsgroup are to be viewed only by authorized members, such as students taking a college course.

To participate in a newsgroup, you must use a program called a **newsreader**, which is included with most browsers. The newsreader enables you to access a newsgroup to read a previously entered message, called an **article** and add an article of your own, called **posting**. A newsreader also keeps track of which articles you have and have not read.

Newsgroup members often post articles as a reply to another article — either to answer a question or to comment on material in the original article. These replies often cause the author of the original article, or others, to post additional articles related to the original article. The original article and all subsequent related replies are called a **thread** or **threaded discussion** [Figure 2-39]. A thread can be short-lived or continue for some time, depending on the nature of the topic and the interest of the participants.

Using the newsreader, you can search for newsgroups discussing a particular subject, such as a type of musical instrument, brand of sports equipment, or educational interests. Newsgroups use a hierarchical naming system with major categories divided into one or more subcategories. A period separates each subcategory. **Figure 2-40** lists major categories for newsgroups. If you like the discussion in a particular newsgroup, you can **subscribe** to it,

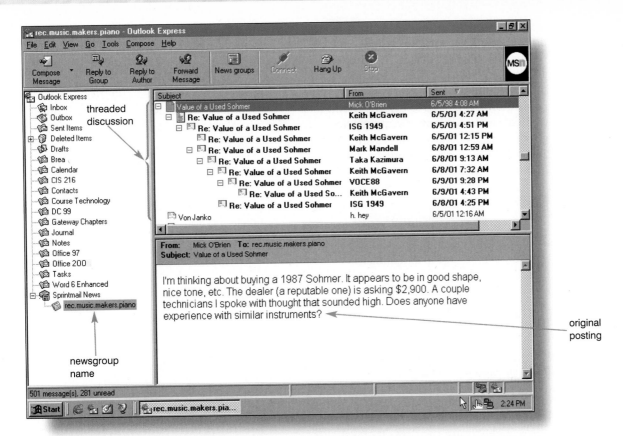

Figure 2-39 A newsgroup is an online area in which users conduct written discussions about a particular subject. Shown is a thread about the value of a used piano model.

Newsgroup Categories

Category	Description	Examples
alt	Alternative	alt.family-names.hendricks alt.music.paul-simon
biz	Business	biz.jobs biz.marketplace.computers
comp	Computer	comp.graphics.animation comp.sys.handhelds
news	Newsgroups	news.announce.newsgroups news.groups.reviews
rec	Recreation	rec.autos.antique rec.travel.misc
soc	Social	soc.college.gradinfo soc.culture.spain
talk	Talk	talk.environment talk.politics.misc

Figure 2-40 Major categories of newsgroups.

which means your newsreader saves the location so you can access it easily in the future.

In some newsgroups, when you post an article, a **moderator** reviews the contents of the article and posts it, if appropriate. The moderator may choose to discard or edit inappropriate articles. Many educational newsgroups have moderators who ensure messages are appropriate for K-12 students.

Mailing Lists

A **mailing list** is a group of e-mail names and addresses given a single name. When a user sends a message to a mailing list, every person on the list receives a copy of the message in his or her mailbox. To add your e-mail name and address to a mailing list, you subscribe to it; to remove your name, you **unsubscribe** from the mailing list. **LISTSERV** is a popular software program used to manage many educational mailing lists.

The basic difference between a newsgroup and a mailing list is that users on the mailing list discuss topics using e-mail, whereas newsgroup members use a newsreader for discussions. Thousands of mailing lists exist on a variety of topics in areas of entertainment, business, computers, society, culture, health, recreation, and education. To locate a mailing list dealing with a particular topic, you can use your Web browser to search for, mailing lists or LISTSERV.

Chat Rooms

A **chat** is a real-time typed conversation that takes place on a computer. **Real-time** means that something occurs immediately. With chat, when you enter a line of text on your computer screen, your words immediately display on one or more participant's screens. To conduct a chat, you and the people with whom you are conversing must be online at the same time.

A **chat room** refers to the communications medium, or channel, that permits users to chat with each other. Anyone on the channel can participate in the conversation, which usually deals with a specific topic.

To start a chat session, you must connect to a chat server through a **chat client**, which is

a program on your computer. Today's browsers usually include a chat client. If yours does not, you can download a chat client from the Web. Some chat clients are text-based only, such as Internet relay chat (IRC) and ichat, while others, such as Microsoft Chat, support graphical and text-based chats.

Once you install a chat client, you then can create or join a conversation on a chat server. The channel name should indicate the topic of discussion. The person who creates a channel acts as the channel operator and has responsibility for monitoring the conversation and disconnecting anyone who becomes disruptive. Users can share operator status or transfer operator status to someone else.

Numerous controlled and monitored chat rooms are available for K-12 students and teachers. Several Web sites also exist for the purpose of conducting chats. Some chat sites even allow participants to assume the role or appearance of a character.

Portals

A **portal** is a Web site designed to offer a variety of Internet services from a single, convenient location. Most portals offer the following services: search engines; local, national, and worldwide news, sports, and weather; references such as yellow pages and maps; shopping malls; e-mail; and chat rooms. Some portals also provide Internet access.

Popular portals include AltaVista, Excite, Infoseek, Lycos, Microsoft Internet Start, Netscape Netcenter, Snap, and Yahoo!. The goal of these portals is to be designed as the Web page in your browser.

Netiquette

Netiquette, which is short for **Internet etiquette,** is the code of acceptable behaviors users should follow while on the Internet; that is, the conduct expected of individuals while online. Netiquette includes rules for all aspects of the Internet, including the Web, e-mail, FTP, Telnet, newsgroups, mailing lists, and chat rooms. **Figure 2-41** outlines the rules of netiquette.

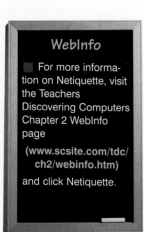

WebInfo

For more information on Netiquette, visit the Teachers Discovering Computers Chapter 2 WebInfo page

(www.scsite.com/tdc/ch2/webinfo.htm)

and click Netiquette.

Netiquette

Golden Rule: *Treat others as you would like them to treat you.*

1. In e-mail, newsgroups, and chat rooms:
    - Keep message brief using proper grammar and spelling.
    - Be careful when using sarcasm and humor, as it might be misinterpreted.
    - Be polite. Avoid offensive language.
    - Avoid sending or posting **flames**, which are abusive or insulting messages. Don't participate in **flame wars**, which are exchanges of flames.
    - Avoid sending spam, which is the Internet's version of junk mail. **Spam** is an unsolicited e-mail message or newsgroup posting sent to many recipients or newsgroups at once.
    - Do not use all capital letters, which is the equivalent of SHOUTING!
    - Use **emoticons** to express emotion. Popular emoticons include

:)	Smile
:(	Frown
:|	Indifference
:\	Undecided
:o	Surprised

    - Use abbreviations and acronyms for phrases such as

BTW	by the way
FYI	for your information
FWIW	for what it's worth
IMHO	in my humble opinion
TTFN	ta ta for now
TYVM	thank you very much

    - Clearly identify a **spoiler**, which is a message that reveals a solution to a game or ending to a movie or program.
2. Read the **FAQ** (frequently asked questions), if one exists. Many newsgroups and Web sites have an FAQ.
3. Use user name for your personal purposes only.
4. Do not assume material is accurate or up-to-date. Be forgiving of other's mistakes.
5. Never read someone's private e-mail.

Figure 2-41 The rules of netiquette.

Using the Internet: Cookies and Security

While it is a vast and exciting resource, the Internet also is a public place. As with all other public places, students and teachers should use common sense while there. The following sections explain guidelines for the use of cookies and security precautions.

Cookies

Many Web sites rely on cookies to track information about viewers, customers, and subscribers. A **cookie** is a small file that contains data about you, such as your login name or viewing preferences. Some Web sites send a cookie to your browser, which stores it on your computer's hard disk **[Figure 2-42]**. The next time you visit the Web site, your browser retrieves the cookie from your hard disk and sends the data in the cookie to the Web site.

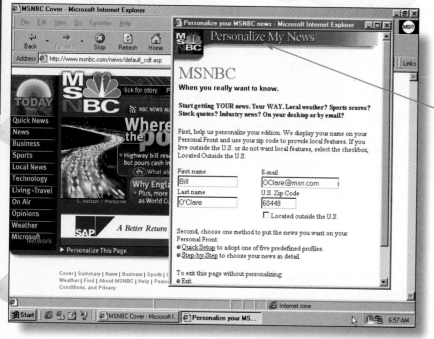

some Web sites use cookies to personalize Web pages for visitors

Figure 2-42 An example of a cookie and where it is saved.

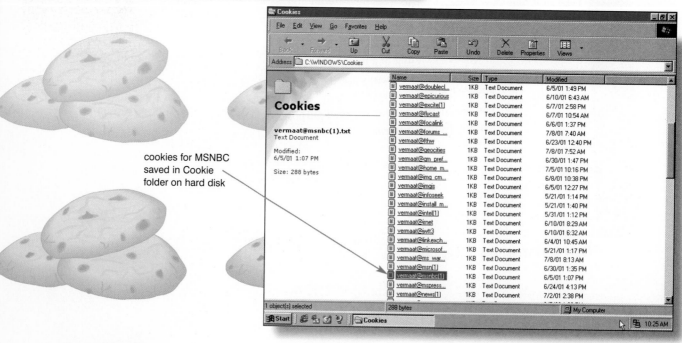

cookies for MSNBC saved in Cookie folder on hard disk

Cookies are used by different types of Web sites.

- Web sites that allow for personalization often use cookies to track user preferences. On such sites, you may be asked to fill in a form requesting personal information, such as your name and site preferences. A news site, for example, might allow you to customize your viewing preferences to display business and sports news only. Your preferences are stored in a cookie on your hard disk.

- Online shopping sites generally use cookies to keep track of items in your shopping cart. This way, you can start an order during one Web session and finish it on another day in another session.

- Some Web sites use cookies to track how often you visit a site and the Web pages you visit while at the site.

- Web sites also use cookies to target advertisements based on your interests and browsing habits.

Although many believe that cookies allow other Web sites to read information on your computer, a Web site can read data only from its own cookie file; that is, it cannot view any other data on your hard disk — including another cookie file. Some sites do, however, sell or trade information stored in your cookie to advertisers — a practice many believe to be unethical. If you do not want your personal information distributed to other companies, you should limit the amount of information you provide to a Web site. You also can set your browser to accept cookies automatically, prompt you if you wish to accept a cookie, or disable cookie use altogether.

Internet Security

Any time a school district or business connects its private network to a public network such as the Internet, it must consider security concerns such as unauthorized access to confidential information. To prevent unauthorized access, schools and businesses implement one or more layers of security. A **firewall** is a general term that refers to both hardware and software used to restrict access to data on a network. Firewalls deny network access to unauthorized personnel. For example, firewalls restrict students from access to inappropriate materials or sensitive information such as student grades and attendance records.

Even with netiquette guidelines, the Internet still opens up the possibility for inappropriate behaviors and content. For example, amidst the wealth of information and services on the Internet, some content may be inappropriate for certain people. Some Web sites, newsgroups, and chat rooms, for instance, contain content or discussions that are unsuitable for children. Schools have a responsibility to ensure that students do not gain access to inappropriate or objectionable materials.

To assist schools and parents with these types of issues, many browsers include software that can screen out unacceptable content. You also can purchase stand-alone Internet **filtering software**, which allows parents, teachers, and others to block access to certain materials on the Internet.

Schools help protect students from the negative aspects of the Internet by using filtering software, firewalls, and teacher observation. Most schools also use an **Acceptable Use Policy (AUP)**, which is an outline of user standards that reminds teachers, students, and parents that they are guests on the Internet and that they need to use it appropriately. Most schools require students, teachers, and parents to sign AUPs.

Confidentiality is another important consideration on the Internet. For example, when shopping online, you should be sure that confidential or personal information such as your credit card number is *encrypted*, or coded, during transmission. Reputable companies have secure servers that automatically encrypt this type of information while it is being transmitted.

One way to identify a secure Web page is to see if its URL begins with **https://**, instead of http:// **[Figure 2-43 on the next page]**. Web browsers usually include encryption software that allows you to encrypt e-mail messages or other documents.

WebInfo

For more information on filtering software, visit the Teachers Discovering Computers Chapter 2 WebInfo page

(www.scsite.com/tdc/ch2/webinfo.htm) and click Filtering Software.

WebInfo

For more information on Acceptable Use Policy (AUP), visit the Teachers Discovering Computers Chapter 2 WebInfo page

(www.scsite.com/tdc/ch2/webinfo.htm) and click AUP.

The Impact of the Internet and the World Wide Web on Education

More than 500 years ago, Johannes Gutenberg developed a printing press that made the written word accessible to the public and

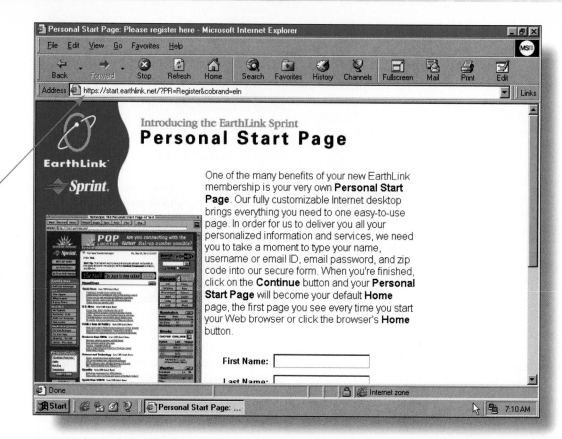

many secure Web pages begin their Web address with https

Figure 2-43 Reputable companies provide secure Web pages.

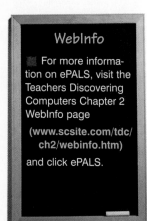

WebInfo

For more information on ePALS, visit the Teachers Discovering Computers Chapter 2 WebInfo page **(www.scsite.com/tdc/ch2/webinfo.htm)** and click ePALS.

revolutionized the way people shared information. The World Wide Web is the Gutenberg printing press of modern times — opening doors to new learning resources and opportunities and allowing for sharing of information and knowledge such as never before. Ten years ago, most students were unable to visit the Library of Congress, the White House, the Smithsonian Institution, the National Art Gallery, or the Louvre Museum. Today, students around the world can visit these historic places and thousands of others on the Web, exploring these locales on interactive and sometimes even virtual tours.

Not only does the Internet provide access to extensive text and multimedia resources, it also allows teachers and students to communicate with other teachers and students all over the world. For example, **ePALS** Classroom Exchange is a project designed to enable students to develop an understanding of different cultures through student e-mail exchanges **[Figure 2-44]**. The mission of ePALS is to have students creatively write in primary and secondary languages, as well as

do research and gather information about other cultures and individuals. Project ePALS is adaptable for any grade level in any country.

As the Internet expanded and evolved from a text-based communications system into the powerful multimedia communications system of today, educators quickly recognized the tremendous potential of the Internet — and especially the Web — to revolutionize the classroom. By providing a variety of learning tools, the Internet and the Web is transforming the way teachers instruct and the way students are learning basic skills and core subjects. These changes have brought the Web to the forefront of instructional strategies in education in a very short period of time.

The potential of the Web for improving the way to teach K-12 students is enormous, is still growing, and will continue to expand for many years to come. Throughout this textbook, hundreds of links and dozens of exercises will help you understand the incredible possibilities the Web offers for K-12 education in general and your classroom in particular.

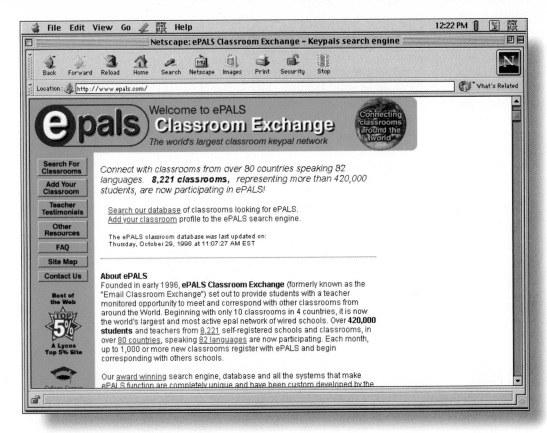

Figure 2-44 An online project, ePals, allows students from all over the world to communicate with each other.

How to Connect to the Internet and the World Wide Web

Today, many institutions of higher education provide Internet access and e-mail accounts for their students. Many also offer off-campus dial-up Internet access, although some schools do charge a fee for this service. Some K-12 school districts and state departments of education provide free dial-up Internet access and e-mail accounts for their teachers, administrators, and staff employees. In Florida, for example, the Florida Information Resource Network (FIRN) provides free dial-up Internet access, an e-mail system, and educational support services for all K-12 teachers and administrators.

The following steps describe how you can connect to the Internet and the World Wide Web.

1. **Determine how you will obtain Internet access.** Three common ways people connect to the Internet are through school or work,

an online service, or an Internet service provider (ISP).

Through school or work: Many schools and organizations have direct, high-speed connections to the Internet. Check with your university, school, or school district's technology coordinator to obtain details about obtaining an Internet account.

Through an online service: Online services, such as America Online and MSN offer Internet access as one of their services. If you already use an online service, this is an excellent way to begin using the Internet.

Through an ISP: As described earlier in the chapter, an ISP has a permanent connection to the Internet and provides temporary connections to others for a fee. The most common fee arrangement is a fixed amount, but you may receive a discounted fee if you sign up for an extended period of time, such as a year. As with online services, most ISPs allow unlimited Internet usage for their monthly fee **[Figure 2-45 on the next page]**.

Before choosing an ISP or online service, be sure you will be dialing to a local telephone number to connect to the ISP. If you live in a medium to large city, most ISPs provide a local telephone number. If you know existing ISP or online users, ask them how often they are unable to log on to the network and the level and quality of technical support. Most ISPs and online services provide free technical support and a local, 800, or 888 number.

Digital Network (ISDN), a cable modem, or a Digital Subscriber Line (DSL) described earlier in this chapter. As noted, these provide an alternative to dial-up access and provide users with higher-speed Internet connections.

3. **Obtain any necessary software**. You need at least two pieces of software to access the Internet and the World Wide Web using an ISP; a communications program and a Web browser program. You also may want software

National Internet Service Providers

Providers	Name	Telephone	Web Site
	AT&T WorldNet^{SM}	(800) 967-5363	www.att.net
	Earthlink Network	(800) 395-8425	www.earthlink.net
	network MCI	(800) 550-0927	www.mci.com
	NETCOM	(800) 638-2661	www.netcom.com
	SPRYNET	(800) 777-9638	www.sprynet.com

Figure 2-45 Examples of national Internet service providers (ISPs). You can find local ISPs in your telephone book yellow pages under Computers-Networks.

2. **Obtain the necessary equipment**. You already may have the equipment necessary to connect to the Internet. At a minimum, you need a computer, a modem, and a telephone line. The speed of the computer, modem, and telephone line affect how rapidly you access and display information.

For the computer, any system less than three-years old should suffice. If your system is more than three-years old, consult your ISP. For the modem, the higher your modem speed the better. As a minimum, you will need a 28.8 Kbps modem; however, to enjoy most of the features of the Internet, you need a 56K modem. Most home computers sold since early 1998 include a 56K modem. If you do not have a modem, purchase a 56K and if you have a slower modem, consider replacing it. A slow modem will act as a bottleneck and lead to frustrating delays as Web pages and information downloads.

For most users, an analog telephone line will be sufficient. You may want to consider adding a second telephone line so your regular telephone line is not tied up while you are online. If you plan to do serious work using the Internet, you may want to consider newer technologies such as Integrated Services

for e-mail, FTP, and other Internet services, although most Web browsers include some or all of these programs. If your browser does not have these options, your ISP may provide the programs free. You can also download these programs from the Internet or purchase them from software retailers.

4. **Install the software**. Read the installation instructions carefully before starting installation. If you run into any problems, immediately call your ISP for assistance.

5. **Explore the Internet and the World Wide Web**. The best way to learn how to use the Internet and the Web is to log on and explore. Pick a subject and use a search tool to see what is on the Web. Look up your school's home page and see if it describes the place you know. Many schools have staff development programs to train teachers, staff, and administrators to use the Internet and the Web. Many tutorials on how to use the Web and software applications also are available on the Web. To help you explore, the special feature following this chapter lists some useful, interesting, and unusual Web sites.

Following other chapters in this textbook are two additional Special Features that will provide you with links to, and information on, hundreds of educational-related Web sites. The Guide to Educational Sites and Professional Organizations is located after Chapter 6 and the Guide to State and Federal Government Educational Web Sites is located after Chapter 8.

The Future of the Internet and the World Wide Web

What is the future of the Internet and the World Wide Web? Without question, the Web will continue to evolve as a primary communications channel for people around the world. As the Web grows in size and operates at higher speeds, it also will continue to have a major influence on restructuring K-12 education. Other predictions regarding the future of the Internet and the World Wide Web and its impact on education include the following:

- In the next few years, the Internet will connect 80 percent of the world's computers.

- Most K-12 teachers will have access to the Internet in their classrooms.

- Everyday home and office appliances and other devices that use embedded computers, such as automobiles, will have built-in Internet access capabilities.

- Web search capabilities will be more intelligent and focused.

- Within a few years, the Web will operate at speeds 100 to 1,000 times faster than today.

- Businesses will continue to be the driving force behind the Web's expansion.

- Increased access speeds and greater availability will allow teachers and students to view thousands of full-motion videos over the Web.

- The Web will become an integral part of all education and will revolutionize the way students learn core subjects.

Finally, many experts believe that separate, proprietary networks used for telephone, television, and radio will merge with the Internet. Eventually, a single, integrated network will exist, made up of many different media that will carry all communications traffic.

Summary of Communications, Networks, the Internet, and the World Wide Web

Communications will continue to impact how you work, learn, teach, access information, and use computers. Because of communications technology, individuals, schools, and organizations no longer are limited to local data resources; they instantly can obtain information from anywhere in the world. Installing communications networks is just one way that school districts will use communications technology to meet current instructional and management challenges. In just a few years, the Internet and World Wide Web may redefine education, just as it has transformed modern businesses and today's society. As educators all over the world integrate the Internet and the World Wide Web into their classroom curricula, their efforts are effecting an educational revolution in today's schools — one that can have a significant positive impact on the quality of graduating students.

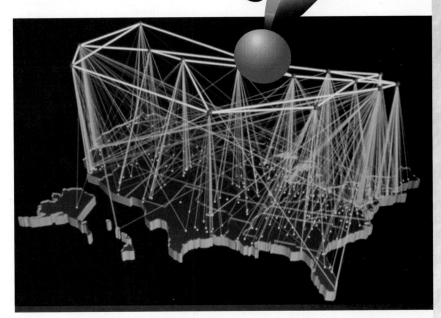

Figure 2-46 The World Wide Web will continue to evolve as the world's primary means of communications. Nobody really knows exactly how the Web will influence the human race during the first decade of the twenty-first century.

CHAPTER 2

www.scsite.com/tdc/ch2/brief.htm

InBrief

Web Instructions: To display this page from the Web, launch your browser and enter the URL, www.scsite.com/tdc/ch2/brief.htm. Click the links for current and additional information. To listen to an audio version of this InBrief, click the Audio button below the title, InBrief, at the top of the page. To play the audio, RealPlayer must be installed on your computer (download by clicking here).

InBrief

KeyTerms

AtTheMovies

CheckPoint

TeacherTime

CyberClass

EdIssues

NetStuff

SPECIAL FEATURES

TimeLine 2000

Guide to WWW Sites

Buyer's Guide 2000

Educational Sites

State/Federal Sites

Chat

News

Home

1. What Is Communications?

Communications, sometimes called **telecommunications**, refers to the transmission of data and information between two or more computers using a communications channel. **Electronic mail (e-mail)**, **voice mail**, **facsimile (fax)**, **telecommuting**, **online services**, **videoconferencing**, the **Internet**, and the **World Wide Web** are examples of applications that rely on communications technology.

2. Communications Networks

A communications **network** is a collection of computers and other equipment organized to share data, information, hardware, and software. Networks also require **communications software**.

3. Local and Wide Area Networks

A **local area network (LAN)** is a communications network that covers a limited geographical area such as a school, an office, a building, or a group of buildings. A LAN consists of a number of computers connected to a central computer, or server. A **wide area network (WAN)** covers a large geographical region (such as a city or school district) and uses regular telephone cables, digital lines, microwaves, wireless systems, and satellites.

4. Benefits of Computer Networks

One benefit of networking is that administrators, teachers, and students can share computer hardware, software, and data resources. The most important benefit of networking school computers is that administrators, teachers, and students instantly can access the unlimited educational resources available on the Internet and communicate with other educators and students all over the world.

5. The Internet

The **Internet** is a worldwide collection of networks that link together millions of businesses, governments, educational institutions, and individuals via modems, telephone lines, and other communications devices and media. Each of these networks provides resources and data that add to the abundance of goods, services, and information accessible via the Internet.

6. How the Internet Works

The Internet operates by dividing data into separate parts, called **packets**, and sending the packets along the best route available to a destination computer. The software used to perform this technique, called **packet switching**, is a communications protocol named **transmission control protocol/Internet protocol (TCP/IP)**. People can connect to the Internet through an organization such as a school or company, an **online service**, or an **Internet service provider (ISP)**.

7. Connecting to the Internet

Most home users use dial-up access to connect to the Internet. **Dial-up access** involves using a computer and a modem to dial into an ISP or online service over regular telephone lines. Newer technologies such as **Integrated Services Digital Network (ISDN)**, **cable modems**, and **Digital Subscriber Line (DSL)** offer an alternative to dial-up access and provide users with higher-speed connections.

8. The World Wide Web

The **World Wide Web (WWW)**, or simply **Web**, consists of a worldwide collection of electronic documents that have built-in hyperlinks to other related documents. These **hyperlinks**, also called **links**, allow users to navigate quickly from one Web page to another, regardless of whether the Web pages are located on the same computer or on different computers in different countries.

1 2 3 4 5 6 7 8

www.scsite.com/tdc/ch2/brief.htm

InBrief

InBrief

KeyTerms

AtTheMovies

CheckPoint

TeacherTime

CyberClass

EdIssues

NetStuff

SPECIAL FEATURES

TimeLine 2000

Guide to WWW Sites

Buyer's Guide 2000

Educational Sites

State/Federal Sites

Chat

News

Home

9. How a Web Page Works

A **Web page** is an electronic document viewed on the Web. A Web page is a **hypertext** document (document with text hyperlinks) or **hypermedia** document (document with text, graphics, video, or sound hyperlinks) residing on an Internet computer. The three types of hyperlinks are **target hyperlinks** that move from one location in a document to another location in the same document; **relative hyperlinks** that move from one document to another document on the same Internet computer; and **absolute hyperlinks** that move from one document to another document on a different Internet computer. Displaying pages from one Web site after another is called **Web surfing**. Web pages are created using **hypertext markup language** (**HTML**), which is a set of special instructions that specifies links to other documents and how the page is displayed.

10. Web Browser Software

Web browser software is a program that interprets and displays Web pages and enables you to link to other Web pages. Each time a browser is launched, a **home page** displays. The browser retrieves Web pages using a **Uniform Resource Locator** (**URL**), which is an address that points to a specific resource on the Internet. Browsers display hyperlinks either as underlined text of a different color or as a graphical image. Linked documents can be displayed by clicking the hyperlink or by typing its URL in the location text box.

11. Web Search Tools

Search tools enable users to locate information found at Web sites all over the world. Two basic types of search tools exist: search engines and search directories. A **search engine** is a specific type of search tool that finds Web sites, Web pages, and Internet files that match one or more keywords you enter. A **search directory** allows users to navigate to areas of interest without having to enter keywords.

12. Multimedia on the Web

Some of the more exciting Web developments involve multimedia. Most browsers have the capability of displaying basic multimedia elements on a Web page. Sometimes, however, the browser needs an additional program called a **plug-in** or **helper application**, which extends the capability of the browser. Web pages include the following multimedia elements: **graphics**, **animation**, **audio**, **video**, and **virtual reality** (**VR**).

13. Other Internet Services

Although the Web is the most talked about service on the Internet, many other Internet services are available. These services include e-mail, FTP, Telnet, newsgroups, mailing lists, and chat rooms. **E-mail** (**electronic mail**) is the transmission of messages and files via a computer network. **File transfer protocol** (**FTP**) is an Internet standard that allows you to exchange files with other computers on the Internet. A **newsgroup** is an online area in which users conduct written discussions about a particular subject. A **chat** is a real-time typed conversation that takes place on a computer.

14. Netiquette, Cookies, and Security

Netiquette is the code of acceptable behaviors users should follow while on the Internet. Many Web sites rely on cookies to track information about viewers, customers, and subscribers. A **cookie** is a small file that contains data about you, such as your login name or viewing preferences. To prevent unauthorized access, schools and businesses implement one or more layers of security. A **firewall** is a general term that refers to both hardware and software used to restrict access to data on a network. Internet **filtering software** allows parents, teachers, and others to block access to certain materials on the Internet.

1 2 3 4 5 6 7 8

www.scsite.com/tdc/ch2/terms.htm

InBrief

KeyTerms

AtTheMovies

CheckPoint

TeacherTime

CyberClass

EdIssues

NetStuff

SPECIAL FEATURES

TimeLine 2000

Guide to WWW Sites

Buyer's Guide 2000

Educational Sites

State/Federal Sites

Chat

News

Home

KeyTerms

Web Instructions: To display this page from the Web, launch your browser and enter the URL, www.scsite.com/tdc/ch2/terms.htm. Scroll through the list of terms. Click a term to display its definition and a picture. Click KeyTerms on the left to redisplay the KeyTerms page. Click the TO WEB button for current and additional information about the term from the Web. To see animations, Shockwave and Flash Player must be installed on your computer (download by clicking here).

absolute hyperlinks **[2.18]**
Acceptable Use Policy (AUP) **[2.35]**
Advanced Research Projects Agency (ARPA) **[2.11]**
analog signal **[2.4]**
animated GIF **[2.24]**
animation **[2.24]**
anonymous FTP **[2.30]**
ARPANET **[2.11]**
article **[2.30]**
AU **[2.24]**
audioconferencing **[2.25]**

backbone **[2.12]**
bookmark **[2.21]**
browser **[2.19]**

cable modem **[2.14]**
chat **[2.32]**
chat client **[2.32]**
chat room **[2.32]**
communications **(2.2)**
communications channel **[2.3]**
communications protocol **[2.13]**
communications software **[2.3]**
cookie **[2.34]**

dial-up access **[2.14]**
digital signals **[2.4]**
digital subscriber line (DSL) **[2.14]**

discovery learning **[2.18]**
domain name **[2.16]**

e-mail address **[2.28]**
electronic mail (e-mail) **[2.28]**
ePALS **[2.36]**
external modem **[2.5]**

favorites **[2.21]**
file transfer protocol (FTP) **[2.28]**
filtering software **[2.35]**
firewall **[2.35]**
FTP server **[2.28]**
FTP site **[2.28]**

graphics **[2.23]**

helper application **[2.22]**
history list **[2.21]**
home page **[2.17]**
host **[2.11]**
http:// **[2.17]**
https:// **[2.35]**
hyperlinks **[2.17]**
hypermedia **[2.18]**
hypertext **[2.18]**
hypertext markup language (HTML) **[2.18]**
hypertext transfer protocol **[2.17]**

Integrated Services Digital Network (ISDN) **[2.14]**
internal modem **[2.5]**
Internet **[2.9]**
Internet backbone **[2.15]**
Internet etiquette **[2.32]**
Internet service provider (ISP) **[2.13]**
Internet telephone service **[2.25]**
Internet telephone software **[2.25]**
Internet telephony **[2.25]**

links **[2.17]**
LISTSERV **[2.32]**
local area network (LAN) **[2.6]**
local ISP **[2.14]**

mailbox **[2.28]**
mailing list **[2.32]**
mail server **[2.28]**
marquee **[2.24]**
modem **[2.4]**
moderator **[2.32]**
Mosaic **[2.19]**
multimedia **[2.21]**

national ISP **[2.14]**
National Science Foundation (NSF) **[2.12]**
Net **[2.9]**
netiquette **[2.32]**
network **[2.3]**
network interface card **[2.6]**

newsgroup **[2.30]**
newsreader **[2.30]**
news server **[2.30]**
NSFnet **[2.12]**

online service **[2.14]**

packets **[2.12]**
packet switching **[2.13]**
plug-ins **[2.22]**
portal **[2.32]**
posting **[2.30]**

RealAudio **[2.25]**
real-time **[2.32]**
RealVideo **[2.26]**
relative hyperlinks **[2.18]**
routers **[2.13]**

search directory **[2.21]**
search engine **[2.21]**
search tools **[2.21]**
server **[2.6]**
streaming **[2.24]**
streaming audio **[2.25]**
streaming video **[2.26]**
subscribe **[2.30]**

tags **[2.18]**
target hyperlinks **[2.18]**
telecommunications **[2.2]**
Telnet **[2.30]**
thread **[2.30]**
threaded discussion **[2.30]**
thumbnail **[2.23]**
traffic **[2.12]**
transmission control protocol/ Internet protocol (TCP/IP) **[2.13]**
transmission media **[2.3]**
twisted-pair cable **[2.3]**

Uniform Resource Locator (URL) **[2.17]**
unsubscribe **[2.32]**
upload **[2.30]**
Usenet **[2.30]**
user name **[2.28]**

virtual reality (VR) **[2.26]**
VR world **[2.26]**

WAV **[2.24]**
Web **[2.17]**
Web audio applications **[2.24]**
Web browser **[2.19]**
Webmaster **[2.18]**
Web page **[2.17]**
Web publishing **[2.18]**
Web server **[2.17]**
Web site **[2.17]**
Web surfing **[2.18]**
Web video applications **[2.25]**
wide area network (WAN) **[2.6]**
World Wide Web (WWW) **[2.17]**

InBrief

KeyTerms

AtTheMovies

CheckPoint

TeacherTime

CyberClass

EdIssues

NetStuff

SPECIAL FEATURES

TimeLine 2000

Guide to WWW Sites

Buyer's Guide 2000

Educational Sites

State/Federal Sites

Chat

News

Home

www.scsite.com/tdc/ch2/movies.htm

AtTheMovies

WELCOME to
VIDEO CLIPS
from CNN

Web Instructions: To display this page from the Web, launch your browser and enter the URL, www.scsite.com/tdc/ch2/movies.htm. Click a picture to view a video. After watching the video, close the video window and then complete the exercise by answering the questions about the video. To view the videos, RealPlayer must be installed on your computer (download by clicking here).

1. Chat Goes to Work

Many people think of chat as a place for social gathering, where you can talk in real-time with friends and family. Today, chat is a valuable business tool. Companies are using chat to deliver technical support and answer customer questions. Based on the video, what kinds of companies are using chat on their Web sites to support customers? Why do companies want to use chat in this manner? What are the advantages and disadvantages? Do you think using chat is more or less effective than using telephone and/or e-mail support? Can you imagine useful applications for chat in an educational environment? Give an example where as a teacher you might use chat to expand students' learning experiences or to overcome student-learning obstacles. Ask students if they can create scenarios where chat would be beneficial to their education.

2. Internet Spam

Business advertisements take many forms. One form of advertisement and Internet communication that has been difficult for the Federal Trade Commission to regulate and Congress to legislate against is, spam. What is spam? Have you ever received spam? Why would a company prefer e-mail advertisements to hard copy? If one form of advertisement is regulated, should all forms be regulated? What is the difference between unsolicited e-mail and junk mail? Consider how an existing U.S. Constitutional amendment protects the right "to spam". What recourse do you have against spam? Encourage your students to discuss both sides of the "to spam" and "be spammed" issue by bringing examples of spam to class for discussion.

3. WebTV

In any given educational institution's population, WebTV could change individuals' overall use of the World Wide Web. As you learned in the video, WebTV Plus is now part of Microsoft's growing list of online products. Develop in your mind, the possibilities for student access to online information. First, what is WebTV? How expensive is it? How is the user able to interact online by using WebTV? Is it compatible with Windows 98? What is the relationship between the Net Channel and WebTV? Explain how WebTV expands Microsoft's presence in the consumer electronics arena? Would you want to use WebTV to access the Internet? Can you see WebTV as an answer to the need for greater student access to the Internet?

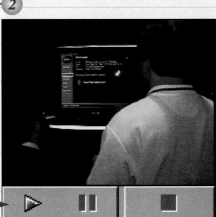

www.scsite.com/tdc/ch2/check.htm

Web Instructions: To display this page from the Web, launch your browser and enter the URL, www.scsite.com/tdc/ch2/check.htm. Click a blank line for the answer. Click the links for current and additional information. To experience the animations and interactivity, Shockwave and Flash Player must be installed on your computer (download by clicking here).

CheckPoint

InBrief

KeyTerms

AtTheMovies

CheckPoint

TeacherTime

CyberClass

EdIssues

NetStuff

SPECIAL FEATURES

TimeLine 2000

Guide to WWW Sites

Buyer's Guide 2000

Educational Sites

State/Federal Sites

Chat

News

Home

1. Label the Figure

Instructions: Identify the components of a communications system.

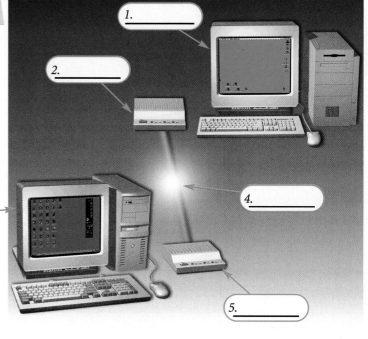

1. _____
2. _____
3. _____
4. _____
5. _____

2. Matching

Instructions: Match each term from the column on the left with the best description from the column on the right.

____ 1. e-mail

____ 2. Webmaster

____ 3. network

____ 4. filtering software

____ 5. search tool

a. an individual responsible for developing Web pages and maintaining a Web site

b. a collection of computers and other equipment organized to share data, hardware, and software

c. the transmission of messages and files via a computer network

d. enables users to locate information found at Web sites all over the world

e. allows parents, teachers, and others to block access to certain materials on the Internet

3. Short Answer

Instructions: Write a brief answer to each of the following questions.

1. How are local area networks (LANs) different from wide area networks (WANs)? _____

2. What is a Web page? What purpose do hyperlinks have on a Web page? What is hypertext markup language (HTML)? _____

3. Explain the process of streaming over the Web. How are streaming audio and streaming video similar? For what purposes is streaming used? _____

4. What is a firewall? What is filtering software? What is an Acceptable Use Policy (AUP)? Why is the use of firewalls, filtering software, and AUPs so important for K-12 networks? _____

5. What is a search tool? Name the two basic types of search tools and describe how each of these works. Which would you use to search for links in the category, Education? _____

www.scsite.com/tdc/ch2/time.htm

TeacherTime

Web Instructions: To display this page from the Web, launch your browser and enter the URL, www.scsite.com/tdc/ch2/time.htm. Click the links for current and additional information.

InBrief

KeyTerms

AtTheMovies

CheckPoint

TeacherTime

CyberClass

EdIssues

NetStuff

SPECIAL FEATURES

TimeLine 2000

Guide to WWW Sites

Buyer's Guide 2000

Educational Sites

State/Federal Sites

Chat

News

Home

1. Many schools are connecting their computers via networks so they can share hardware and software resources, access the Internet, and more. To learn about the considerations regarding a network installation, interview a technology coordinator at a local K-12 school and ask him or her the following questions: For what purpose is the network used? What are the advantages of networking? Are there disadvantages? Are all classroom computers networked? Where is the school's server located? How often is the network down for maintenance reasons?

2. Using the Internet in the classroom has numerous benefits for teachers, who can use it to find current information, online resources for lesson plans and Web-based projects, and interactive content that engages all types of learners. What are some other benefits of using the Internet in the classroom? Are there disadvantages or problems you might encounter in using Internet resources? How might you avoid or solve these problems?

3. Electronic mail (e-mail) is becoming a preferred means of communications for many businesses, schools, and individuals. Whether using an internal network or the Internet for e-mail, you should be cognizant of netiquette guidelines to help ensure that recipients understand the intent behind your e-mail messages. Some users, for example, add emoticons to an e-mail message to communicate intended emotions (by adding a smiley face to a funny comment, for example). How is using e-mail different from writing a letter? What are the similarities, if any? How might you use e-mail in your classroom with students? What benefits might your students experience from using e-mail?

4. The two more popular Web browsers are Netscape Navigator and Microsoft Internet Explorer. Both software companies claim that their browser is the best. Compare these two browsers and form your own opinion. What features are offered in both browsers? Is one browser easier to use than the other browser? If so, how? What capabilities does one have that the other does not? Are both browsers free to anyone who downloads them? Based on your evaluation, which Web browser do you think is better? Why? Which browser would you rather have your students use? Why?

5. The Internet offers teachers, students, and other users around the world almost unlimited resources on virtually any topic. For example, just about everybody agrees that raising children today can be a challenge. Children seem to change almost overnight as they approach adolescence. Is raising daughters different from raising sons? Do you agree that keeping up with teenager's emotional, as well as their physical changes can be tricky? Help and hope are available in many places, and the World Wide Web offers an abundance of information that can help parents and teachers get young people through these roller coaster years. Search the Internet on this topic using a popular search engine tool. To find an array of sources of information, try searching the Internet using different keywords and combinations of keywords, such as raising teenagers, teenage years, and child rearing.

www.scsite.com/tdc/ch2/class.htm

CyberClass

Web Instructions: To display this page from the Web, launch your browser and enter the URL, www.scsite.com/tdc/ch2/class.htm. To start Level I CyberClass, click a Level I link on this page or enter the URL, www.cyber-class.com. Click the Student button, click *Teachers Discovering Computers* in the list of titles, and then click the Enter a site button. To start Level II or III CyberClass (available only to those purchasers of a CyberClass floppy disk), place your CyberClass floppy disk in drive A, click Start on the taskbar, click Run on the Start menu, type a:connect in the Open text box, click the OK button, click the Enter CyberClass button, and then follow the instructions. If you are using a Macintosh, see your instructor.

InBrief

KeyTerms

AtTheMovies

CheckPoint

TeacherTime

CyberClass

EdIssues

NetStuff

SPECIAL FEATURES

TimeLine 2000

Guide to WWW Sites

Buyer's Guide 2000

Educational Sites

State/Federal Sites

Chat

News

Home

1. Flash Cards (<u>Level I</u>, Level II, and Level III)

Click Flash Cards on the Main Menu of the CyberClass Web page. Click the plus sign before the Chapter 2 title. Click What is Communications and answer all the cards in that section. Then, click Communications Networks and answer the cards in that section. If you have less than 85% correct, continue to answer cards in other sections until you have more than 85% correct. All users: Answer as many more Flash Cards as you desire. Close the Electronic Flash Card window and the Flash Cards window by clicking the Close button in the upper-right corner of each window.

2. Practice Test (<u>Level I</u>, Level II, and Level III)

Click Testing on the Main Menu of the CyberClass Web page. Click the Select a book box arrow and then click Teachers Discovering Computers. Click the Select a test to take box arrow and then click the Chapter 2 title in the list. Click the Take Test button. If necessary, maximize the window. Take the practice test and then click the Submit Test button. Click the Display Study Guide button. Review the Study Guide. Scroll down and click the Return To CyberClass button. Click the Yes button to close the Study Guide window. If your score was less than 90%, click the Take another Test button to take another practice test. Continue taking tests until your score is greater than 90%. Then, click the Done button.

3. Web Guide (<u>Level I</u>, Level II, and Level III)

Click Web Guide on the Main Menu of the CyberClass Web page. When the Guide to World Wide Web Sites page displays, click Education and CollegeNET. Search the CollegeNET database for your college or university. Does the information presented accurately reflect the institution you know? When you are finished, write a brief synopsis of what you found. Hand in the synopsis to your instructor.

4. Assignments and Syllabus (Level II and Level III)

Click Assignments on the Main Menu of the CyberClass Web page. Ensure you are aware of all assignments and when they are due. Click Syllabus on the Main Menu of the CyberClass Web page. Verify you are up to date on all activities for the class.

5. CyberChallenge (Level II and Level III)

Click CyberChallenge on the Main Menu of the CyberClass Web page. Click the Select a book box arrow and then click Teachers Discovering Computers. Click the Select a board to play box arrow and then click Chapter 2 in the list. Click the Play CyberChallenge button. Maximize the CyberChallenge window. Play CyberChallenge until your score for a complete game is 500 points or more. Close the CyberChallenge window.

6. Hot Links (Level II and Level III)

Click Hot Links on the Main Menu of the CyberClass Web page. Review the sites in the Hot Links section and then write a brief report indicating which site you like best and why.

www.scsite.com/tdc/ch2/issues.htm

EdIssues

Web Instructions: To display this page from the Web, launch your browser and enter the URL, www.scsite.com/tdc/ch2/issues.htm. Click the links for current and additional information to help you respond to the EdIssues questions.

1. Online Safety

Shortly after you teach your fourth grade students how to use e-mail, one of your students brings in a copy of an e-mail message he received from an unknown toy company. The e-mail message not only advertises product using false claims, it also asks your student to provide personal information — including a parent's credit card number. What is your response? Do you report this to someone? If so, who? At what age do you think educators should start teaching students about online safety? How are you going to teach your students about online safety?

2. Inappropriate Materials

You are grading a middle school student's project that she created in the school's computer lab and saved on a floppy disk. You notice many other files on the floppy disk. You decide to see what they are. The files contain inappropriate materials that you suspect were downloaded from the Web, which is confusing because you thought all of the computers in your school contained Internet filtering programs. What are you going to do? How are you going to approach the student? What are you going to say to the computer lab teacher? Who else should you contact?

3. Online Research Services

When preparing a research report, students often spend a large part of their efforts locating the necessary information. While Internet search tools can help students find relevant information, they often fail to point them to important resources such as journals and books. To ensure that the results of their searches are more comprehensive, some students are turning to Web-based online research services. Visit an online research service to learn about its features. What resources does the service use? How much does it cost? How is using an online research service like using a library? How appropriate is the service for students? Would you want your students using an online research service?

InBrief

KeyTerms

AtTheMovies

CheckPoint

TeacherTime

CyberClass

EdIssues

NetStuff

SPECIAL FEATURES

TimeLine 2000

Guide to WWW Sites

Buyer's Guide 2000

Educational Sites

State/Federal Sites

Chat

News

Home

www.scsite.com/tdc/ch2/issues.htm

InBrief

KeyTerms

AtTheMovies

CheckPoint

TeacherTime

CyberClass

EdIssues

NetStuff

SPECIAL FEATURES

TimeLine 2000

Guide to WWW Sites

Buyer's Guide 2000

Educational Sites

State/Federal Sites

Chat

News

Home

EdIssues

4. Network Security

For the past month, you have had difficulty getting three new computers set up and running in your classroom. Despite your numerous requests for assistance, the district's technology coordinator is just too overwhelmed with other technology-related issues to help. Yesterday during your school's open house, a student's father volunteered to set up the computers, load any needed software, and connect the computers to the school's network. While he is qualified to do the work — he's a computer technician for a local Internet service provider — he will need your password to access the school's network. Giving him your password may compromise network security as he will have access to sensitive information on the school's network, including confidential information on the students. Would you give him your password? Would you let him help you? Would you contact anyone else?

5. Net Censoring

Each day, schools, organizations, and individuals across the country continue in an ongoing debate about Internet censorship. A number of organizations, including the American Library Association, oppose the use of Internet filtering software programs. Some people feel that schools are censoring out valuable information and that students would be better off with unlimited access, coupled with strict teacher observation and guidelines. Others, however, are very concerned about the use of the Internet in schools and do not want children using the Internet — even if filtering programs and Acceptable Use Policies are in place. Do you think schools should limit or ban Internet usage? How could you use effectively the Internet in your classroom without offending or angering parents?

NetStuff

Web Instructions: To display this page from the Web, launch your browser and enter the URL, www.scsite.com/tdc/ch2/net.htm. To use the Connecting to the Internet lab or the World Wide Web lab from the Web, Shockwave and Flash Player must be installed on your computer (download by clicking here).

- InBrief
- KeyTerms
- AtTheMovies
- CheckPoint
- TeacherTime
- CyberClass
- EdIssues
- NetStuff

SPECIAL FEATURES

- TimeLine 2000
- Guide to WWW Sites
- Buyer's Guide 2000
- Educational Sites
- State/Federal Sites
- Chat
- News
- Home

CONNECTING TO THE INTERNET LAB

1. Shelly Cashman Series Connecting to the Internet Lab

Follow the instructions in NetStuff 1 on page 1.34 to start and use the Connecting to the Internet lab. If you are running from the Web, enter the URL, www.scsite.com/sclabs/menu.htm; or display this NetStuff page (see instructions at the top of this page) and then click the CONNECTING TO THE INTERNET LAB button.

WORLD WIDE WEB LAB

2. Shelly Cashman Series World Wide Web Lab

Follow the instructions in NetStuff 1 on page 1.34 to start and use the World Wide Web lab. If you are running from the Web, enter the URL, www.scsite.com/sclabs/menu.htm; or display the NetStuff page (see instructions at the top of this page) and then click the WORLD WIDE WEB LAB button.

WEBTV

3. WebTV

If you are using WebTV and are watching television and an interesting new product is shown, you can click your remote and be connected instantly to the product's Web site. Click the WEBTV button to complete an exercise to learn more about using WebTV.

FACTS AND FUN

4. Search Engine Facts and Fun

Click the FACTS AND FUN button to complete an exercise to learn more about the background of search engines and to learn tips on how to use search engines. This exercise includes a game to test your search engine knowledge.

SEARCH ENGINE TUTORIAL

5. Search Engine Tutorial

Click the SEARCH ENGINE TUTORIAL button to complete an exercise to learn how to conduct Internet searches.

BOOKMARKS

6. Using Bookmarks

Click the BOOKMARKS button to complete an exercise to learn how to make and organize your bookmarks.

REAL-TIME AUCTION

7. Real-time Auction

Today, many real-time auctions are available on the Web. Click the REAL-TIME AUCTION button to complete an exercise to participate in a real-time auction.

WEB CHAT

8. Web Chat

The EdIssues section presents various scenarios on the uses of computers, technologies, and non-technology-related issues in K-12 education. Click the WEB CHAT button to enter a Web Chat discussion related to the EdIssues exercises.

2.50

gUiDE tO wOrLD wIDe wEB sITeS

THE ANDY WARHOL MUSEUM

MUSEUM TOUR

The Underground Cafe

The Underground Cafe at the Andy Warhol Museum, serves light meals - soups, salads, sandwiches, and pastries. Also available are espresso and cappuccino, mineral water and soft drinks, including Coca-Cola in the original glass bottles. It is located in the Underground at the Museum.

The Underground Cafe is open to the public without an admission fee during museum hours. Please call 412.237.8300 for more information.

abn All Business Network

Welcome to the All Business Network- the destination for business on the Web!

Checkout This Great Online Music Catalog

Artist [ ] [go]

Visit:

The Complete Business Resource! [GO!]

plus Keyword Search
Headline News
The Job Bank
Online Databases
Business Services
Online Basics
Business Park

Free Stuff

and why SMALL BUSINESS NEWS chose ABN as one of the **Top 5** business sites!

T he World Wide Web is an exciting and highly dynamic medium. Every day, new Web sites are added, existing ones are changed, and still others cease to exist. Because of this, you may find that a URL listed here has changed or no longer is valid. In order to offer the most up-to-date information available, the *Teachers Discovering Computers* Web site is continually checked and updated.

In later chapters, you will find two additional Special Features that will provide you with links to and information on hundreds of educational-related Web sites. A Guide to Educational Sites and Professional Organizations is located after chapter 6 and a Guide to State and Federal Government Educational Web Sites is located after Chapter 8.

WEB INSTRUCTIONS: *To gain World Wide Web access to the most current version of the sites included in this special feature, launch your browser and enter the URL,* www.scsite.com/tdc/ch2/websites.htm.

JobOptions™

Search Employers | Post Resumes | Job Alert | Career Tools

Job Search

Post Your Resume
Our fast, easy-to-use resume builder gives you professional results that look great online, via email, and on the printed page.

Job Alert
Just sign up, and we'll search our jobs database and email you new openings that match your specifications.

YAHOO! FINANC

Home - Yah

wed Oct 14 10:45am ET - U.S. Markets close in 5 hours 15 m

| Dow 7955.39 +17.25 (+0.22%) | Nasdaq 1523.62 +14.17 (+0.94%) | S&P 500 |
| NYSE Volume 191,485,000 | Nasdaq Volume 184,412,000 | 30-Yr Bon |

Microsoft
HomeAdvisor

CollegeNET

Scholarships
Financial Aid
App

About CollegeNET | College Search | CollegeBOT Crawler

the **computer** museum

HISTORY | GALLERIES | RESOURCES | INFO DESK | STORE

Learn about computers and have fun at the same time!

PLAY INTERACTIVE EXHIBITS
COMPUTER HISTORY RESOURCES
DOWNLOAD EDUCATIONAL MATERIALS

The Virtual FishTank!

Categories

Art	**History**
Business and Finance	**Humor**
Careers and Employment	**Internet**
Computers and Computing	**Museums**
Education	**News Sources**
Entertainment	**Reference**
Environment	**Science**
Government and Politics	**Shopping**
Health and Medicine	**Sports**
	Travel
	Unclassified
	Weather

CATEGORY/SITE NAME	LOCATION	COMMENT

Art

World Wide Arts Resources	wwar.com	Links to many art sites
Fine Art Forum	www.msstate.edu/Fineart_Online/home.html	Art and technology news
Leonardo da Vinci	sunsite.unc.edu/wm/paint/auth/vinci	Works of the famous Italian artist and thinker
The Andy Warhol Museum	www.clpgh.org/warhol	Famous American pop artist
The WebMuseum	mistral.culture.fr/louvre/louvrea.htm	Web version of Louvre Museum, Paris
World Art Treasures	sgwww.epfl.ch/BERGER	100,000 slides organized by civilization

Business and Finance

FinanCenter, Inc.	www.financenter.com	Personal finance information
FINWEB All Business Network	www.all-biz.com	Links to Web business information
PC Quote	www.pcquote.com	Free delayed stock quotes
Yahoo! Finance	quote.yahoo.com	Free delayed stock quotes
Stock Research Group	www.stockgroup.com	Investment information
The Wall Street Journal	interactive.wsj.com	Financial news page

Careers and Employment

CareerMagazine	www.careermag.com	Career articles and information
CareerMosaic®	www.careermosaic.com	Jobs from around the world
E-Span Job Options	www.joboptions.com	Searchable job database
CareerPath	www.careerpath.com	Job listings from U.S. newspapers

Computers and Computing

Computer companies	Insert name or initials of most computer companies between www. and .com to find their Web site. Examples: www.ibm.com, www.microsoft.com, www.dell.com.	
MIT Media Lab	www.media.mit.edu	Information on computer trends
The Computer Museum	www.net.org	Exhibits and history of computing
Virtual Computer Library	www.utexas.edu/computer/vcl	Information on computers and computing
The Virtual Museum of Computing (VMoC)	www.comlab.ox.ac.uk/archive/other/ museums/computing.html	History of computing and online computer based exhibits

Education

CollegeNET	www.collegenet.com	Searchable database of more than 2,000 colleges and universities
EdLinks	webpages.marshall.edu/~jmullens/ edlinks.html	Links to many educational sites
The Open University	www.open.ac.uk	Independent study courses from U.K.

Entertainment

Classics World	www.bmgclassics.com/classics/index.html	Classical music information
Internet Underground Music Archive	www.iuma.com	Underground Music Database
Mr. Showbiz	www.mrshowbiz.com	Information on latest films
Music Boulevard	www.musicblvd.com	Search for and buy all types of music
Playbill On-Line	www.playbill.com	Theater news
Rock & Roll Hall of Fame	www.rockhall.com	Cleveland museum site

CATEGORY/SITE NAME	LOCATION	COMMENT
Environment		
EnviroLink Network	www.envirolink.org	Environmental information
Greenpeace	www.greenpeace.org	Environmental activism
U.S.Environmental Protection Agency (EPA)	www.epa.gov	U.S. government environmental news
Government and Politics		
Canada Info	www.clo.com/~canadainfo/canada.html	List of Canadian Web sites
CIA	www.odci.gov/cia	Political and economic information on countries
FedWorld	www.fedworld.gov	Links to U.S. government sites
The Library of Congress	www.loc.gov	Variety of U.S. government information
The White House	www.whitehouse.gov	Take tour and learn about occupants
United Nations	www.un.org	Latest UN projects and information
U.S. Census Bureau	www.census.gov	Population and other statistics
Health and Medicine		
Centers for Disease Control and Prevention (CDC)	www.cdc.gov	How to prevent and control disease
CODI	codi.buffalo.edu	Resource for disability products and services
The Interactive Patient	medicus.marshall.edu/medicus.htm	Simulates visit to doctor
Women's Medical Health Page	www.cbull.com/health.htm	Articles and links to other sites

CATEGORY/SITE NAME	LOCATION	COMMENT
History		
American Memory	rs6.loc.gov/amhome.html	American history
Historical Text Archive	www.msstate.edu/Archives/History/USA/usa.html	U.S. documents, photos, and database
World History Archives	www.hartford-hwp.com/archives/index.html	Links to history sites
Virtual Library History	history.cc.ukans.edu/history/	Organized links to history sites
Humor		
Calvin & Hobbes Gallery	www.calvinandhobbes.com	Comic strip gallery
Comedy Central Online	www.comcentral.com	From comedy TV network
Late Show Top 10 Archive	marketing.cbs.com/lateshow/topten	David Letterman Top 10 lists
The Dilbert Zone	www.unitedmedia.com/comics/dilbert	Humorous insights about working
Internet		
Beginners Central Internet	northernwebs.com/bc	Beginners guide to the Internet
Internet Glossary	www.matisse.net/files/glossary.html	Definitions of Internet terms
WWW Frequently Asked Questions	www.boutell.com/faq/oldfaq/index.html	Common Web questions and answers

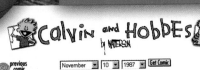

CATEGORY/SITE NAME	LOCATION	COMMENT
Museums		
The Smithsonian	www.si.edu	Information and links to Smithsonian museums
University of California Museum of Paleontology	www.ucmp.berkeley.edu	Great information on dinosaurs and other exhibits
U.S. Holocaust Memorial Museum	www.ushmm.org	Dedicated to World War II victims
News Sources		
C/NET	www.cnet.com	Technology news
CNN Interactive	www.cnn.com	CNN all-news network
Pathfinder	www.pathfinder.com	Excerpts from Time-Warner magazines
The Electronic Newsstand	www.enews.com	Articles from worldwide publications
USA TODAY	www.usatoday.com	Latest U.S. and international news
Wired News	www.wired.com	*Wired* magazine online and HotWired Network
Reference		
Bartlett's Quotations	www.columbia.edu/acis/bartleby/bartlett	Organized, searchable database of famous quotes
Dictionary Library	math-www.uni-paderborn.de/HTML/Dictionaries.html	Links to many types of dictionaries
Internet Public Library	www.ipl.org	Literature and reference works
The New York Public Library	www.nypl.org	Extensive reference and research material
Science		
American Institute of Physics	www.aip.org	Physics research information
Exploratorium	www.exploratorium.edu	Interactive science exhibits
Internet Chemistry Index	www.chemie.de/	List of chemistry information sites
The NASA Homepage	www.nasa.gov	Information on U.S. space program
The Nine Planets	seds.lpl.arizona.edu/nineplanets/nineplanets/	Tour the solar system

2.55

CATEGORY/SITE NAME	LOCATION	COMMENT
Shopping		
Amazon.com	www.amazon.com	Books and gifts
BizWeb	www.bizweb.com	Search for products from more than 1,000 companies
CommerceNet	www.commerce.net	Index of products and services
Consumer World	www.consumerworld.org	Consumer information
Internet Bookshop	www.bookshop.co.uk	780,000 titles on more than 2,000 subjects
Internet Shopping Network	www.internet.net	Specialty stores, hot deals, computer products
The Internet Mall™	www.internet-mall.com	Comprehensive list of Web businesses
Sports		
ESPNET SportsZone	ESPN.SportsZone.com	Latest sports news
NBA Basketball	www.nba.com	Information and links to team sites
NFL Football	www.nfl.com	Information and links to team sites
Sports Illustrated	www.CNNSI.com	Leading sports magazine
Travel		
InfoHub WWW Travel Guide	www.infohub.com	Worldwide travel information
Excite City.Net	www.city.net	Guide to world cities
Lonely Planet Travel Guides	www.lonelyplanet.com	Budget travel guides and stories
Microsoft Expedia	expedia.msn.com	Complete travel resource
Travelocity℠	www.travelocity.com	Online travel agency
TravelWeb℠	www.travelweb.com	Places to stay
Unclassified		
Cool Site of the Day	cool.infi.net	Different site each day
Cupid's Network™	www.cupidnet.com	Links to dating resources
Pizza Hut	www.pizzahut.com	Order pizza online (limited areas)
Weather		
INTELLiCAST Guides	www.intellicast.com	International weather and skiing information
The Weather Channel	www.weather.com	National and local forecasts

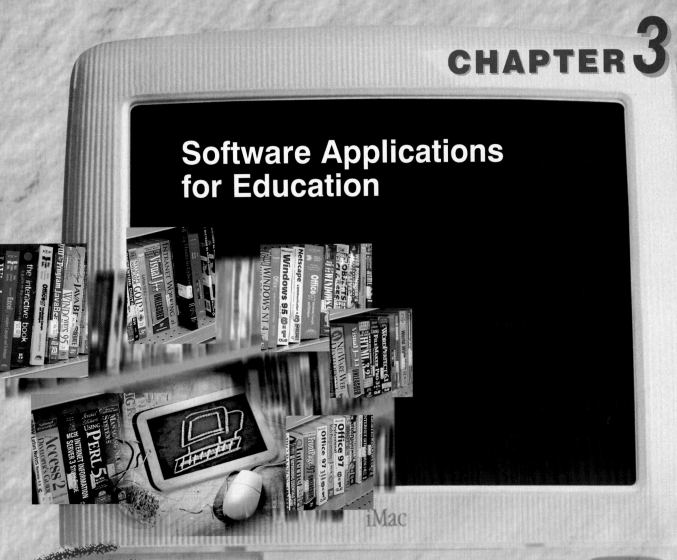

Software Applications for Education

Objectives

After completing this chapter, you will be able to:

- Define and describe a user interface and a graphical user interface

- Identify the important features of widely used software applications

- Describe the advantages of software suites

- Explain how to create Web documents

- Discuss why the use of special needs software is important for K-12 schools

- List and describe learning aids and support tools that help you use and learn software applications

- Explain how to work with different versions of software applications

AN ESSENTIAL ASPECT OF BUILDING COMPUTER LITERACY IS LEARNING ABOUT SOFTWARE, WHICH IS THE SERIES OF INSTRUCTIONS THAT TELL COMPUTER HARDWARE HOW TO PERFORM TASKS. Having a solid understanding of software — especially application software — will help you apprehend how administrators, teachers, students, and other individuals use personal computers in today's society. It also will help you use your computer to be more productive, organized, and well informed.

Application software such as word processing, spreadsheets, and e-mail can help you perform tasks such as creating documents, doing research, and managing projects. Before discussing various software applications used by teachers and students, however, this chapter provides a basic overview of the operating system and the user interface used on both Macintosh computers and PCs. As you have learned, the user interface controls how you work with any software, including application software.

WebInfo

For more information on application software packages, visit the Teachers Discovering Computers Chapter 3 WebInfo page

(www.scsite.com/tdc/ch3/webinfo.htm)

and click Application.

Understanding application software also can help advance your personal and professional goals by helping you manage student records, teach students with different academic needs, and work more productively. In addition, this chapter introduces you to the learning aids and tools available to help you and your students learn to use software applications. Finally, you will learn how to work with different versions of the same software on different computers. Because application software concepts are so important, this book discusses them early so you can refer back to them as you learn more about computers, how they are used today, and how they can help you in your teaching career.

Application Software

Recall that application software consists of programs designed to perform specific tasks for users. Application software, also called a **software application** or **application** can be used for the following purposes:

- As a productivity/business tool

- Supporting school and professional activities
- Assisting with graphics and multimedia projects
- Helping with home and personal activities
- Facilitating communications

The table in **Figure 3-1** categorizes popular types of application software by their general use. These five categories are not all-inclusive or mutually exclusive; for example, e-mail can support productivity, a software suite can include Web page authoring tools, and tax preparation software can be used by a business. In the course of a day, week, or month, you are likely to find yourself using software from many of these categories, whether you are at school, home, or work. Even though personally you may not use all of the applications, you should at least be familiar with their capabilities.

Communications applications such as e-mail, Web browsers, and others were discussed in the previous chapter. The concepts for each application in the other four categories are discussed generally using examples from actual application programs used on Macintosh computers and PCs.

Categories of Application Software

Application Software	Productivity/ Business	Graphics/ Multimedia	School/ Professional	Home/ Personal	Communications
	• Word Processing	• Desktop Publishing	• School/ Student Management	• Personal Finance	• E-mail
	• Spreadsheet	• Paint/Image Editing	• Grade Book	• Tax Preparation	• Browser
	• Database	• Multimedia Authoring	• Education/ Reference	• Legal	
	• Presentation Graphics	• Web Page Authoring	• Special Needs	• Entertainment	
	• Personal Information Management				
	• Software Suite				

Figure 3-1 The five major categories of popular application software. You likely will use software from more than one of these categories.

A huge variety of application software such as word processing is available as packaged software that can be purchased from software vendors in retail stores or on the Web. A particular software product, such as Microsoft Word, for example, often is called a **software package**. Many application software packages also are available as shareware, freeware, and public-domain software; these packages, however, usually have fewer capabilities than retail software packages.

The Role of the Operating System

Like most computer users, you probably are somewhat familiar with application software. To run any application software, however, your computer must be running another type of software — an operating system.

As described in Chapter 1, software can be categorized into two types: system software and application software. **System software** consists of programs that control the operations of the computer and its devices. As shown in **Figure 3-2**, system software serves as the interface between you (the user), your application software, and your computer's hardware. One type of system software, the **operating system**, contains instructions that coordinate all of the activities of the hardware devices in a computer. The operating system also contains instructions that allow you to run application software.

Before either a Macintosh computer or a PC can run any application software, the operating system must be loaded from the hard disk into the computer's memory. Each time you start your computer, the operating system is loaded, or copied, into memory from the computer's hard disk. Once the operating system is loaded, it tells the computer how to perform functions such as processing program instructions and transferring data between input and output devices and memory. The operating system, which remains in memory while the computer is running, allows you to communicate with the computer and other software, such as word processing, grade books, and other application programs. The operating system continues to run until the computer is turned off.

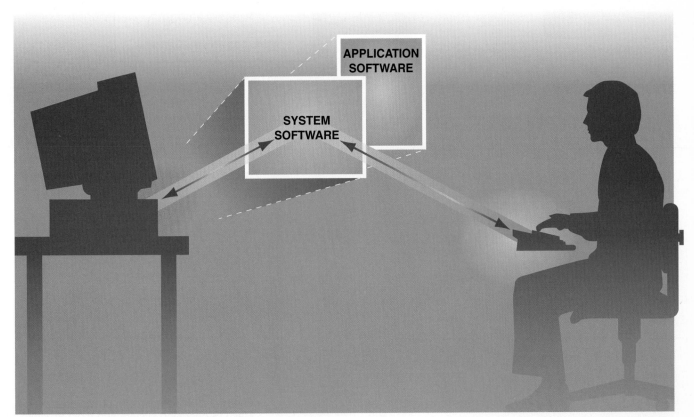

Figure 3-2 A user does not communicate directly with the computer hardware; instead, the user communicates with the system software or with the application software.

WebInfo

For information on Windows, visit the Teachers Discovering Computers Chapter 3 WebInfo page

(www.scsite.com/tdc/ ch3/webinfo.htm)

and click Windows.

WebInfo

For information on Mac OS, visit the Teachers Discovering Computers Chapter 3 WebInfo page

(www.scsite.com/tdc/ ch3/webinfo.htm)

and click Mac OS.

The Role of the User Interface

All software, including the operating system, is designed to communicate with the user in a certain way, through a user interface. A **user interface** controls how you enter data or instructions (input) and how information is presented on the screen (output).

One of the more common user interfaces is a graphical user interface (GUI). A **graphical user interface**, or **GUI** (pronounced gooey), combines text, graphics, and other visual cues to make software easier to use.

In 1984, Apple Computer introduced a new operating system based on a graphical user interface. Recognizing the value of this easy-to-use interface, many software companies followed suit, developing their own GUI software. Since then, Apple has developed several new versions of its original GUI operating system for its Macintosh computers. Today, Macintosh computers use various versions of the Macintosh operating system, called **Mac OS [Figure 3-3a]**. Today's most widely used personal computer operating system and graphical user interface, however, is Microsoft Windows, which often is referred to simply as **Windows** with a capital W **[Figure 3-3b]**.

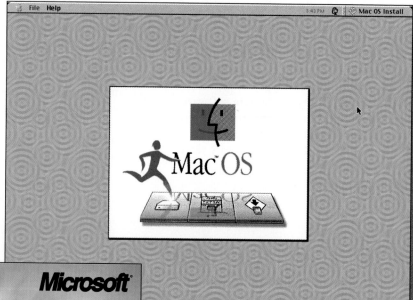

[3-3a] Apple Macintosh operating system

[3-3b] PC operating system

Figure 3-3 Macintosh computers use the Mac OS operating system and most PCs use Microsoft Windows.

Starting a Software Application

Both the Apple Macintosh and Microsoft Windows operating systems use the concept of a desktop to make the computer easier to use. The **desktop** is an on-screen work area that uses common graphical elements such as icons, buttons, windows, menus, and dialog boxes, all of which can display on the desktop **[Figure 3-4]**.

icons

Microsoft Works program window

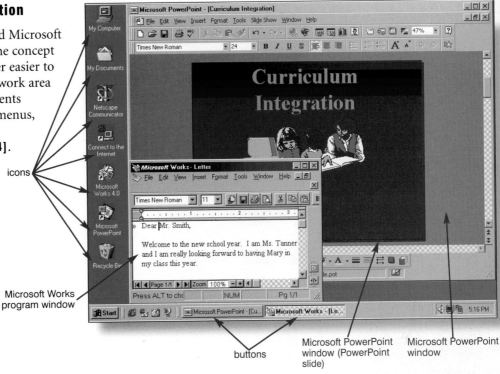

buttons

Microsoft PowerPoint window (PowerPoint slide)

Microsoft PowerPoint window

CHAPTER 3

Figure 3-4 This Windows desktop shows a variety of icons, buttons, and application windows.

An **icon** is a small picture that represents a program, an instruction, or some other object. A **button** is a graphical element (usually a rectangular or circular shape) that when selected, causes a specific action to take place. To select a button, typically you press it, or click it, using a pointing device such as a mouse. You also can select a button using the keyboard. Icons, text, or a combination of both are used to identify buttons.

The Windows desktop contains a Start button in its lower-left corner, which can be used to start an application. When you click the Start button, the Start menu displays on the desktop. A **menu** is a list of commands from which you can select. **Commands** are instructions that cause a computer program to perform a specific action. Some menus have a **submenu**, which is a list of commands that displays when you select a command on a previous menu. For example, as shown in **Figure 3-5**, when you click the Start button and select the Programs command on the Start menu, the Programs submenu displays. Selecting the Accessories command on the Programs submenu displays the Accessories submenu. As shown in the Accessories submenu, Windows includes several applications such as Calculator, Paint, and WordPad.

Start menu

Programs submenu

right arrowhead

Accessories submenu

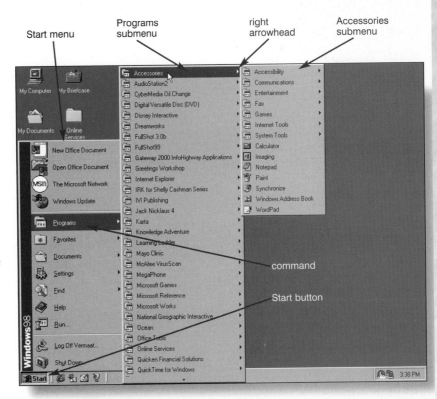

command

Start button

Figure 3-5 The Start menu and the Programs and Accessories submenus display on the Windows desktop. Some commands on menus are followed by a right arrowhead, which indicates that a submenu of additional commands exists.

CHAPTER 3

toolbar title bar Paint window

Figure 3-6 The Paint program displays in a window on the desktop. Paint is an application included with Windows that allows you to create, modify, and print artwork and pictures. Many applications contain a toolbar, which is a row or column of buttons for commonly used tasks.

menus

Figure 3-7 The desktop of the Macintosh operating system consists of an arrangement different from the Windows desktop; however, both operating systems contain similar features.

application windows

You can start an application by clicking its program name on a menu or submenu. Doing so instructs the operating system to start the application by transferring the program's instructions from a storage medium into memory. For example, if you click Paint on the Accessories submenu, Windows transfers the program instructions from the computer's hard disk into memory.

Once started, an application displays in a window on the desktop. A **window** is a rectangular area of the screen that is used to display a program, data, and/or information [Figure 3-6]. The top of a window has a **title bar**, which is a horizontal space that contains the window's name.

One of the major advantages of a graphical user interface is that elements such as icons, buttons, and menus, usually are common across applications. Once you learn the purpose and functionality of these elements, you can apply that knowledge to several software applications. Many of the features just described also are applicable to the desktop of the Macintosh operating system, which is arranged somewhat differently [Figure 3-7].

The features of a user interface make it easier for the user to communicate with a personal computer. You will see examples of these features and how they are used as you learn about various software applications found on school and home Macintosh computers and PCs.

icons

Working with Software Applications

While using many software applications, you have the ability to create, edit, format, print, and save documents. A **document** is a piece of work created with an application program and saved on a disk with a unique file name. Many users think of documents as word processing materials. To a computer, however, data is nothing more than a collection of characters, so a spreadsheet or graphic is as much a document as a letter or report. During the process of developing a document, you likely will switch back and forth between all of the following activities.

Creating involves developing the document by entering text or numbers, designing graphics, and performing other tasks using an input device such as a keyboard or mouse. If you design a map using the graphics tools in Paint, for example, you are creating a document.

Editing is the process of making changes to the document's existing content. Common editing features include inserting, deleting, cutting, copying, and pasting items in a document. For example, using Paint, you can **insert**, or add, text to the map, such as the names of key landmarks. When you **delete**, you remove text. To **cut** involves removing a portion of the document and electronically storing it in a temporary storage location called the **Clipboard**. When you **copy**, a portion of the document is duplicated and stored on the Clipboard. To place whatever is stored on the Clipboard into the document, you **paste** it into the document.

Formatting involves changing the appearance of a document. Formatting is important because the overall look of a document can significantly affect its ability to communicate effectively. For example, you might want to increase the size of the text to improve readability.

One often-used formatting task involves changing the font, font size, or font style of text. A **font** is a name assigned to a specific design of characters. Arial and Times New Roman are examples of fonts. The **font size** specifies the size of the characters in a particular font. Font size is gauged by a measurement system called **points**. A single point is about 1/72 of one inch in height. The text you are reading in this book is ten point. Thus, each character is about 10/72 of an inch in height. A **font style** is used to add emphasis to a font. Examples of font styles are **bold**, *italic*, and underline. Examples of these and additional formatting features are shown in **Figure 3-8**.

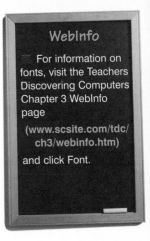

WebInfo

For information on fonts, visit the Teachers Discovering Computers Chapter 3 WebInfo page **(www.scsite.com/tdc/ch3/webinfo.htm)** and click Font.

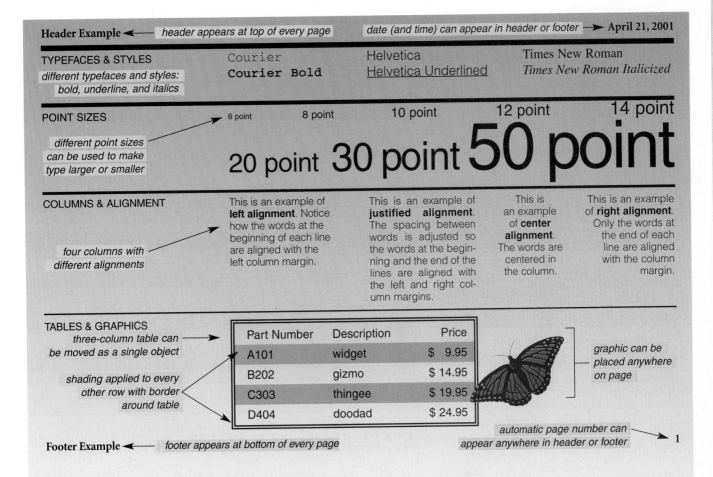

Figure 3-8 Examples of formatting features available with many productivity programs.

While you are creating, editing, and formatting a document, it is held temporarily in memory. Once you have completed these steps, you may want to save your document for future use. **Saving** is the process of copying a document from memory to a storage medium such as a floppy disk or hard disk. You should save the document frequently while working with it so your work will not be lost. Many applications also have an optional **AutoSave** feature that automatically saves open documents at specified time periods.

Any document on which you are working or have saved exists as a file. A **file** is a named collection of data, instructions, or information, such as a document that you create, a program, or a set of data used by a program. To distinguish among various files, each file has a **file name**, which is a unique set of letters, numbers, and other characters that identifies the file.

Once you have created a document, you can print it many times, with each copy looking just like the first. **Printing** is the process of sending a file to a printer to generate output on a medium such as paper. You also can send the document to others electronically, if your computer is connected to a network.

In some cases, when you instruct a program to perform an activity such as printing, a dialog box displays. A **dialog box** is a special window displayed by a program to provide information, present available options, or request a response using command buttons, option buttons, text boxes, and check boxes **[Figure 3-9]**. A Print dialog box, for example, gives you many printing options, such as printing multiple copies, using different printers, or viewing

the document on the screen exactly as it will look when printed.

Productivity Software

Productivity software is designed to make people more effective and efficient while performing daily activities. Productivity software includes applications such as word processing, spreadsheet, database, presentation graphics, personal information management, and software suites. The features and functions of each of these applications are discussed in the following sections.

Word Processing Software

The most widely used application software is **word processing software**, which is used to create, edit, and format documents that consist primarily of text **[Figure 3-10]**. Millions of people use word processing software every day to create documents such as letters, memos,

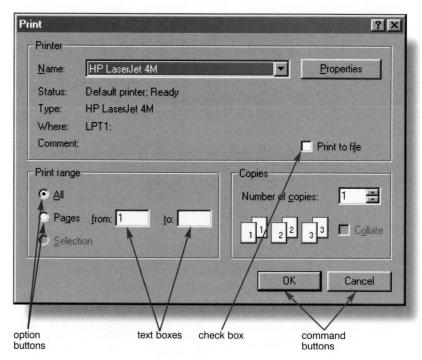

Figure 3-9 This Print dialog box shows elements common to many dialog boxes, such as option buttons, text boxes, check boxes, and command buttons.

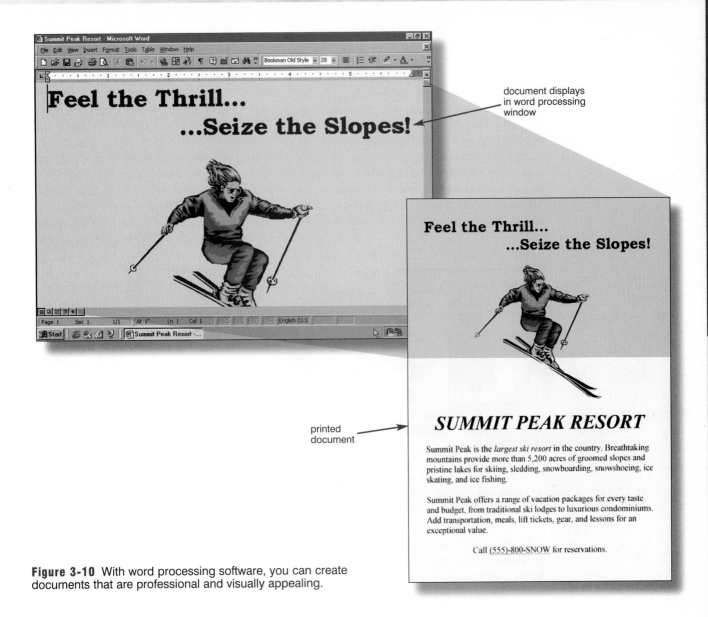

document displays
in word processing
window

printed
document

Figure 3-10 With word processing software, you can create documents that are professional and visually appealing.

reports, fax cover sheets, mailing labels, and newsletters. The more popular word processing programs used in schools today are Microsoft Word and the word processing applications included with AppleWorks, ClarisWorks, and Microsoft Works. By acquiring solid word processing skills, teachers can increase their productivity significantly by using word processing software to create written documents, such as lesson plans and student tests.

In addition to supporting basic text, word processing software has many formatting features to make documents look professional and visually appealing. When developing a newsletter, for example, you can change the font and font size of headlines and headings, change color of characters, or organize text into newspaper-style columns. Any colors used for characters or other formatting will print as black or gray unless you have a color printer.

Most word processing software also can incorporate graphics of many types. For example, you can enhance a document by adding a **border**, which is a decorative line or pattern along one or more edges of a page or graphic. One type of graphic commonly included with word processing software is **clip art**, which is a collection of drawings, diagrams, and photographs that can be inserted in other documents. Clip art collections, which can contain several hundred to several thousand images, usually are grouped by type, such as buildings, nature, or people **[Figure 3-11]**. If you want to use clip art not included in your word processing package, you can create clip art and other graphics using Paint or other applications and **import** (bring into) the clip art into a word processing document. Paint and image editing software is discussed later in this chapter. Once you insert or import a clip art image or other graphic into a document, you can move, resize, rotate, crop, and adjust its color.

on the screen, the top portion of the document moves upward, or scrolls, off the screen. **Scrolling** is the process of moving different portions of the document onto the screen into view.

A major advantage of using word processing software is that you easily can change what you have written. You can insert, delete, or rearrange words, sentences, or entire sections. You can use the **find** or **search** feature to locate all occurrences of a particular character, word, or phrase. This feature can be used in combination with the **replace** feature to substitute existing characters or words with new

Lion 1

Iris

Puppy

Puffin

Conch 1

Trout

Mammoth

Figure 3-11 Clip art consists of previously created illustrations that can be added to documents. Clip art collections include graphic images that are grouped by type. These clip art examples are from an animals and nature collection.

All word processing software provides basic capabilities to help you create, edit, and format documents. For example, you can define the size of the paper on which to print, as well as the **margins** — that is, the portion of the page outside the main body of text, on the top, bottom, and sides of the paper. The word processing software automatically readjusts any text so it fits within the new definitions.

With **wordwrap**, if you type text that extends beyond the page margin or window boundary, the word processor automatically positions text at the beginning of the next line. Wordwrap allows you to type words in a paragraph continually without pressing the ENTER key at the end of each line.

In some instances, such as if you create a several-page document, you can view only a portion of a document on the screen at a time. As you type more lines of text than can display

ones. Current word processing packages even have a feature that automatically corrects errors and makes word substitutions as you type text.

To review the spelling of individual words, sections of a document, or the entire document, you can use a **spelling checker,** also called a **spell checker [Figure 3-12]**. The spelling checker compares the words in the document to an electronic dictionary that is part of the word processing software. You can customize the electronic dictionary by adding words such as names of companies, schools, streets, and cities, and personal names so the software can spell check those words as well. Many word processing software packages allow you to check the spelling of a whole document at one time or check the spelling of single words as you type them.

You also can insert headers and footers into a word processing document. A **header** is

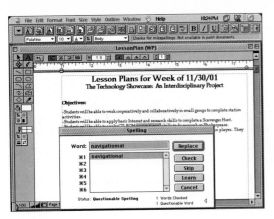

Figure 3-12 Spell checkers are included with most word processors. Shown is the spell checker included with AppleWorks.

text you want at the top of each page; a **footer** is text you want at bottom of each page. Page numbers, as well as company and school names, report titles, or dates, are examples of items frequently included in headers and footers.

Many word processing programs make it quick and easy for teachers and students to create personalized templates using special programs called wizards. A **wizard**, or **assistant**, is an automated tool that helps you complete a task by asking you questions and then automatically performing actions based on your answers. Many software applications include wizards. Word processing software, for example, uses wizards to help you create memorandums, meeting agendas, letters, and other professional looking documents. Word processing wizards also can help you create personalized templates for a letterhead, resume, newsletter, certificate, bibliography, tests, and more [Figure 3-13].

WebInfo

For information on using wizards, visit the Teachers Discovering Computers Chapter 3 WebInfo page **(www.scsite.com/tdc/ch3/webinfo.htm)** and click Wizard.

CHAPTER 3

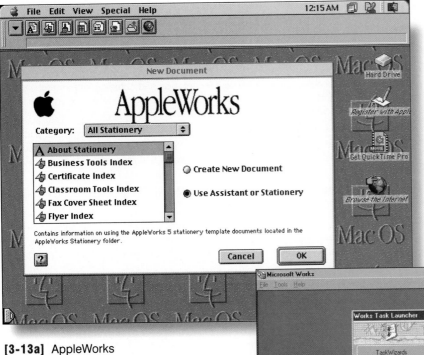

[3-13a] AppleWorks

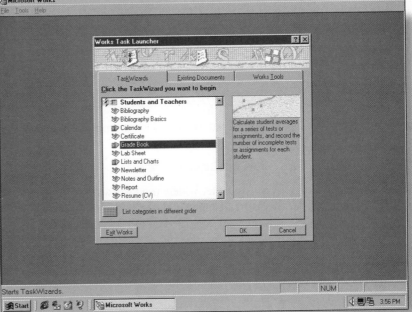

Figure 3-13 A wizard, called an assistant in AppleWorks, allow teachers and students quickly to create personalized flyers, newsletters, certificates, and more. Figure 3-13a shows some of the assistants available in AppleWorks and Figure 3-13b shows some of the wizards available in Microsoft Works.

[3-13b] Microsoft Works

In addition to these basic features, most current word processing packages provide numerous additional features. These additional features are listed in the table in **Figure 3-14**.

manner as it is in a manual spreadsheet **[Figure 3-15]**.

Individuals who frequently work with numbers, for example, financial statements and payroll, use spreadsheets. While many

Word Processing Features

Feature	Description
AutoCorrect	As you type words, the AutoCorrect feature corrects common spelling errors. For example, if you type the word, adn, the word processing software automatically changes it to the correct word, and, AutoCorrect also corrects errors in capitalization. For example, it capitalizes names of days and the first letter in a sentence.
AutoFormat	As you type, the AutoFormat feature automatically applies formatting to your text. For example, it automatically can number a list or convert a Web address to a hyperlink. AutoFormat also automatically creates symbols, fractions, and ordinal numbers. For example, when you type :), it changes to a smiling face symbol ☺; the fraction 1/2 is created when you type 1/2; and the ordinal 2nd is created when you type 2nd.
Columns	Most word processing software can arrange text in two or more columns like a newspaper or magazine. The text from the bottom of one column automatically flows to the top of the next column.
Grammar Checker	You can use the grammar check to proofread documents from grammar, writing style, and sentence structure errors. You can check the grammar of a document all at one time, or instruct the word processing software to check grammar as you enter text.
Tables	Tables are a way of organizing information into rows and columns. With tables, you easily can rearrange rows and columns, change column widths, sort rows and columns, sum the contents of rows and columns, or format the contents of table. Instead of evenly spaced rows and columns, some word processing packages allow you to draw the tables of any size or shape directly into the document.
Templates	A template is a document that contains the formatting necessary for a specific document type. For example, a letter template would contain the proper spacing and indicate the position of elements common to a business letter such as a date, inside address, salutation, body, closing, and signature block. Templates usually exist for documents such as memos, fax cover sheets, and letters.
Thesaurus	With a thesaurus, you can look up synonyms (words with the same meaning) for words in a document while you are using your word processing software.
Tracking Changes/ Comments	If multiple users work with a document, you can instruct the word processing software to highlight or color-code the changes made by various users. This way, you can see easily what changes have been made to the document. You also can add comments to a document, without changing the text itself. These comments allow you to communicate with the other users working on the document.
Voice Recognition	With some of the newer word processing packages, you can speak into your computer's microphone and watch the spoken words display on your screen as you talk. With these packages, you also can edit and format the document by speaking or spelling an instruction.
Web Page Development	Most word processing software supports Internet connectivity, allowing you to create, edit, and format documents for the World Wide Web. You automatically can convert an existing word processing document into the standard document format for the World Wide Web. You also can view and browse Web pages directly from your word processing software.

Figure 3-14 Additional features included with many word processing software packages.

Spreadsheet Software

Another widely used software application is **spreadsheet software,** which allows you to organize numeric data in rows and columns. These rows and columns collectively are called a **spreadsheet**, or **worksheet**. Manual methods, those done by hand, have long been used to organize numeric data. The data in an electronic spreadsheet is organized in the same

teachers do not create their own spreadsheets, many teachers interact with spreadsheet programs on a daily basis. Every time teachers enter a student's grade or attendance information into a computer, they are entering information into a special spreadsheet program, called an electronic grade book. K-12 grade book programs are discussed later in this chapter.

As with word processing software, most spreadsheet software has basic features to help you create, edit, and format electronic spreadsheets. These features, as included in several popular spreadsheet software packages, are described below. Spreadsheet programs typically used in schools are the spreadsheet

Many of the spreadsheet cells shown in **Figure 3-15** contain a number, or a **value**. Other cells, however, contain formulas that are used to generate values. A **formula** performs calculations on the numeric data in the spreadsheet and displays the resulting value in the cell containing the formula. In

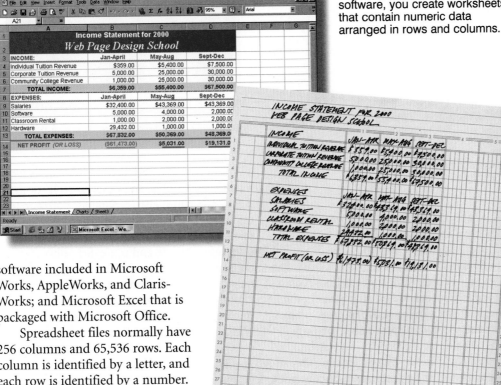

Figure 3-15 With spreadsheet software, you create worksheets that contain numeric data arranged in rows and columns.

software included in Microsoft Works, AppleWorks, and Claris-Works; and Microsoft Excel that is packaged with Microsoft Office.

Spreadsheet files normally have 256 columns and 65,536 rows. Each column is identified by a letter, and each row is identified by a number. The column letters begin with A and row numbers begin with 1. Only a small fraction of these columns and rows display on the screen at one time. To view different parts of a worksheet, you can scroll to display it on your screen.

The intersection of a column and row is called a **cell**. Cells are identified by the column and row in which they are located. For example, the intersection of column B and row 7 is referred to as cell B7. In **Figure 3-15**, cell B7 contains the number $6,359.00, which represents Total Income for the period January through April.

Cells may contain three types of data: labels (text), values (numbers), and formulas. The text, or **label**, entered in a cell is used to identify the data and help organize the spreadsheet. Using descriptive labels such as Total Income, Salaries, and Expenses helps make a spreadsheet more meaningful.

Figure 3-15, for example, cell B7 could contain the formula =B4+B5+B6 to calculate the total income for January through April.

Another standard feature of spreadsheet software is the capability of turning numeric data into a **chart** that graphically illustrates the relationship of the numeric data. Visual representation of data in charts often makes it easier to analyze and interpret information. Most charts are variations of three basic chart types — line charts, pie charts, and bar charts as shown in **Figure 3-16** on the next page. To improve their appearance, most charts can be displayed or printed in a three-dimensional format.

CHAPTER 3

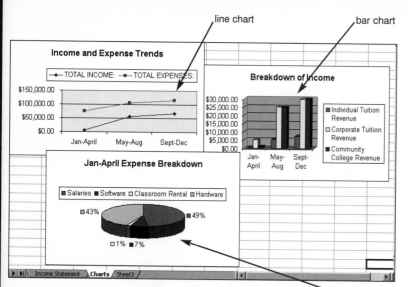

line chart   bar chart

pie chart

Figure 3-16 Three basic types of charts provided with spreadsheet software are line charts, bar charts, and pie charts. The line chart, bar chart, and pie chart shown were created from the data in the spreadsheet shown in Figure 3-15 on the previous page.

Figure 3-17 A database is similar to a manual system, where related data items are stored in files.

As with word processing software, you can quickly create professional looking spreadsheets using wizards. Using the wizards in most popular spreadsheet packages is easy and allows you to create sample grade books, classroom and school schedules, charts, and more. Spreadsheet software also incorporates many of the features of word processing software such as a spelling checker, font formatting, and the capability of converting an existing spreadsheet document into the standard document format for the World Wide Web. Because individual rows, columns, cells, or any combination of cells can be formatted, school districts and businesses often use spreadsheet programs to create their standardized forms.

Database Software

A **database** is a collection of data organized in a manner that allows access, retrieval, and use of that data. In a manual system, schools record information on paper and store it in a filing cabinet **[Figure 3-17]**. In a computerized database, such as the one shown in **Figure 3-20**, data is stored in an electronic format on a storage medium. **Database software** allows you to create a computerized database; add, change, and delete data; sort and retrieve data from the database; and create forms and reports using the data in the database.

Database software is used extensively by businesses, schools, and other organizations. Businesses routinely use database software to organize data and information on customers, employees, equipment, product inventory, sales information, and more. Schools use databases to organize data and information on students, staff members, school policies, equipment inventories, book inventories, purchases, and more. Database programs typically used in schools include database software included in Microsoft Works, Apple-Works, and ClarisWorks and Microsoft Access that is packaged with Microsoft Office.

When you use a database, you need to be familiar with the terms file, record, and field. Just as in a manual system, a **database file** is a collection of related data that is organized in records. Each **record** contains a collection of related facts called **fields**. For example, a student database file might consist of records containing names, address information, and parental or guardian information. All of the data that relates to one student would be considered a record. Each fact, such as the street address or telephone number, is called a field.

Figures 3-18 through **3-20** present the development of a database containing basic information about students enrolled in Ms. Eileen Tanner's second grade class at Martin Luther King Elementary School. This simple database contains the following information on each student — first name, last name, guardian's address, name, and telephone number.

WebInfo

For an example of how athletes use databases for training purposes, visit the Teachers Discovering Computers Chapter 3 WebInfo page

(www.scsite.com/tdc/ ch3/webinfo.htm)

and click Athlete.

Before you begin creating a database, make a list of the data items you want to organize [Figure 3-18]. Each item that you want to keep track of will become a field in the database. To identify the different fields, assign each field a unique name that is short, yet descriptive. For example, the field name for a student's last name could be Last Name, the field name for a student's first name could be First Name and so on. Database programs differ slightly in how they require the user to enter or define fields. A field entry screen from Microsoft Works is shown **Figure 3-19**.

After the database structure is created by defining the fields, data for individual database records can be entered. After data for all records are entered, the database can be used to produce information. **Figure 3-20** shows the

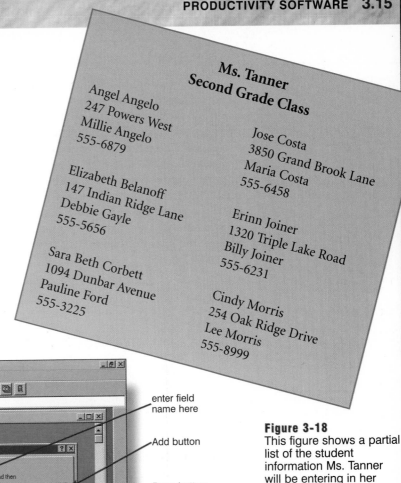

Figure 3-18
This figure shows a partial list of the student information Ms. Tanner will be entering in her student database.

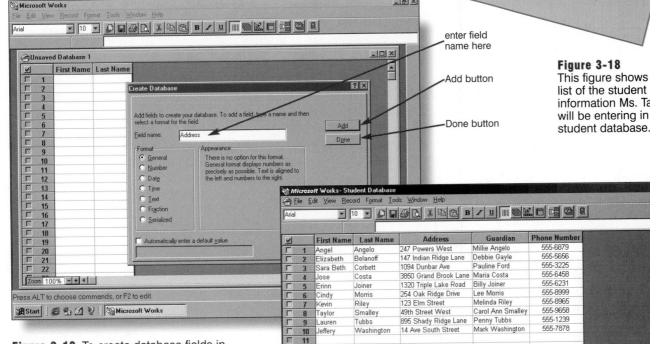

enter field name here

Add button

Done button

Figure 3-19 To create database fields in Microsoft Works, you simply type in each field name and then click the Add button. After entering all the fields you need and clicking the Done button, you are ready to enter the data in the new database.

database after the information on the students has been entered.

As with word processing and spreadsheet software, database software includes wizards that allow teachers and students to create databases for use as address books, directories of parents and students, equipment and book inventories, and so on.

Figure 3-20 Once data has been entered into a database, the records can be arranged in any order specified by users. In this example, the records have been organized alphabetically based on students' last names.

Presentation Graphics Software

WebInfo

For tips on using graphics effectively in a presentation, visit the Teachers Discovering Computers Chapter 3 WebInfo page **(www.scsite.com/tdc/ch3/webinfo.htm)** and click Presentation.

Using **presentation graphics software**, you can create documents called **presentations**, which you then use to communicate ideas, messages, and other information to a group, such as a class or auditorium. The presentations can be viewed as **slides** that display on a large monitor or project onto a screen. Slides can be displayed on a computer's monitor, a large-screen television, or projected on a screen, made into traditional overhead transparencies, or printed and given to students as a handout **[Figure 3-21]**.

Presentation programs typically used in schools are the presentation software included in AppleWorks, ClarisWorks, and Microsoft PowerPoint packaged with Microsoft Office. As with all of the individual software programs in Microsoft Office, you can purchase and use PowerPoint separately.

Presentation graphics software typically provides an array of predefined presentation formats that define complementary colors for backgrounds, text, and other special effects. Presentation graphics software also provides a variety of layouts for each individual slide so you can create a title slide; a two-column slide; a slide with clip art; and others. Any text,

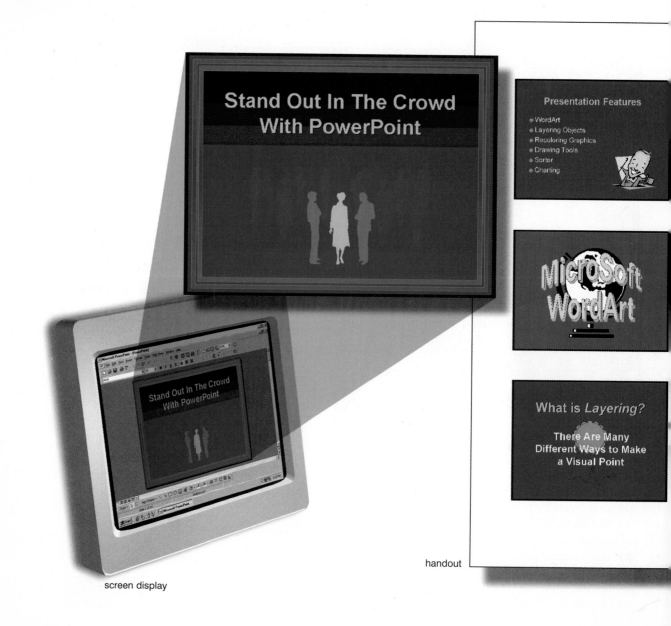

screen display

handout

charts, and graphics used in a slide can be enhanced with 3-D and other effects such as shading, shadows, and textures.

With presentation graphics software, you can incorporate objects from the clip art/image gallery into your slides to create multimedia presentations. A **clip art/image gallery** includes clip art images, pictures, video clips, and audio clips. A clip art/image gallery can be stored on a hard disk, a CD-ROM, or a DVD-ROM; in other cases, you access the clip art/image gallery on the Web. As with clip art collections, a clip gallery typically is organized by categories such as academic, business, entertainment, and transportation. For

example, the transportation category may contain a clip art image of a bicycle, a photograph of a locomotive, a video clip of an airplane in flight, and an audio clip of a Model T car horn.

When building a presentation, you also can set the slide timing so the presentation automatically displays the next slide after a predetermined delay. You can apply special effects to the transition between each slide. For example, one slide might slowly dissolve as the next slide comes into view.

To help organize the presentation, you can view small versions of all the slides in a slide sorter. A **slide sorter** presents a screen view

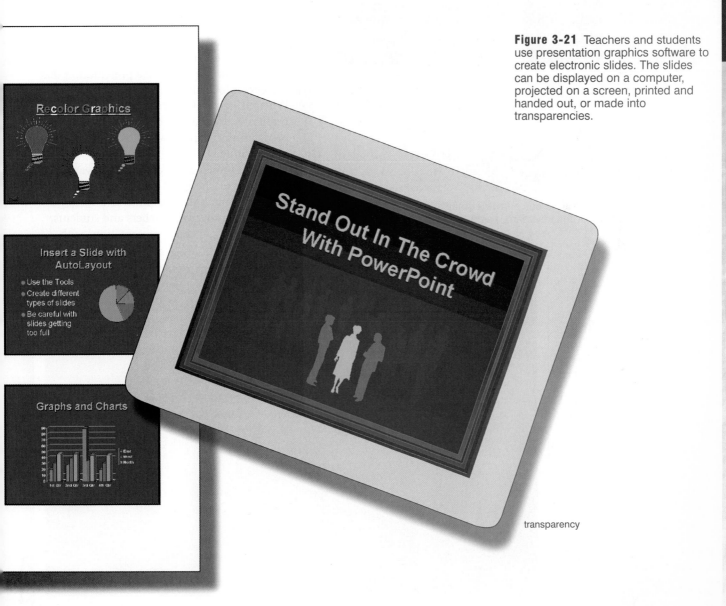

Figure 3-21 Teachers and students use presentation graphics software to create electronic slides. The slides can be displayed on a computer, projected on a screen, printed and handed out, or made into transparencies.

transparency

similar to how 35mm slides would look on a photographer's light table [**Figure 3-22**]. The slide sorter allows you to arrange the slides in any order or display them one at a time by clicking the mouse or pressing a key on the keyboard.

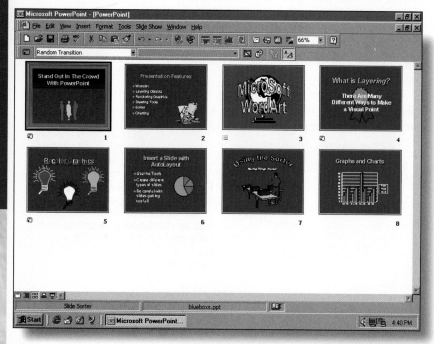

Figure 3-22 This slide sorter screen shows a small version of each slide. Using a pointing device or the keyboard, users can rearrange or change the order of the slides.

Presentation graphics software also incorporates some of the features provided in word processing software such as a spelling checker, font formatting, and the capability of converting an existing slide show into the standard document format for the World Wide Web.

Presentation graphic programs are important software programs for K-12 schools. Electronic presentations easily can be created and integrated into any classroom curriculum and are an exciting alternative to the traditional lecture-only teaching style [**Figure 3-23**]. Students take great pride in creating their own presentations using presentation graphics software. Later chapters provide real-life examples of how teachers integrate presentation graphics software into their instruction and curriculum. A unique feature of presentation graphics software is that it allows you to create a presentation that presents information in a nonlinear format. When using overhead transparencies, teachers traditionally show one slide after another in a predetermined order — that is, linear teaching and learning.

With presentation graphics software programs, teachers and students can easily create presentations with links to a variety of information sources. Teachers and students, for example, can create presentations with

Figure 3-23 Electronic slide presentations are an exciting alternative to the traditional lecture-only teaching style.

links to other slides, other presentations, other files and software programs, animations, audio and video clips, and even sites on the World Wide Web **[Figure 3-24]**. Using these links, teachers and students can branch off in a non-linear fashion at any point in a presentation, to display or access additional information. The ability to modify the presentation content according to student interest makes presentation graphics software a powerful teaching and learning tool.

Personal Information Managers

A **personal information manager** (PIM) is a software application that includes an appointment calendar, address book, and notepad to help you organize personal information such as appointments, task lists, and more, as shown in **Figure 3-25** on the next page. A PIM allows you to take information that previously you tracked in a weekly or daily calendar, and organize and store it on your computer. PIMs can manage many different types of information such as telephone

Figure 3-24 By clicking a hyperlink in a PowerPoint presentation, teachers and students can instantly access another slide, slide presentation, sound clip, video clip, or a Web site anywhere in the world.

hyperlinks
to the Web

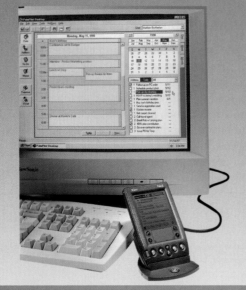

Figure 3-25 Some handheld computers such as the Palm III™ Connected Organizer run PIM software. With these computers, you can transfer information from the handheld computer to your desktop computer so appointments, addresses, and other important information always are available.

Figure 3-26 Two popular software suites are Microsoft Office 2000 and Lotus SmartSuite.

Figure 3-27 Two popular integrated software packages used on home and school computers. Microsoft Works often is found on PCs and contains word processing, spreadsheet, database, and communications software. AppleWorks (formerly ClarisWorks) is used mainly on Macintosh computers and contains word processing, spreadsheet, database, paint, and presentation software.

messages, project notes, reminders, task and address lists, and important dates and appointments.

Precisely defining a PIM is difficult, because personal information managers offer a range of capabilities. As just noted above, however, most include at least an appointment calendar, address book, and notepad. An **appointment calendar** allows you to schedule activities for a particular day and time. With an **address book**, you can enter and maintain names, addresses, and telephone numbers of co-workers, family members, and friends. Instead of writing notes on a piece of paper, you can use a **notepad** to record ideas, reminders, and other important information. Many PIMs also include a calculator or a simple spreadsheet application; some also include e-mail capabilities.

Software Suites and Integrated Software

A **software suite** is a collection of individual application software packages sold as a single package **[Figure 3-26]**. When you install the suite, you install the entire collection of applications at once, rather than installing each application individually. At a minimum, suites typically include: word processing, spreadsheet, database, and presentation graphics.

Integrated software is software that combines applications such as word processing, spreadsheet, and database into a single, easy-to-use package. Unlike a software suite, however, you cannot purchase the applications in the integrated software package individually. Each application in an integrated software package is designed specifically to work as part of a larger set of applications (thus the name, integrated).

The applications within the integrated software package typically do not have all the capabilities of stand-alone productivity software applications. Integrated software thus is less expensive than a more powerful software suite. For many school, home, and personal users, however, the capabilities of an integrated software package more than meet their needs. Popular integrated software packages used in schools include **Microsoft Works** for PCs and **AppleWorks** (formerly ClarisWorks) for Macintosh computers **[Figure 3-27]**.

Both integrated software and software suites offer two major advantages: lower cost and ease of use. Typically, buying a collection of software packages in a suite costs significantly less than that of each of the application packages separately. Software suites provide ease of use because the applications within a suite normally use a similar interface and have some common features. Thus, once you learn how to use one application in the suite, you are familiar with the other applications in the suite. For example, once you learn how to print using the suite's word processing package, you can apply the same skill to the spreadsheet, database, and presentation graphics software in the suite.

Graphics and Multimedia Software

In addition to productivity software, many individuals also work with software designed specifically for their fields of work. Power users such as engineers, architects, desktop publishers, and graphic artists, for example, often use powerful software that allows them to work with graphics and multimedia. Types of graphics and multimedia software include desktop publishing, paint/image editing, multimedia authoring, and Web page authoring software. The features and functions of each of these applications are discussed in the following sections.

Desktop Publishing Software

Desktop publishing (DTP) **software** allows you to design, produce, and deliver sophisticated documents that contain text, graphics, and brilliant colors. Although many word processing packages have some of the capabilities of DTP software, professional designers and graphic artists use DTP software because it is designed specifically to support **page layout,** which is the process of arranging text and graphics in a document. DTP software is ideal for the production of high-quality color documents such as newsletters, marketing literature, catalogs, and annual reports. In the past, documents of this type were created by slower, more expensive traditional publishing methods such as typesetting.

Today's DTP software also allows you to convert a color document into a format for use on the World Wide Web.

Many home, school, and small business users use a much simpler, easy-to-understand DTP software designed for individual desktop publishing projects. Using this DTP software, you can create newsletters, brochures, and advertisements; postcards and greeting cards; letterhead and business cards; banners; calendars; logos; and other such documents. Personal DTP software guides you through the development of these documents by asking a series of questions, offering numerous predefined layouts, and providing standard text you can add to documents. As you enter text, the personal DTP software checks your spelling. You can print your finished publications on a color printer or place them on the Web. Teachers and students use desktop publishing software, such as Microsoft Publisher and Aldus PageMaker to lay out their school yearbooks and create flyers, certificates, and newsletters [Figure 3-28].

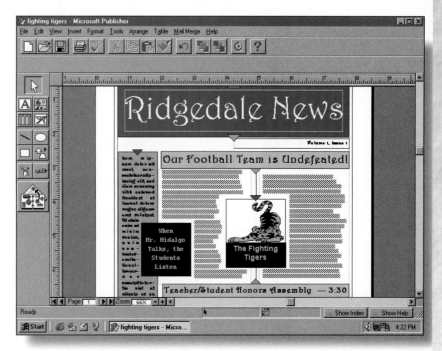

Figure 3-28 Teachers and students use desktop publishing software, such as Microsoft Publisher to lay out school yearbooks and create flyers, certificates, newsletters, and other types of documents.

Paint/Image Editing Software

Graphic artists, multimedia professionals, desktop publishers, and many others use paint software and image editing software to create and modify graphics, such as those used in DTP documents and Web pages [**Figure 3-29**]. **Paint software** allows you to draw pictures, shapes, and other graphics using various tools on the screen such as a pen, brush, eye dropper, and paint bucket. **Image editing software** provides the capabilities of paint software, as well as the capability of modifying existing graphics. For example, you can retouch photographs; adjust or enhance image colors; and add special effects such as shadows and glows.

Many home, school, and small business users opt for personal paint/image editing software. Personal paint/image editing software provides a much easier to use interface and usually has simplified capabilities, with functions tailored to the needs of the home and small business user. As with the professional versions, personal paint software includes various simplified tools that allow

you to draw pictures, shapes, and other graphics.

Personal image editing software provides the capabilities of paint software, and the capability of modifying existing graphics. One popular type of image editing software, called **photo-editing software**, allows you to edit digital photographs by removing red-eye, adding special effects, or creating electronic photo albums. When the photograph is complete, you can print it on labels, calendars, business cards, and banners; or place it on a Web page.

Clip Art/Image Gallery

Although many applications include clip art, you may find that you want a wider selection of graphics. One way to obtain them is to purchase a clip art/image gallery, which is a collection of clip art and photographs. In addition to clip art, many clip art/image galleries provide fonts, animations, sounds, video clips, and audio clips [**Figure 3-30**]. You can use the images, fonts, and other items from

WebInfo

For samples of clip art available on the Internet, visit the Teachers Discovering Computers Chapter 3 WebInfo page (www.scsite.com/tdc/ch3/webinfo.htm) and click Clip Art.

Figure 3-29 With image editing software, artists can create and modify a variety of graphical images.

the clip art/image gallery in all types of documents, such as word processing, desktop publishing, spreadsheets, and presentation graphics.

Multimedia Authoring Software

Multimedia authoring software is used to create electronic presentations that can include text, graphics, video, audio, and animation. **HyperStudio®** is an example of an easy-to-use multimedia authoring software program that allows the author to combine many multimedia elements into a series of interactive cards. The software helps you create presentations by allowing you to control the placement of text and graphics and the duration of sounds, video, and animation. Once created, such multimedia presentations often take the form of interactive computer-based presentations designed to facilitate learning and elicit direct student participation. Commercially produced multimedia presentations usually are stored and delivered via a CD-ROM or DVD-ROM, over a local area network, or via the Internet.

Web Page Authoring Software

Web page authoring software is software designed specifically to help you create Web pages, in addition to organizing, managing, and maintaining Web sites. As noted in previous sections, many application software packages include Web page authoring features that you can use to create basic Web pages consisting of text and graphics [**Figure 3-31**]. Word processing programs, for example, often contain enough features to satisfy the formatting and layout needs of teachers and students for building curriculum pages and other Web documents, as shown in **Figure 3-32** on the next page. A **curriculum page** is a teacher-created document that contains hyperlinks to teacher-selected sites.

Web page authoring software features allow you to create sophisticated multimedia Web pages that include graphics, video, audio, animation, and other special effects. Many school technology coordinators use the popular Web page authoring program, **Microsoft FrontPage**, to create Web pages for schools and school districts. Many teachers and students build their home pages using

Figure 3-30 Clip art/image galleries provide thousands of clip art images and photographs for use in documents such as letters, newsletters, greeting cards, class projects, and presentations.

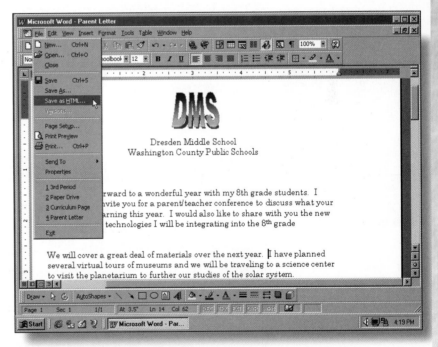

Figure 3-31 This figure shows you how to convert a word processing document automatically into the standard document format for the World Wide Web by saving it in HTML format. Once saved, the document can be published to the Web and viewed in any Web browser.

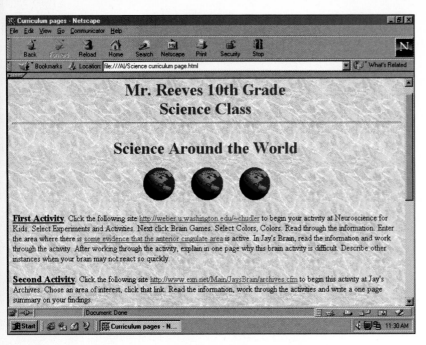

Figure 3-32 An example of a teacher-created curriculum page.

Netscape Composer, which is part of the Netscape Communicator software package **[Figure 3-33]**. With Web page authoring software, both new and experienced users can create fascinating Web pages.

Software for School and Professional Use

Many school districts are undergoing a period of transition in how they maintain student records and other pertinent information. An important key factor driving this transition is the installation of networks: many school districts are networking all of their classrooms and schools into local and wide area networks.

Having networks in schools allows schools to manage and maintain information on students and teachers in various ways. At the

WebInfo

For tips on using Netscape Composer, visit the Teachers Discovering Computers Chapter 3 WebInfo page

(www.scsite.com/tdc/ch3/webinfo.htm)

and click Composer.

Figure 3-33 Many teachers and students build their Web pages using Netscape Composer, which is included with Netscape Communicator.

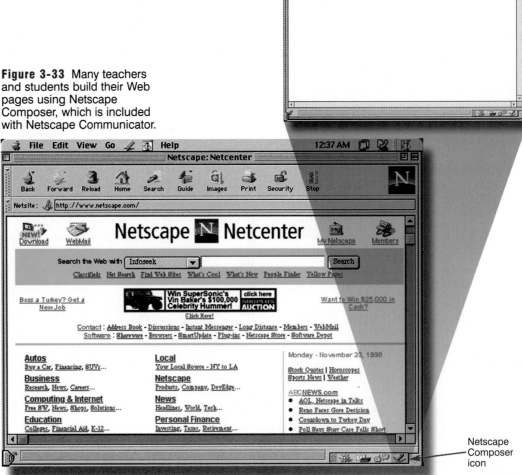

Netscape Composer icon

lower end, some schools still maintain all student records manually or in software programs on individual computers. Teachers and other school personnel then periodically manually input student records into student management software that stores grades and attendance records. Software for schools and professional use includes school management software, student management software, grade book software, educational/reference software, and software for students with special needs.

School and Student Management Software

Schools that have networked at least one computer in each classroom are installing school and student management software. When standardized throughout the school district, these programs can improve dramatically a school's capability of managing and analyzing daily operations, budgets, and student information.

School management software is a centralized program that allows district and school personnel to manage the school district operations, such as budgeting, inventory, technology, and expenses. Most school management software packages allow a school district to keep a database of all district assets, salaries and benefits and food services inventory; manage other school and department budgets; and track transportation vehicle maintenance and use. Some school management software also includes databases for attendance and other student information and has other functions similar to student management software. **Student management software** is a program that allows administrators, teachers, and other staff to manage and track information on students, which includes attendance and academic records.

Recall from Chapter 1, Washington County Public Schools has networked all of its classroom computers **[Figure 3-34]**. Teachers throughout the district enter attendance information into the district's student management software program shortly after classes begin. Within a few minutes, district and school administrators know exactly how many students are present. Teachers also enter student grades into the same grade book and attendance program installed on all district

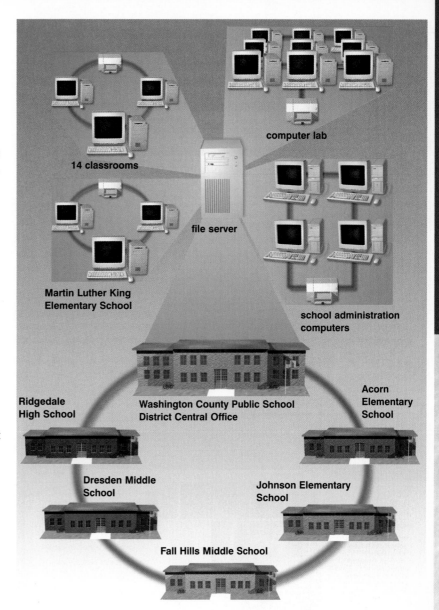

Figure 3-34 Washington County Public Schools uses its wide area network that connects all district classrooms to track student attendance records, grades, and more.

computers. Record keeping at Washington County Schools thus is fully automated.

Grade Book Software

Grade book software is a program that allows teachers to track and organize student tests, homework, lab work, and other scores. Most grade book software allows you to track thousands of students and hundreds of assignments within the same grade book and sort students by name, student number, or

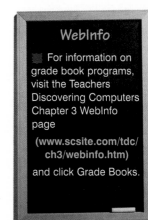

WebInfo

For information on grade book programs, visit the Teachers Discovering Computers Chapter 3 WebInfo page

(www.scsite.com/tdc/ch3/webinfo.htm)

and click Grade Books.

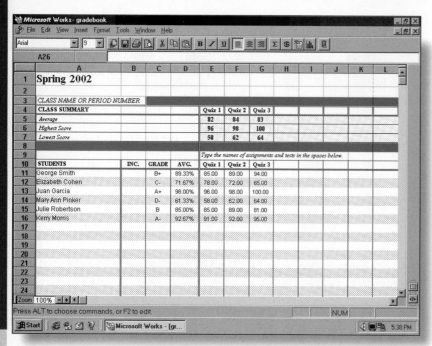

Figure 3-35 An example of a grade book that teachers can create using Microsoft Works.

Figure 3-36 Reference software provides valuable and thorough information for all types of users. For example, Microsoft Encarta includes text, pictures, and videos on earthquakes and thousands of other topics.

current average. The program allows teachers to weight various scores automatically, apply grading curves, adjust letter grade cutoffs, or use a customized grade scale, such as Fair, Good, Excellent, and so on. Grades can be displayed and entered as points, percentages, letter grades, or in a customized grading scale.

Grade book software also integrates with other software packages. Schools that use network-based (online) testing programs, for example, can import student scores directly into the grade book. Teachers also can import and export grades and rosters to a word processing, spreadsheet, or database program.

At some schools, teachers enter attendance and student grades into the same grade book software, which is installed on all district computers. Many schools today, however, have not mandated standard grade book programs for teachers to use; so many teachers choose their own grade book programs. Numerous outstanding grade book and attendance programs are available for teachers. Some of these are shareware programs; others have trial versions that you can download from the Web for evaluation purposes. Popular grade book programs include Grade Book Power, Grade Machine, and Making the Grade. You also can create basic grade book programs using the wizards in Microsoft Works and AppleWorks [Figure 3-35].

Educational/Reference

Educational software is software designed for the learning environment. Educational software exists for just about any subject, from learning a foreign language to learning how to cook. Preschool to high school learners can use educational software to assist them with subjects such as reading and math or to prepare them for class or college entrance exams.

Reference software provides valuable and thorough information for everyone in an educational setting and in the family. Popular reference software includes encyclopedias, dictionaries, health/medical guides, and travel directories [Figure 3-36]. Chapter 5 covers many types of educational and reference software and discusses their features in detail.

Special Needs Software

Special needs software is designed specifically for students with physical impairments or learning disabilities, to assist them in completing school assignments and everyday tasks **[Figure 3-37]**. Special needs software includes such programs as speech synthesis software, text enlargement programs, talking calculators, and more.

Speech synthesis software allows students with speech and vocal muscle disorders to participate in classroom discussions. Students will assign certain keys to reproduce specific frequently used phrases. They use the phrase keys to type in a response; the word processing software then reads the response in a computerized voice.

Students with visual impairments may use software with text enlargement features, which enables them to see the screen better. Other helpful software applications include an onscreen talking calculator that features big, colorful number buttons and high-quality speech synthesis.

Today, teachers have many software options available to use as tools to enhance teaching and learning of students with special needs. Many software applications discussed in this chapter and educational multimedia applications discussed in Chapter 5 also can assist students with special needs. When students use these software programs in combination with assistive devices such as touch screens and adaptive keyboards their ability to succeed increases. These and other special input and output devices designed for use by students with special needs are discussed in Chapter 4. Examples of how teachers can integrate special needs software into their curriculum are covered in later chapters.

Software for Home and Personal Use

Many software applications are designed specifically for use at home or for personal use. Personal software includes packages such as personal finance, tax preparation, and entertainment. Most of the products in this category are relatively inexpensive, often priced at less than $50. The features and functions of some of these applications are discussed in the following sections.

Figure 3-37 Using assistive technology software, teachers help students with disabilities learn subject-related content.

Personal Finance Software

Personal finance software is a simplified accounting program that helps you pay bills; balance your checkbook; track your personal income and expenses, like credit-card bills, track investments; and evaluate financial plans **[Figure 3-38]**. Popular personal finance software includes Quicken and Microsoft Money.

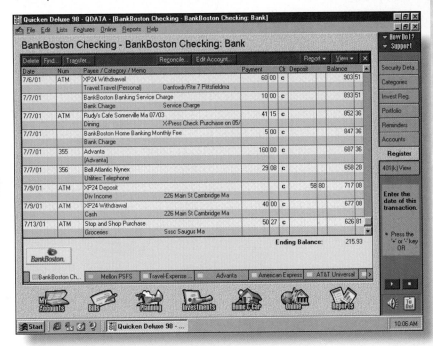

Figure 3-38 Personal finance software assists you with paying bills, balancing your checkbook, tracking credit-card activity, and more.

Using personal finance software can help you determine where, and for what purpose, you are spending money so you can manage your finances. Reports can summarize transactions by category (such as dining), by payee (such as the electric company), or by time period (such as the last two months). Bill-paying features include the ability to print checks on your printer or have an outside service print your checks.

Personal finance software packages usually offer a variety of online services, which require access to the Web. For example, you can track your investments online, compare insurance rates from leading insurance companies, and even do your banking online. With online banking, you can transfer money electronically from your checking to savings or vice versa. To obtain current credit card statements, bank statements, and account balances, you download transaction information from your bank using the Web.

Financial planning features include analyzing home and personal loans, preparing income taxes, and managing retirement savings. Other features included in many personal finance packages include home inventory, budgeting, and tax-related transactions.

Tax Preparation Software

Tax preparation software guides individuals, families, or small businesses through the process of filing federal taxes **[Figure 3-39]**.

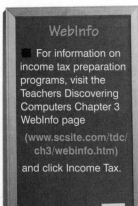

WebInfo

■ For information on income tax preparation programs, visit the Teachers Discovering Computers Chapter 3 WebInfo page

(www.scsite.com/tdc/ch3/webinfo.htm)

and click Income Tax.

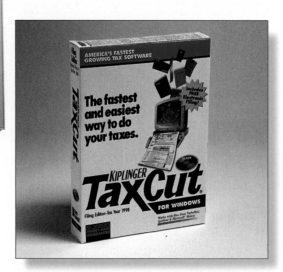

Figure 3-39 Tax preparation software can assist you in preparing your federal and state tax returns efficiently and accurately. You even can file your return electronically using the Internet.

Popular tax preparation software includes TurboTax and TaxCut. These software packages offer money-saving tax tips, designed to lower your tax bill. After you answer a series of questions and complete basic forms, the tax preparation software creates and analyzes your tax forms to search for missed potential errors and deduction opportunities. Once the forms are complete, you can print any necessary paperwork. Most tax preparation software packages even allow you to file your tax forms electronically.

Legal Software

Legal software assists in the preparation of legal documents and provides legal advice to individuals, families, and small businesses **[Figure 3-40]**. Legal software provides standard contracts and documents associated with buying, selling, and renting property; estate planning; and preparing a will. By answering a series of questions or completing a form, the legal software tailors the legal document to your needs.

Once the legal document is created, you can file the paperwork with the appropriate agency, court, or office; or you can take the document to your attorney for his or her review and signature.

Personal Computer Entertainment Software

Personal computer entertainment software includes interactive games, videos, and other programs designed to support a hobby or just provide amusement and enjoyment. For example, you can use personal computer entertainment software to play games, make a family tree, compose music, or fly an aircraft.

Learning Aids and Support Tools

Learning how to use an application software package or the Web effectively involves time and practice. To aid you in that learning process, your school may offer classes or inservice workshops. In addition to these learning opportunities, many software applications and Web sites provide online Help, tutorials, and FAQs. Thousands of books also are available to help you learn specific software packages. Many tutorials are packaged with software or are available free on the Web.

Online Help is the electronic equivalent of a user manual; it usually is integrated into an application software package [**Figure 3-41**]. Online Help provides assistance that can increase your productivity and reduce your frustrations by minimizing the time you spend learning how to use an application software package.

In most packages, a function key or a button on the screen starts the Help feature. When you are using an application and have a question, you can use the online Help feature to ask a question or access the Help topics by subject, keyword, or alphabetical order. Some packages even allow you to type in a question. The online Help evaluates the question and displays a list of related topics.

Often the online Help is **context-sensitive**, meaning that the Help information is related to the current instruction being attempted. Most online Help also points you to Web sites that provide updates and more comprehensive resources to answer your software questions. In many cases, online Help has replaced the user manual altogether, and software developers no longer include user's manuals along with the software.

If printed documentation is included with a software package, often it is organized as reference material rather than structured for learning. This makes it helpful once you know how to use a package, but difficult to use when you are first learning. For this reason, many **trade books** are available to help you learn to use the features of software application packages. These books are available where software is sold, in regular bookstores, or online, as shown in **Figure 3-42** on the next page. Web pages that contain **Frequently Asked Questions** (**FAQs**) about application software abound on the Internet and help you find answers to common questions.

Tutorials are step-by-step instructions using real examples that show you how to use an application. Some tutorials are written manuals; others are software-based or Internet-based, thus allowing you to use your computer to learn about an application software package.

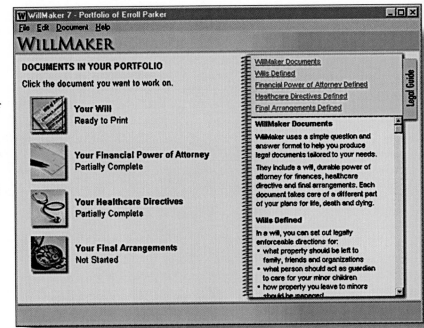

Figure 3-40 Legal software provides legal advice to individual and families and assists in the preparation of legal documents.

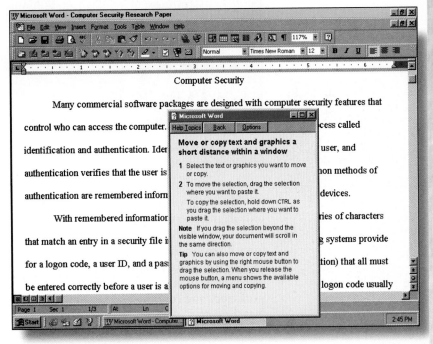

Figure 3-41 Online Help provides assistance without having to leave your application.

Figure 3-42 Many bookstores sell trade books to help you learn to use the features of personal computer application packages.

Many colleges and K-12 school districts provide training on many of the applications discussed in this chapter. If you would like more direction than is provided in online Help, trade books, FAQs, and tutorials; contact your college or school district for a list of workshops and continuing education courses that they offer.

In addition to those discussed here, many other software programs are available for use in schools, homes, and businesses. In the chapters that follow, you will learn more about other types of educational software, including how-to guides, computer-assisted instructional software, educational games, tutorials, educational simulations, multimedia authoring software, and CD-ROM-based and Web-based multimedia applications.

Software Versions and Upgrades

Software programs, including operating systems, usually are designated a **version** number; for example, Microsoft Office 2000, where 2000 indicates the version number. A new version of a software product designed to replace an older version of the same product is called an **upgrade**. As software manufacturers develop a newer version of a software package, the newer version usually is assigned higher numbers. In the past, most manufacturers designate major software releases by increasing the version number by a whole number, for example, version 4.0 to 5.0. To designate minor software improvements, manufacturers usually change the version number by less than a whole number change, such as version 4.0 to 4.2. Today, many manufacturers use calendar years to designate the latest version. For example, in 1998, Microsoft introduced Microsoft Windows 98, which was an upgrade to Windows 95 **[Figure 3-43]**. Using year designations has helped customers track the must current version. Similar versions of software, however, can have different designations when used on Macintosh computers and PCs. Microsoft Office 98 for Macintosh computers, for example, is basically the same as Microsoft Office 97 for PCs.

Using Different Software Versions

Because of the cost of software, most schools do not upgrade their software each time a manufacture releases a new version. When schools purchase new computers, however, the latest versions of operating systems and application software often are pre-installed on the computers.

Teachers and students should know which versions of software applications are installed on their school, classroom, and home computers. Most software includes an About or Information command on the Help menu to indicate the software version **[Figure 3-44]**. Often, teachers and students have different versions of the same software on their home and classroom computers; a teacher might have PowerPoint 97 on a two-year old classroom computer and PowerPoint 2000 on a new home computer.

When working with different versions of the same software, two general rules can help make your work easier. First, an older version of a software package usually will not open a file created in a newer version of the software. Newer versions usually open files created in older versions. Therefore, you cannot open a word processing document created and saved using Microsoft Works 4.5 with Microsoft Works 3.0, an older version of the Microsoft Works program.

To help alleviate this problem, most software programs allow you to save a document in a format compatible with earlier versions of the same software or in a different file format that can be read by another software program. Using Microsoft Works 4.5, for example, you

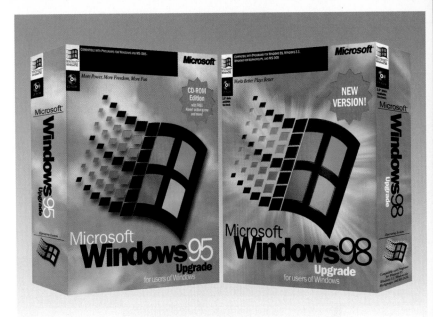

Figure 3-43 Shown are the two versions of Microsoft Windows. Windows 95 was released in 1995 and Windows 98 in 1998.

could save the document in the format of the older version of the software — in this case, Microsoft Works 3.0 **[Figure 3-45 on the next page]**. You then could open the document using the older version of the software.

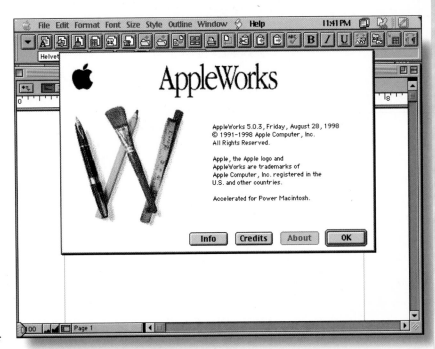

Figure 3-44 To determine the version of a particular software program, on the Help menu click the last command on the menu, which normally provides information about the software you are using. This window, for example, supplies information about AppleWorks.

Working with Macintosh Computers and PCs

When teachers and students try to move between a Macintosh computer and a PC while working on a document or file, many problems can occur. Even experienced users occasionally have problems working with the same document on both Macintosh and PC platforms. Some teachers and students, however, have a PC at home and Macintosh computers in their classrooms or vice versa — and thus have to use files on both platforms.

One source of the problem is that Macintosh computers and PCs format floppy disks differently. While Macintosh computers can access a document or file saved on PC-formatted disk, PCs normally cannot open files saved on a Macintosh-formatted disk. Working with both a Macintosh and a PC, however, is possible. One solution is to save a document or file created on a PC in a Macintosh format **[Figure 3-46]**. Another solution is to install and use a software program specifically designed to support PC to Mac and Mac to PC file conversions, such as MacLink Plus Deluxe or MacOpener **[Figure 3-47]**.

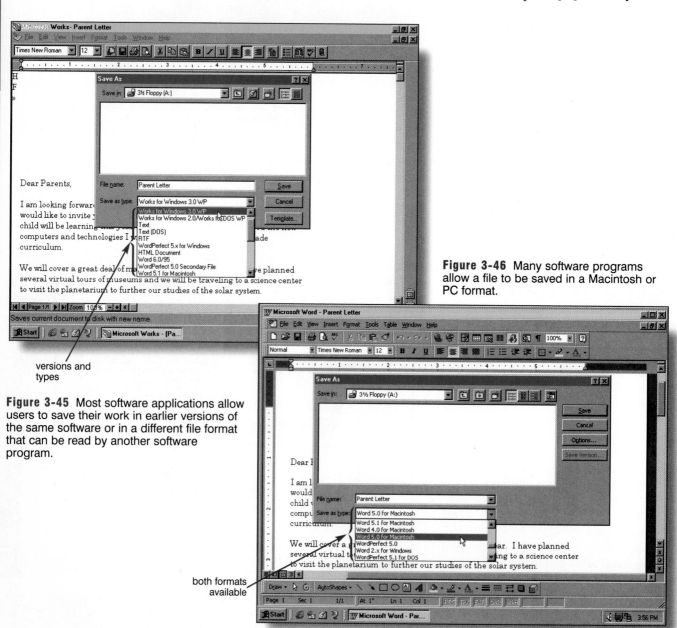

versions and types

Figure 3-45 Most software applications allow users to save their work in earlier versions of the same software or in a different file format that can be read by another software program.

Figure 3-46 Many software programs allow a file to be saved in a Macintosh or PC format.

both formats available

If you have to work with files on both computer platforms, you should speak with experienced teachers and other users in similar circumstances; they can help you find a solution for your situation. You also can ask for assistance from your instructor or school technology coordinator.

Summary of Software Applications for Education

In this chapter, you have learned about user interfaces and several software applications used in schools, businesses, and homes. You also have read about some of the learning aids and support tools that are available for application software. Understanding these software applications increases your computer literacy and helps you to understand how personal computers can help in your career as a teacher, in your classroom instruction, and at home. The next chapter introduces you to hardware applications for education; future chapters provide information on additional software applications used by educators and show you how to integrate various software applications into your classroom curriculum.

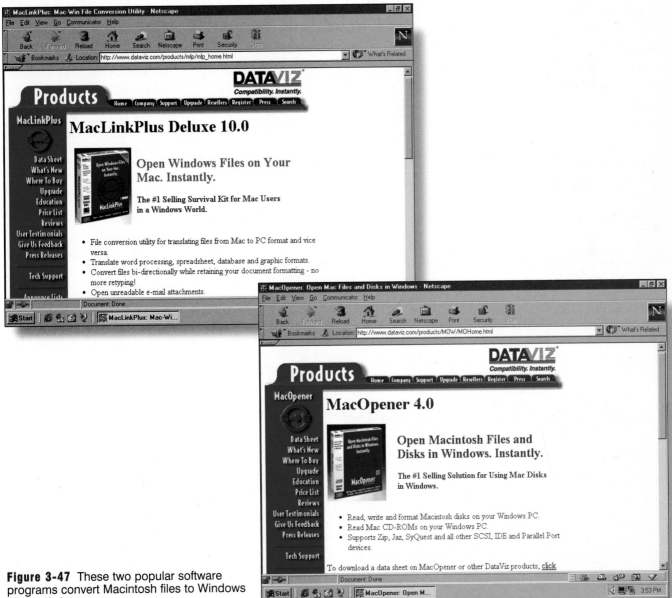

Figure 3-47 These two popular software programs convert Macintosh files to Windows files and vice versa.

www.scsite.com/tdc/ch3/brief.htm

- InBrief
- KeyTerms
- AtTheMovies
- CheckPoint
- TeacherTime
- CyberClass
- EdIssues
- NetStuff

SPECIAL FEATURES

- TimeLine 2000
- Guide to WWW Sites
- Buyer's Guide 2000
- Educational Sites
- State/Federal Sites
- Chat
- News
- Home

InBrief

Web Instructions: To display this page from the Web, launch your browser and enter the URL, www.scsite.com/tdc/ch3/brief.htm. Click the links for current and additional information. To listen to an audio version of this InBrief, click the Audio button below the title, InBrief, at the top of the page. To play the audio, RealPlayer must be installed on your computer (download by clicking here).

1. Application Software

Application software consists of programs designed to perform specific tasks for users. Packaged software can be purchased from software vendors in retail stores or on the Web. A particular software product such as Microsoft Word often is called a **software package**.

2. Role of the Operating System

System software consists of programs that control the operations of the computer and its devices. One type of system software, the **operating system**, contains instructions that coordinate all of the activities of the hardware devices in a computer. The operating system also contains instructions that allow the computer to run application software.

3. Role of the User Interface

All software, including the operating system, is designed to communicate with the user in a certain way, through a user interface. A **user interface** controls how users enter data or instructions (input) and how information is presented on the screen (output). One of the more common user interfaces is a graphical user interface. A **graphical user interface**, or **GUI**, combines text, graphics, and other visual cues to make software easier to use. **Mac OS** and **Windows** are popular graphical user interfaces.

4. Starting a Software Application

Mac OS and Windows use the concept of a desktop to make the computer easier to use. The **desktop** is an on-screen work area that uses common graphical elements such as icons, buttons, windows, menus, and dialog boxes. An **icon** is a small picture that represents a program, an instruction, or some other object. A **button** is a graphical element that when selected, causes a specific action to take place. A **menu** is a list of commands from which you can select. **Commands** are instructions that cause a computer program to perform a specific action.

5. Working with Software Applications

A **document** is a piece of work created with an application program and saved on a disk with a unique file name. **Creating** involves developing the document by entering text and performing other tasks using an input device such as a keyboard. **Editing** is the process of making changes to the document's existing content. **Formatting** involves changing the appearance of a document. **Saving** is the process of copying a document from memory to a storage medium. **Printing** is the process of sending a file to a printer to generate output.

6. Productivity Software

Productivity software is designed to help people work more effectively and efficiently while performing daily activities. Productivity software includes applications such as word processing, spreadsheet, database, presentation graphics, personal information management, and software suites.

7. Word Processing Software

The most widely used software is **word processing software**, which is used to create, edit, and format documents that consist primarily of text. The most popular word processing programs used in schools today are Microsoft Word and the word processing applications included with AppleWorks, ClarisWorks, and Microsoft Works.

8. Spreadsheet Software

Another widely used software application is **spreadsheet software,** which allows you to organize numeric data in rows and columns. These rows and columns collectively are called a **spreadsheet**, or **worksheet**. Individuals who frequently work with numbers; for example financial statements and payroll, use spreadsheets.

www.scsite.com/tdc/ch3/brief.htm

InBrief

- InBrief
- KeyTerms
- AtTheMovies
- CheckPoint
- TeacherTime
- CyberClass
- EdIssues
- NetStuff

SPECIAL FEATURES

- TimeLine 2000
- Guide to WWW Sites
- Buyer's Guide 2000
- Educational Sites
- State/Federal Sites
- Chat
- News
- Home

9. Database Software

A **database** is a collection of data organized in a manner that allows access, retrieval, and use of that data. In a computerized database, data is stored in an electronic format on a storage medium. **Database software** allows you to create a computerized database; add, change, and delete data; sort and retrieve data from the database; and create forms and reports using the data in the database.

10. Presentation Graphics Software

Presentation graphics software allows you to create documents called **presentations**, which are used to communicate ideas, messages, and other information to a group, such as a class or auditorium. The presentations can be viewed as **slides** that display on a large monitor or project onto a screen.

11. Software Suites and Integrated Software

A **software suite** is a collection of individual application software packages sold as a single package. Suites typically include word processing, spreadsheet, database, and presentation graphics software applications. **Integrated software** is software that combines applications such as word processing, spreadsheet, and database into a single, easy-to-use package. Unlike a software suite, however, you cannot purchase the applications in the integrated software package individually.

12. Graphics and Multimedia Software

Graphics and multimedia software include desktop publishing, paint/image editing, multimedia authoring, and Web page authoring software. **Desktop publishing** (DTP) **software** allows you to design, produce, and deliver sophisticated documents that contain text, graphics, and brilliant colors. Paint/image editing software allows you to create and modify graphics such as those used in DTP documents and Web pages. **Multimedia authoring software** is used to create electronic presentations that can include text, graphics, video, audio, and animation. **Web page authoring software** is software designed specifically for creating Web pages and organizing, managing, and maintaining Web sites.

13. Software for School and Professional Use

Software for schools and professional use includes school management software, student management software, grade book software, educational/reference software, and software for students with special needs. **School management software** is a centralized program that allows district and school personnel to manage the school district operations. **Student management software** allows administrators, teachers, and other staff to manage and track information on students. **Grade book software** is a program that allows teachers to track and organize student tests, homework, lab work, and other scores.

14. Educational/Reference Software

Educational software is designed for the learning environment. Educational software exists for just about any subject, from learning a foreign language to learning how to cook. **Reference software** provides valuable and thorough information for everyone in an educational setting and in the family. Popular reference software includes encyclopedias, dictionaries, health/medical guides, and travel directories.

15. Learning Aids and Support Tools

Online Help is the electronic equivalent of a user manual; it usually is integrated into an application software package. **Trade books** are available to help users learn to use the features of software application packages. These trade books are available where software is sold. **Tutorials** are step-by-step instructions using real examples that show users how to use an application.

www.scsite.com/tdc/ch3/terms.htm

KeyTerms

Web Instructions: To display this page from the Web, launch your browser and enter the URL, www.scsite.com/tdc/ch3/terms .htm. Scroll through the list of terms. Click a term to display its definition and a picture. Click KeyTerms on the left to redisplay the KeyTerms page. Click the TO WEB button for current and additional information about the term from the Web. To see animations, Shockwave and Flash Player must be installed on your computer (download by clicking here).

InBrief

KeyTerms

AtTheMovies

CheckPoint

TeacherTime

CyberClass

EdIssues

NetStuff

SPECIAL FEATURES

TimeLine 2000

Guide to WWW Sites

Buyer's Guide 2000

Educational Sites

State/Federal Sites

Chat

News

Home

address book [3.20]
AppleWorks [3.20]
application [3.2]
appointment calendar [3.20]
assistant [3.11]
AutoSave [3.8]

border [3.9]
button [3.5]

cell [3.13]
chart [3.13]
clip art [3.9]
clip art/image gallery [3.17]
Clipboard [3.7]
commands [3.5]
context-sensitive [3.29]
copy [3.7]
creating [3.7]
curriculum page [3.23]
cut [3.7]

database [3.14]
database file [3.14]

database software [3.14]
delete [3.7]
desktop [3.5]
desktop publishing (DTP) software [3.21]
dialog box [3.8]
document [3.6]

editing [3.7]
educational software [3.26]

fields [3.14]
file [3.8]
file name [3.8]
find [3.10]
font [3.7]
font size [3.7]
font style [3.7]
footer [3.11]
formatting [3.7]
formula [3.13]
Frequently Asked Questions (FAQs) [3.29]

grade book software [3.25]
graphical user interface (GUI) [3.4]

header [3.10]
HyperStudio® [3.23]

icon [3.5]
image editing software [3.22]
import [3.10]
insert [3.7]
integrated software [3.20]

label [3.13]
legal software [3.28]

Mac OS [3.4]
margins [3.10]
menu [3.5]
Microsoft FrontPage [3.23]
Microsoft Works [3.20]
multimedia authoring software [3.23]

Netscape Composer [3.23]
notepad [3.20]

online Help [3.29]
operating system [3.3]

page layout [3.21]
paint software [3.22]
paste [3.7]

personal computer entertainment software [3.28]
personal finance software [3.27]
personal information manager (PIM) [3.19]
photo-editing software [3.22]
points [3.7]
presentation graphics software [3.16]
presentations [3.16]
printing [3.8]
productivity software [3.8]

record [3.14]
reference software [3.26]
replace [3.10]

saving [3.8]
school management software [3.25]
scrolling [3.10]
search [3.10]
slide sorter [3.17]
slides [3.16]
software application [3.2]
software package [3.3]
software suite [3.20]
speech synthesis software [3.27]
spell checker [3.10]
spelling checker [3.10]
special needs software [3.27]
spreadsheet [3.12]
spreadsheet software [3.12]
student management software [3.25]
submenu [3.5]
system software [3.3]

tax preparation software [3.28]
title bar [3.6]
trade books [3.29]
tutorials [3.29]

upgrade [3.30]
user interface [3.4]

value [3.13]
version [3.30]

Web page authoring [3.23]
window [3.6]
Windows [3.4]
wizard [3.11]
word processing software [3.8]
wordwrap [3.10]
worksheet [3.12]

www.scsite.com/tdc/ch3/movies.htm

InBrief

KeyTerms

AtTheMovies

CheckPoint

TeacherTime

CyberClass

EdIssues

NetStuff

SPECIAL FEATURES

TimeLine 2000

Guide to WWW Sites

Buyer's Guide 2000

Educational Sites

State/Federal Sites

Chat

News

Home

AtTheMovies

WELCOME to VIDEO CLIPS from CNN

Web Instructions: To display this page from the Web, launch your browser and enter the URL, www.scsite.com/tdc/ch3/movies.htm. Click a picture to view a video. After watching the video, close the video window and then complete the exercise by answering the questions about the video. To view the videos, RealPlayer must be installed on your computer (download by clicking here).

1. Walk Through Computer

What is the idea behind the oversized computer exhibit at the Computer Museum in Boston? How does a museum visitor interact with the computer? Do the creators of this larger-than-life computer describe the interaction between computer software and hardware? Do you think that being inside a computer could help you understand how computers work? To learn more about the museum's latest exhibits, visit the Web site.

2. History Software

Curriculum studies are becoming increasingly computer oriented. Software supports problem solving and effectively crosses the curriculum into science, literature, mathematics, social studies, and history. How are you able to interact with CD curriculum software to research subject matter and prepare reports? Describe the formats of available history reference software. Would you use software like the software in this segment with your history classroom? In what ways could students use integrated application software suites, such as Microsoft Office or AppleWorks, with history software to enhance reports? How would you expect students to reference the multimedia CD in a footnote or endnote? Could you make a case for your educational institution adopting a curriculum that requires the integration of reference and applications' software with the basic disciplines?

3. Knowledge Adventure

Educational enrichment and creative discovery are primary buzzwords in the edutainment software industry. Describe edutainment software. What are some of the types of edutainment software being created by software companies today? What end users and age groups are targeted markets for edutainment software? Do you use any edutainment software in your teaching environment? If so, what is it? Rate the positive and negative aspects of the edutainment software you have used and record your findings. Forward your results and recommendations to software companies or publishers so they are better able to design the essential educational elements that should be contained in their edutainment software.

www.scsite.com/tdc/ch3/check.htm

CheckPoint

Web Instructions: To display this page from the Web, launch your browser and enter the URL, www.scsite.com/tdc/ch3/check.htm. Click a blank line for the answer. Click the links for current and additional information. To experience the animations and interactivity, Shockwave and Flash Player must be installed on your computer (download by clicking here).

InBrief

KeyTerms

AtTheMovies

CheckPoint

TeacherTime

CyberClass

EdIssues

NetStuff

SPECIAL FEATURES

TimeLine 2000

Guide to WWW Sites

Buyer's Guide 2000

Educational Sites

State/Federal Sites

Chat

News

Home

1. Label the Figure

Instructions: Identify each component of the Windows desktop.

2. Matching

Instructions: Match each term from the column on the left with the best description from the column on the right.

____ 1. Clipboard   a. collection of related facts

____ 2. database   b. instructions that cause software to perform specific actions

____ 3. field   c. temporary storage location

____ 4. commands   d. intersection where a column and row meet

____ 5. cell   e. collection of data stored in files

3. Short Answer

Instructions: Write a brief answer to each of the following questions.

1. What is a graphical user interface? Describe some common features of both the Windows and Macintosh graphical user interface. _____

2. Name and describe four different types of productivity software used by K-12 teachers. Which productivity software program do you use the most? Why? _____

3. What are the advantages of integrated software and software suites? Describe three popular integrated software or software suites used in K-12 schools. _____

4. What is a database? How are databases used in K-12 schools? _____

5. What are the advantages of using presentation graphics software programs? What are the disadvantages? How are teachers and students using presentation graphics programs? _____

1 2 3 4 5 6 7 8

www.scsite.com/tdc/ch3/time.htm

TeacherTime

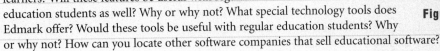

Web Instructions: To display this page from the Web, launch your browser and enter the URL, www.scsite.com/tdc/ch3/time.htm. Click the links for current and additional information.

InBrief

KeyTerms

AtTheMovies

CheckPoint

TeacherTime

CyberClass

EdIssues

NetStuff

SPECIAL FEATURES

TimeLine 2000

Guide to WWW Sites

Buyer's Guide 2000

Educational Sites

State/Federal Sites

Chat

News

Home

1. Your school uses Macintosh computers. Your principal is considering purchasing AppleWorks for all classroom and lab computers. You have never used AppleWorks, however, you are familiar with Microsoft Office 98 for the Macintosh. Your principal has asked you to compare the two software packages and make a presentation to the school's teachers. How are the packages the same? How are the packages different? What type of support does each software package offer? Is one easier to use than the other? Why or why not? Is one easier to learn than the other? Why or why not?

2. Your class is responsible for creating and maintaining your school's new Web page. Your principal purchased a Web publishing program, FrontPage, for you and your students. Your students will learn the program through the software's tutorials and online Help, however, your principal has authorized you to purchase a trade book. How do you locate a good trade book on FrontPage? Review various books available for learning and using FrontPage. Which trade book do you think is the best? Why? How can you use this in your classroom? Will it be easy for your students to learn to use FrontPage using the trade book? Why or why not?

3. You teach third grade and will have students with special needs in your class this year. You are planning to purchase software for your classroom to integrate technology into the curriculum. What software can you purchase that will benefit both your regular students as well as your special needs students? Explore Edmark Software (Figure 3-48). Can you use these products in the classroom described above? What special features do these software packages include for special needs learners? Will these features be useful with regular education students as well? Why or why not? What special technology tools does Edmark offer? Would these tools be useful with regular education students? Why or why not? How can you locate other software companies that sell educational software?

Figure 3-48

4. Many schools create a student/parent newsletter using desktop publishing software. Often these newsletters are enhanced with scanned photographs or graphics representing school events, teachers, and students. Now, the Internet is providing a new resource for desktop publishing. Companies such as ArtToday offer 750,000 images including clip art, photographs, etchings, cartoons, animations, and drawings, 2,150 fonts, and 40,000 Web graphics. ArtToday also features an online search engine for keyword searching. What is the cost of this type of service? How does an online service such as ArtToday differ from purchasing a CD-ROM with clip art images? What are the advantages of an online service? What are the disadvantages? Which gallery would be easier to use in the classroom? Why?

5. Most state Departments of Education negotiate one-year contracts with various vendors for educational software products. This enables schools to acquire software products at substantial discounts. Contact a school in your district or access your state's Department of Education Web page and find out about a few of the software products available through the state purchasing program. Compare these prices to purchasing the same software either online or at a local computer store. What kind of discounts are the schools receiving? How many titles are available through the state catalog? What procedures does a teacher have to go through to purchase software not in the catalog?

www.scsite.com/tdc/ch3/class.htm

CyberClass

Web Instructions: To display this page from the Web, launch your browser and enter the URL, www.scsite.com/tdc/ch3/class.htm. To start Level I CyberClass, click a Level I link on this page or enter the URL, www.cyber-class.com. Click the Student button, click *Teachers Discovering Computers* in the list of titles, and then click the Enter a site button. To start Level II or III CyberClass (available only to those purchasers of a CyberClass floppy disk), place your CyberClass floppy disk in drive A, click Start on the taskbar, click Run on the Start menu, type a:connect in the Open text box, click the OK button, click the Enter CyberClass button, and then follow the instructions. If you are using a Macintosh, see your instructor.

InBrief

KeyTerms

AtTheMovies

CheckPoint

TeacherTime

CyberClass

EdIssues

NetStuff

SPECIAL FEATURES

TimeLine 2000

Guide to WWW Sites

Buyer's Guide 2000

Educational Sites

State/Federal Sites

Chat

News

Home

1. Flash Cards (Level I, Level II, and Level III)

Click Flash Cards on the Main Menu of the CyberClass Web page. Click the plus sign before the Chapter 3 title. Click Application Software and answer all the cards in that section. Choose other selections and continue until you have answered all 20 questions. Record your percentage correct and hand in your score to your instructor. All users: Answer as many more Flash Cards as you desire. Close the Electronic Flash Card window and the Flash Cards window by clicking the Close button in the upper-right corner of each window.

2. Practice Test (Level I, Level II, and Level III)

Click Testing on the Main Menu of the CyberClass Web page. Click the Select a book box arrow and then click Teachers Discovering Computers. Click the Select a test to take box arrow and then click the Chapter 3 title in the list. Click the Take Test button. If necessary, maximize the window. Take the practice test and then click the Submit Test button. Click the Display Study Guide button. Review the Study Guide. Scroll down and click the Return To CyberClass button. Click the Yes button to close the Study Guide window. Then, click the Done button. Hand in your printed Study Guide.

3. Web Guide (Level I, Level II, and Level III)

Click Web Guide on the Main Menu of the CyberClass Web page. When the Guide to World Wide Web Sites page displays, click Science. Go to the Exploratorium and review the site. When you are finished, close the window and then prepare a brief report on what you found and why you would or would not use this Web site in your classroom.

4. Assignments and Syllabus (Level II and Level III)

Click Assignments on the Main Menu of the CyberClass Web page. Ensure you are aware of all assignments and when they are due. Click Syllabus on the Main Menu of the CyberClass Web page. Verify you are up to date on all activities for the class.

5. CyberChallenge (Level II and Level III)

Click CyberChallenge on the Main Menu of the CyberClass Web page. Click the Select a book box arrow and then click Teachers Discovering Computers. Click the Select a board to play box arrow and then click Chapter 3 in the list. Click the Play CyberChallenge button. Maximize the CyberChallenge window. Play CyberChallenge until your score for a complete game is 500 points or more. Close the CyberChallenge window.

6. Hot Links (Level II and Level III)

Click Hot Links on the Main Menu of the CyberClass Web page. Review the sites in the Hot Links section and then write a brief report indicating which site you like best and why.

www.scsite.com/tdc/ch3/issues.htm

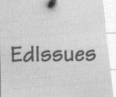
EdIssues

Web Instructions: To display this page from the Web, launch your browser and enter the URL, www.scsite.com/tdc/ch3/issues.htm. Click the links for current and additional information to help you respond to the EdIssues questions.

InBrief

KeyTerms

AtTheMovies

CheckPoint

TeacherTime

CyberClass

EdIssues

NetStuff

SPECIAL FEATURES

TimeLine 2000

Guide to WWW Sites

Buyer's Guide 2000

Educational Sites

State/Federal Sites

Chat

News

Home

1. Word Processing

Many teachers believe that word processing software improves the quality of written work by making it easier for students to create and edit documents. Students can use clip art, scanned images, or other computer graphics to enhance their work. Some people argue, however, that word processing software has become a crutch, eliminating the need to learn the rudiments of language. These people believe students are not forced to know basic grammar and spelling rules because word processing software alerts them to errors. How do you think word processing software has influenced written communication? Does it result in better student work or simply more correct, mediocre work? What word processing features most enhance the quality of written material?

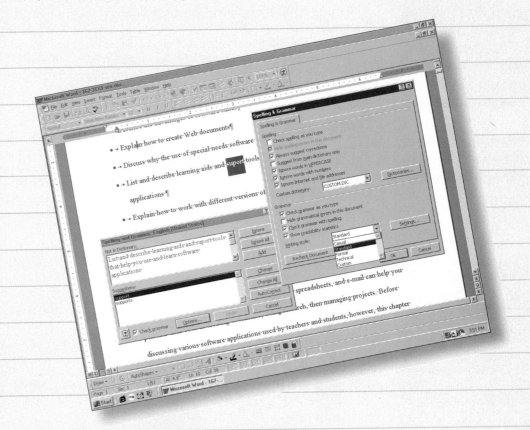

2. Web Publishing

Web publishing software makes creating a Web page as easy as typing a letter. Anyone can create a Web page using a Web editor. Some people, however, believe it is important to know HTML and to teach students how to create Web pages using HTML. They argue that when you have an understanding of HTML, you are able to create more dynamic Web pages, fix problems more easily, and you will possess greater technology skills. Other teachers feel teaching HTML is a waste of time because Web editors do it all for you, and they will continue to improve. Would you teach your students HTML? Why or why not? What are some advantages to knowing HTML? How will knowledge of HTML help your students? What are the advantages of using a Web editor in the classroom? What are some disadvantages of using Web editors? Which Web editor would you use? Why?

EdIssues

InBrief

KeyTerms

AtTheMovies

CheckPoint

TeacherTime

CyberClass

EdIssues

NetStuff

SPECIAL FEATURES

TimeLine 2000

Guide to WWW Sites

Buyer's Guide 2000

Educational Sites

State/Federal Sites

Chat

News

Home

3. Database Software

Increasingly sophisticated software applications not only have impacted business, entertainment, and recreation, but education as well. Database software can give students the opportunity to record, track, and analyze data on virtually any subject matter. Learning about database software also provides students with knowledge of an important software program that is extensively used in business and on the Web. Does learning and using database software help students develop higher-order thinking and problem-solving skills? What other advantages does using database software offer? What are some disadvantages to using database software in the classroom? How might another application described in this chapter be used to teach higher-order thinking skills or problem solving?

4. Computer Use in the Classroom

With the explosion of educational software, multimedia, and the Internet, educators are still learning the best use for computers in the classroom. Drill and practice? Problem solving? Games? A growing number of educators feel that students should be taught the software applications they will have to know to succeed in the workplace. From the applications presented in this chapter, make a list of five applications you think every student should learn, from more important to least important. Explain your ranking. At what level do you think each application should be taught? Why?

5. Learning Styles

With the diversity of the student population today, educators have begun to look at learning styles, which is the belief that people learn things best in different ways. How do you learn things more effectively? If you had to learn one of the software applications described in this chapter, which of the learning aids and support tools (online Help, tutorials, wizards, or trade books) would fit your learning style best? Why? Do you think the type of software application you were learning would affect your choice of learning aid? Why or why not?

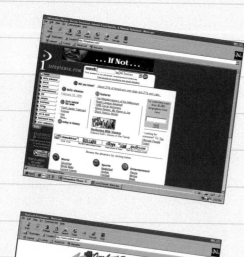

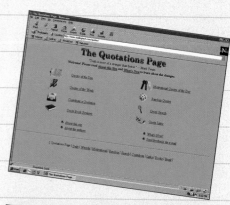

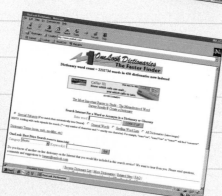

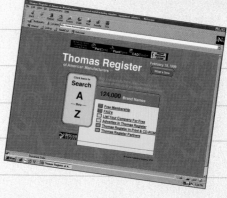

www.scsite.com/tdc/ch3/net.htm

Web Instructions: To display this page from the Web, launch your browser and enter the URL, www.scsite.com/tdc/ch3/net.htm. To use the Word Processing lab or the Setting Up to Print lab from the Web, Shockwave and Flash Player must be installed on your computer (download by clicking here).

InBrief

KeyTerms

AtTheMovies

CheckPoint

TeacherTime

CyberClass

EdIssues

NetStuff

SPECIAL FEATURES

TimeLine 2000

Guide to WWW Sites

Buyer's Guide 2000

Educational Sites

State/Federal Sites

Chat

News

Home

1. Shelly Cashman Series Word Processing Lab

WORD PROCESSING LAB

Follow the instructions in NetStuff 1 on page 1.34 to start and use the Word Processing lab. If you are running from the Web, enter the URL, www.scsite.com/sclabs/menu.htm or display the NetStuff page (see instructions at the top of this page) and then click the WORD PROCESSING LAB button.

2. Shelly Cashman Series Setting Up to Print Lab

SETTING UP TO PRINT LAB

Follow the instructions in NetStuff 1 on page 1.34 to start and use the Setting Up to Print lab. If you are running from the Web, enter the URL, www.scsite.com/sclabs/menu.htm or display the NetStuff page (see instructions at the top of this page) and then click the SETTING UP TO PRINT LAB button.

3. Word Processing Proficiency

WORD PROCESSING PROFICIENCY

Teachers need to be proficient in word processing. Click the WORD PROCESSING PROFICIENCY button to complete an exercise to improve your word processing skills on either a Macintosh computer or PC.

4. Desktop Publishing

DESKTOP PUBLISHING

Desktop publishing software is designed specifically for page composition and layout. Click the DESKTOP PUBLISHING button to complete an exercise to increase your knowledge of desktop publishing software.

5. Mac OS Help

MAC OS HELP

Help refers to additional instructions that are available within application software and a computer's operating system. To learn more about your Macintosh operating system's Help feature, click the MAC OS HELP button and complete this exercise.

6. Windows 98 Help

WINDOWS 98 HELP

To learn more about your Windows 98 operating system's Help feature [Figure 3-49], click the WINDOWS 98 HELP button and complete this exercise.

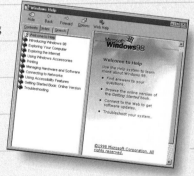

Figure 3-49

7. Financial Information Online

FINANCIAL INFORMATION ONLINE

Online services for up-to-the-minute financial news are widely available on the Web. To see an example of a financial information service, click the FINANCIAL INFORMATION ONLINE button and complete this exercise.

8. Web Chat

WEB CHAT

The EdIssues section presents various scenarios on the uses of computers, technologies, and non-technology-related issues in K-12 education. Click the WEB CHAT button to enter a Web Chat discussion related to the EdIssues exercises.

Creating a Teacher's Web Page

OBJECTIVES:

You will have mastered the material in this project when you can:

- Download image files from the Web
- Start Netscape Composer
- Add a background
- Add text
- Insert a horizontal line
- Create links to other Web pages
- Insert a graphic
- Create an e-mail link
- Save a Web page
- View a Web page

WebInfo

To obtain a free copy of Netscape Communicator, visit the Teachers Discovering Computers Chapter 3 WebInfo page

(www.scsite.com/tdc/ ch3/webinfo.htm)

and click Netscape Communicator.

INTRODUCTION

As you learned in Chapter 2, Web publishing is the development and maintenance of Web pages. Recall also that Web pages are created using **hypertext markup language** (**HTML**), which is a set of special codes, called **tags**, that define the placement and format of text, graphics, video, and sound on a Web page.

Today, teachers and students do not have to learn HTML to create Web pages. Instead, user-friendly programs allow teachers, students, and other users to create their own Web pages easily using basic word processing skills. Numerous software programs specifically designed for creating Web pages, called **HTML editors**, are available for teachers and students. A popular program used by many teachers and students to build their home pages is **Netscape Composer**, which is included with Netscape Communicator and thus already is installed on many school and home computers. If you do not have Netscape Communicator installed on your home or school computer, you can download it easily from the Web.

In this project, you will build a basic teacher's Web page called Ms. Bailey's Home Page (Figure 1). Ms. Bailey is a science teacher at Dresden Middle School. You will find it helpful if you occasionally refer back to Figure 1 to see the completed Web page as you work through the project. Included are step-by-step instructions for creating the project with Netscape Communicator installed on a PC. You also can easily complete this project with Netscape Communicator installed on a Macintosh computer; however, you may encounter slight variations from the step-by-step instructions in this project.

The primary difference between using a Macintosh computer and a PC is how you use a mouse. If you are using a Macintosh computer, when the step-by-step instructions in this project ask you to right-click, you must click and hold down the single Macintosh mouse button for approximately two seconds. Holding down a Macintosh mouse button for approximately two seconds often accomplishes the same command as right-clicking a PC mouse.

Although Web pages can be as distinctive and different as the individuals who create them, a relatively small set of basic features are common to many Web page. The **title** of a Web page is the text that appears on the title bar of the Netscape window when the page is being displayed; the title also can refer to the first line or main heading of a Web page. The background of a Web page is similar to the wallpaper in Windows or the image on the desktop of a Macintosh computer. It provides a backdrop against which other

elements are shown. The background can be either a solid color or a small graphic image that is tiled, or repeated, across the entire page.

Normal text is the text that makes up the main information content of a Web page. Normal text also can be formatted in bold, italic, underlined, or different colors. **Headings** are used to set off different paragraphs of text or different sections of a page. Headings usually are formatted in a larger font size than normal text and often are bold. **Images** are graphics and pictures that are contained on a Web page. Some images are animated and continuously change their appearance. **Links** are areas of the page (text or graphics) that when clicked cause the browser to display another file or Web page or play sounds or videos. **Horizontal rules** normally display across the page and

Figure 1

are used to separate different sections of the page. Finally, many Web pages include an e-mail link so users can send an e-mail message from the Web page.

In this project, you will learn how to download graphics from the Web, open Netscape Composer, select a background image, create a title, insert and format text and headings, insert horizontal rules and graphics, create a linked list of favorite places, create an e-mail link, and save and view Ms. Bailey's Web page. Chapter 3 introduced you to many basic word processing skills. This project assumes you possess basic word processing skills such as entering, selecting, and formatting text.

DOWNLOADING IMAGE FILES

Clip art images are graphical images that are available for you to use on your Web and curriculum pages. Clip art images either may be free or can be purchased. You can insert images into your Web pages from local files; for example, from a floppy disk. To insert the images from local files, however, you must download them from the Web or obtain the images from a clip art gallery. This project requires that you download two images from the Web, marble.jpg and mail.gif. The marble image will be used as a background for the Web page and the mail image will be used to identify the e-mail link. Perform the steps on the next page to download two image files from the Web.

To Download Image Files

1 **Start Netscape Communicator,** enter the URL www.scsite.com/tdc/ sf3.htm **in the location text box, and then press the** ENTER **key.**

The Teachers Discovering Computers Composer project Web page displays.

2 **Right-click the marble image and then point to Save Image As on the shortcut menu.**

The shortcut menu displays (Figure 2). If using a Macintosh computer, click and hold down the mouse button for approximately two seconds to display the shortcut menu.

3 **Insert a floppy disk in drive A and then click Save Image As. When the Save As box displays, click 3½ Floppy (A:) in the Save in list box, type marble in the File name text box, and then click the Save button.**

The marble.jpg file is saved on your floppy disk.

4 **Repeat Steps 2 and 3 for the mail image.**

You should have two image files saved on a floppy disk in drive A. Additional step-by-step instructions for downloading these and other images from the Web are provided at the above listed Web site.

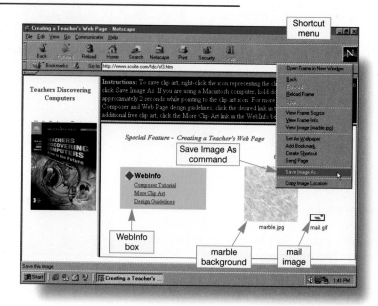

Figure 2

STARTING NETSCAPE COMPOSER

As a result of downloading the image files, the Netscape Navigator browser window already is open on your desktop. The following step shows how to start Netscape Composer so you can begin developing Ms. Bailey's Home Page.

To Start Netscape Composer

1 **Click the Composer icon on the Communicator Component bar.**

Netscape Composer opens displaying a blank page (Figure 3).

Figure 3

SELECTING A BACKGROUND IMAGE

The background of a Web page is created by tiling a small graphic image many times across the page. Users can choose from thousands of graphic images to use for their Web page backgrounds. For this project, you will use the marble image that was downloaded earlier. Perform the following steps to select a background.

 To Select a Background

1 **Click Format on the menu bar and then point to Page Colors and Properties.**

The Format menu displays (Figure 4).

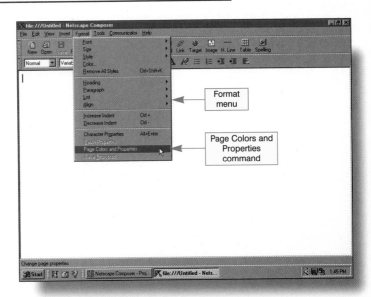

Figure 4

2 Click Page Colors and Properties and then point to the Choose File button.

The Page Properties dialog box and Colors and Background panel display (Figure 5).

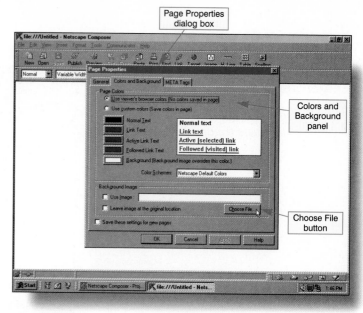

Figure 5

3 Click the Choose File button. When the Choose Image File dialog box displays, if necessary, click 3½ Floppy (A:) in the Look in list, and then point to marble (Figure 6).

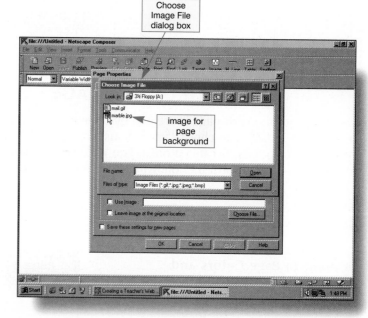

Figure 6

4 **Double-click marble and then point to the OK button.**

The Choose Image File dialog box closes and the file name, marble.jpg, displays in the Use Image text box (Figure 7).

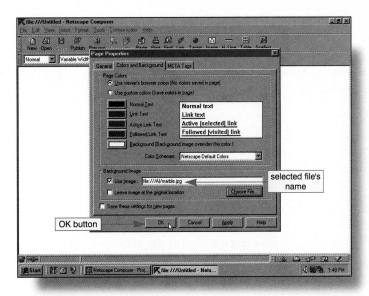

Figure 7

5 **Click the OK button.**

The marble image is tiled across the Web page (Figure 8).

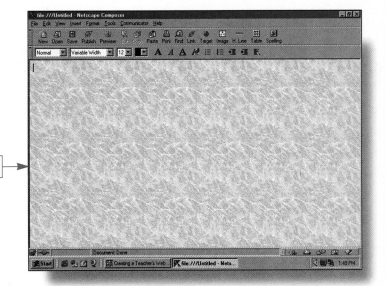

Figure 8

ENTERING AND FORMATTING TEXT

Entering and formatting text in Composer are similar to entering and formatting text using word processing software. In the next sequence of steps, you will enter the title and other information for Ms. Bailey's Home Page.

To Enter and Format Text

1 **Type** Ms. Bailey's Home Page **at the insertion point and then press the ENTER key.**

The title displays in the upper left-hand corner of the page and the insertion point is positioned at the beginning of the next line.

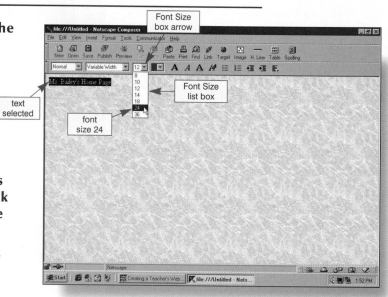

Figure 9

2 **Drag across the text, Ms. Bailey's Home Page to select it, and then click the Font Size box arrow. Point to size 24 in the Font Size list.**

The text is highlighted and the Font Size list box displays (Figure 9).

3 **Click 24 and then click the Alignment button. Point to the Center option button.**

The text is formatted in font size 24 and the Alignment list box displays (Figure 10).

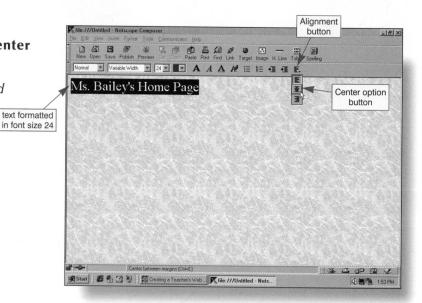

Figure 10

4 Click the Center option button and then click the Font Color box arrow.

The text is centered and the Font Color list box displays (Figure 11).

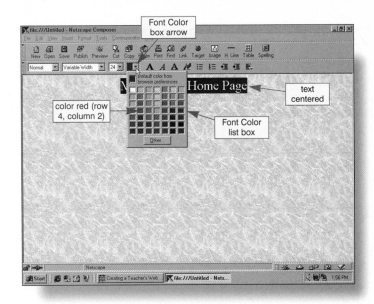

Figure 11

5 Click the color red (row 4, column 2) in the list and then click anywhere outside of the text.

The text displays in the color red, and the insertion point is positioned at the beginning of the next line (Figure 12).

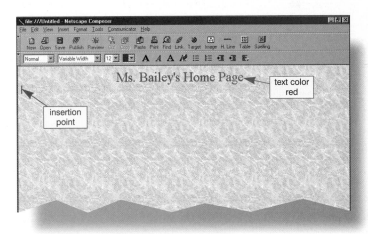

Figure 12

6 Type Dresden Middle School and then press the ENTER key. Type 255 Dresden Drive and then press the ENTER key. Type Amarillo, Texas 34567 and then press the ENTER key. Type (806) 555-9988 and then press the ENTER key. Drag across all the text you just entered beginning with Dresden Middle School, change the font size to 14, the alignment to center, and then click anywhere outside of the text.

The text displays in font size 14 and is centered under Ms. Bailey's Home Page, and the insertion point is positioned at the beginning of the next line (Figure 13).

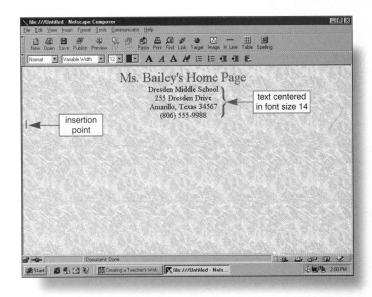

Figure 13

7 **Press the ENTER key. Type** Hi, my name is Ms. Ann Bailey. I teach 6th grade students at Dresden Middle School. I like teaching with technology and my students are motivated beyond belief when they can use computers and the Internet for classroom projects and assignments.

The text displays in the default color black, font size 12, and left alignment (Figure 14).

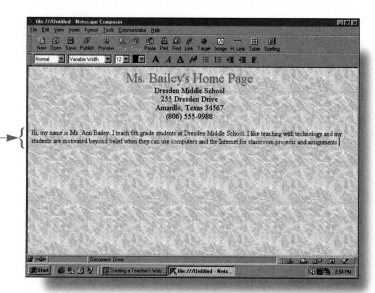

Figure 14

INSERTING A HORIZONTAL RULE AND A HEADING

Horizontal rules are used to set apart different sections of a Web page. Perform the following steps to insert a horizontal rule and then enter the heading.

To Insert a Horizontal Rule and a Heading

1 **Press the ENTER key twice and then click the Insert Horizontal Line button on the Composition toolbar.**

A horizontal rule displays at the insertion point (Figure 15).

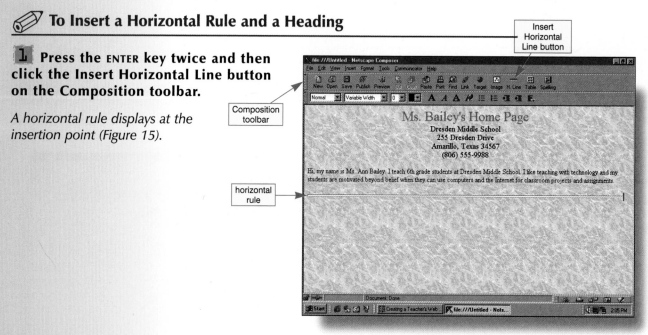

Figure 15

2 Press the ENTER key twice. Type My Favorite Education Links **and then press the ENTER key.**

3 Select the text just entered, change the font size to 18, and then click anywhere outside of the selected text.

The formatted text displays in font size 18, and the insertion point is positioned at the beginning of the next line (Figure 16).

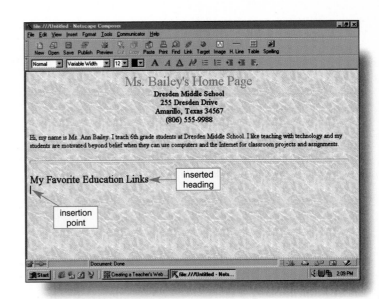

Figure 16

LINKING TEXT TO OTHER WEB PAGES

Using text links, you can create links for your students to other World Wide Web pages. Perform the following steps to enter the names of four education-related Web sites and then link each name to its corresponding Web site by entering the Web site's Uniform Resource Locator (URL).

To Create Links to Other Web Sites

1 Press the ENTER key. Type Education World **and then press the ENTER key. Type** The Texas Education Network **and then press the ENTER key. Type** Web World Wonders **and then press the ENTER key. Type** Museum of Natural History **and then press the ENTER key.**

2 Drag across the text, Education World to select it. Right-click the text and then point to Create Link Using Selected on the shortcut menu.

The Education World text is selected and the shortcut menu displays (Figure 17).

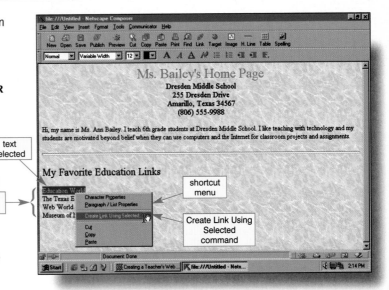

Figure 17

3 **Click Create Link Using Selected.**
Type http://www.education-world.com **in the Link to a page location or local file text box in the Character Properties dialog box and then point to the OK button.**

The Character Properties dialog box displays (Figure 18). The URL displays in the Link to a page location or local file text box.

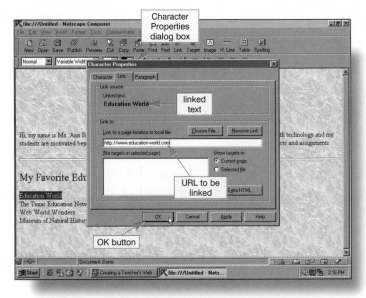

Figure 18

4 **Click the OK button and then click outside of the selected text.**

The dialog box closes and the text now is linked to the entered Web site. The text also displays in the default color blue and may be underlined (Figure 19).

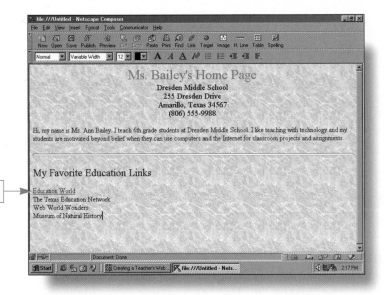

Figure 19

5 Repeat the procedures explained in Steps 2, 3, and 4 for the remaining three named Web sites, using the following URLs:
Texas Education Network
http://www.tenet.edu
Web World Wonders
http://www.firn.edu/fcim/webworld
Museum of Natural History
http://www.fmnh.org/

All four favorite sites now are linked to their respective sites, display in the default color blue, and are underlined (Figure 20). Note: These links will not work while viewing the Web page in Composer, but they will be active when viewing the page in Netscape Navigator. Saving and Viewing the page in Navigator will be discussed later in this project.

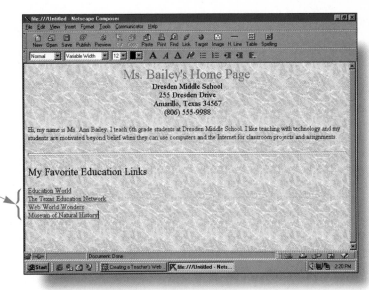

Figure 20

INSERTING AN IMAGE, E-MAIL INFORMATION, AND AN E-MAIL LINK

Adding graphics can enhance a Web page. Thousands of graphic images are available on the Web or in clip art galleries. Some graphics are animated and thus continuously change their appearance while the Web page is viewed in a browser. Many teachers and other users provide e-mail information and an e-mail link on their Web pages so students or others viewing the page can send e-mail messages directly from the page. Perform the following steps to add a graphic image.

 To Insert an Image

1 Position the insertion point at the end of the Museum of Natural History entry and then press the ENTER key. Click the Insert Image button in the Composition toolbar and then point to the Choose File button in the Image Properties dialog box.

The insertion point is positioned below the link text, and the Image Properties dialog box displays (Figure 21).

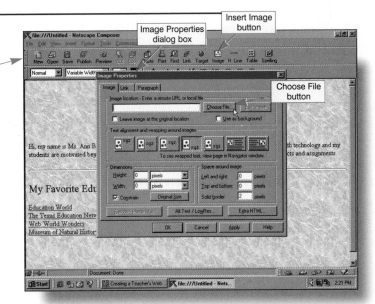

Figure 21

2 **Click the Choose File button. When the Choose Image File dialog box opens, if necessary, click 3½ Floppy (A:) in the Look in list box, and then point to the mail image. Double-click mail and then click the OK button.**

The mail image displays and the insertion point is positioned to the right of the mail image (Figure 22).

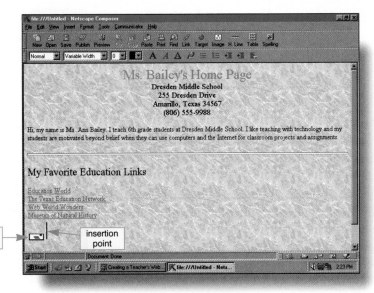

Figure 22

To conclude the e-mail information, perform the following steps to insert the text and link.

To Insert Text and an E-mail Link

1 **Type** My class would like to hear from you. Please e-mail me! **and then select the text. Right-click the selected text and then click Create Link Using Selected on the shortcut menu.**

2 **Type** mailto:AnnBailey@Dresden.k12.tx.us **in the Link to a page location or local file text box and then point to the OK button.**

The character Properties dialog box displays (Figure 23). Ms. Bailey's e-mail address displays in the text box.

3 **Click the OK button and then click anywhere outside of the selected text.**

The text displays as a link.

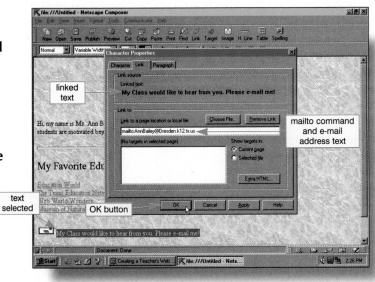

Figure 23

SAVING AND PREVIEWING A WEB PAGE

Before you can preview a Web page you have created, you must save it. Perform the following steps to save Ms. Bailey's Home Page and then view it in a separate Netscape Navigator window.

 To Save and Preview a Web Page

1 Click the Save button on the Composition toolbar. If necessary, click 3½ Floppy (A:) in the Save in list box. Type MsBailey in the File name text box and then point to the Save button in the Save As dialog box.

The Save As dialog box displays and the file name information is entered (Figure 24).

2 Click the Save button. If a Page Title dialog box displays, if necessary, type MsBaily in the title location box and then click the OK button.

The MsBailey.html file is saved on your floppy disk in drive A. The file is given an .html extension automatically, which indicates it is a Web page.

3 Click the Preview in Navigator button on the Composition toolbar.

Ms. Bailey's Web page displays in a Netscape Navigator window (see Figure 1 on page 3.47).

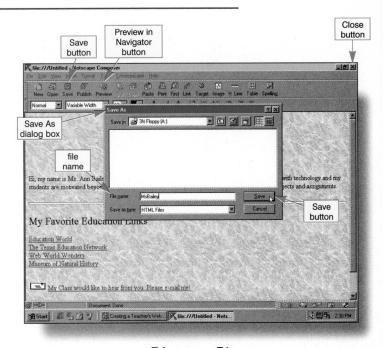

Figure 24

CLOSING COMPOSER AND VIEWING YOUR WEB PAGE

To quit Composer, click the Close button at the upper right corner of the Composer window. To view your Web page file in Netscape Navigator at any time, insert your floppy disk in drive A, type a:/MsBailey.html in the location text box, and then press the ENTER key.

SUMMARY

This project introduced you to the basics of creating a teacher's Web page using Netscape Composer. You have learned how to download images from the Web, open Netscape Composer, select a background image, create a title, insert and format text and headings, insert a horizontal rule and graphics, create a linked list of favorite Web sites, create an e-mail link, and save and view a Web page.

Hardware Applications for Education

Objectives

After completing this chapter, you will be able to:

- Describe the system unit

- Define a bit and describe how a series of bits are used to represent data

- Identify the major components of the system unit and explain their functions

- Explain how the CPU uses the four steps of a machine cycle to process data

- Describe the four types of input and input devices

- List the characteristics of a keyboard and identify various types of keyboards

- Identify various types of pointing devices

- Differentiate between the four types of output

- Identify the different types of output devices

- Explain the differences among various types of printers

- Differentiate between storage and memory

- Identify types of storage media and devices

- Explain how data is stored on floppy and hard disks

- Differentiate between CD-ROMs and DVD-ROMs

DURING YOUR TEACHING CAREER OR PERSONAL ENDEAVORS, YOU MOST LIKELY WILL DECIDE TO PURCHASE A NEW COMPUTER OR UPGRADE AN EXISTING ONE. To be effective in this decision-making process and to be an informed and effective teacher, you should possess a general knowledge of major computer components and how various computer components interact. In addition, the International Society for Technology in Education (ISTE) has developed a series of K-12 national technology standards and skills that K-12 students need to learn throughout their education. One of these technology standards recommends that graduating K-12 students demonstrate a sound understanding of the nature and operation of technology systems. To help you better understand these concepts, this chapter presents a brief look at some of the hardware components used for input, processing, output, and storage. Because Macintosh computers and PCs use similar, and in many cases identical, hardware components, the majority of information presented in this chapter applies to both computer platforms. In instances where Macintosh computers and PCs use slightly different hardware, these differences are explained.

The System Unit

The **system unit** is a box-like case that houses the electronic components a computer uses to process data **[Figure 4-1]**. The system unit is made of metal or plastic and protects the electronic components from damage. On a personal computer, these components and most storage devices reside inside the system unit; other devices, such as a keyboard and monitor usually are located outside the system unit. A laptop computer, on the other hand, houses almost all of its components in the system unit, including the keyboard and monitor.

Figure 4-1 On PCs and many Macintosh computers, the system unit usually is separated from the monitor and keyboard. Some system units are located below the monitor on the desktop, while tower units usually are positioned vertically on the floor. The system unit and monitor are combined in some Macintosh computers such as the iMac. On laptop computers, the keyboard is built into the system unit.

The following explanation of how data is represented in a computer will help you understand how the system unit processes data.

Data Representation

To fully understand how the various components of the system unit work together to process data, you need a basic understanding of how data is represented in a computer. Human speech is **analog**, meaning that it uses continuous signals to represent data and information. Most computers, by contrast, are **digital**, meaning that they understand only two discrete states: on and off. Computers are electronic devices powered by electricity, which has only two states: (1) on or (2) off. These two states are represented easily by electronic circuits using two digits; 0 is used to represent the electronic state of off (absence of an electric charge) and 1 is used to represent the electronic state of on (presence of an electric charge) **[Figure 4-2]**.

When people count, they use the digits 0 through 9, which are digits in the decimal system. Because a computer understands only two states, it uses a number system that has just two unique digits, 0 and 1. This numbering system is referred to as the **binary** system. Using just these two numbers, a computer

BINARY DIGIT (BIT)	ELECTRONIC CHARGE	ELECTRONIC STATE
1		ON
0		OFF

Figure 4-2 A computer circuit represents the binary digits 0 or 1 electronically by the presence or absence of an electronic charge.

can represent data electronically by turning circuits off or on.

Each on or off digital value is called a **bit** (short for **bi**nary dig**it**), and represents the smallest unit of data the computer can handle. By itself, a bit is not very informative. When eight bits are grouped together as a unit, they are called a **byte**. A byte is informative because it provides enough different combination of 0s and 1s to represent 256 individual characters including numbers, uppercase and lowercase letters of the alphabet, and punctuation marks **[Figure 4-3]**.

The combinations of 0s and 1s used to represent characters are defined by patterns called a coding scheme. The most widely used coding scheme to represent data on many personal computers is the **American Standard Code for Information Interchange**, called **ASCII** (pronounced ASK-ee).

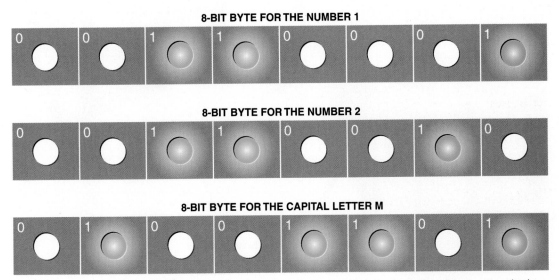

8-BIT BYTE FOR THE NUMBER 1

8-BIT BYTE FOR THE NUMBER 2

8-BIT BYTE FOR THE CAPITAL LETTER M

Figure 4-3 Eight bits grouped together as a unit are called a byte. A byte is used to represent a single character in the computer.

WebInfo

■ For a more detailed description of mother-boards, visit the Teachers Discovering Computers Chapter 4 WebInfo page

(www.scsite.com/tdc/ ch4/webinfo.htm)

and click Motherboard.

Coding schemes such as ASCII make it possible for humans to interact with digital computers that recognize only bits. When you press a key on a keyboard, the keyboard converts that action into a binary form the computer understands. That is, every character is converted to its corresponding byte. The computer then processes that data in terms of bytes, which actually is a series of on/off electrical states. When processing is finished, the computer converts the bytes back into numbers, letters of the alphabet, or special characters to be displayed on a screen or printed **[Figure 4-4]**. All of these conversions take place so quickly that you do not even realize they are occurring.

Figure 4-4 Converting a letter to binary form and back.

The Components of the System Unit

The major components of the system unit discussed in the following sections include the motherboard, the CPU and microprocessor, memory, expansion slots and expansion cards, and ports and connectors.

The Motherboard

Many of the electronic components in the system unit reside on a circuit board called the **motherboard**. **Figure 4-5** shows a photograph of a personal computer motherboard and identifies some of its components, including

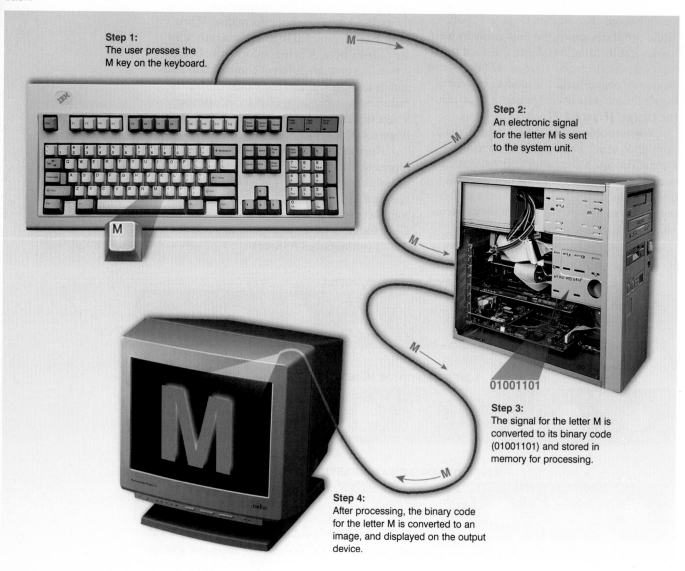

Step 1:
The user presses the M key on the keyboard.

Step 2:
An electronic signal for the letter M is sent to the system unit.

01001101

Step 3:
The signal for the letter M is converted to its binary code (01001101) and stored in memory for processing.

Step 4:
After processing, the binary code for the letter M is converted to an image, and displayed on the output device.

clock chip

connectors
for keyboard,
mouse, monitor,
and printer

expansion
slots

memory slots

memory module
(RAM chips)

CPU chip

Figure 4-5 The motherboard in a personal computer contains many chips and other electronic components.

several different types of chips. A **chip** is a small piece of semiconducting material usually no bigger than one-half-inch square and is made up of many layers of circuits and microscopic components that carry electronic signals. The motherboard in the system unit contains many different types of chips. Of these, one of the most important is the central processing unit (CPU).

CPU and Microprocessor

The **central processing unit** (**CPU**) interprets and carries out the basic instructions that operate a computer. The CPU, also called the **processor**, manages most of a computer's operations. Most of the devices that connect to a computer communicate with the CPU in order to carry out tasks **[Figure 4-6]**.

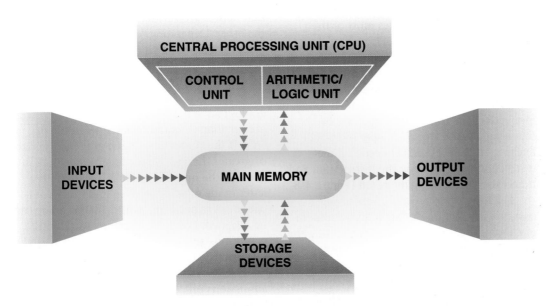

Figure 4-6 Most of the devices connected to a computer communicate with the CPU in order to carry out a task. The arrows in this figure represent the flow of data, instructions, and information.

In a personal computer, a single chip known as the **microprocessor** contains the CPU **[Figure 4-7]**. A microprocessor contains a number of components including a control unit, an arithmetic/logic unit, and a system clock. The following sections describe how these components work together to perform processing operations.

The Arithmetic/Logic Unit

The **arithmetic/logic unit (ALU)**, another component of the CPU, performs the execution part of the machine cycle. Specifically, the ALU performs the arithmetic, comparison, and logical operations.

Arithmetic operations include addition, subtraction, multiplication, and division.

Figure 4-7 Typical microprocessors or CPUs used in PC and Macintosh computers.

The Control Unit

The **control unit**, one component of the CPU, directs and coordinates most of the operations in the computer. The control unit has a role much like a traffic cop. The control unit interprets each instruction issued by a program and then initiates the appropriate action to carry out the instruction. For every instruction, the control unit operates by repeating a set of four basic operations: (1) fetching an instruction, (2) decoding the instruction, (3) executing the instruction, and, if necessary, (4) storing the result **[Figure 4-8]**.

Fetching is the process of obtaining a program instruction or data item from memory. **Decoding** is the process of translating the instruction into commands the computer understands. **Executing** is the process of carrying out the commands. **Storing** is the process of writing the result to memory. Together, these four instructions comprise the **machine cycle** or instruction cycle.

Comparison operations involve comparing one data item to another to determine if the first item is greater than, equal to, or less than the other. Depending on the result of the comparison, different actions may occur. For example, to determine a student's letter grade, the student's numeric grade is compared to a set of numbers corresponding to various letter grades (say, a numeric grade equal to or greater than 90 equates to a letter grade of "A"). If the student's numeric grade is equal to or greater than 90, then a letter grade of A is given; if the numeric grade is less than 90, a letter grade of A is not given and more comparisons are performed until a letter grade can be assigned. **Logical operations** work with conditions and logical operators such as AND, OR, and NOT. For example, if you wanted to search a job database for part-time work in the admissions office, you would search for any jobs classified as part-time AND listed under admissions.

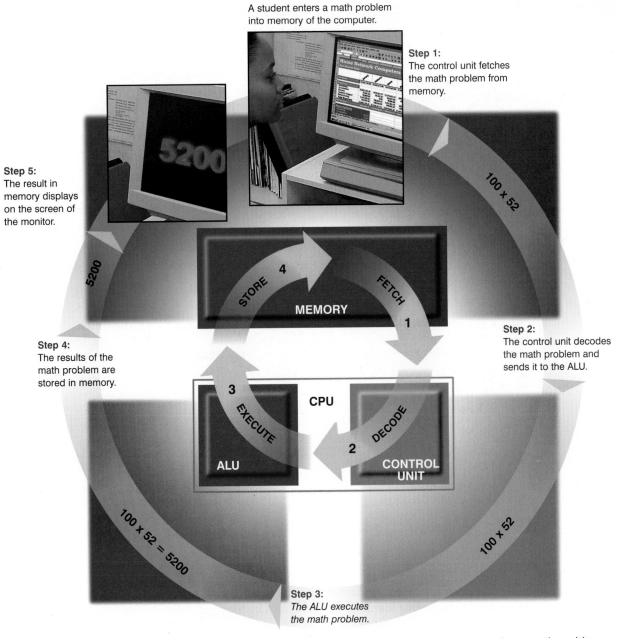

A student enters a math problem
into memory of the computer.

Step 1:
The control unit fetches
the math problem from
memory.

Step 5:
The result in
memory displays
on the screen of
the monitor.

Step 2:
The control unit decodes
the math problem and
sends it to the ALU.

Step 4:
The results of the
math problem are
stored in memory.

Step 3:
The ALU executes
the math problem.

STORE 4   FETCH 1
MEMORY

3 EXECUTE   CPU   DECODE 2
ALU   CONTROL UNIT

100 x 52
100 x 52
100 x 52 = 5200
5200
5200

Figure 4-8 This figure shows the steps involved in a machine cycle for a student wanting to solve a math problem on a computer. Once the result is in memory, it can be displayed on a monitor's screen, printed, or stored on a disk.

The System Clock

The control unit relies on a small chip called the **system clock** to synchronize, or control the timing of, all computer operations. Just as your heart beats at a regular rate to keep your body functioning, the system clock generates regular electronic pulses, or ticks, that set the operating pace of components in the system unit. Think of the components of the CPU as members of a marching band that take their steps to the beat of the system clock drummer.

Clock speed, measured in **megahertz** (**MHz**), is the speed at which a microprocessor executes instructions. One megahertz equates to one million ticks of the system clock. Thus, a computer that operates at 400 MHz has four hundred million clock cycles, or ticks, in one second. The faster the clock speed, the more instructions the CPU can execute per second.

Microprocessor Comparison

A microprocessor often is identified by its model name or model number. **Figure 4-9** summarizes the historical development of microprocessors used in personal computers and the increases in clock speed since 1982.

memory chips on the circuit boards in the system unit perform this function.

Memory stores three basic items: (1) the operating system and other system software that control the computer equipment; (2) application software designed to carry out a specific task such as word

	Name	Date Introduced	Manufacturer	Clock Speed (MHz)
Microprocessors	Pentium® III Xeon	1999	Intel	500 and higher
	Pentium® III	1999	Intel	400-500
	Pentium® II XeonXeon™	1998	Intel	400
	Celeron™	1998	Intel	266-400
	AMD-K6	1998	AMD	300
	Pentium® II	1997	Intel	233-450
	Pentium® with MMX™ technology	1997	Intel	166-233
	Pentium® Pro	1995	Intel	150-200
	Pentium®	1993	Intel	75-200
	80486DX	1989	Intel	25-100
	80386DX	1985	Intel	16-33
	80286	1982	Intel	6-12
	PowerPC	1994	Motorola	50-333
	68040	1989	Motorola	25-40
	68030	1987	Motorola	16-50
	68020	1984	Motorola	16-33
	Alpha	1993	Digital	150-600

Comparison of Widely Used Microprocessors

Figure 4-9 A comparison of some of the more widely used microprocessors.

Intel, the maker of the Pentium family of processors, is the leading manufacturer of CPUs. Other companies such as Cyrix and AMD currently make Intel-compatible microprocessors. These microprocessors have the same internal design and functionality as Intel processors, but often are less expensive. PCs use Intel and Intel-compatible processors and Macintosh computers use processors made by Motorola.

Memory

While performing a processing operation, a processor needs a place to store data and instructions temporarily. A computer uses **memory** to store data and information. The

processing; and (3) the data being processed by the application software.

Recall that a computer stores a character as a series of 0s and 1s, called a byte. Thus, a byte is the basic storage unit in memory. When a computer transfers program instructions and data from a storage device into memory, the computer stores them as bytes. The computer stores each byte in a precise location in memory, called an address. An **address** is simply a unique number identifying the location of the byte in memory. The illustration in **Figure 4-10** shows how seats in a stadium are similar to addresses in memory: (1) a seat holds one person at a time and an address in memory holds a single byte, (2) both a seat and an address can be empty, and

seat #A1 seat #A2 seat #A3 seat #A4 seat #A5 seat #A6

Figure 4-10 This figure shows how seats in a stadium are similar to addresses in memory: (1) a seat holds one person at a time and an address in memory holds a single byte, (2) both a seat and an address can be empty, and (3) a seat has a unique identifying number and so does an address.

(3) a seat has a unique identifying number and so does an address. Thus, to access data or instructions in memory, the computer references the addresses that contain bytes of data.

Because a byte is such a small amount of storage, several terms have evolved to define memory and storage devices [**Figure 4-11**]. A **kilobyte** of memory, abbreviated **KB** or **K**, is equal to 1,024 bytes, but is usually rounded to 1,000 bytes. A **megabyte**, abbreviated **MB**, is equal to approximately one million bytes. A **gigabyte**, abbreviated **GB**, is equal to approximately one billion bytes.

The system unit contains two types of memory: volatile and nonvolatile. The contents of **volatile memory** are lost (erased) when the computer's power is turned off. The contents of **nonvolatile memory**, on the other hand, are not lost when power is removed from the computer. RAM (random access memory) is an example of volatile memory; ROM (read-only memory) is an example of nonvolatile memory. The following sections discuss each of these types of memory.

Random Access Memory (RAM)

The memory chips in the system unit are called **random access memory** (**RAM**). When the computer is powered on, certain operating system files (such as the files that determine how your desktop displays) are loaded from a storage device such as a hard disk into RAM. As long as the power remains on, these files remain in RAM. Because RAM is volatile, the

Memory and Storage Sizes

Term	Abbreviation	Approximate Memory Size	Exact Memory Amount	Approximate Number of Pages of Text
Kilobyte	KB or K	1 thousand bytes	1,024 bytes	50
Megabyte	MB	1 million bytes	1,048,576 bytes	50,000
Gigabyte	GB	1 billion bytes	1,073,741,824 bytes	50,000,000
Terabyte	TB	1 trillion bytes	1,099,511,627,776 bytes	50,000,000,000

Figure 4-11 This table outlines terms used to define storage size.

programs and data stored in RAM are erased when the power to the computer is turned off. Any programs and data needed for future use must be copied from RAM to a storage device such as a hard disk before the power to the computer is turned off.

The most common form of RAM used in personal computers is **dynamic RAM**, or **DRAM** (pronounced DEE-ram). Today, most RAM is installed by using a **dual inline memory module (DIMM)**. A DIMM is a small circuit board that contains multiple RAM chips **[Figure 4-12]**. Common DIMM sizes can hold 16, 32, 64, and 128 megabytes of memory. DIMM chips

are installed in special sockets on the motherboard and can be removed and replaced easily with larger capacity RAM chips.

The amount of RAM a computer requires often depends on the types of applications to be used on the computer. Remember that a computer only can manipulate data that is in memory. RAM is something like the workspace you have on the top of your desk. Just as a desktop needs a certain amount of space to hold papers, pens, and your computer, a computer needs a certain amount of memory to store an application program and files. The more RAM a computer has, the more programs and files it can work on at once. A software package usually indicates the minimum amount of RAM it requires **[Figure 4-13]**. For an application to perform optimally, you usually need more than the minimum specifications on the software package.

dual inline memory module

memory chip

Figure 4-12 This photo shows a dual inline memory module (DIMM).

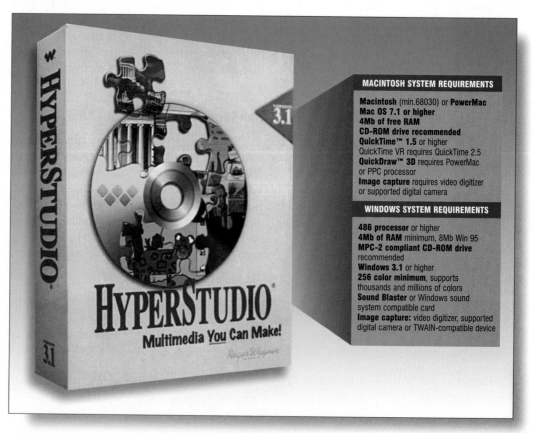

MACINTOSH SYSTEM REQUIREMENTS

Macintosh (min.68030) or **PowerMac**
Mac OS 7.1 or higher
4Mb of free RAM
CD-ROM drive recommended
QuickTime™ 1.5 or higher
QuickTime VR requires QuickTime 2.5
QuickDraw™ 3D requires PowerMac
or PPC processor
Image capture requires video digitizer
or supported digital camera

WINDOWS SYSTEM REQUIREMENTS

486 processor or higher
4Mb of RAM minimum, 8Mb Win 95
MPC-2 compliant CD-ROM drive
recommended
Windows 3.1 or higher
256 color minimum, supports
thousands and millions of colors
Sound Blaster or Windows sound
system compatible card
Image capture: video digitizer, supported
digital camera or TWAIN-compatible device

Figure 4-13 The minimum Macintosh or PC system requirements for many application software programs usually are printed on the side of the box. If the program can be used on both Macintosh computers and PCs, the system requirements usually are listed for both.

Read-Only Memory (ROM)

Read-only memory (**ROM**) devices are chips that store information or instructions that do not change. For example, ROM chips contain the sequence of instructions the computer follows to load the operating system and other files when you first turn it on. Manufacturers permanently record instructions and data on ROM chips. Unlike RAM, ROM memory is nonvolatile because it retains its contents even when the power is turned off. Manufacturers install ROM chips in automobiles, home appliances, toys, educational games, and thousands of other items used by people everyday.

Expansion Slots and Expansion Cards

An **expansion slot** is an opening, or socket, where a circuit board can be inserted into the motherboard. These circuit boards add new devices or capabilities to the computer such as more memory, higher-quality sound devices, a modem, or graphics capabilities. An **expansion card**, **adapter card,** or **expansion board** are terms used to describe

these types of circuit boards. Sometimes a device or feature is built into the expansion card; other times a cable is used to connect the expansion card to a device, such as a scanner, outside the system unit. **Figure 4-14** shows an expansion card being plugged into an expansion slot on a personal computer motherboard.

Three types of expansion cards found in most of today's computers are a video adapter, a sound card, and an internal modem. A video adapter, also called a graphics adapter or card, converts computer output into a video signal that is sent through a cable to the monitor, which displays an image on the screen. A sound card is used to enhance the sound-generating capabilities of a personal computer by allowing sound to be input through a microphone and output through speakers. An internal modem is a communications device that enables computers to communicate via telephone lines or other means.

In the past, installing an expansion card in PCs required setting switches and other elements on the motherboard. Many of today's computers support **Plug and Play**, which refers to the computer's capability to configure

Figure 4-14 This expansion card is being inserted into an expansion slot on the motherboard of a personal computer.

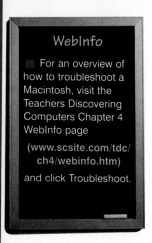

WebInfo

For an overview of how to troubleshoot a Macintosh, visit the Teachers Discovering Computers Chapter 4 WebInfo page **(www.scsite.com/tdc/ ch4/webinfo.htm)** and click Troubleshoot.

automatically expansion cards and other devices as they are installed. Having Plug and Play support means a user can plug in a device, turn on the computer, and then use, or play, the device without having to configure the system manually. Macintosh computers have supported Plug and Play for many years, just one of the reasons many K-12 schools purchased Macintosh computers for use in their offices and classrooms.

Ports and Connectors

A cable often attaches external devices such as a keyboard, monitor, printer, mouse, and microphone to the system unit. A **port** is the point of attachment to the system unit and most computers contain ports on the back of the system unit **[Figure 4-15]**. Ports use

different types of **connectors** that usually are either male or female and come in various sizes and shapes. Male connectors have one or more exposed pins, like the end of an electrical cord you plug into the wall. Female connectors have matching receptacles to accept the pins, like an electrical wall outlet.

Summary of the System Unit

The previous sections presented information about some of the major components of the system unit. You now should be able to identify these components and have a basic understanding about how they operate. The next section will describe several of the major input devices used with computers.

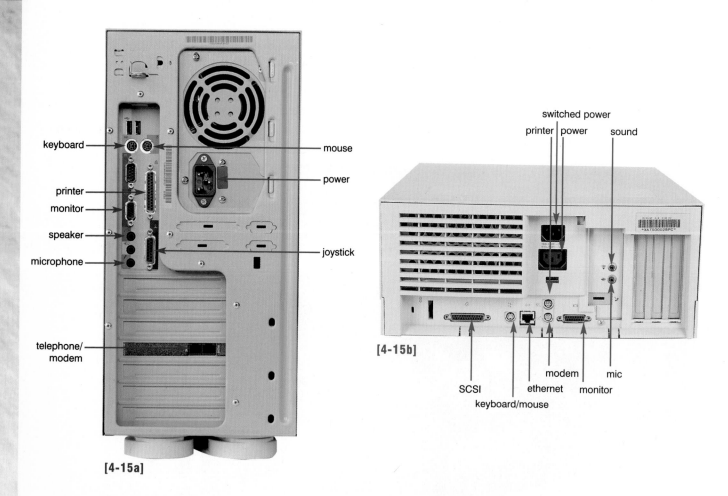

Figure 4-15 Ports are sockets used for cables that connect the system unit with devices such as the mouse, keyboard, and printer. Usually, ports are on the back of the system unit and often are labeled and color coded making it easier for users to plug in various cables. Figure 4-15a shows the back of a PC and Figure 4-15b shows the back of a Macintosh computer.

What Is Input?

Input is any item you enter into the memory of a computer. Once input is in memory, the CPU can access it and process the input into output. Four types of input are data, programs, commands, and user responses [Figure 4-16].

- **Data** is a collection of unorganized facts that can include words, numbers, pictures, sounds, and so on. A computer manipulates and processes data into information, which is useful. Although a single item of data should be called a datum, the term data commonly is used and accepted as both the singular and plural form of the word.

- A **program** is a series of instructions that tells a computer how to perform the tasks necessary to process data into information. Programs are kept on storage media such as a hard disk, CD-ROM, or DVD-ROM. Programs respond to commands issued by a user.

- A **command** is an instruction given to a computer program. Commands can be issued by typing keywords or pressing special keys on the keyboard. A **keyword** is a special word, phrase, or code that a program understands as an instruction. Many programs also allow you to issue commands by selecting graphical objects. Today, most programs have a graphical user interface that uses icons, buttons, and other graphical objects to issue commands.

- Sometimes a program asks you a question that requires a **user response**, such as Do you want to save the changes you made? Based on your response, the program performs specific actions. For example, if you answer, Yes, to this question, the program saves your changed file on a storage device.

WebInfo

To search for a solution to a specific hardware problem for a PC, visit the Teachers Discovering Computers Chapter 4 WebInfo page (www.scsite.com/tdc/ch4/webinfo.htm) and click Search.

CHAPTER 4

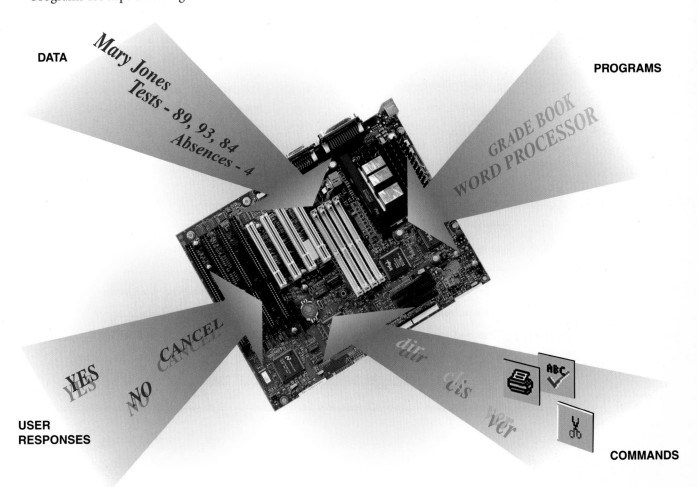

DATA

*Mary Jones
Tests - 89, 93, 84
Absences - 4*

PROGRAMS

GRADE BOOK
WORD PROCESSOR

USER
RESPONSES

YES
NO CANCEL

COMMANDS

Figure 4-16 Four types of input are data, programs, commands, and user responses.

CHAPTER 4

WebInfo

■ To learn more about keyboards, visit the Teachers Discovering Computers Chapter 4 WebInfo page

(www.scsite.com/tdc/ch4/webinfo.htm)

and click Keyboard.

What Are Input Devices?

An **input device** is any hardware component that allows you to enter data, programs, commands, and user responses into a computer. Input devices include keyboards, pointing devices, scanners and reading devices, digital cameras, audio and video input devices, and input devices for physically challenged students. Many of these input devices are discussed in the following pages.

The Keyboard

One of the primary input devices used with a computer is the keyboard. A **keyboard** is a group of switches resembling the keys on a typewriter that allow users to enter input. Most keyboards are similar to the ones shown in **Figures 4-17a** and **4-17b**. You enter data, commands, and other input into a computer by pressing keys on the keyboard.

Personal computer keyboards usually contain from 101 to 105 keys; keyboards for smaller computers, such as laptops, contain

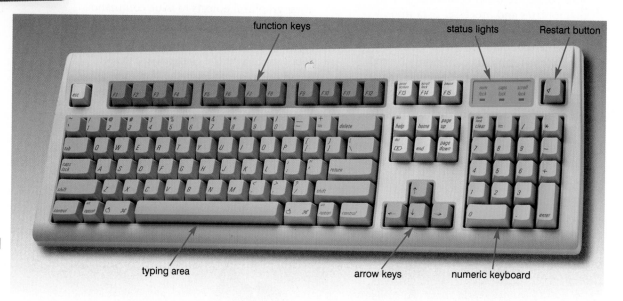

[4-17a]

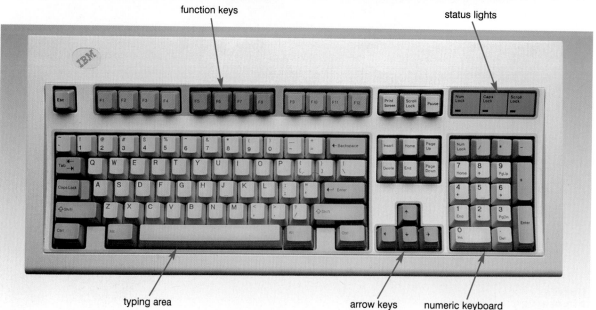

[4-17b]

Figure 4-17 Macintosh and PC keyboards are similar. Figure 4-17a shows a typical Macintosh keyboard and Figure 4-17b shows a typical PC keyboard.

fewer keys. A keyboard includes keys that allow you to type letters, numbers, spaces, punctuation marks, and other symbols such as the dollar sign ($) and an asterisk (*). A keyboard also contains special keys that allow you to enter data and instructions into the computer.

All computer keyboards have a typing area that includes the letters of the alphabet, numbers, punctuation marks, and other basic keys. Because of the layout of its typing area, a standard computer keyboard sometimes is called a QWERTY keyboard. Pronounced KWER-tee, this keyboard layout is named after the first six letters on the top-left alphabetic line of the keyboard.

Many desktop computer keyboards also have a numeric keypad located on the right side of the keyboard. A **numeric keypad** is a calculator-style arrangement of keys representing numbers, a decimal point, and some basic mathematical operators. The numeric keypad is designed to make it easier to enter numbers.

Keyboards also contain keys that can be used to position the insertion point on the screen. The insertion point, or cursor, is a symbol that indicates where on the screen the next character you type will display. Depending on the program, the symbol may be a vertical bar, a rectangle, or an underline. These keys, called arrow keys, allow you to move the insertion point right, left, up, or down. Most keyboards also contain keys such as HOME, END, PAGE UP, and PAGE DOWN that you can press to move the insertion point to the beginning or end of a line, page, or document.

Most keyboards also include toggle keys, which can be switched between two different states. The NUM LOCK key, for example, is a toggle key found on PC keyboards. When you press it once, it locks the numeric keypad so you can use it to type numbers. When you press the NUM LOCK key again, the numeric keypad is unlocked so the same keys serve as arrow keys that move the insertion point. The CAPS LOCK key is another example of a toggle key and is used on both PC and Macintosh computers. Many keyboards have status lights in the upper-right corner that light up to indicate that a toggle key is activated.

Pointing Devices

A **pointing device** is an input device that allows you to control a pointer on the screen. In a graphical user interface, a pointer, or mouse pointer, is a small symbol on the display screen. A pointer often takes the shape of a block arrow ( ), an I-beam (I), or a pointing hand ( ). Using a pointing device, you can position the pointer to move or select items on the screen. For example, you can use a pointing device to move the insertion point; select text, graphics, and other objects; and click buttons, icons, links and menu commands. Common pointing devices include the mouse, trackball, joystick, and touch screen.

Mouse   A mouse is the most widely used pointing device, because it takes full advantage of a graphical user interface. Designed to fit comfortably under the palm of your hand, a **mouse** is an input device used to control the movement of the pointer on the screen and to make selections from the screen. The top of the mouse usually has one or two buttons. The mouse used with PCs usually is a two-button mouse [Figure 4-18]; a one-button mouse is used with Macintosh computers [Figure 4-19].

Figure 4-19 A Macintosh mouse usually has only one button.

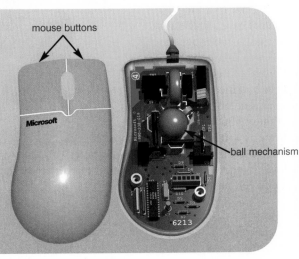

Figure 4-18 A mouse is used to control the movement of a pointer on the screen and make selections from the screen. Electronic circuits in a mouse translate the movement of the mouse into signals that are sent to the computer. Shown is a typical mouse used with PCs.

mouse buttons

ball mechanism

mouse button

The bottom of a mouse is flat and contains a multidirectional mechanism, usually a small ball, which senses movement of the mouse.

The mouse often rests on a **mouse pad**, which usually is a rectangular rubber or foam pad that provides better traction for the mouse than the top of a desk. The mouse pad also protects the ball mechanism from a build up of dust and dirt, which could cause it to malfunction.

As you move the mouse across a flat surface such as a mouse pad, the pointer on the screen also moves. For example, when you move the mouse to the left, the pointer moves left on the screen. When you move the mouse to the right, the pointer moves right on the screen, and so on. If you have never worked with a mouse, you might find it a little awkward at first; with a little practice, however, you will discover that it is quite easy to use.

By using the mouse to move the pointer on the screen and then pressing, or **clicking**, the buttons on the mouse, you can perform actions such as pressing buttons, making menu selections, editing a document, and moving, or **dragging** data from one location in a document to another. To press and release a mouse button twice without moving the mouse is called **double-clicking**. Double-clicking can be used to perform actions such as starting a program or opening a document. The function of the buttons on a two-button mouse can be changed to accommodate right- and left-handed individuals.

Trackball Some users opt for pointing devices other than a mouse, such as a trackball. Whereas a mouse has a ball mechanism on the bottom, a **trackball** is a stationary pointing device with a ball mechanism on its top [Figure 4-20]. The ball mechanism in a larger trackball is about the size of a Ping-Pong ball; laptop computers have small trackballs about the size of a marble. To move the pointer using a trackball, you rotate the ball mechanism with your thumb, fingers, or palm of your hand. Around the ball mechanism, usually a trackball also has one or more buttons that work just like mouse buttons. A trackball is not as accurate as a mouse. If you have limited desk space or use a laptop computer, however, a trackball is a good alternative to a mouse because you do not have to move the entire device.

Figure 4-20 A trackball is like an upside-down mouse. You rotate the ball with your thumb, fingers, or palm of your hand to move the pointer.

trackball

Joystick Users running game software such as a driving or flight simulator may prefer to use a joystick as their pointing device. A **joystick** is a vertical lever mounted on a base [**Figure 4-21**]. You move the lever in different directions to control the actions of a vehicle or a player. The lever usually includes buttons, called triggers, that you can press to activate certain events. Some joysticks also have additional buttons that you can set to perform other actions.

Figure 4-21 A joystick is used with game software to control the actions of a vehicle or player.

Figure 4-22 This kiosk allows you to create personalized Hallmark greeting cards.

Figure 4-23 A typical optical scanner. Items to be scanned are placed on a piece of glass under the top cover, similarly to making a copy on a copier.

Touch Screen   A monitor that has a touch-sensitive panel on the screen is called a **touch screen**. You interact with the computer by touching areas of the screen with your finger. In this case, the screen acts as an input device. To enter data, instructions, and information, you touch words, pictures, numbers, or locations identified on the screen. A touch screen often is used as the input device for a **kiosk**, a freestanding computer that provides information to the user **[Figure 4-22]**. Visitors at museums, for example, can use a kiosk to access and print out maps, facts on tours and exhibits, and other information.

Optical Scanner

An optical scanner, usually simply called a **scanner**, is an input device that electronically can capture an entire page of text or images such as photographs or artwork **[Figure 4-23]**. A scanner converts the text or image on the original document into digital data that can be stored on a disk and processed by the computer. The digitized data can be printed, displayed separately, or merged into another document for editing. Handheld devices that scan only a portion of a page at a time also are available.

WebInfo

To learn more about optical scanners, visit the Teachers Discovering Computers Chapter 4 WebInfo page

(www.scsite.com/tdc/ch4/webinfo.htm)

and click Scanner.

Optical Readers

An **optical reader** is a device that read characters, marks, and codes and then converts them into digital data that can be processed by a computer. There are three types of optical readers. The first is **optical character recognition** (OCR), which is a technology that involves reading typewritten, computer-printed, and in some cases handwritten characters on documents and converting the images into a form that the computer can understand.

For example, the portion of a gas bill that you return with your payment usually has your account number, payment amount, and other information printed in optical characters **[Figure 4-24]**.

this portion is returned with payment

OCR characters indicate amount due and account number

Figure 4-24 OCR is used frequently with turn-around documents. With this gas bill, you tear off the top portion and return it with your payment.

WebInfo

To learn more about digital cameras, visit the Teachers Discovering Computers Chapter 4 WebInfo page

(www.scsite.com/tdc/ ch4/webinfo.htm)

and click Digital Cameras.

WebInfo

For an explanation of speech recognition, visit the Teachers Discovering Computers Chapter 4 WebInfo page

(www.scsite.com/tdc/ ch4/webinfo.htm)

and click Speech Recognition.

Optical mark recognition (OMR) devices read hand-drawn marks such as small circles or rectangles and are used by many schools and colleges. Students place these marks on a form, such as a test, survey, or questionnaire answer sheet.

A bar code scanner uses laser beams to read bar codes **[Figure 4-25]**. A **bar code** is an identification code that consists of a set of vertical lines and spaces of different widths. The bar code, which represents data that identifies the item, is printed on a product's package or label and is read by bar code scanners. Bar codes are printed on virtually all items purchased in retail stores.

Figure 4-25 A bar code scanner uses laser beams to read bar codes on products such as groceries, books, and packages.

Digital Cameras

A **digital camera** allows you to take pictures and store the photographed images digitally instead of on traditional film **[Figure 4-26]**. After you have taken a picture or series of pictures, you download, or transfer a copy of, the pictures to your computer. Once the pictures are stored on your computer, they can be edited with photo-editing software, printed, posted on a Web site, and more.

Figure 4-26 A digital camera is used to take pictures and store the photographed images on a computer.

Audio and Video Input

Although characters (text and numbers) still are the primary forms of input into a computer, individuals increasingly are using other types of input such as images, audio, and video. In the previous sections, you learned about a variety of ways to input image data. The next sections discuss methods used to input audio and video data into a computer.

Audio Input **Audio input** is the process of recording music, speech, or sound effects. To record high-quality sound, your personal computer must have a sound card and most personal computers sold today are equipped with a sound card. Recorded sound is input via a device such as a microphone, tape player, or audio CD player, which plugs into a port on the sound card.

With a microphone plugged into the microphone port on the sound card, you can record sounds using the computer. Once you save the sound as a file, you can play it, add it to a document, or edit it using audio-editing software.

Another use for a microphone is speech recognition. **Speech recognition**, also called voice recognition, is the capability of a computer to distinguish spoken words. Speech recognition programs do not understand speech; they only recognize a vocabulary of certain words. The vocabulary of speech recognition programs can range from two words (such as Yes and No) to more than sixty thousand words.

Speech recognition systems often are used in specialized applications in which a user's hands are occupied or disabled. Instead of typing or using a pointing device, the user speaks into a microphone to dictate words, issue commands, or perform other tasks. Speech recognition software programs are being used by students with certain learning and physical challenges.

Video Input Video input or video capture is the process of entering a full-motion recording into a computer. To capture video, you plug a video camera, VCR, or a similar device into a video capture card, which converts the analog video signal into a digital signal that a computer can understand. Once the device is connected to the card, you can begin recording. Once the video is saved, you can play the video, copy it to a videotape, or edit it using video-editing software.

Input Devices for Challenged Students

The growing presence of computers in everyone's lives has generated an awareness of the need to address computing requirements for those with physical limitations. Today, the Americans with Disabilities Act (ADA) requires that all schools ensure that students who are physically challenged are not excluded from participation in, or denied access to, educational programs or activities. Besides speech recognition, which is ideal for students who are visually impaired, other input devices are available.

Students with limited hand mobility that wish to use a keyboard have several options.

One option is to use a keyguard. A keyguard, when placed over the keyboard, prevents students from inadvertently pressing keys and provides a guide so students strike only one key at a time **[Figure 4-27]**. Keyboards with larger keys also are available. Another option is a screen-displayed keyboard, in which a graphic of a standard keyboard displays on the student's screen. Students then use a pointing device to press the keys on the screen-displayed keyboard. A touch window is a device that attaches to the front of a monitor that allows students to select items by touching the screen instead of using a keyboard **[Figure 4-28]**.

A variety of pointing devices are available for students with motor disabilities. Small trackballs that can be controlled with a thumb or one finger can be attached to a table, mounted to a wheelchair, or held in a student's hand. Students with limited hand movement can use a head-mounted pointer to control the pointer or insertion point. Learning how to integrate software programs and hardware devices into your curriculum that allow challenged students to use computers as tools for learning will be covered in later chapters.

WebInfo

To learn more about alternative keyboards, visit the Teachers Discovering Computers Chapter 4 WebInfo page **(www.scsite.com/tdc/ch4/webinfo.htm)** and click Alternative Keyboards.

Figure 4-27 A keyguard allows students to rest their hands on the keyboard without accidentally pressing any keys. Keyguards also guide a student's fingers so they press only a single key at a time.

Figure 4-28 A touch window allows students who are physically challenged to make inputs into a computer by touching the screen instead of using the keyboard.

Summary of Input

After reading and reviewing the previous sections, you should be familiar with several types of input devices, be able to identify these devices, and have a basic understanding about how they operate. The next section describes some of the major output devices used with computers.

What Is Output?

Output is data that has been processed into a useful form called information. That is, a computer processes input into output.

Computers generate several types of output, depending on the hardware and software being used and the requirements of the user. Four common types of output are text, graphics, audio, and video **[Figure 4-29]**.

■ Text consists of characters that are used to create words, sentences, and paragraphs. A character is a letter, number, punctuation mark, or any other symbol that requires one byte of computer storage space.

■ Graphics are digital representations of nontext information, such as images, drawings, charts, pictures, and photographs. Displaying a series of still graphics creates an animation, a graphic that has the illusion of motion. Many of today's software programs support graphics; others are designed specifically to

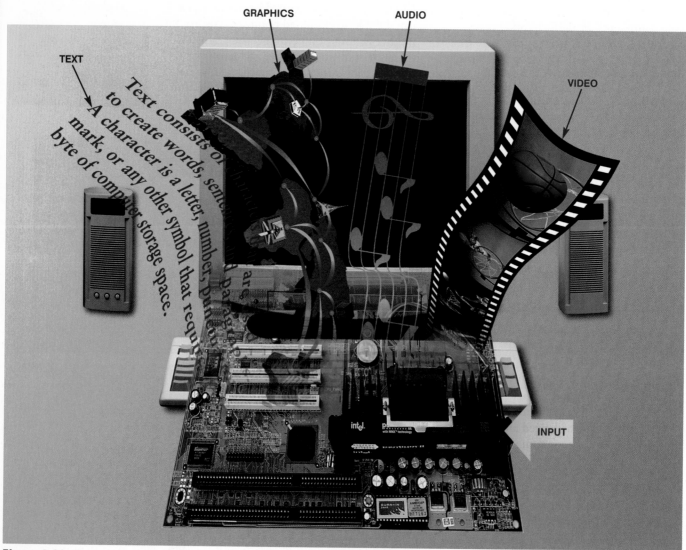

Figure 4-29 Four common types of output are text, graphics, audio, and video.

create and edit graphics. Graphics programs, called image editors, allow you to alter graphics by including enhancements such as blended colors, animation, and other special effects.

- Audio is any music, speech, or other sound that is stored and produced by the computer. Recall that sound waves, such as the human voice or music, are analog. To store such sounds, a computer converts them from a continuous analog signal into a digital format.

- Video consists of photographic images that are played back at speeds that provide the appearance of full motion in real-time. Video often is captured with a video input device such as a video camera or VCR.

What Are Output Devices?

An **output device** is any computer component capable of conveying information to a user. Commonly used output devices include monitors, printers, data projectors, facsimile machines, multifunction devices, speakers, and headsets. Each of these output devices is discussed in the following pages.

Monitors

A **monitor** is a display device that conveys text, graphics, and video information visually and is housed in a plastic or metal case. Information shown on a display device often is called **soft copy**, because the information exists electronically and is displayed for a temporary period of time.

Monitors for personal computers are available in a variety of sizes, with the more common being 15-, 17-, 19-, and 21-inch. The size of a monitor is measured diagonally, from corner to corner. Most monitors are referred to by the diagonal measurement of the large glass tube inside the monitor, which is larger than the actual viewing area provided by the monitor (known as the viewable size). For example, a monitor listed as a 17-inch monitor only may have a viewable size of 15.7 inches.

Determining what size monitor to use depends on your intended use. A larger monitor allows you to view more information at

once, but usually is more expensive. If you work on the Web or use multiple applications at one time, however, you will want to invest in at least a 17-inch monitor.

Like a television set, the core of a monitor is a large glass tube called a **cathode ray tube (CRT) [Figure 4-30]**. The screen, which is the front of the tube, is coated with tiny dots of phosphor material that glow when electrically charged. The CRT moves an electron beam back and forth across the back of the screen, causing the dots to glow, which produces an image on the screen.

WebInfo

For information on monitors, visit the Teachers Discovering Computers Chapter 4 WebInfo page **(www.scsite.com/tdc/ch4/webinfo.htm)** and click Monitor.

cathode ray tube

screen

monitor

Figure 4-30 The core of most personal computer monitors is a cathode ray tube.

Each dot, called a **pixel** (short for picture element), is a single point in an electronic image **[Figure 4-31]**. Monitors consist of hundreds, thousands, or millions of pixels arranged in rows and columns that can be used to create pictures. The pixels are so close together that they appear connected.

Figure 4-31 A pixel is a single dot of color, or point, in an electronic image.

A different type of monitor is an LCD (liquid crystal display) monitor, which is a thin and lightweight monitor used in laptop computers, handheld computers, digital watches, and calculators. An **LCD monitor** uses a liquid crystal display (LCD) to create images on the screen.

Monitor Quality

The quality of a monitor depends largely on its resolution, dot pitch, and refresh rate. The **resolution**, or sharpness and clarity, of a monitor is related directly to the number of pixels it can display. Resolution is expressed as two separate numbers: the number of columns of pixels and the number of rows of pixels a monitor can display. For example, a screen with a 640 x 480 (pronounced 640 by 480) resolution can display 640 columns and 480 rows of pixels (or a total of 307,200 pixels). Most modern monitors can display 800 x 600 and 1024 x 768 pixels. A monitor with a higher resolution displays a greater number of pixels, which provides a smoother but smaller image. The ideal monitor resolution to use is a matter of preference.

Another factor that determines monitor quality is **dot pitch**, which is the distance between each pixel on a monitor. The smaller the distance between the pixels, the sharper the displayed image. To minimize eye fatigue, you should use a monitor with a dot pitch of .28 millimeters or smaller.

Recall that an electron beam moving back and forth behind the screen causes pixels on the screen to glow — thus creating an image. These pixels, however, only glow for a small fraction of a second before beginning to fade. The monitor thus redraws the picture many times per second so that the image does not fade. The speed that the monitor redraws images on the screen is called the **refresh rate**.

Some monitors display an **ENERGY STAR®** label, which identifies the monitor as an energy efficient product as defined by the Environmental Protection Agency (EPA). Monitors usually are equipped with controls to adjust

the brightness, contrast, positioning, height, and width of images. Finally, many monitors sit on a tilt-and-swivel base so you can adjust the angle of the screen to minimize neck strain and reduce glare from overhead lighting.

Printers

A **printer** is an output device that produces text and graphical information on a physical medium such as paper or transparency film. Printed information is called **hard copy** because it is a more permanent form of output than that presented on a monitor. Users can print a hard copy of a file in either portrait or landscape orientation. A page with **portrait orientation** is taller than it is wide, with information printed across the shorter width of the paper. A page with **landscape orientation** is wider than it is tall, with information printed across the widest part of the paper **[Figure 4-32]**. Users typically

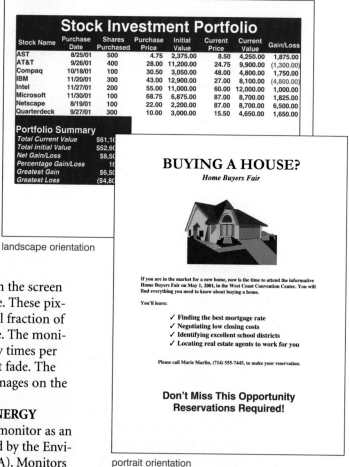

landscape orientation

portrait orientation

Figure 4-32 Portrait orientation is taller than it is wide; landscape orientation is wider than it is tall.

print letters and reports in portrait and spreadsheets and slide shows in landscape.

Because printing requirements vary greatly among users, manufacturers offer printers with varying speeds, capabilities, and printing methods. Generally, printers can be grouped into two categories: impact and nonimpact.

Impact Printers

An **impact printer** forms marks on a piece of paper by striking a mechanism against an ink ribbon that physically contacts the paper. Because of the striking activity, impact printers generally are noisy. Impact printers usually are inexpensive and print relatively quickly, but they do not provide high print quality.

The more commonly used type of impact printer is a dot-matrix printer. A **dot-matrix printer** produces printed images when tiny pins on a print head mechanism strike an inked ribbon **[Figure 4-33]**. When the ribbon presses against the paper, it creates dots that form characters and graphics. The print head mechanism on a dot-matrix printer can contain from nine to twenty-four pins, depending on the manufacturer and the printer model. A higher number of pins means more dots are printed, which results in higher print quality.

Dot-matrix printers typically use 8½-by-11-inch continuous-form paper, in which each sheet of paper is connected together. The pages generally have holes punched along two opposite sides to feed the paper through the printer. Perforations along the inside of the punched holes and at each fold allow you to separate the sheets into standard sizes, such as 8½-by-11-inches. Most dot-matrix printers can print pages in either portrait or landscape orientation.

Nonimpact Printers

A **nonimpact printer** forms marks on a piece of paper without actually striking the paper. Because these printers do not strike the paper, they are much quieter than impact printers. Two common types of nonimpact printers are ink-jet and laser printers.

Because of their reasonable cost and print quality, ink-jet printers often are used in homes and schools **[Figure 4-34]**. An **ink-jet printer** is a type of nonimpact printer that forms marks by spraying tiny drops of liquid ink onto a piece of paper. Ink-jet printers can produce high-quality text and graphics in both black-and-white and color on a variety of media such as paper, envelopes, labels, or transparencies. Some ink-jet printers can print photo-quality images on standard weight paper; others require a heavier weight premium paper. Ink-jet printers use small ink cartridges that are replaced easily or may be refilled using inexpensive ink-jet refill kits. In addition, many ink-jet printers include software to help you create items, such as announcements, banners, cards, and so on.

A **laser printer** is a high-speed, high-quality nonimpact printer. Operating similarly to a copy machine, a laser printer uses powdered ink, called toner, which is packaged in a

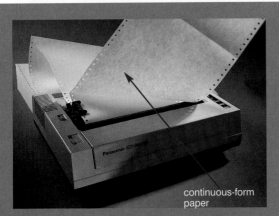

continuous-form paper

Figure 4-33 A dot-matrix printer produces printed images when tiny pins strike an inked ribbon.

Figure 4-34 Most ink-jet printers can print high-quality black-and-white or color documents and are used extensively in homes and schools.

cartridge. When electrically charged, the toner sticks to a special drum inside the printer and then is transferred to the paper through a combination of pressure and heat **[Figure 4-35]**. When the toner runs out, you simply replace the cartridge.

Laser printers, similarly to ink-jet printers, usually use individual sheets of letter and legal-size paper stored in a removable tray that slides into the printer case. Most printers also have a manual feed slot where you can insert individual sheets, transparencies, and envelopes.

Although laser printers cost more than ink-jet printers, laser printers quickly print very high-quality black-and-white text and graphics. Although color laser printers are

available, they are expensive and rarely found in K-12 schools.

Data Projectors

A **data projector** projects the image that displays on a computer screen onto a large screen, so that an audience, such as a classroom or school assembly, can see the image clearly **[Figure 4-36]**. Data projectors range in size from large devices attached to a ceiling or wall in an auditorium to smaller, portable devices. Three types of smaller units are LCD projection panels, LCD projectors, and DLP (digital light processing) projectors. An LCD projection panel uses liquid crystal display technology and is designed to be placed on top

Figure 4-35 A laser printer operates similarly to a copy machine. Electrically charged toner sticks to a special drum inside the printer and then is transferred to the paper through a combination of pressure and heat.

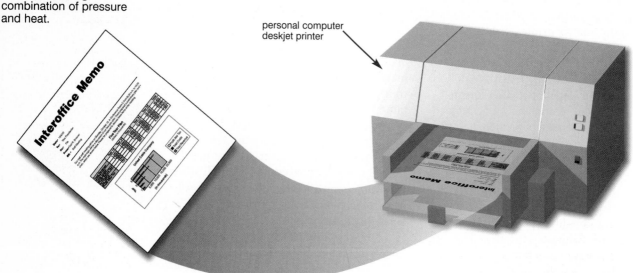

personal computer deskjet printer

Figure 4-36 Data projectors produce sharp, bright images.

of an overhead projector. An LCD projector, which also uses liquid crystal display technology, attaches directly to a computer and uses its own light source to display the information shown on the computer screen. A digital light processing (DLP) projector uses tiny mirrors to reflect light, producing crisp, bright, colorful images that remain in focus and can be seen clearly even in a well-lit room.

Facsimile (Fax) Machine

A **facsimile** (**fax**) **machine** is a device that transmits and receives documents over telephone lines. The documents can contain text, graphics, or photos, or can be handwritten. When a document is sent or received via a fax machine, these documents are known as faxes. A fax machine scans the original document, converts the image into digitized data, and transmits the digitized image [Figure 4-37]. A fax machine at the receiving end reads the incoming data, converts the digitized data into an image, and prints or stores a copy of the original image.

The fax machine described above is a stand-alone fax machine. You also can add fax capability to your computer via a fax modem. A fax modem is a communications device that allows you to send and receive electronic documents as faxes. A fax modem transmits electronic documents, such as a word processing letter or digital photo. A fax modem is like a regular modem except that it transmits documents to a fax machine or to another fax modem. When you receive a fax on your computer, you can view the document on the screen or print it using special fax software.

Multifunction Devices

A **multifunction device** (**MFD**) is a single piece of equipment that provides the functionality of a printer, fax machine, copier, and scanner [Figure 4-38]. The features of multifunction devices vary widely. For example, some use color ink-jet printer technology, while others include a black-and-white laser printer. Small businesses, home offices, and school's administrative offices are using multifunction devices because they take up less space and cost less than a separate printer, scanner, copy machine, and fax machine.

Figure 4-37 A stand-alone fax machine.

Figure 4-38 This OfficeJet by Hewlett-Packard is a color printer, scanner, fax, and copy machine all in one device.

Audio Output

Audio output is any music, speech, or other sound produced by a computer. On your computer, you can listen to music by simply inserting an audio compact disc (CD) into the CD-ROM drive. You can hear sounds of video clips while viewing them on the monitor. Two commonly used devices for audio output are speakers and headsets.

speakers

Figure 4-39 Most computers now include high quality stereo speakers. Some manufacturers build stereo speakers into the monitor or system unit's case.

Figure 4-40 Headsets are used to prevent students from being disturbed by sounds coming from nearby computers.

WebInfo

For information about Braille printers, visit the Teachers Discovering Computers Chapter 4 WebInfo page

(www.scsite.com/tdc/ ch4/webinfo.htm)

and click Braille Printer.

Figure 4-41 A Braille printer.

Most computers have an internal speaker, but they usually produce low-quality sound. For this reason, many personal computers are sold with stereo speakers. **Speakers** either can be separate devices that can be placed on either side of the monitor or built into the monitor or system's unit case **[Figure 4-39]**. Stereo speakers are connected to ports on the sound card. Most speakers have tone and volume controls.

When using speakers, anyone within listening distance can hear the output. Speakers are not always practical in classrooms and computer labs. Often, teachers and students use headsets that can be plugged into a port on the sound card **[Figure 4-40]**. By using headsets, students will not be disturbed by sounds on nearby computers.

Output Devices for Challenged Students

For challenged students, many options with respect to output devices are available. Students who are hearing-impaired, for example, can instruct programs to display words and visual signals instead of sounds. Students who are visually impaired can change screen settings to magnify text, change colors, and so on, to make the words easier to read. Instead of using a monitor, students who are visually impaired also can use speech output, where the computer reads the information that displays on the screen. Another alternative is a Braille printer, which outputs information in Braille onto paper **[Figure 4-41]**. Learning how to integrate software programs and hardware devices into your curriculum that allow students with disabilities to use computers as tools for learning will be covered in later chapters.

Summary of Output

The previous sections have presented information about a few of the major output devices commonly used with computers. You now should be able to identify these components and have a basic understanding about how they operate. The next section will describe some of the major storage devices used in computers.

What Is Storage?

Storage refers to the media on which data, instructions, and information are kept, as well as the devices that record and retrieve these items. To understand storage, you should understand the difference between how a computer uses memory and how it uses storage. As discussed earlier in this chapter, random access memory, called RAM, temporarily stores data and programs that are being processed. You also will recall that RAM is volatile because data and programs stored in memory are lost when the power is turned off or a power failure occurs.

Storage, also called **secondary storage** or **auxiliary storage**, stores data, instructions, and information when they are not being processed. Think of storage as a filing cabinet used to hold file folders, and memory as the top of your desk [Figure 4-42]. When you need to work with a file, you remove it from the filing cabinet (storage) and place it on your desk (memory). When you are finished with the file, you return it to the filing cabinet (storage). Storage is nonvolatile, which means

that data and instructions in storage are retained even when power is removed from the computer.

Storage Media and Devices

A **storage medium** (media is the plural) is the physical material on which data, instructions, and information are kept. One commonly used storage medium is a **disk**, which is a round, flat piece of plastic or metal on which items such as data, instructions, and information can be encoded. A **storage device** is the mechanism used to record and retrieve these items to and from a storage medium.

Storage devices can function as sources of input and output. For example, each time a storage device transfers data, instructions, and information from a storage medium into memory — a process called reading — it functions as an input source. When a storage device transfers these items from memory to a storage medium — a process called writing — it functions as an output source.

The size, or capacity, of a storage device, is measured by the amount of bytes (characters) it can hold. Storage capacity usually is

Figure 4-42 Think of storage as a filing cabinet used to hold file folders and memory as the top of your desk. When you need to work with a file, you remove it from the filing cabinet (storage) and place it on your desk (memory). When you are finished with the file, you return it back in the filing cabinet (storage).

measured in megabytes or gigabytes. Some devices can hold thousands of bytes, while others can store trillions of bytes. For example, a typical floppy disk can store 1.44 MB of data and a typical hard disk can store 8 GB of data.

Storage requirements among users vary greatly. A teacher, for example, might have a list of names, test scores, and average grades for thirty students that requires several hundred bytes of storage. Users of larger computers, such as banks or libraries, might need to store trillions of bytes worth of historical or catalog records. To meet the needs of a wide range of users, numerous types of storage media and storage devices exist, many of which are discussed in the following sections.

Floppy Disks

A **floppy disk** or **diskette** is a portable, inexpensive storage medium that consists of a thin, circular, flexible plastic disk with a magnetic coating enclosed in a square-shaped plastic shell **[Figure 4-43]**. In the early 1970s, IBM introduced a new type of storage medium, called the floppy disk. Because these early, 8-inch wide disks had flexible plastic covers, many users referred to them as floppies or floppy diskettes. The next generation of floppies looked much the same, but were only 5.25-inches wide. Today, the most widely used floppy disk is 3.5-inches wide. The flexible cover of the earlier floppy disks has been replaced with a rigid plastic outer cover. Thus, although today's 3.5-inch disks are not at all floppy, users still refer to them as floppy disks.

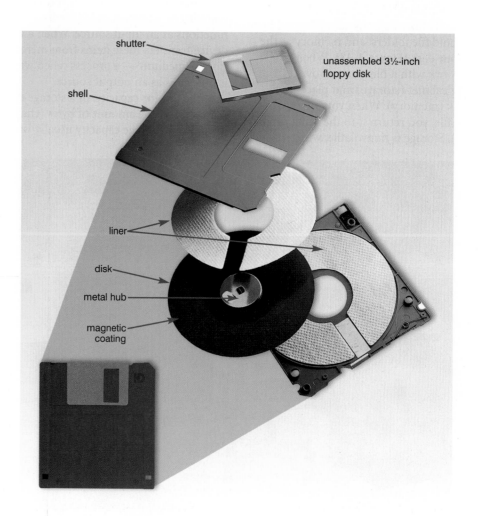

shutter

shell

unassembled 3½-inch floppy disk

liner

disk

metal hub

magnetic coating

Figure 4-43 In a 3.5-inch floppy disk, the thin, circular, flexible disk is enclosed between two liners. A piece of metal called a shutter in the rigid plastic shell covers an opening to the recording surface.

Characteristics of a Floppy Disk

A floppy disk is a type of a magnetic disk, which means it uses magnetic patterns to store data, instructions, and information on the disk's surface. Most magnetic disks are read/write storage media; that is, you can access (read) data from and place (write) data on a magnetic disk any number of times.

A new blank floppy disk has no data, instructions, or information stored on it. Before a computer can write to a new floppy disk, it must be formatted. **Formatting** is the process of preparing a disk (floppy disk or hard disk) for reading and writing by organizing the disk into storage locations called tracks and sectors **[Figure 4-44]**. A **track** is a narrow storage ring around the disk — similar to the annual rings on a tree. A **sector** is a pie-shaped section of the disk, which breaks the tracks into small arcs.

be used in a PC. Many modern Macintosh computers, however, can read PC formatted disks.

To protect them from accidentally being erased, floppy disks have a write-protect notch. A write-protect notch is a small hole in the corner of the disk. By sliding a small tab, you either can cover or expose the notch. On a floppy disk, if the write-protect notch is closed, or covered, the disk drive can write to the floppy disk. If the write-protect notch is exposed, or open, the disk drive cannot write to the floppy disk; it can, however, read from the disk. Some floppy disks have a second hole on the opposite side of the disk that does not have a small tab; this hole identifies the disk as a high-density floppy disk.

A high-density (HD) floppy disk, the most widely used 3.5-inch floppy disk, can store 1.44 MB of data — the equivalent of approximately 700 pages of 2,000 characters each.

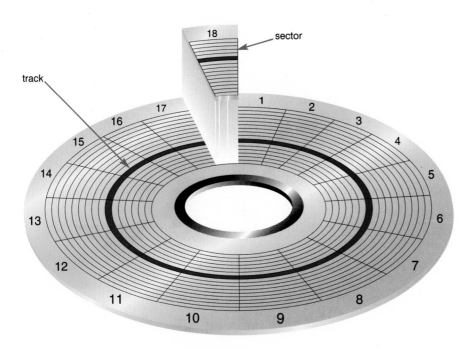

Figure 4-44 A track is a narrow recording band that forms a full circle on the surface of a disk. The disk's storage locations then are divided into pie-shaped sections, which break the tracks into small arcs called sectors.

Most disks are preformatted by the disk manufacturer for use on either a PC or a Macintosh computer. In some cases, however, you must format the disks yourself. Because a Macintosh formats disks differently than PCs, a Macintosh formatted disk cannot normally

With reasonable care, floppy disks can last for many years — providing an inexpensive and reliable form of storage. When handling a floppy disk, you should avoid exposing it to heat, cold, magnetic fields, and contaminants such as dust, smoke, or salt air.

CHAPTER 4

Figure 4-45 outlines some guidelines for the proper care of floppy disks.

A **floppy disk drive** is a device that can read from and write to a floppy disk. Personal computers usually have a floppy disk drive installed inside the system unit. Modern PCs usually have one installed floppy disk drive which is called drive A; if a PC has two floppy drives, the second one usually is called drive B. Macintosh computers also have one installed floppy disk drive and the drive is referred to simply as the floppy disk drive.

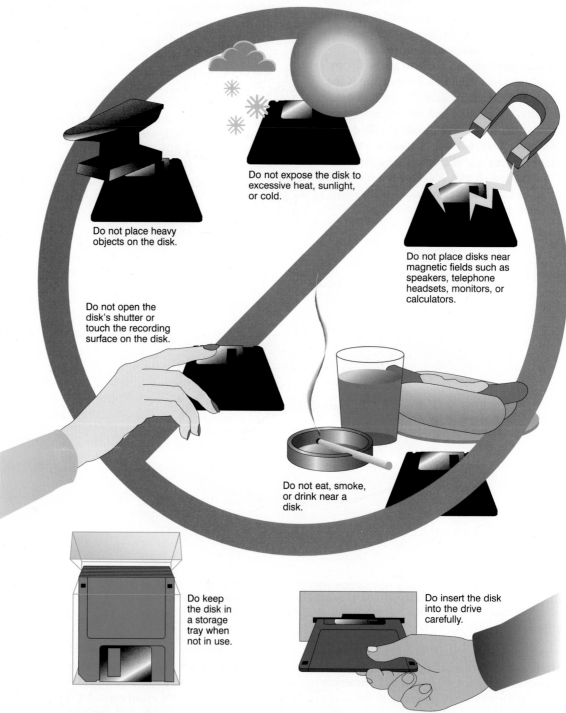

Do not place heavy objects on the disk.

Do not expose the disk to excessive heat, sunlight, or cold.

Do not place disks near magnetic fields such as speakers, telephone headsets, monitors, or calculators.

Do not open the disk's shutter or touch the recording surface on the disk.

Do not eat, smoke, or drink near a disk.

Do keep the disk in a storage tray when not in use.

Do insert the disk into the drive carefully.

Figure 4-45 Guidelines for the proper care of floppy disks.

High-Capacity Disk Drives

Several manufacturers make high-capacity disk drives that use disks with capacities of 100 MB or greater. With these high-capacity disks, you can store large files containing graphics, audio, or video; transport a large number of files from one computer to another; or make a backup of all of your important files. A **backup** is a duplicate of a file, program, or disk that can be used if the original is lost, damaged, or destroyed.

One popular high-capacity drive is the Zip® drive. A **Zip® drive** is a special high-capacity floppy disk drive developed by Iomega Corporation. These drives use a special 3.5-inch Zip® disk, which can store 100 MB of data — equivalent to about 70 high-density floppy disks. Because they are reasonably priced, many new PC and Macintosh computers are equipped with a built-in Zip® drive. You also can add an external Zip®

drive either to a Macintosh computer or PC [**Figure 4-46**]. Just like floppy disks, Macintosh computers format Zip® disks differently than PCs. Macintosh formatted Zip® disks normally cannot be used in a PC. Many modern Macintosh computers, however, can read and write to PC formatted Zip® disks.

Hard Disks

When personal computers were introduced, software programs and their related files required small amounts of storage and files fit easily on floppy disks. As software became more complex and included graphical user interfaces and multimedia, file sizes and storage requirements increased. Today, hard disks, which provide for larger storage capacities and much faster access times than floppy disks, are the primary media for storing software programs and files. Current personal computer hard disks can store from 2 GB to 16 GB of data, instructions, and information.

A **hard disk** usually consists of several inflexible, circular disks, called platters, on which items such as data, instructions, and information are stored electronically. A **platter** in a hard disk is made of aluminum, glass, or ceramic and is coated with a material that allows data to be magnetically recorded on its surface. Although removable hard disks do exist, the hard disks in most personal computers are housed permanently inside the

WebInfo

For a discussion of backup procedures, visit the Teachers Discovering Computers Chapter 4 WebInfo page

(www.scsite.com/tdc/ ch4/webinfo.htm)

and click Backup.

WebInfo

For information about hard disks, visit the Teachers Discovering Computers Chapter 4 WebInfo page

(www.scsite.com/tdc/ ch4/webinfo.htm)

and click Hard Disk.

CHAPTER 4

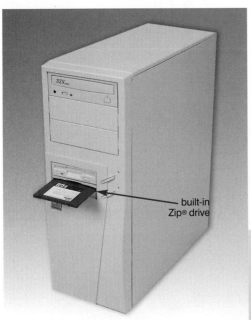

built-in
Zip® drive

external
Zip® drive

Figure 4-46 Many new computers are equipped with a built-in Zip® drive. You also can add an external Zip® drive to a PC or Macintosh computer.

system unit and are enclosed in an airtight, sealed case to protect the platters from contamination **[Figure 4-47]**.

Like a floppy disk, a hard disk is a magnetic disk that stores data, instructions, and information using magnetic patterns. Hard disks also are read/write storage media; that is, you can both read from and write to a hard disk any number of times. Before you can write data, instructions, or information to a hard disk, the hard disk must be formatted. Hard disk manufacturers typically format hard disks before they are installed in computers. Typically, a hard disk is designated drive C on PCs and as the HD Disk on Macintosh computers.

Compact Discs

In the past, when you purchased software, you received one or more floppy disks that contained the files needed to install or run the software program. As software programs became more and more complex, the number of floppy disks required increased, sometimes exceeding 30 disks. These more complex programs required a larger storage medium, which is why many of today's software programs are distributed on compact discs as either a CD-ROM or DVD-ROM.

A **compact disc (CD)** is a flat, round, portable, metal-coated plastic storage medium that is usually 4.75 inches in diameter and less than one-twentieth of an inch thick. CDs store

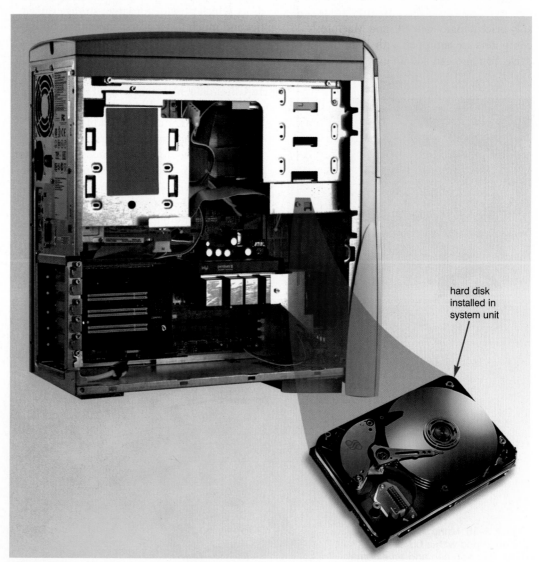

hard disk installed in system unit

Figure 4-47 The hard disk in a personal computer normally is housed permanently inside the system unit.

data, instructions, and information in micro-scopic pits that are on the top surface of the CD under the printed label that most manu-facturers place on the top of the CD so you can identify it. A high-powered laser light cre-ates the pits, and a lower-powered laser reads the data, instructions, and information from the disc by reflecting light through the bottom of the CD. The reflected light is converted into a series of bits that the computer can process.

All multimedia computers have a **CD-ROM drive**, a device than can read CDs **[Figure 4-48]**. On PCs, the drive designation of a CD drive usually follows alphabetically after that of the hard disk. For example, if your hard disk is drive C, then the compact disc will be drive D. When a user places a CD in a Macintosh computer, an icon that looks like a CD displays on the computer desktop.

With proper care, a compact disc is guaranteed to last 5 years, but could last up to 50 years. To protect data on a CD, you should place it in its protective case when you are finished using it. When handling CDs, you should avoid stacking them and exposing them to heat, cold, and contaminants. You can clean the bottom surface of a CD with a soft cloth and warm water or a CD cleaning kit, but never clean the label side of a CD because this is where the data is stored.

Compact discs are available in a variety of formats. The following sections discuss two basic types: CD-ROMs and DVD-ROMs.

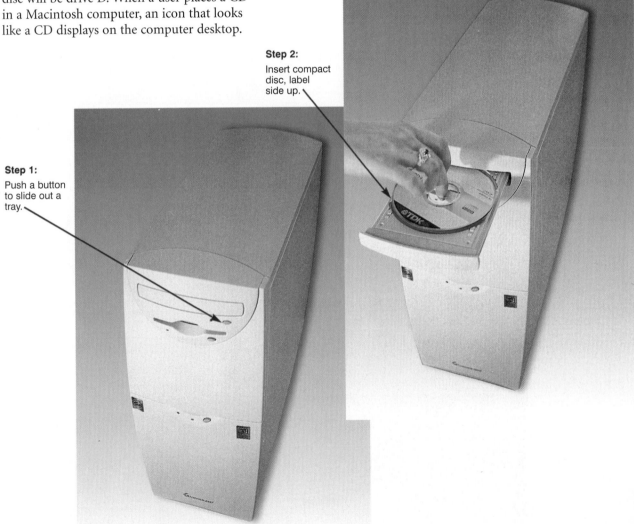

Step 1:
Push a button to slide out a tray.

Step 2:
Insert compact disc, label side up.

Figure 4-48 On most CD-ROM and DVD-ROM drives, you push a button to slide out a tray, insert your disc with the label side up, and then push the same button to close the tray.

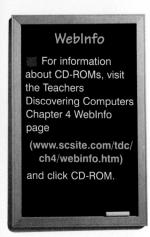

WebInfo

For information about CD-ROMs, visit the Teachers Discovering Computers Chapter 4 WebInfo page

(www.scsite.com/tdc/ ch4/webinfo.htm)

and click CD-ROM.

WebInfo

For information about DVD-ROMs, visit the Teachers Discovering Computers Chapter 4 WebInfo page

(www.scsite.com/tdc/ ch4/webinfo.htm)

and click DVD-ROM.

CD-ROM

Compact disc read-only memory (CD-ROM) (pronounced SEE-DEE-rom), is a compact disc that uses the same laser technology as audio CDs do for recording music. Unlike an audio CD, a CD-ROM can contain text, graphics, and video, as well as sound. The contents of standard CD-ROMs are written, or **recorded**, by the manufacturer and only can be read and used; that is, they cannot be erased or modified — hence, the name read-only.

For a computer to read a CD-ROM, you must place it into a CD-ROM drive. Because audio CDs and CD-ROMs use the same laser technology, you can use your CD-ROM drive to listen to an audio CD while working on your computer.

A CD-ROM can hold 650 MB of data, instructions, and information — about 450 times the capacity of a high-density 3.5-inch floppy disk. Because CD-ROMs have such high storage capacities, they are used to store and distribute today's complex software, such as programs for children, education, games, and reference **[Figure 4-49]**. Most of today's software programs also are sold on CD; some programs even require that the disc be in the drive each time you use the program.

DVD-ROM

Although CD-ROMs have large storage capacities, even these are not large enough for many of today's complex programs. Some software, for example, is sold on five or more

Figure 4-49 CD-ROMs are used to store and distribute multimedia software including programs for children, education, games, and reference.

CD-ROMs. To meet the tremendous storage requirements of today's software, the digital video disc read-only memory (DVD-ROM) format was developed. A **digital video disc read-only memory (DVD-ROM)** is an extremely high capacity CD capable of storing from 4.7 GB to 17 GB, more than enough to hold a telephone book containing every resident in the United States **[Figure 4-50]**. Not only is the storage capacity greater than a CD-ROM, but the quality of a DVD-ROM far surpasses that of a CD-ROM. In order to read a DVD-ROM, you must have a **DVD-ROM drive**. Many computers now are sold with DVD-ROM drives that will read both conventional CDs and DVDs. As the cost of DVD technologies becomes more reasonable, many industry professionals believe that DVDs will eventually replace CDs, VCRs, and VHS tapes in our businesses, homes, and schools.

Summary of Storage

Storage is used to store data and programs that currently are not being processed by the computer. The previous sections discussed the various types of storage used with computers. Adding what you have learned about these storage devices and storage operations in general to what you learned about the input, processing, and output operations will complete your understanding of the information processing cycle.

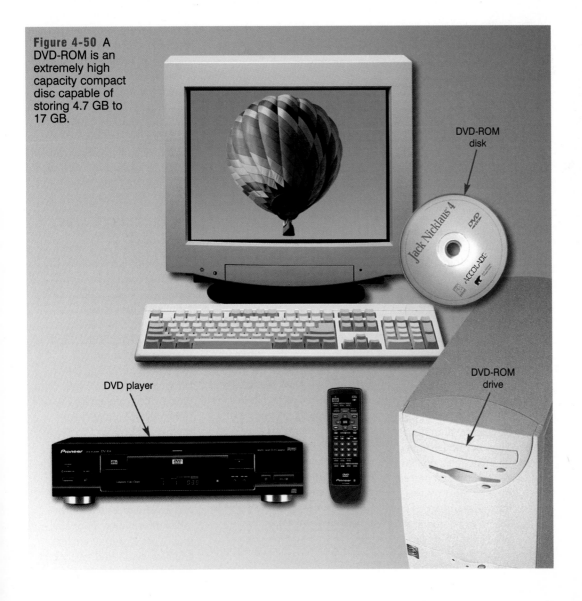

Figure 4-50 A DVD-ROM is an extremely high capacity compact disc capable of storing 4.7 GB to 17 GB.

DVD-ROM disk

DVD-ROM drive

DVD player

1 2 3 4 5 6 7 8

InBrief

- InBrief
- KeyTerms
- AtTheMovies
- CheckPoint
- TeacherTime
- CyberClass
- EdIssues
- NetStuff

SPECIAL FEATURES

- TimeLine 2000
- Guide to WWW Sites
- Buyer's Guide 2000
- Educational Sites
- State/Federal Sites
- Chat
- News
- Home

Web Instructions: To display this page from the Web, launch your browser and enter the URL, www.scsite.com/tdc/ch4/brief.htm. Click the links for current and additional information. To listen to an audio version of this InBrief, click the Audio button below the title, InBrief, at the top of the page. To play the audio, RealPlayer must be installed on your computer (download by clicking here).

1. The System Unit

The **system unit** is a box-like case that houses the electronic components a computer uses to process data. The system unit is made of metal or plastic and protects the electronic components from damage. The major components in the system unit include the motherboard, the CPU and microprocessor, memory, expansion slots and expansion cards, and ports and connectors.

2. Bits and Bytes

Most computers are **digital**, meaning that they understand only two discrete states: on and off. In order to store and process data, a computer must convert the data into a form it understands. Each on or off digital value is called a **bit** (short for binary digit), and represents the smallest unit of data the computer can handle. When eight bits are grouped together as a unit, they are called a **byte**.

3. CPU and Microprocessor

The **central processing unit (CPU)** interprets and carries out the basic instructions that operate a computer. The CPU manages most of a computer's operations. A chip known as the **microprocessor** contains the CPU. A microprocessor contains a number of components including a control unit, an arithmetic/logic unit, and a system clock.

4. Memory

Computers use **memory** to store data and information temporarily. Several terms have evolved to define memory and storage devices. A **kilobyte (KB or K)** of memory is equal to 1,000 bytes, a **megabyte (MB)** is equal to one million bytes, and a **gigabyte (GB)** is equal to one billion bytes. Two common types of memory are RAM and ROM. **RAM** is an example of volatile memory and **ROM** is an example of nonvolatile memory.

5. Types of Input

Input is entering data, programs, commands, and user responses into memory. **Data** is a collection of unorganized facts that include words, numbers, pictures, and sounds. A **program** is a series of instructions that tells a computer how to perform tasks. A **command** is an instruction given to a computer program. **User response** is a user's input to a question from a program.

6. Keyboards

A **keyboard** is a group of switches resembling the keys on a typewriter that allow users to enter input. You enter data, commands, and other input into a computer by pressing keys on the keyboard. A keyboard contains keys that allow you to type letters, numbers, spaces, punctuation marks, and other symbols.

7. Pointing Devices

A **pointing device** is an input device that allows you to control the movement of the pointer on the screen and to make selections from the screen. Common pointing devices include the mouse, trackball, and joystick. A **mouse** is an input device that usually has one or two buttons and a ball mechanism on the bottom. A **trackball** is a stationary pointing device with a ball mechanism on its top. A **joystick** is a vertical lever mounted on a base.

8. Audio and Video Input

Audio input is the process of recording music, speech, or sound effects. Recorded sound is input via a device such as a microphone, tape player, or audio CD player. **Video input** is the process of entering a full-motion recording into a computer. To capture video, you plug a video camera, a VCR, or a similar device into a video capture card.

9. Types of Output

Output is data that has been processed into a useful form called information. Four common types of output are text, graphics, audio, and video. Text

www.scsite.com/tdc/ch4/brief.htm

InBrief

KeyTerms

AtTheMovies

CheckPoint

TeacherTime

CyberClass

EdIssues

NetStuff

SPECIAL FEATURES

TimeLine 2000

Guide to WWW Sites

Buyer's Guide 2000

Educational Sites

State/Federal Sites

Chat

News

Home

InBrief

consists of characters that are used to create words, sentences, and paragraphs. Graphics are digital representations of nontext information, such as images and drawings. Audio is music, speech, or other sound that is stored and produced by the computer. Video consists of photographic images that are played back on a computer at speeds that provide the appearance of full motion in real-time.

10. Output Devices

An **output device** is any computer component capable of conveying information to a user. Commonly used output devices include monitors, printers, data projectors, facsimile machines, multifunction devices, speakers, and headsets.

11. Monitors

A **monitor** is a display device that conveys text, graphics, and video information visually and is housed in a plastic or metal case. Monitors for personal computers are available in a variety of sizes, with the more common being 15-, 17-, 19-, and 21-inch. Like a television set, the core of a monitor is a large glass tube called a **cathode ray tube** (**CRT**). The quality of a monitor depends largely on its resolution, dot pitch, and refresh rate.

12. Printers

A **printer** is an output device that produces text and graphical information on a physical medium such as paper or transparency film. Printers are grouped in two categories: impact and nonimpact. The more commonly used type of impact printer is a dot-matrix printer. A **nonimpact printer** forms marks on a piece of paper without actually striking the paper. Two common types of nonimpact printers are ink-jet and laser printers.

13. Storage

Storage, or **secondary storage**, refers to the media on which data, instructions, and information are kept, as well as the devices that record and retrieve these items. Storage is nonvolatile, which means that data and instructions in storage are retained even when power is removed from the computer.

14. Storage Media and Devices

A **storage medium** is the physical material on which data, instructions, and information are kept. One commonly used storage medium is a **disk**, which is a round, flat piece of plastic or metal on which items such as data, instructions, and information can be encoded. A **storage device** is the mechanism used to record and retrieve items to and from a storage medium.

15. Floppy Disks

A **floppy disk**, or **diskette**, is a portable, inexpensive storage medium that consists of a thin, circular, flexible plastic disk with a magnetic coating enclosed in a square-shaped plastic shell. Floppy disks are read/write magnetic storage media; that is, you can access (read) data from and place (write) data on a floppy disk any number of times.

16. Hard Disks

Hard disks provide for larger storage capacities and much faster access times than floppy disks and are the primary media for storing software programs and files. A **hard disk** usually consists of several inflexible, circular disks, called platters, on which items such as data, instructions, and information are stored electronically.

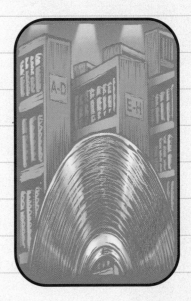

www.scsite.com/tdc/ch4/terms.htm

KeyTerms

InBrief

KeyTerms

AtTheMovies

CheckPoint

TeacherTime

CyberClass

EdIssues

NetStuff

SPECIAL FEATURES

TimeLine 2000

Guide to WWW Sites

Buyer's Guide 2000

Educational Sites

State/Federal Sites

Chat

News

Home

Web Instructions: To display this page from the Web, launch your browser and enter the URL, www.scsite.com/tdc/ch4/terms.htm. Scroll through the list of terms. Click a term to display its definition and a picture. Click KeyTerms on the left to redisplay the KeyTerms page. Click the TO WEB button for current and additional information about the term from the Web. To see animations, Shockwave and Flash Player must be installed on your computer (download by clicking here).

adapter card **[4.11]**
address **[4.8]**
American Standard Code for Information Interchange (ASCII) **[4.3]**
analog **[4.3]**
arithmetic operations **[4.6]**
arithmetic/logic unit (ALU) **[4.6]**
audio input **[4.18]**
audio output **[4.25]**
auxiliary storage **[4.27]**

backup **[4.31]**
bar code **[4.18]**
binary **[4.3]**
bit **[4.3]**
byte **[4.3]**

cathode ray tube (CRT) **[4.21]**
CD-ROM drive **[4.33]**
central processing unit (CPU) **[4.5]**
chip **[4.5]**
clicking **[4.16]**
clock speed **[4.7]**
command **[4.13]**
compact disc (CD) **[4.32]**

compact disc read-only memory (CD-ROM) **[4.34]**
comparison operations **[4.6]**
connectors **[4.12]**
control unit **[4.6]**

data **[4.13]**
data projector **[4.24]**
decoding **[4.6]**
digital **[4.3]**
digital camera **[4.18]**
digital video disc read-only memory (DVD-ROM) **[4.35]**
disk **[4.27]**
diskette **[4.28]**
dot pitch **[4.22]**
dot-matrix printer **[4.23]**
double-clicking **[4.16]**
dragging **[4.16]**
dual inline memory module (DIMM) **[4.10]**
DVD-ROM drive **[4.35]**
dynamic RAM (DRAM) **[4.10]**

ENERGY STAR® **[4.22]**
executing **[4.6]**
expansion board **[4.11]**
expansion card **[4.11]**
expansion slot **[4.11]**

facsimile (fax) machine **[4.25]**
fetching **[4.6]**
floppy disk **[4.28]**
floppy disk drive **[4.30]**
formatting **[4.29]**

gigabyte (GB) **[4.9]**

hard copy **[4.22]**
hard disk **[4.31]**

impact printer **[4.23]**
ink-jet printer **[4.23]**
input **[4.13]**
input device **[4.14]**

joystick **[4.16]**

keyboard **[4.14]**
keyword **[4.13]**
kilobyte (K or KB) **[4.9]**
kiosk **[4.17]**

landscape orientation **[4.22]**
laser printer **[4.23]**
LCD monitor **[4.22]**
logical operations **[4.6]**

machine cycle **[4.6]**
megabyte (MB) **[4.9]**
megahertz (MHz) **[4.7]**
memory **[4.8]**

microprocessor **[4.6]**
monitor **[4.21]**
motherboard **[4.4]**
mouse **[4.15]**
mouse pad **[4.16]**
multifunction device (MFD) **[4.25]**

nonimpact printer **[4.23]**
nonvolatile memory **[4.9]**
numeric keypad **[4.15]**

optical character recognition (OCR) **[4.17]**
optical mark recognition (OMR) **[4.18]**
optical reader **[4.17]**
output **[4.20]**
output device **[4.21]**

pixel **[4.21]**
platter **[4.31]**
Plug and Play **[4.11]**
pointing device **[4.15]**
port **[4.12]**
portrait orientation **[4.22]**
printer **[4.22]**
processor **[4.5]**
program **[4.13]**

random access memory (RAM) **[4.9]**
read-only memory (ROM) **[4.11]**
recorded **[4.34]**
refresh rate **[4.22]**
resolution **[4.22]**

scanner **[4.17]**
secondary storage **[4.27]**
sector **[4.29]**
soft copy **[4.21]**
speakers **[4.26]**
speech recognition **[4.19]**
storage **[4.27]**
storage device **[4.27]**
storage medium **[4.27]**
storing **[4.6]**
system clock **[4.7]**
system unit **[4.2]**

touch screen **[4.17]**
track **[4.29]**
trackball **[4.16]**

user response **[4.13]**

video input **[4.19]**
volatile memory **[4.9]**

Zip® drive **[4.31]**

InBrief

KeyTerms

AtTheMovies

CheckPoint

TeacherTime

CyberClass

EdIssues

NetStuff

SPECIAL FEATURES

TimeLine 2000

Guide to WWW Sites

Buyer's Guide 2000

Educational Sites

State/Federal Sites

Chat

News

Home

www.scsite.com/tdc/ch4/movies.htm

AtTheMovies
WELCOME to
VIDEO CLIPS
from CNN

Web Instructions: To display this page from the Web, launch your browser and enter the URL, www.scsite.com/tdc/ch4/movies.htm. Click a picture to view a video. After watching the video, close the video window and then complete the exercise by answering the questions about the video. To view the videos, RealPlayer must be installed on your computer (download by clicking here).

1. Biz IBM STORAGE

Storage capacity of brand-new IBM microprocessors is on the fast track for growth. What are the emerging trends in processors and storage? How much has the cost of 1 MB of storage fallen since 1991? Storage capacities will continue to increase in the future. How much data will higher-density storage being developed by IBM allow you to store on one-square inch of disk space? Why is greater storage capacity important? Does IBM intend to share this new technology with competitors? Describe the impact these higher-density IBM microprocessors, if licensed to different manufacturers, could have on the computer departments of educational facilities and K-12 schools.

2. Joystick Review

Advances in joystick technology have created exciting new possibilities. Where would you expect to use a joystick? What two types of joysticks are illustrated in the video? Describe the features of each. How do they differ from other input devices, such as a mouse? How are they the same? In relation to the joystick, what is meant by "feedback technology"? Which model of joystick would you purchase? Identify any educational software that you are familiar with that would require joystick technology. Then define the mental and motor skill values of the software and computer interaction involving the joystick. Would your students agree with your opinions, or do you think they are unaware of how much joystick aptitude determines mental acuity?

3. Postage Computer

The United States Postal Service is about to alter the way letters are stamped. Technology to issue e-stamps is being tested and soon will be ready for routine use. What is an e-stamp? How does an e-stamp get on a letter? Do you need a special printer to print them? Can a person handwrite the address on an e-stamped letter? What are the advantages and disadvantages of e-stamps? Examine with your students how e-stamp technology will affect the entire letter delivery process from the time the letter arrives at a postal sorting facility to the time it is delivered to the addressee's mailbox.

As you examine e-stamp technology in practice, find out from your students if they think that any special training should be given to the public so they will know how to use the technology. Do they feel that post offices should supply on-site e-stamp computers and printers for public use?

InBrief

KeyTerms

AtTheMovies

CheckPoint

TeacherTime

CyberClass

EdIssues

NetStuff

SPECIAL FEATURES

TimeLine 2000

Guide to WWW Sites

Buyer's Guide 2000

Educational Sites

State/Federal Sites

Chat

News

Home

CheckPoint

Web Instructions: To display this page from the Web, launch your browser and enter the URL, www.scsite.com/tdc/ch4/check.htm. Click a blank line for the answer. Click the links for current and additional information. To experience the animation and interactivity, Shockwave and Flash Player must be installed on your computer (download by clicking here).

1. Label the Figure

Instructions: Identify these areas or keys on a typical desktop computer keyboard.

2. Matching

Instructions: Match each term from the column on the left with the best description from the column on the right.

_____ 1. byte

_____ 2. scanner

_____ 3. output

_____ 4. Zip® drive

_____ 5. chip

a. small piece of semicoducting material usually no bigger than one-half-inch square

b. eight bits grouped together as a unit

c. data that has been processed into a useful form, called information

d. an input device that can capture an entire page of text electronically

e. a special high-capacity floppy disk drive developed by Iomega Corporation

3. Short Answer

Instructions: Write a brief answer to each of the following questions.

1. What are the components of the system unit? What is the purpose of the central processing unit and system clock? _____

2. How are RAM and ROM similar? How are they different? What terminology is used to describe the storage capacity of RAM chips? _____

3. How is a computer keyboard like a typewriter? What keys can be found on most keyboards but not on traditional typewriters? What is the purpose of these keys? _____

4. How are impact printers different from nonimpact printers? What are examples of each type of printer? Which type of printer is commonly used in schools? _____

5. How does formatting prepare a floppy disk for storage? What is the storage capacity of a 3.5-inch high-density floppy disk? _____

TeacherTime

Web Instructions: To display this page from the Web, launch your browser and enter the URL, www.scsite.com/tdc/ch4/time.htm. Click the links for current and additional information.

InBrief

KeyTerms

AtTheMovies

CheckPoint

TeacherTime

CyberClass

EdIssues

NetStuff

SPECIAL FEATURES

TimeLine 2000

Guide to WWW Sites

Buyer's Guide 2000

Educational Sites

State/Federal Sites

Chat

News

Home

1. While teachers can sometimes select application software packages for use in the classroom, they often do not choose the type of computers used at their school. Suppose you want to purchase Math Workshop, an educational software package that reinforces elementary math concepts. How can you determine if your classroom computers will support the software? Where should you look to find the software's system requirements? How would you determine if your computer meets those requirements? For example, how could you determine if your computer had enough memory, a fast enough CPU, or enough hard disk space?

2. Last year, you received a color ink-jet printer — a Hewlett-Packard DeskJet 697C — for your classroom. Until recently, the printer worked flawlessly. Lately, however, when you print a document, the ink is smearing and the print quality is poor. No one at your school can provide technical assistance or support. Where else might you find technical support? Does the manufacturer (Hewlett-Packard, in this example), provide technical support? Via what methods can you contact the manufacturer or access technical support information — telephone, e-mail, fax, the Web, or all of these? Which type of support would you prefer? Visit Hewlett-Packard's Web site and use their Web-based technical support to determine how to fix the printer problem. How does Web-based support differ from face-to-face support or support via telephone? What are some advantages and disadvantages of Web-based support?

3. In K-12 schools, the high-density 3.5-inch floppy disk is the most widely used portable storage media. Although these disks hold 1.44 MB of information, the storage requirements for software and graphic files continue to increase. If your students create multimedia projects, for example, a floppy disk might not provide sufficient storage space. In light of this disadvantage, do floppy disks still have a place in the classroom? What are the advantages of using floppy disks? What other, high-capacity portable storage media could you use in your classroom?

4. The central processing unit (CPU) sometimes is described as the brains of a computer because the functions it performs are similar to those of the human brain. Can this analogy be reversed? Pick a simple task or activity that teachers or students perform every day in the classroom. In accomplishing this task, which of their actions resemble the machine cycle operations of fetching, decoding, executing, and storing? What actions are different? Could you omit any of these without affecting the completion of the task?

5. Digital video disks (DVDs) are capable of storing more than two million pages of text, seven hours of music, or eight hours of popular movies. The quality of a DVD also surpasses that of a CD. Many computers now include drives that will read both conventional CDs and the newer DVDs. Already, thousands of movies and games are available on DVD; each day, more and more software is made available on DVD-ROM. What software packages currently are available on DVD-ROM? Are any of these DVD-ROM software packages education-related? How does the price of DVD-ROM software packages compare to the same software sold on CD-ROM? What features of DVDs do you think are important in a classroom setting?

Web Instructions: To display this page from the Web, launch your browser and enter the URL, www.scsite.com/tdc/ch4/class.htm. To start Level I CyberClass, click a Level I link on this page or enter the URL, www.cyber-class.com. Click the Student button, click *Teachers Discovering Computers* in the list of titles, and then click the Enter a site button. To start Level II or III CyberClass (available only to those purchasers of a CyberClass floppy disk), place your CyberClass floppy disk in drive A, click Start on the taskbar, click Run on the Start menu, type a:connect in the Open text box, click the OK button, click the Enter CyberClass button, and then follow the instructions. If you are using a Macintosh, see your instructor.

- InBrief
- KeyTerms
- AtTheMovies
- CheckPoint
- TeacherTime
- CyberClass
- EdIssues
- NetStuff

SPECIAL FEATURES
- TimeLine 2000
- Guide to WWW Sites
- Buyer's Guide 2000
- Educational Sites
- State/Federal Sites
- Chat
- News
- Home

1. Flash Cards (<u>Level I</u>, Level II, and Level III)

Click Flash Cards on the Main Menu of the CyberClass Web page. For Level I users, click the plus sign before the Chapter 4 title. Click The System Unit and answer all of the cards in that section. For Level I users, click Data Representation and answer the cards in that section. If you have less than 85% correct, continue to answer cards in other sections until you have more than 85% correct. All users: Answer as many more Flash Cards as you desire. Close the Electronic Flash Card window and the Flash Cards window by clicking the Close button in the upper-right corner of each window.

2. Practice Test (<u>Level I</u>, Level II, and Level III)

Click Testing on the Main Menu of the CyberClass Web page. Click the Select a book box arrow and then click Teachers Discovering Computers. Click the Select a test to take box arrow and then click the Chapter 4 title in the list. Click the Take Test button. If necessary, maximize the window. Take the practice test and then click the Submit Test button. Click the Display Study Guide button. Review the Study Guide. Scroll down and click the Return To CyberClass button. Click the Yes button to close the Study Guide window. If your score was less than 80%, click the Take another Test button to take another practice test. Continue taking tests until your score is greater than 80%. Then, click the Done button.

3. Web Guide (<u>Level I</u>, Level II, and Level III)

Click Web Guide on the Main Menu of the CyberClass Web page. When the Guide to World Wide Web Sites page displays, click Humor. Examine the sites under humor until you find a joke or comic strip related to computers. Based upon what you have learned so far in this course, is the joke or comic strip accurate or inaccurate? Do you think humor helps or hurts an understanding of computers? Hand in a brief synopsis of your answers to your instructor.

4. Assignments and Syllabus (Level II and Level III)

Click Assignments on the Main Menu of the CyberClass Web page. Ensure you are aware of all assignments and when they are due. Click Syllabus on the Main Menu of the CyberClass Web page. Verify you are up to date on all activities for the class.

5. CyberChallenge (Level II and Level III)

Click CyberChallenge on the Main Menu of the CyberClass Web page. Click the Select a board to play box arrow and then click Chapter 4 in the list. Click the Play CyberChallenge button. Maximize the CyberChallenge window. Play CyberChallenge until your score for a complete game is 500 points or more. Close the CyberChallenge window.

www.scsite.com/tdc/ch4/issues.htm

Web Instructions: To display this page from the Web, launch your browser and enter the URL, www.scsite.com/tdc/ch4/issues.htm. Click the links for current and additional information to help you respond to the EdIssues questions.

EdIssues

1. The Paperless Classroom

As computers became popular in business, people predicted the paperless office where nearly all documents would exist only electronically. Yet, much to the dismay of environmentalists, studies show that many of today's offices use more paper than in the past. Why do you think computerized offices use more paper than ever before? What about schools? Will there ever be a paperless school or classroom? Would you want to teach in a paperless classroom? What impact might the increased use of computers and the World Wide Web have on paper usage in your classroom? What could you do to decrease the amount of paper used? Will you let your students print information they find on the Web on your classroom printer?

2. Technology Coordinator

At every educational level, from preschool through advanced academic degrees, there is a movement to integrate technology into the educational environment. In many K-12 schools, the technology coordinator is responsible for technology planning and implementation, staff training, and technical support. Your school is in the process of hiring a technology coordinator and you are on a committee that has to define the responsibilities of the position. What should be the responsibilities of the technology coordinator? What type of staff development would you want the technology coordinator to conduct? What kind of technical support should he or she provide? If you were the technology coordinator, what might be some of your technology plans for the future?

InBrief

KeyTerms

AtTheMovies

CheckPoint

TeacherTime

CyberClass

EdIssues

NetStuff

SPECIAL FEATURES

TimeLine 2000

Guide to WWW Sites

Buyer's Guide 2000

Educational Sites

State/Federal Sites

Chat

News

Home

www.scsite.com/tdc/ch4/issues.htm

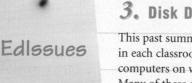

Edlssues

InBrief
KeyTerms
AtTheMovies
CheckPoint
TeacherTime
CyberClass
Edlssues
NetStuff

SPECIAL FEATURES

TimeLine 2000

Guide to WWW Sites

Buyer's Guide 2000

Educational Sites

State/Federal Sites

Chat

News

Home

3. Disk Drives

This past summer, your school purchased and set up three new iMac computers in each classroom. Last year your classroom was equipped with older Macintosh computers on which you had installed many educational software programs. Many of these software packages are stored on floppy disks, as are many of your classroom management tools and files. Your new iMac computers, however, do not have floppy disk drives. What will you do? Can you still use the educational software or your files? Could you use external floppy drives to solve this problem? How might you approach your principal about purchasing external floppy drives? What arguments will you use to persuade your principal to purchase them?

4. Obsolete Equipment

Many businesses, government agencies, and parents donate obsolete computer equipment to schools. Although fully operational, this equipment often is not capable of running multimedia software, due to slow microprocessors, lack of memory, lack of hard disk space, and the lack of a CD-ROM drive. Some teachers feel that any kind of computer is better than no computer. Do you agree or disagree? Is there a use for these types of computers in the classroom or in a school lab? How could you use one in your classroom? Should schools continue to accept older computers? Why or why not?

5. Input Devices

Almost everyone knows someone who feels intimidated when forced to enter data into a computer. Some input devices make it easy for novices to enter data, while others require users to receive training. Which input device would be the easiest for someone to learn who is uncomfortable with computers? Why? Which input devices would you like to use in your classroom? Do you think emerging input technologies, such as voice input will become important in education? Why? Which input device would be the most important for your students to learn to use? Why?

Web Instructions: To display this page from the Web, launch your browser and enter the URL, www.scsite.com/tdc/ch4/net.htm. To use the Understanding the Motherboard lab, Configuring Your Display lab, and Maintaining Your Hard Drive lab from the Web, Shockwave and Flash Player must be installed on your computer (download by clicking here).

InBrief

KeyTerms

AtTheMovies

CheckPoint

TeacherTime

CyberClass

EdIssues

NetStuff

SPECIAL FEATURES

TimeLine 2000

Guide to WWW Sites

Buyer's Guide 2000

Educational Sites

State/Federal Sites

Chat

News

Home

UNDER-
STANDING THE
MOTHERBOARD

1. Shelly Cashman Series Understanding the Motherboard Lab

Follow the instructions in NetStuff 1 on page 1.34 to start and use the Understanding the Motherboard lab. If you are running from the Web, enter the URL, www.scsite.com/sclabs/menu.htm or display the NetStuff page (see instructions at the top of this page) and then click the UNDERSTANDING THE MOTHERBOARD LAB button.

CONFIGURING
YOUR DISPLAY
LAB

2. Shelly Cashman Series Configuring Your Display Lab

Follow the instructions in NetStuff 1 on page 1.34 to start and use the Configuring Your Display lab. If you are running from the Web, enter the URL, www.scsite.com/sclabs/menu.htm or display the NetStuff page (see instructions at the top of this page) and then click the CONFIGURING YOUR DISPLAY LAB button.

MAINTAINING
YOUR HARD
DRIVE LAB

3. Shelly Cashman Series Maintaining Your Hard Drive Lab

Follow the instructions in NetStuff 1 on page 1.34 to start and use the Maintaining Your Hard Drive lab. If you are running from the Web, enter the URL, www.scsite.com/sclabs/menu.htm or display the NetStuff page (see instructions at the top of this page) and then click the MAINTAINING YOUR HARD DRIVE LAB button.

TROUBLE-
SHOOTING

4. Troubleshooting Hardware Problems

Teachers need to develop troubleshooting skills so they can identify and fix basic computer-related hardware problems. To learn more about fixing basic hardware problems, click the TROUBLESHOOTING button and complete this exercise.

DIGITAL
CAMERAS

5. Digital Cameras

Digital cameras record photographs in the form of digital data. Click the DIGITAL CAMERAS button to complete an exercise to learn more about digital cameras and to see them in action.

DATA
COMPRESSION

6. Data Compression

One way to store more data on a disk is to use data compression. Click the DATA COMPRESSION button to complete an exercise to learn how data compression works and how you can compress files.

WEB CHAT

7. Web Chat

Winnie the Pooh may be less "rumbley in the tumbley." Toy makers have put something in the stomach of stuffed versions of the bear — microprocessors. The stuffed Pooh chatters through 20 minutes of talk and song and can be programmed to use a child's name, discuss favorite foods and activities, and play games both at and away from a computer. Yet, some parents are not impressed with the bear's accomplishments. They maintain that a simple stuffed toy develops creativity through imaginary conversations and fanciful play, but the processor-enriched bear promotes little more than passive observation. Stuffed toys with microprocessors are available for about $100. Would you buy one for your child? Why or why not? Click WEB CHAT button to enter a Web Chat discussion related to this topic.

4.46

WEB INSTRUCTIONS: *To gain World Wide Web access to additional and up-to-date information regarding this special feature, launch your browser and enter the URL shown at the top of this page.*

The decision to buy a personal computer system is an important one – and finding and purchasing a personal computer system suited to your needs will require an investment of both time and money. In general, personal computer buyers fall into three categories: first-time buyers, replacement buyers, and upgrade buyers. A recent survey of North American consumers found that the

Buyer's Guide 2000
How to Purchase, Install, and Maintain a Personal Computer

largest of the three categories, first-time buyers, make up 40 percent of the personal computer market. Surprisingly, the survey also discovered that most first-time buyers have little computer experience. In fact, more than 70 percent of first-time home computer buyers do not even use a computer at work.

As with many buyers, you may have little computer experience and find yourself unsure of how to proceed. The following guidelines are presented to help you purchase, install, and maintain a computer system. These guidelines also apply to the purchase of a laptop computer. Purchasing a laptop also involves some additional considerations, which are addressed later in this special feature.

How to Purchase a Personal Computer

1. Determine what application software products you will use on your computer. Knowing what software applications you plan to use will help you decide on the type of computer to buy, as well as to define the memory, storage, and other requirements. Certain software products, for example, can run only on Macintosh computers, while others run only on a PC with the Windows operating system. Further, some software products require more memory and disk space than others, as well as additional input/output devices.

When you purchase a computer system, it may come bundled with several software products (although not all will). At the very least, you probably will want software for word processing and a browser to access the World Wide Web. If you need additional applications, such as a spreadsheet, database, or presentation graphics, consider purchasing a software suite that offers reduced pricing on several applications.

Before selecting a specific package, be sure the software contains the features necessary for the tasks you want to perform. Many Web sites and magazines, such as those listed in Figure 1, provide reviews of software products. These sites also frequently have articles that rate computer systems and software on cost, performance, and support.

Type of System	Web Site	URL
PC	PC Comparison	www.computers.com/scoreboard
	Computer Shopper	www.zdnet.com/computershopper/edit/howtobuy/C0000001
	PC World Magazine	www.pcworld.com
	Tech Web Buyer's Guides	www.techweb.com/infoseek/shopper/bguides.html
	Byte Magazine	www.byte.com
	PC Computing Magazine	www.zdnet.com/pccomp
	PC Magazine	www.zdnet.com/pcmag
	Ziff-Davis	www.zdnet.com/product
	Yahoo! Computers	computers.yahoo.com
	Family PC Magazine	www.zdnet.com/familypc/filters/fpc.hardware.html
	Compare.Net	compare.net
	Tips on Buying a PC	www.css.msu.edu/pc-guide.html
Macintosh	Byte Magazine	www.techweb.com/wire/apple/
	Ziff-Davis	www.zdnet.com/mac
	Macworld Magazine	www.macworld.com
	Apple	www.apple.com

For an updated list of hardware and software reviews and their Web sites, visit www.scsite.com/tdc/ch4/buyers.htm.

Figure 1 Hardware and Software Reviews

2. Before buying a computer system, do some research. Talk to friends, coworkers, and instructors about prospective computer systems. What type of computer system did they buy? Why? Would they recommend their system and the company from which they bought it? You also should visit the Web sites or read reviews in the magazines listed in Figure 1. As you conduct your research, consider the following important criteria:

- Speed of the processor

- Size and types of memory (RAM) and storage (hard disk, floppy disk, CD-ROM, DVD-ROM, Zip® drive)

- Input/output devices included with the system (e.g., mouse, keyboard, monitor, printer, sound card, video card)

- Communications devices included with the system (modem, network interface card)

- Any software included with the system

- Overall system cost

3. Look for free software. Many system vendors include free software with their systems. Some sellers even let you choose which software you want. Remember, however, that free software has value only if you would have purchased the software even if it had not come with the computer.

4.48

	XPS R450	XPS R450	XPS R450	XPS R400
Purchase Price	**$3399** BUY IT	**$2499** BUY IT	**$2299** BUY IT	**$1999** BUY IT
Personal Lease Price	$127/Mo. 36 Months¹ LEASE IT	$94/Mo. 36 Months¹ LEASE IT	$86/Mo. 36 Months¹ LEASE IT	$75/Mo. 36 Months¹ LEASE IT
Processor	Pentium® II Processor at 450MHz	Pentium® II Processor at 450MHz	Pentium® II Processor at 450MHz	Pentium® II Processor at 400MHz
Chassis	Mini Tower	Mini Tower	Mini Tower	Mini Tower
RAM	128MB 100MHz SDRAM Memory	128MB 100MHz SDRAM Memory	128MB 100MHz SDRAM Memory	96MB 100MHz SDRAM Memory
Cache	512KB Integrated L2	512KB Integrated L2	512KB Integrated L2	512KB Integrated L2
Hard Drive	16.8GB Ultra ATA	10GB Ultra ATA	10GB Ultra ATA	13.6GB Ultra ATA
Monitor	1600HS 21" (19.8" viewable, .26dp) Trinitron® Monitor	1200HS 19" (17.9" viewable, .26dp) Monitor	1000LS 17" (15.9" viewable) Monitor	1000LS 17" (15.9" viewable) Monitor
Video Card	16MB STB nVidia TNT 3D AGP Graphics Card	16MB STB nVidia TNT 3D AGP Graphics Card	ATI Xpert 98D 8MB 3D 2X AGP Graphics Card	ATI Xpert 98D 8MB 3D 2X AGP Graphics Card
CD-ROM / DVD	NEW 4.8X DVD-ROM Drive and Decoder Card	NEW 40X Max Variable CD-ROM Drive	NEW 40X Max Variable CD-ROM Drive	NEW 40X Max Variable CD-ROM Drive
Sound	Turtle Beach A3D 64V Sound Card	Turtle Beach A3D 64V Sound Card	Crystal 3D 64V Wavetable Sound	Crystal 3D 64V Wavetable Sound
Speakers	Altec Lansing ACS-495 Speakers	NEW harman/kardon HK-195 Speakers	Altec Lansing ACS-295 Speakers with Subwoofer	NEW harman/kardon HK-195 Speakers
Modem	NEW 3Com® USRobotics V.90* PCI WinModem ConnectDirect Internet Service	NEW 3Com® USRobotics V.90* PCI WinModem ConnectDirect Internet Service	NEW 3Com® USRobotics V.90* PCI WinModem ConnectDirect Internet Service	NEW 3Com® USRobotics V.90* PCI WinModem ConnectDirect Internet Service
Additional Storage Devices	Optional	Optional	Iomega Zip 100MB Internal Drive with One Cartridge	Optional
Software	Microsoft Home Essentials 98 with Money 98	Microsoft Home Essentials 98 with Money 98	Microsoft Home Essentials 98 with Money 98	Microsoft Home Essentials 98 with Money 98
Operating System	Microsoft Windows® 98	Microsoft Windows® 98	Microsoft Windows® 98	Microsoft Windows® 98
Keyboard	QuietKey® Keyboard	QuietKey® Keyboard	QuietKey® Keyboard	QuietKey® Keyboard
Mouse	Microsoft IntelliMouse®	Microsoft IntelliMouse®	Microsoft IntelliMouse®	Microsoft IntelliMouse®
Warranty	3 Year Limited Warranty With 1 Year On-Site Service***	3 Year Limited Warranty With 1 Year On-Site Service***	3 Year Limited Warranty With 1 Year On-Site Service***	3 Year Limited warranty With 1 Year On-Site Service***
Price	$3,399	$2,499	$2,299	$1,999
Personal Lease Price¹	$127/mo. 36 months¹	$94/mo. 36 months¹	$86/mo. 36 months¹	$75/mo. 36 months¹
Order Code #	501001	501013	501018	501071
Go to the Dell Online Store	BUY IT	BUY IT	BUY IT	BUY IT

Figure 2 Some mail-order companies, such as Dell Computer, sell computers online.

Figure 4 Used computer mail-order companies

Company	URL	Telephone Number
American Computer Exchange	www.amcoex.com	1-800-786-0717
Boston Computer Exchange	www.bocoex.com	1-617-625-7722
United Computer Exchange	www.uce.com	1-800-755-3033
Used Computer Exchange	www.usedcomputerexchange.com	1-888-256-0481

For an updated list, visit www.scsite.com/tdc/ch4/buyers.htm

4. If you are buying a new computer system, you have several purchasing options: buying from your school bookstore, a local computer dealer, a local large retail store; or ordering by mail via telephone or the World Wide Web. Each purchasing option has certain advantages. Many college bookstores, for example, sign exclusive pricing agreements with computer manufacturers and, thus, can offer student discounts. Local dealers and local large retail stores, however, more easily can provide hands-on support. Mail-order companies that sell computer systems by telephone or online via the Web (Figure 2) often provide the lowest prices but extend less personal service. Some major mail-order companies, however, have started to provide next-business-day, onsite services. A credit card usually is required to buy from a mail-order company. Figure 3 lists some of the more popular mail-order companies and their Web site addresses.

Type of System	Company	URL	Telephone Number
PC	Computer Shopper	www.computershopper.com	
	Compaq	www.compaq.com	1-800-888-0220
	CompUSA	www.compusa.com	1-800-266-7872
	Dell	www.dell.com	1-800-678-1626
	Gateway	www.gateway.com	1-800-846-4208
	IBM	www.ibm.com	1-800-426-7235
	Micron	www.micron.com	1-800-964-2766
	Packard Bell	www.packardbell.com	1-888-474-6772
	Quantex	www.quantex.com	1-800-346-6685
Macintosh	Apple Computer	store.apple.com	1-800-795-1000
	Club Mac	www.clubmac.com	1-800-258-2622
	MacBase	www.macbase.com	1-800-951-1230
	Mac Wholesale	www.macwholesale.com	1-800-531-4622
	Mac Exchange	www.macx.com	1-888-650-4488

For an updated list of new computer mail-order companies and their Web sites, visit www.scsite.com/tdc/ch4/buyers.htm.

Figure 3 New computer mail-order companies

5. If you are buying a used computer system, stick with name brands. Although brand-name equipment can cost more, most brand-name systems have longer, more comprehensive warranties, are better supported, and have more authorized centers for repair services. As with new computer systems, you can purchase a used computer from local computer dealers, local large retail stores, or mail order via the telephone or the Web. Classified ads and used computer brokers offer additional outlets for purchasing used computer systems. Figure 4 lists several major used computer brokers and their Web site addresses.

6 . Use a worksheet to compare computer systems, services, and other considerations. You can use a separate sheet of paper to take notes on each vendor's computer system and then summarize the information on a spreadsheet, such as the one shown in Figure 5. Most companies advertise a price for a base system that includes components housed in the system unit (processor, RAM, sound card, video card), disk drives (floppy disk, hard disk, CD-ROM, and DVD-ROM), a keyboard, mouse, monitor, printer, speakers, and modem. Be aware, however, that some advertisements list prices for systems with only some of these components. Monitors, printers, and modems, for example, often are not included in a base system price. Depending on how you plan to use the system, you may want to invest in additional or more powerful components. When you are comparing the prices of computer systems, make sure you are comparing identical or similar configurations.

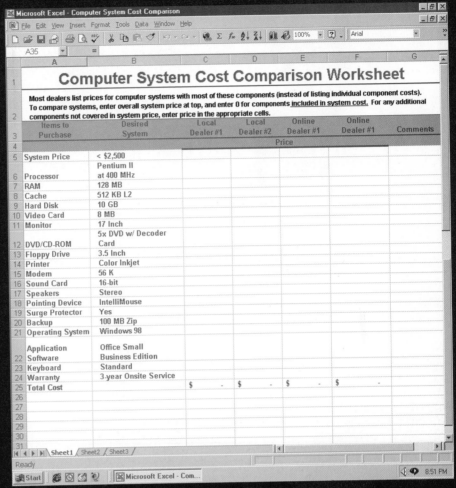

Items to Purchase	Desired System	Local Dealer #1	Local Dealer #2	Online Dealer #1	Online Dealer #1	Comments
		Price				
System Price	< $2,500					
Processor	Pentium II at 400 MHz					
RAM	128 MB					
Cache	512 KB L2					
Hard Disk	10 GB					
Video Card	8 MB					
Monitor	17 Inch					
DVD/CD-ROM	5x DVD w/ Decoder Card					
Floppy Drive	3.5 Inch					
Printer	Color Inkjet					
Modem	56 K					
Sound Card	16-bit					
Speakers	Stereo					
Pointing Device	IntelliMouse					
Surge Protector	Yes					
Backup	100 MB Zip					
Operating System	Windows 98					
Application Software	Office Small Business Edition					
Keyboard	Standard					
Warranty	3-year Onsite Service					
Total Cost		$ -	$ -	$ -	$ -	

Figure 5 A spreadsheet is an effective tool for summarizing and comparing the prices and components of different computer vendors.

7 . Be aware of hidden costs. Before purchasing, be sure to consider any additional costs associated with buying a computer, such as an additional telephone line, an uninterruptible power supply (UPS), computer furniture, floppy disks and paper, or computer training classes you may want to take. Depending on where you buy your computer, the seller may be willing to include some or all of these in the system purchase price.

8. Consider more than just price. The lowest cost system may not be the best buy. Consider such intangibles as the vendor's time in business, the vendor's regard for quality, and the vendor's reputation for support. If you need to upgrade your computer often, you may want to consider a leasing arrangement, in which you pay monthly lease fees but upgrade or add on to your computer system as your equipment needs change. If you are a replacement buyer, ask if the vendor will buy your old system; an increasing number of companies are taking trade-ins. No matter what type of buyer you are, insist on a 30-day, no questions-asked return policy on your computer system.

9. Select an Internet service provider (ISP) or online service. You can access the Internet in one of two ways: via an ISP or an online service. Both provide Internet access for a monthly fee that ranges from $5 to $20. Local ISPs offer Internet access through local telephone numbers to users in a limited geographic region. National ISPs provide access for users nationwide (including mobile users), through local and toll-free telephone numbers. Because of their size, national ISPs offer more services and generally have a larger technical support staff than local ISPs. Online services furnish Internet access as well as members-only features for users nationwide. Figure 6 lists several national ISPs and online services. Before you choose an Internet access provider, compare such features as the number of access hours, monthly fees, available services (e-mail, Web page hosting, chat), and reliability.

Figure 6 National ISPs and online services

Company	Service	URL	Telephone Number
America Online	ONLINE	www.americaonline.com	1-800-827-6364
AT&T Network Commerce Services	ISP	www.att.com/work-net	1-800-467-8467
CompuServe	ONLINE	www.compuserve.com/ gateway/default.asp	1-800-394-1481
Earthlink Network	ISP	www.earthlink.com	1-800-395-8425
GTE Internet	ISP	www.gte.net	1-888-GTE-SURF
IBM Internet Connection Services	ISP	www.ibm.net	1-800-455-5056
MCI	ISP	www.mciworldcom.com	1-800-888-0800
The Microsoft Network	ONLINE	www.msn.com	1-800-386-5550
Prodigy/Prodigy Classic	ISP/ONLINE	www.prodigy.com	1-800-PRODIGY
The UUNet Technologies	ISP	www.uu.net	1-800-4UUNET4

For information on local ISPs or to learn more on any ISPs and online services listed here, visit The List™ at thelist.internet.com. The List™ — the most comprehensive and accurate directory of ISPs and online services on the Web — compares dial-up services, access hours, and fees for over 5,000 access providers.

For an updated list of ISPs and online service providers, visit www.scsite.com/tdc/ch4/buyers.htm.

10. Buy a system compatible with the ones you use elsewhere. If you use a personal computer at school or in some other capacity, make sure the computer you buy is compatible. For example, if you use a PC at school, you may not want to purchase a Macintosh for home use. Having a computer compatible with the ones at home or school will allow you to transfer files and spend time at home on school-related projects.

11. Consider purchasing an onsite service agreement.

If you use your computer system for business or are unable to be without your computer, consider purchasing an onsite service agreement through a local dealer or third-party company. Most onsite service agreements state that a technician will come to your home, work, or school within 24 hours. If your system includes onsite service only for the first year, think about extending the service for two or three years when you buy the computer.

13. Avoid buying the smallest system available.

Computer technology changes rapidly, meaning a computer that seems powerful enough today may not serve your computing needs in a few years. In fact, studies show that many users regret they did not buy a more powerful system. Plan to buy a system that will last you for two to three years. You can help delay obsolescence by purchasing the fastest processor, most memory, and largest hard drive you can afford. If you must buy a smaller system, be sure you can upgrade it with additional memory and auxiliary devices as your system requirements grow.

12. Use a credit card to purchase your system.

Many credit cards now offer purchase protection and extended warranty benefits that cover you in case of loss of or damage to purchased goods. Paying by credit card also gives you time to install and use the system before you have to pay for it. Finally, if you are dissatisfied with the system and are unable to reach an agreement with the seller, paying by credit card gives you certain rights regarding withholding payment until the dispute is resolved. Check your credit card agreement for specific details.

Figure 7 Many credit cards offer purchase protection and extended warranty benefits.

4.52

How to Purchase a Laptop Computer

If you need computing capability when you travel, you may find a laptop computer to be an appropriate choice. The guidelines mentioned in the previous section also apply to the purchase of a laptop computer (Figure 8). The following are additional considerations unique to laptops.

1. Purchase a laptop with a sufficiently large active-matrix screen. Active-matrix screens display high-quality color that is viewable from all angles. Less expensive, passive matrix screens sometimes are hard to see in low-light conditions and cannot be viewed from an angle. Laptop computers typically come with a 12.1-inch, 13.3-inch, or 14.1-inch display. For most users, a 13.3-inch display is satisfactory. If you intend to use your laptop as a desktop replacement, however, you may opt for a 14.1-inch display. If you travel a lot and portability is essential, consider that most of the lightest machines are equipped with a 12.1-inch display. Regardless of size, the resolution of the display should be at least 800 x 600 pixels.

2. Experiment with different pointing devices and keyboards. Laptop computer keyboards are far less standardized than those for desktop systems. Some laptops, for example, have wide wrist rests, while others have none. Laptops also use a range of pointing devices, including pointing sticks, touchpads, and trackballs. Before you purchase a laptop, try various types of keyboard and pointing devices to determine which is easiest for you to use. Regardless of the pointing device you select, you also may want to purchase a regular mouse unit to use when you are working at a desk or other large surface.

Figure 8 Laptop computer

3. Make sure the laptop you purchase has a CD-ROM or DVD-ROM drive. Loading software, especially large software suites, is much faster if done from a CD-ROM or DVD-ROM. Today, most laptops come with either an internal or external CD-ROM drive; others have an internal and external unit that allows you to interchange the 3.5-inch floppy drive and the CD-ROM drive. An advantage of a separate CD-ROM drive is that you can leave it behind to save weight. Some users prefer a DVD-ROM drive to a CD-ROM drive. Although DVD-ROM drives are more expensive, they allow you to read CD-ROMs and play movies using your laptop.

4. If you plan to use your laptop both on the road and at home or at school, consider a docking station. A docking station usually includes a floppy disk drive, a CD-ROM or DVD-ROM drive, and a connector for a full-sized monitor. When you work both at home and at school, a docking station is an attractive alternative to buying a full-sized system. A docking station essentially turns your laptop into a desktop, while eliminating the need to transfer files from one computer to another.

5. **If necessary, upgrade memory and disk storage at the time of purchase.** As with a desktop computer system, upgrading your laptop's memory and disk storage usually is less expensive at the time of initial purchase. Some disk storage systems are custom designed for laptop manufacturers, meaning an upgrade might not be available two or three years after you purchase your laptop.

6. **If you are going to use your laptop on an airplane, purchase a second battery.** Two batteries should provide enough power to last through most airplane flights. If you anticipate running your laptop on batteries frequently, choose a system that uses **lithium-ion batteries** (they last longer than nickel cadmium or nickel hydride batteries).

7. **Purchase a well-padded and well-designed carrying case.** An amply padded carrying case will protect your laptop from the bumps it will receive while traveling. A well-designed carrying case will have room for accessories such as spare floppy disks; an external floppy disk, CD-ROM, or DVD-ROM drive; a user manual; pens; and paperwork (Figure 9).

8. **If you travel overseas, obtain a set of electrical and telephone adapters.** Different countries use different outlets for electrical and telephone connections. Several manufacturers sell sets of adapters that will work in most countries (Figure 10).

Figure 10
Set of electrical and telephone adapters

9. **If you plan to connect your laptop to a video projector, make sure the laptop is compatible with the video projector.** Some laptops will not work with certain video projectors; others will not allow you to display an image on the laptop and projection device at the same time (Figure 11). Either of these factors can affect your presentation negatively.

Figure 11 Video projector

Figure 9 Well-designed carrying case

4.54 How to Install a Personal Computer

1. Read the installation manuals before you start to install your equipment. Many manufacturers include separate installation instructions with their equipment that contain important information. You can save a great deal of time and frustration if you make an effort to read the manuals.

2. Do some research. To locate additional instructions on installing your computer, review the computer magazines or Web sites listed in Figure 12 to search for articles on installing a computer system.

WEB SITE	URL
Getting Started/Installation	
Once You've Bought It	www.newsday.com/plugin/ c101main.htm
HelpTalk Online	www.helptalk.com
Ergonomics	
Ergonomic Computing	cobweb.creighton.edu/training/ergo.htm
Healthy Choices for	
Computer Users	www-ehs.ucsd.edu/vdttoc.htm
Video Display Health Guidelines	www.uhs.berkeley.edu/facstaff/ergonomics/ ergguide.html

For an updated list of reference materials, visit www.scsite.com/tdc/ch4/buyers.htm.

Figure 12 Web references on setting up and using your computer

3. Set up your computer in a well-designed work area, with adequate workspace around the computer. Ergonomics is an applied science devoted to making the equipment and its surrounding work area safer and more efficient. Ergonomic studies have shown that using the correct type and configuration of chair, keyboard, monitor, and work surface will help you work comfortably and efficiently, and help protect your health. For your computer workspace, experts recommend an area of at least two feet by four feet. Figure 13 illustrates additional guidelines for setting up your work area.

4. Install bookshelves. Bookshelves above and/or to the side of your computer area are useful for keeping manuals and other reference materials handy.

5. Have a telephone outlet and telephone near your workspace so you can connect your modem and/or place calls while using your computer. To plug in your modem to dial up and access the World Wide Web, you will need a telephone outlet close to your computer. Having a telephone nearby also helps if you need to place business or technical support calls while you are working on your computer. Often, if you call a vendor about a hardware or software problem, the support person can talk you through a correction while you are on the telephone. To avoid data loss, however, do not place floppy disks on the telephone or near any other electrical or electronic equipment.

Figure 13 A well-designed work area should be flexible to allow adjustments to the height and build of different individuals. Good lighting and air quality also are important considerations.

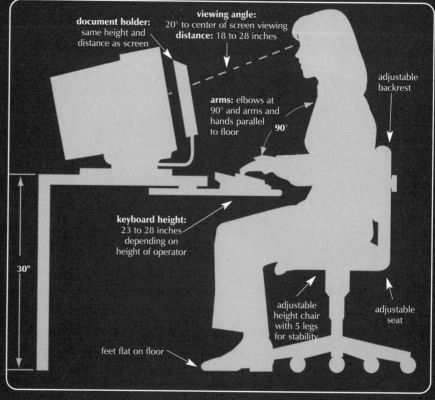

document holder: same height and distance as screen

viewing angle: 20° to center of screen viewing distance: 18 to 28 inches

arms: elbows at 90° and arms and hands parallel to floor

90°

adjustable backrest

keyboard height: 23 to 28 inches depending on height of operator

30"

adjustable seat

adjustable height chair with 5 legs for stability

feet flat on floor

6. While working at your computer, be aware of health issues. Working safely at your computer requires that you consider several health issues. To minimize neck and eye discomfort, for instance, obtain a document holder that keeps documents at the same height and distance as your computer screen. To provide adequate lighting that reduces eye strain, use non-glare light bulbs that illuminate your entire work area. Figure 14 lists additional computer user health guidelines.

Computer User Health Guidelines

1. Work in a well-designed work area. See Figure 13 on the previous page.

2. Alternate work activities to prevent physical and mental fatigue. If possible, change the order of your work to provide some variety.

3. Take frequent breaks. Every fifteen minutes, look away from the screen to give your eyes a break. At least once per hour, get out of your chair and move around. Every two hours, take at least a fifteen-minute break.

4. Incorporate hand, arm, and body stretching exercises into your breaks. At lunch, try to get outside and walk.

5. Make sure your computer monitor is designed to minimize electromagnetic radiation (EMR). If it is an older model, consider adding EMR reducing accessories.

6. Try to eliminate or minimize surrounding noise. Noisy environments contribute to stress and tension.

7. If you frequently use the telephone and the computer at the same time, consider using a telephone headset. Cradling the telephone between your head and shoulder can cause muscle strain.

8. Be aware of symptoms of repetitive strain injuries: soreness, pain, numbness, or weakness in neck, shoulders, arms, wrists, and hands. Do not ignore early signs; seek medical advice.

Figure 14 Following these health guidelines will help computer users maintain their health.

7. Obtain a computer tool set. Computer tool sets include any screwdrivers and other tools you might need to work on your computer. Computer dealers, office supply stores, and mail-order companies sell these tool sets. To keep all the tools together, get a tool set that comes in a zippered carrying case.

8. Save all the paperwork that comes with your system. Keep the documents that come with your system in an accessible place, along with the paperwork from your other computer-related purchases. To keep different-sized documents together, consider putting them in a manila file folder, large envelope, or sealable plastic bag.

9. Record the serial numbers of all your equipment and software. Write the serial numbers of your equipment and software on the outside of the manuals packaged with these items. As you will note in Figure 16 on page 4.57, you also should create a single, comprehensive list that contains the serial numbers of all your equipment and software.

10. Complete and send in your equipment and software registration cards. When you register your equipment and software, the vendor usually enters you in its user database. Being a registered user not only can save you time when you call with a support question, it also makes you eligible for special pricing on software upgrades.

11. Keep the shipping containers and packing materials for all your equipment. Shipping containers and packing materials will come in handy if you have to return your equipment for servicing or must move it to another location.

12. Identify device connectors. At the back of your system, you will find a number of connectors for your printer, monitor, mouse, telephone line, and so forth (Figure 15). If the manufacturer has not identified them for you, use a marking pen to write the purpose of each connector on the back of the computer case.

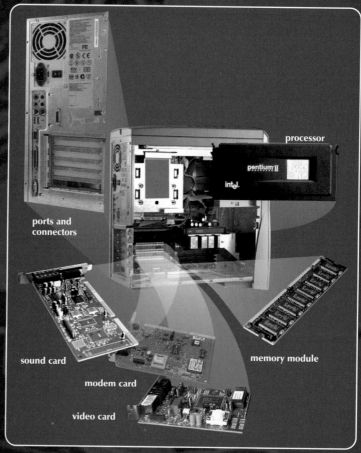

Figure 15 Inside the system unit and the connectors at the back

13. Install your system in an area where you can maintain the temperature and humidity. You should keep the system in an area with a constant temperature between 60°F and 80°F. High temperatures and humidity can damage electronic components. Be careful when using space heaters, for example, as the hot, dry air they generate can cause disk problems.

14. Keep your computer area clean. Avoid eating and drinking around your computer. Also, avoid smoking. Cigarette smoke can cause damage to the floppy disk drives and floppy disk surfaces

15. Check your home or renter's insurance policy. Some renter's insurance policies have limits on the amount of computer equipment they cover. Other policies do not cover computer equipment at all if it is used for business. In this instance, you may want to obtain a separate insurance policy.

How to Maintain Your Personal Computer

1. **Start a notebook that includes information on your system.** Keep a notebook that provides a single source of information about your entire system, both hardware and software. Each time you make a change to your system, such as adding or removing hardware or software or altering system parameters, record the change in your notebook. Include the following items in your notebook.

- Vendor support numbers from your user manuals
- Serial numbers of all equipment and software
- User IDs, passwords, and nicknames for your ISP or online service, network access, Web sites, and so on
- Vendor and date of purchase for all software and equipment
- Trouble log that provides a chronological history of equipment or software problems
- Notes on any discussions with vendor support personnel

Figure 16 provides a suggested outline for the contents of your notebook.

PERSONAL COMPUTER OWNER'S NOTEBOOK OUTLINE

1. Vendors
Vendor
City/State
Product
Telephone #
URL

2. Internet and online services information
Service provider name
Logon telephone number
Alternate logon
  telephone number
Technical support
  telephone number
User ID
Password

3. Web site information
Web site name
URL
User ID
Password
Nickname

4. Serial numbers
Product
Manufacturer
Serial #

5. Purchase history
Date
Product
Manufacturer
Vendor
Cost

6. Software log
Date installed/uninstalled

7. Trouble log
Date
Time
Problem
Resolution

8. Support calls
Date
Time
Company
Contact
Problem
Comments

9. Vendor paperwork

2. **Before you work inside your computer, turn off the power and disconnect the equipment from the power source.** Working inside your computer with the power on can affect both you and the computer adversely. Thus, you should turn off the power and disconnect the equipment from the power source before you open a computer to work inside. In addition, before you touch anything inside the computer, you should touch an unpainted metal surface such as the power supply. Doing so will help discharge any static electricity that could damage internal components.

Figure 16 To keep important information about your computer on hand and organized, use an outline such as this sample outline.

4.58

How to Maintain Your Personal Computer

3. Keep the area surrounding your computer dirt and dust free. Reducing the dirt and dust around your computer will reduce the need to clean the inside of your system. If dust builds up inside the computer, remove it carefully with compressed air and a small vacuum. Do not touch the components with the vacuum.

4. Back up important files and data. Use the operating system or utility program to create an emergency or rescue disk to help you restart your computer if it crashes. You also regularly should copy important data files to disks, tape, or another computer.

5. Protect your system from computer viruses. A computer virus is a potentially damaging computer program designed to infect other software or files by attaching itself to the software or files with which it comes in contact. Virus programs are dangerous because often they destroy or corrupt data stored on the infected computer. You can protect your computer from viruses by installing an antivirus program.

6. Keep your system tuned. Most operating systems include several system tools that provide basic system maintenance functions. One important system tool is the disk defragmenter. Defragmenting your hard disk reorganizes files so they are in contiguous (adjacent) clusters, making disk operations faster. Some programs allow you to schedule system maintenance tasks for times when you are not using your computer. If necessary, leave your computer on at night so the system can run the required maintenance programs. If your operating system does not provide the system tools, you can purchase a stand-alone utility program to perform basic system maintenance functions.

7. Learn to use system diagnostic tools. Diagnostic tools help you identify and resolve system problems, thereby helping to reduce your need for technical assistance. Diagnostic tools help you test system components, monitor system resources such as memory and processing power, undo changes made to system files, and more. As with basic maintenance tools, most operating systems include system diagnostic tools; you also can purchase or download many stand-alone diagnostic tools.

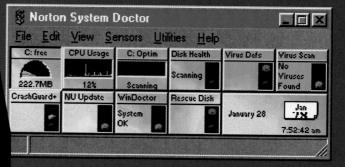

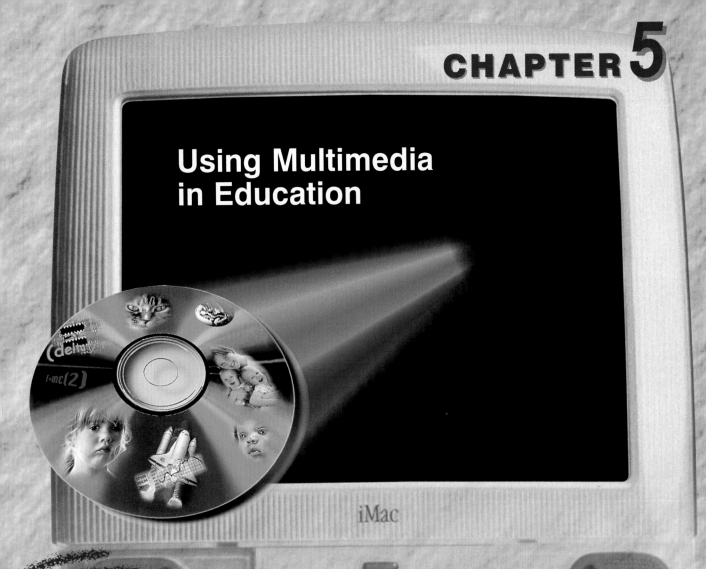

Using Multimedia in Education

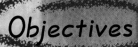

Objectives

After completing this chapter, you will be able to:

■ Define multimedia

■ Describe types of media used in multimedia applications

■ Explain the different uses of multimedia applications

■ Discuss multimedia applications on the Web

■ Identify various K-12 software applications

■ Describe different components of multimedia computers

■ Specify what is meant by an interactive multimedia application

■ Examine the uses of multimedia authoring software programs

■ Explain why multimedia applications are important for education

TODAY, MULTIMEDIA PLAYS AN INCREASINGLY IMPORTANT ROLE IN EDUCATION, BUSINESS, AND ENTERTAINMENT. MULTIMEDIA INVOLVES THE USE OF COMPUTERS TO PRESENT TEXT, GRAPHICS, VIDEO, ANIMATION, AND SOUND IN AN INTEGRATED WAY. Unlike television, which combines and presents these media elements in a set order, most multimedia applications are interactive. An interactive multimedia application allows you to choose the material you want to view, define the order in which it is presented, and receive feedback on your actions. **Interactivity**, which is one of the essential features of multimedia applications, also allows for individualized instruction and exploration, both of which enrich the educational experience.

This chapter introduces you to many basic multimedia concepts, discusses educational applications of multimedia, and describes various media components used in multimedia applications. First, you will learn about the different types and uses of multimedia applications. Next, the chapter will cover the various hardware components needed to create and view multimedia applications. Finally, you will learn how software developers, teachers, and students create multimedia applications using various multimedia authoring software packages.

WebInfo

■ For more information on multimedia applications, visit the Teachers Discovering Computers Chapter 5 WebInfo page (www.scsite.com/tdc/ch5/webinfo.htm) and click Multimedia Applications.

What Is Multimedia?

Multimedia is the combination of the following elements: text, color, graphics, animation, audio, and video. **Multimedia software** refers to any computer-based presentation or application software that uses multimedia elements. **Interactive multimedia** describes a multimedia application that accepts input from the user by means of a keyboard, voice, or a pointing device such as a mouse; and performs an action in response. Most interactive multimedia applications allow you to move through materials at your own pace. As you progress through the application or complete certain tasks, you receive feedback in the form of a sound, points, or other response.

The multimedia application shown in **Figure 5-1**, for example, allows students to interact with and learn about the human body. The ability of users to interact with a multimedia application is perhaps its most unique and important feature — a feature that has the potential to change dramatically the way K-12 students learn. Interactive multimedia allows students to define their own learning paths, investigate topics in depth, and get immediate feedback from drill-and-practice or exploration activities. Multimedia applications also tend to engage and challenge students, thus encouraging them to think creatively and independently.

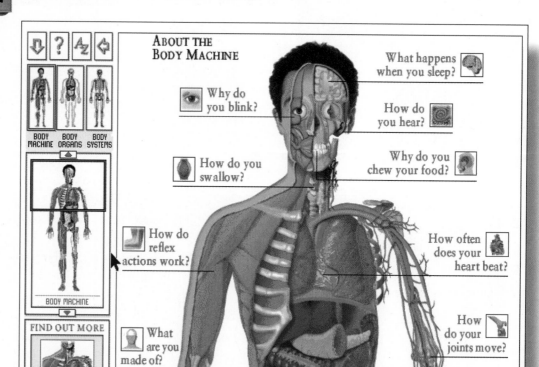

Figure 5-1 The Ultimate Human Body by DK Multimedia is a popular educational program that allows students to interact with and learn about the human body. Clicking the heart, for example, allows students to see and hear a human heart in action.

With many multimedia applications, you navigate through the content by clicking links with a pointing device such as a mouse. Recall from Chapter 2 that Web pages use links to allow users to navigate quickly from one document to another. In a multimedia application, a **link** serves a similar function, allowing users to access information quickly and navigate from one topic to another in a nonlinear fashion. For example, while reading about Marco Polo, you might click the keyword, Travels, to display a map of his journeys or listen to a reading from his travel journals.

In a multimedia application, any clickable object — text, graphics, animation, and even videos — can function as a link. **Figure 5-2** shows the main menu of a multimedia application that uses text, graphics, and animations as links to additional sources of information. The following sections provide an introduction to the different media elements contained in multimedia applications.

barometer
image link

Figure 5-2 The left screen shows the main menu for a popular nature encyclopedia. The menu provides text, buttons, and graphics that allow students or teachers quickly to choose a particular topic. Every object on the main menu is a link to discovery learning. The right screen shows what happens when a user clicks the barometer. An enlarged barometer now provides numerous additional links to other multimedia sources of information.

CHAPTER 5

Text

Text consists of characters that are used to create words, sentences, and paragraphs and is a fundamental element used in all multimedia applications. Multimedia applications not only use ordinary text to convey basic information, they also use a variety of textual effects to emphasize and clarify information. A different font size, color, or style, for example, often is used to emphasize certain words or phrases. Many multimedia applications use text-based menus that allow you to select and display information on a certain topic **[Figure 5-3]**.

Graphics

Recall from Chapter 4 that a **graphic** is a digital representation of nontext information such as a drawing, chart, or photograph. A graphic, also called a picture or image, contains no movement or animation.

In multimedia applications, graphics serve several functions. For one, graphics can illustrate certain concepts more vividly than text. A picture of Saturn, for example, clearly depicts the planet's rings in a way that text cannot. Graphics also play an important role in the learning process: many individuals — who are **visual learners** — learn concepts faster or retain a higher percentage of material if they *see* the information presented graphically. Graphics also serve as navigational elements in many software packages. Multimedia applications, for one, often use graphics as buttons that link to more information. The graphical user interfaces used on Macintosh computers and PCs and graphical Web browsers also demonstrate the importance of graphics when using computers.

If you are creating a multimedia application, you can obtain graphics in several ways. You can purchase a **clip art collection**, which is a set of previously created digital graphics

WebInfo

For information on free clip art, visit the Teachers Discovering Computers Chapter 5 WebInfo page (www.scsite.com/tdc/ch5/webinfo.htm) and click Clip Art.

A TEACHER'S GUIDE TO THE HOLOCAUST
Timeline • People • Arts • Activities • Resources

Teacher Resources

 Articles. Abstracts from the Educational Resources Information Center (ERIC) database.

 Books. A bibliography of Holocaust works for students and teachers.

 Documents. Primary source materials related to the Holocaust.

 Films. An annotated list of films and videos about the Holocaust.

 Images. A selection of Holocaust photographs, drawings, and paintings.

 Museums. Descriptions of Holocaust museums and resource centers in Florida and elsewhere.

 Plays. An annotated list of educational plays with a Holocaust theme.

 Professional Development. Announcements of upcoming conferences and institutes for Holocaust educators.

Figure 5-3 The main menu from A TEACHER'S GUIDE TO THE HOLOCAUST CD-ROM provides text and buttons that allow teachers quickly to access the listed topic.

that you can insert into a document. Many clip art collections are grouped by themes, such as Academic, Maps, and People **[Figure 5-4]**. You also can create your own graphics using a paint or drawing program. Many presentation graphics and multimedia authoring software packages, for example, include drawing tools for creating graphics as shown in **Figure 5-5** on the next page. As you will learn later in the chapter, you can obtain photographs for use in a multimedia application by using a color scanner to digitize photos; taking photographs with a digital camera; or using a collection of photographs on a CD-ROM. Some stock photograph agencies even let you purchase and download photographs from the Web.

Figure 5-4 Most computer stores carry several different clip art collections to assist users in creating multimedia projects.

CHAPTER 5

Figure 5-5 Microsoft PowerPoint provides an AutoShapes palette on the Drawing toolbar that allows you to draw a 24-point star or other shapes to include in a multimedia presentation. This type of graphic image is a resizable, movable object that can be colored in a variety of different ways or combined with other clip art, graphics, or text.

Animation

Displaying a series of still graphics creates an **animation**, which is a graphic that has the illusion of motion. Animations range in scope from a basic graphic with a simple motion (for example, a blinking icon) to a detailed image with complex movements (such as a simulation of how an avalanche starts). As with graphics, animations can convey information more vividly than text alone. An animation showing the up-and-down movement of pistons and engine valves, for example, provides a better illustration of the workings of an internal combustion engine than a written explanation as shown in **Figures 5-6a** through **5-6c**.

The use of animation has improved the quality of educational software dramatically and made Web sites more interesting for users. You can create your own detailed and highly dynamic animations using a graphics animation software package. In addition, you can obtain previously created animations from a CD-ROM or on the Web.

[5-6b] Piston down motion

[5-6c] Piston up motion

[5-6a] Piston

Figure 5-6 Microsoft's Encarta Encyclopedia contains numerous media animations, including a demonstration of how an internal-combustion engine works. Figure 5-6a is a snapshot of the initial screen, Figure 5-6b shows that the piston has moved down during the intake stroke, and Figure 5-6c shows the piston moving up during the compression stroke.

Audio

Audio is any digitized music, speech, or other sounds that are stored and produced by the computer. As with animation, audio allows developers to provide information in a manner not otherwise conveyed in the computer environment. The vibration of a human heartbeat or the melodies of a symphony, for example, are concepts difficult to convey without the use of sound. Using audio in a multimedia application to supplement text and graphics enhances understanding. An actor's narration added to the text of a Shakespearean play, for example, reinforces a student's grasp of the passage [**Figure 5-7**].

You can obtain audio files for use in multimedia applications in several different ways. One method is to capture sounds digitally using a microphone, tape or audio CD player, or any other audio input device that is plugged into a port on a sound card. Recall from Chapter 4 that you also can play and store music from a synthesizer, keyboard, or other musical device that is connected to a sound card using a MIDI port.

In addition to being a port, **Musical Instrument Digital Interface** (**MIDI**) is the electronic music industry's standard that defines how digital musical devices electronically represent sounds. Software programs that conform to the MIDI standard allow you to compose and edit music and other sounds. For example, you can change the speed, add notes, or rearrange the score to produce an entirely new sound. As with graphics and animations, you also can purchase audio clips on a CD-ROM or download them from the Web.

Video

Video consists of photographic images that are played back at speeds of 15 to 30 frames per second and provide the appearance of full motion in real-time. The integration of video into classroom curricula has

WebInfo

For an overview of digital video software, visit the Teachers Discovering Computers Chapter 5 WebInfo page

(www.scsite.com/tdc/ch5/webinfo.htm)

and click Digital Video.

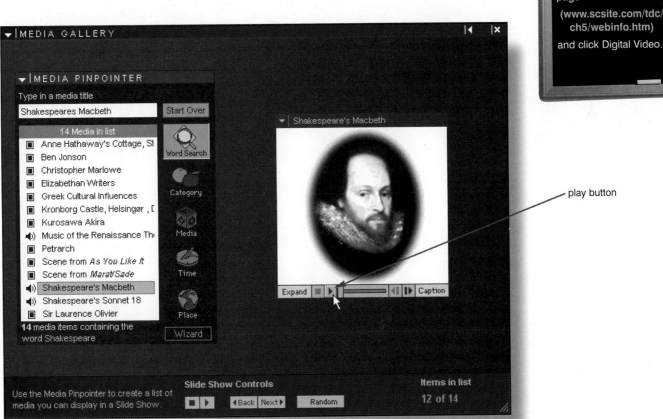

play button

Figure 5-7 Interactive encyclopedias offer students many opportunities to hear the words and passages of great historical events and literary works, such as Shakespeare's Macbeth. By clicking the play button, students hear passages from Macbeth.

significantly impacted the way that students learn core subjects. Videos can reinforce lectures and readings, provide a common base of knowledge, and show things that students would not otherwise experience. For example, after reading the text of one of Martin Luther King's speeches, students can watch a video of King delivering that same speech to an enthusiastic crowd.

To use video in a multimedia application, you first must capture, digitize, and edit the video segment using special video production hardware and software. As described in Chapter 4, video often is captured digitally with a video input device such as a video camera or VCR.

Due to the size of video files, incorporating video into a multimedia application often is a challenge. Video files require tremendous amounts of storage space: a three-minute segment, or **clip**, of high-quality video can take an entire gigabyte of storage. To decrease the size of the files, video often is compressed.

Video compression works by taking advantage of the fact that only a small portion of the image changes from frame to frame. A video compression program thus might store the first reference frame and then, assuming that the following frames will be almost identical to it, store only the changes from one frame to the next **[Figure 5-8]**. Prior to viewing, video compression software decompresses the video segment. The **Moving Pictures Experts Group** has defined a popular standard for video compression and decompression, called **MPEG** (pronounced em-peg). These standardized compression methods reduce the size of video files up to 95 percent, while retaining near-television quality.

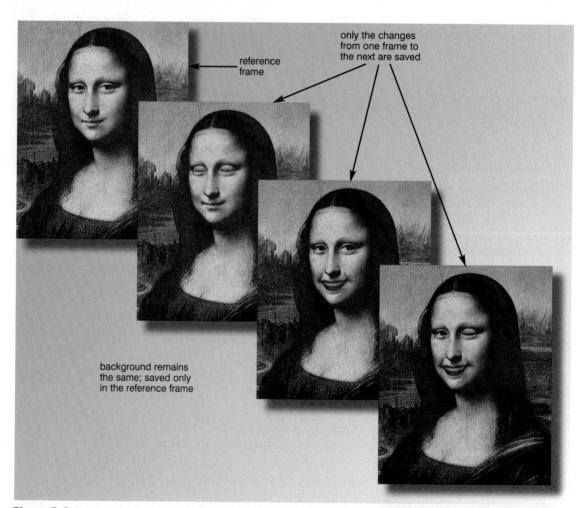

reference frame

only the changes from one frame to the next are saved

background remains the same; saved only in the reference frame

Figure 5-8 In many video clips, only a small portion of the image changes from frame to frame. In a clip of a person talking, for example, the facial expressions will change, but the background remains the same. A video compression program first will store a reference frame and then store only the changes from one frame to the next.

Video compression and other improvements in video technology have allowed video to play a more important role in multimedia applications. Technologies such as streaming video also have made video a viable part of multimedia on the Web.

Multimedia Applications

A **multimedia application** involves the use of multimedia technology for education, business, and entertainment. Businesses use multimedia, for example, in interactive advertisements and for job- and skill-training applications. Teachers use multimedia applications to deliver classroom presentations that enhance student learning. Students, in turn, use multimedia applications to learn by reading, seeing, hearing, and interacting with the subject content. Multimedia also is used in a huge variety of computer games and other types of entertainment.

Another important application of interactive multimedia is to create **simulations**, which are computer-based models of real-life situations. Multimedia simulations often replace costly and sometimes hazardous demonstrations and training in areas such as chemistry, biology, medicine, and aviation.

The following sections provide a more detailed look at different types of well-known multimedia applications, including computer-based training, electronic books and references, how-to guides, and magazines. These sections also address the use of multimedia in entertainment; virtual reality; information kiosks; and the importance of multimedia on the World Wide Web. After learning about the various types of well-known multimedia applications, you will learn about specific K-12 educational software applications used to improve teaching and learning by virtually all schools.

Computer-Based Training (CBT)

Computer-based training (CBT) is a tool in which individuals learn by using and completing exercises using instructional software on computers. Computer-based training is popular in business and industry to teach new

skills or enhance the existing skills of employees. Athletes, for example, use multimedia computer-based training programs to practice baseball, football, soccer, tennis, and golf skills, while airlines use multimedia CBT simulations to train employees **[Figure 5-9]**. Interactive CBT software called **courseware** usually is available on CD-ROM, DVD-ROM, or the Web.

One important advantage of computer-based training is that it allows for flexible, on-the-spot training. Businesses and schools, for

Figure 5-9 Boeing uses flight CBT to train new pilots and maintenance personnel. Clicking the right-pointing arrow displays the next screen.

Figure 5-10 Teachers can learn innovative uses of technology, teaching strategies, and various subject-related software packages in a school district's professional development center.

example, can set up corporate training or teacher professional development labs so employees can update their skills without leaving the workplace **[Figure 5-10]**. Installing CBT software on an employee's computer or on the company network provides even more flexibility — allowing employees to update their job skills right at their desks, at home, or while traveling.

Computer-based training provides a unique learning experience because learners receive instant feedback — in the form of positive response for correct answers or actions, additional information on incorrect answers, and immediate scoring and results. Testing and self-diagnostic features allow instructors to verify that an individual has mastered curriculum objectives and identify students who need additional instruction or practice. Computer-based training is especially effective for teaching software skills if the CBT is integrated with the software application because it allows students to practice using the software as they learn.

Electronic Books and References

Electronic books are digital texts that use links to give the user access to information. Electronic books have many of the elements of a regular book, including pages of text and graphics. You generally turn the pages of an electronic book by clicking icons **[Figure 5-11]**. A table of contents, glossary,

WebInfo

To learn more about electronic books, visit the Teachers Discovering Computers Chapter 5 WebInfo page

(www.scsite.com/tdc/ch5/webinfo.htm)

and click Electronic Books.

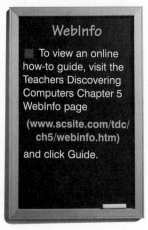

WebInfo

To view an online how-to guide, visit the Teachers Discovering Computers Chapter 5 WebInfo page

(www.scsite.com/tdc/ch5/webinfo.htm)

and click Guide.

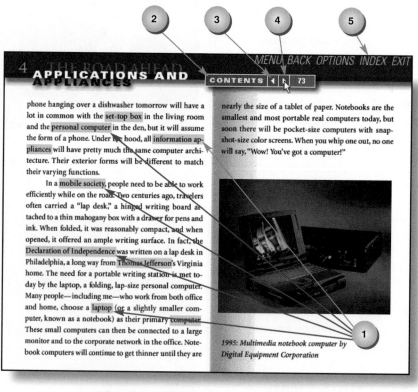

1. hyperlinks to additional information (hotwords)
2. to table of contents
3. to previous page
4. to next page
5. to index

Figure 5-11 The complete text of *The Road Ahead* by Bill Gates is contained on a CD-ROM. In addition to the text, the CD-ROM includes numerous hyperlinks, audio and visual clips showing future technologies, and more. This figure shows a page from the CD-ROM version of the book.

and index also are available at the click of a button. To display a definition or a graphic, play a sound or a video sequence, or connect to a Web site, you simply click a link (often a bold or underlined word).

One popular type of electronic book is an electronic reference, such as a multimedia encyclopedia on CD-ROM. An **electronic reference** is a digital version of a reference text, which uses text, graphics, sound, animation, and video to explain a topic or provide additional information. The multimedia encyclopedia, Microsoft Encarta, for example, includes the complete text of a multivolume encyclopedia. In addition to text-based information, Microsoft Encarta includes thousands of photos, animations, audiandand detailed illustrations. This array of multimedia information is accessible via menus and links.

Health and medicine are two areas in which electronic references play an important role. Instead of using volumes of books, health professionals and students rely on electronic references for articles, photographs, illustrations, and animations that cover hundreds of health and first aid topics. Physical education, science, and medical students, for example, use the reference CD-ROM, A.D.A.M. (Animated Dissection of Anatomy for Medicine), to learn about the human body. Practicing physicians also use the CD-ROM to communicate information to their patients **[Figure 5-12]**.

How-To Guides

Today, many interactive multimedia applications are available to help individuals in their daily lives. These multimedia applications fall into the broad category of how-to guides. **How-to guides** are multimedia applications that include step-by-step instructions and interactive demonstrations to teach you practical new skills **[Figure 5-13]**. Similarly to the computer-based training applications used by schools and businesses, how-to guides allow you to acquire new skills, become more productive, and try out your skills in a risk-free environment. The skills you learn with a how-to guide, however, usually apply to enhancing talents outside of your job.

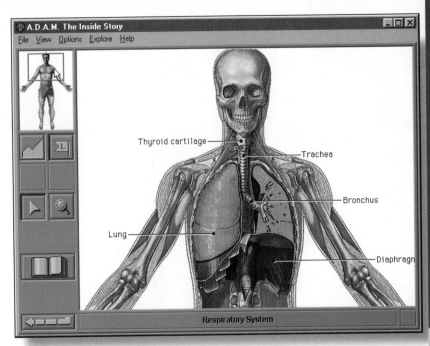

Figure 5-12 Interactive CD-ROMs such as A.D.A.M. can be used to study the respiratory system and other systems of the body.

Figure 5-13 An example of a do-it-yourself guide available on CD-ROM from *Reader's Digest*.

Figure 5-14 A 3-D view of a house with plants, trees, patio, and garden area.

WebInfo

To access an online educational magazine, visit the Teachers Discovering Computers Chapter 5 WebInfo page

(www.scsite.com/tdc/ ch5/webinfo.htm)

and click Educational Magazine.

Figure 5-15 The contents screen for this issue of the *NautilusCD* multimedia magazine shows the different departments, such as Entertainment and Education.

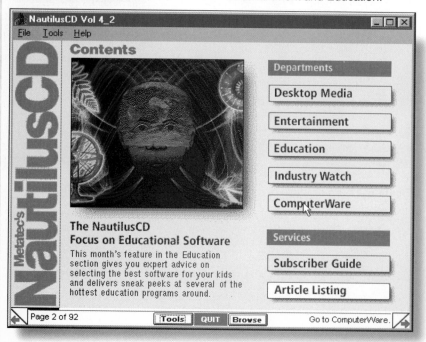

How-to guides can help you buy a home or a car; design a garden; plan a vacation; repair your home, car, or computer; and more. Landscaping how-to guides, for example, allow you to design a landscape; place trees, shrubs, and flowers; and then add features such as pathways, fences, and retaining walls to complete the design **[Figure 5-14]**. Many gardening how-to guides allow you to explore a database of plants with color photographs and the growth attributes of each one. Multimedia how-to guides are available on CD-ROM, DVD-ROM, and the Web.

Multimedia and Electronic Magazines (E-Zines)

A **multimedia magazine**, also called an **electronic magazine** or **e-zine,** is a digital version of a magazine, which is distributed on CD-ROM or via the World Wide Web. The term, e-zine, refers specifically to Web-based digital magazines.

Multimedia magazines usually include the sections and articles found in a print-based magazine, such as departments, editorials, and more. Unlike printed publications, however, electronic magazines use many types of media to convey information. Audio and video clips can be included to showcase recent album releases or movies; animations can depict weather patterns or election results. The magazine, *NautilusCD*, for instance, has the appearance of a printed publication but presents the content of articles with multimedia elements such as sound, graphics, videos, and animations **[Figure 5-15]**.

Some multimedia magazines exist only in their digital format, whereas others are simply electronic versions of existing print magazines. Today, many print-based journals and magazines have companion Web sites that provide some or all of the magazine's printed content. Up-to-the-minute news, interactive polls, and multimedia elements such as audio and video clips enhance the content found in the printed magazine **[Figure 5-16]**.

Entertainment and Edutainment

As described, multimedia combines the media elements of television *and* interactivity — thus making it ideal for

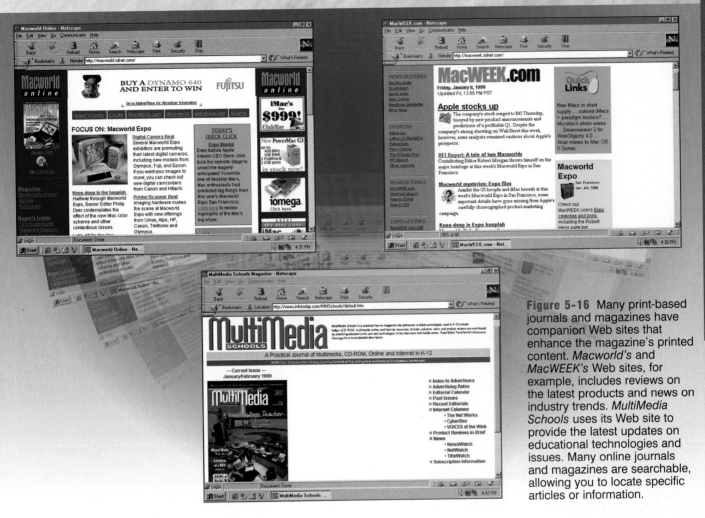

Figure 5-16 Many print-based journals and magazines have companion Web sites that enhance the magazine's printed content. *Macworld's* and *MacWEEK's* Web sites, for example, includes reviews on the latest products and news on industry trends. *MultiMedia Schools* uses its Web site to provide the latest updates on educational technologies and issues. Many online journals and magazines are searchable, allowing you to locate specific articles or information.

entertainment. Multimedia **computer games**, for example, use a combination of graphics, sound, and video to create a realistic and entertaining game situation. Often, the game simulates a real or fictitious world, in which you play the role of a character and have direct control of what happens in the game.

The music industry also sells interactive multimedia applications on CD-ROM and DVD-ROM. Some interactive music CD-ROMs, for example, let you play musical instruments along with your favorite musician, read about the musician's life and interests, and even create your own version of popular songs. Like interactive games, these applications give you a character role and put you in control of the application. Many multimedia applications are used for **edutainment**, which is an experience meant to be both educational and entertaining [Figure 5-17].

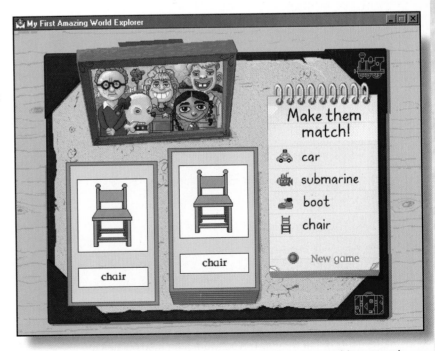

Figure 5-17 Interactive multimedia computer games use graphics, sound, and video to create an entertaining game experience for all age groups.

Figure 5-18 Virtual Glider by Intel takes the rider on a hang-gliding trip through the Grand Canyon

Figure 5-19 A virtual reality body suit allows the VR software to interpret the body movements of the wearer. The software then manipulates the image in the virtual environment, which is displayed in the headset.

Virtual Reality

Virtual reality (VR) is the use of a computer to create an artificial environment that appears and feels like a real environment and allows you to explore space and manipulate the setting **[Figure 5-18]**. In its simplest form, a virtual reality application displays a view that appears to be a three-dimensional view of a place or object, such as a landscape, a building, a molecule, or a red blood cell, which users can explore. Architects are using this type of software to show clients how a proposed construction or remodeling will appear.

Advanced forms of VR software require you to wear specialized headgear, body suits, and gloves to enhance the experience of the artificial environment **[Figure 5-19]**. The headgear displays the artificial environment in front of your eyes. The body suit and gloves sense your motion and direction, allowing you to move through and pick up and hold items displayed in the virtual environment. Experts predict that body suits eventually will provide tactile feedback so you can experience the touch and feel of the virtual world.

Your first encounter with VR is likely to be a Web-based virtual reality game. In such games, as you walk around the game's electronic landscape, the site notes your movements and changes your view of the landscape accordingly. Other VR Web sites allow you to take VR tours of a city, view hotel accommodations, or interact with local attractions. The United States Senate Web site provides a virtual tour of the U.S. Capitol building. Students can take a guided tour or venture out on their own to tour the Capitol **[Figure 5-20]**.

Companies are using VR for more practical, commercial applications as well. Office furniture companies have created virtual showrooms in which customers wander among and inspect available products. Automobile and airplane manufacturers are using virtual prototypes to test new models and shorten product design time. Telecommunications firms and others are using computer-based VR applications for employee training. As computing power and the use of the Web increase, practical applications of VR continue to emerge for education, business, and entertainment.

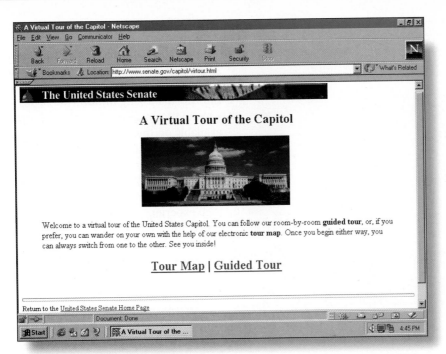

Figure 5-20 The Web allows students to take virtual tours of many historical places all over the world. At this government Web site, students can take a guided tour of the United States Capitol or they may venture on their own to explore the Capitol.

Information Kiosks

An **information kiosk** is a computerized information or reference center that allows you to select various options to browse through or find specific information. A typical information kiosk is a self-service structure equipped with computer hardware and software. Kiosks often use touch screen monitors or keyboards for input devices and have all of the data and information needed for the application stored directly on the computer.

Information kiosks provide information in public places where visitors or customers have common questions. Locations such as shopping centers, hotels, airports, colleges and universities for example, use kiosks to provide information on available services, product locations, maps, and other information **[Figure 5-21]**. Museums and libraries use kiosks to allow visitors to find the location of a specific exhibit. Kiosks providing Internet access also are expected to be popular in the near future.

Figure 5-21 Using information kiosks in airports, travelers can check on hotel location and availability, confirm car rentals, read about local attractions, and more. Some kiosks even print out local maps and directions to specific sites.

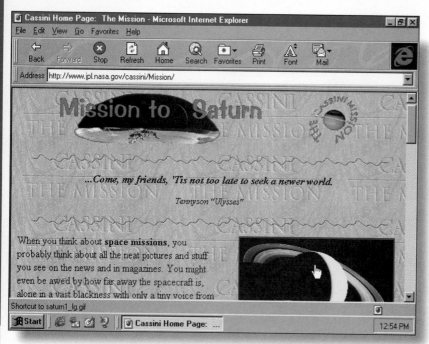

Figure 5-22 A NASA Web server offers textual and graphical information about the Mission to Saturn. By clicking the thumbnail picture, you can obtain a larger, more detailed image of Saturn and Saturn's rings.

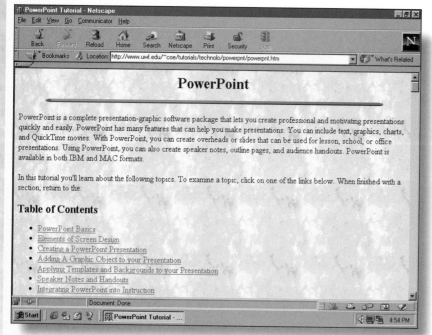

Figure 5-23 An example of one of the dozens of PowerPoint tutorials that are available on the Web.

The World Wide Web

Multimedia applications also play an important role on the **World Wide Web**, which is the part of the Internet that supports multimedia. Using multimedia brings a Web page to life, increases the types of information available on the Web; expands the Web's potential uses; and makes the Internet a more entertaining place to explore. As described in Chapter 2, the Web uses many types of media to deliver information and enhance a user's Web experience **[Figure 5-22]**. Graphics and animations reinforce text-based content. Online radio stations, movie rental sites, and games use audio and video clips to provide movie and music clips or deliver continuously updated information.

Web-based training (WBT) is an approach to computer-based training that uses the technologies of the Internet and the World Wide Web. As with CBT, Web-based training typically consists of self-directed, self-paced instruction on a topic. Because it is delivered via the Web, however, WBT has the advantage of being able to offer up-to-date content on any type of computer platform.

Over the past few years, the number of organizations using Web-based training has exploded. Today, almost every major corporation in the United States provides employees with some type of Web-based training to teach new skills or upgrade their current skills.

Web-based training also is available for individuals at home or at work. Many school districts are using the Web to deliver all types of training to their teachers. This media offers anytime, anyplace training.

Today, anyone with access to the Web can take advantages of hundreds of multimedia tutorials offered online. Such tutorials cover a range of topics, from how to change a flat tire to creating presentations in PowerPoint **[Figure 5-23]**. Many of these Web sites are free; others ask you to register and pay a fee to take the complete Web-based training course.

Many of the multimedia applications previously described, including computer- and Web-based training, e-zines, games, and virtual reality, are deliverable via the Web. As you will learn, most multimedia authoring software packages include tools for creating and delivering multimedia applications via the World Wide Web.

K-12 Educational Software Applications

As noted in the descriptions in previous sections, multimedia is important not only for business and entertainment, but also for education. An **educational software application** refers to computer software products used to support teaching and learning of subject-related content. Interactive multimedia applications enrich the learning process by providing individualized instruction and exploration; allowing students to examine their skills in a risk-free environment; and providing instant feedback, testing, and review [Figure 5-24].

The number and quality of educational software applications designed specifically for the K-12 learning environment have increased dramatically in the past few years. Educational software applications are available in many different designs, forms, and curriculum levels as shown in **Figures 5-25a** and **5-25b**.

The next sections discuss computer-assisted instruction, drill-and-practice, educational games, tutorials, educational simulations, integrated learning systems, and Web-based education. Information in Chapters 6 and 7 will provide you with ways to integrate these types of software programs into your classroom curriculum.

CHAPTER 5

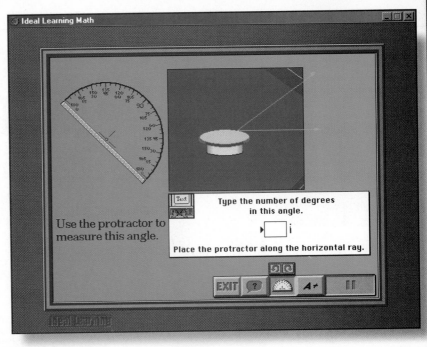

Figure 5-24 An interactive math practice test provides numerous nontraditional ways for students to assess their knowledge of geometry in a nonthreatening learning environment. In this geometry test by Ideal Learning Inc., students have the option of rotating the protractor over the angle to determine the number of degrees before answering the question. Feedback is instantaneous, once the student fills in the number of degrees.

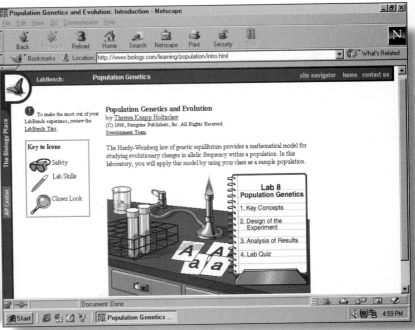

[5-25a] Math site

[5-25b] Science site

Figure 5-25 Multimedia applications are great tools to help teach difficult math and science concepts. The interactive math program shown in Figure 5-25a allows teachers to pretest students' knowledge before they enter a particular level of instruction. Science Web sites, such as the biology site shown in Figure 5-25b, help students learn the basic tools and procedures before entering the lab so they can focus on the actual hands-on experiment once in the lab.

WebInfo

For links to popular education-related computer-based applications, visit the Teachers Discovering Computers Chapter 5 WebInfo page **(www.scsite.com/tdc/ch5/webinfo.htm)** and click Educational Applications.

Figure 5-26 An educational multimedia application designed to teach young learners basic reading skills.

Computer-Assisted Instruction (CAI)

Computer-assisted instruction (CAI) has been used in education for more than two decades. Computer-assisted instruction is software designed to help teach facts, information, and/or skills associated with subject-related materials. For practical purposes, using a computer to enhance instruction could be called computer-assisted instruction. Most educators, however, do not feel that computer-assisted instruction accurately describes the many different computer-based educational software programs available today. With the growth of educational technology, the teaching profession has seen the emergence of other names used to refer to education software, such as computer-based instruction (CBI), computer-based learning (CBL), and computer-aided learning (CAL). For the purposes of this textbook, educational software applications are being used to refer to computer software products that support teaching and learning of subject-related content **[Figure 5-26]**.

Drill-and-Practice Software

Drill-and-practice software is software that first supplies factual information and then through repetitive exercises allows students to continue to work on the specific materials to remember the information, or memorize. Another name is **skills-reinforcement software**. Drill-and-practice software is effective for learning basic skills and for remediation.

Remediation is reviewing content many times until a student grasps the concepts being taught. One of the important features of drill-and-practice software and other educational software is that students receive instant feedback on correct and incorrect answers. Using drill-and-practice can increase students' performance in areas that are weak. Drill-and-practice software usually has built-in features that once a student masters a level, the computer will move the student to the next level automatically. Drill-and-practice software is effective when used with students who require extra assistance in content instruction.

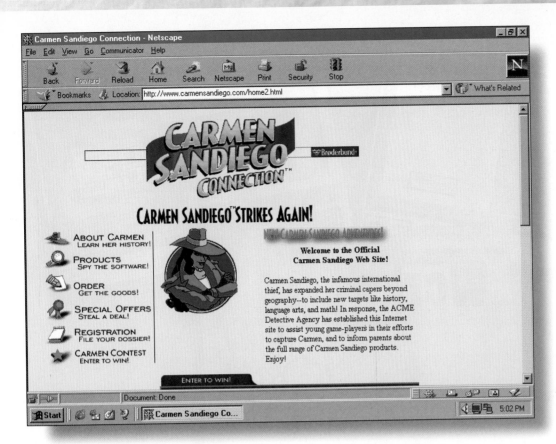

Figure 5-27 For more than a decade, students of all ages have been chasing the elusive Carmen Sandiego and her counterparts, while learning about geography, cultures, astronomy, music, and history.

Educational Games

Today, the majority of educational games are available on CD-ROMs and on the Web. **Educational games** usually include a set of rules, and students can compete against other students or the game itself. Games can be an effective way to teach information through repetition and practice.

Many students find educational games a fun way to learn. Various educational games create problem-solving environments forcing students to use high-order thinking skills to find solutions. The Carmen Sandiego series has become a front-runner in educational software games that clearly contains nonlinear subject-related content **[Figure 5-27]**. For more than ten years, young people have been chasing the fleeting Carmen Sandiego and her counterparts, while learning about geography, cultures, astronomy, music, and history.

Tutorials

A **tutorial** is a teaching program designed to help individuals learn to use a product or concepts. Tutorials are designed to tutor, or instruct. Many software products contain built-in tutorials to teach the user how to use the software, such as Microsoft Windows 98, Microsoft Works, HyperStudio, word processing programs, and many others as shown in **Figure 5-28** on the next page. Developers create educational tutorials that use the computer to provide an entire instructional area and are created so students can work their way through the tutorial to learn content without any help or other materials. The teaching solutions provided by tutorials range from a very structured linear approach with specific content objectives to a nonlinear approach that offers alternative paths through the lesson based on students' responses, called **branching**. Branching reflects classroom learning theory by allowing students to excel

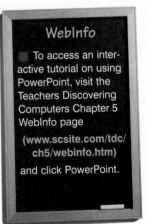

WebInfo

To access an interactive tutorial on using PowerPoint, visit the Teachers Discovering Computers Chapter 5 WebInfo page

(www.scsite.com/tdc/ ch5/webinfo.htm) and click PowerPoint.

Figure 5-28 Many software products contain built-in tutorials to teach the user how to use the software, such as Microsoft Works and HyperStudio.

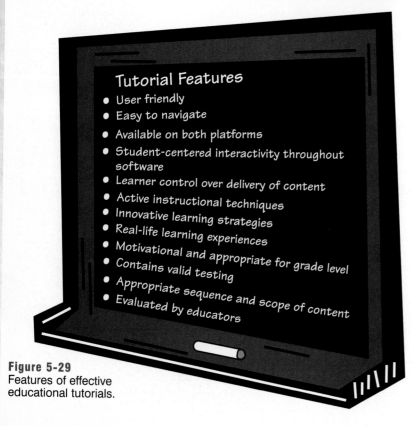

Figure 5-29
Features of effective educational tutorials.

at their own pace, provide feedback, and remediation when needed. The table in **Figure 5-29** provides some of the features of effective educational tutorials.

Educational Simulations

An **educational computer simulation** is a computerized model of real life that represents a physical or simulated process. These programs are unique because the user can cause things to happen, change the conditions, and make decisions based on the criteria provided to simulate real-life situations. These interactive programs model some event, reality, real-life circumstances, or phenomenon. Simulations offer learners the opportunity to manipulate variables that effect the outcomes of the experience. Using simulation is not a new teaching strategy. As you learned earlier in this chapter, business and industry have been using simulation for many years.

Interest is growing in programs such as SimCity and SimEarth, which let students design, interact, and provide more accurate explanations and examples of real life. **SimCity** is a very popular simulation program for education **[Figure 5-30]**. Students design cities, communities, neighborhoods, and businesses, including infrastructure, such as telephone lines, buildings, and more. As the cities grow in size and complexity, natural disasters and other realistic problems occur continuously requiring students to use all available city resources, including financial resources to keep the cities running.

The availability of educational computer simulations on the Web also is experiencing dramatic growth. A student can learn how a building is demolished, dissect a frog, see a real heart in action, and more.

Integrated Learning Systems

An **integrated learning system (ILS)** is a sophisticated software package usually developed by an established educational software corporation as a complete educational software solution in one package. These software solutions provide individual student diagnostic data through pre-tests, instruction based on the diagnostic data, continuous monitoring of student performance with automatic adjustments in instruction when needed, a variety of formats for teaching content, and multilevels and multigrade of content **[Figure 5-31]**. Most integrated learning systems also offer a comprehensive management solution for maintaining the software and for tracking student use and progress. Although expensive, integrated learning systems are praised as a comprehensive software solution for low-achieving schools. Integrated learning systems are appealing to school administrators, school boards, and principals because of their one package, one solution.

Applications for Students with Disabilities

Educational software applications offer unique advantages to students who have physical impairments or learning disabilities. Students who are visually impaired, for example, benefit from the audio capabilities of

Figure 5-30 SimCity, a popular simulation program, creates a real-life environment for development of problem-solving skills.

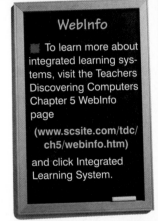

WebInfo

To learn more about integrated learning systems, visit the Teachers Discovering Computers Chapter 5 WebInfo page

(www.scsite.com/tdc/ch5/webinfo.htm)

and click Integrated Learning System.

Figure 5-31 Jostens Learning software is a popular integrated learning system used in thousands of schools.

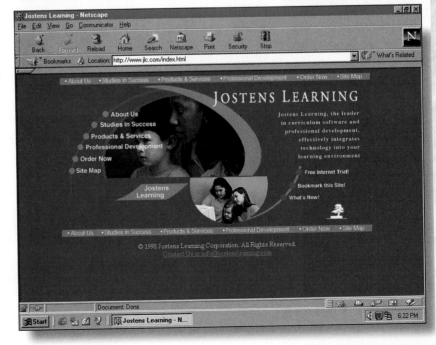

WebInfo

For more information on multimedia applications for students with disabilities, visit the Teachers Discovering Computers Chapter 5 WebInfo page

(www.scsite.com/tdc/ch5/webinfo.htm)

and click Disabilities.

multimedia applications, as well as the use of graphics and large font sizes. Visual materials such as graphics, animation, and video also make learning easier for students who are hearing impaired. Many educational software companies offer multimedia products with closed captioning or sign language to enhance the learning experience for hearing impaired students **[Figure 5-32]**.

For students with learning disabilities, the ability to work at their own pace is a major benefit of interactive multimedia applications. Students are able to interact with the software, practice, and review at their own pace, which alleviates the pressure to keep up with peers.

Web-Based Education

Many colleges and universities offer numerous Web-based or Web-enhanced courses. A **Web-based course** is a course that is taught mostly or completely on the Web, rather than in a traditional classroom. A

Web-enhanced course is a course that uses the Web to enhance the content of the course. Web-based courses offer many advantages for students that live far from a college or university campus or work full time, allowing them to attend class from home or at any time that fits their schedule. A number of colleges and universities now offer complete degree programs taught over the Web.

Some high schools are beginning to offer Web-based courses. For high schools, Web-based courses can help ease overcrowding and provide instruction for homebound students. Web-based courses also allow less-populated districts, and schools in rural areas, to share teachers. By using the Web, these areas can offer specialized classes, such as French, Latin, calculus, and numerous advanced placement courses. By pooling resources and linking students from more than one school into a Web-based course, school districts can expand the number and type of classes they offer.

Figure 5-32 The *Aesop Fables* multimedia application provides access to the visual language through sign language and the printed word for students who are hearing impaired. In the corner of the screen, a teacher signs all the printed words on the screen.

A relatively new benefit of using the Web in the classroom is having students interact with subject area experts using Web Resources. Many scientists want to increase educational opportunities for students, who someday may decide to become scientists. The Smithsonian Institution, for example, permits teachers and students to interact with the actual scientists who work for the Smithsonian via the Web.

The previous sections introduced you to a number of different applications of multimedia in education, business, and entertainment. The next sections describe the multimedia components of modern computers; first, asking you, what is a multimedia computer?

Multimedia Personal Computers

A PC or Macintosh **multimedia personal computer [Figures 5-33a** and **5-33b]** is a computer system that uses specific hardware and software components to input, process, and output various types of media. In general, any multimedia personal computer purchased in the past three years will have the capability of running most CD-ROM and Web-based multimedia applications. Many K-12 schools, however, have older multimedia computers, which may not be able to run all multimedia applications.

Teachers can verify that their classroom computers can run a particular multimedia application by reviewing the minimum hardware and software requirements needed to run the software for the appropriate platform, whether PC or Macintosh. These system requirements usually are printed on the side or back panel of the software packaging or on the CD-ROM or DVD-ROM insert **[Figure 5-34]**.

In addition to their many devices and components, multimedia computer systems use **multimedia extensions**, which are a type of system software that operates in the background of an application and are responsible for the playing or displaying of media. These multimedia extensions communicate with and control the operations of the devices in a multimedia computer, such as the sound card and CD-ROM or DVD-ROM drive. The following

[5-33a] iMac

[5-33b] PC

Figure 5-33 Most multimedia Macintosh computers and PCs are equipped with devices such as a microphone, a CD-ROM drive, stereo speakers, and a high-resolution monitor. Figure 5-33a shows a Macintosh iMac multimedia computer and Figure 5-33b shows a multimedia PC.

Broderaund Education Software Sampler

Macintosh and PowerPC; System 7.1 or higher; 25 MHz 68030 processor or faster; 5.5 MB RAM free; 2X CD-ROM drive or faster; 640 x 480 display, 256 colors

Windows 3.1 or Windows 95; 33 MHz 486SX or faster; 8 MB RAM required, 16 MB RAM recommended for Windows 95; 2X CD-ROM drive or faster; 640 x 480 display; 256 colors; Windows compatible sound device.

Figure 5-34 The minimum hardware and software system requirements to install and run multimedia applications usually are printed on the side or back panel of software packaging or on the insert that comes with a CD-ROM.

WebInfo

To learn more about multimedia computers, visit the Teachers Discovering Computers Chapter 5 WebInfo page

(www.scsite.com/tdc/ch5/webinfo.htm)

and click Multimedia Computers.

section describes the different equipment needed to develop and display a multimedia presentation or application.

Sound Card

As described in Chapter 4, a **sound card** is an expansion card that enhances the sound-generating capabilities of a computer by supporting audio input and output **[Figure 5-35]**. A sound card can record or digitize most audio signals. The sound card usually has two input jacks. One jack accepts input from your microphone. The other jack accepts input from a radio, stereo, tape player, external CD player, or other audio sources. A sound card also contains an output jack that connects devices such as speakers, headphones, or a stereo sound system. A sound card allows you to manipulate a sound stored on a disk. Sound cards are necessary for nearly all CD-ROMs and have become standard components of today's personal computers.

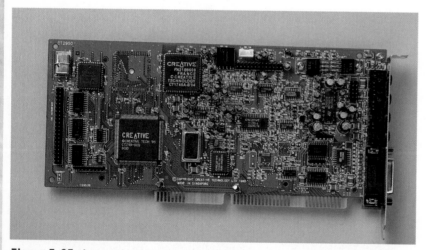

Figure 5-35 A sound card is used to provide both audio input and output.

CD-ROM and DVD-ROM Drives

In Chapter 4, you learned that a **CD-ROM** is an optical storage medium that can hold 650 MB of data, instructions, and information. A CD-ROM's large storage capacity makes it an excellent medium for storing and distributing multimedia applications that contain graphics, audio, and short video clips. Recall that a **DVD-ROM** is an extremely high-capacity CD capable of storing from

4.7 GB to 17 GB. Storing interactive multimedia applications on DVD-ROMs has the dual advantage of greater capacity to store longer video clips and higher-quality playback.

Today, all multimedia computer systems include a CD-ROM drive as standard equipment, although increasingly more include a DVD-ROM drive. Recall that a **DVD-ROM drive** plays both DVD-ROMs and CD-ROMs. The CD-ROM or DVD-ROM drive connects to the computer's sound card and stereo speakers to produce high-quality audio output.

Speakers and Microphones

Small stereo **speakers**, such as those shown in **Figure 5-33b** on page 5.23, provide an easy and inexpensive way to play audio on a multimedia personal computer. Speakers are sometimes built into or attach to the monitor. The speakers connect to a port on the sound card.

As with speakers, a microphone can be either a stand-alone device that plugs into the back of the sound card or built into the monitor **[Figure 5-36]**. A **microphone** is an inexpensive device that allows teachers, students, and other users to record their voices and other sounds.

microphone

speakers

Figure 5-36 Most Macintosh computers have both the stereo speakers and microphone built into the monitor.

Video Capture Card

A **video capture card** is an expansion card that enables users to connect a video input device to a computer. As noted in Chapter 4, to input or capture video, you plug a video camera, VCR, or a similar device into the video capture card, which converts the analog video signal into a digital signal that a computer can understand. Once the device is connected to the card, you can begin recording. **Video capture software** used with the card compresses video data so the video files are small enough to be stored on a computer's hard disk. Once the video is saved, you can play the video, copy it to videotape, or manipulate it using special video editing software. Most multimedia computers do not come with preinstalled video capture cards; instead, users must purchase and install video capture cards and associated software. Some teachers and students are beginning to use video capture technology to enhance teaching and learning.

Monitor and Video Adapter

A **monitor** is an important part of a multimedia personal computer system. When choosing a monitor for your multimedia personal computer, you should consider both the monitor and the video adapter. As noted in Chapter 4, a **video adapter**, also called a **graphics adapter** or **display adapter**, is an expansion card that plugs into a computer to give it display capabilities. The video adapter converts the computer's output into a video signal that is sent through a cable to the monitor, which displays an image on the screen. The display capabilities of a computer depend on both the video adapter and the display monitor.

Data Projectors and Projection Systems

Delivering a multimedia presentation to an audience often requires a data projector or projection system so the audience can see and hear the presentation clearly. For individual multimedia presentations or presentations to small groups, a large monitor often is appropriate.

Many school districts are providing teachers with a 27- or 32-inch television set for classroom presentations. These large-screen television sets often are mounted on rolling carts so teachers can use them in more than one classroom [Figure 5-37]. Connecting a multimedia computer to a television requires a special converter that converts the

Figure 5-37 Using a large-screen television set connected to a computer is a common way to project the computer images in a classroom so all students can view a multimedia presentation or interactive software program. These systems also can be used to show videotapes using a VCR.

digital signal of a computer to an analog signal required by television sets.

For presenting to larger groups, an overhead projection system often is used. One such system uses a liquid crystal display (LCD) projector panel [Figure 5-38]. A **liquid crystal display (LCD) projector panel** is a flat-screen panel that a user places on top of a high-intensity overhead projector. A computer connects to the LCD

Figure 5-38 An LCD projector panel, such as this InFocus color LCD panel, can be used with a laptop and overhead projector to deliver an effective multimedia presentation for classroom instruction.

Figure 5-39 A video projector uses a self-contained light source to display a multimedia application or presentation onto a screen. Many projectors have audio output capabilities as well and are ideal for multimedia presentations in large classrooms or auditoriums.

projector panel, which uses the overhead projector as a light source to project the images onto a screen. You can view the presentation on the computer monitor and projection screen at the same time.

Another type of projection system is a **data projector**, which connects directly to a computer with a cable and uses its own light source to display a multimedia application or presentation on a screen **[Figure 5-39]**. Recall

from Chapter 4 that two types of data projectors are LCD projectors and DLP projectors. An **LCD projector** attaches directly to a computer and uses its own light source to display the information shown on the computer screen. A **digital light processing (DLP) projector** uses tiny mirrors to reflect light, producing crisp, bright, colorful images that remain in focus and can be seen clearly even in a well lighted room. Both LCD and DLP projectors usually have audio capabilities, as well.

Videodisc Players

A **videodisc**, also called a **laserdisc**, is an optical disk used to store and provide up to 60 minutes of high-quality audio, video, and other multimedia presentations. Videodiscs require a videodisc player for playback of stored audio and video **[Figure 5-40]**. Teachers have been using videodisc technology in their classrooms since the 1980s. Because of dramatic improvements in Web-based, CD-ROM, and DVD-ROM multimedia applications, use of videodiscs in many K-12 schools is on the decrease.

Figure 5-40 A typical videodisc player used by teachers. One advantage of a videodisc player is you do not have to have a computer to show multimedia presentations or software.

Creating Multimedia Applications

Creating or developing multimedia applications involves producing various media elements, defining the elements' relationships to each other, and then sequencing them in an appropriate order. Individuals often use multimedia authoring software to help complete these tasks.

Obtaining Graphics for a Multimedia Application

Graphics, including illustrations, photos, and animations, are essential elements in any multimedia application. Teachers and students easily can add color images and photos to multimedia applications using color scanners, digital cameras, and PhotoCDs.

A **color scanner** converts images into a digitized format for use in multimedia applications **[Figure 5-41]**. The basic software that comes with scanners **[Figure 5-42]** allows users to conduct basic editing of scanned images and also save scanned images in different file formats. Sophisticated image editing programs are available for users requiring a wider variety of image-editing possibilities.

Another easy and effective way to obtain color photographs for a multimedia application is by using a digital camera **[Figure 5-43]**. As discussed in Chapter 4, **digital cameras** work much like regular cameras, except they use a small reusable disk or internal memory to store digital photographs. You easily can transfer photographs taken with a digital camera to a computer's hard disk and then incorporate them into a multimedia application.

Another way of obtaining digital images for use in a multimedia application is from a PhotoCD as shown in **Figure 5-44** on the next page. The **PhotoCD system** uses compact discs to store photographic images. After you take photos with any camera, the film is developed and the images are transferred to a PhotoCD master disc, which you can view on almost any computer equipped with a CD-ROM drive. Once you have obtained the appropriate graphics, you can incorporate them into a multimedia application.

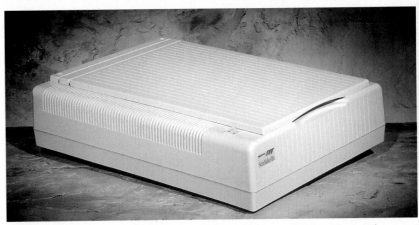

Figure 5-41 A color scanner can convert images into digitized format for multimedia applications and are easy to use.

Figure 5-42 The basic software that comes with scanners allows users to edit scanned images and save the images in different file formats.

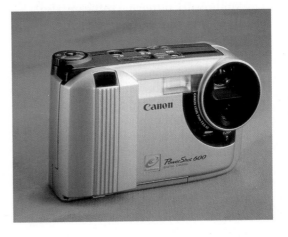

Figure 5-43 An easy and effective way to obtain digitized color photographs is by using a digital camera. Once the photographs are input into a computer, they can be incorporated into a multimedia application.

Figure 5-44 PhotoCDs are write-once compact discs that can store about 100 photographic images. Photos taken on any camera are transferred to the PhotoCD master disk when the film is developed.

Multimedia Authoring Software

Multimedia authoring software, also called an **authoring tool,** allows an individual to create an interactive multimedia presentation that includes text, graphics, sound, animation, or video. A multimedia presentation, however, is more than just a combination of these elements. Multimedia authoring software lets you create the application or presentation by controlling the placement of text and graphics and the duration of sounds, video, and animations.

Recall that a multimedia application also is interactive, meaning you can decide the

amount and order of the material you cover. Multimedia authoring programs allow you to create interactivity by defining places in the program that respond to user input. In a multimedia application, for example, you might, include a screen on which users can choose to click a video button to play a video or skip the video and move to the next screen.

Multimedia developers in corporations and businesses use multimedia authoring software programs such as Asymetrix Multimedia **ToolBook**, Macromedia **Authorware**, and Macromedia **Director**. Developers use these high-end programs to produce many of the hundreds of educational multimedia applications used in schools today.

Very few teachers use ToolBook or Authorware to develop their own multimedia applications, as these high-end programs are expensive and more tailored to a commercial environment. Many easy-to-use and less expensive authoring programs, however, are widely available and currently are used by K-12 teachers and students in schools all over the world. Two of the more popular multimedia authoring tools used in K-12 schools are Microsoft PowerPoint and HyperStudio®.

While not considered a true multimedia authoring software program, Microsoft **PowerPoint** does allow teachers and students to create multimedia presentations that can incorporate text, graphics, animation, audio, video, links, and most importantly interactivity. You learned the basics of PowerPoint in Chapter 3. A popular multimedia authoring program used by teachers, students and businesses is HyperStudio by Roger Wagner Publishing, Inc. **[Figure 5-45]**.

HyperStudio® is an easy-to-use multimedia authoring software program that allows the author to combine all of the multimedia elements described in this chapter into a series of interactive cards. Originally, the developers of HyperStudio created the authoring program for use on Macintosh computers. As with many other educational multimedia programs and applications, however, HyperStudio now is available for the Macintosh and PCs. Today, more than two million K-12 and college students, including thousands of elementary school students, have developed interactive multimedia presentations using HyperStudio. Other multimedia authoring programs used in schools include

Digital Chisel by Pierian Springs Software, **Astound** by Astound, Inc., **SuperLink** and **Multimedia Scrapbook** by IBM, **HyperCard** by Apple Computers, and **Teach** by Acrux Software.

Why Are Multimedia Applications Important for Education?

Multimedia applications are changing the traditional dynamics of learning in classrooms. As previously noted, interactivity is one of the major features of multimedia applications. The ability of users to interact with a multimedia application is perhaps the single-most critical feature of multimedia and has enormous potential to improve learning in K-12 schools.

Research has shown that, when properly evaluated and integrated into teaching at the point of instruction, multimedia applications are a highly effective teaching tool. Studies indicate that students retain approximately 20 percent of what they see; 30 percent of what they hear; and 50 percent of what they see *and* hear. When a student has a chance to hear, see, *and* interact with a learning environment, he or she can retain as much as 80 percent of the information. Multimedia applications provide that interactive learning environment, which makes them powerful tools for teaching and learning.

An important reason for students' increased retention is that they become actively involved in the learning process instead of passive recipients of information. Interactive multimedia applications engage students by asking them to define their own paths through an application, which often leads them to explore many related topics.

An additional benefit of integrating multimedia into the classroom is that students take great pride in authoring their own multimedia applications. Many teachers have noted that students are motivated by and enjoy the process of creating their own interactive multimedia applications using multimedia authoring software. Many students enjoy conducting research and writing when their writing projects involve the creation of a multimedia application — and they will more readily practice those skills. Further, the completion

Figure 5-45 HyperStudio®, developed by Roger Wagner Publishing, Inc., is a popular K-12 multimedia authoring program.

of a multimedia project is a self-esteem and confidence booster for many students.

For multimedia applications to reach their full potential in the classroom, teachers must evaluate multimedia applications for content and appropriateness. Chapter 7 provides additional guidance on evaluating educational software and Web resources for the classroom.

Summary of Multimedia in Education

This chapter examined the field of multimedia and introduced you to different elements used in multimedia applications. After discussing a variety of uses of multimedia applications, this chapter covered the components of a multimedia personal computer with a focus on the hardware and software needed to develop and deliver a multimedia application. Finally, the chapter reviewed how to develop a multimedia application and the value of multimedia in education. As more teachers integrate multimedia applications into their classroom curriculum, CD-ROM-, DVD-ROM-, and Web-based multimedia applications have the potential to impact public education dramatically and positively.

WebInfo

To view student projects created with HyperStudio, visit the Teachers Discovering Computers Chapter 5 WebInfo page **(www.scsite.com/tdc/ch5/webinfo.htm)** and click Student Projects.

InBrief

KeyTerms

AtTheMovies

CheckPoint

TeacherTime

CyberClass

EdIssues

NetStuff

SPECIAL FEATURES

TimeLine 2000

Guide to WWW Sites

Buyer's Guide 2000

Educational Sites

State/Federal Sites

Chat

News

Home

www.scsite.com/tdc/ch5/brief.htm

InBrief

Web Instructions: To display this page from the Web, launch your browser and enter the URL, www.scsite.com/tdc/ch5/brief.htm. Click the links for current and additional information. To listen to an audio version of this InBrief, click the Audio button below the title, InBrief, at the top of the page. To play the audio, RealPlayer must be installed on your computer (download by clicking here).

1. What Is Multimedia?

Multimedia is the combination of the following elements: text, color, graphics, animation, audio, and video. **Multimedia software** refers to any computer-based presentation or application software that uses multimedia elements. **Interactive multimedia** describes a multimedia application that accepts input from the user by means of a keyboard, voice, or a pointing device such as a mouse; and performs an action in response.

2. Media Elements

Text consists of characters that are used to create words, sentences, and paragraphs and is a fundamental element used in all multimedia applications. A **graphic** is a digital representation of nontext information such as a drawing, chart, or photograph. Displaying a series of still graphics creates an **animation**, which is a graphic that has the illusion of motion. **Audio** is any digitized music, speech, or other sounds that are stored and produced by the computer. **Video** consists of photographic images that are played back at speeds of 15 to 30 frames per second and give the appearance of full motion in real time.

3. Multimedia Applications

A **multimedia application** involves the use of multimedia technology for education, business, and entertainment. Businesses use multimedia, for example, in interactive advertisements and for job- and skill-training applications. Another important application of interactive multimedia is to create **simulations**, which are computer-based models of real-life situations. Multimedia applications include computer-based training; electronic books and references; how-to guides; and magazines. Multimedia also is used in entertainment, virtual reality, information kiosks, and on the Web.

4. Computer-Based Training

Computer-based training (CBT) is a tool in which individuals learn by using and completing exercises using instructional software on computers. Computer-based training is popular in business and industry to teach new skills or enhance the existing skills of employees. Computer-based training is effective especially for teaching software skills if the CBT is integrated with the software application, because it allows students to practice as they learn.

5. Electronic Books

Electronic books are digital texts that use links to give the user access to information. Electronic books have many of the elements of a regular book, including pages of text and graphics. Generally, you turn the pages of an electronic book by clicking icons. **How-to guides** are multimedia applications that include step-by-step instructions and interactive demonstrations to teach you practical new skills. A **multimedia magazine** is a digital version of a magazine, which is distributed on CD-ROM or via the World Wide Web.

6. Entertainment

Multimedia combines the media elements of television and interactivity, making it ideal for entertainment. Multimedia **computer games** use graphics, sound, and video to create a realistic and entertaining game situation. Many multimedia applications are used for **edutainment**, which is an experience meant to be both educational and entertaining. **Virtual reality** (**VR**) is the use of a computer to create an artificial environment that appears and feels like a real environment and allows a user to explore space and manipulate the setting. As computing power and the use of the Web increase, practical applications continue to emerge for education, business, and entertainment. An **information kiosk** is a computerized information or reference center that provides information in public locations.

www.scsite.com/tdc/ch5/brief.htm

InBrief

InBrief

KeyTerms

AtTheMovies

CheckPoint

TeacherTime

CyberClass

EdIssues

NetStuff

SPECIAL FEATURES

TimeLine 2000

Guide to WWW Sites

Buyer's Guide 2000

Educational Sites

State/Federal Sites

Chat

News

Home

7. World Wide Web

Multimedia applications also play an important role on the **World Wide Web**, which is the part of the Internet that supports multimedia. The Web uses many types of media to deliver information and enhance a user's Web experience. **Web-based training (WBT)** is an approach to computer-based training that uses the technologies of the Internet and the World Wide Web.

8. K-12 Educational Software Applications

Multimedia is important not only for business and entertainment, but also for education. An **educational software application** refers to computer software products used to support teaching and learning of subject-related content. Educational software applications are available in several different designs, forms, and curriculum levels. Educational applications include computer-assisted instruction, drill-and-practice, educational games, tutorials, educational simulations, integrated learning systems, and Web-based education.

9. Drill-and-Practice, Games, and Tutorials

Drill-and-practice software is software that first supplies factual information and then through repetitive exercises allows students to continue to work on the specific materials to remember the information. **Educational games** usually include a set of rules, and students can compete against other students or the game itself. Games can be an effective way to teach information through repetition and practice. A **tutorial** is a teaching program designed to help individuals learn to use a product or concepts.

10. Simulations and Integrated Learning Systems

An **educational computer simulation** is a computerized model of real life that represents a physical or simulated process. An **integrated learning system (ILS)** is a sophisticated software package usually developed by an established educational software corporation as a complete educational software solution in one package.

11. Web-Based Education

Many colleges and universities and some high schools offer Web-based or Web-enhanced courses. A **Web-based course** is a course that is taught mostly or completely on the Web, rather than in a traditional classroom. A **Web-enhanced course** is a course that uses the Web to enhance the content of the course.

12. Multimedia Personal Computers

A PC or Macintosh **multimedia personal computer** is a computer system that uses specific hardware and software components to input, process, and output various types of media. Media devices include a **sound card**, **CD-ROM** or **DVD-ROM drive**, **speakers**, and a **monitor**.

13. Creating Multimedia Applications

Creating or developing multimedia applications involves producing various media elements, defining the elements' relationships to each other, and then sequencing them in an appropriate order. **Multimedia authoring software** allows an individual to create an interactive multimedia presentation that includes text, graphics, sound, animation, or video. Two of the more popular multimedia authoring tools used in K-12 schools are Microsoft PowerPoint and HyperStudio.

14. PowerPoint and HyperStudio

Microsoft **PowerPoint** allows teachers and students to create multimedia presentations that can incorporate text, graphics, animation, audio, video, links, and interactivity. **HyperStudio** is an easy-to-use multimedia authoring software program that allows the author to combine all of the multimedia elements described in this chapter into a series of interactive cards.

KeyTerms

InBrief

KeyTerms

AtTheMovies

CheckPoint

TeacherTime

CyberClass

EdIssues

NetStuff

SPECIAL FEATURES

TimeLine 2000

Guide to WWW Sites

Buyer's Guide 2000

Educational Sites

State/Federal Sites

Chat

News

Home

Web Instructions: To display this page from the Web, launch your browser and enter the URL, www.scsite.com/tdc/ch5/terms.htm. Scroll through the list of terms. Click a term to display its definition and a picture. Click KeyTerms on the left to redisplay the KeyTerms page. Click the TO WEB button for current and additional information about the term from the Web. To see animations, Shockwave and Flash Player must be installed on your computer (download by clicking here).

animation [5.6]
Astound [5.29]
audio [5.7]
authoring tool [5.28]
Authorware [5.28]

branching [5.19]

CD-ROM [5.24]
clip [5.8]
clip art collection [5.4]
color scanner [5.27]
computer-assisted instruction (CAI) [5.18]
computer-based training (CBT) [5.9]
computer games [5.13]
courseware [5.9]

data projector [5.26]
Digital Chisel [5.29]
digital cameras [5.27]
digital light processing (DLP) projector [5.26]
Director [5.28]
display adapter [5.25]
drill-and-practice [5.18]
DVD-ROM [5.24]
DVD-ROM drive [5.24]

educational computer simulation [5.20]
educational games [5.19]
educational software application [5.17]
edutainment [5.13]
electronic books [5.10]
electronic magazine [5.12]
electronic reference [5.11]
e-zine [5.12]

graphic [5.4]
graphics [5.27]
graphics adapter [5.25]

how-to guides [5.11]
HyperCard [5.29]
HyperStudio® [5.28]

information kiosk [5.15]
integrated learning system (ILS) [5.21]
interactive multimedia [5.2]
interactivity [5.1]

laserdisc [5.26]
LCD projector [5.26]
link [5.3]
liquid crystal display (LCD) projector panel [5.25]

microphone [5.24]
monitor [5.25]
Moving Pictures Experts Group (MPEG) [5.8]
multimedia [5.2]
multimedia application [5.9]
multimedia authoring software [5.28]

multimedia extensions [5.23]
multimedia magazine [5.12]
multimedia personal computer [5.23]
Multimedia Scrapbook [5.29]
multimedia software [5.2]
Musical Instrument Digital Interface (MIDI) [5.7]

PhotoCD system [5.27]
PowerPoint [5.28]

remediation [5.18]

SimCity [5.21]
simulations [5.9]
skills-reinforcement software [5.18]
sound card [5.24]
SuperLink [5.29]

Teach [5.29]
text [5.4]
ToolBook [5.28]
tutorial [5.19]

video [5.7]
video adapter [5.25]
video capture card [5.25]
video capture software [5.25]
video compression [5.8]
videodisc [5.26]
virtual reality (VR) [5.14]
visual learners [5.4]

Web-based course [5.22]
Web-based training (WBT) [5.16]
Web-enhanced course [5.22]
World Wide Web [5.16]

www.scsite.com/tdc/ch5/movies.htm

AtTheMovies

WELCOME to VIDEO CLIPS from CNN

Web Instructions: To display this page from the Web, launch your browser and enter the URL, www.scsite.com/tdc/ch5/movies.htm. Click a picture to view a video. After watching the video, close the video window and then complete the exercise by answering the questions about the video. To view the videos, RealPlayer must be installed on your computer (download by clicking here).

InBrief

KeyTerms

AtTheMovies

CheckPoint

TeacherTime

CyberClass

EdIssues

NetStuff

SPECIAL FEATURES

TimeLine 2000

Guide to WWW Sites

Buyer's Guide 2000

Educational Sites

State/Federal Sites

Chat

News

Home

1. SBT Tech Guide (DVD)

This video revealed that CD-ROM technology is on the move toward DVD technology. Because of DVD's storage and playing capacity, some believe that CDs soon will be replaced. One very enticing possibility presented by DVD technology is the ability to turn your television set and computer into one complete system. According to what you have learned, what is a DVD-ROM? What is the storage capacity of a DVD? How does a DVD differ from a CD? What are the advantages and disadvantages of DVD? Conduct research to find out more about DVD technology. Then decide whether you would "future proof" your educational facilities' computer systems now, or whether you would budget for the upgrade later.

2. SBT Online/Netflix

Online access to DVD movies is not uncommon in this age of Web shopping pages. Popularity is growing for sites such as the NetFlix.com movie Web site where you can search for your favorite movie, and then either rent or buy it in DVD-ROM format. Do you or your students know anyone who owns a DVD player? What would it cost to rent a DVD movie online, and how would you receive and return the movie? What are the advantages and disadvantages of an online DVD movie rental? What movie companies are strong players in the DVD movie market? As an educator, do you see how Web shopping pages such as the one shown in the video could benefit students or you in an academic setting? Are you or your students aware of other DVD movie sites? Do any of the sites focus on distributing educational movies? If so, how are the online transactions handled?

3. SBT Tech Guide Animation

Multimedia applications often use a blend of media elements to present information in a variety of ways. What kinds of media are used on the Web site to bring jazz to life? What types of multimedia Web technologies are used? Of the media and Web technologies used, which do you think is the most effective? What other media could you add to the site to make it more interesting and informative? Does your educational facility's technical environment support multimedia and personal Web site capabilities? How could you incorporate into your teaching paradigm the multimedia features found in the video whether or not you had access to a Web page? What output devices would you find useful and how would they parallel business office uses?

www.scsite.com/tdc/ch5/check.htm

InBrief

KeyTerms

AtTheMovies

CheckPoint

TeacherTime

CyberClass

EdIssues

NetStuff

SPECIAL FEATURES

TimeLine 2000

Guide to WWW Sites

Buyer's Guide 2000

Educational Sites

State/Federal Sites

Chat

News

Home

CheckPoint

Web Instructions: To display this page from the Web, launch your browser and enter the URL, www.scsite.com/tdc/ch5/check.htm. Click a blank line for the answer. Click the links for current and additional information. To experience the animation and interactivity, Shockwave and Flash Player must be installed on your computer (download by clicking here).

1._____

2._____

3._____

4._____

5._____

1. Label the Figure

Instructions: Identify the multimedia devices.

2. Matching

Instructions: Match each term from the column on the left with the best description from the column on the right.

____ 1. text

____ 2. graphic

____ 3. animation

____ 4. audio

____ 5. video

a. a graphic that has the illusion of motion

b. photographic images played back at speeds of 15 to 30 frames per second to provide the appearance of motion in real time

c. digitized music, speech, or other sound stored and produced by a computer

d. characters used to create words, sentences, and paragraphs; a fundamental element in multimedia

e. digital representation of nontext information such as a drawing, chart, or photograph

3. Short Answer

Instructions: Write a brief answer to each of the following questions.

1. What is interactive multimedia software? Why is interactive multimedia software important for K-12 education? _____

2. Name four media components of multimedia software? Briefly describe each. _____

3. What are the differences between electronic reference books and how-to guides? Which one is used more often in education? Why? _____

4. What is virtual reality? How do teachers, students, and others use virtual reality? Is virtual reality available on the Web? _____

5. What is meant by educational software applications? Briefly describe four different categories of educational software applications. _____

www.scsite.com/tdc/ch5/time.htm

TeacherTime

Web Instructions: To display this page from the Web, launch your browser and enter the URL, www.scsite.com/tdc/ch5/time.htm. Click the links for current and additional information.

InBrief

KeyTerms

AtTheMovies

CheckPoint

TeacherTime

CyberClass

EdIssues

NetStuff

SPECIAL FEATURES

TimeLine 2000

Guide to WWW Sites

Buyer's Guide 2000

Educational Sites

State/Federal Sites

Chat

News

Home

1. Many schools are using multimedia applications and the Web to help students better understand the past or gain a greater appreciation of other cultures. For example, using a multimedia application called Oregon Trail, students learn about westward expansion by experiencing the hardships and making decisions similar to those facing nineteenth-century settlers. At the Web site for Educational Web Adventures, students can participate in adventures such as, Tracking The Tiger Trade, in which they go undercover to Asia to explore the illegal trade of tiger parts, or Amazon Interactive, a project focusing on the people and geography of the Ecuadorian Amazon. Are these kinds of multimedia applications and Web adventures appropriate for all grade levels? How does their use compare with traditional approaches to instruction and learning? How do you think students feel about using these types of resources? How could you best use these types of resources in your classroom? What supplemental materials would you need?

2. You have been teaching your students about famous eighteenth- and nineteenth-century artists. As a final activity, you want to take your students on a field trip to an art museum. The nearest museum, however, is three hours away, so the trip requires bus transportation. Due to the cost of the proposed field trip, your principal has asked you to explore other possibilities. What other options do you have? Could you take your class on a virtual field trip to an art museum? How would you and your students feel about taking that type of field trip? What are some advantages of a virtual field trip? What are some disadvantages?

3. Multimedia reference books are a popular alternative to printed reference books. Not only are they updated more frequently than printed resources, many multimedia encyclopedias have easy-to-use indexes, links to related topics, and audio and video enhancements. Many people, however, believe that printed reference books supply more in-depth information than multimedia references. How and when would you want your students to use multimedia reference books? When would you want your students to use printed reference materials? Describe a situation in which a multimedia reference book would be more appropriate than a printed reference, and vice versa. Which type of reference resource is easier for your students to use — a multimedia or printed reference book?

4. You are beginning to use multimedia software in your classroom and you have received $500 to purchase additional software. Before making a decision, you would like to review a list of popular educational software programs and get other educators' opinions on the software. Where might you locate such a list within your school district? Where might you locate such a list on the Web? Do any of these lists provide other teachers' reviews of the software? What other actions might you take to ensure that you make an informed decision about the multimedia software that is best for you and your students?

5. You are teaching geography to your sixth grade class. For their final project, the students are to select an area they would like to visit and then prepare a multimedia presentation describing the country or region, its culture, major landmarks, and famous sites. To gather information, the students will use multimedia reference books and visit geography Web sites. Using the Web for your research, list five or six reference books and Web sites that you might suggest as resources. What other multimedia resources could your students use? How do multimedia resources support student learning?

CyberClass

Web Instructions: To display this page from the Web, launch your browser and enter the URL, www.scsite.com/tdc/ch5/class.htm. To start Level I CyberClass, click a Level I link on this page or enter the URL, www.cyber-class.com. Click the Student button, click *Teachers Discovering Computers* in the list of titles, and then click the Enter a site button. To start Level II or III CyberClass (available only to those purchasers of a CyberClass floppy disk), place your CyberClass floppy disk in drive A, click Start on the taskbar, click Run on the Start menu, type a:connect in the Open text box, click the OK button, click the Enter CyberClass button, and then follow the instructions. If you are using a Macintosh, see your instructor.

InBrief

KeyTerms

AtTheMovies

CheckPoint

TeacherTime

CyberClass

EdIssues

NetStuff

SPECIAL FEATURES

TimeLine 2000

Guide to WWW Sites

Buyer's Guide 2000

Educational Sites

State/Federal Sites

Chat

News

Home

1. Flash Cards (<u>Level I</u>, Level II, and Level III)

Click Flash Cards on the Main Menu of the CyberClass Web page. Click the plus sign before the Chapter 5 title. Select all the subjects under the Chapter 5 title and answer all the flash cards. Hand in the number right, the number wrong, and the percentage score to your instructor. All users: Close the Electronic Flash Card window and the Flash Cards window by clicking the Close button in the upper-right corner of each window.

2. Practice Test (<u>Level I</u>, Level II, and Level III)

Click Testing on the Main Menu of the CyberClass Web page. Click the Select a book box arrow and then click Teachers Discovering Computers. Click the Select a test to take box arrow and then click the Chapter 5 title in the list. Click the Take Test button. If necessary, maximize the window. Take the practice test and then click the Submit Test button. If you miss more than one question, take another test by clicking the Take another Test button. Continue to take tests until you miss no more than one question.

3. Web Guide (<u>Level I</u>, Level II, and Level III)

Click Web Guide on the Main Menu of the CyberClass Web page. When the Guide to World Wide Web Sites page displays, click Art and World Art Treasures. Review this site and determine if it is appropriate for use in K-12 education. Would you use it in your classroom? Why? When you are finished, hand in a brief summary of your conclusions to your instructor.

4. Assignments and Syllabus (Level II and Level III)

Click Assignments on the Main Menu of the CyberClass Web page. Ensure you are aware of all assignments and when they are due. Click Syllabus on the Main Menu of the CyberClass Web page. Verify you are up to date on all activities for the class.

5. CyberChallenge (Level II and Level III)

Click CyberChallenge on the Main Menu of the CyberClass Web page. Click the Select a board to play box arrow and then click Chapter 5 in the list. Click the Play CyberChallenge button. Maximize the CyberChallenge window. Play CyberChallenge until you correctly answer the 20, 30, 40, and 50 point questions diagonally left or right across the playing board.

6. Hot Links (Level II and Level III)

Click Hot Links on the Main Menu of the CyberClass Web page. Click Add a Link. Click New Link Topic. Type your name and the word, Multimedia, in the Link Topic Name box. Click the Create Link Topic button. Type the link name in the Link Name box, the URL in the URL (Internet address) box, and the link description in the Link Description box to revisit a multimedia Web site you think is outstanding. Click the Add Link button.

1 2 3 4 5 6 7 8

www.scsite.com/tdc/ch5/issues.htm

EdIssues

Web Instructions: To display this page from the Web, launch your browser and enter the URL, www.scsite.com/tdc/ch5/issue.htm. Click the links for current and additional information to help you respond to the EdIssues questions.

1. Virtual Dissection

Most people remember dissecting a frog in their high school biology class — the odor of formaldehyde, the nervous laughter, the unsuspecting classmate who finds a webbed foot in his lunch bag. For many students, conventional dissections are being replaced by virtual dissections using multimedia applications. Students use computers to view color graphics of a frog's anatomy and videos of biological systems, and to take interactive quizzes. Although these CD-ROM multimedia programs and Web activities are supported by animal rights activists and squeamish students, many biology teachers believe there is no substitute for genuine dissection. Should multimedia applications replace traditional dissection? Why or why not? Who should make the choice between virtual and traditional dissection? Why? On what basis should the choice be made?

InBrief

KeyTerms

AtTheMovies

CheckPoint

TeacherTime

CyberClass

EdIssues

NetStuff

SPECIAL FEATURES

TimeLine 2000

Guide to WWW Sites

Buyer's Guide 2000

Educational Sites

State/Federal Sites

Chat

News

Home

External Features

Click on the name of each part of the frog's external

amphibian

frog

Preparation

Purpose

This section shows the steps necessary to prepare your frog for the

Getting Read

(1.3MB) An Overview of the Dissection Process.

Procedure

AMPHIBIAN 1999

SPRING SOFTWARE

FEATURES

AWARDS

SYSTEM REQUIREMENTS

PRODUCT SHEET

PRICING

BACK TO SCIENCE

helping young, E mind

BioLab Frog
Our most popular "real-life" dissection simulation! *BioLab Frog* provides an in-depth lab experience in the physiology of amphibians. Students can explore the frog's external mouth and its digestive, circulatory, reproductive, and skeletal systems.

The program includes lab simulations, post-lab reinforcement, and a final test for each unit. Up-close graphics and colorful animations illustrate functions that are normally hard to view. *BioLab Frog* is an ideal dissection alternative and supplement to anatomy instruction. AGE 11+ / GRADE 6+ / MAC/WIN CD-ROM SCREEN

HOW TO ORDER

AWARDS

er Apple Award

- Mini-labs
- Post-lab activities and final test
- On-screen log to track progress
- Realistic graphics
- Video and full-color photography

Virtual Frog Dissection Kit - - - Lawrence Berkeley National Laboratory

www.scsite.com/tdc/ch5/issues.htm

1 2 3 4 5 6 7 8

EdIssues

InBrief

KeyTerms

AtTheMovies

CheckPoint

TeacherTime

CyberClass

EdIssues

NetStuff

SPECIAL FEATURES

TimeLine 2000

Guide to WWW Sites

Buyer's Guide 2000

Educational Sites

State/Federal Sites

Chat

News

Home

2. Bringing the Past to the Present

A simulation on a popular multimedia application lets students assume the role of a prominent <u>Civil War</u> general in an actual battle. Students direct and position their army. Confrontations are accompanied by video of battle reenactments. Critics argue that the use of these kinds of multimedia applications lack the insight and detail of a traditional textbook. Supporters claim that, by being immersed in the battle, students gain a better understanding of the Civil War. What place do multimedia applications have in learning history? Why? What are the advantages and disadvantages of multimedia applications compared with traditional textbooks? In what historical studies, if any, would multimedia applications be particularly appropriate? Why?

3. Educational Technology Funding

Multimedia applications are motivating, capture students' attention, and appeal to students with different learning styles — and they have been shown to have a positive effect on student performance. As multimedia applications continue to expand and improve, however, they require more computer memory and faster microprocessors. Eighteen months ago, your school purchased 70 new multimedia computers. At the time, they were considered high-powered computers; today, they cannot run some of the new multimedia applications. You want the school to increase the computers' memory and purchase DVD-ROM drives. Should schools budget for the costs of upgrading computer equipment? Why or why not? How can schools stay on the cutting edge of technology without incurring unexpected expenses? Where else can classroom teachers locate educational <u>technology funding</u> to purchase new or upgrade older computer hardware?

4. Information Overload

The amount of information available to people is growing every day — as scientists uncover new facts; physicians develop improved treatments; technology firms design unprecedented products; and journalists record history in the making. Technologies such as multimedia CD-ROMs, DVD-ROMS, and the World Wide Web make this vast — some say overwhelming — amount of information easily available to teachers and students. As a result of this potential <u>information overload</u>, experts worry that students might be spending more time sifting through information than actually applying and utilizing information. What do you think? Can there ever be too much information? Why or why not? How could too much information adversely affect teachers and students? What can be done about information overload? How can teachers help students avoid this?

5. Multimedia Realism

One benefit of multimedia applications is the realistic quality of the media elements such as graphics, animations, audio, and video. Today, multimedia applications on CD-ROMs, DVD-ROMs, and the Web artfully combine these elements to provide students with real-life experiences. Students can observe how blood circulates throughout the body; watch from <u>Apollo 11</u> as Neil Armstrong walks on the moon; or take a virtual tour of the <u>Smithsonian Institution</u>, all without ever leaving the classroom. Are there times, however, when multimedia applications are too real? One educational CD-ROM about dinosaurs, for example, shows a Tyrannosaurus Rex killing another dinosaur, complete with blood and dramatic sound effects. Would this type of CD-ROM be appropriate for an elementary classroom? Why or why not? How can you determine what types of multimedia applications are appropriate for your classroom? Should teachers always preview multimedia programs before using them with students? Should school districts have one person who reviews and approves all multimedia software purchases? Why or why not?

www.scsite.com/tdc/ch5/net.htm

NetStuff

InBrief

KeyTerms

AtTheMovies

CheckPoint

TeacherTime

CyberClass

EdIssues

NetStuff

SPECIAL FEATURES

TimeLine 2000

Guide to WWW Sites

Buyer's Guide 2000

Educational Sites

State/Federal Sites

Chat

News

Home

Web Instructions: To display this page from the Web, launch your browser and enter the URL, www.scsite.com/tdc/ch5/net.htm. To use the Understanding Multimedia lab or the Scanning Documents lab from the Web, Shockwave and Flash Player must be installed on your computer (download by clicking here).

UNDER-
STANDING
MULTIMEDIA
LAB

1. Shelly Cashman Series Understanding Multimedia Lab

Follow the instructions in NetStuff 1 on page 1.34 to start and use the Understanding Multimedia lab. If you are running from the Web, enter the URL, www.scsite.com/sclabs/menu.htm or display the NetStuff page (see instructions at the top of this page) and then click the UNDERSTANDING MULTIMEDIA LAB button.

SCANNING
DOCUMENTS
LAB

2. Shelly Cashman Series Scanning Documents Lab

Follow the instructions in NetStuff 1 on page 1.34 to start and use the Scanning Documents lab. If you are running from the Web, enter the URL, www.scsite.com/sclabs/menu.htm or display the NetStuff page (see instructions at the top of this page) and then click the SCANNING DOCUMENTS LAB button.

SEARCHING
FOR GRAPHICS

3. Searching for Graphics

Graphics can enhance your students' multimedia presentations dramatically. Fortunately, an abundance of clip art and animated graphics are available free on the Web. Click the SEARCHING FOR GRAPHICS button to complete an exercise to locate free graphics on the Web.

VR ON
THE WEB

4. Virtual Reality on the Web

Web-based virtual reality applications have the potential to positively impact K-12 education. Click the VR ON THE WEB button to complete an exercise and learn more about virtual reality.

SEARCHING
FOR SOUND
FILES

5. Searching for Sound Files

Sound clips also can enhance a multimedia presentation. As with graphics, an abundance of free sound clips is available on the Web. Click the SEARCHING FOR SOUND FILES button and complete an exercise to learn how to find and dowload free sounds clips from the Web.

MULTIMEDIA
ON THE WEB

6. Multimedia on the Web

The World Wide Web offers high-quality multimedia products for teachers and students. To learn more about this topic and see the various media elements used in a sophisticated Web site, click the MULTIMEDIA ON THE WEB button and complete this exercise.

WEB CHAT

7. Web Chat

Have you or any of your classmates used multimedia simulations in classes or any other places? Were your experiences positive or negative? If given the option in a chemistry class lab, would you choose to use a multimedia simulation to complete an experiment, instead of actually doing the experiment in the lab? Why? In chemistry labs, the liquids, gases, and solids used often have an odor and can be slightly dangerous if not handled properly. Do you think the lack of smell and not handling the chemicals detracts from the knowledge gained in an experiment? Click the WEB CHAT button to enter a Web Chat discussion related to this topic.

Creating a HyperStudio Project

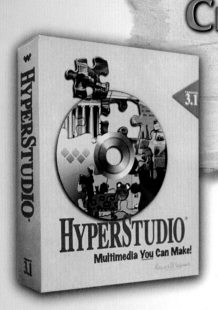

OBJECTIVES:

You will have mastered the material in this project when you can:

- Start HyperStudio
- Create a new stack
- Add a text object
- Create a graphic
- Add a new card
- Add a background
- Save a stack
- Add a navigation button
- Use a navigation button

WebInfo

For more information on how to obtain an evaluation copy of HyperStudio, visit the Teachers Discovering Computers Chapter 5 WebInfo page **(www.scsite.com/tdc/ch5/webinfo.htm)** and click Evaluation Copy.

WHAT IS HYPERSTUDIO?

HyperStudio is an easy-to-use multimedia authoring software program that allows the author to combine many multimedia elements into a series of interactive cards. A card is one of the most basic elements of HyperStudio. Much like a slide in a PowerPoint presentation, each individual screen within a Hyper-Studio project is a **card**. Every card has a background and can have one or more objects such as text, graphics, and other elements. Creating a HyperStudio project involves entering text, adding backgrounds, and inserting graphics, sounds, buttons, and animation to a variety of cards.

A HyperStudio project is called a stack. A HyperStudio **stack** is a file that consists of one or more linked cards, along with any graphics, sounds, buttons, or other media elements. Individual cards in a stack are linked with buttons. **Buttons** are small graphical icons that allow a user to navigate from card to card in any sequence, as defined by the author. An author can use buttons to link the cards in a non-linear way, for example, to create a stack that allows for discovery learning. Buttons also allow the user to initiate actions such as playing sound, viewing an animation, launching other stacks, and connecting to the World Wide Web.

HyperStudio originally was developed for Macintosh computers. As with most other educational software, however, HyperStudio now can be used on both Macintosh computers and PCs. Today, more than two million students, including elementary students, are proud developers of interactive multimedia presentations using HyperStudio.

PROJECT — MARS THE RED PLANET STACK

In this project, you will learn the basic steps involved in creating a HyperStudio stack. This project uses HyperStudio to create a two-card stack about the planet Mars (Figures 1a and 1b). The first card in the stack lists the project title and includes a graphic and a button that links to the next card. The second card uses text and a solar system background graphic to present information about Mars. As you work through the project, you may find it helpful to refer back to Figures 1a and 1b to see the finished stack.

This project provides step-by-step instructions for creating the project using HyperStudio installed on a Macintosh computer. You also can complete this project using HyperStudio installed on a PC. In addition, you can complete this project using the Preview

Figure 1a

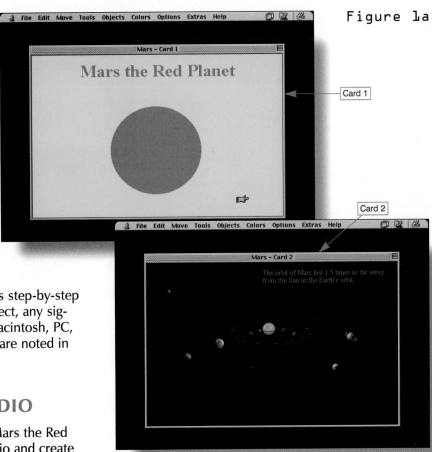

Version of HyperStudio. You can obtain a free Preview Version on an Evaluation CD from Roger Wagner Publications.

When completing this project using HyperStudio installed on a PC or the HyperStudio Preview Version, you may encounter slight variations from the project's step-by-step instructions. Throughout the project, any significant differences among the Macintosh, PC, and Preview Version instructions are noted in the steps.

STARTING HYPERSTUDIO

The first step in developing the Mars the Red Planet stack is to start HyperStudio and create a new stack. Perform the following steps to start HyperStudio and create a new stack.

Figure 1b

 ### To Start HyperStudio and Create a New Stack

1 **If the HyperStudio icon is not on your desktop, ask your instructor how to start HyperStudio. If the HyperStudio icon is on your desktop, double-click it and then click the New Stack button. Point to the Yes button.**

The HyperStudio window and the main menu display. A dialog box displays, asking you if you are sure you want to leave the Home Stack (Figure 2).

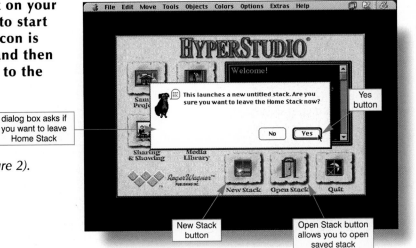

Figure 2

2 **Click the Yes button. When the next dialog box displays, click the Yes button. Click Edit on the menu bar and then point to Preferences.**

The Untitled - Card 1 window and the Edit menu display (Figure 3).

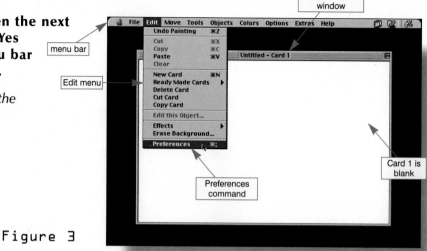

Figure 3

3 **Click Preferences.**

The Preferences dialog box displays.

4 **Click I'm an experienced HyperStudio user and then click Show card number with stack name. Point to the OK button.**

Selecting I'm an experienced HyperStudio user prevents future Help messages from displaying and allows you to choose more options. Selecting Show card number with stack name displays the card number and stack name on the title bar (Figure 4).

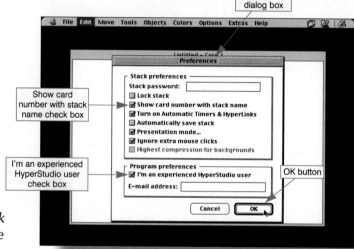

Figure 4

5 **Click the OK button and then click Tools on the menu bar. While holding down the mouse button, drag the Tools menu to the left edge of the Untitled - Card 1 window. Click Colors on the menu bar. While holding down the mouse button, drag the Colors menu to the right edge of the Untitled - Card 1 window.**

*Dragging a menu to the edge of a window — an operation called **tearing away** — causes the menu items to display as a palette. The Tools menu and Colors menu display as palettes on the edges of the Untitled - Card 1 window (Figure 5).*

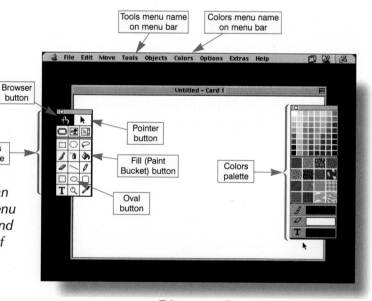

Figure 5

Once you have torn away these menus, you can choose a tool or color without clicking the menu name. Only the Tools menu and Colors menu can be torn away from the menu bar.

ADDING A BACKGROUND COLOR, TEXT OBJECT, AND A GRAPHIC

Next, you will begin formatting and adding content to the first card in the stack. The following steps show you how to add a yellow background color, add a text object in which to type the card title, and add a graphic of the planet Mars to the first card.

To Add a Background Color, Text Object, and a Graphic

1 **Click the Fill button on the Tools palette. Click yellow (row 5, column 2) on the Colors palette and then click anywhere on Card 1.**

The Fill tool (Paint Bucket) and the color yellow are selected. Clicking anywhere on Card 1 changes the background of the card to yellow (Figure 6).

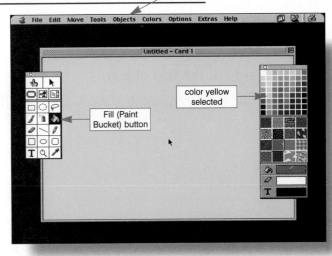

Figure 6

2 **Click Objects on the menu bar and then click Add a Text Object. If a dialog box displays, click the OK button.**

*HyperStudio displays flashing dots in the shape of a rectangle to represent the default size and location of the text object (Figure 7). A **text object** is an area where you can add text. The **flashing dots** indicate that the text object is selected and you can resize or move it.*

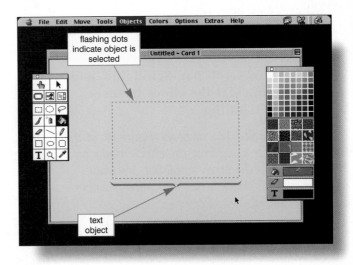

Figure 7

3 Point to an open area in the text object. When the mouse pointer changes to a double two-headed arrow, drag the text object to position the top of the text object at the top of the card. Point to the bottom line of the text object. When the mouse pointer changes to a two-headed arrow, drag the bottom line up until the text object occupies about one quarter of Card 1. Next, stretch the left and right side of the text object.

The text object is moved and resized to display at the top of Card 1 (Figure 8a).

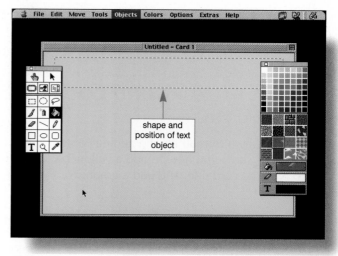

Figure 8a

4 Click outside of the text object.

The Text Appearance dialog box displays (Figure 8b).

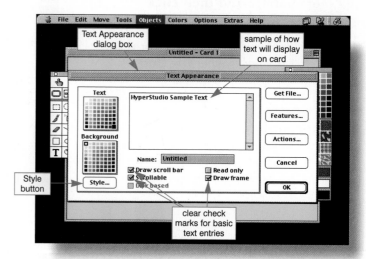

Figure 8b

5 Click Draw scroll bar, Scrollable, and Draw frame to clear the check boxes. Click the Style button.

The Text Style dialog box displays (Figure 9). In the Text Appearance dialog box, the check marks no longer display in the Draw scroll bar, Scrollable, and Draw frame check boxes indicating the check boxes are cleared.

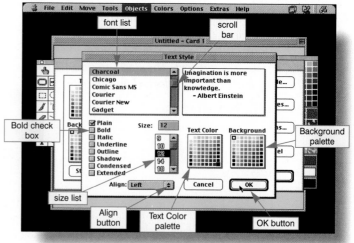

Figure 9

6 Use the scroll bar to scroll through the font list and then click Times New Roman. Click Bold, click 36 in the size list, and then click the Align button. Click Center in the Align list. Click red (row 4, column 4) in the Text Color palette and then click yellow (row 5, column 2) in the Background palette. Click the OK button in the Text Style dialog box. Click the OK button in the Text Appearance dialog box.

The dialog boxes no longer display. The insertion point displays in the text object.

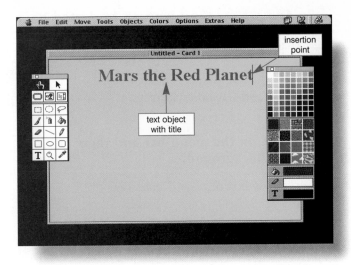

Figure 10

7 Type `Mars the Red Planet` in the text object as the card title.

The title displays in 36-point Times New Roman red, bold font. The title is centered in the text object (Figure 10).

8 Click the Oval button on the Tools palette and then click red (row 4, column 4) on the Colors palette. Point to an open area in the bottom center of the window. While holding down the SHIFT key, drag the mouse pointer up diagonally to draw a two-inch circle. If the circle is not where you want it on your card, immediately click Undo on the Edit menu and redraw the circle. Click the Fill button on the Tools palette and then click anywhere in the circle.

A red circle displays in the center of Card 1, below the title (Figure 11).

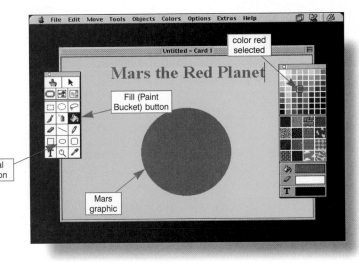

Figure 11

The red circle shown in Figure 11 represents Mars the Red Planet. Card 1 of the HyperStudio stack is now complete.

ADDING A NEW CARD WITH AN IMPORTED BACKGROUND

Now that you have completed your first HyperStudio card, the next step is to create a second card with an imported background. HyperStudio includes many clip art images you can use to create a background for the cards in a stack. The second card in this HyperStudio stack uses a solar system background. Perform the steps on the next page to add a new card with an imported solar system background.

To Add a New Card with an Imported Background

1 **Click Edit on the menu bar and then click New Card.**

The Untitled - Card 2 window displays.

2 **Click File on the menu bar and then click Import Background.**

The HS Art dialog box displays (Figure 12).

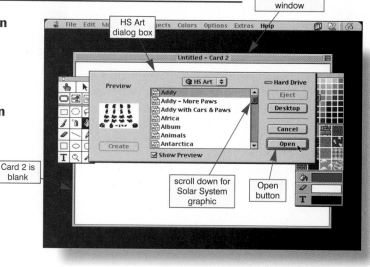

Figure 12

3 **Scroll down and click Solar System in the HS Art list. (If you are using a PC, click solrsstm.bmp in the HS Art list). Click the Open button.**

The solar system graphic displays as the background of Card 2 (Figure 13).

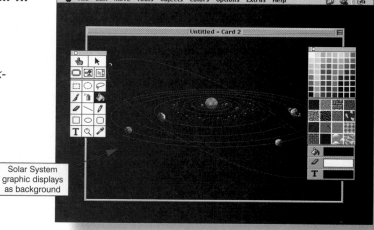

Figure 13

ADDING A TEXT OBJECT TO CARD 2 AND SAVING A STACK

You already have learned how to add a text object to a HyperStudio card. In the next sequence of steps, you will add a text object and then enter text that provides additional information about Mars. Then, you will save your HyperStudio stack. Perform the following steps to add a new text object and then save the HyperStudio stack.

To Add a Text Object and Save the HyperStudio Stack

1 **Click Objects on the menu bar and then click Add a Text Object. Resize and move the text object to display in the top-right corner of the card (refer to Figure 1b on page 5.41 for the size and placement of the text object). Click outside of the text object.**

2 **When the Text Appearance dialog box displays, click Draw scroll bar, Scrollable, and Draw frame to clear the check boxes. Click the Style button. In the Text Style dialog box, click Times New Roman in the font list, click Plain, click 14 in the size list, and then click Left in the Align list. Click red (row 4, column 4) in the Text Color palette and then click black (row 8, column 8) in the Background palette. Click the OK button twice. Type** `The orbit of Mars lies 1.5 times as far away from the Sun as the Earth's orbit.` **in the text object.**

The text object displays in the top-right corner of Card 2. The text displays in 14-point Times New Roman red font.

3 **Insert a floppy disk in the disk drive. Click File on the menu bar and then click Save Stack. When the save dialog box displays, type** `Mars` **in the Please name this STACK text box, click the Desktop button, click the Floppy icon in the list, and then click the Open button.**

The save dialog box displays (Figure 14). When you click the Desktop button in the save dialog box, a list of drives displays where you can choose the drive on which you will save the stack. Clicking the Open button returns you to the save dialog box.

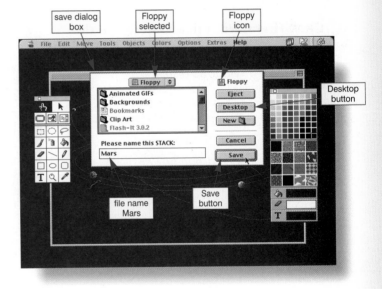

Figure 14

4 **Click the Save button.**

HyperStudio saves the file on a floppy disk with the file name, Mars.

ADDING A NAVIGATION BUTTON

The capability of adding navigation buttons is a very important feature of HyperStudio. Adding navigation buttons allows an author to link cards in a non-linear way to promote discovery learning. Perform the steps on the next page to add a navigation button to Card 1 in the HyperStudio stack.

✏️ To Add a Navigation Button

1 **Click Move on the menu bar and then point to First Card.**

The Move menu displays with the First Card command highlighted. Other commands on the Move menu allow users to display different cards (Figure 15).

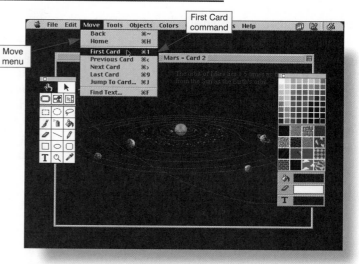

Figure 15

2 **Click First Card. Click Objects on the menu bar.**

The Mars – Card 1 windows displays.

3 **Click Add a Button on the Objects menu.**

The Button Appearance dialog box displays (Figure 16).

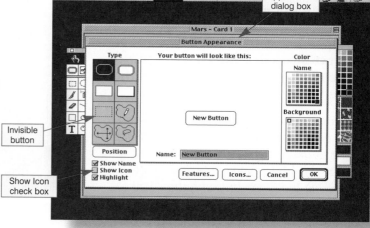

Figure 16

4 **Click the Invisible button in the Type palette (row 3, column 1) and then click Show Icon to select it.**

The Icons dialog box displays (Figure 17). This dialog box allows you to select an icon to represent the navigation button.

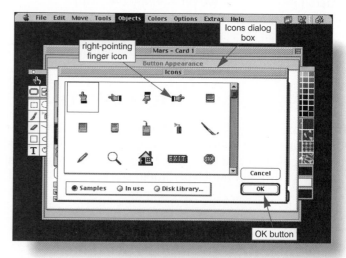

Figure 17

5 Click the right-pointing finger icon (row 1, column 4) and then click the OK button twice. If a dialog box displays, click the OK button.

The right-pointing finger icon displays in the center of Card 1, surrounded by flashing dots (Figure 18).

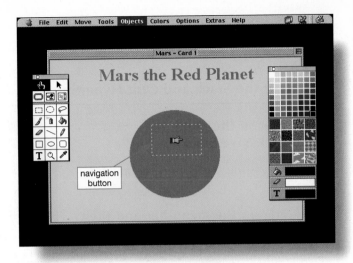

Figure 18

6 Click anywhere inside the flashing dots and then drag the right-pointing finger icon to the bottom-right corner of the card. Click outside of the flashing dots.

The Actions dialog box displays.

7 In the Actions dialog box, click Next Card, click Fastest, click the OK button, and then click the Done button.

The right-pointing finger navigation button displays on Card 1 (Figure 19). Clicking this navigation button with the Browser button selected displays the next card in the HyperStudio stack.

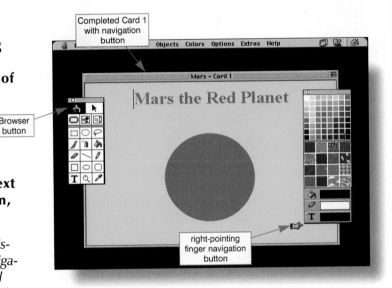

Figure 19

USING A NAVIGATION BUTTON

Students interact with a HyperStudio stack by clicking navigation buttons. Students' ability to interact with a HyperStudio stack actively engages them in the learning process — and is one of the many features that makes HyperStudio a powerful learning tool. To use a navigation button, perform the following step.

 To Use a Navigation Button

1 Click the Browser button on the Tools palette. Click the right-pointing finger navigation button.

Card 2 of the HyperStudio stack displays.

QUITTING HYPERSTUDIO

Perform the following steps to save your stack again and quit HyperStudio.

 To Save the Stack and Quit HyperStudio

1 **Click File on the menu bar and then click Save Stack.**

HyperStudio saves the stack on the floppy disk.

2 **Click File on the menu bar and then point to Quit HyperStudio.**

The File menu displays and the Quit HyperStudio command is highlighted (Figure 20).

3 **Click Quit HyperStudio (if you are using a PC, click Exit).**

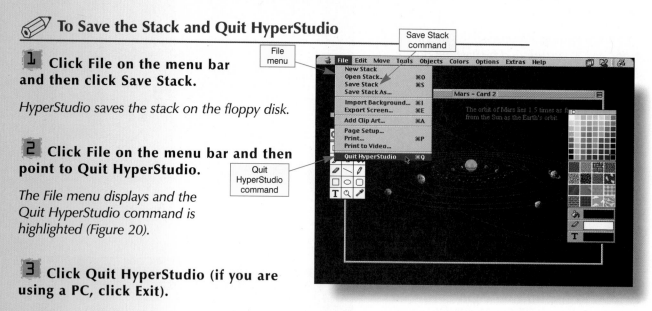

Figure 20

SUMMARY

HyperStudio is a powerful multimedia authoring software program that allows teachers and students to create projects that contain text, graphics, sound, video, animations, and even hyperlinks to Web sites and other sources of information. In completing this project, you learned how to use some of the basic features of HyperStudio to create a simple two-card HyperStudio stack.

Many teachers also have their students create an **About the Author Card**, which allows students to take ownership of their work. Students usually are very proud of their HyperStudio stacks. Including an About the Author card gives them the opportunity to tell others about themselves. About the Author cards often contain brief facts and a picture of a student; some even include a recorded audio file that tells about the student. The audio file can be linked to a scrolling text object or set to play when the About the Author card displays.

HyperStudio contains a multitude of additional features, which you easily can learn on your own or with the help of your instructor. Some of the many sources that can help you learn more about using HyperStudio include the following:

  HyperStudio contains an extensive Help system, Show Me How tutorials, and dozens of student-created sample stacks to help you build your own HyperStudio stack. You can access these tools from the HyperStudio main menu (Figure 21).

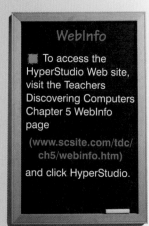

WebInfo

 To access the HyperStudio Web site, visit the Teachers Discovering Computers Chapter 5 WebInfo page

(www.scsite.com/tdc/ ch5/webinfo.htm)

and click HyperStudio.

Figure 21

- HyperStudio's Web site provides numerous resources, including tutorials, lesson plans, and sample stacks. The Web site also contains an online form you can use to request a free Preview Version of HyperStudio.
- Many schools offer beginning and advanced HyperStudio workshops. Check with your college or school district to see if they offer HyperStudio workshops.
- Various schools maintain libraries of books, tutorials, and other materials that can help you learn more about using HyperStudio. Ask your college or university instructor or your school's technology coordinator or media specialists for HyperStudio learning products.

One other way to learn more about HyperStudio is to review the student-created sample stacks provided with HyperStudio and the additional stacks that are available at the HyperStudio Web site. These student-created stacks clearly demonstrate the many features of HyperStudio — and can help you better understand how multimedia authoring software programs such as HyperStudio can make a difference in the way students learn.

CHAPTER 6

Education and Technology Integration

Objectives

After completing this chapter, you will be able to:

- Define curriculum and explain curriculum standards and benchmarks

- Explain technology integration

- Describe the use of computers in computer labs versus classroom instruction

- Identify ways in which technology can positively influence learning

- Identify ways to plan for technology integration

- Explain various planning tools and instructional models

- Describe the steps of the ASSURE Instructional Model

- Identify ways to get started using technology at a new school

- Describe the use of learning centers

THROUGHOUT THIS TEXTBOOK, YOU LEARNED ABOUT COMPUTERS AND OTHER EDUCATIONAL TECHNOLOGIES, AND YOU HAVE SEEN THE IMPACT TECHNOLOGY HAS ON PEOPLE'S LIVES, SCHOOLS, AND CLASSROOMS. Everyday, computers help many individuals accomplish many job-related tasks more efficiently and effectively. For educators, computers and other technologies serve as the tools needed to implement new and evolving teaching strategies.

The first five chapters of this textbook focused on building computer and information literacy skills. This chapter builds upon your computer and information literacy and provides you with a basic understanding of how to integrate technology across the curriculum. As you learned in Chapter 1, integration literacy is the ability to use computers and other technologies combined with a variety of teaching and learning strategies to enhance students' learning. Integration literacy means that teachers can determine how to match appropriate technologies to learning objectives, goals, and outcomes. Just as computer and information literacy are linked, integration literacy relies on a solid foundation of computer and information literacy, all of which help teachers successfully integrate technology into their classroom curriculum.

What Is Curriculum?

Education literature defines the term, curriculum, in many ways. Often, curriculum is defined simply as that which is taught. For the purpose of this textbook, **curriculum** is defined as all of the experiences a learner has under the supervision and guidance of teachers **[Figure 6-1]**. Curriculum consists of a plan or written document that includes a series of required goals and learning

outcomes. **K-12 curriculum** is any and all subject areas offered or taught in a K-12 school environment.

Many countries have Departments of Education or educational organizations that serve as the governing association for educational regulations and reform. Agencies in the United States include the federal Department of Education (DOE), and each state has its own Department of Education **[Figure 6-2]**.

The federal Department of Education is the governing body for public education in the United States. State Departments of Education provide their school districts with policies, directives, and updates to state public education issues. In addition, state DOEs provide access to up-to-date statistics, information about standards and accountability, teacher certification, scholarships, grants and funding sources, resources, and more.

State Departments of Education also provide their school districts with documents that describe curriculum goals and objectives for learning. These documents often are called **curriculum guides [Figure 6-3]**. While curriculum guides usually include subject specific

WebInfo

For numerous curriculum links, visit the Teachers Discovering Computers Chapter 6 WebInfo page

(www.scsite.com/tdc/ch6/webinfo.htm)

and click Curriculum Links.

Figure 6-1 Using computers in the classroom helps teachers achieve the learning outcome defined by the curriculum.

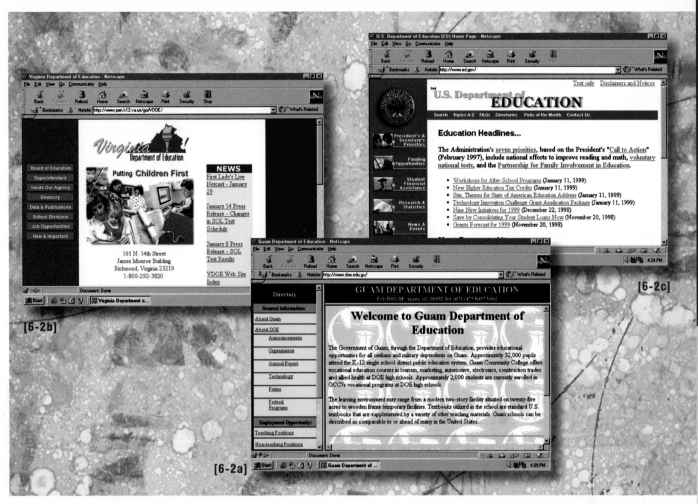

[6-2b]

[6-2c]

[6-2a]

Figure 6-2 Figure 6-2a displays the home page of Guam's Department of Education. The Virginia state Department of Education [Figure 6-2b] and the U.S. Department of Education [Figure 6-2c] have Web sites that provide information and statistics on certification, scholarships, and more.

goals and standards, they often include direction for specific content areas, benchmarks, activities, and forms of evaluation.

School curriculum guides not only include recommendations, but examples that teachers can use to develop curriculum-based lesson plans and they usually are organized by grade level and subject. Curriculum guides may include specific curriculum standards and benchmarks to assist teachers in meeting curriculum objectives.

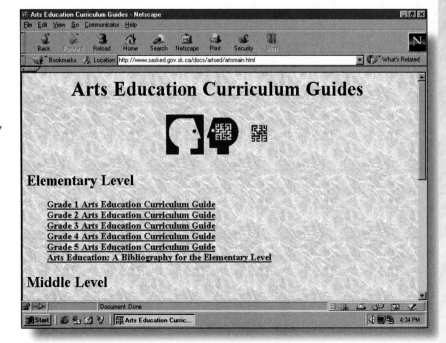

Figure 6-3 Curriculum guides usually outline specific learning objectives by grade level and subject.

Curriculum Standards and Benchmarks

A **curriculum standard**, also called a **curriculum goal** or **learning goal**, defines what a student is expected to know at certain stages of education. Curriculum standards for K-12 education are a collection of general concepts that school districts expect students to learn as they progress through grade levels.

Curriculum standards vary from state to state and usually cover core subjects, such as language arts, mathematics, science, social studies, art, health, and foreign languages. A **benchmark** is a specific, measurable learning objective or indicator that usually is tied to a curriculum standard. **Figure 6-4** lists a sample curriculum standard and appropriate and measurable benchmarks for language arts for different grade levels.

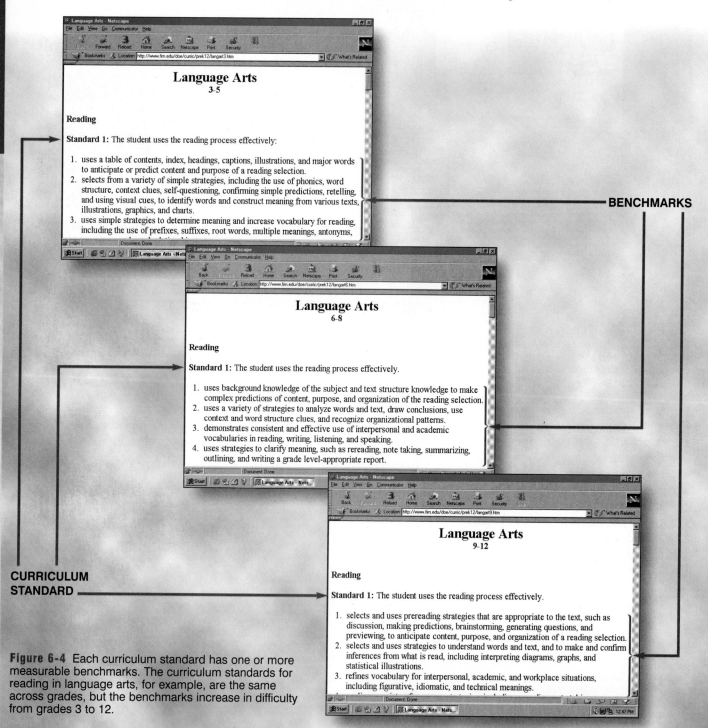

Figure 6-4 Each curriculum standard has one or more measurable benchmarks. The curriculum standards for reading in language arts, for example, are the same across grades, but the benchmarks increase in difficulty from grades 3 to 12.

What Is Technology Integration?

Defining curriculum is easy when compared to defining technology integration. First, **integration** by itself is defined as bringing different parts together to combine into a whole. Therefore, **technology integration** is the combination of all technology parts, such as hardware and software, together with each subject-related area of curriculum to enhance learning. Furthermore, technology integration is using technology to help meet the curriculum standards and learner outcomes of each lesson, unit, or activity.

Mastering technology integration is not easy. Extensive formal training and practical experiences are imperative for successful integration of technology at all levels of K-12 education. Technology cannot enhance learning unless teachers know how to use and integrate technology into subject-specific areas.

First and foremost, teachers must remember that technology is only a tool to enhance or support new instructional strategies. Educators should take steps to integrate technology throughout classroom experiences — and find ways to use technology to teach subject-specific information while establishing connections between those subjects and the real world **[Figure 6-5]**. This chapter will assist you in learning the basics necessary to integrate technology into your classroom and provide the understanding needed to promote integration literacy.

A critical issue related to technology integration is that technology should not drive the curriculum. The curriculum, rather, should drive the technology; that is, teachers should use the appropriate technologies to enhance learning at the appropriate times **[Figure 6-6]**. In the next section, you will learn the pros and cons of using computers located in a centralized computer lab or in individual classrooms.

Classroom Integration versus Computer Labs

Educational technologists have become the advocates in integrating computers into content areas. For years, teachers and

Figure 6-5 When a teacher integrates virtual reality technology in his or her classroom curriculum, students are introduced to many unique and positive learning experiences.

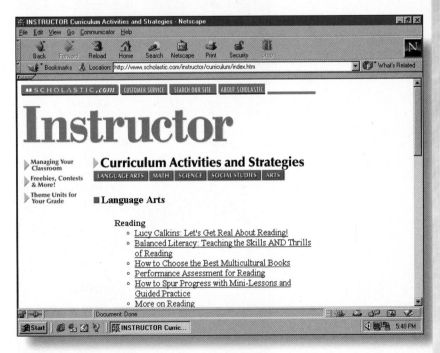

Figure 6-6 Many Web sites provide teachers with curriculum integration activities and strategies.

Figure 6-7 At many schools, computer labs give students access to computers and other technologies.

Figure 6-8 This teacher knows by using computers at the point of instruction she can enhance the students' learning experiences.

Figure 6-9 A teacher often can identify a teachable moment just by looking in the faces of excited students who are motivated to learn!

administrators have focused their efforts on getting technology or computer labs into the schools. A **computer lab**, or **technology lab**, usually is a designated classroom filled with computers and technology for groups of students to use **[Figure 6-7]**. Lab computers usually are connected to the school's local area network (LAN) and provide many resources in a centralized area.

Teachers can schedule time in computer labs for an entire class period and use the labs for many purposes. In addition to computer labs, school media centers contain computers and also can be scheduled for use by classroom teachers. Computer labs are a popular approach to getting technology into K-12 schools. The primary reason administrators usually opt for computer labs first is due to cost and location. When computers are installed in the same location, they are easier to maintain and connect to a school network. Popular uses for networked school computer labs are for students to work through tutorial software and integrated learning systems software, which you learned about in Chapter 5.

Computer labs clearly provide solutions to some educational dilemmas and are an excellent addition to any school. Research shows that computers and related technologies, however, are more effective when integrated into subject content and placed in the classroom — at the point of instruction. **Point of instruction** is having the technology in the teachers' classroom at the teachers' and students' fingertips **[Figure 6-8]**.

If technology is readily available, teachers and students will use the technology more. An example would be an elementary teacher teaching a lesson on frogs. Students want to see and learn more about frogs, so they start asking questions. Teachers can turn to the technologies in their classrooms, such as multimedia software programs or the Web to show how a frog jumps, where frogs live, and more.

Convenience is important and so is the availability of the technology at the time of instruction. Many educators refer to this as a teachable moment. When students are interested and ready to learn more about a topic, teachers have a **teachable moment**, which is an open window of opportunity for the information to be comprehended in greater detail by students **[Figure 6-9]**. Computers, when placed in the hands of teachers and students, provide unique, effective, and powerful opportunities for many different types of teaching and learning.

The Classroom In Action

To illustrate the benefits of having technology at the point of instruction, this section takes you into Mr. Balado's fourth grade classroom at Martin Luther King Elementary School. Just as Mr. Balado finished reading his class a fictional story about a little boy and his secret dinosaur, several students raise their hands to ask questions. "Is the dinosaur a T-Rex?" asked one student. Another student inquired, "Did people and dinosaurs live at the same time?" "How did dinosaurs grow so big?" asked a third. Mr. Balado smiled, because he expected these types of questions and knew they would open the door for a wonderful opportunity for learning. The questions clearly lead to a teachable moment, which he could maximize by using the classroom technologies.

Mr. Balado's classroom contains five multimedia student computers networked to the school's local area network and the World Wide Web. In addition, Mr. Balado has an instructional computer with access to the Web and connected to a large screen television set [Figure 6-10]. Projecting the computer's image onto the larger screen of the television set is an excellent way to allow all students to see what displays on the computer's monitor, to see and hear interactive multimedia applications, and to interact with the Web and educational software, while at the same time asking questions. These questions create enthusiasm and a quest for additional knowledge by the students.

Mr. Balado already had planned and prepared for the integration of various technologies into his lesson on dinosaurs. First, he had looked on the Web for sites that would be appropriate for the fourth-grade curriculum and would provide detailed information and graphics about dinosaurs. Locating the sites in advance allowed him to identify several excellent sites and eliminated the need to search for Web sites during class instruction time. In addition, Mr. Balado evaluated all of the Web sites in advance for their content and appropriateness for his fourth grade students. Evaluation of technology resources is an important element in technology integration and is covered in detail in Chapter 7.

Figure 6-10 Teachers easily can connect a computer to a television set to display a computer monitor's image to the entire class.

While interacting with the Web sites, students asked more questions such as, How fast can dinosaurs run? Are all fossils dinosaurs? How long ago did they live? and How are dinosaurs named? This was all part of Mr. Balado's master plan and their questions continued as Mr. Balado actively engaged his students in exploration and discovery learning at selected dinosaur Web sites. The students were genuinely excited while exploring the Web sites of famous natural history museums; they were discovering new concepts while Mr. Balado guided their learning **[Figure 6-11]**.

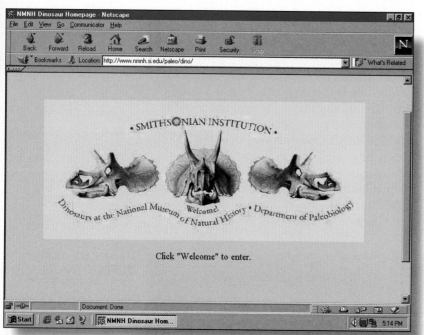

Figure 6-11 The Web provides vast amounts of information that allow students and teachers to discover innovative ways to enhance learning.

WebInfo

■ To discover more about learning styles, visit the Teachers Discovering Computers Chapter 6 WebInfo page
(www.scsite.com/tdc/ch6/webinfo.htm) and click Learning Styles.

With computers placed in his classroom at the point of instruction, Mr. Balado has his students' full attention as together they explore interesting Web sites while traveling through interactive virtual tours of dinosaurs. **Virtual tours** are tours that allow you to walk through doorways, down halls, and let you see everything in a three-dimensional world via a computer; as if being there. Mr. Balado's students no longer were only hearing a story read to them about a fictional dinosaur, they and the teacher now were seeing, hearing, and interacting with the topic. After they looked at many dinosaur facts and pictures, Mr. Balado

sent his students to their desks to write their own stories about dinosaurs and what they learned today.

Integrating Technology into the Curriculum

As this example illustrates, computers and other technologies can provide unique, effective, and powerful opportunities for many different types of teaching and learning. Many educators also recognize that technology can serve as an extremely powerful tool that can help alleviate some of the problems of today's schools. Motivating students to learn is one area that all educators constantly are trying to achieve. Technology has the potential to increase student motivation and class attendance. Using these technology tools with students with varying abilities has helped to address different learning styles. With the right approach, educators can integrate technologies such as computers, CD-ROMs, DVD-ROMs, application software, multimedia applications, electronic books and references, laserdisc, and communications applications into almost any classroom situation. For technology to enhance student learning, however, it must be integrated into the curriculum.

The key to successful technology integration is identifying what you are trying to accomplish within your curriculum. First, you must consider what the learning goals and standards are and then you must identify an appropriate technology tool that will help you accomplish your goals. While this process sounds simple, complete integration of technology in all subject areas is complex and takes a great deal of planning. A later section of this chapter will discuss how to plan for technology integration.

Once you have determined specific learning goals and objectives and identified technologies appropriate for areas of the curriculum, you then can begin to develop innovative ways to teach a diverse population of learners with different learning styles **[Figure 6-12]**. A **learning style** refers to how individuals learn, including how they prefer to receive information, express themselves, and process information. Learning styles vary among individuals. For example, some people learn better alone while others learn better in groups. Many different types of learning styles exist and most individuals learn using a combination of several styles. The use of technologies such as multimedia and the Web can help address learning styles typically neglected by traditional teaching methods. By engaging students in different ways, technology encourages students to take a more active role in the learning process.

Figure 6-12 Technology is a tool that creates valuable learning experiences for many different types of learners.

Changing Instructional Strategies

When students play a more active role in the learning process, the teacher's role must change. Teachers are transitioning from the conventional lecture-practice-recall teaching methods — often called the sage on the stage — to a classroom in which teachers engage students in activities that allow them opportunities to construct knowledge — a new role called the guide on the side. That is, teachers are beginning to shift from being the dispenser of knowledge to being the facilitator of learning. Rather than dictating a learning process, a **facilitator of learning** motivates students to want to learn, guides the student learning process, and promotes a learning atmosphere and an appreciation for the subject.

Several assumptions must be considered as teachers become facilitators of learning. The first is that students can accomplish learning and that the teachers' role is to assist their students in this process. A second assumption is that academic work extends beyond the mere storage of information. Instead, teachers want their students to be able to assimilate information and become problem solvers.

As teachers become facilitators of learning and incorporate technology into their instructional strategies, they will progress through several developmental stages. **Wellivers Instructional Transformation Model**, for example, describes five hierarchical stages of technology integration through which all teachers must progress to integrate technology effectively **[Figure 6-13]**.

Wellivers Instructional Transformation Model

1. **Familiarization** is when teachers become aware of technology and its potential uses.

2. **Utilization** is when teachers use technology, but minor problems will cause teachers to discontinue its use.

3. **Integration** is when technology becomes essential for the educational process and teachers are constantly thinking of ways to use technology in their classrooms.

4. **Reorientation** is when teachers begin to rethink the educational goals of the classroom with the use of technology.

5. **Revolution** is the evolving classroom that becomes completely integrated with technology in all subject areas. Technology becomes an invisible tool that is seamlessly woven into the teaching and learning process.

Figure 6-13 Wellivers Instructional Transformation Model describes five hierarchical stages for technology integration, through which all teachers must progress in order to integrate technology effectively.

CHAPTER 6

Barriers to Technology Integration

With all change comes barriers, and technology integration is no exception. In 1995, Bill Gates stated, "In all areas of the curriculum, teachers must teach an information-based inquiry process to meet the demands of the Information Age. This is the challenge for the world's most important profession. Meeting this challenge will be impossible unless educators are willing to join the revolution and embrace the new technology tools available." Even after several years, these words are still true.

For over two decades, several barriers have hindered technology integration in many schools. Such barriers include a lack of teacher training, lack of administration support, limited time for teacher planning, computer placement in remote locations making it difficult for teachers to have access, budget constraints, and a basic resistance to change by many educators.

Every educator looks at the integration of technology — and its challenges — from a different perspective. Technology coordinators view the problems of insufficient hardware, software, and training as major obstacles. Teachers consider the lack of time to develop computer-based lessons a concern. Administrators identify teachers' lack of experience using computers in instruction as a consideration. Teachers and schools, however, can and are beginning to overcome these barriers with proper training, planning, and a commitment to enhancing teaching and learning using technology **[Figure 6-14]**.

Figure 6-14 With proper training and planning, educators can overcome many of the barriers to effective technology integration.

With Proper Technology Training, Teachers:

- Create relationships between active learning and active teaching.

- Develop an appreciation and an understanding of the potential of technology.

- Learn to be authors of multimedia software.

- Develop leadership skills and become role models for successful integration.

- Understand the power of technology integration.

- Design integrated curriculum.

- Learn the benefits of technology in the classroom.

- Develop ownership of the technology through authentic experiences.

- Learn to motivate students with technology.

- Achieve success by becoming informed and reflective decision makers.

- Become advocates for technology integration.

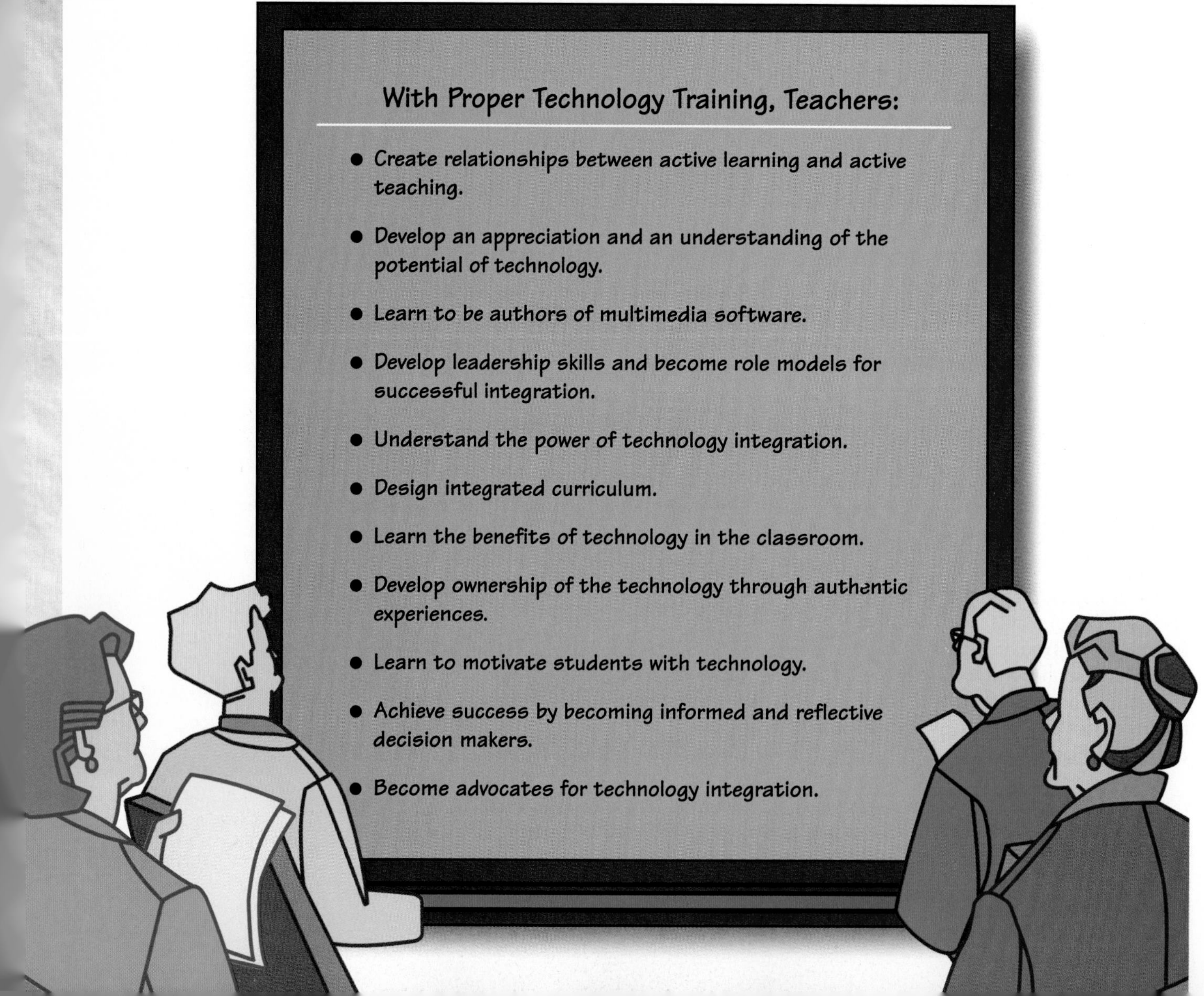

Technology Integration and the Learning Process

Before teachers can begin to develop integration skills, they must realize and understand how integration of technology can enhance teaching and learning. Research shows that using technology in the classroom motivates students, encourages them to become problem solvers, and creates new avenues to explore information. Teachers also have found that using computers or computer-related technologies can capture and hold students' attention. Interactive technologies, such as software applications, multimedia software, reference guides, tutorials, simulations, and the Web, are especially engaging, as they allow students to determine the flow of information, review concepts, practice skills, do in-depth research, and more.

Technologies capable of providing interactivity, learner control, and student engagement are a natural choice for improving instruction. When used properly, technology is extremely beneficial in the learning process.

The Learning Process

For learning to take place, learners must be engaged in the process of education. One way to engage learners is to motivate them through authentic learning experiences. **Authentic learning** experiences are instructional activities that demonstrate real-life connections by associating the concept being taught with a real-life activity or event **[Figure 6-15]**. For authentic learning to take place, teachers must involve students in the process of gathering information, analyzing information, and using information to make informed decisions that relate to real life.

When possible, teachers also should promote active learning, which is particularly appropriate for K-12 students. **Active learning** provides students with the opportunity to be involved and interested in their own learning and gives them a sense of ownership of the information with which they are presented because they are actively involved in the learning process.

WebInfo

For more information about authentic learning experiences, visit the Teachers Discovering Computers Chapter 6 WebInfo page

(www.scsite.com/tdc/ch6/webinfo.htm)

and click Authentic Learning.

CHAPTER 6

Figure 6-15 Learners are motivated to learn through authentic real-life experiences.

A lesson on the human digestive system, for example, presents concepts that are difficult for students to understand. Students have never seen the digestive system, nor can they feel or touch it. For students to understand these new concepts, they must have background information or a knowledge base on which to build. Providing a knowledge base on which students can build is called **anchored instruction**. Through anchored instruction, learning and teaching activities are designed around an anchor (or situation) that provides a scenario or problem enhanced with curriculum materials that allow exploration by the learner. Anchored instruction also includes the component of **problem-based instruction**, in which students use the background (anchor) information to begin to solve and understand complex problems or concepts.

By providing students with opportunities to expand their knowledge base, students can experience visionary exploration or discovery learning. Recall that **discovery learning** is an inquiry-based method for teaching and learning. Exploration offers opportunities for discovery learning.

Technology and the Learning Process

Technology can provide numerous tools to support many types of instruction and learning. To teach students about the human heart, for example, a teacher could integrate a multimedia educational software application such as Body Works or Microsoft Encarta into the lesson. **Body Works** is a multimedia product for teaching all related concepts about the human body. As you learned in the previous chapter, **Microsoft Encarta** is an interactive multimedia encyclopedia. These multimedia applications provide working visual models of how the various parts of the human heart interact **[Figure 6-16]**. These multimedia applications thus allow students to see and experience clearly things they could never experience by reading a textbook. Multimedia applications such as these also allow students to build a **cognitive scaffold**, which is a mental bridge to build an understanding of complicated concepts.

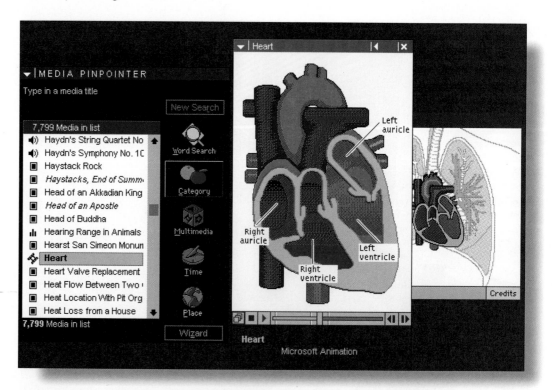

Figure 6-16 Microsoft Encarta is an educational software program that allows students to interact with a myriad of subjects. In this example, students see and hear how the human heart works.

Another benefit of integrating educational multimedia applications is that they encourage students to think not only in words and pictures, but also in colors, sounds, animations, and more. Adults and children think in multimedia, or in colors, sounds, animation, and movements. A young child, for example, will describe a fire engine by imitating the sounds of a siren, describing its color, and demonstrating the sounds and movements of fire engines going to a fire [Figure 6-17]. Most traditional instruction, however, uses words and pictures only, often in two-color textbooks. Multimedia allows students to have learning experiences in which concepts are brought to life with a variety of representations — sounds, colors, pictures, and animations.

of climbing in high altitudes, or how avalanches start.

Computers, multimedia, and especially the Web create numerous opportunities for discovery learning. Many students may never be able to visit an extraordinary museum such as the Smithsonian Institution. The Web, however, can transport them to a world beyond their own filled with infinite amounts of

Figure 6-17 Everyone thinks in colors, sounds, and animations. A young child, for example, will describe a fire engine by imitating the sounds of a siren, describing its color, and demonstrating the sounds and movements of fire engines going to a fire.

WebInfo

To take a virtual tour of a museum, visit the Teachers Discovering Computers Chapter 6 WebInfo page (www.scsite.com/tdc/ch6/webinfo.htm) and click Tour.

Technology helps teachers promote active learning and create authentic learning experiences by allowing students to conduct Web-based research, explore concepts in a multimedia presentation, create a slide show for a history presentation, create a database of results from a group science project, and so on. Technology also provides opportunities for anchored instruction. Students can watch a Web-based video clip of a Himalayan mountain-climbing expedition, for example, and then move on to examine the history of Tibet, the Sherpa culture, the physical effects

information — visually, audibly, and even virtually. Using discovery learning you can break down classroom walls with technology, the Web, and most importantly — imagination. Properly integrated technology allows students to understand concepts clearer and learn no matter who or where they are.

The Internet and the World Wide Web have been called the **educational equalizer** — that is, they give students of all backgrounds, socioeconomic levels, learning styles, and learning abilities access to the same information. **Figure 6-18** on the next page

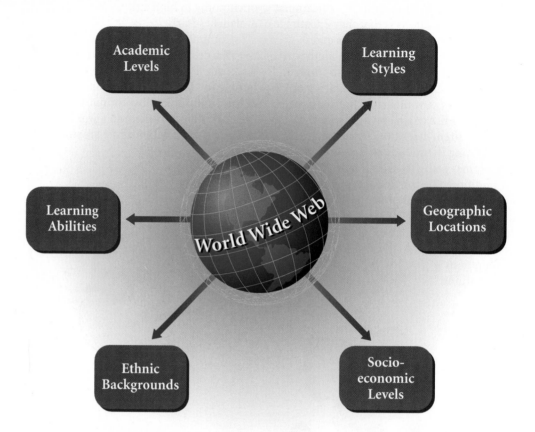

Figure 6-18 The Web has the capability of transporting students to a world beyond their own filled with an infinite amount of information.

WebInfo

To learn more about cooperative learning, visit the Teachers Discovering Computers Chapter 6 WebInfo page

(www.scsite.com/tdc/ch6/webinfo.htm)

and click Cooperative Learning.

illustrates how the Web brings these elements together to provide valuable learning experiences.

The Web allows children to experience educational opportunities previously not available. Students can publish their work, meet students with similar interests across the globe, and participate in shared learning experiences with classrooms around the world. The Internet and Web also support projects in which students interact with authors, elected officials, or scientists doing research. E-mail and Web-based projects are perfect for teacher-monitored school projects that involve language arts, cultural learning, history, geography, social studies, science, or communications with friends around the world [Figure 6-19].

As illustrated by these examples, computers can provide many unique, effective, and powerful opportunities for teaching and learning. Such opportunities include skill-building practice, interactive learning, and linking learners to instructional technology

resources. In adddition, computers support communications beyond classroom walls, thus enabling schools and communities to provide an environment for cooperative learning and the development of innovative opportunities for learning.

Cooperative learning refers to a method of instruction where students work collaboratively in groups to achieve learning objectives and goals. Instead of working alone on activities and projects, students benefit from sharing ideas, learn teamwork skills, and begin to help one another to accomplish tasks or achieve learning goals. Cooperative classroom activities are student-centered, with the teacher serving as a facilitator and the students as information seekers. **High-order thinking skills** are problem solving, critical thinking, and the ability to interpret and solve complex issues. Teachers need to create activities for students to promote the use of high-order thinking skills throughout their educational experiences [Figure 6-20].

Figure 6-19 Using computers and the World Wide Web, students can join various projects to learn about other cultures and communicate with other students around the world.

Figure 6-20 Computers support communications beyond classroom walls thus providing an environment that allows for cooperative learning, development of high-order thinking skills, and solving complex problems.

WebInfo

For more ideas about how to use e-mail in the class-room, visit the Teachers Discovering Computers Chapter 6 WebInfo page

(www.scsite.com/tdc/ch6/webinfo.htm)

and click E-mail Projects.

CHAPTER 6

By promoting new and enhanced learning experiences, properly integrated technology offers limitless possibilities for instruction and learning. Computers, multimedia, the Web, and other technologies help students to understand concepts more clearly and help teachers develop unique activities that maximize every teachable moment. Students become knowledge seekers and active learners who acquire knowledge and find different ways to interpret what they discover. Finally, technology can help improve students' abilities as independent thinkers and encourage them to become lifelong learners.

Strategies for Teaching with Technology

The best strategy for technology integration is to put the technology into the hands of trained teachers, make it easily accessible, and let them decide how best to use it in their classrooms at the point of instruction. Teachers then can use an array of teaching strategies to develop a learning environment in which students are encouraged to be independent learners and take responsibility for their own learning.

The main goal of such teaching strategies is to provide a consistent application of

technology tools to support instructional curriculum areas. Also, it is important to give every student the opportunity to work with computers and related technologies. When proper strategies are used for technology integration, students enjoy learning to use technology as well as the content in the subject-related curriculum areas.

Already, many experienced educators are integrating technology into subject-related instruction — and have seen the benefits technology integration can bring to the learning experience. One critically important element in effective technology integration is continuous planning. Planning for technology integration must take place on many levels, including planning by the school district, planning for integration of technology in the classroom, and planning to integrate technology into your lesson plans.

The Role of the School District

Effective technology integration cannot take place if support for technology integration does not come from several sources within the school district. School district administrators must plan carefully for every aspect of technology integration, from purchase to installation to teacher and staff training. Almost every school district has a detailed technology plan for technology integration. A **technology plan** is an outline that specifies the school district's procedures for purchasing equipment and software and training teachers to use and then integrate technology into their classroom curriculum. Because of emerging and changing technologies, many school districts update their technology plans annually.

To prepare educators to use the technology once it is implemented, administrators provide technology training with mentorship programs and follow-up staff development after training **[Figure 6-21]**. A **mentorship program** teams new teachers with experienced teachers to encourage new teachers to learn to integrate technology resources. Collaboration is promoted by sharing planning time and e-mail with other teaching professionals inside and outside the district. Experienced teachers guide new teachers by providing information and suggestions. In-house workshops are

WebInfo

To view a school district's technology plan, visit the Teachers Discovering Computers Chapter 6 WebInfo page

(www.scsite.com/tdc/ ch6/webinfo.htm)

and click Technology Plan.

Figure 6-21 Mentorship programs allow teachers to learn computer and technology integration concepts from experienced teachers in a nonthreatening environment.

provided so teachers learn to use and integrate the available technologies in their schools and classrooms.

Today, many federal, public, and state grant funding sources now are requiring that the majority of funding must be spent on teacher training. This increase in funding should increase the number of teachers using and integrating technology.

Planning for Technology Integration in the Classroom

Teachers must plan carefully for the use and integration of computers and technologies in the classroom. Just as planning is essential to effective instruction, it is required for effective use and integration of technology in the classroom. One important consideration is deciding on the most appropriate technology to achieve desired learner outcomes. Teachers must plan how they will teach the curriculum, what areas they need to cover for content, and where they can use technology to meet learning objectives.

Another important consideration in the planning stage is preparing the classroom environment **[Figure 6-22]**. The way in which you integrate technology into the curriculum will depend largely on how many computers are in your classroom or in your school. Whether you use one computer, two computers, or 30 computers, however, you must plan how and when you will use those computers and how you will enable your students to use those computers. The amount of planning will vary according to the arrangement of computers in your classroom and school and the scope of your lesson. Chapter 7 discusses these and other planning issues.

Using a Computer Lab

Because few classrooms include a computer for every student, using a computer lab allows teachers to provide learning opportunities that are not possible in a one-, two-, or even five-computer classroom. The most important advantage of using a computer lab is that all students are provided hands-on experience with using computer technology **[Figure 6-23]**. Computer labs can be used

Figure 6-22 Teachers must prepare their classrooms carefully for the integration of computers and other technologies.

Figure 6-23 The biggest advantage of computer labs is they allow all students to have hands-on experience with computers.

WebInfo

For assistance with creating lesson plans, visit the Teachers Discovering Computers Chapter 6 WebInfo page **(www.scsite.com/tdc/ ch6/webinfo.htm)** and click Lesson Plans.

CHAPTER 6

successfully by teachers for tutorials, remediation, cooperative learning, computer skill instruction (such as word processing, spreadsheets, and databases), Internet research, whole class instruction, and integrated learning systems (ILS). Computer labs have an added benefit of allowing students to interact with technology and software that is student-centered. Taking your class to a computer lab, however, requires careful planning to use the allocated time efficiently and effectively. Managing instruction in a lab environment also requires that teachers carefully plan their learning strategies for this multi-computer environment.

One-Computer Classroom

In classrooms with only one computer, teachers must plan to maximize the effectiveness of that one computer. In such classrooms, the computer most commonly is used for classroom presentations and demonstrations. To allow students to view the presentation or demonstration, teachers easily can project the monitor's image on a large screen television set. Using a television set with a 27-inch or 32-inch screen usually is sufficient. If you do not have a large screen television set in your classroom, the school's media center should be able to provide one. Television sets normally are available, as long as you plan ahead.

Another option is to project the image onto a projection screen or classroom wall using a liquid crystal display (LCD) panel and an overhead projector; again, you may have to plan ahead to schedule the use of an LCD panel through the school's media center.

A good instructional strategy for the classroom computer is to introduce students to various types of software and create learning paths prior to taking the class to the computer lab. Using this instructional strategy optimizes the time students spend on computers while in the lab. Rather than spending time learning basic software skills, students can devote time to interacting with the computer to experience discovery learning.

In addition, teachers in a one-computer classroom can use the computer for the same purposes as described in the next sections on two or more computer classrooms. With only one computer available, however, additional planning is required.

Two-Computer Classroom

In classrooms with two computers, teachers must develop a strategy to manage their use. One computer could be used mainly for research on the Internet, presentations, Web-based projects, and e-mail. The other computer might be used as a writing center or for students to create multimedia projects.

Regardless of how you use the computers, you should develop a strategy for how you will allocate computer use and how students' computer time will be managed. Questions that can assist with planning are:

- Will both computers have the same hardware, software, and network access?

- Will one or both computers be connected to the Web?

- Will students rotate through using one or both computers on a daily basis?

- How much time will each student be allowed on each computer?

- Is it better to have the students work together on projects?

- How are you going to observe your students using the Internet?

- How will you evaluate student learning?

More Than Two Computers

Teachers who have several computers may find that arranging their classrooms in a single learning center or several learning centers through which groups of students can rotate as they complete projects or activities provides an environment for productive use of the computers [Figure 6-24]. Other technologies also can be organized into learning centers, such as a video center, using video tapes; a CD-ROM and DVD-ROM center; a listening center; a laserdisc; or a digital camera center.

Before setting up a computer center or centers teachers should ask the planning questions previously cited, in addition to considering how many computers will be in each center and what, if any, other technologies might be included in the center. As noted, the technologies a teacher utilizes will depend on the learning objectives. Furthermore, part of preparing the classroom environment and determining learning

WebInfo

For additional strategies and applications for one-computer classrooms, visit the Teachers Discovering Computers Chapter 6 WebInfo page (www.scsite.com/tdc/ch6/webinfo.htm) and click One Computer.

Figure 6-24 A networked computer with Internet access provides stations for students to use while working on projects and for exploration on the Web.

objectives is being aware of the prerequisite skills necessary for students to be successful.

Planning Lessons with Technology

One of the more important parts of technology planning is developing classroom lessons and activities that utilize technology. Most students do not begin school knowing a great deal about computers. As students use computers in the classroom, however, they gain a familiarity with computers. Many educators have stated that, by using computers and related technologies, students are given new reasons to get excited and motivated about learning and, at the same time, have the opportunity to develop their own computer literacy. Students should, at some point, be taught basic computer concepts and operations, but they will learn many basic computer skills just from everyday use.

When planning lessons that use technology, teachers must consider the skills and knowledge level required for students to start and complete the lesson successfully. If technology is part of the lesson, teachers need to consider student technology skills. Many different tools are available to assess students'

skill levels, such as a skill assessment survey. A **skill assessment survey** is designed to identify individual students' academic and technology skill levels and then create a starting point for developing instructional strategies. Another simple and effective tool to help in the planning process is a KWL chart.

KWL Charts

A **KWL chart** is an instructional planning chart to assist a teacher in identifying curriculum objectives by stating what students already **K**now, what they **W**ant to know, and what they will **L**earn as shown in **Figure 6-25** on the next page. A KWL chart is a very helpful planning tool in determining skill and knowledge levels of students prior to beginning almost any project. Once a teacher has established the learner objectives, the KWL chart can be used as a survey tool to determine what students already know about a topic and what technology skills they will need for a project. The teacher and students then can determine what they will learn from the project and the technologies best suited to mastering the learning objectives.

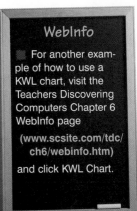

WebInfo

For another example of how to use a KWL chart, visit the Teachers Discovering Computers Chapter 6 WebInfo page (www.scsite.com/tdc/ch6/webinfo.htm) and click KWL Chart.

Figure 6-25 A KWL chart is an instructional planning tool that assists a teacher in creating specific curriculum objectives based on the knowledge of their students.

KNOW/WANT TO KNOW/LEARNED

KNOW	WANT TO KNOW	LEARNED
Dinosaurs lived a long time ago.	Did all the dinosaurs live during the same time period?	Different dinosaurs lived in different time periods.
Some dinosaurs ate meat.	How many different dinosaurs were meat eaters?	Each time period had meat-eating dinosaurs.
Other dinosaurs ate plants.	What kinds of plants did dinosaurs eat? Were they the same kinds of plants we have today?	Different plants grew during the different time periods.
Some dinosaurs were very large.	What was the largest dinosaur?	The largest dinosaurs were the sauropods.
Other dinosaurs were very small.	What was the smallest dinosaur?	The smallest dinosaurs were the compsognathus and the saltopus. They were the size of a chicken.
Some dinosaurs flew.	Which dinosaurs flew in addition to the pterodactyl?	Dinosaurs did not really fly. Bird-like dinosaurs had feathers, but could not fly. Some prehistoric birds with dinosaur characteristics flew. They include the pterodactyl, the archaeopteryx, and the quetzalcoatlus.
Dinosaurs became extinct.	Why did the dinosaurs become extinct?	Scientists can speculate only about how and why the dinosaurs became extinct.
Scientists learn about dinosaurs when they find fossils.	How do scientists know what dinosaurs ate, how they looked, and the noises they made?	Scientists form ideas about dinosaurs based on bone structure and teeth. They compare these to animals of today.
	Where have the majority of fossils been found? Where did dinosaurs live?	Many fossils have been found in Wyoming. Dinosaurs lived in many areas of the United States, but not all across the U.S.
	What are scientists who study dinosaurs called?	Scientists who study dinosaurs are called paleontologists.
	What kinds of tools do scientists use when they find dinosaur fossils?	Scientists use shovels, picks, plaster, measurement tools, computers, small brooms and brushes, magnifying glasses, and many other tools.

CHAPTER 6

As the project progresses, students are encouraged to list the objectives and skills learned on the KWL chart. Not only will students be learning subject-related matter, they will be learning new and different types of technology skills when using technology to accomplish tasks.

Instructional Models

Before you start a lesson, you plan the lesson, which is a process that involves using an instructional design or model. Effective teaching with technology also involves using an instructional model. An **instructional model** is a systematic guide for planning instruction or a lesson. When using technology, an instructional model and planning takes on a more important role. Which technology you use is not the critical issue; what is important is that you use the technology effectively and the technology is appropriate to the learning objective. Many instructional models are available from which you can choose. For the purpose of this textbook, the popular educational instructional model called the ASSURE Model is described.

The ASSURE Model

The **ASSURE Model** is a procedural guide for planning and delivering instruction that integrates technologies and media into the teaching process **[Figure 6-26]**. The ASSURE Model is a well-known guide for developing a lesson or any other instructional lessons. The following is a description of the steps of the ASSURE Model and an explanation of how to use the model in your classroom.

Analyze the Learner Knowing your learner's skill level is important. Some students may come into your classroom with academic and computer skills that others do not possess. Teachers should plan for this situation. Know your audience and consider the diverse differences in the student population you are teaching.

State Your Objectives or Identify Your Objectives or Purpose Student objectives are a statement of the type of performance you

expect students to be able to demonstrate at the end of instruction. When you have clear student objectives, you can select your materials and determine the focus and purpose of your project more wisely. Be sure to match student objectives to curriculum goals.

Select Media and Materials Selection of media and materials includes three processes, which are (1) decide on the method of instruction, (2) choose the media format that is appropriate for the method, and (3) select, modify, update, or design materials for the instruction. Media and materials include all items you choose to meet the curriculum goals, such as print, technology, information resources, and related components. Media can take many forms, including laserdisc, CD-ROM, DVD-ROM, the Internet or the Web, a video, an overhead projector, a calculator, special technology devices for learning, or

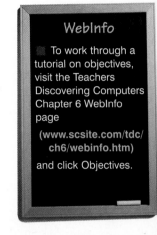

WebInfo

To work through a tutorial on objectives, visit the Teachers Discovering Computers Chapter 6 WebInfo page

(www.scsite.com/tdc/ch6/webinfo.htm)

and click Objectives.

Figure 6-26 This table shows the steps of the ASSURE Model, which is an instructional model used by educators to develop technology-based lessons.

ASSURE Model
Analyze the Learners
State Objectives
Select Media and Materials
Utilize Media and Materials
Require Learner Participation
Evaluate and Revise

any combination of these and other items [**Figure 6-27**]. The first step is to decide which method best meets your needs, such as discovery, tutorials, or demonstration. Next, you need to decide on the media, how you are going to use the media, and what you want the learners to do. Again, refer back to your objectives to assist you in determining this step. Make sure those materials are available and list what you are planning to use. Finally, determine if you need to modify any of the media or materials or design new media or materials.

Utilizing Media and Materials Teachers should preview all media and materials they are planning to use, including videos, multimedia applications, and Web sites. While a software company may advertise that a particular software product contains the correct content for your objectives, you, as the teacher, must evaluate the content of all software. Next, you will need to prepare the classroom environment. Use these questions to guide you in making preparations:

Figure 6-27 Teachers must choose which technology to use and when it is appropriate to use the technology.

- What equipment or devices are required to use the media?

- Do you need to reserve extra equipment that you may not have in your classroom?

- How do you prepare your classroom to use the equipment?

- How do you prepare the students to use the media and materials?

Require Learner Participation As previously discussed, the most effective learning situations are those that require active learning and ask learners to complete activities that build mastery toward the objectives. Classroom lessons should motivate students to be active learners who are involved in the process of learning, such as practicing, performing, solving, building, creating, and manipulating. As you develop these lessons, you must decide what information to include in the activities. If students are doing a research project using the Web, for example, they need guidelines of what to incorporate and how you will assess the outcome of the project. Chapter 7 discusses assessment tools in more detail.

Evaluate and Revise At the end of a project, it is important to evaluate all aspects of the lesson or instruction. This evaluation process includes assessing the media and materials used, the effectiveness of the project, and learner outcomes. Teachers should conduct thoughtful reflection on all aspects of the instructional process. **Reflective evaluation** is thinking back on the components of the teaching and learning process and determining the effectiveness of the learner outcomes and the use of technology during the process. **Figure 6-28** lists a number of questions that teachers should consider during the evaluation and revision of a project.

Students should also be asked to reflect on their learning experiences, their perceptions on the content learned, and their evaluation of the learning process. Emerging technologies will expand our potential to communicate effectively, to convey ideas, and to amuse, encourage, and educate students. As you revise your lesson plans, you will need to evaluate and consider using new and emerging technologies.

The ASSURE Model is an example of one popular educational model that teachers can use to plan for technology integration into instruction. As you can see, planning is important on all levels — from the district, to

---

Critical Questions to Ask During the Evaluate and Revise Step of the ASSURE Model

- Did students learn what you wanted them to learn?

- Can students demonstrate understanding of the content?

- Was the chosen technology effective?

- Were the learning objectives met using the technology?

- Should learning objectives be taught in a different format?

- Would these learning objectives be better taught without technology or with another technology?

- Can students work cooperatively with a partner on this lesson?

- Would parts of the content be better understood if students worked individually?

- What would you change?

- What would you keep the same?

- How will you revise this lesson?

Figure 6-28 Technology can create powerful opportunities for many different types of teaching and learning; however, teachers must evaluate and revise the use of technology.

the classroom, to planning individual lessons. As a new teacher, planning for technology integration will present its challenges. The next section provides information on where to go for guidance and materials to help you plan for technology integration in your classroom.

Getting Started at a New School

You are a new teacher and it is the first day of preplanning week for teachers. You are excited to get that first glimpse of your new classroom. When you finally do, you discover you have a new networked Power Macintosh and a color inkjet printer in your classroom. Fortunately, you learned about Macintosh computers and PCs during your teacher education courses. While you feel comfortable using computers, you immediately wonder how to get started and begin to consider ways to integrate this computer into your classroom curriculum [Figure 6-29]. As you start to plan for technology integration, you will need to consider many issues related to technology information and support, technology training, hardware, software, other technologies, and technology supplies.

Information About Technology

One of the first items to investigate is who else in the school is using technology in their classroom. Individuals to consult are your principal, media specialist, technology committee members, or other teachers. Any of these educators usually will know who else actively is integrating technology in their classrooms. Check to see if your school has a mentorship program.

Ascertain if your school has a technology committee — and who the members are. You can get this information from your principal or assistant principal. Consult your teacher's manual for a list of various school committees and their members [Figure 6-30]. A **teacher's manual** is a booklet that contains information, rules and regulations, rights and responsibilities, and policies and procedures that will provide answers to many of your questions.

Figure 6-29 New teachers need to ask a lot of questions on how to get started using and integrating technology in their new classrooms.

Ridgedale High School
Teachers Manual

Administration and Support Staff

Principal	Tony Hidalgo	555-4589
Assistant Principal	Latisha Smith	555-4590
Assistant Principal	Betty Rice	555-4591
Technology Coord.	Jenny Marcus	555-4567
Media Specialist	Chris Finley	555-4534
School Secretary	Clara Rich	555-4587
Administrative Asst.	Dana Gerhardt	555-4586
Cafeteria Manager	Kim Johnson	555-4512

Technology Committee

Jenny Marcus	Chair
Betty Rice	Administration Representative
Chris Finley	Media Center Representative
Regina Susol	9th Grade Representative
Gary Roberts	10th Grade Representative
Mike Holt	11th Grade Representative
Gary Orwig	12th Grade Representative
Dick Cornell	Special Education Rep.
Mari Yoshida	Student Government Rep.
Tonya Naar	PTA Representative
Kristen Myers	Community Representative

Figure 6-30 A teacher's manual provides teachers with information on a variety of subjects, such as names and telephone numbers of school personnel and members of various committees.

Finally, you should determine where you should go to get technology support. The principal, media specialist, school or district technology coordinator, and other teachers who use technology can either offer you support or guide you to where you can find support.

Technology Training

Take time to find out if your school offers any professional development or inservice training for using technology or learning software. **Inservice** means training teachers after they have entered the profession of teaching. Your principal, curriculum coordinator, technology coordinator, or district instructional/technology coordinators are able to provide information on inservice training opportunities. Sometimes, school secretaries also will be up to date on this information.

For information about technology workshops, talk with your principal, curriculum coordinator, or district technology coordinator. Let these people know you are interested in any technology or other training that becomes available. If you have students with learning disabilities in your classroom, check with the district exceptional student education program specialist about training opportunities. Many school districts post the dates and times of inservice training and workshops on the district's Web site and on teacher bulletin boards.

Hardware

Another item to consider is determining how can you obtain additional hardware or upgrade your classroom computers. As soon as you can, join your school's technology committee. Technology committees help make the decisions on what new technologies will be purchased, where these new technologies get placed, and establishes how the technology plan for the school is implemented. You also may need to look into educational grants for additional funds. Your principal and curriculum coordinator usually receive notification of grant opportunities. Let them know you are interested in writing a grant and they will provide you with the information. If your district

has a person responsible for grant writing for the district or county, he or she can serve as a good source of information. Additionally, you will find numerous grant opportunities on the Internet and the Web. Chapter 7 provides more information on locating and writing educational grants.

A question to consider is what type of equipment can you purchase if you receive grant funds. Before you write a grant, determine what kind of equipment you can purchase. Your principal, technology coordinator, curriculum coordinator, or members of the technology committee should be able to provide you with this information. If your school is networked, also check with the network administrator at the district level.

Software

With hardware requirements decided, you will need to determine what kind of software is available to you and where you can find it. First, you should check your classroom computer for software that is already installed. To learn more about the software available at your school or on the school's network, ask the school media specialist or curriculum coordinator, or the district technology coordinator. If you are a special education teacher, you might check with your district exceptional student education coordinator, who should know what software is available for students with disabilities.

Next, determine the procedure for purchasing additional software. The school secretary or other teachers can direct you to the right person for this information. If your school is networked, it is important to check with the network coordinator prior to purchasing software so you can avoid buying software that already may be installed on the network or may conflict with the network. Many schools install computer-assisted instructional software programs on their network server for use by all teachers.

Finally, you need to determine if your school district or state Department of Education has an adopted state bid list for purchasing software. Many states contract with companies to purchase specific software applications at reduced prices and these are included on a **state bid list**. Be sure to find out

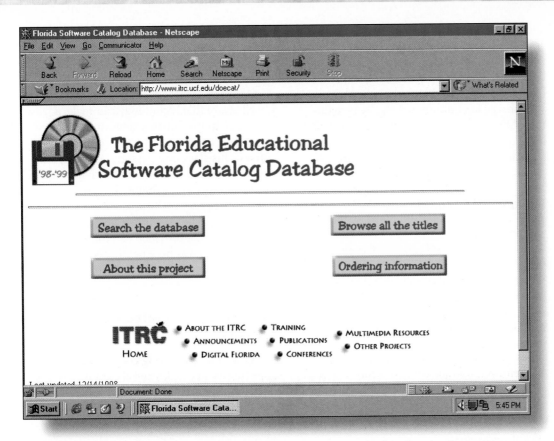

Figure 6-31 Many states provide online access to state-approved educational software titles.

if your state has a special catalog of software titles that they have adopted **[Figure 6-31]**. Curriculum coordinators, technology coordinators, or media specialists are good sources for this information. Your district office should maintain this information as well.

Other Technologies

Consider other technologies and where you can find them, such as a VCR or a presentation television set. Your media specialist usually handles scheduling and distribution of VCRs and other equipment **[Figure 6-32]**. Reserve early because a sign-up sheet and allocation usually is based on a first-come, first-served basis. Ask about the length of time that you are allowed to keep checked-out equipment.

You also should ask where you can find a listing of educational programs or laserdisc titles offered throughout the school district for use in the classroom. The media specialist usually has a list of software programs, laserdisc,

Figure 6-32 A school's media specialist usually assists teachers with checking out VCRs, overhead projectors, projection panels, and other equipment.

and CD-ROM and DVD-ROM titles for teachers to use in the classroom. A listing of instructional television programs and broadcast times, and any videotapes the school has or that are available to the school through interlibrary loan programs usually is maintained by the media specialist. He or she can inform you of the procedures for checking out laserdiscs, VCRs, and other equipment.

Technology Supplies

A basic, but often overlooked, question to consider is how you can obtain additional supplies for use with computers and other technologies. If the bulb in your overhead projector burns out, for example, or you need paper or ink cartridges for your printer, to whom do you speak about replacing it? Generally, the media specialist can replace burned out bulbs and solve other supply problems with projectors. The school secretary or the bookkeeper usually handles orders for general supplies. Ask the school secretary and he or she will direct you to the appropriate person.

Now, that you have some basic knowledge of where to go for guidance and materials to help you integrate technology into your classroom, consider how one teacher is putting it all together.

Figure 6-33 Learning centers are a great way to organize a classroom to optimize learning opportunities.

Putting It All Together

As described earlier in this chapter, Mr. Balado is well aware that technology can make a difference in his fourth grade students' learning — and has been using technology to enhance his classroom lessons. After the students completed their writing activity/exercise, Mr. Balado planned a highly integrated classroom strategy of teaching science to his fourth graders. As part of the integrated learning environment, he provided carefully planned centers, which was how he divided his classroom for group activities and inquiry learning.

Creating an Integrated Learning Environment

Centers, or **learning centers,** give you the opportunity to break your classroom into many different types of learning environments without ever leaving the room. Just as an office building has different offices in which work is accomplished, learning centers allow students to rotate around the classroom to complete a project or activities **[Figure 6-33]**. Mr. Balado had a plan for how the students would work through the centers in his classroom. He had five computers in his classroom for student use and 26 students. He divided the students into groups of two and three; these students would work together throughout the levels of the project. Mr. Balado then assigned each group a dinosaur to research.

Students were excited and surprised, because most did not even know how to pronounce the name of their dinosaurs. Their assignment was to find out what the name of their dinosaurs meant and uncover as many facts as they could about their dinosaurs. Instead of writing a report, students would create an electronic report using HyperStudio.

Mr. Balado gave each group the same guidance and questions to think about for their project, such as, What does your dinosaur look like? What period of time did your dinosaur live in? What did your dinosaur eat? How big was it and how much did it weigh? He also asked each of them to gather all the information they felt important for them and others in the class to understand their dinosaur. Students also were asked to create their own questions and then find answers to those questions.

The Classroom Centers

For his lesson on dinosaurs, Mr. Balado set up seven learning centers in his classroom, which included the discovery computer center, the Web search center with a computer connected to the Internet, the modeling center, the great explorers library center, the science center, the scanning center with a computer set up for scanning pictures and other objects, and the HyperStudio center.

The discovery computer center included two computers and a number of different CD-ROMs Mr. Balado checked out from the media center that covered dinosaurs. He purchased two CD-ROMs at his own expense. At the Web search center was one computer that students could use to investigate various Web sites for which Mr. Balado had provided links on his curriculum Web page. To locate these Web sites and other available media,

Mr. Balado worked with the media specialist at his school. Once he had collected and evaluated a list of sites for the students to conduct their dinosaur research, Mr. Balado created a curriculum Web page so students would not be wasting time surfing the Net without supervision **[Figure 6-34]**. Mr. Balado was quite aware of the dangers of inappropriate or inaccurate information available at some Web sites.

In the modeling center were all types of modeling tools, modeling clay, paper, rocks, and all types of different-shaped items. This center was for students to create a model of their dinosaurs and other objects related to the project. At the next center, the great explorers library center, as shown on the next page in **Figure 6-35**, Mr. Balado provided a collection of books, journals, and magazines for students to use to research dinosaurs and become great research explorers. The media specialist was instrumental in locating books and print materials through the interlibrary loan program, which was established in the state to assist teachers in obtaining resources from media centers throughout the state.

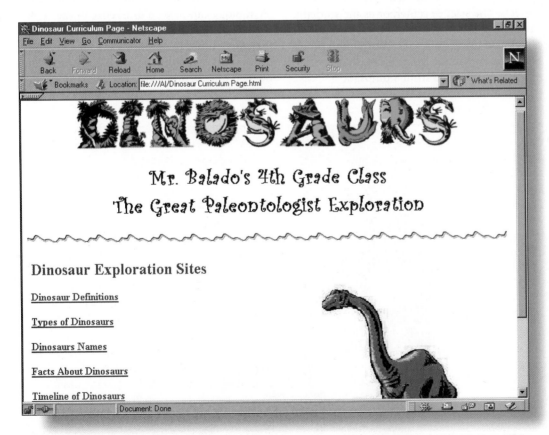

Figure 6-34 Teacher-created curriculum pages allow students to link directly to appropriate Web sites.

Figure 6-35 This learning center contains a variety of print resources for students to use to develop their research projects.

The Results of Technology Integration

Students worked though the centers and created some of the most interesting and creative projects Mr. Balado had ever seen. One group had seen a picture of a dinosaur in the woods, so for their model they decided to create a dinosaur and the woods in which it lived.

Most students could describe in detail all of the information they had learned about their dinosaurs — and all of the groups had given their dinosaurs a nickname. The HyperStudio stacks were outstanding; most of them contained many pictures and dinosaur stories with actual research and details about the dinosaur **[Figure 6-36]**.

Mr. Balado knew that his students were involved actively in their own learning and had interacted with numerous resources, Web sites, and software programs. By using Hyper-Studio to let his students create their own multimedia projects, his young students presented their findings in a new medium — one that enhanced their learning through the development and use of higher-level thinking skills. As Mr. Balado and his students learned, technology can make a difference in the classroom if used appropriately and integrated into the curriculum. In addition, Mr. Balado noticed that his students' self-esteem, self-confidence, and writing skills improved as a result of creating their own projects **[Figure 6-37]**.

WebInfo

For more information on the benefits of technology integration, visit the Teachers Discovering Computers Chapter 6 WebInfo page **(www.scsite.com/tdc/ ch6/webinfo.htm)** and click Benefits.

The scanning center had a computer set up with a flatbed scanner so students could scan pictures from books, magazines, and other sources for use in their HyperStudio projects. The science center, or as the students liked to call it, Mr. Fossil and Mrs. Bones center, had real fossils, rocks, and different types of bones made from plastic that Mr. Balado obtained from a dinosaur education package. The last center was the HyperStudio center, which had one computer set up for students to create their Hyper-Studio projects. HyperStudio also was installed on all of the classroom computers so students could work on their HyperStudio stacks as they progressed through the various centers.

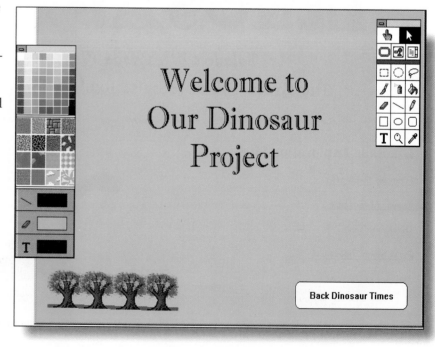

Welcome to Our Dinosaur Project

Back Dinosaur Times

Figure 6-36 Using HyperStudio, students can create electronic projects.

Figure 6-37 Students feel an amazing sense of pride and ownership when they complete their projects.

Summary of Education and Technology Integration

As you have learned in this chapter, the best strategy for technology integration is to place technology into the hands of trained teachers, make it easily accessible, and let them decide how best to use it in their classrooms at the point of instruction. Teachers are the content experts who should evaluate all resources used in classrooms. This chapter first discussed curriculum and technology issues as they apply to technology integration and then provided teachers with ideas, an instructional model, and effective planning strategies. The chapter then provided an introduction to the concept of technology integration that will help you build your integration literacy skills. Finally, this chapter showed you how one teacher, Mr. Balado, fully integrated technology into a science lesson. In Chapter 7, you will build upon the skills you have learned in this chapter and increase your integration literacy skills by learning implementation strategies and integration activities that are curriculum directed.

www.scsite.com/tdc/ch6/brief.htm

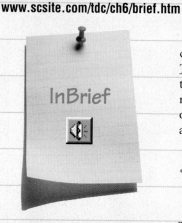

InBrief

Web Instructions: To display this page from the Web, launch your browser and enter the URL, www.scsite.com/tdc/ch6/brief.htm. Click the links for current and additional information. To listen to an audio version of this InBrief, click the Audio button below the title, InBrief, at the top of the page. To play the audio, RealPlayer must be installed on your computer (download by clicking here).

1. Curriculum, Curriculum Standards, and Benchmarks

Curriculum is defined as all of the experiences a learner has under the supervision and guidance of teachers. A **curriculum standard**, also called a **curriculum goal** or **learning goal**, defines what a student is expected to know at certain stages of education. A **benchmark** is a specific, measurable learning objective that usually is tied to a curriculum standard.

2. What Is Technology Integration?

Technology integration is the combination of all technology parts, such as hardware and software, together with each subject-related area of curriculum to enhance learning. Technology integration is using technology to help meet the curriculum standards and learner outcomes of each lesson, unit, or activity.

3. Integrating Technology into the Curriculum

The key to successful technology integration is identifying what you are trying to accomplish within your curriculum. Teachers must consider what the learning goals and standards are, identify an appropriate technology, and develop innovative ways to teach a diverse population of learners with different learning styles. A **learning style** refers to how individuals learn, including how they prefer to receive information, express themselves, and process information.

4. Changing Instructional Strategies

As students begin to play a more active role in the learning process, the teacher's role must change. Teachers are transitioning from the conventional lecture-practice-recall teaching methods to being the facilitator of learning. Rather than dictating a learning process, a **facilitator of learning** motivates students to want to learn, guides the student learning process, and promotes a learning atmosphere and an appreciation for the subject.

5. Barriers to Technology Integration

With all change comes barriers, and technology integration is no exception. Barriers include a lack of teacher training, lack of administration support, limited time for teacher planning, computer placement in remote locations making it difficult for teachers to have access, budget constraints, and a basic resistance to change by many educators.

6. Technology Integration and the Learning Process

For learning to take place, learners must be engaged in the process of education. **Authentic learning** experiences are instructional activities that demonstrate real-life connections by associating the concept being taught with a real-life activity or event. **Active learning** provides students with the opportunity to be involved and interested in their own learning process. **Discovery learning** is an inquiry-based method for teaching and learning.

7. Strategies for Teaching with Technology

The best strategy for technology integration is to put the technology into the hands of trained teachers, make it easily accessible, and let them decide how best to use it in their classrooms at the point of instruction. When proper strategies are used for technology integration, students enjoy learning to use technology as well as learning content in subject-related curriculum areas.

8. The Role of the School District

School district administrators must plan carefully for every aspect of technology integration,

InBrief
KeyTerms
AtTheMovies
CheckPoint
TeacherTime
CyberClass
EdIssues
NetStuff

SPECIAL FEATURES

TimeLine 2000
Guide to WWW Sites
Buyer's Guide 2000
Educational Sites
State/Federal Sites
Chat
News
Home

www.scsite.com/tdc/ch6/brief.htm

- InBrief
- KeyTerms
- AtTheMovies
- CheckPoint
- TeacherTime
- CyberClass
- EdIssues
- NetStuff

SPECIAL FEATURES

- TimeLine 2000
- Guide to WWW Sites
- Buyer's Guide 2000
- Educational Sites
- State/Federal Sites
- Chat
- News
- Home

InBrief

from purchase, to installation, to teacher and staff training. Almost every school district has a detailed technology plan for technology integration. A **technology plan** is an outline that specifies the school district's procedures not only for purchasing equipment and software, but also for training teachers to use and then integrate technology into their classroom curriculum.

9. Planning for Technology Integration in the Classroom

Teachers must plan carefully for the use and integration of computers and technologies in the classroom. They must plan how they will teach the curriculum, what areas they need to cover for content, and where they can use technology to meet learning objectives. Whether teachers use one computer, two computers, or 30 computers, however, they must plan how and when to use the computers and how they will enable students to use the computers.

10. Planning Lessons with Technology

When planning lessons that use technology, teachers must consider the skills and knowledge level required for students to start and complete the lesson successfully. A **KWL chart** is a helpful planning tool in determining the skill and knowledge level of students prior to beginning almost any project. An **instructional model** is a systematic guide for planning instruction or a lesson. The **ASSURE Model** is a procedural guide for planning and delivering instruction that integrates technologies and media into the teaching process.

11. Getting Started at a New School

Teachers need to consider many issues related to technology information and support, technology training, hardware, software, other technologies, and technology supplies. A **teacher's manual** is a booklet that contains information, rules and regulations, rights and responsibilities, and policies and procedures that will provide answers to many questions.

12. Putting It All Together

Creating an integrated learning environment with centers is a great way to put it all together. **Centers**, or **learning centers**, give teachers the opportunity to break their classrooms into many different types of learning environments without ever leaving the room. Technology can make a difference in the classroom if used appropriately and integrated into the curriculum.

www.scsite.com/tdc/ch6/terms.htm

KeyTerms

- InBrief
- KeyTerms
- AtTheMovies
- CheckPoint
- TeacherTime
- CyberClass
- EdIssues
- NetStuff

SPECIAL FEATURES

- TimeLine 2000
- Guide to WWW Sites
- Buyer's Guide 2000
- Educational Sites
- State/Federal Sites
- Chat
- News
- Home

Web Instructions: To display this page from the Web, launch your browser and enter the URL, www.scsite.com/tdc/ch6/terms.htm. Scroll through the list of terms. Click a term to display its definition and a picture. Click KeyTerms on the left to redisplay the KeyTerms page. Click the TO WEB button for current and additional information about the term from the Web. To see animations, Shockwave and Flash Player must be installed on your computer (download by clicking here).

active learning **[6.11]**
anchored instruction **[6.12]**
ASSURE Model **[6.21]**
authentic learning **[6.11]**

benchmark **[6.4]**
Body Works **[6.12]**

centers **[6.28]**
cognitive scaffold **[6.12]**
computer lab **[6.6]**
cooperative learning **[6.14]**
curriculum **[6.2]**
curriculum goal **[6.4]**
curriculum guides **[6.2]**
curriculum standard **[6.4]**

discovery learning **[6.12]**

educational equalizer **[6.13]**

facilitator of learning **[6.9]**

high-order thinking skills **[6.14]**

inservice **[6.26]**
instructional model **[6.21]**
integration **[6.5]**

K-12 curriculum **[6.2]**
KWL chart **[6.19]**

learning centers **[6.28]**
learning goal **[6.4]**
learning style **[6.8]**

mentorship program **[6.16]**
Microsoft Encarta **[6.12]**

point of instruction **[6.6]**
problem-based instruction **[6.12]**

reflective evaluation **[6.23]**

skill assessment survey **[6.19]**
state bid list **[6.26]**
student objectives **[6.21]**

teachable moment **[6.6]**
teacher's manual **[6.25]**
technology integration **[6.5]**
technology lab **[6.6]**
technology plan **[6.16]**

virtual tours **[6.8]**

Wellivers Instructional
    Transformation Model **[6.9]**

www.scsite.com/tdc/ch6/movies.htm

AtTheMovies

**WELCOME to
VIDEO CLIPS
from CNN**

Web Instructions: To display this page from the Web, launch your browser and enter the URL, www.scsite.com/tdc/ch6/movies.htm. Click a picture to view a video. After watching the video, close the video window and then complete the exercise by answering the questions about the video. To view the videos, RealPlayer must be installed on your computer (download by clicking here).

InBrief

KeyTerms

AtTheMovies

CheckPoint

TeacherTime

CyberClass

EdIssues

NetStuff

SPECIAL FEATURES

TimeLine 2000

Guide to WWW Sites

Buyer's Guide 2000

Educational Sites

State/Federal Sites

Chat

News

Home

1. Distance Learning

Simultaneously at separate educational facilities, students are taught important lessons each day. What type of communications equipment is used to connect the schools and how is it used? How does a distance-learning environment differ from a regular classroom? Would you want to teach or moderate in a classroom like this? In your opinion, what unique situations might teachers and students face while participating in a distance-learning program?

2. Kid Scientists

By viewing this video of a science class investigation in action you discovered that students take greater ownership for their learning when they have access to top-notch science equipment and computer technology. What technologies are used to help teach science? How does using technology foster collaboration? Do you agree that using technology helps to get the attention, devotion, interest, and fascination of students? What challenges can you see in using technology to teach science?

3. Plugged In

Some suggest that computers create a class of haves and have nots, where some have computer access and others clearly do not. In East Palo Alto, California, however, computers are being made available to everyone in the community — a policy of universal access that is helping to forge stronger community bonds. What are some benefits of providing universal access to computers? How can understanding computers help strengthen an individual's self-identity? Specifically, describe how computer and Internet access such as that at the East Palo Alto drop-in center could erase the dividing lines between the different strata of society in your community.

www.scsite.com/tdc/ch6/check.htm

CheckPoint

Web Instructions: To display this page from the Web, launch your browser and enter the URL, www.scsite.com/tdc/ch6/check.htm. Click a blank line for the answer. Click the links for current and additional information. To experience the animation and interactivity, Shockwave and Flash Player must be installed on your computer (download by clicking here).

InBrief

KeyTerms

AtTheMovies

CheckPoint

TeacherTime

CyberClass

EdIssues

NetStuff

SPECIAL FEATURES

TimeLine 2000

Guide to WWW Sites

Buyer's Guide 2000

Educational Sites

State/Federal Sites

Chat

News

Home

1. Label the Figure

Instructions: Identify the five hierarchy stages of the Wellivers Instructional Transformation Model.

2. Matching

Instructions: Match each term from the column on the left with the best description from the column on the right.

Wellivers Instructional Transformation Model

1. _____ is when teachers become aware of technology and its potential uses.

2. _____ is when teachers use technology, but minor problems will cause teachers to discontinue its use.

3. _____ is when technology becomes essential for the educational process and teachers are constantly thinking of ways to use technology in their classrooms.

4. _____ is when teachers begin to rethink the educational goals of the classroom with the use of technology.

5. _____ is the evolving classroom that becomes completely integrated with technology in all subject areas. Technology becomes an invisible tool that is seamlessly woven into the teaching and learning process.

____ 1. ASSURE Model

____ 2. authentic learning

____ 3. curriculum standards

____ 4. mentorship program

____ 5. KWL chart

a. lessons connected to real-life events

b. instructional planning tool to assist teachers in identifying curriculum objectives

c. procedural guide for planning and delivering instruction that integrates technology

d. collection of general concepts that school districts expect their students to learn

e. new teachers team with experienced teachers

3. Short Answer

Instructions: Write a brief answer to each of the following questions.

1. What is the difference between a curriculum standard and a benchmark? Are both curriculum standards and benchmarks measurable? Why or why not? _____

2. What are learning styles? How can a teacher be a facilitator of learning and at the same time address various students' learning styles? _____

3. Name five barriers to technology integration. In your opinion, which barrier is the most important? Why? _____

4. Name three people who can help teachers find information on available technologies in their schools. Describe other sources that can assist teachers in locating technology resources. _____

5. Name three areas teachers must address when planning for technology integration in a one-computer classroom. Can these same planning strategies also work for a two-computer classroom? _____

www.scsite.com/tdc/ch6/time.htm

TeacherTime

Web Instructions: To display this page from the Web, launch your browser and enter the URL, www.scsite.com/tdc/ch6/time.htm. Click the links for current and additional information.

InBrief

KeyTerms

AtTheMovies

CheckPoint

TeacherTime

CyberClass

EdIssues

NetStuff

SPECIAL FEATURES

TimeLine 2000

Guide to WWW Sites

Buyer's Guide 2000

Educational Sites

State/Federal Sites

Chat

News

Home

1. After using technology in your classroom, you are beginning to understand that using technology is different from integrating technology. You would like to begin integrating technology into your social studies curriculum. Where do you begin? Are resources available on the Internet that can help you? Where can you locate examples of lesson plans that integrate technology but still support your curriculum? Can you modify these lessons to use in your classroom?

2. The school where you teach participated in a technology pilot project four years ago. The entire school was networked, and each classroom received three IBM multimedia computers to be used as student workstations. The applications your students can access at the workstations are not multimedia software applications, instead they are older, text-based programs. While you see the benefit of skill reinforcement that these text-based applications offer, you would like to use more multimedia software and would like to start with HyperStudio. You are not allowed to purchase software on your own; you must have the approval of your principal. How can you convince your principal that multimedia authoring software would benefit your students? What would you say? Can you provide any research to support your position?

3. Your school is located in a rural area, and technology funds are limited. You have used technology with students before and were encouraged by the results. You have one computer in your classroom and would really like to provide your students with greater access to technology. You have decided to explore possible grant opportunities. Your district is small, however, and does not have any grant programs. Very few large businesses in your community offer grants opportunities. Where can you learn about other grant opportunities? Are grants available that are specific to your circumstances for which you can apply? What are some other funding options? What other organizations in your community could you contact?

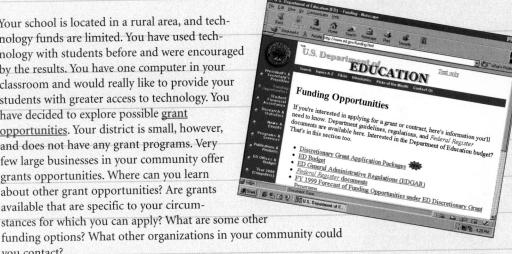

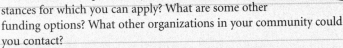

4. You would like to integrate technology into your math curriculum, but you do not know where to start. You want to provide the students with authentic activities and you need ideas. You consider talking to a math teacher who integrates technology, but you do not know anyone. You have heard of a Web site where teachers can receive mentoring from other teachers and ask for advice and ideas. What are some advantages to finding assistance online? What are some disadvantages? Could you use this type of assistance for any subject? Why or why not? Could your students benefit from this type of interaction? Why or why not? How can you locate more resources such as this for yourself and for your students?

5. As a teacher of students with special learning needs, you are very concerned about finding software that appeals to different learning styles. You would like to find a Web resource that will give you information about what learning styles are addressed by specific software products. Does this exist? How can this information assist regular education teachers? How could you evaluate software packages to see what learning styles they appeal to? Are learning styles important to consider when making software purchases? Why or why not?

www.scsite.com/tdc/ch6/class.htm

InBrief

KeyTerms

AtTheMovies

CheckPoint

TeacherTime

CyberClass

EdIssues

NetStuff

SPECIAL FEATURES

TimeLine 2000

Guide to WWW Sites

Buyer's Guide 2000

Educational Sites

State/Federal Sites

Chat

News

Home

Web Instructions: To display this page from the Web, launch your browser and enter the URL, www.scsite.com/tdc/ch6/class.htm. To start Level I CyberClass, click a Level I link on this page or enter the URL, www.cyber-class.com. Click the Student button, click *Teachers Discovering Computers* in the list of titles, and then click the Enter a site button. To start Level II or III CyberClass (available only to those purchasers of a CyberClass floppy disk), place your CyberClass floppy disk in drive A, click Start on the taskbar, click Run on the Start menu, type a : connect in the Open text box, click the OK button, click the Enter CyberClass button, and then follow the instructions. If you are using a Macintosh, see your instructor.

1. Flash Cards (<u>Level I</u>, Level II, and Level III)

Click Flash Cards on the Main Menu of the CyberClass Web page. Click the plus sign before the Chapter 6 title. Click What Is Curriculum and answer all the cards in that section. Then, click What Is Technology Integration and answer the cards in that section. If you have less than 85% correct, continue to answer cards in other sections until you have more than 85% correct. All users: Answer as many more Flash Cards as you desire. Close the Electronic Flash Card window and the Flash Cards window by clicking the Close button in the upper-right corner of each window.

2. Practice Test (<u>Level I</u>, Level II, and Level III)

Click Testing on the Main Menu of the CyberClass Web page. Click the Select a book box arrow and then click Teachers Discovering Computers. Click the Select a test to take box arrow and then click the Chapter 6 title in the list. Click the Take Test button. If necessary, maximize the window. Take the practice test and then click the Submit Test button. Click the Display Study Guide button. Review the Study Guide. Scroll down and click the Return To CyberClass button. Click the Yes button to close the Study Guide window. If your score was less than 80%, click the Take another Test button to take another practice test. Continue taking tests until your score is greater than 80%. Then, click the Done button.

3. Web Guide (<u>Level I</u>, Level II, and Level III)

Click Web Guide on the Main Menu of the CyberClass Web page. When the Guide to World Wide Web Sites page displays, click Museums and review the sites. Are Web museum sites appropriate for use in K-12 education? Would you use these sites in your classroom? Why? When you are finished, hand in a brief summary of your conclusions to your instructor.

4. Assignments and Syllabus (Level II and Level III)

Click Assignments on the Main Menu of the CyberClass Web page. Ensure you are aware of all assignments and when they are due. Click Syllabus on the Main Menu of the CyberClass Web page. Verify you are up to date on all activities for the class.

5. CyberChallenge (Level II and Level III)

Click CyberChallenge on the Main Menu of the CyberClass Web page. Click the Select a book box arrow and then click Teachers Discovering Computers. Click the Select a board to play box arrow and then click Chapter 6 in the list. Click the Play CyberChallenge button. Maximize the CyberChallenge window. Play CyberChallenge until your score for a complete game is 500 points or more. Close the CyberChallenge window.

6. Text Chat (Level II and Level III)

Arrange for your instructor to conduct office hours using CyberClass Text Chat. Then, at the appointed time, click Text Chat on the Main Menu of the CyberClass Web page and ask any questions you may have about the course so far.

Edlssues

Web Instructions: To display this page from the Web, launch your browser and enter the URL, www.scsite.com/tdc/ch6/issues.htm. Click the links for current and additional information to help you respond to the EdIssues questions.

InBrief
KeyTerms
AtTheMovies
CheckPoint
TeacherTime
CyberClass
Edlssues
NetStuff

SPECIAL FEATURES

TimeLine 2000
Guide to WWW Sites
Buyer's Guide 2000
Educational Sites
State/Federal Sites
Chat
News
Home

1. Computer-Assisted Instruction

Your school district has spent a great deal of money on computer-assisted instruction software. The software is available for use by all teachers throughout the district. This software generates tests and automatically tracks student progress. The software is not interactive, however. Students follow a set order and progress systematically through the programs. What are some of the benefits of this type of software? What are some disadvantages? Does this type of software appeal to different learning styles? Can students with learning disabilities use this type of software? Which group of students might benefit the most from this type of software?

2. Levels of Integration

It is the second month of the semester, and you are teaching seventh-grade science. The parents of one of your students contact you. They are upset because when their son was in elementary school, the majority of teachers were using technology in their classrooms. At your middle school, however, their son has not had the same opportunities. The parents are very concerned about the lack of technology. What can you do about this situation? To whom can you refer the parents? Do greater barriers to technology integration exist in middle schools than in elementary or high schools? Why or why not? How could you integrate technology into your seventh-grade science curriculum?

3. Integrating the Internet

In your school district, Internet access is available in all classrooms. Most teachers use the Internet for research. You would like to integrate the Internet in a meaningful way, however, you need some ideas about how to start. Where can you find suggestions on how to integrate the Internet into your classroom? What kinds of projects are the best to start with? What are other appropriate uses for the Internet, besides conducting research? Does your district offer training on Internet technology integration issues or just on how to use technology? How can you integrate the Internet to stimulate authentic learning? Is it appropriate to integrate the Internet for every subject area? Why or why not?

4. Gender Issues

Reports show that while females are beginning to take more science and math courses, they still are not as likely to enroll in technology courses as male students. Teachers' attitudes towards females using technology can have an effect as well. Perceptions of successful computer users and a lack of positive role models also reinforce this gender gap. What can you do to encourage gender equity with technology usage? What other factors contribute to this problem? Can integrating technology in your classroom have a positive effect and reduce the gender gap? Why or why not? What other areas of education, if any, reinforce and perpetuate the gender gap?

5. The Internet

You are teaching statistics and probability. You want your students to access the Internet and gather data to create graphs. The students then will create Web pages to display their information. One student's parents do not want their daughter to use the Internet. They are concerned about Internet safety and do not allow their daughter to access the Internet at home. What can you say to these parents? What procedures can you have in place to make the parents more comfortable? Should you give the student an alternative assignment? How? What other resources could the student use? How could you provide access to Web information without the student being online?

www.scsite.com/tdc/ch6/net.htm

NetStuff

Web Instructions: To display this page from the Web, launch your browser and enter the URL, www.scsite.com/tdc/ch6/net.htm. To use the Working at Your Computer lab from the Web, Shockwave and Flash Player must be installed on your computer (download by clicking here).

InBrief

KeyTerms

AtTheMovies

CheckPoint

TeacherTime

CyberClass

EdIssues

NetStuff

SPECIAL FEATURES

TimeLine 2000

Guide to WWW Sites

Buyer's Guide 2000

Educational Sites

State/Federal Sites

Chat

News

Home

WORKING AT YOUR COMPUTER LAB

1. Shelly Cashman Series Working at Your Computer Lab

Follow the instructions in NetStuff 1 on page 1.34 to start and use the Working at Your Computer Lab. If you are running from the Web, enter the URL, www.scsite.com/sclabs/menu.htm or display the NetStuff page (see instructions at the top of this page) and then click the WORKING AT YOUR COMPUTER LAB button.

TEACHING STYLE

2. Teaching Style

When integrating technology into the curriculum you use different teaching strategies. Click the TEACHING STYLE button and complete an online assessment to learn more about your teaching style, learning styles, and classroom strategies.

TECHNOLOGY SKILLS

3. Technology Skills

What is your technology skill level? Click the TECHNOLOGY SKILLS button and complete an online assessment to learn more about your current skill level.

REALITY CHECK

4. Reality Check

Students often have unrealistic ideas about money, lifestyles, and future employment. Click the REALITY CHECK button to complete an exercise that shows you how to help your students learn more about what kinds of jobs they will need in the future to support their desired lifestyles.

FREE

5. FREE

The federal government provides teachers with many free resources. Click the FREE button and complete this exercise to see what government resources are free for teachers.

INFORMATION MINING

6. Information Mining

Click the INFORMATION MINING button and complete this exercise to improve your Web research skills by using an education search engine to find examples of how other teachers have integrated World Wide Web sites into specific lesson plans.

ONE-COMPUTER CLASSROOM

7. One-Computer Classroom

Click the ONE-COMPUTER CLASSROOM button to complete an exercise to find information on how to use and integrate one computer into classroom instruction.

WEB CHAT

8. Web Chat

The EdIssues section presents various scenarios on the uses of computers, technologies, and non-technology-related issues in K-12 education. Click the WEB CHAT button to enter a Web Chat discussion related to the EdIssues exercises.

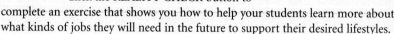

Categories

Art

Biology

Business Education

Chemistry

Education Search Engines

Foreign Language

Fun Stuff for Kids

Grant Sources

Health & Physical Education

Internet Information

Language Arts & Literature

Magazines & News

Mathematics

Museums

Music & Performing Arts

Professional Organizations

Reference Sources

Science & Technology

Social Studies & History

Vocational Education

Web Projects

Guide to Educational Sites and Professional Organizations

WEB INSTRUCTIONS: *To gain World Wide Web access to the most current version of the sites included in this special feature, launch your browser and enter the URL, www.scsite.com/ tdc/ch6/edsites.htm.*

The World Wide Web offers almost unlimited educational resources for teachers and students. Everyday, hundreds of new and exciting educational Web sites are added, existing ones are changed, and still others cease to exist. Because of this, you may find that a URL listed here has changed or no longer is valid. A continually updated Guide to Educational Sites and Professional Organizations, which links to the most current versions of these sites, can be found at www.scsite.com/tdc/ ch6/edsites.htm. A Guide to State and Federal Government Educational Web Sites is located following Chapter 8.

6.42

CATEGORY/SITE NAME	LOCATION	COMMENT
Art		
Art Room	www.arts.ufl.edu/art/rt_room/@rtroom_home.html	A virtual learning environment for exploring the world of art
The Art Teacher Connection	www.primenet.com/~arted/	Encouraging innovation in art education through technology
World Wide Arts Resources	wwar.world-arts-resources.com/default.html	Guide to visual arts information
The Refrigerator	www.artcontest.com/	An art contest for kids
Biology		
The Biology Project	www.biology.arizona.edu/default.html	An online interactive resource for learning biology
The Heart: Online Exploration	sln.fi.edu/biosci/heart.html	Interactive tour of the human heart
Virtual Frog Dissection Kit	george.lbl.gov/ITG.hm.pg.docs/dissect/info.html	An interactive frog dissection
Neuroscience for Kids	weber.u.washington.edu/~chudler/neurok.html	For teachers and students who want to learn more about the nervous system
BioChemNet	schmidel.com/bionet.htm	Biology and chemistry educational resources
Business Education		
Business Education Lesson Plans and Resources	www.angelfire.com/ks/tonyaskinner/index.html	Links to all areas of business education
Great Ideas for Teaching Marketing	www.swcollege.com/mm/gitm/gitm.html#4e8	Lesson plans dealing with marketing
EduStock	portia.advanced.org/3088/	Designed to teach young and old alike how the stock market works
Investing for Kids	tqd.advanced.org/3096/	Examines stocks, bonds, mutual funds, and more
Learning@Web.Sites	www.ecnet.net/users/gdlevin/bized.html	Great links to business-related sites
Chemistry		
ChemCenter	www.ChemCenter.org/	Directory of chemistry for researchers and students
Chemical Elements.com	www.chemicalelements.com/	Interactive periodic table of elements
Chemistry Teaching Resources	www.anachem.umu.se/eks/pointers.htm	A comprehensive list of chemistry teaching resources
Chemistry: Links for Chemists	www.liv.ac.uk/Chemistry/Links/links.html	Searchable index of more than 4,200 chemistry resources
Education Search Engines		
Kathy Schrock's Guide for Educators	discoveryschool.com/schrockguide/	Everything dealing with education and more. This is a must-bookmark site!
Busy Teachers' Web Site K-12	www.ceismc.gatech.edu/busyt/	Links of interest to educators
Blue Web'n	www.kn.pacbell.com/wired/bluewebn/	Educational links arranged by subject
Education Index	www.educationindex.com/	An annotated guide to education-related sites on the Web
K-5 CyberTrail	www.wmht.org/trail/trail.htm	Educational resources on the Web available to K-5 teachers
Education World	www.education-world.com/	Links to educational pages, searchable by topic and grade level
K-12 World	www.k-12world.com/	A collection of links to educational sites and resources

(continued)

CATEGORY/SITE NAME	LOCATION	COMMENT
Education Search Engines (continued)		
The New Teacher Page	www.geocities.com/~newteach/	A great site if you have been teaching for years or if you are thinking of starting
Theme-Related Resources on the World Wide Web	www.stemnet.nf.ca/CITE/themes.html	Resources classified by themes
Web Sites and Resources for Teachers	www.csun.edu/~vceed009/	A variety of valuable information
Foreign Language		
Internet Activities for the Foreign Language Class	members.aol.com/maestro12/web/wadir.html	Series of lesson plans that use the resources on the Internet
Language Learning	www.ozemail.com.au/~cdug/	Information and resources for teachers and students of English as a second language
Teaching Resources: Foreign Languages	www.tcom.ohiou.edu/OU_Language/teacher/index.html	A list of links for the world language educator
Learning@Web.Sites: Foreign Languages Department	www.ecnet.net/users/gdlevin/flanguages.html	A list of annotated educational resources
Fun Stuff for Kids		
Too Cool for Grownups	www.tcfg.com/	Interactive searches, reviews, student writings, and more for ages 10 to 14
Kids Domain	www.kidsdomain.com/	Everything for kids from clip art to downloads; a parent section, too!
Kid Info	www.kidinfo.com/Index.html	Collection of sites selected by students, for students; parents and teachers, too!
Cyberhaunts for Kids	www.freenet.hamilton.on.ca/~aa937/Profile.html	This site is full of great links and activities
Funbrain	www.funbrain.com/	Online interactive quizzes and activities
Grant Sources		
U.S. Department of Education	http://www.ed.gov/funding.html	Extensive information on federal funding sources
National Endowment for the Humanities	www.neh.fed.us/	Grants for history, languages, and other humanities
GrantsWeb	web.fie.com/cws/sra/resource.htm	Great source for federal and non-federal grant sources.
Looking for Partners	www.ed.gov/free/partner.html	Great source to partner with a federal agency to help develop learning activities and instructional materials
Health & Physical Education		
Cyber-Active!	www.tc.umn.edu/nlhome/g032/arnt0008/kara/	Physical education resource in the areas of P.E., adapted P.E., and gross motor development, with links
A Great Physical Education Site	educ.ubc.ca/dept/cust/pe/	A resource for both current and future physical educators
Spring 4 Health	www.directcon.net/spring4/index.html	A great nutrition site with plenty of ideas for curriculum integration
You Are What You Eat	hyperion.advanced.org/11163/gather/cgi-bin/wookie.cgi/?id=M2gZ	Information about nutrition and the ability to create a nutritional profile
PE Links 4 U	www.cwu.edu/~jefferis/jeff_prorg.html	List of physical education associations, sites, vendors, and lessons

6.44

CATEGORY/SITE NAME	LOCATION	COMMENT
Internet Information		
Integrating the Internet	l2l.ed.psu.edu/linktuts/intemain.htm	A tutorial for educators with ideas and a foundation for Internet use in the classroom
Newbie-U: New User University	www.newbie-u.com/	Tutorials that introduce the Web, e-mail, FTP, news, and IRC
Site Seeing on the Internet	www.ftc.gov/bcp/conline/pubs/online/sitesee/index.html	Introduces middle school kids to the Net
Safe Surfing for Kids	www.kidsdomain.com/kids/surfsafe.html	Internet safety tips for young surfers
Digital Education Network	www.actden.com/	Great tutorials on e-mail and other applications as well as activities for grades 6 to 12
Language Arts & Literature		
Carol Hurst's Children's Literature Site	www.carolhurst.com/	Tips on how to use children's literature in the classroom
Learning@Web.Sites: English/Language Arts Department	www.ecnet.net/users/gdlevin/engdept.html	Great links to curriculum sites
CyberGuides	www.sdcoe.k12.ca.us/score/cyberguide.html	Web-delivered units of instruction centered on core works of literature
Guide to Grammar and Writing	webster.commnet.edu/HP/pages/darling/grammar.htm	Source for secondary students and educators
Poetry Pals	www.geocities.com/EnchantedForest/5165/lessonplans.html	Links to support teaching poetry in the classroom
Magazines & News		
Educast	www.educast.com	Latest education-related news delivered directly to your computer
Electronic Learning	www.scholastic.com/el/	A great magazine with information about technology and the classroom
TIME for Kids	pathfinder.com/TFK/	*TIME* magazine just for kids
TIME.com	cgi.pathfinder.com/time/	*TIME* magazine for adults
NewsCentral	www.all-links.com/newscentral/	More than 3,500 newspaper links
Mathematics		
Ask Dr. Math	forum.swarthmore.edu/dr.math/drmath.html	Math questions, searchable and arranged by grade level
Explorer	explorer.scrtec.org/explorer/	A collection of educational resources for K-12 mathematics
Educator Resources	www.mcrel.org/resources/links/math.asp	Links with educational standards in math
Awesome Library Math	www.awesomelibrary.org/Library/Materials_Search/Lesson_Plans/Math.html	A collection of hundreds of math lesson plans for grades K to 12

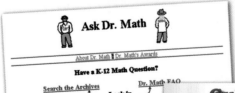

CATEGORY/SITE NAME	LOCATION	COMMENT
Museums		
MC Carlos Museum	www.cc.emory.edu/CARLOS/carlos.html	Online museum tour
Musee'	www.musee-online.org/	An interactive directory to museum collections
Museum of Science, Boston	www.mos.org/mos/onlinemuseum.html	Great online exhibits
Smithsonian Institution	www.si.edu/	Links to the Smithsonian's electronic exhibits
Music & Performing Arts		
Arts Edge	artsedge.kennedy-center.org/ artsedge.html	Information about the visual and performing arts
K-12 Resources for Music Educators	www.isd77.k12.mn.us/resources/ staffpages/shirk/k12.music.html	Resources for music educators
Music Education Resource Links (MERL)	jarl.cs.uop.edu/~cpiper/musiced.html	Well-arranged list of music education sites
The Puppetry Home Page	www.sagecraft.com/puppetry/	List of links to all types of puppetry resources on the Internet
Professional Organizations		
International Society for Technology in Education (ISTE)	www.iste.org	ISTE is dedicated to the improvement of education through technology
American Federation of Teachers (AFT)	www.aft.org/index.htm	AFT is a 900,000-member union of public and professional employees
National Education Association (NEA)	www.nea.org/	More than 2.3 million members dedicated to helping students achieve
American Association of School Administrators (AASA)	www.aasa.org/	A professional organization of educational leaders with more than 16,500 members
National Parent Teachers Association (PTA)	www.pta.org/index.stm	An organization dedicated to helping students through the cooperation of teachers and parents
National Science Teachers Association	www.nsta.org/	An organization dedicated to the improvement of science education
Reference Sources		
Acceptable Use Policies	chico.rice.edu/armadillo/acceptable.html	Extensive list of sample acceptable use policies (AUP)
Copyright & Fair Use	fairuse.stanford.edu/	Links to sites, articles, and information regarding copyright laws
Electronic Reference Desk	scholes.alfred.edu/Ref.html	List of useful reference tools on the Net
Encyclopedia.com	www.encyclopedia.com/	Quick and useful information on almost any topic
Maintaining a Healthy Computer	pip.ehhs.cmich.edu/healthy/index.html	How to manage one or more computers and prevent problems

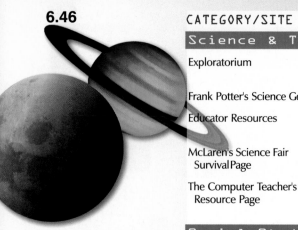

CATEGORY/SITE NAME	LOCATION	COMMENT
Science & Technology		
Exploratorium	www.exploratorium.edu/	Electronic exhibits and resources for teachers, students, and science enthusiasts
Frank Potter's Science Gems	www-sci.lib.uci.edu/SEP/SEP.html	A collection of 2,000 science references
Educator Resources	www.mcrel.org/resources/links/ science.asp	List of links with educational standards in science
McLaren's Science Fair Survival Page	www.ri.net/schools/East_Greenwich/ sciencefair.html	Tips, tricks, and links to a successful project
The Computer Teacher's Resource Page	nimbus.temple.edu/~jallis00/	Links to educational sites, lesson plans, and ideas for using computers in grades K to 8
Social Studies & History		
History/Social Studies Web Site for K-12 Teachers	www.execpc.com/~dboals/boals.html	Extensive, annotated links to help social studies teachers find information
The History Net	www.thehistorynet.com/	Well set-up site includes world and U.S. history
Social Studies Sources	education.indiana.edu/~socialst/	List of social studies resources for teachers
This Day in History	www.historychannel.com/thisday/	Information on events for any day of the year
Vocational Education		
WWW Virtual Library: Autos	www.car-nection.com/classic/vl/auto.htm	An extensive list of links to everything auto-related
Construction Trades Resources	www.educationindex.com/construct/	A list of sites to support vocational construction classes
Fabric Link	www.FabricLink.com/	A Web resource for fabrics and textiles
Aunt Edna's Kitchen	www.cei.net/~terry/auntedna/	Home life skills site that includes measurements, recipes, and more
Better Homes and Gardens Home Improvement Encyclopedia	www.bhglive.com/homeimp/docs/ index.htm	Basic plumbing, electrical, landscape, and household tips and tricks
Web Projects		
Web66: A K12 World Wide Web Project	web66.coled.umn.edu/	A project to help teachers integrate the Internet into their classroom curriculum
Cool Teaching Lessons, Units and Educational Resources	www.cl.ais.net/rlevine/coolunits.htm	A resource for teachers who want ready-made units and lessons
TrackStar	scrtec.org/track/	An awesome series of Internet integration curriculum tracks
Wired Learning in the Classroom & Library	www.kn.pacbell.com/wired/wiredApps .html#Projects	A very useful site with activities, processes, resources, and tools
Youth Net	www.youth.net/	Links to many online interactive projects for grades K to 12

Welcome to Aunt Edna's Kitchen!
Come in and see what's cooking.

Integrating Educational Technology into the Curriculum

Objectives

After completing this chapter, you will be able to:

Identify the sources of information for evaluating technology

Describe the considerations and tools used to evaluate software applications

List and explain the key criteria used to evaluate Web resources

Describe the tools for evaluating the effectiveness of technology

Describe the methods used to evaluate student projects

Identify the different technology integration strategies by classroom layout

Define and describe the value of a curriculum page

Describe ways to integrate technology into specific curriculum subject areas

Identify possible sources of funding for classroom technology

As you learn about the various types of emerging technology and methods of integrating it into your classroom curriculum, undoubtedly you will be called upon to evaluate the appropriateness of this technology and the effectiveness of its integration into the learning process. Several technology-integration strategies based on the number of computers available to you and your students, subject-specific examples of curriculum integration activities, such as creating and using curriculum pages, and the possibilities available for providing funding for your future classroom plans are presented to assist you in providing state-of-the-art technology for your students.

Evaluating Educational Technology

Evaluating the appropriateness and effectiveness of educational technology is an important aspect of integrating current technology into the classroom. To **evaluate** an item is to determine its value or judge its worth. Evaluating educational technology involves determining if the technology is appropriate and enhances the teaching and learning process. To be considered **appropriate**, educational technology must be suitable for the educational situation and promote learning at the correct levels of ability and academic achievement.

It is important to evaluate educational technology before instruction begins, during the instructional period, and after instruction has taken place [**Figure 7-1**]. Before integrating any technology into the curriculum, classroom teachers should thoroughly evaluate it. Before using software or sites on the World Wide Web, for example, teachers should determine if this technology meets their curriculum needs and if the product or content is developmentally and age appropriate for their classroom learning situation. Information from many sources helps teachers evaluate the appropriateness of educational technologies.

Sources of Information

Finding the right educational technology can be difficult, especially for new users of technology, because each year, developers create hundreds of new educational software packages and Web sites for K-12 classroom use [**Figure 7-2**]. To avoid confusion in this important task, teachers may rely on a variety of resources to help them identify and evaluate the appropriateness of educational technologies. These resources include material from school districts, state Departments of Education, catalogs, and sites on the Web.

School Districts and State Departments of Education   Many school districts compile software evaluations that provide guidance on subject-specific software. In addition, many state Departments of Education provide lists of software that are recommended and evaluated by educators. Teachers access these lists and evaluations at state-sponsored Web sites, or they may request them in printed form.

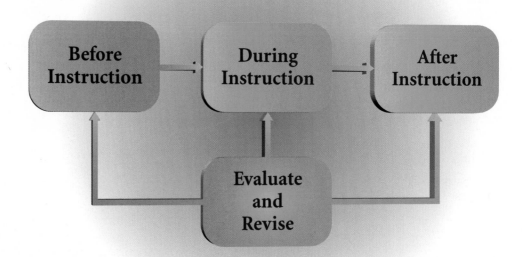

The Evaluation Cycle

Before Instruction → **During Instruction** → **After Instruction**

Evaluate and Revise

Figure 7-1 Successful technology integration requires evaluation during all phases of instruction.

Figure 7-2 Numerous high-quality educational software packages are available for classroom use.

To assist you in locating these sources of information from your school district and state Departments of Education, contact your technology coordinator, principal, media specialist, or other teachers.

Professional Educational Organizations

Many regional, national, and international educational organizations provide extensive information on how to evaluate educational resources **[Figure 7-3]**. Many of these groups provide Web sites with details related to software programs, such as grade, academic or ability level, content, and pricing.

catalogs from most companies by calling a toll-free number or completing an online form at the company's Web site.

Recommendations of Colleagues

A good way to identify software and other technology that has potential for your classroom is to talk to other educators. Colleagues can offer advice on outstanding products as well as those to avoid — unbiased advice that often is based upon first-hand experience.

Published Evaluations

Departments of Education, professional organizations, and

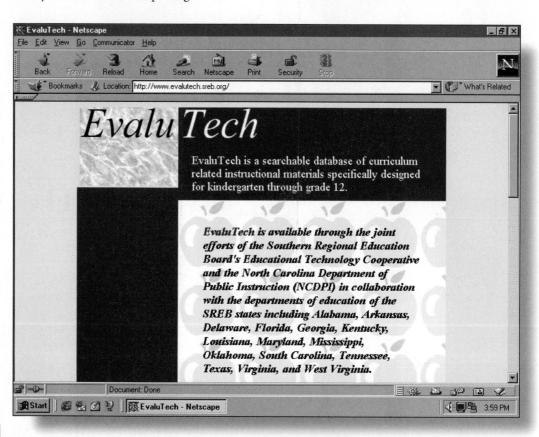

Figure 7-3 Many regional, national, and international educational organizations maintain Web sites that provide teachers with evaluations of educational technologies.

WebInfo

▢ To preview Tom Synder software products, visit the Teachers Discovering Computers Chapter 7 WebInfo page

(www.scsite.com/tdc/ ch7/webinfo.htm)

and click Tom Synder.

Catalogs Often, companies list their hardware and software suited for educational use in catalogs. These catalogs are a valuable resource to help identify technologies for your classroom. In addition to providing information about existing and new products, many software firms also provide information on how their products relate to curriculum and learning standards. You may order free

other educational groups publish evaluations of new products. Numerous software developers include evaluations completed by educators on their Web sites. Many educational publications and journals also have sections dedicated to reviews of educational technologies **[Figure 7-4]**.

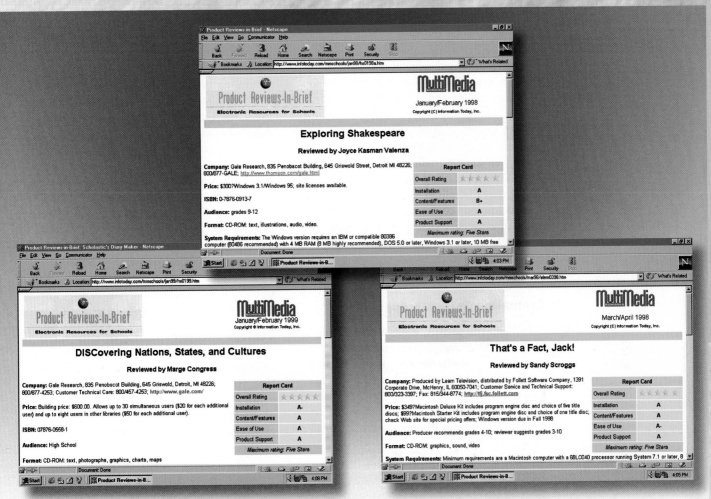

Figure 7-4 Numerous educational publications and journals have sections dedicated to reviews of educational technologies. MultiMedia Schools, for example, provides reviews of educational software in its Product Reviews-In-Brief section.

Technology Conferences Every year, dozens of national and state organizations host educational technology conferences [Figure 7-5]. A **technology conference** is a meeting dedicated to provide a vast array of information and resources for teachers. This gathering may be large or small and includes workshops and presentations by educators on hundreds of technology topics. In addition, software and hardware vendors usually have booths staffed by representatives to provide teachers with demonstrations and information on their products.

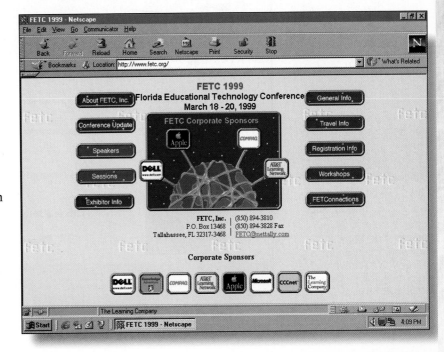

Figure 7-5 Technology conferences provide teachers with valuable resources, information, and opportunities to discuss educational technology issues with other educators.

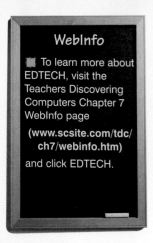

WebInfo

To learn more about EDTECH, visit the Teachers Discovering Computers Chapter 7 WebInfo page

(www.scsite.com/tdc/ ch7/webinfo.htm)

and click EDTECH.

The Web By far, the Web is the most comprehensive source of tools and resources to help you evaluate educational technology. Teachers may visit thousands of Web sites dedicated to educational topics. Mailing lists, forums, newsgroups, discussion groups, and bulletin boards available on the Web also provide vast sources of information. One of the larger well-known mailing lists is EDTECH. The EDTECH mailing list allows educators from many disciplines — teachers, administrators, technology coordinators, media specialists, and university faculty — to exchange information, comments, and ideas on educational issues.

Evaluating Software Applications

When you identify a software package that is potentially suited to your curriculum needs, you should evaluate the software for appropriateness; review the accuracy of the content; and consider its relevance to the curriculum standards and goals. A cost-effective way to evaluate software is to download a free trial version [Figure 7-6] and use it for the specified period of time. Many software companies allow you to download these trial versions from their Web or FTP sites.

Software evaluation rubrics also help you evaluate educational software. A **rubric** is a detailed assessment tool that provides a number of important evaluation criteria, including content, documentation and technical support, ability and academic levels, technical quality, and ease of use to help assess the quality of software or other items. A two-page Software Evaluation Rubric is shown opposite in **Figure 7-7a** and on page 7.8 in **Figure 7-7b**. Many schools develop their own software evaluation rubrics for teachers to use, while in other locations, teachers create their own software evaluation rubrics.

Content When evaluating educational software, content is the most important area to consider. When examining software content, you need to determine if the software is valid. **Valid** means the software has well-grounded instructional properties, provides appropriate content, and teaches what is intended.

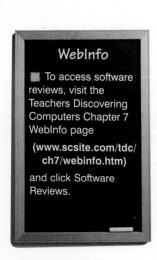

WebInfo

To access software reviews, visit the Teachers Discovering Computers Chapter 7 WebInfo page

(www.scsite.com/tdc/ ch7/webinfo.htm)

and click Software Reviews.

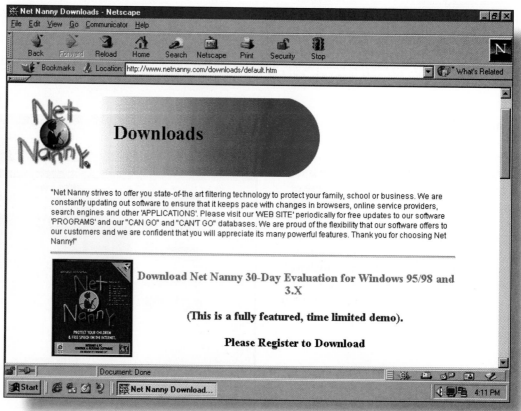

Figure 7-6 Many software companies allow you to download free evaluation copies of their software.

Rubric

Software Evaluation Rubric

Application Title: _____ Subject Area: _____

Version: _____ Producer/Publisher: _____

Purchased From: _____

Goal(s): _____

Objective(s): _____

Prerequisite Skills: _____

Configuration

Hardware/System Requirements: _____

_____

Type of Drive Required: DVD-ROM _____ CD-ROM _____ 3-1/2" _____

Hard Drive Space Required: _____ Memory Required: _____

Content

<u>Program Categories</u>: (Check all that apply)

☐ Presentation   ☐ Remediation   ☐ Word Processing

☐ Authoring   ☐ Simulation   ☐ Database

☐ Problem Solving   ☐ Tutorial   ☐ Spreadsheet

Other: _____

Skill/Ability/Grade Levels: _____

_____

_____

Use the following system to rate the software

1 = Strongly disagree   2 = Disagree
3 = Agree   4 = Strongly agree
NA = Not applicable

	1	2	3	4	NA
1. The content is accurate and factual.	1	2	3	4	NA
2. The content is educationally appropriate.	1	2	3	4	NA
3. The content is free of errors.	1	2	3	4	NA
4. The content meets learning goals and objectives.	1	2	3	4	NA
5. The content is valid.	1	2	3	4	NA
6. The content is free of stereotypes and racial bias.	1	2	3	4	NA

Figure 7-7a A software evaluation rubric helps teachers evaluate educational software packages.

Rubric

Software Evaluation Rubric

Ease of Use

1. Directions are clear.	1	2	3	4	NA
2. Students can exit the program at any time.	1	2	3	4	NA
3. Students can restart the program where they stopped.	1	2	3	4	NA
4. The software is reliable and free of disruption by system errors.	1	2	3	4	NA

Documentation and Support

1. The software manual is clear and thorough.	1	2	3	4	NA
2. The software has an 800/888 support number.	1	2	3	4	NA
3. Online technical support is available.	1	2	3	4	NA
4. Help and tutorials are clear and easy to use.	1	2	3	4	NA

Ability Levels

1. The user level can be set by the teacher.	1	2	3	4	NA
2. The user level automatically advances.	1	2	3	4	NA
3. The software covers a variety of ability/skill levels.	1	2	3	4	NA

Technical Quality

1. Animation and graphics are used well.	1	2	3	4	NA
2. Audio, voice input/output, is used well.	1	2	3	4	NA
3. Feedback and prompts are appropriate.	1	2	3	4	NA
4. The application allows branching.	1	2	3	4	NA
5. Student interest is maintained.	1	2	3	4	NA
Overall Quality:	1	2	3	4	NA

RECOMMENDATION

☐ Purchase Immediately   ☐ Priority (as funds become available)

☐ Do Not Purchase   ☐ Other (specify)

Comments: _____

_____

_____

Evaluator: _____ Date: _____

Teachers Discovering Computers

Figure 7-7b

page 2 of 2

Most software companies and distributors provide a description of the content and learning skills addressed for their software packages; some software firms even match the skills the software teaches with specific curriculum standards and learning objectives. When evaluating the contents of a software application, always relate them to your school's specific learning standards and curriculum goals.

Documentation and Technical Support

When evaluating software, consider the technical support and documentation the software offers. **Documentation** is any printed or online information that provides assistance in installing, using, and maintaining the software. You should review the documentation for readability and depth of coverage. **Technical support** is a service that hardware and software manufacturers and third-party service companies offer to customers to provide answers to questions, repairs, and other assistance. Companies usually provide technical support over the phone or via the Web [Figure 7-8]. Some firms even provide on-site

support, in which a technician comes to the school, home, or business to solve hardware and software problems.

In addition to reviewing the available documentation and technical support, you also should determine if any other kinds of support are available, such as clear, easy-to-use aids and tutorials. Some software companies, for example, provide instructor resource guides and lesson plans to assist in integrating their software into curriculum areas.

Ability and Academic Levels   Educators need to evaluate whether the software can be used with more than one ability or academic level. An **ability level** refers to a student's current competency level or the skill level they can achieve for a specific learning objective. The **academic level** is based on the grade level with increments to determine if a student is performing at the appropriate level. Several software applications, such as math and reading software, adjust the academic level as students successfully move through specific skills. Numerous software applications allow you to set the academic, skill, or ability levels at which you wish the students to work.

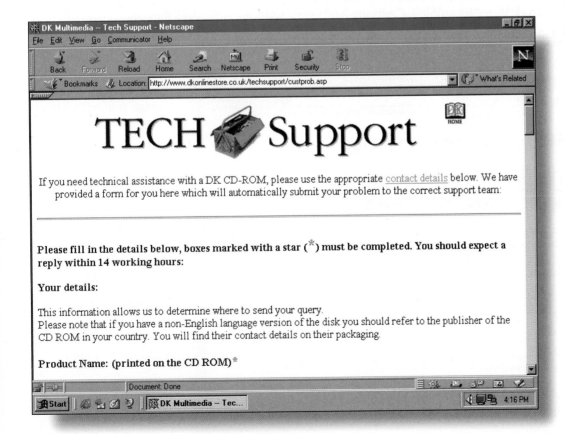

Figure 7-8 Many software manufacturers provide technical support for their products via the Web. In this example, DK Multimedia provides support within 14 working hours.

Technical Quality and Ease of Use

Technical quality refers to how well the software presents itself and how well it works. Items to evaluate are the clarity of the screen design; appropriateness of feedback and student prompts; and use of graphics, animations, sound, and other media elements. **Ease of use**, or user-friendliness, refers to anything that makes the software easy to use. Software should be easy for both you and the students to use, while at the same time maintaining the students' interest.

Student opinions also play an important role in successfully integrating new technology. After you complete your evaluation, you may wish to obtain feedback from students by allowing them to use and test the software. If students dislike the software, they will not enjoy using it even though they may learn. This dislike will limit the effectiveness of the software in classroom use.

Evaluating Web Resources

The Web is an incredible resource for teachers. Not all of the information on the Web, however, is placed there by reliable sources. Web page authoring software has made it easy for anyone to create, or publish, a Web page or Web site that contains personal opinions, ideas, theology, and philosophy. In contrast, before a book is published, the content is reviewed for accuracy and objectivity and the author's credentials are verified. Once published, the book's copyright date and table of contents allow users to determine the currency of the information and the book's depth of coverage. A Web site offers no such safeguards.

Because Web sites often contain inaccurate, incomplete, or biased information, evaluating Web resources presents a unique challenge. Teachers must know how to evaluate Web sites and teach their students how to do the same. When evaluating a Web site as an instructional source, you should consider criteria such as authority, affiliation, content, audience, timeliness, and Web site design.

Authority   When evaluating Web sites, **authority** refers to the credibility of the person or persons who author and create the site. A Web site on asteroids by a distinguished astronomy professor, for example, has more authority than an astronomy Web site created by an amateur stargazer. When reviewing a Web site, answer the following questions.

- Is the author identified? If you cannot identify the creator of the Web page, you may wish to avoid this Web site.

- Examine the credentials of the author, or creator, of the Web site. What evidence is there the author qualifies to publish on this topic? The authority of the Web page shown in **Figure 7-9**, for example, is based on the credibility of several organizations and corporations.

Figure 7-9 Teachers can consider this Web site authoritative because it was created by a number of major organizations and corporations.

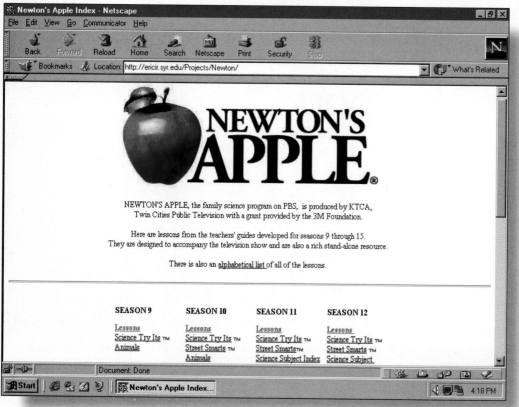

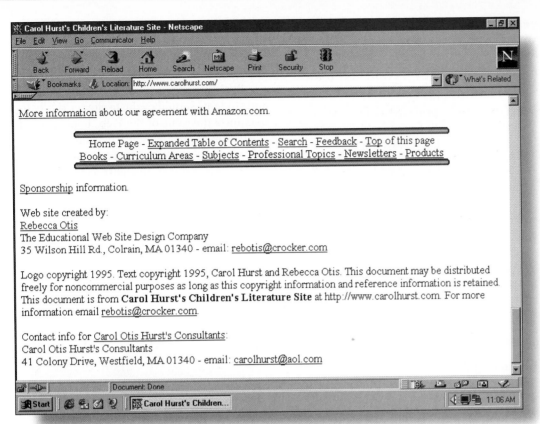

Figure 7-10 Information on the author, or creator, of a Web site often is found at the bottom of the Web site's home page.

WebInfo

To learn the "10 C's for evaluating Internet resources," visit the Teachers Discovering Computers Chapter 7 WebInfo page **(www.scsite.com/tdc/ ch7/webinfo.htm)** and click 10 C's.

Has the author listed his or her occupation, years of experience, position, education, or other credentials? If you do not see this information immediately, refer to the bottom of the home page, which often provides additional information about the creator, or author, and affiliation **[Figure 7-10]**.

Affiliation **Affiliation** refers to the professional organization, school, school district, university, company, or government office with which a particular Web site is associated. A simple way to determine a site's affiliation is to examine the URL and domain name to identify what type of organization maintains the Web page. A site with a .com domain, for example, is operated by a commercial business; an .edu domain is controlled by an educational institution **[Figure 7-11]**. Well known sources of information such as the U.S. government, universities, school districts, newspapers, and non-profit organizations usually have reliable facts on their Web sites.

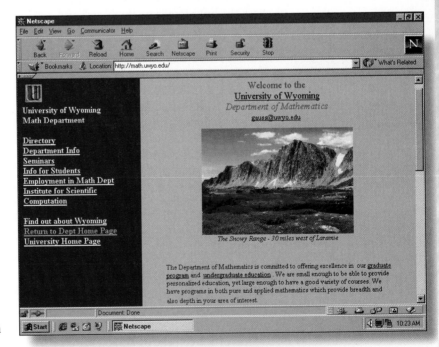

Figure 7-11 This Web site's affiliation is easily identifiable as the University of Wyoming.

WebInfo

For more examples of Web site evaluation rubrics for students, visit the Teachers Discovering Computers Chapter 7 WebInfo page (**www.scsite.com/tdc/ch7/webinfo.htm**) and click Rubrics.

Content   **Content** is the information the Web page provides. Web pages use a variety of media to convey facts, opinions, and news. As you evaluate the content of a Web page, consider the following questions.

- Is the content provided as a public service? Is it free from bias? Why is the author, or creator, providing the information? If it is not clearly stated, attempt to determine the purpose of the Web page.

- Does the information on the page relate to your curriculum and instructional standards?

- What topics are covered? Is the information clearly labeled and well organized?

- For what level is the information written? How thorough is the information?

- Do the links within the site add value and assist you in meeting your instructional goals?

As you evaluate the content of a Web page, you always should keep the learning objectives and curriculum standards of the classroom in mind. Also, take the time to check the links to ensure they work and are appropriate for your intended audience.

Audience and Currency   The **audience** is the individual or group intended to view the Web page. You should review the Web page to determine if it is suitable for an audience such as your students. Is the content appropriate for your students? Can you use this Web page in your classroom? Again, keep your learning objectives in mind as you examine the Web page. **Currency** is the measure of how up to date, or timely, the Web page content is and how often it is updated. A good Web page will state clearly when the page was last revised or updated.

WebInfo

To explore technology assessment further, visit the Teachers Discovering Computers Chapter 7 WebInfo page (**www.scsite.com/tdc/ch7/webinfo.htm**) and click Assessing Technology.

Design   The **design** of a Web site is the way it is arranged — that is, the way it uses instructional design principles to deliver content to the user. Web site design determines the effectiveness of a Web page by enhancing it or detracting from it. **Web effectiveness** is defined as producing an appropriate effect in an efficient manner. An effective Web page loads in a reasonable amount of time, has a good general appearance, is pleasing to the eye, and is easy to navigate. Links should be well organized, clearly marked, work properly, and lead to related materials.

Both in and out of the classroom, teachers and students should evaluate sites critically to maximize the value of the Web. To assist in the evaluation of Web sites, teachers often find rubrics useful. A Web Page Evaluation Rubric for teachers is shown in **Figure 7-12**. Teachers should use rubrics that reflect the evaluation criteria just discussed. Students also benefit from a rubric. **Figure 7-13** shown on page 7.14 illustrates a user-friendly, engaging Student Web Site Evaluation Form. No matter which method you choose, the key is to have a pre-determined way of effectively evaluating the information found on the Web.

Evaluating the Effectiveness of Technology Integration

To effectively integrate technology into the curriculum requires planning, time, dedication, and resources. Teachers, schools, and school districts need to know if their integration strategies are working, so after approximately a year, a teacher, school, or district should take steps to evaluate the effectiveness of their technology integration.

Evaluating the effectiveness of technology can be challenging; there is no simple way to evaluate what works in all situations — all students, all technology, all schools, and all classrooms. Nor do any standard types of evaluation show the relationship between the technology and student achievement. Educators should not rely, therefore, on the assumption that technology tools are having some impact. Instead, teachers and administrators must locate or develop alternative techniques to measure the effectiveness of integrating technology.

The first step in evaluating educational technology's impact on student achievement is to develop indicators that measure a student's performance, skills acquired, and academic and ability levels obtained. Test scores are not the only, or even the best, indicators of the successful integration of technology. The types of learning best supported by technology are those not easily measured by traditional assessments such as standardized tests.

Web Page Evaluation Rubric

Title of site: _____

Curriculum area: _____

URL: _____

Objectives that will be supported by this site:_____

_____

_____

Notes:_____

_____

_____

	Level 1	Level 2	Level 3	Level 4
Authority	No author is listed and no e-mail contact is provided.	No author is listed but an e-mail contact is provided.	An author is listed with no credentials, but you cannot tell if the author is the creator of the material.	An author is listed with appropriate credentials, and is the creator of the material.
Affiliation	It is unclear what institution supports this information.	A commercial Internet provider supports the site, but it is unclear if the author has any connection with a larger institution.	The site is supported by a larger institution, but some bias is apparent in the information from the institution.	The site is supported by a reputable institution without bias in the information.
Objectivity	The Web page is a Virtual Soapbox.	The Web page contains some bias and a great deal of advertising.	The Web page contains some advertising and minimal bias.	The Web page contains little advertising and is free of bias.
Audience	The Web page is not appropriate for my audience.	The Web page is written above the level of my audience, but some of the information is useful.	The Web page is written at an appropriate level for my audience and some of the information is useful.	The Web page is written at an appropriate level and the information is suitable for my classroom.
Currency	Information on the page has not been revised since 1998, or no date can be located.	Information on the page has not been updated since 1998, but the information is still of good quality.	Information has been updated in the last year. Seems to reflect currency.	Information has been updated in the last three months, is current, and up to date.
Content	The information on the Web page does not relate to my objectives.	The information relates to my objectives, but many of the links do not work.	The information relates to my objectives, links work, but the site is not well organized.	The information relates to my objectives, links work, and the site is well organized.
Web Site Design	The Web site does not load well and is difficult to read.	The Web site loads slowly, and the general appearance is poor.	The Web site loads well, but the site is not easy to navigate.	The Web site loads well, is easy to navigate, is visually pleasing, and easy to read.

Figure 7-12 A rubric is helpful in evaluating the educational value of Web sites.

Rubric

Student Web Site Evaluation Form

Student team members: _____

DESIGN

Can move easily from page to page

Good use of graphics (pictures and color)

CONTENT

Information is useful

How this site compares in content to similar sites

TECHNICAL ELEMENTS

This site loads quickly (within 30 seconds)

All links work

CREDIBILITY

Contact person is stated with his or her e-mail address

States the name of the host school or organization

Tells when this site was last updated

Figure 7-13 Students enjoy rubrics that are fun and user-friendly when evaluating Web sites.

Due to the nature of technology and the way the learning environment is changing, educators must create and use different types of evaluation tools.

Tools for Evaluating the Effectiveness of Technology Integration

Evaluating the effectiveness of educational technology can help you assess whether the technology is appropriate for the learner, meets learning objectives, and enhances the learning process. Traditionally, teachers use many different evaluation techniques in the final stage of instruction or when assessing **student performance**. To ensure that students meet the learning objectives, teachers generally use the traditional means of testing to assess student performance. **Assessment** is any method used to understand the current knowledge a student possesses; it can range from a teacher's subjective judgment based on a single observation of a student's performance to a state-mandated standardized test.

Reliable assessment information provides accurate estimates of student performance, permits appropriate generalizations about the students' skills and abilities, and enables teachers or other decision-makers to make appropriate decisions. Traditional forms of assessment include testing in the form of multiple choice, fill-in-the blank, true/false, short answer, and essay questions.

Traditional forms of assessment also can be used to evaluate the effectiveness of technology. Just as technology opens many new and exciting doors for teaching and learning, technology also opens new doors for evaluating student performance. When integrating technology, some teachers and schools move toward a nontraditional approach of student assessment, known as alternative assessment. **Alternative assessment** uses nontraditional methods to determine whether students have mastered the appropriate content and skill level. Educators may adopt several approaches to alternative assessment, such as authentic, or performance-based, assessment.

Authentic assessment, or **performance-based assessment,** refers to alternative ways to evaluate students' performances to determine how well and in what way they meet learning objectives and standards. Authentic assessment can be formal or informal and aims to present the student with tasks that mirror the priorities and challenges typical of their instructional activities. They answer open-ended questions, conduct hands-on experiments, do research, write, revise and discuss papers, and create portfolios of their work over a period of time. **Authentic learning** presents learning experiences that demonstrate real-life connections between students' lessons and the world.

Authentic assessment measures this learning by testing a student's ability to master practical learning standards. Using authentic assessment, for example, a student may be asked to explain historical events, generate scientific hypotheses, solve math problems, create portfolios or presentations, or converse in a foreign language. When using authentic assessment, many teachers use a checklist or rating scale.

A **checklist** is a predetermined list of performance criteria. A Project Evaluation Checklist is shown on the next page in **Figure 7-14**. Once a student has met a criterion, the criterion is marked as complete. A **rating scale** is a more complex form of checklist that lists a numerical value, or rating, for each criterion. Assessment involves rating each student on his or her achievement for each criterion and specifying the total based on all criteria.

Another very popular form of alternative assessment is the rubric. A **rubric** is a detailed assessment tool that makes it easier for teachers to assess the quality of an item, such as a learning project. As used in assessment, a rubric is a set of criteria that specifies the required achievements for each level of quality, which is usually identified by the number, or level, of points earned. Although a rubric is similar to a checklist, it describes in greater detail the criteria and components that must be achieved.

When evaluating technology integration, one of the more widely used authentic assessment techniques is teacher observation. **Teacher observation** as shown in **Figure 7-15** on page 7.17 is the result of teachers actively observing their students during the learning process.

WebInfo

To learn more about portfolio assessment, visit the Teachers Discovering Computers Chapter 7 WebInfo page **(www.scsite.com/tdc/ch7/webinfo.htm)** and click Portfolios.

CHAPTER 7

Checklist

Project Evaluation Checklist

Date: _____

Student name: _____

Project Title: _____

	YES	NO
The project is creative.	☐	☐
The project is eye appealing.	☐	☐
The project is organized.	☐	☐
Content is presented well.	☐	☐
Multimedia features are used effectively.	☐	☐
The project is complete.	☐	☐
The project storyboard was pre-approved.	☐	☐
The project is easy to navigate.	☐	☐
Grammar and spelling are used correctly.	☐	☐
The text is easy to read and follow.	☐	☐
The project was well planned.	☐	☐
The project has an author's section.	☐	☐

Teachers Discovering Computers

Figure 7-14 Teachers often use alternative assessment tools such as checklists and rating scales to evaluate student performance.

Teachers notice whether students are highly motivated during the learning process when technology is used, observe how long the students work on a given objective, and observe the length of time students continue working on a task in order to master its content and skills. Teacher observation is a powerful assessment tool, and it often is used in combination with other assessment tools. All of these tools can be used to evaluate individual student projects.

Others, such as HyperStudio and PowerPoint, do not provide assessment components. These multimedia authoring applications, however, are ideal for students to use to create projects that are innovative and motivational. Teachers who use these software programs for technology-based students' projects need to develop effective assessment tools to measure their achievements.

Before a teacher presents a project's requirements to students, he or she should

Figure 7-15 This teacher knows that teacher observation is critical when integrating technology.

Evaluating Technology-Based Student Projects

Today, skills in technology are essential in order for students to learn. Technology-based student projects help facilitate integrating technology and multimedia into the curriculum. In the process, students learn how to use, manage, and understand technology and how it is used to synthesize and present information on a variety of subjects.

Some software programs, such as those provided with integrated learning systems (ILS), automatically track student progress.

create an assessment rubric. **Figure 7-16** on the next page illustrates a Student Project Evaluation Rubric that guides students on how they will be evaluated on projects. To determine the criteria to include in the rubric, ask yourself what the students should learn and how this learning will be evidenced in their projects. In the rubric, be sure to specify what students need to include in their projects and clearly inform the students how they will be evaluated. Checklists, rating scales, and teacher observation also are valid assessment tools for technology-based student projects. Your goals and objectives should define and guide the selection and creation of your assessment tool.

Rubric

Student Project Evaluation Rubric

Group Members: _____

Project Title: _____

	Poor	Fair	Good	Excellent
Planning				
Student completed project outline for stack.	4 5	6 7	8 9	10
Student completed storyboard sheets for stack.	4 5	6 7	8 9	10
Students used reference materials and Web sites in gathering information.	4 5	6 7	8 9	10
Stack Design				
Stack design reflects planning.	4 5	6 7	8 9	10
Visual contrast between text and background is present.	4 5	6 7	8 9	10
Text used is easy to read and is Read Only.	4 5	6 7	8 9	10
Navigation buttons link and work logically.	4 5	6 7	8 9	10
Stack is easy to navigate.	4 5	6 7	8 9	10
Buttons are located consistently on the cards and are easy to find.	4 5	6 7	8 9	10
Colors, clip art and artwork are complementary to stack content.	4 5	6 7	8 9	10
Consistency				
The stack design reflects consistency and creativity.	4 5	6 7	8 9	10
No more than two fonts are used on a card.	4 5	6 7	8 9	10
Transitions from card to card are not distracting.	4 5	6 7	8 9	10
Creativity				
The stack is interesting to use and holds your attention.	4 5	6 7	8 9	10
Graphics are used well.	4 5	6 7	8 9	10
Special effects, including animations, are used well.	4 5	6 7	8 9	10
Content				
Understanding of the topic is evidenced by factual and interesting information.	4 5	6 7	8 9	10
Complete sentences with correct punctuation, grammar, and spelling are used.	4 5	6 7	8 9	10
Information is presented accurately and logically.	4 5	6 7	8 9	10
The stack contains a title card, reference card, and author card.	4 5	6 7	8 9	10

Figure 7-16 A rubric guides students in determining how they will be evaluated on projects. This rubric, for example, is designed to evaluate students' HyperStudio stacks.

Evaluating Content Your goals and objectives will help determine the content to include in student projects and how to assess this content. For technology-based student projects, content may include factual information on a historical figure; the key points included in a multimedia presentation; biology lab data in a spreadsheet; and other pertinent information. In addition, evaluation of the content also should include a review of punctuation, grammar, spelling, coverage of material, presentation of the material in a logical order, and specific information such as a title, references, and about the author.

Evaluating Planning Effective teaching involves planning. Students also must plan a project prior to creating it, if it is to be effective. When assigning technology-based projects, establish how you want students to plan and what tools they will use. A software planning tool such as **Inspiration®** helps students and teachers quickly develop and communicate ideas using flowcharts, concept maps, and story webs **[Figure 7-17]**.

Flowcharts are diagrams that show the step-by-step actions that must take place by plotting a sequence of events. Flowcharts are useful in helping students outline the individual tasks that must be performed to complete an action, a story, or an experiment and the sequence in which they must be performed. A **concept map** or **story web** helps students use flowcharting to understand the attributes and relationships of the main subject and provides a visual tool for brainstorming and planning **[Figure 7-18]**. Another useful planning tool is a **storyboard**, which is a drawing that allows students to design and lay out a project or assignment before creating it on a computer.

Evaluating Creativity When evaluating student projects, teachers should consider students' originality, imaginative and innovative approach, and artistic abilities — all aspects of **creativity**. Creative student projects should be interesting and unique. Students should demonstrate an understanding of how to use the special effects offered by multimedia authoring software to enhance their projects, instead of distracting from its content. Color, clip art, and artwork should strengthen content.

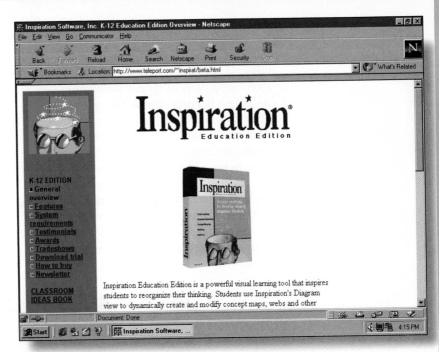

Figure 7-17 Inspiration® is an excellent tool for teaching students how to organize their ideas.

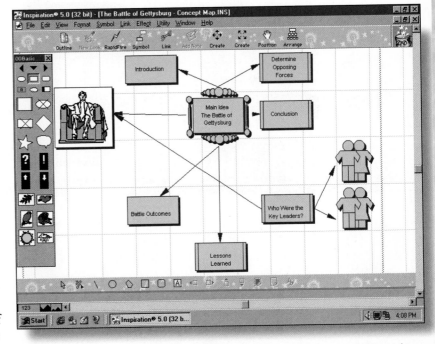

Figure 7-18 Using Inspiration® software, students create a concept map to plan an undertaking such as this history project on the Battle of Gettysburg.

Putting it All Together — Evaluating Technology Integration

Ms. Vicki Osborne teaches social studies and other subjects at Fall Hills Middle School.

CHAPTER 7

CHAPTER 7

She has one computer in her classroom and 26 students. Her middle school is on a **block schedule**, which is an alternative way of scheduling classes. This means the social studies class meets every other day for 88 minutes. Because it is a presidential election year, Ms. Osborne would like her social studies students to research one of the presidential candidates and then prepare a HyperStudio stack to present their findings to the class.

She has six objectives for the lesson. The students will: (1) work cooperatively in groups with three or four students in each group; (2) use reference materials and Web resources to research the candidate; (3) create a HyperStudio project to present their research; (4) identify three major campaign issues for their candidate; (5) provide personal facts about the candidate, such as education, occupation prior to politics, and military service; and (6) use correct grammar, spelling, and punctuation in their presentation. She will use a rubric to evaluate the students' projects.

Ms. Osborne began her social studies lesson by displaying her slides on a 32" television for easy viewing by all students. The first step was to brainstorm with her students about the lesson and create a concept map about the election process and the candidates **[Figure 7-19]**. She also passed out a copy of

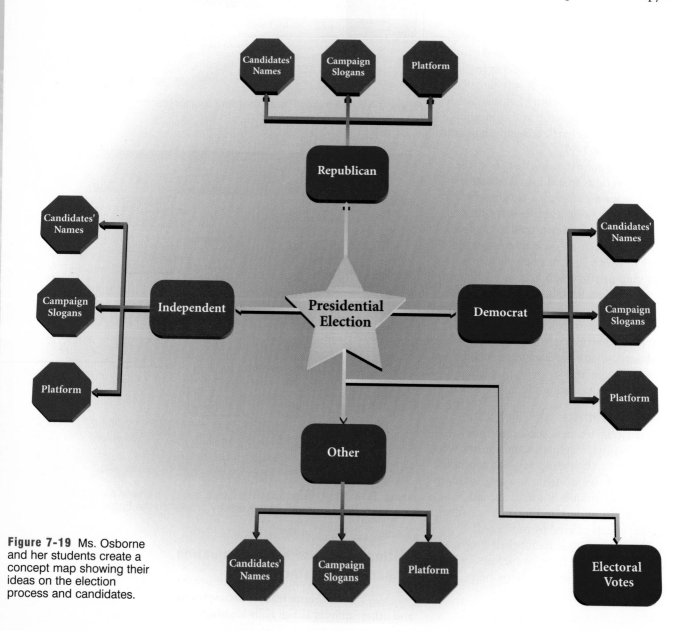

Figure 7-19 Ms. Osborne and her students create a concept map showing their ideas on the election process and candidates.

her evaluation rubric, discussed the rubric with her students, and answered their questions. Students then were divided into groups to complete their first task.

Students were required to create a flowchart or storyboard of their project on paper before they began working on the computers. Ms. Osborne must approve their flowchart drawings and storyboards. When the groups were ready to begin creating their projects on the computer, Ms. Osborne borrowed an additional computer from another teacher and arranged for two groups to use computers in the Media Center. This allowed four groups to work on computers at the same time. Groups rotated through the four computers in 40-minute blocks [Figure 7-20].

make this an authentic learning experience, Ms. Osborne's students created voting boxes and placed them all over the school, so the students at Fall Hills Middle School could vote. After the actual presidential election three weeks later, her students planned to compare the school election results to the results of the actual election.

To successfully integrate technology, teachers must continuously evaluate educational technology before instruction begins, during the instructional period, and after instruction has taken place. Technology not only changes the learning process but also the teaching and evaluation processes. Teachers have the responsibility to evaluate and update assignments and activities continuously: on a

Figure 7-20 Centers allow students to work collaboratively in groups on subject-directed projects.

When the groups finished their projects, Ms. Osborne had each group present their project to the class in the media center. She also invited the principal, a local politician, the media specialist, and another social studies class to participate in the presentations. The students were very proud of their projects and enjoyed showing them to their peers, teachers, and school administrators. The school newspaper highlighted some of the projects. To

daily, weekly, monthly, or semester basis, depending on the project or assignment.

To make the learning more effective, often only minor changes and improvements are necessary. In other instances, however, teachers need to implement major revisions to reflect content, curriculum, or technology changes. The next few sections introduce you to other integration strategies, such as using technology in various classroom configurations and developing curriculum pages.

Integration Strategies

To help meet the constant challenge of motivating students to learn, teachers must change their traditional roles and become facilitators of learning. Technology plays a key role in easing this change because it allows teachers to use technology tools to enhance the learning environment, motivate students, guide students in an active learning process, and encourage them to learn. The most effective way to integrate technology is to place the technology at the point of instruction — the classroom. In the ever-increasing need to motivate students to learn, teachers have a mandate to use the powerful tools of technology to enhance the learning environment.

Many different technologies, availability of computer labs, and different kinds and numbers of computers in the classroom are found in schools today **[Figure 7-21]**. The following instructional strategies describe techniques to integrate technology into a one-computer classroom, a multi-computer classroom, and a computer lab.

One-Computer Classroom

Most classrooms are equipped with one multimedia computer and are referred to as a **one-computer classroom**. There are many ways to integrate educational technology with only one computer in the classroom. In this scenario, the most common practice is to use the computer for classroom presentations and demonstrations. By projecting the computer's image on a projection screen or large-screen television, you can use the computer to supplement and enhance your traditional lectures to accomplish whole-class instruction of learning objectives. You also can use the computer to introduce new concepts, prepare students for a lesson, describe background information for assignments, and explain evaluation criteria.

Another strategy permits students to work on the computer in small groups to foster collaboration and cooperative learning opportunities. Students also may use the computer to present their assignments, projects, and research activities to the entire class. In addition, you can use the computer to maintain records, create presentations and projects,

Figure 7-21
Technology can be integrated into many different classroom environments.

do research, and communicate with other teachers [Figure 7-22].

To integrate technology in a one-computer classroom follow these guidelines.

- Obtain Internet access. Use the Web's many educational resources, such as audio, video, and multimedia applications to enhance instruction and learning.

- Utilize educational multimedia application software. Both teachers and students can make use of the abundance of educational software available on CD-ROM, DVD-ROM, and school networks.

- Enhance lectures and presentations. Connect the computer to a television monitor, and use the computer to enhance lectures, create and give presentations, and take students on virtual Web tours.

- Use the computer as a teaching assistant. Tutor individual students by having them use drill and practice software, tutorials, simulations, and problem-solving software.

- Foster group and cooperative learning. Students can use the computer as an informational resource or a creation tool for group projects, such as multimedia presentations.

- Write an ongoing story. Begin a story on the computer, which serves as a creative writing center, and allow student authors to add to it daily. Before you begin, explain the rules for acceptable behavior, the types of content to be included in the story, and the types of entries that are satisfactory.

- Start a class newsletter. Allow students to write articles and use word processing or desktop publishing software to create a class newsletter. For example, as an adjunct to a history class, students can collaborate to create a newsletter with sections on various aspects related to that period of history [Figure 7-23].

- Maintain a student database. Instead of having students fill out emergency information forms, let them enter the information into a database on the computer. Students also may enter

Figure 7-22 Teachers benefit from using a classroom computer to maintain grades and other important files.

Figure 7-23 Students gain real-world skills by creating a class or school newsletter.

information on a variety of content-related subject areas, such as information on science projects, vocabulary words, historical places, and so on.

- Utilize the computer as a teacher productivity tool. The computer is an excellent tool on which to create tests and lesson plans, maintain grades and attendance records, write letters to parents, and create achievement certificates. Purchasing grade book or student information management software helps to streamline many daily management responsibilities.

- Optimize computer lab time. Use the computer to introduce students to various types of software and thus create learning paths before taking them to the school's computer lab. This will optimize the time students spend on computers while in the computer lab.

Multi-Computer Classroom

Having two or more computers in your classroom fosters additional learning opportunities that allow flexibility in computer usage and make technology integration an integral part of the curriculum. Remember, one-computer classroom strategies also are applicable to a classroom with two or more computers.

One way to use two or more computers is to set up the computers as separate learning centers for student use. Teachers can divide the centers by subject area and then create activities that continuously change to match the curriculum or lessons being taught. A math center, for example, may include CD-ROM/DVD-ROM and network-based tutorials to reinforce math skills. A language arts center may include word processing software for creative writing projects, HyperStudio and PowerPoint to create multimedia presentations, as well as reading and spelling software skill programs.

A social science center may allow students to use the Web as a research tool and correspond with other classrooms via the Internet to learn more about the culture, language, history, and geography of other regions. Multimedia CD-ROMs like the Carmen Sandiego series help reinforce mapping and geography skills in relation to other curriculum areas.

Learning centers are an effective way to create a flexible learning environment with many options for students. Teachers can integrate technologies into learning centers to create specialized centers such as a video center, a listening center, and a digital camera center.

To illustrate how one teacher is integrating technology into a science curriculum, consider the middle school classroom of Ms. Julie Davis. At the beginning of class, she takes her students for a nature walk on school property to learn about trees, plants, changing seasons, and photosynthesis. During the nature walk, students notice a lot of trash on the school property. She lets her students use a digital camera to take pictures of the trash, plants, trees, and other items of interest [Figure 7-24]. In a follow-up discussion in class, the students decide the trash is a form of pollution — and they should do something to make the school cleaner. Ms. Davis recognizes this as a teachable moment and shows the students a short CNN video on global warming.

The next day, Ms. Davis continues the learning process by dividing the students into groups to begin their research projects on trees, plants, air, and waste associated with the environment. She is fortunate to have four multimedia computers in her classroom. Two of the computers are used as Web research centers, while the other two are set up as creation centers. To complete group projects, students rotate through the Web centers and use her curriculum page to locate resources from agriculture, environmental protection, and other related Web sites [Figure 7-25]. Then they use the creation centers to create PowerPoint presentations that suggest ways to protect the environment. The students incorporate their digital pictures into the PowerPoint presentations.

While completing the projects, the students learn about citizenship and that everyone is responsible for protecting the environment. They then decide to start a school-wide cleanup project. The class creates flyers using Microsoft Publisher and posts them throughout the school so all the students and teachers will be aware of the environment.

Figure 7-24 Using a digital camera, students can take pictures to enhance their electronic projects.

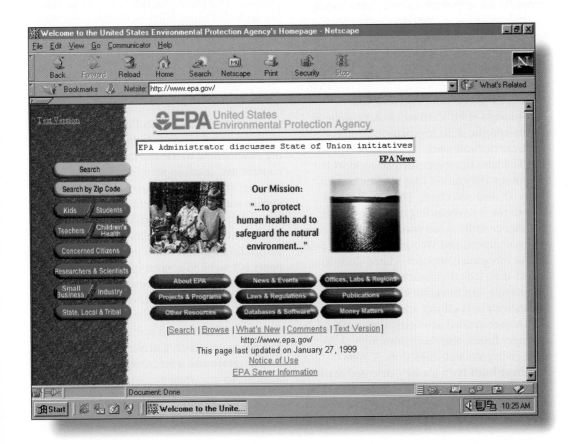

Figure 7-25 Students can locate information dealing with pollution, global warming, and other environmental issues easily on the Web.

As this example illustrates, using computers and other technologies in the classroom promotes active learning, involves the students, and provides a sense of ownership, or authentic learning, of the information being presented. Having two or more computers in the classroom — especially used as learning centers — requires more planning and attention to detail than having just one computer. Before setting up a learning center or centers, teachers should consider how many computers will be in each center and what, if any, other technologies may be included in the center. Once the centers are set up, teachers can work on managing and planning activities, scheduling rotation times through each center for the students as they complete projects and activities. Teachers may create a sign-up list or use a timing device so all students have a fair amount of time on the computers.

Computer Lab

A computer lab offers teachers instructional opportunities that are not possible in a one-, two-, or even a five-computer classroom. The most important advantage of using a computer lab is that all students have hands-on experience using computer technology. Teachers may successfully use computer labs for drill and practice, remediation, collaborative learning, computer skill instruction (for example, word processing), Internet research, whole class instruction, and tutorials.

Students often learn technology skills or subject-specific skills in isolation from the rest of the curriculum while in school computer labs. The labs, however, can also support the technology integration that teaches curriculum goals and objectives. They are not just a place to teach keyboarding, remedial math, and science drills. A lab with multimedia computers, scanners, and Web access makes it possible to integrate computer-related skills into subject-directed curriculum areas. Teachers, for example, can integrate specific software applications into subject area content.

Teacher-created activities, such as Web scavenger hunts, also teach computer skills, while giving students direction. A **Web scavenger hunt** is an inquiry-oriented activity in which students explore the resources of the Web using discovery learning to find the

answers to teacher-created questions **[Figure 7-26]**. While searching for the answers, students use their higher-order thinking skills. When teachers plan creative instructional activities in advance, the computer lab, along with other technologies and the Internet, can bring authentic excitement and enthusiasm to students who otherwise might be uninterested in their daily school work.

Curriculum Integration Activities

Many teachers already use computers and technology in their classrooms and computer labs to help meet curriculum standards. For technology integration to be effective, however, the curriculum should drive the technologies used in the classroom; that is, teachers should use the applicable technologies to enhance learning at the appropriate times.

As teachers use technology in the classroom, they are finding many different ways to integrate it into subject-specific learning objectives. Learning to integrate technology effectively, however, requires planning and practice. The more practice you have in teaching with and integrating technology, the more you will discover innovative ways to use technology to facilitate all types of instruction.

Curriculum Pages

One of the biggest technology integration challenges that teachers face today is determining exactly how to use the Internet in their classrooms. Teachers who integrate the Internet successfully are using it in ways that engage students in problem solving, locating research information, and developing high-order thinking skills. Supervising students and controlling Web activities with curriculum pages is crucial to success in the classroom use of the Internet. As previously described, a **curriculum page** is a teacher-created document that contains hyperlinks to teacher-selected-and-evaluated sites that are content and age appropriate. Curriculum pages are easy to create and a valuable teaching tool for students to use when accessing the World Wide Web.

WebInfo

■ For a tutorial on creating Web treasure hunts, visit the Teachers Discovering Computers Chapter 7 WebInfo page **(www.scsite.com/tdc/ch7/webinfo.htm)** and click Treasure Hunt.

WebInfo

■ To learn more about curriculum pages and projects for the one-computer classroom, visit the Teachers Discovering Computers Chapter 7 WebInfo page **(www.scsite.com/tdc/ch7/webinfo.htm)** and click WebQuest.

Roller Coaster Scavenger Hunt

To learn more about the forces behind the fun, visit the Amusement Park Physics Web site at:

http://www.learner.org/exhibits/parkphysics

1. Do roller coasters have engines? _____

2. What drives a roller coaster? _____

3. What is the difference between running wheels and friction wheels? _____

   _____

4. How do roller coasters stop? _____

5. What is centripetal force? _____

6. What is gravitational force? _____

7. What were the forerunners of present day roller coasters? _____

8. What type of materials did they use? _____

9. What was the first American roller coaster introduced?_____

10. What year and where did the nation's first theme park open? _____

11. What was the name of the first tubular steel coaster and what year was it introduced?

    _____

12. Have you been on a roller coaster before? _____

    If yes, what was the name of it, where was it, and what did you like most about it?

    _____

    _____

    If no, would you go on one now that you know more about them? Why?

    _____

    _____

    On the back of this paper, list four additional facts that you have learned.

    Good Luck!

Figure 7-26 A scavenger hunt is a great way to have students explore the resources of the Web while using their higher-order thinking skills at the same time.

Simple curriculum pages contain hyperlinks to teacher-selected sites. More detailed curriculum pages provide hyperlinks to sites and instructions for constructive and purposeful activities that students may complete when they get to the selected Web sites. **Figure 7-27** shows examples of teacher-created curriculum pages.

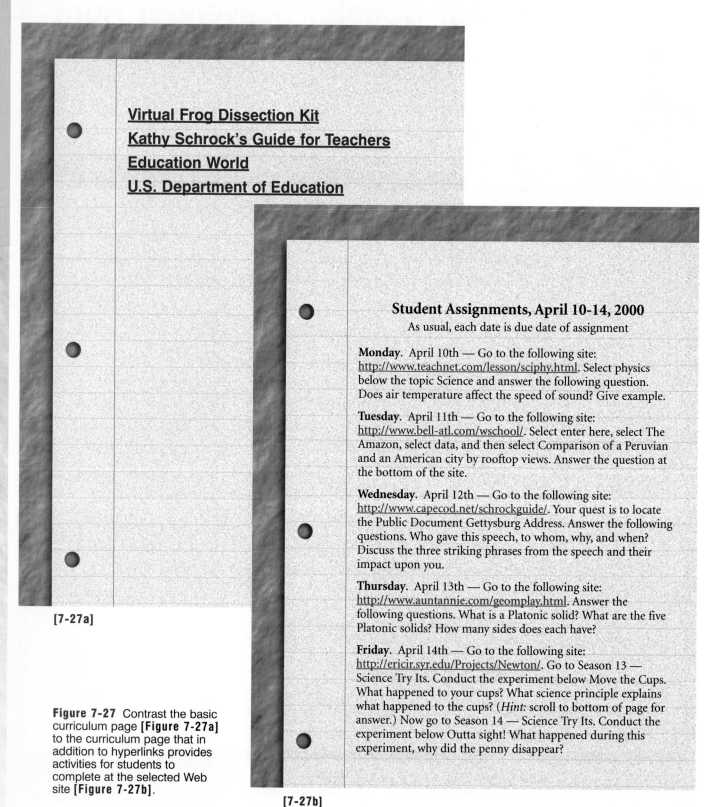

Virtual Frog Dissection Kit

Kathy Schrock's Guide for Teachers

Education World

U.S. Department of Education

[7-27a]

Student Assignments, April 10-14, 2000
As usual, each date is due date of assignment

Monday. April 10th — Go to the following site: http://www.teachnet.com/lesson/sciphy.html. Select physics below the topic Science and answer the following question. Does air temperature affect the speed of sound? Give example.

Tuesday. April 11th — Go to the following site: http://www.bell-atl.com/wschool/. Select enter here, select The Amazon, select data, and then select Comparison of a Peruvian and an American city by rooftop views. Answer the question at the bottom of the site.

Wednesday. April 12th — Go to the following site: http://www.capecod.net/schrockguide/. Your quest is to locate the Public Document Gettysburg Address. Answer the following questions. Who gave this speech, to whom, why, and when? Discuss the three striking phrases from the speech and their impact upon you.

Thursday. April 13th — Go to the following site: http://www.auntannie.com/geomplay.html. Answer the following questions. What is a Platonic solid? What are the five Platonic solids? How many sides does each have?

Friday. April 14th — Go to the following site: http://ericir.syr.edu/Projects/Newton/. Go to Season 13 — Science Try Its. Conduct the experiment below Move the Cups. What happened to your cups? What science principle explains what happened to the cups? (*Hint:* scroll to bottom of page for answer.) Now go to Season 14 — Science Try Its. Conduct the experiment below Outta sight! What happened during this experiment, why did the penny disappear?

[7-27b]

Figure 7-27 Contrast the basic curriculum page [**Figure 7-27a**] to the curriculum page that in addition to hyperlinks provides activities for students to complete at the selected Web site [**Figure 7-27b**].

Creating Lesson Plans

Planning is one of the most important variables for good instruction, and technology integration demands a great deal of planning. When first introducing technology into the classroom, many teachers try to incorporate technology into their existing lesson plans and activities. Because of the nature of the new technology tools, however, and because teaching and learning approaches must change, most teachers quickly learn this initial approach is only partially effective. To be successful in integrating technology, teachers must rethink and redesign activities and create new teaching and learning strategies as they progressively integrate technology across their curriculum. In other words, new technology tools require new instructional lessons.

Teachers do not have to rely solely on their own resourcefulness to create technology-enriched lesson plans and activities. Today, teachers may receive online advice from other educators by joining educational mailing lists, forums, newsgroups, discussion groups, and bulletin boards. Teachers also may refer to **AskERIC**, which is a federally funded Internet-based service providing educational information to teachers, media specialists, administrators, parents, and other interested persons throughout the world **[Figure 7-28]**. In addition to providing a question-and-answer service, the AskERIC Web site also provides a virtual library, lesson plans, and searchable database that contains more than 950,000 abstracts of documents and journal articles on educational research and application.

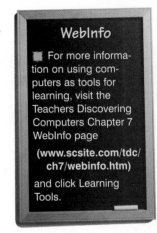

WebInfo

For more information on using computers as tools for learning, visit the Teachers Discovering Computers Chapter 7 WebInfo page **(www.scsite.com/tdc/ch7/webinfo.htm)** and click Learning Tools.

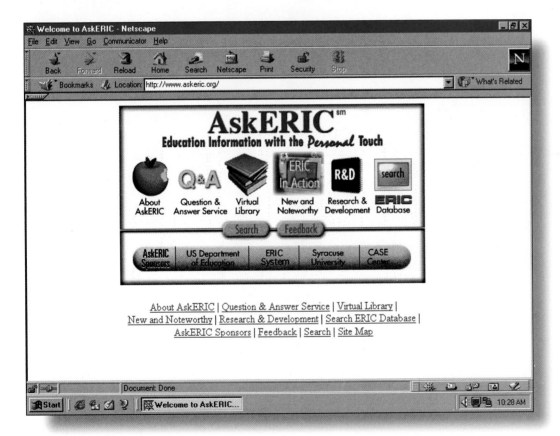

Figure 7-28 When teachers need educational information, all they have do is AskERIC!

A multitude of lesson plans and activities at thousands of educational Web sites are also available for teachers to use **[Figure 7-29]**. Many such sites provide search engines to locate curriculum-specific lesson plans and activities for almost any K-12 curriculum area.

Figure 7-29 Teachers can locate an almost unlimited supply of lesson plans and activities at thousands of Web sites.

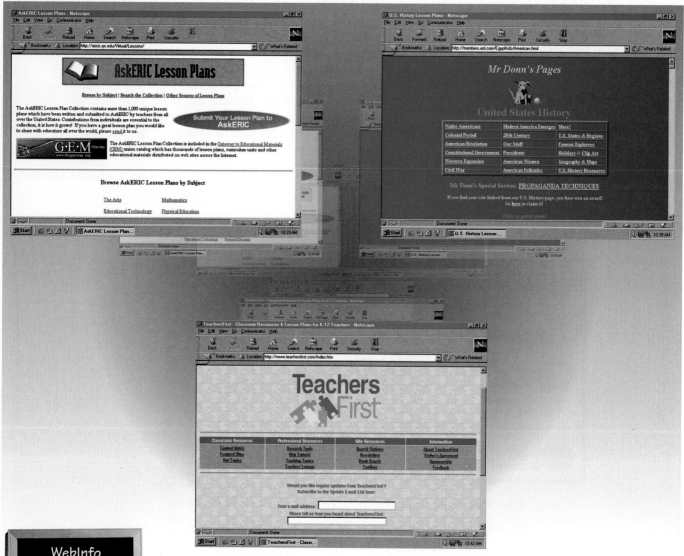

WebInfo

For a lesson plan template on integrating the Internet, visit the Teachers Discovering Computers Chapter 7 WebInfo page **(www.scsite.com/tdc/ch7/webinfo.htm)** and click Template.

The following sections describe seven subject-specific teacher-created curriculum integration activities that provide examples of integration activities. The purpose of these curriculum integration activities is to provide a basic understanding of how to integrate technology into the classroom. You may wish to adapt these examples to subject areas covered in your classroom or use them in other curriculum areas for thematic instruction.

Language Arts Integration **Language arts curriculum** usually includes instruction in reading, writing, listening, viewing, speaking, and literature. **Figure 7-30** shows a curriculum integration activity, called *Oh Where, Oh Where Can Information Be Found?*, that integrates technology into the subject areas of research and writing.

Language Arts

Curriculum Area:	Language Arts
Subject Area:	Research and Writing
Lesson Title:	Oh Where, Oh Where Can Information Be Found?
Suggested Grade Level:	8 - 12
Equipment Needed:	Technology: One computer or more, television monitor, access to a computer lab, Internet and WWW access Software: Inspiration, AppleWorks or word processor, HyperStudio or PowerPoint, Multimedia Encyclopedias such as, Encarta, Microsoft Bookshelf, and Grolier's Encyclopedia Other: Access to media center
Learning Objectives:	Students will determine content for their projects by using a variety of research resources, including indexes, magazines, newspapers, and journals. Students will use a variety of tools, including card catalogs and computer catalogs, and the Internet to gather information for research topics. Students will create a multimedia research report using PowerPoint, AppleWorks, or HyperStudio.
Instructions:	Introduce the task to the students. Allow the students to select the topic they would like to research. Distribute a predetermined assessment rubric and cover information that needs to be included in the multimedia research report, and how the report will be evaluated. With a computer connected to a television monitor, use Inspiration and brainstorm with the students about the various resources available for this project. Compare and contrast the type of information found in the different resources, create a concept map as students give ideas. Examine the currency of information on the Internet compared to information found in books. Have the students explain how the information found on the Internet is accurate. Students create an outline describing their topic. Once the outline has been approved, the students may begin the project using the Internet, CD-ROMs, and the media center as resources for finding their information. Using the computers in the classroom and media center, students will create a multimedia project.
Evaluation of Content:	The students will be evaluated on their multimedia research projects with a rubric created prior to the project. They will be evaluated throughout the project by teacher observation, their planning outline, and usage of technology tools.
Evaluation of Technology:	By using teacher observation, students will be evaluated on time on task and length of time students work to master content and technology skills. Students will be evaluated on the information they included in their projects. Teacher observation will help to verify if the technology assisted in meeting various learning styles of students. Evaluation of technology skills while creating a multimedia project from the research found will be assessed.

Figure 7-30 A sample lesson plan for *Oh Where, Oh Where Can Information Be Found?*

CHAPTER 7

Social Studies Integration Social studies curriculum usually encompasses instruction in history, geography, civics, and economics. **Figure 7-31** shows a curriculum integration activity, called *What Wonderful Webs We Weave,* that integrates technology into the subject area of Ancient Egypt.

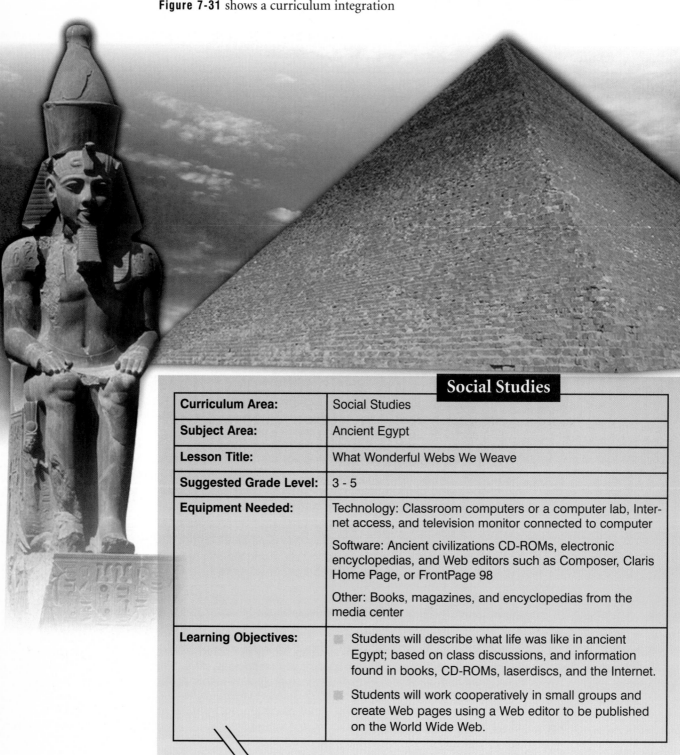

Social Studies

Curriculum Area:	Social Studies
Subject Area:	Ancient Egypt
Lesson Title:	What Wonderful Webs We Weave
Suggested Grade Level:	3 - 5
Equipment Needed:	Technology: Classroom computers or a computer lab, Internet access, and television monitor connected to computer Software: Ancient civilizations CD-ROMs, electronic encyclopedias, and Web editors such as Composer, Claris Home Page, or FrontPage 98 Other: Books, magazines, and encyclopedias from the media center
Learning Objectives:	▪ Students will describe what life was like in ancient Egypt; based on class discussions, and information found in books, CD-ROMs, laserdiscs, and the Internet. ▪ Students will work cooperatively in small groups and create Web pages using a Web editor to be published on the World Wide Web.

(continued)

Instructions:	Introduce the activity to the students and create a KWL chart about ancient Egypt. As a class, decide on five or six broad topics of study relating to ancient Egypt; mummies, pyramids, Pharaohs, etc. Connect a classroom computer to a television monitor and view teacher-created Web curriculum pages about ancient Egypt. Discuss what makes a Web site interesting and attractive. Distribute an evaluation rubric for the students' Web page project. Review the rubric with the students so they will understand how their Web page will be evaluated. Next, divide students into small groups of three to four. Have each group select one of the broad topics the class listed. Allow students to research their particular topic. They may use the CD-ROMs, laserdiscs, books, magazines, and encyclopedias from the media center, and the Internet. After students have finished their research, they will complete a planning worksheet. Students will plan their Web page layout, background, attention-getting titles, animated gifs, pictures, and links to related Web sites. Once students have created their Web page on paper, they may create it using a Web editor. When the Web pages are complete, they can be posted on your school's server or on a free Web server site.
Evaluation of Content:	Teacher observation along with the project rubric will be used to evaluate this activity. Additionally, students planning worksheets will be used for assessment purposes. Quality of research and information utilized on the Web page also will be assessed.
Evaluation of Technology Integration:	Learning to access, analyze and apply information from different resources is a necessary skill for students and will be observed. How well students locate information, determine what information is valuable and apply that information will be examined. Student motivation and enthusiasm when creating a Web page will also assist with evaluating the technology.

Figure 7-31 A sample lesson plan for *What Wonderful Webs We Weave.*

CHAPTER 7

Mathematics Integration **Mathematics curriculum** usually includes instruction in basic number concepts, measurements, geometry, algebra, calculus, and data analysis. **Figure 7-32** shows a curriculum integration activity, called *The Business of Professional Sports,* that integrates technology into the subject areas of measurement, problem solving, and geometry.

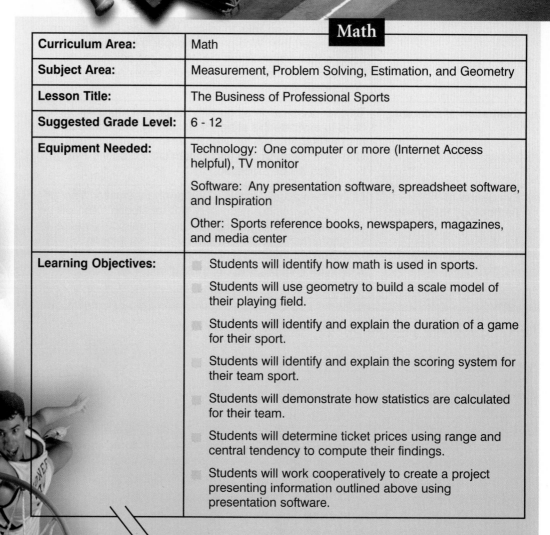

Math	
Curriculum Area:	Math
Subject Area:	Measurement, Problem Solving, Estimation, and Geometry
Lesson Title:	The Business of Professional Sports
Suggested Grade Level:	6 - 12
Equipment Needed:	Technology: One computer or more (Internet Access helpful), TV monitor
	Software: Any presentation software, spreadsheet software, and Inspiration
	Other: Sports reference books, newspapers, magazines, and media center
Learning Objectives:	Students will identify how math is used in sports.
	Students will use geometry to build a scale model of their playing field.
	Students will identify and explain the duration of a game for their sport.
	Students will identify and explain the scoring system for their team sport.
	Students will demonstrate how statistics are calculated for their team.
	Students will determine ticket prices using range and central tendency to compute their findings.
	Students will work cooperatively to create a project presenting information outlined above using presentation software.

(continued)

Instructions:	Have the students list all the team sports they know. Create a concept map using Inspiration, projected to the class on the television monitor with Math as the center. Brainstorm with the class about how math is used in sports and add these to your concept map. Allow students to select their favorite team sport. Separate the students into groups on interest. The group must decide what type of project to create that will include each of the items outlined in the objectives.
	Provide the students with class time to research their team sport. Allow them to use the Internet for research, as well as any resources from the media center including newspapers to calculate statistics. Provide each group with a designated time to use the computer. When groups are not using the computer, they may be using other resource materials to develop their project.
	Coordinate with the media specialist to allow students access to other computers, or schedule time in the computer lab when the groups are working on their presentations. Students create graphs using any spreadsheet software application, and these may be included in their projects. When groups have completed their projects, share them with the class.
Evaluation of Content:	Design a rubric to assess student performance. Include all of the major points of the project. Be sure to discuss the rubric prior to beginning the project. Teacher observation, student motivation, and an increased understanding of statistics also will be examined for evidence of student learning.
Evaluation of Technology Integration:	Evaluate problem-solving skills when students use the concept map with brainstorming as a visual model. Furthermore, assess students gaining technology skills and problem-solving skills with the types of software applications. Evaluate the use of spreadsheet software to learn how to organize information and see graphical representation of that information. Evaluate student presentations to determine if this process reinforces skills in communication, organization, problem solving and critical-thinking skills.

Figure 7-32 A sample lesson plan for *The Business of Professional Sports.*

Science Integration   **Science curriculum** usually contains instruction in physical sciences, earth and space sciences, and life sciences. **Figure 7-33** shows a curriculum integration activity, called *Let's Think As a Scientist*, that integrates technology into the subject area of physical science.

Science

Curriculum Area:	Science
Subject Area:	Physical Sciences
Lesson Title:	Let's Think As a Scientist
Suggested Grade Level:	K - 3
Equipment Needed:	Technology: One computer and a television monitor or large screen Software: Thinkin' Science (published by Edmark). This lesson can be adapted with other software-specific products Other: Student computers if available
Learning Objectives:	Students will practice observation and memory skills. Students will demonstrate understanding of content. Students will interpret data. Students will determine cause and effect between two events.
Instructions:	Thinkin' Science explores the earth, life, and physical sciences. Connect the computer to a television monitor or large screen. For this activity, go to Animal Tracking. Students will need to observe animals and then apply problem-solving skills. Students will explore animal behavior and then interpret data that is presented. Guide students by asking questions and drawing their attention to important events. To provide further practice of observation skills, and to increase visual memory, use the activity, *What Did You See?* The students will be presented with a scene. The scene will disappear and students will have to recreate the scene. All students should tell you what needs to be placed in the scene. After you have used the software with the whole class, you may set it up in a learning center. NOTE: Software comes with a Teacher's Guide and reproducible activity sheets. You may place these in the learning center to support the students.
Evaluation of Content:	Students will be quizzed on content provided to determine if memorization and observation skills were mastered. The number of correctly answered questions from each student will determine attainment of content.
Evaluation of Technology Integration:	Thinkin' Science is an excellent multimedia application. The software provides positive continuous feedback for students and is interactive. Teacher observation will be used to measure student attention and motivation. Both of these are used as assessment tools. An additional evaluation will be how many students utilize the software in the learning center.

Figure 7-33 A sample lesson plan for *Let's Think As a Scientist*.

Physical Education And Health Integration

Physical education and health curriculum usually includes instruction in basic health and physical education literacy. **Figure 7-34** shows a curriculum integration activity, called *Eating Healthy!*, that integrates technology into the subject area of nutrition.

Physical Education and Health

Curriculum Area:	Physical Education and Health
Subject Area:	Nutrition
Lesson Title:	Eating Healthy!
Suggested Grade Level:	3 - 6 (Could be adapted for any grade level)
Equipment Needed:	Technology: 3 computers, at least 1 with Internet access Software: HyperStudio, Database and Draw program such as ClarisWorks, AppleWorks, or Microsoft Works Other: Nutrition Brochure (from Hospital/Health Dept.) and Website http://www.dole5aday.com
Learning Objectives:	■ Students will be able to use the Internet to take the Dole 5 A Day Challenge. ■ Students will create a 5-day menu, which must include at least five fruits/vegetables each day. ■ Students will be able to enter one of their menu items into the class cookbook database. ■ Students will be able to work cooperatively and collaboratively to locate facts about their assigned fruit/vegetable using the Dole Fruit and Vegetable Encyclopedia. ■ Students will be able to use HyperStudio to create and present a stack on their fruit/vegetable.
Instructions:	Individually students will go to the Dole Web site to take the 5-Day Challenge. Students will be given time to browse the Web page to learn more about why it is so important to eat at least five fruits/vegetables. Using what they learned from the Web and using their Nutrition brochure, students will create a 5-day menu. From his or her menu, each student will select one item to submit to the class cookbook database. Copies of the recipe will be printed for students to share with their families. Before students take them home, however, they need to create a cookbook cover using a drawing program. Students working in groups of two to three will use the Dole Fruit and Vegetable Encyclopedia and their nutrition brochure to create a HyperStudio stack on their assigned item.
Evaluation of Content:	Each student's menu item will be evaluated using a rubric (spelling and grammar included). Group HyperStudio stack/presentations also will be evaluated using a rubric (spelling and grammar included).
Evaluation of Technology Integration:	The effectiveness of the technology will be evaluated by testing students' content retention in a culminating quiz. Effectiveness will be apparent in student presentations. Students will gain valuable experience exploring Internet resources and learning how to use them to complete an assignment.

Figure 7-34 A sample lesson plan for *Eating Healthy!*

Arts Integration **Arts curriculum** usually incorporates instruction in the visual and performing arts of drawing, painting, dance, music, and theater. **Figure 7-35** shows a curriculum integration activity, called *The Theory of Color,* that integrates technology into the subject area of color theory.

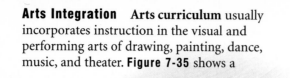

Art	
Curriculum Area:	Art
Subject Area:	Color-Theory — Reinforcing Basic Reading, Writing, and Math Skills
Lesson title:	The Theory of Color
Suggested Grade Level:	Grade 5, easily adapted to higher levels
Equipment Needed:	Technology: Requires access to a student computer lab Requires computer connected to large monitor or TV Software: PowerPoint and any paint program
Learning Objectives:	Increased understanding of color theory. Increased use of reading, math and writing in the art classroom. Demonstration of abstract conceptualization of written materials. Demonstrate skills in computer paint accessories.

(continued)

Instructions:	Students are given a brief introductory lecture explaining the goals of the lessons. They are told that an important part of the lesson is their own reading and writing skills. A simple pretest is given to allow students to demonstrate any pre-existing knowledge of the content area.
	Color mixing: Using basic math skills and written directions, students prepare a series of diagrammatic color charts that teach basic color mixing and theory. The blank charts are prepared with the paint software. The color formulas will be written in a mathematical or fractional way; i.e., Orange = ½ Yellow + ½ Red. Students will use eyedroppers to mix tempera paints to the proper proportion and paint samples as a permanent record in their portfolio.
	Relating reading and color theory: Based on the belief that children should be taught to visualize color as described in books or stories, children will read a series of excerpts from stories that include written descriptions of colors. Students will create color samples that show an understanding of the written excerpt and the colors described.
	Relating color to written descriptions: In contrast to the previous activity, students will be given blank lined pages for writing text. Each blank paragraph will have a pre-printed block of color. Students will be directed to create brief descriptive paragraphs that relate to each of the attached colors.
	Integrating technology: This lesson will be spread over a period of time to allow adequate computer access time. Students will engage in a computer-oriented lesson that integrates what they have learned about colors with both reading and technology.
	Students will create a drawing with the paint program. The requirement for this piece of art will be that it clearly shows three primary colors, three secondary colors, one tint, and one shade.
Evaluation of Content:	A critique rubric will be used that the students easily can understand. Students will engage in critiques of each other's work. Critiques will be consolidated and students and instructors jointly will discuss the results of the exercises. The teacher also will assign individual student work. This will be based on the rubric to ensure consistency and reliability of results. Final results are compared to the pretest, where marked improvement in the students' understanding of color and color theory should be identified.
Evaluation of Technology Integration:	As a first time computer graphics assignment, teacher observation should be used to determine the quality of the projects. Higher levels of complexity or variance in the final project can be evaluated.

Figure 7-35 A sample lesson plan for *The Theory of Color*.

Exceptional Education Integration

Exceptional education curriculum, or **special education curriculum**, usually contains instruction in all curriculum areas with adaptations made for students with unique characteristics or special needs. These students include those who are gifted, learning disabled, physically disabled, emotionally disabled, or mentally disabled. Instruction for regular-education students and exceptional-educational students is merging as teachers find many of the technology resources and integration activities dramatically enhance the instruction of students with special needs.

Teachers easily can modify many of the integration activities illustrated in **Figure 7-30** through **Figure 7-35** to meet the needs of exceptional-educational students. **Figure 7-36** shows a curriculum integration activity, called *Rainforests Are in Trouble,* that integrates technology into the subject area of current events and can be used for students with special needs.

Special Education	
Curriculum Area:	Science, Social, Studies, Math and Language Arts for special education students.
Subject Area:	Current Events
Lesson Title:	Rainforests Are In Trouble
Suggested Grade Level:	3 - 5 (This lesson has been developed for grade levels 3 to 5 special education students. This lesson can be used with 3rd to 12th grade with appropriate adaptations.)
Equipment Needed:	Technology: Computer and a television monitor or large screen, Internet access and use Welcome to the Amazon Web site located at http://sunsite.doc.ic.ac.uk/netspedition/amazon.html Software: Encarta 99 or electronic encyclopedias, Tom Synder's Rainforest Researchers or Rainforest CD-ROMs Other: *The Lost Compound* video, 3x5 index cards, notebooks, pencils, pens
Learning Objectives:	☐ Students will collect information about the rainforests. ☐ Students will take a Web expedition to the Amazon using the Internet. ☐ Students will understand current research efforts on tropical rainforest, learn adaptations of organisms, and demonstrate knowledge gained of tropical rainforest issues, and explore plant life cycles. ☐ Students will create a multimedia research report

(continued)

Instructions:	Students will work in groups of four. They will be given a list of Web sites about rainforests. They will access at least three different sites and take notes (3x5 index cards) about five different aspects of the rainforests. If there is an e-mail address, students will write a short note asking a specific question they want to know about the rainforest.
	Students will work with their same partners and venture into the Amazon Web site. While there, they enter the options available at the Web site; Research, The Team, Map, About Netspedition, Equipment, and Venezuela and document a brief description of each. Next, the team will give a brief description about one of the butterfly surveys, indicating date, location, and what types of butterflies were caught. The team will then access the log book and choose one specific day on the calendar. They will record the date, location, temperature, a description of one of the photographs, a description of author's feelings, and the name of the person entering the information.
	Students still work in their cooperative teams taking turns at the computer. Each student plays the role of a scientific expert, chemist, ecologist, botanist, or taxonomist using one of four unique student reference books. Teams watch the video on *The Lost Compound* and use on-screen instructions to guide them in analyzing information, collaborating, and making decisions. Students will create research projects on the computer with drawings, maps, etc.
Evaluation of Content:	The projects the students completed will indicate whether the students grasped the concepts indicated by the above objectives. In addition, PowerPoint or HyperStudio can be completed by individual students on a particular species or rainforest to present to the class. This project could be used as an additional or follow-up assignment.
Evaluation of Technology Integration:	Teacher observation will help to verify if the technology assisted in meeting various learning styles and needs of special education students. Teacher observation will determine if technology assisted in student attention and motivation. Students will be evaluated on time on task and length of time students work to master content and technology skills. An additional evaluation will be looking at each student and his or her individual needs throughout the lesson.

Figure 7-36 A sample lesson plan for *Rainforests Are in Trouble*.

Finding Funds to Support Classroom Technology Integration

One of the most difficult aspects of implementing technology in schools is finding and obtaining the funds for new technologies and the associated ongoing expenses. At present, many school districts do not have sufficient funding to incorporate technology at all levels throughout the district. For this reason, a classroom may not contain all the hardware and software to fully integrate technology into the curriculum.

While the continued drop in computer and educational software prices lessens the problem, obtaining funding for classroom technology often is challenging. Many teachers, however, find that persistence often produces dramatic results. To increase the quantity and quality of technology in a classroom, a teacher first should ask the principal and other district administrators for additional classroom equipment and software. If you still need to obtain additional technology funding, you can turn to numerous other sources, including the public, industry, and the government.

Fundraising Drives and Contest

Class car washes, cookie drives, and other activities can help raise money to purchase additional computers, other hardware components, and software for classrooms. Local businesses such as banks, car dealerships, grocery stores, and department stores often respond to solicitations to improve the educational quality of the schools in their areas with donations. Corporations frequently are eager to get involved in active school technology programs — whether it is to contribute equipment, funds, or expertise. Teachers regularly write letters to local school business partners stating the school's needs in order to enlist their support. Even relatively small amounts of acquired funding can make a difference in the availability of technology in your classroom. Raising $100.00 will fund a new ink jet printer, numerous educational CD-ROMs, or a color scanner; $500.00 will allow a purchase of a multimedia computer [Figure 7-37].

Figure 7-37 Teachers organize all kinds of class events, such as car washes and cookie sales, to raise funds to purchase computers, printers, scanners, digital cameras, educational software, and other items for use in integrated classrooms.

Another way to obtain hardware and software for the classroom is to enter contests. Teachers may locate information on hundreds of contests on the Web and in educational journals and magazines.

Teachers should involve the community — especially parents — in fundraising. The local school community holds its schools accountable for everything that goes on in the classroom, so enlisting the help of parents and business partners will broaden the base of support for the school's educational technology efforts. In addition, parent may have contacts or affiliations with local businesses or be able to provide further information on how to obtain funding. Another avenue of locating potential sources for technology funding is to showcase your classroom's use of technology for parents, business leaders, and school board members at your school's Parent Teacher Association (PTA), Parent Teacher Organization (PTO), or Parent Teacher Student Organization (PTSO) meetings.

Schools also should consider asking for volunteer services from the community in addition to or instead of asking for funds to pay for services. If funding for equipment maintenance is not available, for example, a local consultant may be willing to donate services. Many schools find a combination of financial and volunteer support demonstrates the community's commitment to technology integration and strengthens the long-term community-school partnerships.

Grants

The majority of outside funding sources for technology fall under a general category called grants. **Grants** are funds provided by a funding source that transfers money, equipment, or services to the grantee. The **grantee** is the teacher, school, or organization to which the grant funds or equipment are transferred. Grants can be obtained from school districts, state Departments of Education, federal sources, foundations, and corporations. Grants range from a few hundred to millions of dollars. Many corporations maintain or support foundations that provide grants, both large and small, for creative projects.

To obtain a grant, a school district, school, or teacher must submit a grant proposal in response to a request for proposal (RFP). A **request for proposal (RFP)** is a document provided by the grant source that details the information teachers and schools need to provide to write a successful grant proposal. A **grant proposal** is the document the potential grantee sends to the funding source. Grant proposals can vary from a simple one-page application to an extensive multi-page document.

When writing a grant, schools can take one of several approaches. A single person may write the grant proposal; teachers may write grant proposals with other teachers, media specialists, technology coordinators, and school district personal; or if the proposal is extensive, the school districts may even employ a grant writing specialist or consultant to write the proposal to increase the availability of technology in their classrooms.

The principal and curriculum coordinator usually receive notification of grant opportunities. In addition, teachers can locate many grant opportunities on the Web [Figure 7-38].

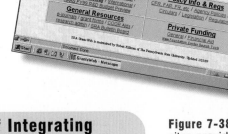

Summary of Integrating Educational Technology into the Curriculum

Technology will not make a difference in the quality of students graduating from K-12 schools unless teachers learn how to use it as an integration tool to enhance learning. This chapter first introduced the various tools and resources teachers use to evaluate the appropriateness of educational technology and the effectiveness of technology integration. Next, a number of strategies were presented for integrating technology into one-computer classrooms and other K-12 instructional settings along with seven subject-specific curriculum integration activities. Finally, the chapter provided information on how to obtain funding to increase the availability of technology in your classroom.

WebInfo

For more information on how to get equipment for your classroom, visit the Teachers Discovering Computers Chapter 7 WebInfo page

(www.scsite.com/tdc/ ch7/webinfo.htm)

and click Free Equipment.

Figure 7-38 Many Web sites provide teachers and administrators with current, extensive information on grants for education.

WebInfo

For more information on grant opportunities for educators, visit the Teachers Discovering Computers Chapter 7 WebInfo page

(www.scsite.com/tdc/ ch7/webinfo.htm)

and click Grants.

www.scsite.com/tdc/ch7/brief.htm

- InBrief
- KeyTerms
- AtTheMovies
- CheckPoint
- TeacherTime
- CyberClass
- EdIssues
- NetStuff

SPECIAL FEATURES
- TimeLine 2000
- Guide to WWW Sites
- Buyer's Guide 2000
- Educational Sites
- State/Federal Sites
- Chat
- News
- Home

InBrief

Web Instructions: To display this page from the Web, launch your browser and enter the URL, www.scsite.com/tdc/ch7/brief.htm. Click the links for current and additional information. To listen to an audio version of this InBrief, click the Audio button below the title, InBrief, at the top of the page. To play the audio, RealPlayer must be installed on your computer (download by clicking here).

1. Evaluating Educational Technology

Evaluation of educational technology is important before instruction begins, during the instructional period, and after the instruction takes place. Educators can rely on a variety of resources to help them identify and evaluate the appropriateness of educational technologies, including resources available from school districts, state Departments of Education, professional educational organizations, catalogs, and Web sites.

2. Evaluating Software Applications

Teachers should evaluate software for appropriateness and accuracy of content, and consider its relevance to curriculum learning objectives. Software evaluation rubrics help teachers evaluate educational software. A **rubric** is a detailed assessment tool that allows individuals to assess the quality of software or other items. A software evaluation rubric should list a number of important evaluation criteria, including content, documentation and technical support, ability and academic levels, technical quality, and ease of use.

3. Evaluating Web Resources

When evaluating a Web site as an instructional source, teachers should consider characteristics such as authority, affiliation, audience, currency, and Web site design. **Authority** refers to the credibility of both the author and creator (if not the same person) of the Web page or Web site. **Affiliation** refers to the professional organization, school, school district, university, company, or government office with which a particular Web site is connected. **Content** is the information provided on a Web page. The **audience** is the individual or group intended to view the Web page. **Currency** is a measure of how up to date, or timely, the Web page content is and how often it is updated.

4. Evaluating the Effectiveness of Technology Integration

When integrating technology, some teachers and schools are moving towards a non-traditional approach of student assessment, known as alternative assessment. **Alternative assessment** is using nontraditional methods to determine if students have mastered content and skill level. **Authentic assessment,** or **performance-based assessment**, refers to alternative ways to evaluate student performance to determine how well and in what way students are able to accomplish learning objectives and standards.

5. Evaluation Tools

When using authentic assessment, many teachers use checklists, rating scales, rubrics, and teacher observation. A **checklist** is a predetermined list of performance criteria. A **rating scale** is a more complex form of a checklist that lists a numerical value, or rating, for each criterion. A **rubric** is a detailed assessment tool that makes it easier for teachers to assess the quality of an item, such as a learning project. **Teacher observation** is when teachers actively observe their students during the learning process.

InBrief

6. Evaluating Technology-Based Student Projects

Checklists, rating scales, and teacher observation are valid assessment tools for technology-based student projects. Curriculum goals and objectives should define and guide the selection and creation of the assessment tool. Student projects should be evaluated for content, planning, and creativity. Planning tools include flowcharts and concept maps. **Flowcharts** are diagrams that show the step-by-step actions that must take place through a sequence of events. A **concept map** or **story web** helps students use flowcharting to understand the attributes and relationships of the main subject and provides a visual tool for brainstorming and planning.

7. Integration Strategies

To help meet the constant challenge of motivating students to learn, teachers must change their traditional roles to become facilitators of learning. Instructional strategies help teachers integrate technology into a one-computer classroom, a multi-computer classroom, and a computer lab. Most teachers will teach in a classroom with one multimedia

computer, often referred to as the **one-computer classroom**. The most common usage of one computer is for classroom presentations and demonstrations. The most important advantage of using a computer lab is that all students are provided hands-on experience with using computer technology.

8. Curriculum Pages

Teachers who integrate the Internet successfully are utilizing it in ways to engage students in problem solving, finding research information, and developing high-order thinking skills. Crucial to the successful use of the Internet in the classroom is supervising students and controlling Web activities by using curriculum pages. A **curriculum page** is a teacher-created document that contains hyperlinks to teacher-selected sites that have been evaluated for content and age appropriateness.

9. Creating Lesson Plans

To be successful when integrating technology, teachers must rethink and redesign activities and create new teaching and learning strategies. New technology tools require new instructional lessons. Teachers do not have to originate and create technology-enriched lesson plans and activities. They may find a multitude of lesson plans and activities at thousands of educational Web sties. Many educational Web sites provide search engines that allow teachers to locate curriculum-specific lesson plans and activities for almost any K-12 curriculum area.

10. Finding Funds to Support Integration

Teachers can obtain funding for classroom technology from a number of sources, including persons within their school district, businesses, private organizations, foundations, and the government. Class car washes, cookie drives, and other activities raise money to purchase additional computers, other hardware components, and software for classrooms. Other ways to obtain these tools are to solicit corporate donations and enter contests.

11. Grants

The majority of outside funding sources for technology fall under a general category called grants. **Grants** are funds provided by a funding source that transfers money, equipment, or services to the grantee. The **grantee** is the teacher, school, or organization to which the grant funds or equipment are transferred. To obtain a grant, a school district, school, or teacher must submit a grant proposal in response to a request for proposal. A **request for proposal** (RFP) is a document provided by the grant source that details the information teachers and schools need to provide to write a successful grant proposal. A **grant proposal** is the document sent to the funding source.

InBrief

KeyTerms

AtTheMovies

CheckPoint

TeacherTime

CyberClass

EdIssues

NetStuff

SPECIAL FEATURES

TimeLine 2000

Guide to WWW Sites

Buyer's Guide 2000

Educational Sites

State/Federal Sites

Chat

News

Home

www.scsite.com/tdc/ch7/terms.htm

KeyTerms

InBrief

KeyTerms

AtTheMovies

CheckPoint

TeacherTime

CyberClass

EdIssues

NetStuff

SPECIAL FEATURES

TimeLine 2000

Guide to WWW Sites

Buyer's Guide 2000

Educational Sites

State/Federal Sites

Chat

News

Home

Web Instructions: To display this page from the Web, launch your browser and enter the URL, www.scsite.com/tdc/ch7/terms.htm. Scroll through the list of terms. Click a term to display its definition and a picture. Click KeyTerms on the left to redisplay the KeyTerms page. Click the TO WEB button for current and additional information about the term from the Web. To see animations, Shockwave and Flash Player must be installed on your computer (download by clicking here).

ability level [7.9]
academic level [7.9]
affiliation [7.11]
alternative assessment [7.15]

appropriate [7.2]
arts curriculum [7.38]
AskERIC [7.29]
assessment [7.15]
audience [7.12]
authentic assessment [7.15]
authentic learning [7.15]
authority [7.10]

block schedule [7.19]

checklist [7.15]
concept map [7.19]
content [7.12]
creativity [7.19]
currency [7.12]
curriculum page [7.26]

design [7.12]
documentation [7.9]

ease of use [7.10]
evaluate [7.2]
exceptional education curriculum [7.40]

flowcharts [7.19]

grant proposal [7.43]
grantee [7.43]
grants [7.43]

Inspiration® [7.19]

language arts curriculum [7.31]

mathematics curriculum [7.34]

one-computer classroom [7.22]

performance-based assessment [7.15]
physical education and health curriculum [7.37]

rating scale [7.15]
reliable assessment [7.15]
request for proposal (RFP) [7.43]
rubric [7.6, 7.15]

science curriculum [7.36]
social studies curriculum [7.32]
special education curriculum [7.40]
story web [7.19]
storyboard [7.19]
student performance [7.15]

teacher observation [7.15]
technical quality [7.10]
technical support [7.9]
technology conference [7.5]

valid [7.6]

Web effectiveness [7.12]
Web scavenger hunt [7.26]

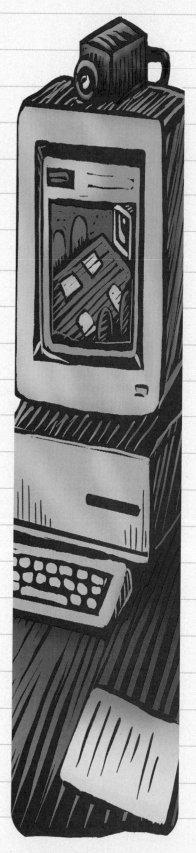

www.scsite.com/tdc/ch7/movies.htm

AtTheMovies

WELCOME to VIDEO CLIPS from CNN

Web Instructions: To display this page from the Web, launch your browser and enter the URL, www.scsite.com/tdc/ch7/movies.htm. Click a picture to view a video. After watching the video, close the video window and then complete the exercise by answering the questions about the video. To view the videos, RealPlayer must be installed on your computer (download by clicking here).

InBrief

KeyTerms

AtTheMovies

CheckPoint

TeacherTime

CyberClass

EdIssues

NetStuff

SPECIAL FEATURES

TimeLine 2000

Guide to WWW Sites

Buyer's Guide 2000

Educational Sites

State/Federal Sites

Chat

News

Home

1. Electronic Libraries

Does your school library use computers? Have you or your students used a computer in the past year to do research in the library? Have you or your students used a library computer to do research on the Web? Over the next decade, many libraries will begin to convert hard-copy documents into digital form, much like the University of Florida's effort depicted on the video. What are the advantages and disadvantages of this shift to electronic data? Some suggest that in the future, traditional libraries will exist only to house publicly accessible computers and a collection of texts required for verifying digitized versions. Do you agree with this vision? Do you think print-based books will ever disappear? Why or why not?

2. Illicit Term Papers

Some Web sites now sell prewritten term papers for students to download, customize, and turn in on their own. In this way, does the Internet facilitate cheating? In late 1997, Boston University sued eight online term-paper vendors for distributing and selling term papers and contributing to cheating. They also listed as an example of academic misconduct, Purchased term papers and turned in as own work. Should it be against the law to have a business selling term papers over the Net? Why or why not? As a teacher, what steps would you take to prevent students from turning papers in that have been downloaded from the Internet? How would you penalize a student who did?

3. Parents Online

Parents' involvement in their children's day-to-day education has taken a giant step forward thanks to an Internet student information system (ISIS) and EduLink. What is an ISIS? What information does it provide to a parent? What family and school changes have made such an information system more valuable? For a parent and for a student, what are the advantages and disadvantages of using such a system? If you were a student at a school that used an ISIS, how would you feel about the system? Would your need as an educator who wishes to keep parents informed outweigh any negative feelings a student might have about an ISIS?

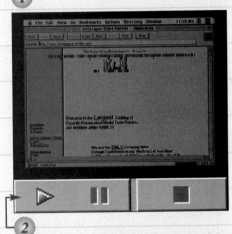

www.scsite.com/tdc/ch7/check.htm

CheckPoint

Web Instructions: To display this page from the Web, launch your browser and enter the URL, www.scsite.com/tdc/ch7/check.htm. Click a blank line for the answer. Click the links for current and additional information. To experience the animation and interactivity, Shockwave and Flash Player must be installed on your computer (download by clicking here).

InBrief

KeyTerms

AtTheMovies

CheckPoint

TeacherTime

CyberClass

EdIssues

NetStuff

SPECIAL FEATURES

TimeLine 2000

Guide to WWW Sites

Buyer's Guide 2000

Educational Sites

State/Federal Sites

Chat

News

Home

1. Label the Figure

Instructions: Identify the various categories used to evaluate Web sites.

2. Matching

Instructions: Match each term from the column on the left with the best description from the column on the right.

____ 1. curriculum page

____ 2. request for proposal

____ 3. checklist

____ 4. evaluate

____ 5. concept map

a. to determine the value or to judge the worth

b. provides a visual tool for brainstorming and planning

c. teacher created document that contains hyperlinks to teacher-selected Web sites

d. predetermined list of performance criteria

e. a document provided by a grant source that details the information needed to write a grant

Level 1
1. _____   No author is listed and no e-mail contact is provided.
2. _____   It is unclear what institution supports this information.
3. _____   The Web page is a Virtual Soapbox.
4. _____   The Web page is not appropriate for my audience.
5. _____   Information on the page has not been revised since 1998, or no date can be located.
6. _____   The information on the Web page does not relate to my objectives.
7. _____   The Web site does not load well and is difficult to read.

3. Short Answer

Instructions: Write a brief answer to each of the following questions.

1. Describe four resources where teachers can find information on how to evaluate educational software. Why is it important for teachers to evaluate software prior to using it in the classroom? _____

2. Should teachers evaluate Web resources for instructional value in the same way they evaluate print resources? Why or why not? _____

3. Describe three techniques for evaluating students' technology projects. _____

4. Briefly describe three uses of technology in a one-computer classroom. Why does having more than one computer in a classroom allow for more flexibility and greater integration of technology?
_____

5. Briefly describe grant funding for K-12 schools. Why are grants so important for many K-12 schools? Describe three ways in which teachers can obtain funding for classroom technology. _____

1 2 3 4 5 6 7 8

www.scsite.com/tdc/ch7/time.htm

TeacherTime

Web Instructions: To display this page from the Web, launch your browser and enter the URL, www.scsite.com/tdc/ch7/time.htm. Click the links for current and additional information.

InBrief

KeyTerms

AtTheMovies

CheckPoint

TeacherTime

CyberClass

EdIssues

NetStuff

SPECIAL FEATURES

TimeLine 2000

Guide to WWW Sites

Buyer's Guide 2000

Educational Sites

State/Federal Sites

Chat

News

Home

1. As a member of the technology committee, you have been asked to make recommendations for software purchases to enhance the sixth-grade math curriculum at your school. Your principal asked you to supply her with five different titles and a detailed evaluation of each title. Where can you find software reviews for math applications? Are these reviews helpful? What type of information can you gather about the software from these reviews? Based on what you have learned in this chapter, what would be your next step in identifying and evaluating the five different multimedia math applications?

2. In your elementary classroom you have one Macintosh computer. You want to use the computer and multimedia software but are unsure where to begin. The Web offers many suggestions by other teachers on which software works best in the one-computer classroom. What type of software do these teachers suggest? Describe the ways these teachers use the software? What are some other uses for the recommended software? Which of the products offer a free trial version you can download and test? Were you able to evaluate the software effectively based on the free trial version? Why or why not?

3. You teach students with special needs in a middle school. You want to integrate multimedia software applications into your curriculum to enhance your students' learning. You are looking for software applications that can be used in more than one curriculum area. You are familiar with multimedia authoring programs such as PowerPoint and HyperStudio and already are using them in different curriculum areas. Describe the ways in which the other applications described in this chapter may be used in more

than one curriculum area? Explore subject-specific software such as WHERE IN THE U.S.A. IS CARMEN SANDIEGO? (social studies software). Can this type of software be used in other curriculum areas as well? Why or why not?

4. As you begin to integrate technology into your curriculum, you need alternative ways to assess student performance. In this chapter, you read about the rubrics that teachers use to assess performance. Itemize the key points to remember when evaluating student work. What alternative assessment tools can you use in your classroom? When is using alternative assessment tools most appropriate? When are other types of assessment tools most appropriate?

5. You want to write a grant to purchase additional technology for your classroom. You never have written a grant before and do not know where to begin. You know that searching the Internet will produce numerous funding sources and instructions covering the basic elements of grant writing. Explore the pros and cons of working with another teacher when seeking additional funding. Is another partner available whom you could include when writing a grant? Are you limited to working with teachers at your school? What are the advantages of working with another person when seeking grant funds?

www.scsite.com/tdc/ch7/class.htm

CyberClass

Web Instructions: To display this page from the Web, launch your browser and enter the URL, www.scsite.com/tdc/ch7/class.htm. To start Level I CyberClass, click a Level I link on this page or enter the URL, www.cyber-class.com. Click the Student button, click *Teachers Discovering Computers* in the list of titles, and then click the Enter a site button. To start Level II or III CyberClass (available only to those purchasers of a CyberClass floppy disk), place your CyberClass floppy disk in drive A, click Start on the taskbar, click Run on the Start menu, type `a:connect` in the Open text box, click the OK button, click the Enter CyberClass button, and then follow the instructions. If you are using a Macintosh, see your instructor.

InBrief

KeyTerms

AtTheMovies

CheckPoint

TeacherTime

CyberClass

EdIssues

NetStuff

SPECIAL FEATURES

TimeLine 2000

Guide to WWW Sites

Buyer's Guide 2000

Educational Sites

State/Federal Sites

Chat

News

Home

1. Flash Cards (Level I, Level II, and Level III)

Click Flash Cards on the Main Menu of the CyberClass Web page. Click the plus sign before the Chapter 7 title. Click Evaluation of Educational Technology and answer all the cards in that section. Then, click Evaluating the Effectiveness of Technology Integration and answer the cards in that section. If you have less than 85% correct, continue to answer cards in other sections until you have more than 85% correct. All users: Answer as many more Flash Cards as you desire. Close the Electronic Flash Card window and the Flash Cards window by clicking the Close button in the upper-right corner of each window.

2. Practice Test (Level I, Level II, and Level III)

Click Testing on the Main Menu of the CyberClass Web page. Click the Select a book box arrow and then click Teachers Discovering Computers. Click the Select a test to take box arrow and then click the Chapter 7 title in the list. Click the Take Test button. If necessary, maximize the window. Take the practice test and then click the Submit Test button. Click the Display Study Guide button. Review the Study Guide. Scroll down and click the Return To CyberClass button. Click the Yes button to close the Study Guide window. If your score was less than 80%, click the Take another Test button to take another practice test. Continue taking tests until your score is greater than 80%. Then, click the Done button.

3. Web Guide (Level I, Level II, and Level III)

Click Web Guide on the Main Menu of the CyberClass Web page. When the Guide to World Wide Web Sites page displays, click Government and Politics and review the White House and Library of Congress sites. Are these sites appropriate for use in K-12 classrooms? Would you use these sites in your classroom? What kind of resources are available at the Library of Congress site? When you are finished, hand in a brief summary of your conclusions and findings to your instructor.

4. Assignments and Syllabus (Level II and Level III)

Click Assignments on the Main Menu of the CyberClass Web page. Ensure you are aware of all assignments and when they are due. Click Syllabus on the Main Menu of the CyberClass Web page. Verify you are up to date on all activities for the class.

5. CyberChallenge (Level II and Level III)

Click CyberChallenge on the Main Menu of the CyberClass Web page. Click the Select a book box arrow and then click Teachers Discovering Computers. Click the Select a board to play box arrow and then click Chapter 7 in the list. Click the Play CyberChallenge button. Maximize the CyberChallenge window. Play CyberChallenge until your score for a complete game is 500 points or more. Close the CyberChallenge window.

6. Hot Links (Level II and Level III)

Click Hot Links on the Main Menu of the CyberClass Web page. Review the sites in the Hot Links section and then write a brief report indicating which site you like best and why.

Edlssues

Web Instructions: To display this page from the Web, launch your browser and enter the URL, www.scsite.com/tdc/ch7/issues.htm. Click the links for current and additional information to help you respond to the EdIssues questions.

InBrief

KeyTerms

AtTheMovies

CheckPoint

TeacherTime

CyberClass

Edlssues

NetStuff

SPECIAL FEATURES

TimeLine 2000

Guide to WWW Sites

Buyer's Guide 2000

Educational Sites

State/Federal Sites

Chat

News

Home

1. Simulation Software

Increasingly sophisticated software applications not only have impacted business, entertainment, and recreation, but education as well. Simulation software gives students experience with designing a city, constructing buildings, flying airplanes, or saving a forest. Many educators feel simulation software assists students in developing higher-order thinking skills and problem-solving skills. Opponents argue, however, that using these types of software merely leads students and does not help develop problem-solving skills. Opponents stress that simulation software programs are no more than fancy games. Do you agree with either side? Why? Why not? Support your position with documentation. What advantages, if any, do simulation software applications offer? Do you think disadvantages may become evident when using the simulation software in the classroom? How might another application described in this chapter be used to teach higher-order thinking skills or problem solving?

2. Parental Concerns

You teach high school English. Your students create multimedia research reports and other projects using the World Wide Web and other technologies. You use teacher-created rubrics and other alternative assessment tools to assess student learning. The parents of one of your students are upset and do not believe that creating electronic research reports will prepare their child for college English or for producing written research reports. How will you convince these parents about the benefits of integrating modern multimedia software programs into the classroom curriculum? How can you demonstrate that students are using higher-order thinking skills when they create electronic projects? Describe other ways in which you can ease the fears of these parents.

www.scsite.com/tdc/ch7/issues.htm

- InBrief
- KeyTerms
- AtTheMovies
- CheckPoint
- TeacherTime
- CyberClass
- EdIssues
- NetStuff

SPECIAL FEATURES

- TimeLine 2000
- Guide to WWW Sites
- Buyer's Guide 2000
- Educational Sites
- State/Federal Sites
- Chat
- News
- Home

Edlssues

3. Evaluating Web Sites

A great deal of <u>information exists on the Internet</u> that is not what it appears to be. Sometimes material seems authoritative and well written, but upon closer inspection, the material is biased, inaccurate, or out of date. Your school board feels it is a teacher's responsibility to teach students to recognize the quality and authority of information they find on the Internet. Do you agree or disagree? Why? How will you teach your students to do this? What criteria should students use when evaluating Web sites? Do students need to evaluate all Web sites? Support your answer with illustrations from exiting Web sites.

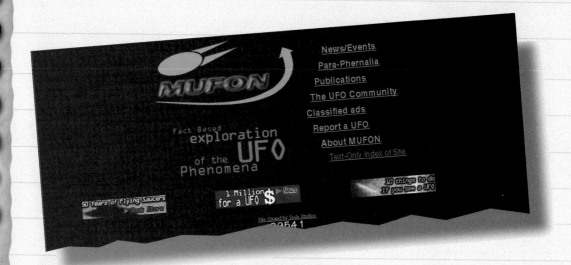

4. Grants for Training

You locate a request for proposal (RFP) to fund a grant for laptop computers for all the teachers in your school. The grant will provide the laptops, but the school has to provide the teacher training. You want to develop the proposal with the help of the technology committee. You recognize this is a great opportunity to get technology into the hands of all teachers through the use of their own laptop computers. You think your school has an extremely good chance of being funded. The principal immediately says, "NO!" She feels the teachers should write grants only to get student computers. She also states that no funds are available for teacher training. Do you see a solution to this dilemma? What should you do? Where can you go to get more information and creative ideas for <u>writing the grant</u> and solving the <u>training issues</u>? How will you convince the principal that putting a computer in each teacher's hands is an important initial step toward technology integration?

5. Alternative Assessment

Your first teaching job is at a very progressive new school that has technology in every classroom. During your college education, you learned a great deal about assessing student achievement through testing. You learned how to create appropriate traditional tests for subjects. This new school, however, has no traditional testing program. It has implemented an innovative approach to learning that uses only alternative assessment. No grades are assigned and all assessment is based on mastery learning. Do you think this is a good strategy? Support your position with reasons based on educational research. What <u>alternative assessment tools</u> can you use to meet the school's standards? Itemize the advantages and disadvantages of this type of assessment.

www.scsite.com/tdc/ch7/net.htm

Web Instructions: To display this page from the Web, launch your browser and enter the URL, www.scsite.com/tdc/ch7/net.htm.

InBrief

KeyTerms

AtTheMovies

CheckPoint

TeacherTime

CyberClass

EdIssues

NetStuff

SPECIAL FEATURES

TimeLine 2000

Guide to WWW Sites

Buyer's Guide 2000

Educational Sites

State/Federal Sites

Chat

News

Home

NetStuff

1. The Rubricator

The Web offers teachers opportunities to purchase numerous software programs to help accomplish their daily tasks. Click the RUBRICATOR button to complete an exercise that will let you download a trial version of a software program to assist you in creating checklists and rubrics for authentic assessment.

EVALUATING INTERNET RESOURCES

2. Evaluating Internet Resources

Evaluating information found on the World Wide Web is a critical skill that teachers and students must possess. Click the EVALUATING INTERNET RESOURCES button to complete an exercise and learn how to evaluate the quality of Internet resources.

EVALUATING STUDENT PROJECTS

3. Evaluating Student Projects

Designing effective evaluation tools to assess student learning requires thought and preparation. One popular assessment tool is an assessment rubric. Click the EVALUATING STUDENT PROJECTS button to complete an exercise on how to create effective rubrics.

INTEGRATION STRATEGIES

4. Integration Strategies

When integrating technology into the curriculum, teachers use different strategies depending on the number of computers in their classrooms. Many teachers have only one modern multimedia computer in their classroom. Click the INTEGRATION STRATEGIES button to complete an exercise and learn more about integration strategies in the one-computer classroom.

CURRICULUM PAGES

5. Creating Curriculum Pages

Teachers find that creating curriculum pages is an easily learned skill. Curriculum pages are also an important tool for integrating the Web into the curriculum. Click the CURRICULUM PAGES button and complete an exercise to learn more about creating curriculum pages.

GRAPHIC ORGANIZERS

6. Graphic Organizers

Concept maps, flowcharts, story webs, storyboards, and other graphic organizers assist students with visualizing concepts and organizing information. Click the GRAPHIC ORGANIZERS button and complete an exercise to learn more about these concepts.

WEB SCAVENGER HUNT

7. Web Scavenger Hunt

A Web scavenger hunt is an excellent method of allowing students to explore the resources of the Web using discovery learning. Click the WEB SCAVENGER HUNT button and complete an exercise to learn more about Web scavenger hunts.

WEB CHAT

8. Web Chat

The EdIssues section presents various scenarios on the uses of computers, technologies, and non-technology-related issues in K-12 education. Click the WEB CHAT button to enter a Web Chat discussion related to the EdIssues exercises.

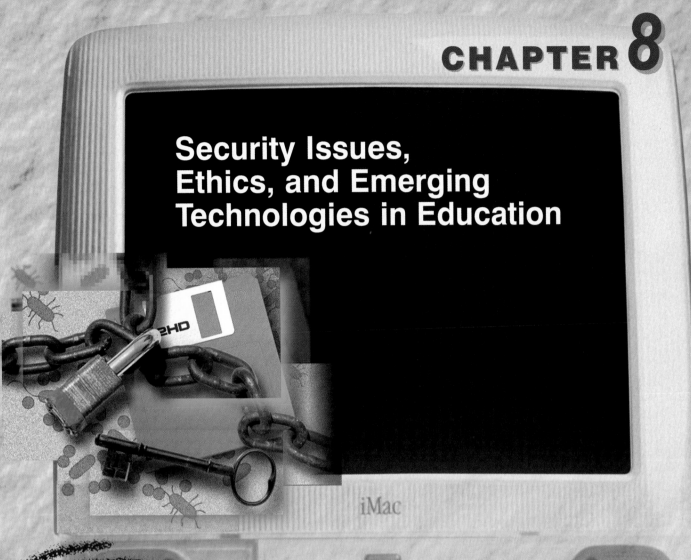

Security Issues, Ethics, and Emerging Technologies in Education

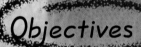

After completing this chapter, you will be able to:

- Identify security risks that threaten school computers

- Describe how a computer virus works and the steps you can take to prevent viruses

- Describe different ways schools safeguard computers and networks

- Explain why computer backup is important and how it is accomplished

- Define what is meant by information privacy and its impact on schools

- Identify the components of copyright that impact education

- Describe the ethical issues related to Internet usage and steps schools are taking to address them

- Describe the emerging technologies that will transform traditional classrooms

EVERY DAY, BUSINESSES, SCHOOLS, AND INDIVIDUALS DEPEND ON COMPUTERS TO PERFORM A VARIETY OF SIGNIFICANT TASKS, SUCH AS TRACKING SALES, RECORDING STUDENT GRADES, CREATING REPORTS, AND SENDING E-MAIL. Because increasingly we rely on computers to create, store, and manage critical information, it is important to ensure that computers and software are protected from loss, damage, and misuse. School districts, for example, must take precautions to guarantee that student information such as grades, attendance rates, and personal, family, and learning problems, is protected from loss and kept confidential.

This chapter identifies some potential risks to computers and software and describes a number of safeguards that schools, businesses, and individuals can implement to minimize these risks. The chapter also discusses information privacy, including the current laws that keep certain data confidential. The chapter then reviews concerns about the ethical use of computers and which activities are right, wrong, or even criminal. Finally, the chapter covers security, privacy, and the ethical issues that relate to how teachers and students use the information they find on the Internet.

WebInfo

For more information on computer viruses, visit the Teachers Discovering Computers Chapter 8 WebInfo page (www.scsite.com/tdc/ch8/webinfo.htm) and click Viruses.

Computer Security: Risks and Safeguards

Any event or action that has the potential of causing a loss of computer equipment, software, data and information, or processing capability is a **computer security risk**. Some of these risks, such as viruses, unauthorized access and use, and information theft, are a result of deliberate acts that are against the law. Any illegal act involving a computer generally is referred to as a **computer crime**. The following sections describe some of the more common computer security risks and the measures schools can take to minimize or prevent their consequences.

Computer Viruses

At 4:30 in the afternoon, Ms. Vicki Reamy of Ridgedale High School is in her classroom making last-minute adjustments to the Excel spreadsheet she plans to use in tomorrow's third period business education class. As she opens the spreadsheet file to make one last change, the top of the spreadsheet displays the message, "Something wonderful has happened, your PC is alive." Dismayed, she realizes that a computer virus has corrupted her spreadsheet and she has lost all her work.

A **computer virus** is a potentially damaging computer program designed to affect your computer negatively without your knowledge or permission by altering the way it works. More specifically, a virus is a segment of program code that implants itself in a computer file and spreads systematically from one file to another. **Figure 8-1** shows how a virus spreads from one computer to another.

Computer viruses, however, do not generate by chance. Creators of virus programs write them for a specific purpose — usually either to spread from one file to another or to implement the specific symptom or damage. Many viruses, for example, are designed to destroy or corrupt data stored on the infected computer. The symptom or damage caused by a virus, called the **virus payload**, can be harmless or cause significant damage, as planned by the creator.

Unfortunately, Vicki Reamy's experience is not unusual. Although viruses are a serious problem for both PC and Macintosh computer users, the majority of virus programs are intended to infect PCs. Currently, more than 13,000 known viruses or variants exist, and approximately 100 new viruses or variants are identified every month. The increased use of networks and the Internet makes the spread of viruses easier than ever.

Although users know of numerous variations, four main types of viruses exist: boot sector viruses, file viruses, Trojan horse viruses, and macro viruses. A **boot sector virus** replaces the boot program used to start the computer with a modified, infected version of the boot program. When the computer runs the infected boot program, it loads the virus into the computer's memory. Once a virus is in memory, it spreads to any disk inserted into the computer. A **file virus** inserts virus code into program files; the virus then spreads to any program that accesses the infected file. A **Trojan horse virus** (named after the Greek myth) is a virus that hides within or is designed to look like a legitimate program. A **macro virus** uses the macro language of an application, such as word processing or spreadsheet, to hide virus codes. When you open a document with an infected macro, the macro virus loads into memory. Certain actions, such as saving the document, activate the virus. Macro viruses often are part of templates, so they will infect any document created using one of the templates. Viruses normally are spread between computers by inserting an infected floppy disk in a computer or downloading an infected file from the Internet via e-mail or a web page.

Some viruses are relatively harmless pranks that temporarily freeze a computer or

A COMPUTER VIRUS: WHAT IT IS AND HOW IT SPREADS

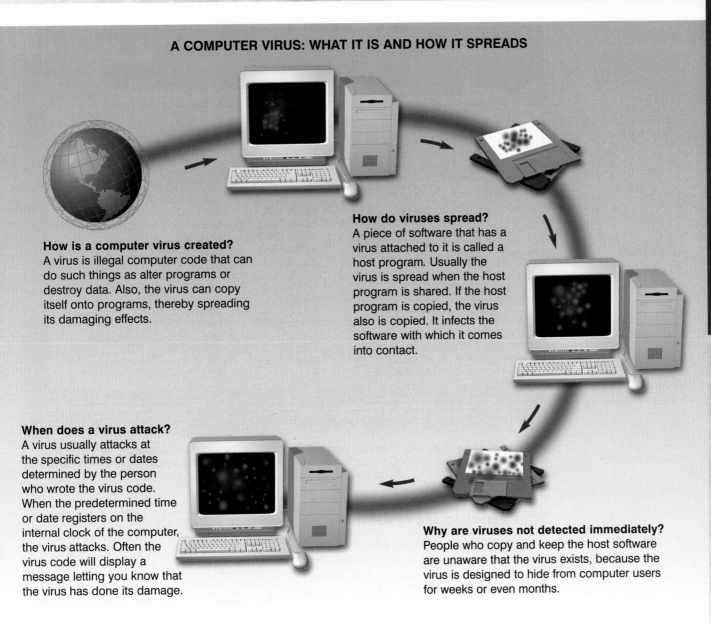

How is a computer virus created?
A virus is illegal computer code that can do such things as alter programs or destroy data. Also, the virus can copy itself onto programs, thereby spreading its damaging effects.

How do viruses spread?
A piece of software that has a virus attached to it is called a host program. Usually the virus is spread when the host program is shared. If the host program is copied, the virus also is copied. It infects the software with which it comes into contact.

When does a virus attack?
A virus usually attacks at the specific times or dates determined by the person who wrote the virus code. When the predetermined time or date registers on the internal clock of the computer, the virus attacks. Often the virus code will display a message letting you know that the virus has done its damage.

Why are viruses not detected immediately?
People who copy and keep the host software are unaware that the virus exists, because the virus is designed to hide from computer users for weeks or even months.

Figure 8-1 A virus spreads from one computer to another as illustrated in this figure.

cause it to display sounds or messages. The computer plays a few chords of music when the Music Bug virus is triggered, for example. Other viruses cause extensive damage to computer files and spread quickly throughout a network. For example, if a state administrator e-mails an Excel spreadsheet infected with a macro virus to every school district in the state, the virus can quickly infect hundreds of computers.

Some viruses are considered logic bombs or time bombs. A **logic bomb** is a program that activates when it detects a certain condition. One disgruntled worker, for example, planted a logic bomb that began destroying files when his name was added to a list of terminated employees. A **time bomb** is a type of logic bomb that activates on a particular date. A well-known time bomb is the **Michelangelo virus**, which destroys data on your hard disk on March 6, the date of Michelangelo's birthday. **Figure 8-2** on the next page lists information on some common viruses.

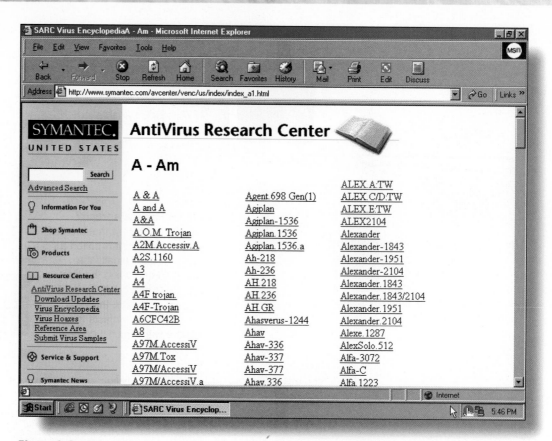

Figure 8-2 Many Web sites maintain lists of the thousands of viruses in existence, so you can obtain information on a specific virus if your computer is infected. The Symantec AntiVirus Research Center Web page, for example, organizes the virus names alphabetically.

Virus Detection and Removal

There are no completely effective ways to keep a computer or network safe from computer viruses. You can, however, take precautions to protect your home and classroom computers from virus infections. **Figure 8-3** lists a number of safe computing tips that may help you minimize the risk of viruses.

Using an antivirus program is one of the most effective ways to protect against computer viruses. An **antivirus program** is designed to detect, disinfect, and protect computers and networks from viruses. Antivirus programs, also called **vaccines**, work by looking for programs that attempt to modify the boot program, the operating system, or other programs that normally are read from but not written to [**Figure 8-4**].

In addition to providing protection from viruses, most antivirus programs also have utilities to remove or repair infected programs and files. If the virus has infected the boot program, however, the antivirus program may require you to restart the computer with a rescue disk. A **rescue disk** is a floppy disk that contains an uninfected copy of key operating system commands and startup information that enables the computer to restart correctly. Once you have restarted the computer using a rescue disk, you can run repair and removal programs to remove infected files and repair damaged files. If the program cannot repair the damaged files, you may have to replace or restore them with uninfected backup copies of the files. Later sections in the chapter explain backup and restore procedures.

To help protect against viruses, most schools install antivirus programs on their networks and on individual computers throughout the school. Two popular antivirus programs used in schools and homes, shown in **Figure 8-5** on page 8.6, are McAfee VirusScan and Symantec Norton AntiVirus.

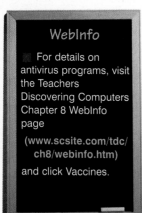

WebInfo

For details on antivirus programs, visit the Teachers Discovering Computers Chapter 8 WebInfo page

(www.scsite.com/tdc/ ch8/webinfo.htm)

and click Vaccines.

Safe Computing Tips

A number of simple steps teachers can take will protect their home and classroom computers from viruses.

- **Purchase reliable antivirus software.** Most programs offer free virus updates. Upgrade antivirus software every three to six months.

- **Scan all disks.** Floppy disks are the number-one culprit for carrying viruses from one computer to another and spreading throughout networks. If someone hands you a disk that has been used in another system — scan it.

- **Scan all files downloaded from the Internet.** One of the more common sources for viruses is downloaded files. To be safe, download all files into a special folder on your hard drive and scan immediately after downloading.

- **Scan all attached files before reading them.** You cannot get a virus from reading your e-mail, but it is possible to transfer a virus to your system by opening an attachment.

- **Scan all software before using even if it is shrink-wrapped.** Viruses have been found in manufacturer-supplied software. Scan before installing software.

- **Avoid pirated, illegal copies of copyrighted software.** Not only is using them illegal, but they are a favorite source of viruses.

- **Install programs on computers from the original disks.** Do not try to move copies from one computer to another. Viruses can hide on one system and wait for a free ride to another computer. The extra seconds you spend may save you days of recovery time and lost data.

- **Have a bootable system disk.** Always have a clean, bootable system disk available.

- **Back up your files often.** Even with the best virus software, realize that your computer's files can be infected. Be prepared to deal with the problem.

- **Set your antivirus program to scan automatically.** Most antivirus programs can be set up to scan the system automatically when booted and check it whenever floppy drives are accessed or files are opened.

Figure 8-3 Teachers can use a number of safe computing tips to minimize the risk of viruses.

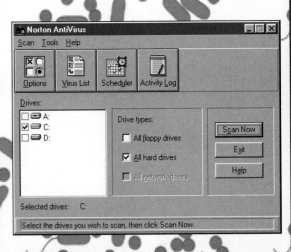
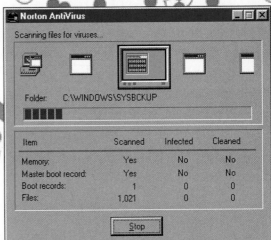
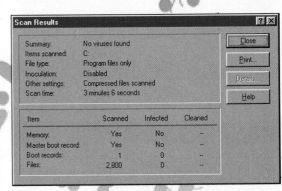

Figure 8-4 Antivirus programs check disk drives and memory for computer viruses. The top screen allows you to select the disk drives to be scanned. The middle screen displays the status during the scan, and the bottom screen shows the results.

When you install an antivirus program, you should set up the program to continuously monitor a computer for possible viruses, including continual scans of all floppy disks and files downloaded from the Internet [Figure 8-6].

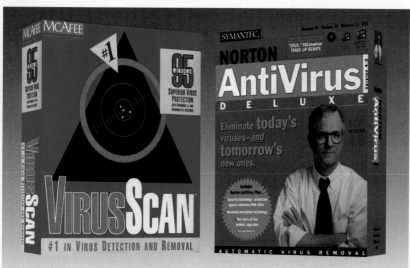

Figure 8-5 McAfee VirusScan and Symantec Norton AntiVirus are two popular antivirus programs used in schools, businesses, and homes.

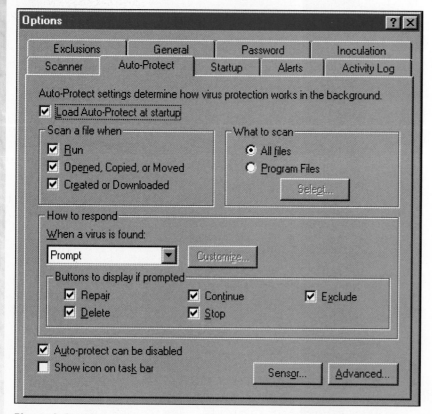

Figure 8-6 Using Norton AntiVirus Auto-Protect, users can opt for several different virus protection options, such as scanning all Created or Downloaded files.

False warnings about viruses often spread via e-mail and over the Internet. Known as **virus hoaxes**, these warnings describe viruses that are not actually known to exist. Given the damage viruses cause, however, you should take the time to research the validity of any virus warnings you receive, in the event they are real.

Unauthorized Access and Use

Unauthorized access is the use of a computer or network without permission. An individual who tries to access a computer or network illegally is called a **cracker** or hacker. The term, **hacker**, although originally a complimentary word for a computer enthusiast, now has a derogatory connotation because it refers to people who try to break into a computer often intending to steal or corrupt its data. Crackers and hackers typically break into computers by connecting to the system via a modem and logging in as a user. Some intruders have no intent of causing damage to computer files; they merely wish to access data, information, or programs on the accessed computer before logging off. Other intruders leave some evidence of their presence with a message or by deliberately altering data.

Unauthorized use is the use of a computer or data for unapproved or possibly illegal activities. Unauthorized use ranges from an employee using a company computer to send personal e-mail or track his or her child's soccer league scores to someone gaining access to a bank system and completing an unauthorized transfer.

One way to prevent unauthorized access to and use of computers is to implement **access controls**, which are security measures that define who can access a computer, when they can access it, and what actions they can take while using the computer. To prevent unauthorized use and access to sensitive information, schools install different levels and types of access controls. Schools set up their network so that users have access only to those programs, data, and information for which they are approved. Most schools and businesses provide authorized users with unique user identification (user ID) and a password that allows them to log on to the network to use e-mail, transfer files, and access other shared resources [Figure 8-7]. When a user logs on to a computer or network by entering a user ID and a password, the operating system checks to see if the user ID and password match the entries stored in an authorization file. If the entries match, the computer or network grants access.

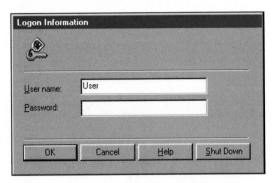

Figure 8-7 Many schools require administrators, teachers, staff, and students to log on the school's network with a unique User ID and password.

Often you are asked to select your own password by choosing a word or series of characters that will be easy to remember. If your password is too simple or obvious, such as your initials or birthday, however, others may guess it easily. Some suggestions to follow when you create a password are:

- Choose names of obscure places in other countries

- Make the password at least eight characters (if supported by the software)

- Join two words together

- Mix initials and dates together

- Add one or more numbers at the beginning, middle, or end of a word

- Choose words from other languages

- Choose family names far back in your family tree

- Add letters to or subtract letters from an existing word

Generally, the more creative your password, the harder it is for someone else to figure out. Even long and creative passwords,

however, do not provide complete protection against unauthorized access. Some basic precautions to take include:

- Do not post passwords near your computer

- Use a password that is easy to remember, so that you do not have to write it down

- Use a password you can type quickly without having to look at the keyboard

- Do not share your password with other users

Following these guidelines helps to ensure that others will not use your password to access data, programs, or sensitive information stored on your computer or a school network.

At many schools, each user ID and password is associated with a specific level of computer and network access. The following is a brief description of some basic access levels schools use to prevent unauthorized access and use of sensitive information.

- Students usually can access only instructional materials and software. Many schools also provide student access to the Internet and Web — although many schools install filtering software on the network to prevent students from viewing inappropriate Web sites. Students do not have network access to grades, attendance rates, and other sensitive and personal information.

- Teachers typically have access to all the programs, data, and information to which students have access; they usually also have access to selected information about their students, such as grades and attendance. Teachers normally do not have access to information on other teachers' students or any administrative files.

- Principals and assistant principals normally have access to all information that pertains to students enrolled at their school; they may not, however, access information on students attending other schools in the district.

- School district administrators and superintendents usually have access to all information stored on the district's network servers.

WebInfo

For more information on unauthorized access, visit the Teachers Discovering Computers Chapter 8 WebInfo page (www.scsite.com/tdc/ch8/webinfo.htm) and click Unauthorized Access.

CHAPTER 8

Hardware Theft and Vandalism

For schools, hardware theft and vandalism present a difficult security challenge. To help minimize the theft of computers and associated equipment, schools can implement a variety of security precautions. In addition to installing security systems, many schools also install additional physical security devices such as cables that lock the equipment to a desk, cabinet, or floor [**Figure 8-8**]. Schools also normally install deadbolt locks and alarm systems to protect the equipment in their computer labs.

against theft of laptop computers and other portable equipment. You should never, for example, leave a laptop computer unattended or out in the open in a public place, such as the cafeteria, or on the seat of a car. Some schools install physical devices such as cables that temporarily lock laptops to a desk or table. As a precaution in case of theft, you also should back up the files stored on your laptop computer regularly.

In addition to hardware theft, another area of concern for K-12 schools is vandalism. **Computer vandalism** takes many forms, from a student cutting a computer cable or deleting

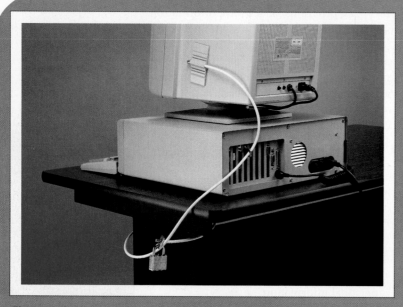

Figure 8-8 Using cables to lock computers can help prevent the theft of desktop and portable computer equipment.

Figure 8-9 The size and weight of laptop computers make them easy to steal, and their value makes them tempting targets for thieves. Schools and teachers need to take special precautions to prevent the theft of their laptop computers.

WebInfo

For an overview of software and technology law, visit the Teachers Discovering Computers Chapter 8 WebInfo page (www.scsite.com/tdc/ch8/webinfo.htm) and click Software.

With the use of portable equipment such as laptop computers, hardware theft now poses a more serious risk. Increasingly, K-12 schools and colleges are providing laptop computers for teachers and loaning them to students for short periods of time. Some universities and colleges even require that each entering student purchase a laptop computer. Users must take special care to protect their laptop computers. The size and weight of these smaller computers make them easy to steal, and their value makes them tempting targets for thieves [Figure 8-9].

Common sense and a constant awareness of the risks are the best preventive measures

files to individuals breaking in a school and randomly smashing computers. Schools usually have written policies and procedures for handling the various types of vandalism.

Software Theft

Like hardware theft and vandalism, software theft takes many forms — from a student physically stealing a CD-ROM or floppy disk to intentional piracy of software. **Software piracy** — the unauthorized and illegal duplication of copyrighted software — is by far the most common form of software theft.

When you purchase software, you actually do not *own* the software; instead, you have purchased the right to use the software, as outlined in the software license. A **software license** is an agreement that provides specific conditions for use of the software, which users must accept before using the software. Manufacturers usually print the terms of a software license on the software packaging, or in the case of software downloaded via the Web, a page at the manufacturer's site. The same agreement generally displays on a licensing acceptance screen during the software's setup program **[Figure 8-10]**. Installation and use of the software constitutes the user's acceptance of the terms.

The most common type of license included with software packages purchased by individual users is a **single-user license** or **end-user license agreement (EULA)**. An end-user license agreement typically includes numerous conditions, including the following:

- Users may install the software on only one computer

- Users may not install the software on a network, such a school computer lab network

- Users may make *one* copy for backup purposes

- Users may not give copies to friends and colleagues.

Unless otherwise specified by a software license, you do not have the right to loan, rent, or in any way distribute software you purchase. This means you cannot install the software on both your home and classroom computer or on more than one classroom computer. Doing so not only is a violation of copyright law, it also is a federal crime.

Software piracy introduces a number of risks into the software market: it increases the chance of viruses; reduces your ability to receive technical support; and significantly drives up the price of software for all users. Experts estimate that, for every authorized copy of software in use, at least one unauthorized copy is made.

One recent study reported that software piracy results in worldwide losses of more than $12 billion per year. Software piracy continues for several reasons. Some countries do

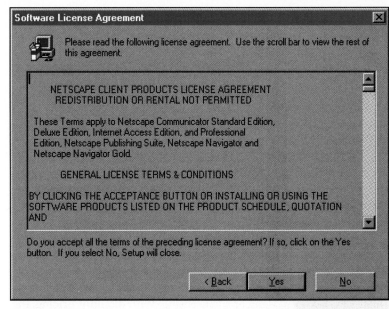

Figure 8-10 Purchasers of single-use software usually have to accept all the terms of the licensing agreement during installation of the software.

not provide legal protection for software, while other countries rarely enforce laws. In addition, many buyers believe they have the right to copy the software for which they have paid hundreds, even thousands of dollars — particularly when it is on an inexpensive floppy disk, CD-ROM, or DVD-ROM.

Software companies, by contrast, take illegal copying seriously and prosecute some offenders (including school districts, school administrators, and teachers) to the fullest extent of the law. Penalties include fines up to $250,000 and up to five years in jail. Most schools have strict policies governing the installation and use of software and enforce their rules by periodically checking classroom and lab computers to ensure that all software is properly licensed. Teachers who are not completely familiar with their school's policies governing installation of software should always check with the school's technology coordinator before installing any software on a classroom computer.

Two additional types of software, shareware and freeware, also require license agreements and are protected under copyright law. As you learned in Chapter 1, **shareware** is software that is distributed free for a trial use period. If you wish to use a shareware program beyond the trial period, the developer

WebInfo

For a list of freeware for the PC, visit the Teachers Discovering Computers Chapter 8 WebInfo page **(www.scsite.com/tdc/ch8/webinfo.htm)** and click PC Freeware.

WebInfo

For a list of free-ware for the Macintosh, visit the Teachers Discovering Computers Chapter 8 WebInfo page **(www.scsite.com/tdc/ch8/webinfo.htm)** and click Mac Freeware.

CHAPTER 8

(person or company) expects you to send a small fee. **Freeware**, by contrast, is software provided at no cost to a user by an individual or company. You should carefully read the license included with any shareware or freeware to familiarize yourself with the usage terms and conditions. Some shareware licenses, for example, allow you to install the software on several computers for the same fee, while others allow you to install the software on an unlimited number of computers in the same school for a minimal additional fee. You also should always scan shareware and freeware programs for viruses prior to installation and use.

To reduce software costs for schools and businesses with large numbers of users, software vendors often offer special discount pricing or site licensing. With discount pricing, the more copies of a program a school district purchases, the greater the discount. Purchasing a software **site license** gives the buyer the right to install the software on multiple computers at a single site. Site licenses usually cost significantly less than purchasing an individual copy of the software for each computer; many school districts, in fact, purchase software site licenses that allow for use on computers throughout the district, thus gaining substantial savings.

Network site licenses for many software packages also are available. A **network site license** allows network users to share a single copy of the software, which resides on the network server. Network software site licenses are priced based on a fixed fee for an unlimited number of users, a maximum number of users, or per user.

A **community site license** gives an entire region or state the right to install an unlimited number of educational copies of a particular software program on individual computers or a network. As with other site licenses, a community site license provides substantial savings. **Figure 8-11** summarizes the various types of software licenses used in education. A number of major software companies, such as Microsoft, provide site licenses for some of their software to K-12 schools at drastically reduced rates.

Type of License	Characteristics	Use in Schools
Single-user	Can be installed on only one computer.	Used when a school needs only a few copies of a particular software. Commonly found in small schools and when purchasing specialized software programs.
Multiple-user	Software can be installed on a set number of computers, typically 5, 10, 50, or more.	Cost-effective method to install software on more than one computer. Commonly found in schools.
Network License	Software is installed on the school's network. The license will specify and the software will control a specific number of simultaneous users, such as 50, 100, 250, or 500.	Cost-effective method of allowing students and teachers throughout the school to have access to an application software program. As schools continue to install networks, network licenses are becoming very common.
Community/State License	Frequently used with software distributed on CD-ROMs/DVD-ROMs. Any number of programs can be purchased for either Macintosh or PC platforms.	Very cost-effective method for schools to purchase large quantities of software. Savings can be significant over individual CD-ROM or DVD-ROM pricing.

Figure 8-11 A summary of the various types of software licenses used in education.

Information Theft

As you have learned, information is a valuable asset to an organization, such as a school district. The deliberate theft of information, thus, causes as much or more damage than the theft of hardware. Information theft typically occurs for a variety of reasons — from organizations stealing or buying stolen information to learn about competitors to individuals stealing credit card and telephone charge card numbers to make purchases. Information theft often is linked to other types of computer crime. An individual, for example, first may gain unauthorized access to a computer and then steal credit card numbers stored in a firm's accounting files.

Most organizations prevent information theft by implementing the user ID controls previously mentioned. Another way to protect sensitive data is to use encryption. **Encryption** is the process of converting readable data into unreadable characters by applying a formula that uses a code, called an **encryption key**. The person who receives the message uses the same encryption key to decrypt it (convert it back to readable data). Both the sender and receiver computers use the same encryption software. Any person illegally accessing the information sees only meaningless symbols [Figure 8-12].

School networks do contain a great deal of important and confidential information on students, teachers, and staff. While information theft is not a major problem in schools, the potential is taken seriously. As a result, schools implement many of the security precautions described in this chapter.

WebInfo

For more information on encryption software, visit the Teachers Discovering Computers Chapter 8 WebInfo page **(www.scsite.com/tdc/ ch8/webinfo.htm)** and click Encryption.

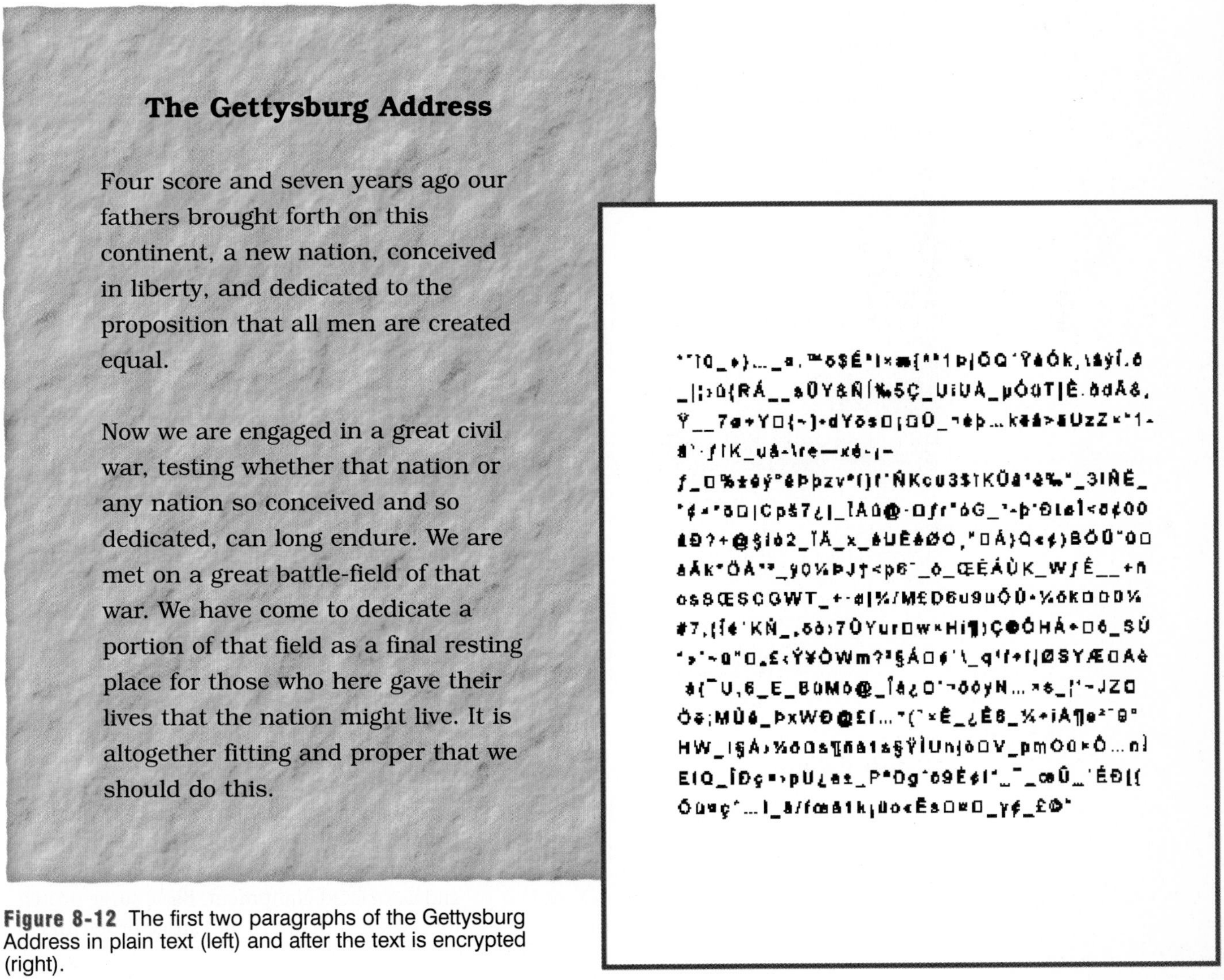

The Gettysburg Address

Four score and seven years ago our fathers brought forth on this continent, a new nation, conceived in liberty, and dedicated to the proposition that all men are created equal.

Now we are engaged in a great civil war, testing whether that nation or any nation so conceived and so dedicated, can long endure. We are met on a great battle-field of that war. We have come to dedicate a portion of that field as a final resting place for those who here gave their lives that the nation might live. It is altogether fitting and proper that we should do this.

Figure 8-12 The first two paragraphs of the Gettysburg Address in plain text (left) and after the text is encrypted (right).

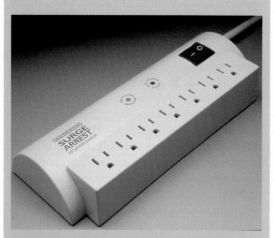

Figure 8-13 Circuits inside a surge protector safeguard equipment against overvoltages.

in-out telephone line connections for modem

Figure 8-14 Home users should purchase a surge protector that includes an in-and-out connection for the telephone line to the computer's modem.

System Failure

Theft is not the only cause of hardware, software, data, or information loss. Any of these also can occur during a **system failure**, which is a malfunction of a computer. System failures occur because of electrical power

problems, hardware component failure, or software error.

One of the more common causes of system failures in schools and homes is an abrupt variation in electrical power. A variation in electrical power can cause data loss or damage computer components. In a school network, for example, a single power disturbance can damage multiple computers and their associated equipment. Two more common electrical power variations that cause system failures are undervoltages or overvoltages.

An **undervoltage** occurs when the electrical power supply drops. In North America, electricity normally flows from the wall plug at approximately 120 volts. Any significant drop below 120 volts is considered an undervoltage. A **brownout** is a prolonged undervoltage; a **blackout** is a complete power failure. Undervoltages cause data loss and computer crashes but generally do not cause serious equipment damage.

An **overvoltage**, or **power surge**, occurs when the incoming electrical power increases significantly above the normal 120 volts. A momentary overvoltage, called a **spike**, occurs when the power increase lasts for less than one millisecond (one thousandth of a second). Spikes are caused by uncontrollable disturbances, such as lightning, or controllable disturbances, such as turning on a piece of equipment that uses the same electrical circuit. Overvoltages can cause immediate and permanent equipment damage.

To protect your computer equipment from overvoltages, you should use surge protectors. A **surge protector** is a device that uses special electrical components to smooth out minor voltage errors, provide a stable current flow, and keep an overvoltage from damaging computer equipment **[Figure 8-13]**. Schools should use surge protectors for all classroom and lab computers and printers.

Electrical power surges can also occur over communications lines, such as telephone lines. Home users thus should purchase a surge protector that includes a connection for the phone line connected to your modem **[Figure 8-14]**. Overall, surge protectors provide an inexpensive way to protect computers and associated equipment. Basic surge protectors cost less than $15 and surge protectors that include protection from power surges over telephone lines cost less than $20.

While a surge protector absorbs a small overvoltage without damage, a large overvoltage, such as that caused by a lightning strike, will cause the surge protector to fail in order to protect the computer components. Surge protectors also are not completely effective; large power surges may bypass the surge protector and repeated small overvoltages weaken a surge protector permanently.

For additional electrical protection, many home and school users connect their computers and printers to an uninterruptable power supply, instead of a surge protector. An **uninterruptable power supply (UPS)** is a device that contains surge protection circuits and one or more batteries that provide power during a temporary or permanent loss of power **[Figure 8-15]**. The amount of time a UPS allows you to continue working depends on the electrical requirements of the computer and the size of the batteries in the UPS. A less expensive UPS provides enough time for users to save their current work and properly shut down the computer after a power outage (about ten minutes).

To ensure that their networks will continue to operate in the event of a power loss, most schools and businesses install UPSs to protect their network servers. Home users also should consider investing in a UPS, especially if they live in an area prone to power surges, power failures, and lightning strikes. For home users, the $75 to $150 investment in a UPS can prevent user frustration associated with most power-related computer problems, crashes, and loss of data. Some UPS manufacturers pay for any damage your computer sustains from power surges, including lightning strikes.

Backup Procedures

To prevent data loss caused by a system failure or a computer virus, many schools, businesses, and home users back up their important files. A **backup** is a duplicate of a file, program, or disk that maybe used if the original is lost, damaged, or destroyed. When a file is corrupted or destroyed, a user uses the backup copy to **restore**, or reload, the file on a computer or network file server. Schools and home users often overlook storing backup

WebInfo

To learn more about Microsoft Backup, visit the Teachers Discovering Computers Chapter 8 WebInfo page

(www.scsite.com/tdc/ ch8/webinfo.htm)

and click Backup.

Figure 8-15 If power fails, an uninterruptible power supply (UPS) uses batteries to provide electricity for a limited amount of time. A UPS also contains circuits that safeguard against overvoltages.

copies at another location, called an **offsite location**, as an additional precaution. This simple precaution prevents a single disaster, such as a fire, from destroying both the primary and backup copies of important files.

Most schools have a **backup procedure** that outlines a regular plan of copying and backing up important data and program files. At many schools, the backup procedures cover only essential school programs, information, and data, such as student grades, attendance, and other personal information. Schools normally do not back up the files individual teachers or students create on their classroom computers. If your school does not provide backups for the files you create in your classroom, you should make backup copies of your school files periodically and store them on floppy or Zip® disks. Educators also should periodically back up the files they create on their home computers. Whether at school or home, backing up your important files prevents loss of lesson plans, curriculum pages, handouts, tests, and more — files that represent years of work. Teachers also should teach their students how to back up their homework, projects, and other files.

Creating backup copes of your files is not a difficult procedure. Today, most personal computer operating systems include an easy-to-use backup utility program **[Figure 8-16]**. Such utilities not only allow users to back up their important files, they also compress the backed up files so that they require less storage space than the original files.

Ethics and the Information Age

As with any powerful technology, individuals can use computers for both good and bad actions. The standards that determine whether an action is good or bad are called **ethics**. **Computer ethics** are the moral guidelines that govern the use of computers, networks, and information systems **[Figure 8-17]**. Five areas of computer ethics frequently discussed are: (1) unauthorized use of computers; (2) hardware, software, and information theft; (3) information privacy; (4) copyright; and (5) the existence of objectionable materials on the Internet.

Unauthorized use of computers and hardware, copying software, and information theft were discussed earlier in this chapter. The following sections present the issues surrounding information privacy and copyright. The ethical issues related to objectionable materials on Internet will be discussed later in this chapter.

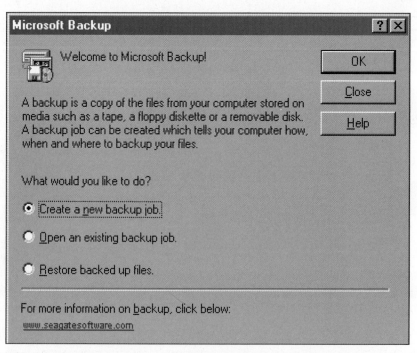

Figure 8-16 Microsoft Backup is a utility program that comes with Microsoft Windows and is an easy way to back up your important computer files.

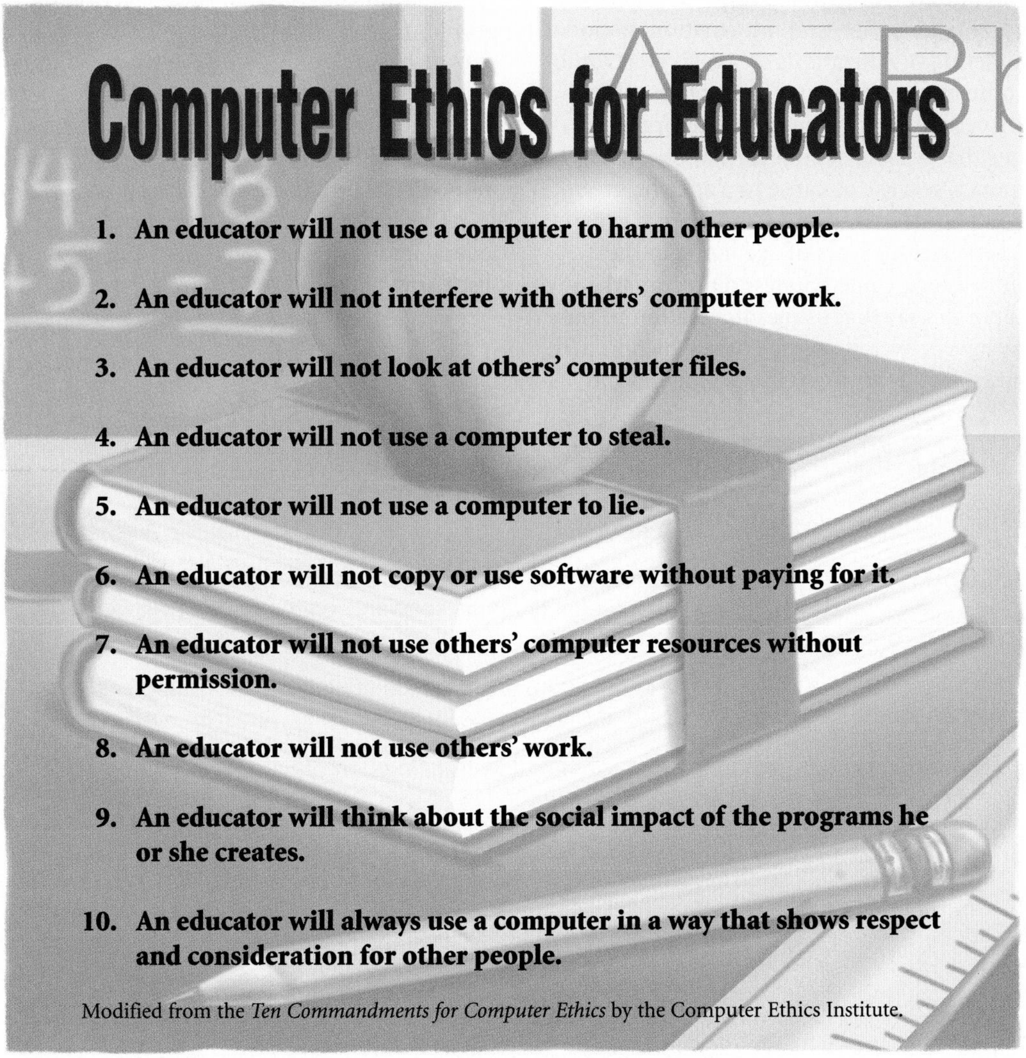

Computer Ethics for Educators

1. An educator will not use a computer to harm other people.

2. An educator will not interfere with others' computer work.

3. An educator will not look at others' computer files.

4. An educator will not use a computer to steal.

5. An educator will not use a computer to lie.

6. An educator will not copy or use software without paying for it.

7. An educator will not use others' computer resources without permission.

8. An educator will not use others' work.

9. An educator will think about the social impact of the programs he or she creates.

10. An educator will always use a computer in a way that shows respect and consideration for other people.

Modified from the *Ten Commandments for Computer Ethics* by the Computer Ethics Institute.

Figure 8-17 Computer ethics are the guidelines that govern the use of computers and information systems. This table lists computer ethics for educators.

Information Privacy

Information privacy is the right of individuals and organizations to deny or restrict the collection and use of information about them. In the past, information privacy was easier to control because information was kept in separate locations; individual schools of a large school district maintained their own files; individual stores had their own credit files; government agencies had separate records; doctors had separate files; and so on. Now it is feasible, both technically and economically, for schools, businesses, and other organizations to store large amounts of related data in a database or on one network server because of the widespread use of networks and increased storage capacity. These organizations also use computers to monitor student and employee activities. As a result, many people have concerns about how the unauthorized collection and use of data and monitoring affects their privacy.

Unauthorized Collection and Use of Information Most individuals are surprised to learn that national marketing organizations often purchase information individuals provide for magazine subscriptions, product warranty registration cards, contest entry forms, and other documents. By combining this acquired data with other information obtained from public sources, such as driver's licenses and vehicle registration information, national marketing organizations create an **electronic profile** of an individual. The organizations then sell this electronic profile to organizations that wish to send information on a product, service, or cause to a specific group of individuals (for example, all sports car owners over 40 years of age living in the southeastern United States). Direct marketing supporters say that using information in this way lowers overall selling costs, which in turn, lowers product prices. Critics contend the

information combined in these electronic profiles reveals more about individuals than anyone has a right to know. These same individuals believe that, at a minimum, companies should inform individuals they intend to sell or release personal information and give the individual the right to deny such use.

The concern about privacy has led to federal and state laws regarding storing and disclosing personal data [Figure 8-18].

Figure 8-18 Summary of the major U.S. government laws concerning privacy.

U.S. Government Laws Concerning Privacy

Date	Law	Purpose
1997	No Electronic Theft (NET) Act	Closes a narrow loophole in the law that allowed people to give away copyrighted material (such as software) on the Internet without legal repercussions.
1996	National Information Infrastructure Protection Act	Penalizes theft of information across state lines, threats against networks, and computer system trespassing.
1994	Computer Abuse Amendments Act	Amends 1984 act to outlaw transmission of harmful computer code such as viruses.
1992	Cable Act	Extends privacy of Cable Communications Policy Act of 1984 to include cellular and other wireless services.
1991	Telephone Consumer Protection Act	Restricts activities of telemarketers.
1988	Computer Matching and Privacy Protection Act	Regulates the use of government data to determine the eligibility of individuals for federal benefits.
1988	Video Privacy Protection Act	Forbids retailers from releasing or selling video-rental records without customer consent or a court order.
1986	Electronic Communications Privacy Act (ECPA)	Provides the same right of privacy protection for the postal delivery service and telephone companies to the new forms of electronic communications, such as voice mail, e-mail, and cellular telephones.
1984	Cable Communications Policy Act	Regulates disclosure of cable TV subscriber records.
1984	Computer Fraud and Abuse Act	Outlaws unauthorized access of federal government computers.
1978	Right to Financial Privacy Act	Strictly outlines procedures federal agencies must follow when looking at customer records in banks.
1974	Privacy Act	Forbids federal agencies from allowing information to be used for a reason other than the one for which it was collected.
1974	Family Educational Rights and Privacy Act	Gives students and parents access to school records and limits disclosure of records to unauthorized parties.
1970	Fair Credit Reporting Act	Prohibits credit reporting agencies from releasing credit information to unauthorized people and allows consumers to review their credit records.

Common points in some of these laws include the following:

- A business or government agency collecting data should limit the information collected and only store what is necessary to carry out the organization's functions.

- Once it has collected data, an organization must make provisions to restrict data access to those employees who must use it to perform their job duties.

- An organization should release an individual's personal information outside the organization only after the individual has agreed to its disclosure.

- When an organization collects information about an individual, the organization must inform the individual that it is collecting data and give him or her the opportunity to determine the accuracy of the data.

Schools and school districts have a legal and moral responsibility to protect sensitive information, whether in printed form or stored electronically on school computers. Just like any other business, school districts must follow state and federal laws concerning storage and release of personal information about students, teachers, and staff personnel. For these reasons, school districts generally restrict access to sensitive information stored on their networks and printed materials on a strict need-to-know basis. Teachers also must follow federal and state laws concerning the storage and release of information on their students. Teachers should carefully read and make sure they understand all school district policies concerning the release of sensitive information as related to their students.

Employee and Student Monitoring

Employee monitoring uses computers to observe, record, and review an individual's use of a computer, including communications such as e-mail, keyboard activity (used to measure productivity), and Internet sites visited. A frequently discussed issue is whether or not an employer has the right to read an employee's e-mail messages. Actual policies vary widely, with some organizations declaring they will review e-mail messages regularly,

while others state they consider e-mail private and will protect it just like a letter sent through ground mail.

Most schools usually have very specific rules governing the use of e-mail and school networks by teachers, administrators, staff, and students. Some schools randomly monitor e-mail messages and the Internet sites visited by teachers, administrators, staff, and students, while other schools do not. In either case, teachers should familiarize themselves with all school policies concerning e-mail, computer, and Internet usage. To ensure that individuals understand these policies, most schools require that teachers, students, staff, and parents sign an Acceptable Use Policy (AUP) that provides specific guidance for using school computers, networks, and the Internet. Teachers also should ensure that students fully understand school personnel or their future employers may monitor their use of the organization's computer resources.

Copyright Laws

As discussed earlier in this chapter, copyright laws cover software programs to protect them from piracy. There are many other aspects of copyright law, however, that teachers need to understand. The Copyright Act of 1976 and its numerous amendments apply to all creative works. A **copyright** means the original author or creator of the work retains ownership of the work and has the exclusive right to reproduce and distribute the creative work. All educators need to understand how the copyright law impacts the manner in which they and their students use information created by others. Such an understanding is important because the building blocks of education use the creative works of others: books; videos; newspapers, magazines, and other reference materials; software; and information located on the World Wide Web.

Three areas of copyright directly impact today's classrooms: (1) illegally copying or use of copyrighted software programs; (2) fair use laws and their application to the use of both printed copyrighted materials and copyrighted materials accessible on the Internet; and (3) use of copyrighted materials on teacher and student Web pages. The first area (illegally copying or using licensed and copyrighted software) was covered earlier in this chapter; the following sections cover the other two areas of copyright.

Fair Use The Copyright Act of 1976 established **fair use**, or guidelines that allow educators to use and copy certain copyrighted materials for non-profit educational purposes. **Figure 8-19** shows Section 107 of the Copyright Act of 1976, which deals with fair use. Copyright issues are complex and sometimes the laws are vague. School districts thus provide teachers with specific guidelines for using copyrighted materials in their classrooms. Schools can interpret copyright issues differently, so school policies concerning the use of copyrighted materials vary widely.

Teachers need to read school policies concerning copyright carefully and understand them.

In addition to providing printed school policies on copyright issues, most schools have two individuals who provide teachers with information and answer questions about copyright issues. For information or answers to questions concerning software copyright issues, teachers should ask their school or district technology coordinator. For all other issues concerning copyright, fair use, and associated school district policies, teachers should speak with their media specialist. Media specialists receive training on copyright issues and deal with them on a daily basis. If in doubt, teachers should contact the creator of the

WebInfo

■ To learn more about Fair Use, visit the Teachers Discovering Computers Chapter 8 WebInfo page (www.scsite.com/tdc/ch8/webinfo.htm) and click Fair Use.

U.S. Copyright Law: Fair Use

(U.S. Code, Title 17, Chapter 1, Section 107)

§ 107. Limitations on exclusive rights: Fair use

Notwithstanding the provisions of sections 106 and 106A, the fair use of a copyrighted work, including such use by reproduction in copies or phonorecords or by any other means specified by that section, for purposes such as criticism, comment, news reporting, teaching (including multiple copies for classroom use), scholarship, or research, is not an infringement of copyright. In determining whether the use made of a work in any particular case is a fair use, the factors to be considered shall include:

(1) the purpose and character of the use, including whether such use is of a commercial nature or is for nonprofit educational purposes;

(2) the nature of the copyrighted work;

(3) the amount and substantiality of the portion used in relation to the copyrighted work as a whole; and

(4) the effect of the use upon the potential market for or value of the copyrighted work. The fact that a work is unpublished shall not itself bar a finding of fair use if such finding is made upon consideration of all the above factors.

Figure 8-19 Section 107 of The Copyright Act of 1976, which defines Fair Use.

work and ask for written permission to use his or her material.

Fair use guidelines apply to copyrighted materials on the Internet just as they apply to a copyrighted article published in a magazine. Basically, Web sites include two kinds of information: original copyrighted information and information without copyright restriction. Web pages that contain original information generally include a copyright statement at the bottom of the page; the copyright statement normally contains the copyright symbol, year, and creator's name **[Figure 8-20]**.

If a teacher uses copyrighted materials from the Internet, he or she must follow fair use guidelines, school policies, and any restrictions listed on the Web site. If the information located on the Web site does not include copyright restriction, it does not mean the creator is waiving his or her privileges under copyright. To be safe, you should assume everything on the Web is copyrighted and always follow fair use guidelines and school policies when using Web materials for educational purposes in a classroom. In addition, you always should give proper credit and use citations, if appropriate.

These guidelines do not apply only to text-based materials on the Web. The Web also contains a multitude of graphics, animations, and audio and video files teachers can download and use for educational purposes or classroom presentations. When teachers download and use these materials, they must adhere to fair use guidelines, school policies, and any other restrictions noted on the Web site. Also, teachers always should scan all downloaded files for viruses.

Teacher and Student Web Pages Teachers and students in school districts all over the country are creating and publishing their own Web pages **[Figure 8-21]**. As previously discussed, **Web publishing** is the development and maintenance of Web pages. When developing these pages, teachers and students must take care to respect copyright laws and follow the guidelines outlined in the previous section.

Copyright laws do protect any original materials created by students and teachers and published on the Web. To ensure that this is clear, however, teachers and students may want to include a copyright statement at the bottom of their home page.

The use of copyrighted materials (text, graphics, animations, audio, and video) on

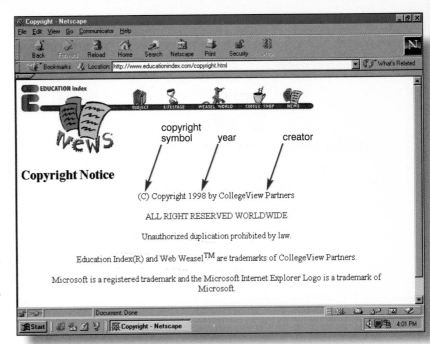

Figure 8-20 This educational Web page has a copyright statement. The copyright statement includes basic copyright information as well as the company contact information and other information.

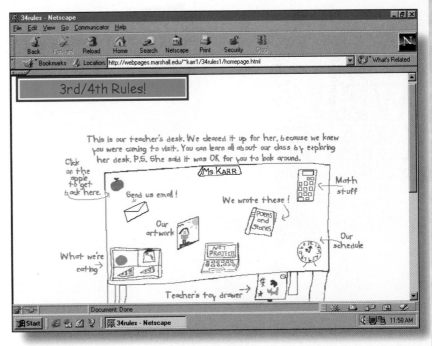

Figure 8-21 Teachers and students in school districts all over the country are creating and publishing their own Web pages.

CHAPTER 8

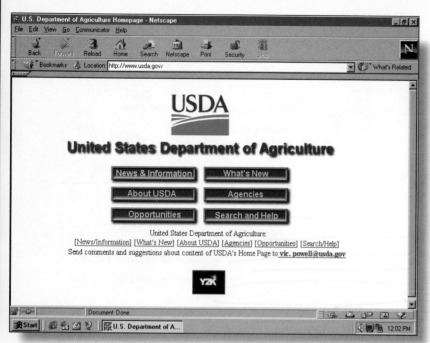

Figure 8-22 An example of a public domain government Web page. Government Web pages usually have a URL that ends in .gov.

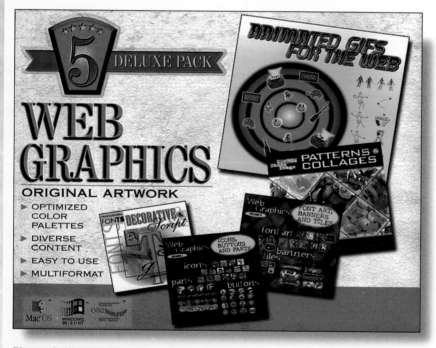

Figure 8-23 Web Graphics is a popular software package that provides teachers and students with thousands of graphics they can use on their published Web pages.

teacher or student Web pages requires permission from the creator of the materials. Most Web pages include an e-mail link to use when asking for permission to use copyrighted materials. To use the materials on the Web, simply send a short e-mail message to the creator of the work, explaining how you will use his or her work on your Web page. Many authors are more than willing to allow teachers to use their original text or artwork for educational purposes as long as they receive proper credit.

Many school districts have specific guidelines that teachers and students must follow when publishing Web pages on school servers. Teachers should carefully read all school rules prior to publishing any teacher or student Web pages. Some schools, for example, prohibit using any copyrighted materials on Web pages. In such instances, students and teachers must use only original material or material that is not copyrighted. The school district may provide it, or it may be from government-sponsored Web sites, which are considered public domain **[Figure 8-22]**. Anything considered **public domain** — including software or creative works — is free from copyright restrictions.

School districts are also purchasing copyright-free CD-ROMs that contain thousands of clipart images, graphics, and audio and video clips for teachers and students to use on their Web pages and in class presentations and projects **[Figure 8-23]**. In addition to respecting copyright law, teachers also must consider other issues related to Web page publishing. Teachers, for example, must protect their students from Internet users who might want to harm them. **Figure 8-24** lists some basic guidelines that teachers should consider when creating Web pages.

Internet Ethics and Objectionable Materials

As you already have learned in this chapter, the widespread use of the Internet — especially in today's schools and classrooms — raises many issues regarding security, privacy, and ethics. Of all of these, one issue is of particular concern for teachers and parents: the availability of **objectionable material** on the Internet, including racist literature, obscene pictures and videos, and even gambling.

Guidelines

- Always protect the identity of your students.

- Never list student last names, telephone numbers, home addresses, or e-mail addresses.

- Use only first names of students on a Web site, but never in conjunction with other identifying information, such as a photograph.

- Use caution when including digital pictures of classrooms; avoid pictures that show close-ups of students.

- Never provide links to sites that are not appropriate for K-12 students or educational settings.

- List the function of all linked Web pages. Link only to pages that inform, explain, or teach a concept or curriculum area to students. Beware of linking to Web sites that persuade students.

- Avoid providing links to sites whose primary purpose is selling non-educational products and services, unless relevant to the subject under discussion.

- Avoid linking to Web pages that are not updated on a regular basis.

- Provide links to sites that help you achieve instructional and curriculum goals.

- Avoid discussing controversial issues on your Web site or linking to Web sites that discuss controversial issues.

- Carefully read and follow all guideline and policies that your school district provides.

WebInfo

- For more information on Web page guidelines, visit the Teachers Discovering Computers Chapter 8 WebInfo page

(www.scsite.com/tdc/ ch8/webinfo.htm)

and click Guidelines.

Figure 8-24 Guidelines that teachers should consider when creating teacher and student Web pages.

Teachers and other school personnel must be concerned with three different types of Internet materials that fall under the general term, objectionable material. The first area includes all materials that most people consider pornographic, such as obscene pictures, stories, graphics, articles, cartoons, and videos. The second area includes racist literature, controversial subjects such as gambling, and other similar materials. Teachers and parents usually easily identify Web sites that contain materials in these first two areas.

The third area includes Web sites that contain incorrect material and thus are inappropriate for K-12 students. Identifying this type of Web page is more difficult than identifying the first two. Because anyone may create and publish a Web page or Web site, some people deliberately create and publish materials on Web pages to fool unsuspecting people. Young students are extremely vulnerable to being fooled by these sites. These Web sites appear perfectly appropriate for K-12

students, but contain information that is historically and otherwise inaccurate. An elementary student may not know the difference between a site that is historically inaccurate about our founding fathers and an educational site that is accurate.

Prior to the explosive growth of the Internet, it was difficult for most K-12 students to obtain and view objectionable materials, such as pornographic magazines. Today, anybody with Internet access may view a vast array of obscene and other inappropriate materials on the Web. Many people want to ban such materials from the Internet, while others would only restrict objectionable materials so they are not available to minors. Opponents argue that banning any material violates the constitutional right of free speech. Instead of limiting Internet access and materials, state these opponents, schools should teach students right from wrong.

While the ethical debate continues, many K-12 schools and parents have taken proactive

CHAPTER 8

steps to protect their students and children from the negative aspects of the Internet. While only a small percentage of the information available on the Internet is unsuitable for children at home or in K-12 schools, educators agree that such materials have no place in our classrooms. Teachers and parents need to ensure that children understand inappropriate materials exist on the Internet, and some individuals may try to exploit them via e-mail messages or in chat room conversations.

Federal Government and Organizational Controls

Responding to pressure for restrictions, President Clinton signed the **Communications Decency Act** in February 1996, making it a criminal offense to distribute indecent or patently offensive material online. Opponents appealed immediately and, in June 1996, the law was declared unconstitutional. Today, the U.S. government and the governments of other nations continue to explore ways to prevent or limit objectionable materials from being distributed on the Internet.

Many organizations and businesses also recognize that individuals and companies need specific standards for the ethical use of computers and information systems. To help establish these standards, a number of computer-related organizations established **codes of conduct**, which are written guidelines that help determine whether a specific computer action is ethical or unethical **[Figure 8-25]**. Many businesses adopt codes of conduct and make them known to their employees. Establishing codes of conduct that apply to an entire organization helps employees make ethical decisions by providing a standard against which they can measure their actions.

Parental Controls

Parents may take a number of steps to prevent children from accessing pornographic and other objectionable materials on the Internet. First, parents need to ensure that their children understand some Internet sites contain objectionable materials, and some people who use the Internet would like to harm them.

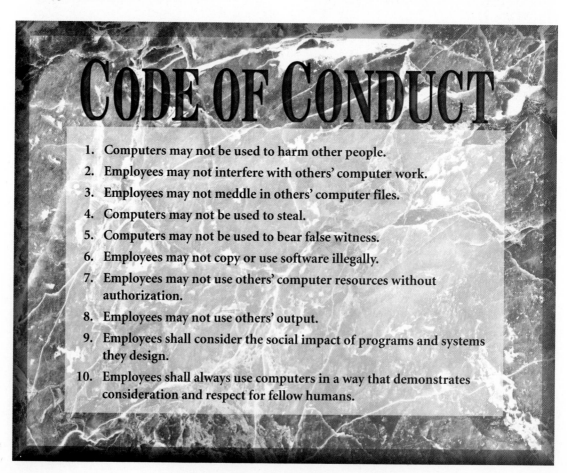

CODE OF CONDUCT

1. Computers may not be used to harm other people.
2. Employees may not interfere with others' computer work.
3. Employees may not meddle in others' computer files.
4. Computers may not be used to steal.
5. Computers may not be used to bear false witness.
6. Employees may not copy or use software illegally.
7. Employees may not use others' computer resources without authorization.
8. Employees may not use others' output.
9. Employees shall consider the social impact of programs and systems they design.
10. Employees shall always use computers in a way that demonstrates consideration and respect for fellow humans.

Figure 8-25 An example of a code of conduct that an employer may distribute to employees.

One approach to restricting access to certain material uses a rating system similar to those used for videos, movies, and television shows. The rating system is understood by your Web browser, which allows you to set limits on the types of material available for viewing [**Figure 8-26**]. If content at the Web site goes beyond the rating limitations you set in the Web browser, the site will not display. You prevent the rating limitations from being changed by using a password.

content their Web browser will display. America Online, for example, allows home users to establish different accounts for adults and children. When a user logs on using the child's account, only appropriate pages will display.

Another protective measure parents and schools may take is to install programs that prevent children from accidentally providing personal information in e-mail messages or in chat rooms.

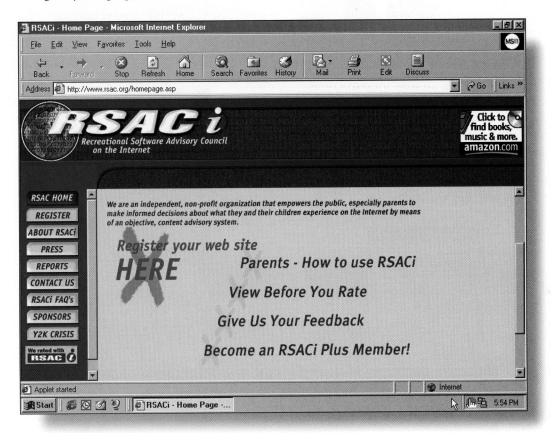

Figure 8-26 Many Web browsers use the ratings of the Recreational Software Advisory Council on the Internet (RSACi), which allows you to specify a rating level for material unsuitable for minors.

A more effective approach to blocking objectionable materials is for parents to install filtering software programs on any computer with Internet access. As you learned in Chapter 2, **filtering software programs** prevent your browser from displaying materials from targeted sites or that contain certain keywords or phrases. Popular filter programs such as NetShepherd, NetNanny, SurfWatch, and SafeSurf are shown in **Figure 8-27** on the next page.

Many Internet service providers also provide software that allows users to control the

One such program, CyberPatrol, shown on the next page in **Figure 8-28**, allows parents to enter sensitive information, such as names, phone numbers, addresses, and credit card numbers, into the software program. If a child enters any of these protected words or numbers in an e-mail message or during a chat room conversation, the software program substitutes a series of Xs for the protected words or numbers.

Finally, the best way for parents to protect children is to monitor their children's activities while on the Internet both by direct and indirect observations.

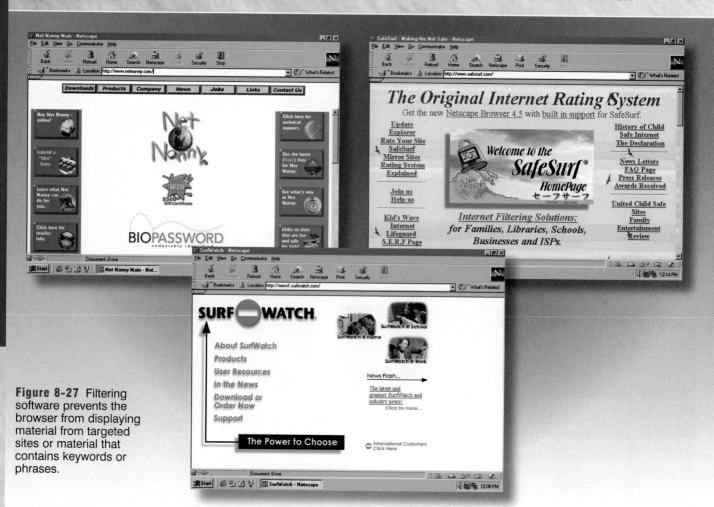

Figure 8-27 Filtering software prevents the browser from displaying material from targeted sites or material that contains keywords or phrases.

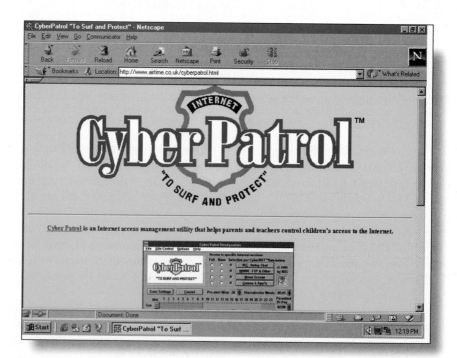

Figure 8-28 Some filtering software programs can be set to prevent children from giving out sensitive information, such as names, phone numbers, addresses, and credit card numbers over the Internet.

Because it is difficult to always monitor or observe children's Internet activities directly, you can check which Internet sites children are visiting by viewing the browser's history list. The history list may be set to record information on all the sites visited for any number of previous days [**Figure 8-29**]. This simple, but effective technique, however, is useless if children are able to clear the history list.

Filtering Software As previously discussed, filtering software programs prevent the browser from accepting material from targeted sites or material that contains keywords or phrases. Schools install Internet filtering software on their networks and then constantly update the software programs to keep them as current as possible. While very effective, these filtering software programs do not prevent

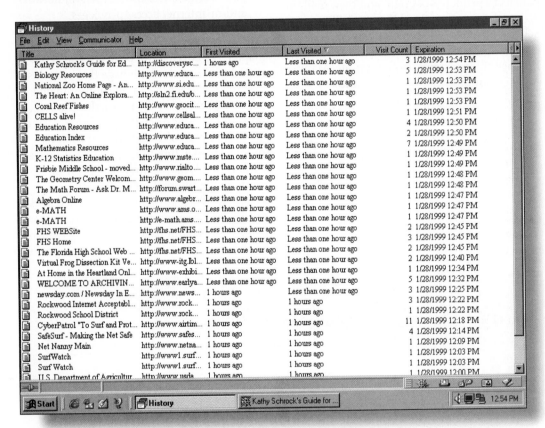

Figure 8-29 A browser's history list records information on all the sites visited for a predetermined number of days.

Educational Controls

As you have learned, businesses and parents have several available options to use to control access to inappropriate Internet sites. Most school districts also control student access to objectionable materials by implementing these controls and a few additional ones. For schools, attacking this problem uses a four-pronged approach: filtering software, Acceptable Use Policies, use of curriculum pages, and teacher observation. All four prongs of the approach are discussed in the following sections.

access to all objectionable and inappropriate materials. Filtering software programs is the first level of protection that many school districts use.

Acceptable Use Policies Recognizing that teachers, students, administrators, and staff personnel need guidance, most schools develop specific standards for the ethical use of computers, school networks, and the Internet. These standards are called Acceptable Use Policies. As discussed in Chapter 1, an **Acceptable Use Policy (AUP)** is a set of rules that governs the use of school and school district computers, networks, and the Internet by teachers, administrators, staff, and students.

Acceptable Use Policies vary greatly from school district to school district. Many schools have separate AUPs for students, teachers, and staff personnel. Many school districts require both students and their parents to sign student AUPs. Some schools publish student AUPs on their Web sites, which allows new students and parents to print, review, sign, and then mail or deliver them to the school **[Figure 8-30]**. Schools normally will not allow students or teachers to access the school's network or Internet unless a signed AUP is on file. Many AUPs contain the following guidelines:

- Notice that use of school networks and the Internet is a privilege, not a right

- Notice that students should behave as guests when on the Internet — that is, they should use good manners and be courteous

- List of rules concerning accessing objectionable Internet sites

- List of rules dealing with copyright issues

- Outline of proper use of all networks and computers

- List of rules covering online safety and release of personal information

- Notice that students who violate AUPs will face disciplinary action and possible permanent cancellation of school network and/or Internet access privileges

Curriculum Pages   As you learned in Chapter 7, a **curriculum page** is a teacher-created document or Web page that contains hyperlinks to teacher-chosen-and-evaluated Web sites that match the curriculum, goals, and learning indicators of their classes. Using a curriculum page offers several advantages. Students quickly link to excellent sites, instead of the varied locations they may get from searching the Internet for information. Because the teacher evaluates the linked sites for content and appropriateness before posting them, a curriculum page significantly reduces the chance students will view an inappropriate

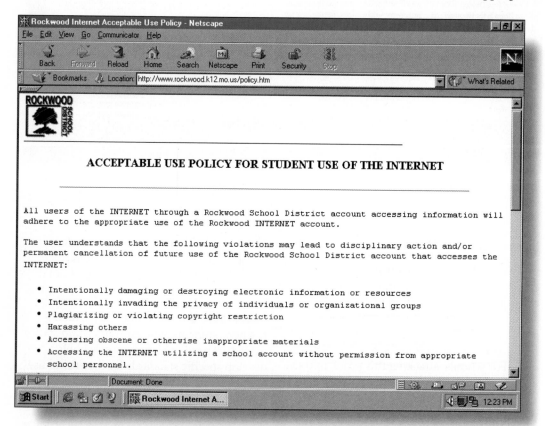

Figure 8-30 Many schools include AUPs on their Web sites, so that new teachers, students, and parents can print and review, sign, and mail or deliver them to the school.

site. Furthermore, by providing links for students to click, a curriculum page eliminates the need for students to type URLs. Students often make mistakes typing in URLs, which, in addition to wasting time, sometimes link them to inappropriate or incorrect sites.

Teacher Observation Teacher observation or supervision permits teachers to actively and continuously monitor their students while they are on the Internet [Figure 8-31]. Teacher observation is extremely important and, in most cases, a final measure to prevent students from accessing objectionable and inappropriate materials on the Internet. For teacher observation to be effective, teachers must constantly and actively watch what their students are doing in the classroom and viewing on the Internet. Teachers should direct students that, if they access an Internet site that contains objectionable material, they should immediately click their browser's Back button to return to the previous page or simply close the browser. Either is a quick and easy way to prevent objectionable material from displaying in the browser. You also may want students to notify you if such a situation arises, so that you may add that site to the sites restricted by the filtering software.

As a final note, all educators should understand clearly the ethical issues covered in this chapter in order to model these concepts for their students and teach them to be ethical computer users. The questionnaire shown in **Figure 8-32** on the next page will help you further understand these ethical concepts.

Emerging Technologies

The classrooms and schools you attended throughout your twelve years of K-12 education probably were similar to the classrooms in which your parents sat — for some of you, the schools and furniture were exactly the same. More importantly, your educational experience and the educational experiences of your parents also probably were very similar. Unlike society, which has dramatically changed, many schools and school curriculum have been slow to change during the past few decades.

Fortunately, the infusion of modern multimedia computers, high-speed networks and Internet access, higher-quality educational software, and a realization by administrators that teachers must receive extensive and appropriate technology training is beginning to transform many classrooms. In some cases, the transformation is remarkable.

Figure 8-31 Teacher observations can prevent students from viewing objectionable or inappropriate material on the Internet.

Figure 8-32 Indicate whether you think the described situation is ethical, unethical, or a crime. Discuss your answers with other teachers as well as your students.

Computer Ethics

	Ethical	Unethical	Crime
1. A teacher uses her computer at school to send e-mail to her friends and family.	☐	☐	☐
2. A teacher uses the Web at school to access stock market reports. So that he can periodically check the market, he leaves the Web connection running in the background all day.	☐	☐	☐
3. A principal installs a new version of a word processing program on her office computer. Because no one will be using the old version of the program, she takes it home and installs it on her home computer so her husband and children can use it.	☐	☐	☐
4. While checking teachers' e-mail messages, the principal finds that one of his teachers is using the district's e-mail system to bet on football games.	☐	☐	☐
5. A school technology facilitator has his students develop HyperStudio tutorials. When the projects are completed, he offers to sell the tutorials to another school.	☐	☐	☐
6. A principal tells a teacher to install a piece of software on numerous computers on campus. The teacher knows the software has a single user license, but because the principal said to install it, he does.	☐	☐	☐
7. Personnel in the district's computer center occasionally monitor computer use in the schools. They monitor how often and for what lengths of time particular teachers are connected to the Internet, as well as what sites have been visited.	☐	☐	☐
8. The media specialist uses photo retouching software to put her school name on another school's logo.	☐	☐	☐
9. A teacher downloads a piece of shareware software. He uses it for the allotted time and when asked to pay for the software, he simply closes the window and continues to use it.	☐	☐	☐
10. An educational learning company contacts a principal requesting information on students, including names and addresses. The company offers to provide students with free learning supplements. The principal sends the company her student database.	☐	☐	☐
11. Your students are creating Web pages of their own. They search the Internet for ideas. One of them finds a very cool home page and decides to copy the page, change the name, and use it.	☐	☐	☐
12. You are doing a unit on famous cartoon characters and go to the Disney Web site to get clip art for your curriculum page.	☐	☐	☐

Due to the infusion of informational technologies and the World Wide Web, teachers are no longer bound by the four walls of traditional classrooms and the two covers of traditional textbooks [Figure 8-33]. Furthermore, technology has helped a number of schools significantly improve the quality of their graduates.

Because of the strong commitment of federal, state, and local governments, thousands of organizations dedicated to improving education, and millions of concerned parents, the infusion of computer technologies into schools will continue — and continue explosively. Technology has only begun to influence the way teachers instruct and students learn. The following sections summarize five emerging areas of educational technology that will continue to significantly influence our system of public education: the World Wide Web, the next generation of software on DVDs, assistive technologies, Web-enhanced textbooks, and Web-based training and distance learning.

The World Wide Web

In 1996, only a small percentage of K-12 schools and public libraries had Internet access; even fewer classrooms had Internet access. In two years, at the start of the 1998 school year, the majority of K-12 schools and public libraries had Internet connections — and more are soon to follow. The federal government is committed to ensuring that every K-12 classroom has high-speed Internet access and is investing billions of dollars to meet the goal. The following specific Internet improvements will directly influence the quality of the K-12 educational experience:

- The speed of the Internet will increase dramatically.

- Students will be able to access full-motion videos on demand. Streaming video technology will allow teachers to bring live video footage of current and historical events into their classrooms, simply by clicking a video link. Teachers and students will have thousands of videos from which to choose.

Figure 8-33 The Web has enormous potential to change the way teachers instruct and students learn due to the vast amount of current and education-related information available at thousands of Web sites.

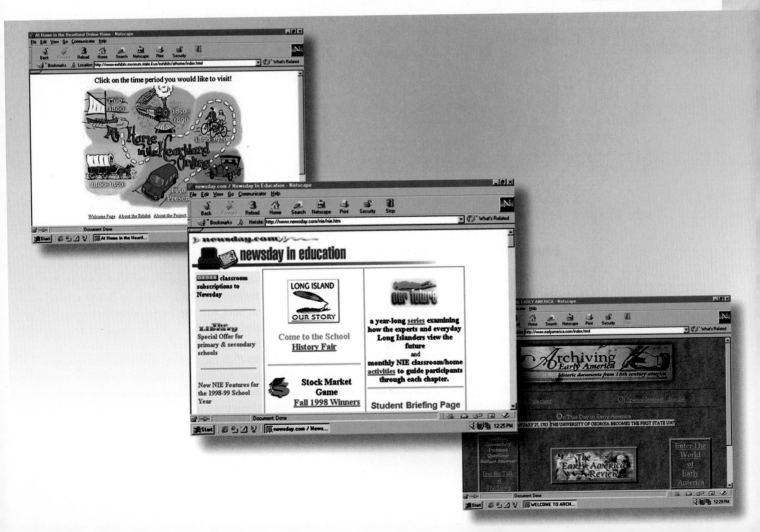

■ Teachers and students will have instant access to tens of thousands of interactive Web-based educational programs, including tutorials, exercises, virtual reality tours, science experiments, and other subject-related activities. Many of these online educational programs will be fully interactive, thus opening up incredible opportunities for discovery learning [**Figure 8-34**].

information, graphics, animations, video, and interactive links. These next-generation educational software programs on DVDs will include hours of high quality full-motion video that teachers and students may access instantly.

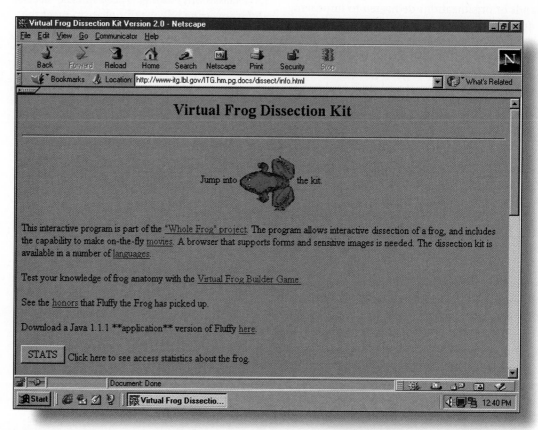

Figure 8-34 Many educational Web sites are offering students and teachers opportunities to explore education topics interactively. This Web site, for example, allows students to actually dissect a frog, just as if they were in a school biology lab.

Educational Software on DVD-ROM

During the last five years, the influx of multimedia computers with CD-ROM drives and the availability of hundreds of high-quality CD-ROM-based educational software programs impacted education significantly.

During the next five years, the availability of DVD-based education software programs will have an even greater impact on education. The huge storage capacity of the DVD-ROM will allow educational software developers to build programs that contain vast amounts of

Assistive Technologies

Dramatic improvements are being made in hardware, software, and Web-based tools that teachers will use to help instruct students with special needs. As you learned earlier, **assistive technologies** are innovative technologies that modify or adapt the classroom for special learning needs. Assistive technologies aid in teaching students who are visually or hearing impaired, have Down's syndrome, cerebral palsy, or other needs that make learning challenging. Emerging assistive technologies will provide teachers with new and innovative tools to help students with special needs overcome the disability that blocks or impedes their learning process.

Nationwide, funding for assistive technologies is increasing significantly. Teacher education programs and K-12 schools are placing more emphasis on assistive technologies, due to the number of students with disabilities who are mainstreamed into regular classrooms. According to the Individuals with Disabilities Act (IDEA) Amendment of 1997, regular classroom teachers must be part of the cross-curriculum and interdisciplinary team that teaches all students. Technology is the bridge that provides new strategies for all students to learn and succeed **[Figure 8-35]**.

In addition, many leaders express concern that current technologies are widening the gap between the economic haves and have-nots. Federal funding, private funding, and emerging technologies will help slow this crisis facing America. Schools will be provided funding and guidance to ensure that at-risk students have equal access to current and emerging technologies.

Figure 8-35 Technology can be the bridge that provides new strategies for all students to learn and succeed, including students with physical and other challenges.

Web-Enhanced Textbooks

For many years, K-12 textbooks remained basically unchanged. Recently, however, this began to change as the Web became an integral part of K-12 textbooks. Traditional textbooks will fade into history as all areas of education create increasingly interactive and extensive Web-enhanced textbooks. Many of these textbooks will correlate to national and state curriculum standards and benchmarks.

Imagine teaching social studies, biology, or English literature using a Web-enhanced textbook with an extensive Web site that is continuously updated and maintained by a team of experienced educators and provides students with discovery learning avenues and information on thousands of topics from thousands of sources all over the world. These exciting and interactive Web-enhanced textbooks will crumble the concrete and brick walls of traditional classrooms and remove the covers of traditional textbooks.

Web-Based Distance Learning

Due to the increasingly diverse population of students, education is changing in an effort to meet the needs of this dissimilar and changing student body. These changes bring the Web to the forefront of instructional strategies in education — specifically, the use of Web-based distance learning.

Web-based distance learning has already experienced phenomenal growth in institutions of higher education, and it is just beginning to emerge as an additional option K-12 schools use to improve the quality of their students. During the past few years, a few newly opened high schools began to provide students with all of their instruction via the Web. The more common approach for schools to take, however, is to use the Web to enhance classes and instruction.

These Web-based teaching strategies are new and will continue to evolve for many years. Web-based strategies offer creative solutions for homebound students, home-schooled students, at-risk students, students who are physically challenged, and shortages of teachers for specialized positions. Because many small or rural schools cannot offer students courses such as Latin, French, or

WebInfo

To see an example of a Web-enhanced science textbook, visit the Teachers Discovering Computers Chapter 8 WebInfo page

(www.scsite.com/tdc/ch8/webinfo.htm)

and click Textbook.

WebInfo

To learn more about a Web-enhanced high-school class, visit the Teachers Discovering Computers Chapter 8 WebInfo page

(www.scsite.com/tdc/ch8/webinfo.htm)

and click Class.

WebInfo

🔲 To learn more about a Web-based high school, visit the Teachers Discovering Computers Chapter 8 WebInfo page **(www.scsite.com/tdc/ch8/webinfo.htm)** and click High School.

advanced placement courses in math and science, states and school districts now offer students these specialized courses using the Web. Depending upon the situation and school district policies, students take these Web-based courses at home, at a public library, or in a classroom — Internet access is the common agent for this remote instruction **[Figure 8-36]**.

employees, teachers, and students also have an obligation to use computers responsibly and not abuse the power computers provide. This responsibility presents constant challenges, which sometimes weigh the rights of the individual against increased efficiency and productivity. Schools have the added responsibility and challenge of protecting their students from unethical practices and people.

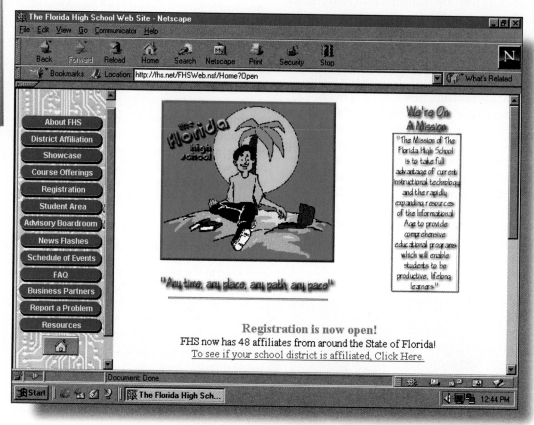

Figure 8-36 Web-based distance learning is just beginning to be used by K-12 schools. The Florida High School project, for example, will allow students to take all high school courses online by 2001. All courses will be approved by the state and tied to national and state standards.

Summary of Security Issues, Ethics, and Emerging Technologies in Education

The livelihood of businesses, schools, and individuals depends on the computers and networks Americans use every day. This increased reliance on computers and information sent over networks makes it essential to take steps to protect the systems and information from known risks. At the same time,

The computer is a tool whose effectiveness is determined by the knowledge, skill, experience, level of training, and ethics of the user. The computer knowledge you acquire should help you be better able to participate in decisions on how to use computers, other educational technologies, and the Internet efficiently and ethically.

Summary of Teachers Discovering Computers

To be effective in using technology in their classrooms, teachers must be computer literate, information literate, and most importantly, integration literate. This textbook provided you with knowledge and skills in all three areas. What you have learned is only a beginning.

Teachers must continuously update their technology and technology-integration skills. The teachers of America have an incredible responsibility — a far greater responsibility than any previous generation of teachers. The amount of knowledge that teachers must instill in their students is enormous and continues to expand at a phenomenal rate. To continue to prosper in the twenty-first century, educational institutions must provide America's students with a solid foundation of the basic skills and other core subjects. Used as instructional and productivity tools, current and emerging technologies help teachers make a difference in the quality of their students. Teachers will be able to use and integrate technology to influence future generations in immensely positively ways — the possibilities really are limitless [Figure 8-37].

Figure 8-37 Teachers make a difference in the quality of their students' education when they integrate technology effectively.

1 2 3 4 5 6 7 8

www.scsite.com/tdc/ch8/brief.htm

InBrief

InBrief

KeyTerms

AtTheMovies

CheckPoint

TeacherTime

CyberClass

EdIssues

NetStuff

SPECIAL FEATURES

TimeLine 2000

Guide to WWW Sites

Buyer's Guide 2000

Educational Sites

State/Federal Sites

Chat

News

Home

Web Instructions: To display this page from the Web, launch your browser and enter the URL, www.scsite.com/tdc/ch8/brief.htm. Click the links for current and additional information. To listen to an audio version of this InBrief, click the Audio button below the title, InBrief, at the top of the page. To play the audio, RealPlayer must be installed on your computer (download by clicking here).

1. Computer Security Risks

A **computer security risk is** any event or action that can cause a loss of computer equipment, software, data and information, or processing capability or damage to them. A **computer crime** is any illegal act involving a computer.

2. Computer Viruses

A **computer virus** is designed to affect computers negatively by altering the way they work. Many viruses are designed to destroy or corrupt data. A **boot sector virus** replaces the boot program used to start the computer with a modified, infected version of the boot program. A **file virus** inserts virus code into program files. A **Trojan horse virus** hides

within or is designed to look like a legitimate program. A **macro virus** uses the macro language of an application to hide virus codes.

3. Virus Detection and Removal

Antivirus programs are designed to detect, disinfect, and protect computers and networks from viruses. Antivirus programs work by looking for programs that attempt to modify the boot program, the operating system, and other programs that normally are read from but not written to. Most antivirus programs also have utilities to remove or repair infected programs and files.

4. Unauthorized Access and Use

Unauthorized access is the use of a computer or network without permission. The term, **cracker** or **hacker,** refers to a person who tries to break into a computer often with the intent of stealing or corrupting its data. **Unauthorized use** is the use of a computer or data for unapproved or possibly illegal activities. Unauthorized access is prevented by establishing **access controls**, which are security measures that define who may access a computer or information.

5. Theft

Common sense and a constant awareness of the risks are the best preventive measures against theft of laptop computers and other portable equipment. **Software piracy** is the unauthorized and illegal duplication of copyrighted software. Software piracy

is a violation of copyright law and is a federal crime. A **software license** is an agreement that provides specific conditions for use of the software, which users must accept before using the software.

6. System Failure

A **system failure** is a malfunction of a computer system. System failures occur because of electrical power problems, hardware component failure, or a software error. An **undervoltage** occurs when the electrical power supply drops. An **overvoltage**, or **power surge**, occurs when the incoming electrical power increases significantly above the normal 120 volts. A **surge protector** keeps an overvoltage from damaging computer equipment.

7. Copyright Laws

The Copyright Act of 1976 applies to all creative works. A **copyright** means the original author or creator of the work retains exclusive ownership of the work. **Fair use** guidelines allow educators to use and copy certain copyrighted materials for non-profit educational purposes.

8. Internet Ethics

Objectionable materials on the Internet include racist literature and obscene pictures and videos. **Codes of conduct** are written guidelines that help determine whether a specific computer action is ethical or unethical. **Filtering software programs** prevent browsers from displaying materials from targeted sites or materials that contain certain keywords or phrases.

9. Educational Controls

<u>Controls</u> to prevent student access to inappropriate Internet sites include filtering software, Acceptable Use Policies, use of curriculum pages, and teacher observation. An **Acceptable Use Policy (AUP)** is a set of rules that governs the use of school and school district computers, networks, and the Internet. A **curriculum page** is a teacher-created document or Web page that contains links to teacher-chosen-and-evaluated Web sites that match curriculum goals. **Teacher observation** involves teachers actively and continuously monitoring their students while they are on the Internet.

10. Emerging Technologies

Emerging educational technologies that will significantly influence public education include the World Wide Web, the next generation of software on DVDs, <u>assistive technologies</u>, Web-enhanced textbooks, and Web-based training.

- InBrief
- KeyTerms
- AtTheMovies
- CheckPoint
- TeacherTime
- CyberClass
- EdIssues
- NetStuff

SPECIAL FEATURES

- TimeLine 2000
- Guide to WWW Sites
- Buyer's Guide 2000
- Educational Sites
- State/Federal Sites
- Chat
- News
- Home

KeyTerms

Web Instructions: To display this page from the Web, launch your browser and enter the URL, www.scsite.com/tdc/ch8/terms.htm. Scroll through the list of terms. Click a term to display its definition and a picture. Click KeyTerms on the left to redisplay the KeyTerms page. Click the TO WEB button for current and additional information about the term from the Web. To see animations, Shockwave and Flash Player must be installed on your computer (download by clicking here).

Acceptable Use Policy (AUP) **[8.25]**
access controls **[8.6]**
antivirus program **[8.4]**
assistive technologies **[8.30]**

backup **[8.13]**
backup procedure **[8.14]**
blackout **[8.12]**
boot sector virus **[8.2]**
brownout **[8.12]**

codes of conduct **[8.22]**
Communications Decency Act **[8.22]**
community site license **[8.10]**
computer crime **[8.2]**
computer ethics **[8.14]**
computer security risk **[8.2]**
computer vandalism **[8.8]**
computer virus **[8.2]**
copyright **[8.17]**
cracker **[8.6]**
curriculum page **[8.26]**

electronic profile **[8.16]**
employee monitoring **[8.17]**
encryption **[8.11]**
encryption key **[8.11]**
end-user license agreement (EULA) **[8.9]**
ethics **[8.14]**

fair use **[8.18]**
file virus **[8.2]**
filtering software programs **[8.23]**
freeware **[8.10]**

hacker **[8.6]**

information privacy **[8.15]**

logic bomb **[8.3]**

macro virus **[8.2]**
Michelangelo virus **[8.3]**

network site license **[8.10]**

objectionable material **[8.20]**
offsite location **[8.14]**
overvoltage **[8.12]**

power surge **[8.12]**
public domain **[8.20]**

rescue disk **[8.4]**
restore **[8.13]**

shareware **[8.9]**
single-user license **[8.9]**
site license **[8.10]**
software license **[8.9]**
software piracy **[8.8]**
spike **[8.12]**
surge protector **[8.12]**
system failure **[8.12]**

teacher observation **[8.27]**
time bomb **[8.3]**
Trojan horse virus **[8.2]**

unauthorized access **[8.6]**
unauthorized use **[8.6]**
undervoltage **[8.12]**
uninterruptable power supply (UPS) **[8.13]**

vaccines **[8.4]**
virus hoaxes **[8.6]**
virus payload **[8.2]**

Web publishing **[8.19]**

www.scsite.com/tdc/ch8/movies.htm

Web Instructions: To display this page from the Web, launch your browser and enter the URL, www.scsite.com/tdc/ch8/movies.htm. Click a picture to view a video. After watching the video, close the video window and then complete the exercise by answering the questions about the video. To view the videos, RealPlayer must be installed on your computer (download by clicking here).

AtTheMovies
WELCOME to
VIDEO CLIPS
from CNN

- InBrief
- KeyTerms
- AtTheMovies
- CheckPoint
- TeacherTime
- CyberClass
- EdIssues
- NetStuff

SPECIAL FEATURES

- TimeLine 2000
- Guide to WWW Sites
- Buyer's Guide 2000
- Educational Sites
- State/Federal Sites
- Chat
- News
- Home

1. Biz Software Snoop

Employee monitoring involves the use of computers to observe, record, and review an individual's use of a computer, including game playing, e-mail, keyboard activity, and Internet sites visited. Is employee monitoring ethical? How much money do firms lose each year due to workers playing games or doing personal tasks during work time? Some suggest that this is not a new problem — workers always have spent some time at work being unproductive. Do you think computers have made the situation better or worse? If you knew your school used employee monitoring, how might it alter your behavior? Discuss with your students or other teachers some of the negative repercussions for either the employer or the employee involved in computer monitoring.

2. Internet Crimes

Inappropriate adult dialog with minors often takes place in chat rooms on the Internet. Unfortunately, clandestine meetings sometimes result from these online conversations. This video indicates that these incidents on the adults' part are categorized as "Predatory Adult Behavior." When you log onto a chat room, should it be illegal to use a false identity (name, gender, age, etc)? What precautions can a school or parent take to restrict access to sites? What tips would you offer? According to the video, to whom on the Web can you report inappropriate behavior?

3. Library Censors

Many libraries are concerned about providing access to objectionable materials on the Internet to children from computers located on library premises. As a result, some librarians are using filtering software and other approaches to limit and monitor the sites accessed from library computers. Critics consider this censorship. Do you think filtering software can prevent worthwhile research on censored sites? Why or why not? If you were a librarian and had to choose an Internet-filtering approach, which would you advocate and why? What are the downfalls of the approaches currently in use? In your opinion, should filtering software be used at both public and school libraries? Would filtering software need to be used at all school levels, or just in elementary, middle, or junior high schools? What is the reasoning behind your opinion for filter use in the schools?

www.scsite.com/tdc/ch8/check.htm

InBrief

KeyTerms

AtTheMovies

CheckPoint

TeacherTime

CyberClass

EdIssues

NetStuff

SPECIAL FEATURES

TimeLine 2000

Guide to WWW Sites

Buyer's Guide 2000

Educational Sites

State/Federal Sites

Chat

News

Home

CheckPoint

Web Instructions: To display this page from the Web, launch your browser and enter the URL, www.scsite.com/tdc/ch8/check.htm. Click a blank line for the answer. Click the links for current and additional information. To experience the animation and interactivity, Shockwave and Flash Player must be installed on your computer (download by clicking here).

1. Label the Figure

Instructions: Identify each type of software license.

Type of License	Characteristics	Use in Schools
1. _____	Can be installed on only one computer.	Used when a school needs only a few copies of a particular software. Commonly found in small schools and when purchasing specialized software programs.
2. _____	Software can be installed on a set number of computers, typically 5, 10, 50, or more.	Cost-effective method to install software on more than one computer. Commonly found in schools.
3. _____	Software is installed on the school's network. The license will specify and the software will control a specific number of simultaneous users, such as 50, 100, 250, or 500.	Cost-effective method of allowing students and teachers throughout the school to have access to an application software program.
4. _____ _____	Frequently used with software distributed on CD-ROMs or DVD-ROMs. Any number of programs can be purchased for either Macintosh or PC platforms.	Very cost-effective method for schools to purchase large quantities of software. Savings can be significant over individual CD-ROM or DVD-ROM pricing.

2. Matching

Instructions: Match each term from the column on the left with the best description from the column on the right.

____ 1. filtering software
____ 2. curriculum page
____ 3. Trojan horse
____ 4. Web publishing
____ 5. computer ethics

a. teacher-created Web page that contains links to teacher-chosen-and-evaluated Web sites

b. moral guidelines that govern the use of computers, networks, and information systems

c. prevents computer browser from displaying materials from certain Web sites

d. a virus designed to look like a legitimate program

e. the development and maintenance of Web pages

3. Short Answer

Instructions: Write a brief answer to each of the following questions.

1. What are computer security risks? What different types of security risks threaten school computer systems? What are some safeguards that minimize security risks? _____

2. What is a computer virus? Describe three types of computer viruses. Why are computer viruses commonly found in schools? What can teachers do to minimize the impact of computer viruses both at home and at school? _____

3. What is a single-user software license? How is a single-user software license different from a network site license? What types of software licenses are typically found in schools? _____

4. What is an overvoltage? What precautions should teachers take to protect their computers and other electronic equipment from overvoltages, both at home and at school? _____

5. What are Acceptable Use Policies (AUP)? Why are AUPs so important for K-12 schools? Describe two other ways to limit student access to inappropriate Internet sites. _____

www.scsite.com/tdc/ch8/time.htm

TeacherTime

InBrief

KeyTerms

AtTheMovies

CheckPoint

TeacherTime

CyberClass

EdIssues

NetStuff

SPECIAL FEATURES

TimeLine 2000

Guide to WWW Sites

Buyer's Guide 2000

Educational Sites

State/Federal Sites

Chat

News

Home

Web Instructions: To display this page from the Web, launch your browser and enter the URL, www.scsite.com/tdc/ch8/time.htm. Click the links for current and additional information.

1. The school at which you are doing your internship is being networked and each classroom will have Internet access. Your principal has asked you to help the newly created technology committee create an Acceptable Use Policy (AUP) for teachers, staff, students, and parents. What key components do you think the committee should include? Will the teachers, staff, and student AUPs be the same? Why or why not? What are some consequences that you think students should face for violating AUP rules? What consequences should teachers face? How should your principal educate all school personnel and students about the new AUPs? What suggestions do you have that the principal could use to educate parents about the new AUPs for students?

2. Based on Section 107 of the Copyright Act of 1976, also known as Fair Use, teachers are allowed to photocopy and use copyrighted materials in their classrooms for educational purposes. With the advent of the Internet and the Web, legislators have had to reexamine Fair Use. Do Fair Use rules apply to the Internet and the Web? Is using materials found on the Web different from using materials found in a copyrighted book? Do you need to teach your students about Fair Use? Why or why not? How can you determine if your use of copyrighted materials is governed by Fair Use rules?

3. Recently, you have been hearing a lot about viruses. You have two Macintosh computers in your classroom and they are connected to the Internet. In the past, you have not worried about viruses, because Macintosh computers do not get them as often as PCs. Other teachers, however, have been discussing a new virus affecting their Macintosh computers. Where can you get reliable information about Macintosh viruses? What kind of support is available on the Internet? Can you get a virus from the Internet? How can you protect your computers from getting a virus?

4. You are a high school math teacher, and your school is installing a school-wide network. Your new principal is concerned about networking and is not willing to allow you to use a networked computer and the Internet in your classroom. He has heard about other schools that have problems with students breaking into the network and causing serious problems. The principal feels that more control is possible in a lab setting than in the classroom. How can you convince your principal to let you use the new network in your classroom? What network security procedures can you suggest that prevent students from unauthorized access and use? Do you know of a way to prevent students from gaining unauthorized access to the network but still allows them to use the network and the Internet?

5. Parents are concerned about objectionable materials found on the Internet and are looking for some kind of protection. Your district is considering installing filtering software. What are the benefits of filtering software? Is filtering software foolproof? Why or why not? What are the disadvantages of filtering software? What type of report would you make to your school board about installing filtering software? How could an Acceptable Use Policy address the issue of objectionable materials?

Security Issues

www.scsite.com/tdc/ch8/class.htm

Web Instructions: To display this page from the Web, launch your browser and enter the URL, www.scsite.com/tdc/ch8/class.htm. To start Level I CyberClass, click a Level I link on this page or enter the URL, www.cyber-class.com. Click the Student button, click *Teachers Discovering Computers* in the list of titles, and then click the Enter a site button. To start Level II or III CyberClass (available only to those purchasers of a Cyber-Class floppy disk), place your CyberClass floppy disk in drive A, click Start on the taskbar, click Run on the Start menu, type a:connect in the Open text box, click the OK button, click the Enter CyberClass button, and then follow the instructions. If you are using a Macintosh, see your instructor.

InBrief

KeyTerms

AtTheMovies

CheckPoint

TeacherTime

CyberClass

EdIssues

NetStuff

SPECIAL FEATURES

TimeLine 2000

Guide to WWW Sites

Buyer's Guide 2000

Educational Sites

State/Federal Sites

Chat

News

Home

1. Flash Cards (<u>Level I</u>, Level II, and Level III)

Click Flash Cards on the Main Menu of the CyberClass Web page. Click the plus sign before the Chapter 8 title. Click Computer Security: Risks and Safeguards and answer all the cards in that section. Then, click Ethics and the Information Age and answer the cards in that section. If you have less than 85% correct, continue to answer cards in other sections until you have more than 85% correct. All users: Answer as many more Flash Cards as you desire. Close the Electronic Flash Card window and the Flash Cards window by clicking the Close button in the upper-right corner of each window.

2. Practice Test (<u>Level I</u>, Level II, and Level III)

Click Testing on the Main Menu of the CyberClass Web page. Click the Select a book box arrow and then click Teachers Discovering Computers. Click the Select a test to take box arrow and then click the Chapter 8 title in the list. Click the Take Test button. If necessary, maximize the window. Take the practice test and then click the Submit Test button. Click the Display Study Guide button. Review the Study Guide. Scroll down and click the Return To CyberClass button. Click the Yes button to close the Study Guide window. If your score was less than 80%, click the Take another Test button to take another practice test. Continue taking tests until your score is greater than 80%. Then, click the Done button.

3. Web Guide (<u>Level I</u>, Level II, and Level III)

Click Web Guide on the Main Menu of the CyberClass Web page. When the Guide to World Wide Web Sites page displays, click History and review the sites. Are these history Web sites appropriate for use in K-12 education? Are these Web sites a good resource for history teachers to integrate into their classroom curriculum? Why? When you are finished, hand in a brief summary of your conclusions to your instructor.

4. Assignments and Syllabus (Level II and Level III)

Click Assignments on the Main Menu of the CyberClass Web page. Ensure you are aware of all assignments and when they are due. Click Syllabus on the Main Menu of the CyberClass Web page. Verify you are up to date on all activities for the class.

5. CyberChallenge (Level II and Level III)

Click CyberChallenge on the Main Menu of the CyberClass Web page. Click the Select a book box arrow and then click Teachers Discovering Computers. Click the Select a board to play box arrow and then click Chapter 8 in the list. Click the Play CyberChallenge button. Maximize the Cyber-Challenge window. Play CyberChallenge until your score for a complete game is 500 points or more. Close the CyberChallenge window.

6. Hot Links (Level II and Level III)

Click Hot Links on the Main Menu of the CyberClass Web page. Review the sites in the Hot Links section and then write a brief report indicating which site you like best and why.

InBrief

KeyTerms

AtTheMovies

CheckPoint

TeacherTime

CyberClass

EdIssues

NetStuff

SPECIAL FEATURES

TimeLine 2000

Guide to WWW Sites

Buyer's Guide 2000

Educational Sites

State/Federal Sites

Chat

News

Home

www.scsite.com/tdc/ch8/issues.htm

Web Instructions: To display this page from the Web, launch your browser and enter the URL, www.scsite.com/tdc/ch8/issues.htm. Click the links for current and additional information to help you respond to the EdIssues questions.

1. Computer Viruses

You have heard about computer viruses but have never had any problems with them. You do not have any virus scanning software installed on your classroom computer, but you have considered purchasing this type of software. One day, one of your students brings in a floppy disk from home and puts it in the classroom computer — and the disk contains a virus. The virus corrupts a number of system files on your hard drive, so your computer will not boot properly. What should you do now? Is it possible to recover any of the lost information? Should students be allowed to bring disks from home? Should schools require that each computer have antivirus software? What policies and procedures can you follow to minimize this type of problem in the future?

2. Term Papers

For years, the only way to write a term paper was to visit the library, walk through shelves of texts and journals to find what you needed — before you even started to write. Today, obtaining a paper is as easy as clicking a button. Several sites on the Web now provide a searchable database of term papers gathered from college and high school students. Students can download a term paper, make any necessary changes, print a copy, and then turn it in as their own. How can instructors keep students from claiming the work of others as their own? Can you explain how using the Web for research differs from using it to copy someone's work? What should be the consequences for plagiarizing from a Web site?

3. Teacher and Student Monitoring

Your school district maintains a policy that states classroom computers and Internet access are to be used for instructional purposes only. The district instructs teachers not to send or receive personal messages, surf the Internet for fun, or play games on classroom computers. The district observes Internet activities with monitoring software. Some teachers feel they should be allowed to use the Internet or play games during their lunch periods. What limits, if any, should be placed on teachers' use of classroom computers? How closely should the school district be able to monitor teacher and student use? Why? Should administrative personnel be allowed to monitor your e-mail messages to other teachers? Why or why not? Should you be allowed to monitor your students' e-mail messages? Why or why not?

4. Distance Learning

You have been asked to be part of a committee of teachers that is interested in starting a distance learning project at your high school. You know that one of the major drawbacks of distance learning in high schools is accountability. Your principal wants to know how to be sure the registered student actually is doing the work. You express concern as well. What solutions can you offer for this problem? Do teachers have this same type of problem in a face-to-face classroom as well? Explain why or why not? What other problems are unique to distance learning? Is distance learning appropriate at the high school level? What about middle schools? Elementary schools? Why or why not?

5. Software Piracy

Software manufacturers are watching school districts closely for evidences of illegal use of software. Recently, a major school district was fined $300,000 for having multiple copies of non-licensed software installed on classroom computers. Teachers often illegally install multiple copies of single-user programs on their classroom computers. What are some of the ethical issues regarding software piracy? Why is illegally installing software so prevalent in K-12 schools? How does the software industry deal with violators of software copyright law? Describe several ways in which school districts can prevent illegal software from being installed on school computers.

NetStuff

Web Instructions: To display this page from the Web, launch your browser and enter the URL, www.scsite.com/tdc/ch8/net.htm. To use the Exploring the Computers of the Future lab and the Keeping Your Computer Virus Free lab from the Web, Shockwave and Flash Player must be installed on your computer (download by clicking here).

InBrief

KeyTerms

AtTheMovies

CheckPoint

TeacherTime

CyberClass

EdIssues

NetStuff

SPECIAL FEATURES

TimeLine 2000

Guide to WWW Sites

Buyer's Guide 2000

Educational Sites

State/Federal Sites

Chat

News

Home

EXPLORING THE COMPUTERS OF THE FUTURE LAB

1. Shelly Cashman Series Exploring the Computers of the Future Lab

Follow the instructions in NetStuff 1 on page 1.34 to start and use the Exploring the Computers of the Future lab. If you are running from the Web, enter the URL, www.scsite.com/sclabs/menu.htm or display the NetStuff page (see instructions at the top of this page) and then click the EXPLORING THE COMPUTERS OF THE FUTURE LAB button.

KEEPING YOUR COMPUTER VIRUS FREE LAB

2. Shelly Cashman Series Keeping Your Computer Virus Free Lab

Follow the instructions in NetStuff 1 on page 1.34 to start and use the Keeping Your Computer Virus Free lab. If you are running from the Web, enter the URL, www.scsite.com/sclabs/menu.htm or display the NetStuff page (see instructions at the top of this page) and then click the KEEPING YOUR COMPUTER VIRUS FREE LAB button.

COPYRIGHT

3. Web Copyrights

Web browsers and Web editors make it easy for you to copy elements from other Web pages for your own use. Having the ability, however, does not make it legal. To learn more about copyright law and the Web, click the COPYRIGHT button and complete this exercise.

FILTERING SOFTWARE

4. Internet Filtering Software

Internet filtering software allows parents and teachers to block students from having Internet access to objectionable materials. To learn more about Internet filtering software, click the FILTERING SOFTWARE button and complete this exercise.

COMPUTER CRIME

5. Computer Crime

Many computer crimes fall under the jurisdiction of the Federal Bureau of Investigation (FBI). To learn about the computer crimes the FBI investigates, click the COMPUTER CRIME button and complete this exercise.

SOFTWARE PIRACY

6. Software Piracy

Software piracy is a problem in K-12 schools. The Business Software Alliance (BSA) Web site provides the latest information about software piracy. BSA fights against software piracy by conducting educational programs and operating antipiracy hotlines. To learn more, click the SOFTWARE PIRACY button and complete this exercise.

WEB CHAT

7. Web Chat

Schools use a four-pronged approach to prevent students from accessing inappropriate Internet sites; an approach that includes filtering software, AUPs, use of curriculum pages, and teacher observation. To enter a Web Chat discussion related to this issue, click the WEB CHAT button.

Guide to State and Federal Government Educational Web Sites

WEB INSTRUCTIONS: *To gain World Wide Web access to the most current version of the sites included in this special feature, launch your browser and enter the URL,* www.scsite.com/ tdc/ch8/govsites.htm.

The federal government, state governments, and state institutions and organizations provide a multitude of Web resources for K-12 teachers and students. Everyday, hundreds of new and exciting educational Web resources are added, existing ones are changed, and still others cease to exist. Because of this, you may find that a URL listed here has changed or no longer is valid. A continually updated Guide to State and Federal Government Educational Web Sites, which links to the most current versions of these sites, can be found at www.scsite.com/tdc/ch8/govsites.htm.

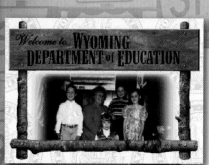

State Departments of Education

Site Name	Location (all site locations begin with http://)
Alabama	www.alsde.edu
Alaska	www.educ.state.ak.us
Arizona	ade.state.az.us
Arkansas	arkedu.state.ar.us
California	www.cde.ca.gov/iasa/
Colorado	www.cde.state.co.us
Connecticut	www.state.ct.us/sde
Delaware	www.doe.state.de.us
District of Columbia	www.k12.dc.us
Florida	www.firn.edu/doe/index.html
Georgia	www.doe.k12.ga.us
Hawaii	www.k12.hi.us
Idaho	www.sde.state.id.us/Dept/
Illinois	www.isbe.state.il.us
Indiana	www.doe.state.in.us
Iowa	www.state.ia.us/educate
Kansas	www.ksbe.state.ks.us
Kentucky	www.kde.state.ky.us
Louisiana	www.doe.state.la.us
Maine	www.state.me.us/education/homepage.htm
Maryland	www.msde.state.md.us
Massachusetts	www.doe.mass.edu
Michigan	www.mde.state.mi.us
Minnesota	www.educ.state.mn.us
Mississippi	mdek12.state.ms.us
Missouri	services.dese.state.mo.us
Montana	www.metnet.mt.gov/
Nebraska	www.nde.state.ne.us
Nevada	www.nsn.k12.nv.us/nvdoe/
New Hampshire	www.state.nh.us/doe/education.html
New Jersey	www.state.nj.us/education
New Mexico	sde.state.nm.us
New York	www.nysed.gov
North Carolina	www.dpi.state.nc.us
North Dakota	www.dpi.state.nd.us/
Ohio	www.ode.ohio.gov
Oklahoma	sde.state.ok.us
Oregon	www.ode.state.or.us
Pennsylvania	www.cas.psu.edu/pde.html
Rhode Island	instruct.ride.ri.net
South Carolina	www.state.sc.us/sde
South Dakota	www.state.sd.us/deca/
Tennessee	www.state.tn.us/education/
Texas	www.tea.state.tx.us
Utah	www.usoe.k12.ut.us
Vermont	www.state.vt.us/educ
Virginia	www.pen.k12.va.us/go/VDOE
Washington	www.ospi.wednet.edu
West Virginia	wvde.state.wv.us
Wisconsin	www.dpi.state.wi.us
Wyoming	www.k12.wy.us/wdehome.html

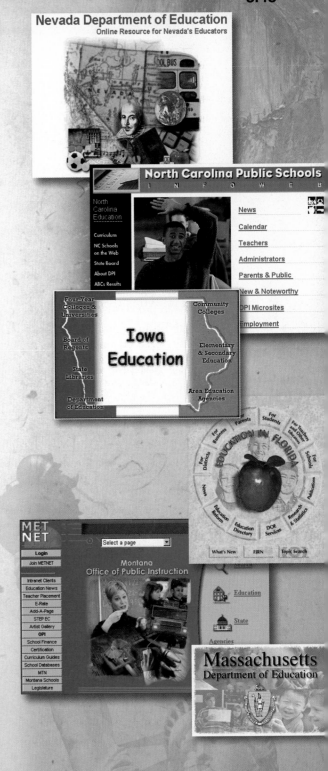

Federal Government

Site Name	Location (all site locations begin with http://)	Comment
U.S. Department of Education	www.ed.gov/	A necessary first stop for all teachers
Welcome to the White House	www.whitehouse.gov	Provides links to many other collections, programs, and products of significant educational benefit
Department of Defense (DoD)	www.acq.osd.mil/ddre/edugate/	Your gateway to education efforts sponsored by the DoD
Department of Energy (DOE)	www.sandia.gov/ESTEEM/	Education resources in science, technology, energy, and math
Environmental Protection Agency (EPA)	www.epa.gov/epahome/students.htm	Everything from asbestos hazards to acid rain, this site has it all
Federal Communications Commission (FCC)	www.fcc.gov/learnnet/	LearnNet — the FCC is working to bring every school in America into the information age
National Aeronautics and Space Administration (NASA)	www.hq.nasa.gov/office/codef/ education/index.html	NASA's extensive education program — awesome
National Archives and Records Administration (NARA)	www.nara.gov/education/classrm.html	Digital Classroom encourages teachers of students at all levels to use archival documents in the classroom
National Endowment for the Humanities	www.neh.fed.us/html/online.html	Online projects that support learning in history, literature, philosophy, and other areas of the humanities
National Park Service (NPS)	www.nps.gov/interp/learn.htm	The Learning Place is your one stop for finding education materials on national parks
National Science Foundation	www.nsf.gov/	A must stop for science teachers
Peace Corps	www.peacecorps.gov/wws/index.html	World Wise Schools is designed to help students gain a greater understanding of other cultures and countries
Smithsonian Education	educate.si.edu/	Essential source for all educators; includes lesson plans, resource guide, and more
United States Department of Agriculture (USDA)	www.reeusda.gov/	Extensive sources of research and education information about many subjects

Smithsonian Education

Federal Government

Site Name	Location (all site locations begin with http://)	Comment
United States Geological Survey	www.usgs.gov/education/	Learning Web — dedicated to K-12 education, exploration, and life-long learning
The Kennedy Center for the Performing Arts	artsedge.kennedy-center.org/	ArtsEdge — linking the arts and education through technology
Federal Resources for Educational Excellence (FREE)	www.ed.gov/free/	FREE — hundreds of Internet-based education resources supported by federal agencies available at one Web site
Bureau of Land Management	www.blm.gov/education/index.html	Education site for teachers looking for resources when teaching about the environment
Library of Congress	www.loc.gov	An incredible library resource
Educational Resources Information Center (ERIC) and Other Clearinghouses	www.ed.gov/EdRes/EdFed/ERIC.html	A nationwide information network that acquires, catalogs, summarizes, and provides access to education information from many sources
AskERIC	www.askeric.org/	Education information with the personal touch — simply AskERIC
FedWorld	www.fedworld.gov/	A comprehensive central access point for searching, locating, ordering, and acquiring government information
National Development and Research Centers	www.ed.gov/offices/OERI/ResCtr.html	List of links to national educational research and development centers
Regional Assistance Centers	www.ed.gov/EdRes/EdFed/EdTechCtrs.html	Department of Education funded K-12 regional assistance centers
Regional Education Laboratories	www.ed.gov/EdRes/EdFed/RegLab.html	Department of Education funded K-12 laboratories to help schools solve problems
Regional Technology in Education Consortia (R*TEC)	www.rtec.org/	Department of Education funded program to help K-12 schools integrate technology

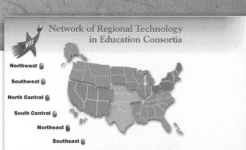

INDEX

INDEX

Community site license: Software site license that gives an entire region or state the right to install an unlimited number of educational copies of a particular software program on individual computers or a network. **8.10**

Compact disc (CD): Flat, round, portable, metal-coated plastic storage medium that stores items in microscopic pits that are on the top surface of the CD. A high-powered laser light creates the pits, and a lower-powered laser reads items by reflecting light through the bottom of the CD; the reflected light is converted into a series of bits the computer can process. Types of compact discs are CD-ROMs and DVD-ROMs. **1.9, 4.32-34**

Compact disc read-only memory, *see* **CD-ROM**

Compaq, history of, 1.40

Comparison operations: Operations performed by the arithmetic/logic unit that involve comparing one data item to another to determine if the first item is greater than, equal to, or less than the other. **4.6**

Compression, video, 5.8

Computer(s): Electronic machine, operating under the control of instructions stored in its own memory, that can accept data (input), manipulate the data according to specified rules (process), produce results (output), and store the results for future use (storage). **1.6.** *See also* Macintosh computers; Personal computer(s)

components, 1.6-9

example of use, 1.21-25

history of, 1.36-45

installing, 4.54-56

maintaining, 4.57-58

power of, 1.9-10

purchasing, 4.47-53

software, *see* **Application software; Software**

speed of, 1.10

Computer-assisted instruction (CAI): Software designed to help teach facts, information, and/or skills associated with subject-related materials. **5.18, 6.39**

Computer-based training (CBT): Type of education in which students learn by using and completing exercises with instructional software. **5.9**

Computer crime: Any illegal act involving a computer. **8.2**

Computer ethics: Moral guidelines that govern the use of computers and information systems. **8.14**

Computer games: Games that use a combination of graphics, sound, and video to create a realistic and entertaining game situation. **5.13**

Computer lab: Designated classroom filled with computers and technology for groups of students to use. Also called technology lab. **6.6, 6.17-18, 7.26**

Computer literacy: A knowledge and understanding of computers and their uses. **1.4, 6.2**

Computer program: A series of instructions that tells the hardware of a computer what to do. **1.10-17, 4.13.** *See also* **Application program; Software**

Computer programmers, *see* **Programmers**

Computer security risk: Any event or action that has the potential of causing a loss of computer equipment, software, data and information, or processing capability. **8.2-14**

Computer vandalism: The intentional causing of damage to computers. **8.8**

Computer virus, *see* **Virus**

Concept map: Planning tool that helps students use flowcharting to understand the attributes and relationships of the main subjects and provides a visual tool for brainstorming and planning. **7.19**

Confidentiality, Internet and, 2.35

Connector: Used to attach a cable to a device, such as an external device to the system unit. **4.12**

Content: The information provided by a Web page. **7.12**

Context-sensitive: Help information related to the current instruction being attempted. **3.29**

Control unit: Component of the CPU that directs and coordinates most of the computer's operations; interprets each instruction issued by a program, then initiates the appropriate action to carry out the instruction. For every instruction, the control unit repeats a set of four basic operations called the machine cycle or instruction cycle: (1) fetching an instruction, (2) decoding the instruction, (3) executing the instruction, and if necessary (4) storing the result. **4.6**

Cookie: Small file stored by a Web server on a user's computer that contains data about the user, such as the user's name or viewing preferences; used to track information about Web site viewers, customers, and subscribers. **2.34**

Cooperative learning: Method of instruction where students work collaboratively in groups to achieve learning objectives and goals. 1.20, **6.14,** 7.22, 7.23

Copy: Editing function in which a portion of the document is duplicated and stored on the Clipboard. **3.7**

Copyright: Ownership of a creative work that is retained by the original author or creator, who has the exclusive right to reproduce and distribute the creative work. 8.9, **8.17**-20

Core subjects, curriculum standards for, 6.4

Corporations, school partnerships with, 7.42

Country code abbreviations, 2.17

Courseware: Interactive computer-based training software, usually available on CD-ROM, DVD-ROM, or shared over a network. **5.9**

Cracker: Person who tries to access a computer or network illegally. **8.6**

Creating (document): Process of developing a document by entering text or numbers, inserting graphical images, and performing other tasks using an input device such as a keyboard or mouse. **3.7**

Creativity: Originality, imaginative and innovative approach, and artistic abilities demonstrated by students' projects. **7.19**

Currency: Measure of how up to date, or timely, the Web page content is and how often it is updated. **7.12**

Curriculum: All of the experiences a learner has under the supervision and guidance of teachers; consists of a plan or written document that includes a series of required goals and learning outcomes. **6.2-4**

integrating technology into, 6.8-9

integrating technology, 6.5, 7.1-43

Web site, 7.12

Curriculum goal, *see* **Curriculum standard**

Curriculum guides: Documents provided by State Departments of Education to school districts that describe curriculum goals and objectives for learning; often include direction for specific content areas, benchmarks, activities, and forms of evaluation. **6.2**

Curriculum objectives, 6.19

Curriculum page: Teacher-created document that contains hyperlinks to teacher-selected sites. **3.23, 7.26, 8.26**

Curriculum standard: Definition of what a student is expected to know at certain stages of education. **6.4**

Custom software: Application software developed at a user's request to perform specific functions. **1.16**

Cut: Editing function in which a portion of the document is removed and electronically stored in a temporary storage location called the Clipboard. **3.7**

Data: Collection of items such as words, numbers, images, and sounds that are not organized and have little meaning individually. Data is processed into information. **1.6, 4.13**

representation of, 4.3-4

Database: Collection of data organized in a manner that allows access, retrieval, and use of that data. **3.14**-15

student, 7.23-24

Database file: Collection of related data that is organized in records. **3.14**

Database software: Software used to create a computerized database; add, change, and delete data; sort and retrieve data from the database; and create forms and reports using the data in the database. 1.15-16, **3.14**-15, 3.41

Data projector: Output device that takes an image displayed on a computer screen and projects it onto a larger screen so an audience can see the image clearly. 4.24-25, **5.26,** 7.22

Decoding: Second operation in the machine cycle, performed by the control unit; the process of translating the instruction into commands the computer understands. **4.6**

Delete: Editing function that involves removing a portion of the document. **3.7**

Design: The way a Web site is arranged; that is, the way it uses instructional design principles to deliver content to the user. **7.12**

Desktop: Onscreen work area that uses common graphical elements such as icons, buttons, windows, menus, links, and dialog boxes, all of which can display on the desktop. **3.5**

PHOTO CREDITS

Cover: *Images* Courtesy of PhotoDisc, Inc; **Chapter 1:** *Figure 1-0a* © 1999 PhotoDisc, Inc.; *Figure 1-0b* Courtesy of Apple Computer, Inc.; *Figure 1-1* Courtesy of International Business Machines; *Figure 1-2* Courtesy of Apple Computer, Inc.; *Figure 1-3a* Courtesy of Apple Computer, Inc.; *Figure 1-3b* Courtesy of Dell Computer; *Figure 1-4a* Anthony Wood/Stock Boston; *Figure 1-4b* Andy Sacks/Tony Stone Images; *Figure 1-4c* Mark Richards/PhotoEdit; *Figure 1-4d* David Young-Wolff/PhotoEdit; *Figure 1-4e* Charles Gupton/Tony Stone Images; *Figure 1-5* Scott Goodwin Photography; *Figure 1-7a* © 1999 PhotoDisc, Inc.; *Figure 1-7b,c,d,* Courtesy of Intel Corporation; *Figure 1-7e* Phil A. Harrington/Peter Arnold, Inc.; *Figure 1-7f* courtesy of Motorola; *Figure 1-8* © 1999 PhotoDisc, Inc.; *Figure 1-9* Courtesy of Toshiba America Information Systems, Inc.; *Figure 1-11a* Courtesy of Apple Computer, Inc.; *Figure 1-11b* Courtesy of EDMARK; *Figure 1-11c* Courtesy of HyperStudio; *Figure 1-11d* Courtesy of Apple Computer, Inc.; *Figure 1-14b* Courtesy of Apple Computer, Inc.; *Figure 1-16* Scott Goodwin Photography; *Figure 1-23* Jose L. Pelaez/The Stock Market; *Figure 1-24* © 1999 PhotoDisc, Inc.; *Figure 1-25* Courtesy of Hewlett Packard Company; *Figure 1-26* © 1999 PhotoDisc, Inc.; *Figure 1-27* Bob Daemmrich/The Image Works; *Figure 1-28* Seth Resnick/Liaison Agency; *Figure 1-29* Nancy Sheehan/PhotoEdit; *Figure 1-30* Tom McCarthy/PhotoEdit; *Figure 1-31* Jeff Greenberg/PhotoEdit; *Figure 1-32* Gary Wagner/Stock Boston; *Figure 1-33* © 1999 PhotoDisc, Inc.; *Figure 1-00i* Reproduced by Special Permission from the December 15, 1998 edition of *The New York Times* on the Web, © 1998 by *The New York Times*; *Figure 1-00i* © *USA Today*. Reprinted with permission; **Timeline:** *1937* Courtesy of Iowa State University; *1937* Courtesy of Iowa State University; *1937* Courtesy of Iowa State University; *1943* The Computer Museum; *1943* The Computer Museum; *1945* Courtesy of the Institute for Advanced Studies; *1946* Courtesy of the University of Pennsylvania Archives; *1947* Courtesy of International Business Machines; *1951* Courtesy of Unisys Corporation; *1952* Courtesy of the Hagley Museum and Library; *1953* Courtesy of M.I.T. Archives; *1957* Courtesy of International Business Machines; *1957* Courtesy of the Department of the Navy; *1958* Courtesy of M.I.T. Archives; *1958* Courtesy of International Business Machines; *1959* Courtesy of International Business Machines; *1960* Courtesy of The Hagley Museum and Library; *1961* Courtesy of International Business Machines; *1965* Courtesy of Dartmouth College News Services; *1965* Courtesy of Digital Equipment Corporation; *1968* Courtesy of International Business Machines; *1970* Courtesy of International Business Machines; *1971* Courtesy of Intel Corporation; *1971* The Computer Museum; *1975* Courtesy of InfoWorld; *1976* Courtesy of Apple Computer, Inc.; *1976* Courtesy of Apple Computer, Inc.; *1976* Courtesy of Apple Computer, Inc.; *1979* The Computer Museum; *1980* Courtesy of International Business Machines; *1980* Courtesy of Microsoft Corporation; *1981* Courtesy of International Business Machines; *1982* Courtesy of Hayes; *1983* Courtesy of Lotus Development Corporation; *1983* © 1982, Time, Inc.; *1984* Courtesy of International Business Machines; *1984* Courtesy of Hewlett Packard Company Archives; *1984* Courtesy of Apple Computer Company; *1987* Courtesy of Compaq Computer Corporation; *1989* © 1997-1998 W3C (MIT, INRIA, Keio), All Rights Reserved.; *1989* Courtesy of Intel Corporation; *1992* Courtesy of Microsoft Corporation; *1993* Courtesy of Intel Corporation; *1993* Jim Clark/The Liaison Agency; *1993* Courtesy of Netscape Communications ; *1994* Courtesy of Netscape Communications Corporation; *1995* Courtesy of Microsoft Corporation; *1995* Courtesy of Sun Microsystems, Inc.; *1996* © 1999 PhotoDisc, Inc.; *1996* Reuters/Rick T. Wilking/Archive Photos; *1996* © 1999 PhotoDisc, Inc.; *1996* Courtesy of Web TV Networks Inc.; *1996* Courtesy of Web TV Networks Inc.; *1997* Courtesy of Intel Corporation; *1997* I. Uimonen/Sygma; *1997* Courtesy of International Business Machines; *1997* Motion Picture and Television Archives; *1997* © 1999 PhotoDisc, Inc.; *1998* Courtesy of Microsoft Corporation; *1998* Courtesy of Dell Computer; *1998* © Corel Corporation; *1998* Courtesy of Apple Computer Company; *1998* © 1999 PhotoDisc, Inc.; *1998* © 1999 PhotoDisc, Inc.; *1999* Courtesy of Microsoft Computer Corporation; **Chapter 2:** *Figure 2-0a* Courtesy of Apple Computer, Inc.; *Figure 2-0a* © 1999 PhotoDisc, Inc.; *Figure 2-1* Kevin Horan/Tony Stone Images; *Figure 2-5* Scott Goodwin Photography; *Figure 2-6* Courtesy of U.S. Robotics; *Figure 2-11* Amy Etra/PhotoEdit; *Figure 2-15* Courtesy of Donna Cox & Robert Patterson/NCSA/UIUC; *Figure 2-46* Courtesy of Donna Cox & Robert Patterson/NCSA/UIUC; **Chapter 3:** *Figure 3-0a* Scott Goodwin Photography; *Figure 3-0a* Courtesy of Apple Computer, Inc.; *Figure 3-17* Scott Goodwin Photography; *Figure 3-23* James Schnepf/Liaison Agency; *Figure 3-25* Courtesy of Palm Computing, Inc., a 3COM Company; *Figure 3-26a* Courtesy of Microsoft Corporation; *Figure 3-26b* Courtesy of Lotus Development Company; *Figure 3-27a* Courtesy of Microsoft Corporation; *Figure 3-27b* Courtesy of Apple Computer, Inc.; *Figure 3-37* Russell D. Curtis/Photo Researchers, Inc.; *Figure 3-39* Courtesy of Block Financial Group Corp., makers of Kiplinger TaxCut; *Figure 3-40* Courtesy of Nolo Press, Inc.; *Figure 3-42* Figure Scott Goodwin Photography; *Figure 3-43* Courtesy of Microsoft Corporation; **Creating a Web Page:** *Cartoon illustrations* Courtesy of Dynamic Graphics, Inc.; **Chapter 4:** *Figure 4-0a* Lester Lefkowitz/The Stock Market; *Figure 4-0b* Courtesy of Apple Computer, Inc.; *Figure 4-1b* Courtesy of International Business Machines; *Figure 4-1c* Courtesy of Apple Computer, Inc.; *Figure 4-5* Scott Goodwin Photography; *Figure 4-7a, c, d* Courtesy of Intel Corporation; *Figure 4-7b* Courtesy of Motorola, Inc.; *Figure 4-8* David Young Wolff/Tony Stone Images; *Figure 4-10* AP/Wide World Photos; *Figure 4-12* Scott Goodwin Photography; *Figure 4-13* Courtesy of HyperStudio; *Figure 4-14* Scott Goodwin Photography; *Figure 4-15 a, b* Scott Goodwin Photography; *Figure 4-16* Scott Goodwin Photography; *Figure 4-17a* Courtesy of Apple Computer, Inc.; *Figure 4-17b* Courtesy of International Business Machines; *Figure 4-19* © 1999 PhotoDisc, Inc.; *Figure 4-20* David Young Wolf/PhotoEdit; *Figure 4-21* Courtesy of Gravis Gaming Devices/Kensington Technology Group; *Figure 4-22* Michael Newman/PhotoEdit; *Figure 4-23* Courtesy of Visioneer Inc. PaperPort 6100; *Figure 4-24* Scott Goodwin Photography; *Figure 4-25a* Cassey Cohen/PhotoEdit; *Figure 4-25b* Courtesy of Symbol Technologies, Inc.; *Figure 4-25c* Novastock/PhotoEdit; *Figure 4-26* Courtesy of Casio; *Figure 4-27* Will & Deni McIntyre/Photo Researchers, Inc.; *Figure 4-28* Eric Sander/Liaison Agency; *Figure 4-33* Scott Goodwin Photography; *Figure 4-34* Courtesy of Hewlett Packard Company; *Figure 4-36a* Courtesy of InFocus, Inc.; *Figure 4-36b* InFocus LP735 data/video projector, Jerome Hart Photography/Courtesy of InFocus, Inc.; *Figure 4-37* Bob Daemmrich/The Image Works; *Figure 4-38* Courtesy of Hewlett Packard Company; *Figure 4-39* Courtesy of Apple Computer, Inc.; *Figure 4-40* © 1999 PhotoDisc, Inc.; *Figure 4-41* Courtesy of Index; *Figure 4-46a* Scott Goodwin Photography; *Figure 4-46b* Courtesy of Iomega Corporation; *Figure 4-47* Courtesy of Seagate Technology; *Figure 4-48* Courtesy of Misty Vermaat; *Figure 4-50* Courtesy of Pioneer Electronics; *Figure eoc4a* Courtesy of Broderbund Software; *Figure eoc4b* Tim Flach/Tony Stone Images; *Figure eoc4c* Jon Gray/Tony Stone Images; **Buyer's Guide:** *Figure CO* © 1999 PhotoDisc, Inc.; *Figure 1* © 1999 PhotoDisc, Inc.; *Figure 1* Jeff Zaruba/The Stock Market; *Figure 8* Courtesy of International Business Machines; *Figure 9* Courtesy of Toshiba America, Inc; *Figure 10* Courtesy of Xircom Corporation; *Figure 11* Courtesy of In Focus Systems, Inc.; *Figure 12* © 1999 PhotoDisc, Inc. **Chapter 5:** Figure 5-0a Peter Steiner/The Stock Market; *Figure 5-0b* Courtesy of Apple Computer, Inc.; *Figure 5-4* Scott Goodwin Photography; *Figure 5-8* SuperStock; *Figure 5-9* Courtesy of AMR Training Group; *Figure 5-10* Michael Newman/PhotoEdit; *Figure 5-18a* © 1999 PhotoDisc, Inc.; *Figure 5-18b* Courtesy of Intel Corporation; *Figure 5-19* Christian Zachariasen/Sygma; *Figure 5-21* Courtesy of Touchnet Systems, Inc.; *Figure 5-33a* Courtesy of Apple Computer, Inc.; *Figure 5-33b* Courtesy of Ast Research, Inc.; *Figure 5-35* Scott Goodwin Photography; *Figure 5-36* Courtesy of Apple Computer, Inc.; *Figure 5-37* Mark Richards/PhotoEdit; *Figure 5-38* Courtesy of In Focus Systems, Inc.; *Figure 5-39* Courtesy of In Focus Systems, Inc.; *Figure 5-40* Courtesy of Pioneer Electronics; *Figure 5-41* Courtesy of Microtek; *Figure 5-43* Courtesy of Canon Computer Systems, Inc.; *Figure 5-44* Courtesy of Corel Corporation; *Figure eoc3* ©1994-1999 by Lawrence Berkeley National Laboratory; **Chapter 6:** *Figure 6-0a* John Lamb/Tony Stone Images; *Figure 6-0b* Courtesy of Apple Computer, Inc.; *Figure 6-1* Courtesy of Gateway 2000; *Figure 6-5* Corbis/Roger Ressmeyer; *Figure 6-7* Matt Klicker/The Image Works; *Figure 6-8* Spencer Grant/PhotoEdit; *Figure 6-9* David Young-Wolff/PhotoEdit; *Figure 6-12* Will & Deni McIntyre/Photo Researchers, Inc.;

Figure 6-15 David Young-Wolff/Tony Stone Images; *Figure 6-19* Alan Levenson/Tony Stone Images; *Figure 6-20* Ed Bock/Stock Market; *Figure 6-21* Corbis /Bob Rowan; Progressive Image; *Figure 6-22* Mark Richards/PhotoEdit; *Figure 6-23* Tom Stewart/Stock Market; *Figure 6-24* Jim Pickerell/FPG International; *Figure 6-27* © 1999 PhotoDisc, Inc.; *Figure 6-29* © 1999 PhotoDisc, Inc.; *Figure 6-30a* Walter Hodges/Tony Stone Images; *Figure 6-30b* Ian Shaw /Tony Stone Images; *Figure 6-30c* © 1999 PhotoDisc, Inc.; *Figure 6-30d* © 1999 PhotoDisc, Inc.; *Figure 6-30e* Peter Cade/Tony Stone Images; *Figure 6-30f* © 1999 PhotoDisc, Inc.; *Figure 6-30g* © 1999 PhotoDisc, Inc.; *Figure 6-32* Tony Freeman/PhotoEdit; *Figure 6-33* Ed Bock/Stock Market; *Figure 6-35* Peter Cade/Tony Stone Images; *Figure 6-37* Mark Richards/PhotoEdit; **Educational Sites:** *pages 6.41-46* teachers/children and computer, hand with sphere, school books and apple, teacher on desk with computer and student, abacus, stack of books Courtesy of PhotoDisc, Inc; framed picture, frog, beanie, newspapers, plaque, sheet music, tools, Courtesy of Corel Professional Photos CD-ROM Image usage; lab beakers, runner, planets, Lincoln, Courtesy of Digital Stock; hand, Courtesy of ClipArt Warehouse; window, Courtesy of Expert Software; **Chapter 7:** *Figure 7-0* © 1999 PhotoDisc, Inc.; *Figure 7-0* Courtesy of Apple Computer, Inc.; *Figure 7-15* Bruce Ayers/Tony Stone Images; *Figure 7-20* Richard T. Nowitz/Corbis; *Figure 7-21a* Seth Resnick/Stock Boston; *Figure 7-21c* Michael Newman/PhotoEdit; *Figure 7-21a* Robert E. Daemmrich/Tony Stone ImagEs; Figure 7-21d Porter Gifford/The Liaison Agency; *Figure 7-22* David Young-Wolff/PhotoEdit; *Figure 7-23* Michael Newman/PhotoEdit; *Figure 7-24* James Wilson/Woodfin Camp & Associates; *Figure 7-31* © Corel Corporation; *Figure 7-32b* © KPT; *Figure 7-32c, d* © 1999 PhotoDisc, Inc.; *Figure 7-33* © Corel Corporation; *Figure 7-34* © KPT; *Figure 7-35b* © DigitalStock; *Figure 7-35a* © 1999 PhotoDisc, Inc.; *Figure 7-36* © Corel Corporation; **Chapter 8:** *Figure 8-0* Courtesy of Apple Computer, Inc.; *Figure 8-5* Courtesy of Network Associates; *Figure 8-5b* Courtesy of Symantec Corporation; *Figure 8-8* Courtesy of Global Computer Supplies; *Figure 8-9* Courtesy of Apple Computer, Inc.; *Figure 8-10* © 1999 PhotoDisc, Inc.; *Figure 8-13* Courtesy of American Power Conversion; *Figure 8-14* Courtesy of Panamax; *Figure 8-15* Courtesy of American Power Conversion; *Figure 8-24* Courtesy of Forest Technologies, Inc.; *Figure 8-31* Michael Newman/PhotoEdit; *Figure 8-35* Will & Deni McIntyre/Photo Researchers, Inc.; *Figure 8-37* A. Ramey/Woodfin Camp & Associates; **Chapter 1-8:** *end-of-chapter graphics* Courtesy of Artville, Chet Phillips; *WebInfo, post a note,* Courtesy of PhotoDisc, Inc.

PRIMARY MATHEMATICS 4B
WORKBOOK

U.S. EDITION

Original edition published under the titles
Primary Mathematics Workbook 4B (Part One) and 4B (Part Two)
© 1983 Curriculum Planning & Development Division
Ministry of Education, Singapore
Published by Times Media Private Limited
This American Edition
© 2003 Times Media Private Limited
© 2003 Marshall Cavendish International (Singapore) Private Limited
© 2014 Marshall Cavendish Education Pte Ltd

Published by Marshall Cavendish Education
Times Centre, 1 New Industrial Road, Singapore 536196
Customer Service Hotline: (65) 6213 9688
US Office Tel: (1-914) 332 8888 | Fax: (1-914) 332 8882
E-mail: cs@mceducation.com
Website: www.mceducation.com

First published 2003
Second impression 2003
Third impression 2005
Reprinted 2005, 2006 (thrice), 2007, 2008 (twice), 2009, 2010, 2011,
          2012 (twice), 2014, 2015, 2016, 2017, 2018 (thrice), 2019 (twice), 2020 (thrice)

ISBN 978-981-01-8509-1

Printed in Singapore

ACKNOWLEDGEMENTS

Our special thanks to Richard Askey, Professor of Mathematics (University of Wisconsin, Madison), Yoram Sagher, Professor of Mathematics (University of Illinois, Chicago), and Madge Goldman, President (Gabriella and Paul Rosenbaum Foundation), for their indispensable advice and suggestions in the production of Primary Mathematics (U.S. Edition).